"*Let Us Draw Near* is a book we've needed for de[...] students from around the world in transcultural [...] always relied on Ron Man's insightful, biblical instruction and his global experience as a missionary and ethnodoxologist. Now his many great articles have been integrated into a cohesive, rich resource on the theology and practice of worship. It should be required reading for pastors, seminary educators, missionaries, ethnodoxologists, and worship leaders of all kinds."

—ROBIN HARRIS, president, Global Ethnodoxology Network

"Worship focused on God's story of redemption in Christ, God's covenantal table of grace, and God's mission of love to the world is the source and summit of the very life and hope of all humankind. Ron Man presents a superb magnum opus that delineates multiple aspects and principles of this great climactic act of reconciling friendship with God. This book is a must-have for any serious theologian's library."

—JAMES R. HART, president, Robert E. Webber Institute for Worship Studies

"If you are looking for a biblically grounded, thoroughly comprehensive, meticulously researched, historically connected, vibrantly relevant, and engagingly written work on Christian worship, look no further than Ron Man's *Let Us Draw Near*. While he expertly teaches *about* worship, Man masterfully guides the reader through biblical, theological, historical, cultural, and global tributaries that engage the reader to respond *as* worshipers of Jesus Christ, to the glory of God the Father in the power of the Holy Spirit."

—JOSEPH R. CRIDER, dean of the school of church music and worship, Southwestern Baptist Theological Seminary

"The best resource on the crucial subject of godly worship is the Bible. And now, the best guide to those scriptural resources is Ron Man's newly published book, *Let Us Draw Near*. Thorough enough for theologians, pastors, and worship leaders, yet readable enough for people in the pew, may this faithful investigation of biblical truth richly inform—and thereby *transform*—the worship of many a Christian for years to come."

—A. DUANE LITFIN, president emeritus, Wheaton College

"Ron Man's years of global worship education have honed this pastoral, practical, biblical study of worship. He is clear, systematic, and thorough; professorial, without being pedantic; and generous, with quotations from the many authors, in his extensive, select, up-to-date bibliography. I am eager to use *Let Us Draw Near* in my undergraduate and seminary teaching."

—CHARLES KING, adjunct music and worship educator, Trinity International University and Wheaton College

"From a lifetime as both worship leadership practitioner and theological thinker, Ron has compiled a valuable, complete resource for all worshipers, whether pastors, leaders of worship, or congregants. This large volume of writing offers important perspectives not often found in a single volume, such as the primacy of worship throughout the Scriptures, local and global perspectives, and practical applications for everyday church ministry. *Let Us Draw Near* will be a go-to resource for both academic and ministry applications."

—EDWIN (ED) M. WILLMINGTON, director, Fred Bock Institute of Music

"*Let Us Draw Near* is a gift with the heart of a sage and the mind of a scholar who has invested his life in educating, engaging, and equipping in cross-cultural contexts. Ron Man invites all seekers of true worship to quench their thirst from the well of theologically truthful, culturally curated, and missionally motivated resources. The book will be an ideal resource for students and scholars of Christian worship, practical theology, and biblical studies, as well as for interested laypersons."

—ERIC SARWAR, president, Tehillim School of Church Music & Worship, Pakistan

"With this book, Ron Man adds his voice to the number of quality studies dealing with the biblical material on worship; and his is a welcome voice for the church today. Ron's helpful 'examination of the centrality of worship to all of life and ministry' encourages us in our responses of worship to God's revelation, both as individuals and as the church. *Let Us Draw Near* is sure to become an essential text for the study and understanding of biblical worship."

—STEVEN BROOKS, director, Worship Quest Ministries

"Drawing on a career traveling the planet and teaching on worship, Ron Man has sifted through his lectures, his years of monthly updates, his exhaustive quotations files, along with his in-depth survey of the Scriptures to create a monumental, comprehensive volume, a go-to manual, a virtual encyclopedia of the major themes of biblical and theological worship. Like a huge orchestral score, Man weaves the Revelation-Response continuum along with other recurring motifs throughout this remarkable book."

—FRANK FORTUNATO, co-director, GROW (Global Renewal of Worship) Center for the Robert E. Webber Institute of Worship Studies

"Ron Man provides a fresh, systematic, thorough, and distinctive survey of biblical teaching about worship, especially with reference to its congregational expression. He writes as one who is passionate for the glory of God and offers practical advice to those responsible for leading God's people in this vital pursuit."

—DAVID G. PETERSON, author of *Engaging with God*

"The reader senses in *Let Us Draw Near* an undercurrent of music—Ron Man's passion for the beautiful, expressed via voice and instrument, bears his narrative along with a cadence that makes his writing not only substantive, but memorable. Biblically based and rooted in a lifetime of practical ministry experience, here is a manual you can *use*. It will inspire you to experience the freedom that can come with deep and theologically consistent worship—worship that leads us to the throne of grace as we magnify the Lord Jesus Christ."

—REG GRANT, chair and senior professor of media arts and worship, Dallas Theological Seminary

"As a musician working in Japan, I sat under Ron Man's teaching of the principles laid out in these pages and participated in the lively discussions that followed. Various debates erupted, but Man continually brought us back to the biblical foundations of worship—which remain the same, no matter the place or situation. This perspective is so needed for those of us leading worship around the globe and trying to navigate issues as numerous and nuanced as the nations of the earth."

—ROGER W. LOWTHER, founder and director, Community Arts Tokyo

"Ron Man's *Let Us Draw Near* shows us that 'worship is central' in God's program—from the Old Testament to the New Testament and in the mission of the church today. It is a book with biblical and theological depth that provides foundational principles for worship applicable to a wide range of church contexts, including cross-cultural ministry contexts. I recommend this as an invaluable resource, textbook, and guidebook for the study, teaching, and practice of Christian worship."

—JOSHUA A. WAGGENER, professor of church music and worship, Southwestern Baptist Theological Seminary

"*Let Us Draw Near* contains a rich exploration of biblical worship. With tremendous facility, Ron Man has provided a synthesis of heart and mind, spirit and truth, beauty and reason. For those desiring greater understanding, this substantive manual provides both rigor and clarity regarding the nature of Christian worship."

—STEPHEN MARTIN, director of worship studies, Azusa Pacific University

"We are created to worship God. Most of the time, we human beings miss this important truth. In his book *Let Us Draw Near*, Ron Man expounds worship in a captivating way as a response given by God's creation to his revelation. The book brings the reader close to true biblical worship. It is a treasure that can be used for personal edification or a textbook in theological institutions."

—FREW TAMRAT, principal, Evangelical Theological College of Addis Ababa, Ethiopia

"Ron Man lives what he has written in these pages. Having served with him over many years in numerous international contexts, I've also witnessed Ron's heart for mission-related ministry—an important aspect found in this book. Ron's love for God and his word shines brightly in his teaching as well as in this volume—a culmination of years of faithful service all over the world."

—RICHARD MAUNEY, Jubilate Foundation, Romania

"For anyone wondering what the Bible has to say about worship, Ron Man delivers a comprehensive and balanced guide. *Let Us Draw Near* is a God-centered, Bible-saturated resource rife with significant implications for the church. Moreover, this book does what good conversations about Christian worship should do—it stirs postures and practices of heartfelt devotion to God. Here are essential ideas for church leaders and students of Christian worship today."

—JONATHAN S. WELCH, assistant professor of Christian worship, Southeastern Baptist Theological Seminary

"Ron Man has likely taught worship courses at the seminary and Bible college level in more nations than anyone else. I love his commitment to both theological orthodoxy and methodological flexibility. In this book, he presents a rigorous exploration of God's transcultural instruction on worship. A combination of biblical and systematic theology, historical survey, and practical advice, this book is a treasure trove for those pursuing more biblically faithful worship."

—KEN BOER, pastor of worship, First Evangelical Church of Memphis, TN

"*Let Us Draw Near* thoroughly unfolds core elements of worship and the purpose of Christ's Church. Ron Man is deeply committed to the responsorial implications of evangelical thought. This work is very much his while it successfully amalgamates the thoughts of dozens of our most trusted voices in the tradition regarding worship. He accomplishes this while framing New Testament paradigms that call for the pursuit of God's glory. Highly recommended!"

—PAUL RUMRILL, associate dean, Center for Music and Worship, Liberty University

"One of the great needs of our day is a renewal in understanding biblical and theological foundations of worship. I am thankful that Ron Man has curated his wisdom and life work into a comprehensive volume. I trust this book will be a helpful guide for any who seek to grow both as worshipers and leaders of worship."

—MATT BOSWELL, hymnwriter

"I am overjoyed that Ron Man has finally written this book. *Let Us Draw Near* is the fruit of countless hours mining the riches of Scripture and hundreds of books and articles on the topic of worship. It is at once biblically faithful, comprehensive, thoughtful, Christ-centered, and pastorally driven. I have no doubt that Ron's book will serve pastors, music leaders, musicians, and church members as a resource on worship for decades to come."

—BOB KAUFLIN, director, Sovereign Grace Music

"Expansive in scope and grounded in years' worth of hard-earned wisdom, Ron Man's book is a beautiful invitation to the breadth, length, height, and depth of worship and to the God whom we worship as Father, Son, and Holy Spirit. May it invigorate and inspire you afresh."

—W. DAVID O. TAYLOR, associate professor of theology and culture, Fuller Theological Seminary

"Ron Man has uniquely combined biblical theology of worship through both Testaments, worship in church history, and practical considerations for church worship in a global context. This book is a gift and a welcomed resource for all of us who teach God-centered, biblical worship to seminarians and aspiring church worship leaders."

—CHUCK STEDDOM, pastor for worship and ministry development, Bethlehem Baptist Church

"We have been honored by Ron Man providing the pinnacle of his study of the Scriptures and twenty-five years of experience in a valuable book, *Let Us Draw Near*. Its message has impacted students at our seminary over many years, as it traces the repeated pattern of divine revelation and human response through the Scriptures. Man stresses the danger of the church losing the reality of the present work of Christ: the Savior is present at every church meeting as the real teacher about the nature of God, leader of worship, energizer of trust, and motivator for service."

—IMAD SHEHADEH, founder and president, Jordan Evangelical Theological Seminary

# LET US DRAW NEAR

# WORSHIP AND WITNESS

The Worship and Witness series seeks to foster a rich, interdisciplinary conversation on the theology and practice of public worship, a conversation that will be integrative and expansive. Integrative, in that scholars and practitioners from a wide range of disciplines and ecclesial contexts will contribute studies that engage church and academy. Expansive, in that the series will engage voices from the global church and foreground crucial areas of inquiry for the vitality of public worship in the twenty-first century.

The Worship and Witness series demonstrates and cultivates the interaction of topics in worship studies with a range of crucial questions, topics, and insights drawn from other fields. These include the traditional disciplines of theology, history, and pastoral ministry—as well as cultural studies, political theology, spirituality, and music and the arts. The series focus will thus bridge church worship practices and the vital witness these practices nourish.

We are pleased that you have chosen to join us in this conversation, and we look forward to sharing this learning journey with you.

**Series Editors:**
John D. Witvliet
Noel Snyder
Maria Cornou

# LET US DRAW NEAR

## Biblical Foundations of Worship

Ron Man

*Foreword by John D. Witvliet*

CASCADE *Books* · Eugene, Oregon

LET US DRAW NEAR
Biblical Foundations of Worship

Worship and Witness

Copyright © 2023 Ron Man. All rights reserved. Except for brief quotations in
critical publications or reviews, no part of this book may be reproduced in any
manner without prior written permission from the publisher. Write: Permissions,
Wipf and Stock Publishers, 199 W. 8th Ave., Suite 3, Eugene, OR 97401.

Cascade Books
An Imprint of Wipf and Stock Publishers
199 W. 8th Ave., Suite 3
Eugene, OR 97401

www.wipfandstock.com

PAPERBACK ISBN: 978-1-6667-6277-8
HARDCOVER ISBN: 978-1-6667-6278-5
EBOOK ISBN: 978-1-6667-6279-2

*Cataloguing-in-Publication data:*

Names: Man, Ron, author. | Witvliet, John D., foreword.

Title: Let us draw near : biblical foundations of worship / by Ron Man;
foreword by John D. Witvliet.

Description: Eugene, OR: Cascade Books, 2023. | Worship and Witness. |
Includes bibliographical references and index.

Identifiers: ISBN 978-1-6667-6277-8 (paperback). | ISBN 978-1-6667-6278-5
(hardcover). | ISBN 978-1-6667-6279-2 (ebook).

Subjects: LCSH: Worship. | Worship—Biblical teaching.
Classification: BV10.3 M36 2023 (print). | BV10.3 (epub).

11/08/23

*This book is gratefully dedicated to the congregation and the Worship Choir of First Evangelical Church in Memphis, Tennessee.*

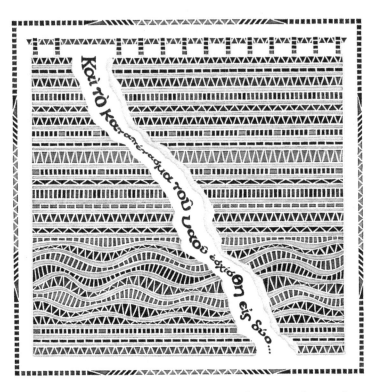

The curtain of the temple was torn in two, from top to bottom.[1]

Matt 27:51; also Mark 15:38; Luke 23:45

Therefore, brethren, since we have confidence
to enter the holy places by the blood of Jesus,
by the new and living way that he opened for us
through the curtain, that is, through his flesh,
and since we have a great priest over the house of God,
*let us draw near*
with a true heart in full assurance of faith,
with our hearts sprinkled clean from an evil conscience
and our bodies washed with pure water.

Heb 10:19–22

1. Artwork by Kirsten Malcolm Berry.

# CONTENTS

# Part 4 | Worship in the Old Testament

# Part 5 | Worship in the New Testament

# Part 6 | Worship in Church History

# Part 7 | Worship in the Church

# FOREWORD

This book is the result not only of careful study of what the Bible teaches about worship. It is also a field-tested guide for a variety of effective ways to teach that material to others. The vast majority of the teaching ministry does not consist of learning new things to teach—as important as continual learning is. Rather, the vast majority of teaching ministry consists of teaching the same things again and again more effectively and faithfully. This work is enriched by noticing which ideas, themes, or ways of explaining things either inspire or confuse students; by experimenting with different ways of getting at essential considerations; by discerning which topics are truly of central concern and which ones could be trimmed from a course that has grown a bit too complex. Ron Man has been doing this work for many years, and the fruit of this learning is reflected here.

It is of great value that Ron began this work as a deeply curious pastoral musician, who realized early on that to prepare and lead God's people in worship is a formidable priestly, pastoral, and prophetic task, one that invites us into lifelong prayerful engagement with the Bible and theological reflection (see the preface). This kind of reflection invites us over time to treat our task as a weighty and significant one, with lifelong spiritual implications for those with whom we work and minister. It also teaches us to rest more diligently and trustingly, entrusting the ultimate fruit of our work to the operation of the Holy Spirit. The Christian life is an invitation to invest deeply and hold on loosely, a graced way to live as we walk in step with the Holy Spirit.

One of the themes I have especially appreciated in Ron's teaching over the years has been his exposition of Heb 2:12 and the importance of Jesus Christ as a true priestly leader of our worship. The priestly role of the ascended Jesus—so central to the book of Hebrews—challenges us to look to Jesus in a new and dramatic way, utterly grateful for the way that Jesus's priestly ministry inspires us to praise God with profound gratitude and wonder, but without the burden of thinking that divine blessing depends on the perfection of our all-too-meager liturgical offerings. The gospel of grace is central here.

In any number of single session workshops and in his earlier work, *Proclamation and Praise: Hebrews 2:12 and the Christology of Worship* (Wipf & Stock, 2007), Ron explained the life-changing implications of attending to that heavenly vision. Now we have the advantage of seeing more clearly how that compelling conviction fits inside a larger vista of theological reflection (ch. 26). So much of our Bible reading is like that: we focus intently on a particular image, theme, narrative, or conviction, and then we set it inside a larger context. This helps us practice the hermeneutical maxim "Scripture interprets Scripture." And it also provides *many* points of entry into a larger theological vision.

I suspect that as Ron has taught his twelve Biblical Principles of Worship (ch. 39) over the years, each of them has been singled out by different students as being particularly helpful. I suspect that with his students, as with mine, their own unique cultural context affects which principle—and which related exegetical investigation—was particularly illuminating for them. Some students come from a context starved for the transcendent vision of Isa 6; others are starved for the gracious news about the Holy Spirit's presence with us in our weakness.

Some are challenged by the Revelation-Response paradigm (ch. 4), because all they have been asked to do as worshipers is to listen to God's word, with relatively little emphasis on the response. Others are challenged because they have been asked to sing and pray and testify and give and dedicate themselves, but with a relatively modest diet of liturgical Bible readings to prompt and guide these actions.

Some students are shocked to realize how robust the transcultural aspects of Christianity are (ch. 37)—how much there is to translate into local languages and cultural sensibilities. Others are shocked by the astonishing pluriformity that results across cultures when the sixty-six books of the Bible are translated into local languages and when careful attention to these texts starts its inevitable process of inspiring renewed ways of approaching preaching, prayer, music, and patterns of leadership (ch. 38).

A volume like this offers many opportunities for us to pay Ron Man the compliment of drawing on his insights, echoing his language, and reflecting our thanks to God by saying, "I'm grateful to Ron Man for helping me learn how to explain this point." A volume like this can also prompt each of us to stretch to do what he has done here, to hone and sharpen our own symphonic approach to teaching, building on his work.

In closing, let me also commend the value of a comprehensive account of what the Bible teaches about worship. There is also merit, of course, in comprehensive approaches to the history of worship, to worship in various Christian traditions, to worship in various cultural contexts, to the complementary roles and functions of multiple art forms which engage each of our senses in biblically informed ways. There is merit in developing comprehensive collections of liturgical resources. So many gifts enrich the field of worship. Thanks to be God for a host of pastoral leaders around the world who take up one or more of the callings. Each of these other kinds of books, however, ultimately depends on lifelong, faithful engagement with the Bible, the ever-renewing source of our knowledge of God. That also means that a book like this—and the study it reflects—is a key kind of resource to ground and inspire all these other kinds of work. May this foundational work be used by God's Spirit to instruct, inspire, encourage, and deeply ground the work of a new generation of teachers of Christian worship.

JOHN D. WITVLIET
Director, Calvin Institute of Christian Worship
Grand Rapids, Michigan

# PREFACE

There is a kind of book about which you may say, almost without exaggeration, that it is the whole of a man's literary life, the unique child of his thought. Other writings he may have published, on this or that occasion; please God, the work was not scamped, nor was he indifferent to the praise or blame of his critics. But it was all beside the mark. The Book was what mattered—he had lived with it all these years, fondled it in his waking thoughts, used it as an escape from anxiety, a solace in long journeys, in tedious conversations. Did he find himself in [a] library, he made straight for the shelves which promised light on one cherished subject; did he hit upon a telling quotation, a just metaphor, an adroit phrase, it was treasured up, in miser's fashion, for the Book. The Book haunted his daydreams. . . . Such a thing, for better or worse, is this book which follows. I have been writing it for thirty years and a little more.[1]

This is that kind of book for me.

When I became Pastor of Worship and Music at First Evangelical Church in Memphis, Tennessee, in 1988, I had seminary training behind me as well as musical training. However, these two tracks had never been integrated in any way, and I really did not understand anything about worship. Over the ensuing years worship became more and more important in our church—not because of something I brought, but because the Lord was teaching me and the congregation about the importance and practice of worship. After a few years I started looking around and doing some reading and discovered that God was doing much the same thing in many different churches in many different places

---

1. Knox, *Enthusiasm*, v.

around the world: God through his Spirit seemed to be bringing a revival, or reformation, of worship to his church.

Back in 1961, A. W. Tozer wrote a little book in which he asserted:

> Now, worship is the missing jewel in modern evangelicalism. We're organized; we work; we have our agendas. We have almost everything, but there's one thing that the churches, even the gospel churches, do not have: that is the ability to worship. We are not cultivating the art of worship. It's the one shining gem that is lost to the modern church, and I believe that we ought to search for this until we find it.[2]

Tozer said God's people were busy doing many good things; they were just neglecting the most important thing: the worship of Almighty God. Tozer was a lonely prophetic voice at a time when no one else was talking about worship.[3] If he were alive today, he would undoubtedly be amazed at how that situation has changed in the meantime: worship is certainly not being overlooked in today's church! It is very much a point of discussion in the evangelical church. There are many, many worship songs that have been written; there are conferences on worship; there are courses on worship being taught in schools and churches around the world; and there are many books on worship.

Worship is very much at the forefront of congregational thought in our day: that's the *good* news. The *bad* news is that worship has become a primary source of conflict, strife, even division among our churches (the so-called worship wars). It is a travesty that the worship of Almighty God should have become a source of division and conflict in the church of Jesus Christ! As a result of this situation, I became convinced that pastors, worship leaders, and churchgoers need more grounding in a *theology of worship* (more on that below) to inform their thinking and discussions about worship. As I pursued my own personal study of the biblical

---

2. Tozer, *Worship*, 20.

3. "I think that God has given me a bit of a spirit of a crusader and I am crusading where I can that Christians of all denominations and shades of theological thought might be restored again to our original purpose. We're here to be worshipers first and workers second" (Tozer, *Worship*, 10). In 1998 I was on a three-month sabbatical from my church worship ministry, and during that time had the opportunity to sit down and visit with two prominent teachers of worship. I asked them both the same question, "How did you first become interested in worship?" Remarkably, they answered my question in almost exactly the same way: something along the lines of, "When I was a student in Bible school, A. W. Tozer came and spoke on campus about worship, and it opened up a whole new world to me . . ." Such was the legacy of Tozer.

foundations of worship, God opened up opportunities for teaching in Bible schools and seminaries overseas, and within a few years I moved overseas with my family to pursue this teaching ministry full-time (and continued it full-time, and then part-time, after returning to the US a few years later). I have had rich times of teaching in such places as Tyndale Theological Seminary (Netherlands), Odessa Theological Seminary (Ukraine), Jordan Evangelical Theological Seminary, and Singapore Bible College.

This book is a distillation of some twenty-five years of teaching on the biblical foundations of worship in close to forty countries; the basic survey course that forms the basis, and provides the structure, for this book I have taught more than fifty times in fifteen countries. Invariably, I have found students in which God had already instilled true hearts for worship; so I have never had to convince them of the importance of the subject. But I also found that, as I presented the material found in this book, adding real biblical depth to their understanding of worship, the students responded with wonder and enthusiasm. For heart *and* mind— if you will, spirit *and* truth—both have a vital role to play in Christian worship.

There are a number of fine studies dealing with the biblical material on worship (referenced elsewhere in this book), to which this author and many others are indebted. Some of the distinctives of the present treatment include:

1. The consistent emphasis throughout the work on the pervasive *revelation and response* paradigm of Scripture and its foundational significance for worship

2. The development in depth of the crucial theme of Jesus Christ as the true leader of our worship (the topic of a previous book of mine, *Proclamation and Praise: Hebrews 2:12 and the Christology of Worship* [Wipf & Stock, 2007])

3. The focus on missions and worship, including a look at the new and developing field of *ethnodoxology* (drawing upon my involvement in that movement)

4. The concluding synthesis of twelve "Biblical Principles of Worship" distilled from the inductive study, and the emphasis on their application to personal and corporate worship

5. The perspective brought from being a church worship leader for more than forty years, as well as a student and teacher of worship on the academic level

6. A more extensive treatment of the New Testament material than in some other works of the sort

7. The marshaling of quotations from a wide array of authors, adding richness and depth to the treatment of the topics covered

It should be added that the book does not deal a lot with specific *practices*, because its focus is on identifying unifying principles that transcend cultures and ecclesiastical traditions. I pray that this work, building on the shoulders of others, will be, through its systematic, thorough, and distinctive treatment of biblical worship, a help, blessing, and inspiration to many students of worship, leaders of worship, pastors, and Christian worshipers of all kinds.

> O come, let us sing for joy to the LORD,
> Let us shout joyfully to the rock of our salvation!
> Let us come before his presence with thanksgiving,
> Let us shout joyfully to him with psalms.
>
> For the LORD is a great God
> and a great King above all gods,
> In whose hand are the depths of the earth,
> The peaks of the mountains are his also.
> The sea is his, for it was he who made it,
> And his hands formed the dry land.
>
> Come, let us worship and bow down,
> Let us kneel before the LORD our Maker.
> For he is our God, and we are the people of his pasture
> and the sheep of his hand.
>
> (Ps 95:1–7 NASB)

# ACKNOWLEDGMENTS

T here have been many who have impacted my life and my teaching along the pilgrimage that led to the writing of this book. I will mention just a few.

Tom and Marilyn Dumm modeled for me a life of both spiritual commitment and musical excellence when the things of the Lord were still strange and foreign to me. David Stevens, missionary to Germany, inspired this baby Christian with his zeal for the word and with his lending library. Donald E. Hurlbert was the first great expositor I got to sit under (in York, Pennsylvania).

Dallas Theological Seminary instilled in me a deep commitment to rigorously handling the word of God. John W. Reed, in his dual roles at Dallas Seminary and Sherman Bible Church, was a mentor and an exemplar of a true shepherd. The people of Sherman Bible Church loved and encouraged and supported me in my early, fumbling attempts at ministry (and a number have continued to follow and support my ministry).

Duane Litfin, formerly Senior Pastor of First Evangelical Church in Memphis, Tennessee, insisted on a worship pastor with theological as well as musical training, opening the way for my now thirty-five-year association with that wonderful church. He also patiently walked with me through the (often trial-and-error) design of worship services that sought to be God-honoring. Twyla Dixon painstakingly transcribed my teaching notes (the foundation of this book), with all of their virtually illegible marginal scratchings, and put them into a much more usable form; she also helped me greatly to clean up the manuscript to this book with her very keen and thorough editor's eye. Judi Simpson helped with another edit.

The congregation and the Worship Choir of First Evan have for a long time loved us and supported us through all our comings and goings, and it is to those two groups that this book is gratefully dedicated. First Evan has a been a huge part of our support team, along with others outside: without all your prayers, encouragement, and financial support through many years of worship ministry, both near and far, the years of teaching and the writing of this book would not have been possible.

John Piper, from our earliest email discussions and through his teaching and writings, has impacted my understanding of worship more than anyone else (and I quote him in this book more than any other author).

The writings of the late James B. Torrance first introduced me to the wonderful truths about the Lord Jesus Christ as the Leader and Perfecter of our worship. His hospitality for a couple of days in Edinburgh were very memorable as well.

Thank you to the editors and staff of Wipf & Stock publishing, and the editors of the Worship and Witness series in their Cascade Books imprint, for seeing this project through to completion. A special thanks to John Witvliet for his generous foreword, and to all those dear colleagues who provided endorsements.

I also owe a great debt to the hundreds of students in numerous countries who have field-tested this material over the past twenty-five years.

My wife Betsy has faithfully gone with me through this long pilgrimage, with all its twists and turns. And my children Grace, Lily, and Christian have been along for quite a ride as well! I am profoundly thankful for their Christian marriages and for the delightful spouses (Duke, Brandon, and Brooke) and grandchildren they have brought into our lives.

Finally, of course, I owe great praise to the Lord Jesus Christ, the Leader of our worship; to the Holy Spirit, the Motivator of our worship; and to the Father, who has lavished his grace, mercy, and patience upon me.

> For from him and through him and to him are all things.
> To him be glory forever! Amen. (Rom 11:36)

# ABBREVIATIONS

ANF        *Ante-Nicene Fathers*

BCOTWP     Baker Commentary on the Old Testament Wisdom and Psalms

*BSac*       *Bibliotheca Sacra*

*CurTM*      *Currents in Theology and Mission*

ICC        International Critical Commentary

*JETS*       *Journal of the Evangelical Theological Society*

NICNT      New International Commentary on the New Testament

*NIDNTT*     *New International Dictionary of New Testament Theology.* Edited by Colin Brown. 4 vols. Grand Rapids: Zondervan, 1975–1978.

TOTC       Tyndale Old Testament Commentaries

*SJT*        *Scottish Journal of Theology*

*WTJ*        *Westminster Theological Journal*

# Part 1

# Introduction

# 1

# THE PRIVILEGE OF DRAWING NEAR

The curtain of the temple was torn in two, from top to bottom.

MATT 27:51; ALSO MARK 15:38; LUKE 23:45

Therefore, brethren, since we have confidence

to enter the holy places by the blood of Jesus,

by the new and living way that he opened for us

through the curtain, that is, through his flesh,

and since we have a great priest over the house of God,

*let us draw near*

with a true heart in full assurance of faith,

with our hearts sprinkled clean from an evil conscience

and our bodies washed with pure water.

HEB 10:19–22

"Let us draw near" is the climactic pronouncement ("Therefore . . .") of the book of Hebrews, and in a sense of the new covenant itself. This invitation, challenge, and command goes to the very heart of what God has accomplished for us through the work of Christ: extending to us sinners the inestimable privilege of entering into the very presence of God in worship through, in, and with our Lord Jesus Christ, who has opened the way through his atoning death and even *takes us with him* to the Father's throne of grace (Heb 4:16). This free and open access means that we can come with "confidence" and "full assurance of faith."

This mind-boggling reality sets us on our course in this book, as we delve into God's word to see more of his heart and to relish his mercy and grace in allowing the likes of us to *draw near*.

# 2

# DEFINING WORSHIP

## Worship: A Biblical Definition

Worship, in its most basic understanding, presupposes a fundamental distinction between the worshiper and the object of worship. Even in the most banal use of the term, e.g., where famous athletes or musicians are said to be worshiped by their fans, there is still the idea that those persons' abilities or appeal are far superior to those of normal people. When it comes to God, of course, the distance is infinite: God is totally unique. He made the universe, and everything that exists besides him owes to him its existence; only he has no beginning, no cause, no limits or limitations. In spite of our exalted stature of being created in the image of God, there is still an infinite chasm that separates us as creatures from the one Creator.

Yet sin foolishly seeks to mar that distinction, to bridge that chasm. This was the fundamental issue in the serpent's temptation of Eve in the garden: "you will be like God" (Gen 3:5). The attack was on God's utter uniqueness as the Creator and Lord of all, on the fundamental distinction between him and all his creatures, including Eve (and Adam, and Satan). There was in the garden (and has been ever since) a presumptuous attempt to lower God to a more creaturely level, and so to raise humans to Godlike status. Needless to say, this is an affront to God; and it also constitutes a denial of humans' proper place in the created order, and a refusal to acknowledge God's unique place and to respond appropriately. (More on this in ch. 7.)

This is exactly what we see in Rom 1. In v. 21 Paul states that sinful humanity "did not honor him as God or give thanks." And this in spite of being able to observe God's power and greatness in the works of nature (v. 20). Paul's phrase in v. 21, though used in the negative of what natural humans steadfastly refuse to do, suggests what the appropriate response of human creatures should be to their Maker: they should "honor him as God" (i.e., accord to him the unique place that he as the Creator God rightly holds, "[ascribing] to the LORD the glory due his name" [Ps 96:8]), and "give thanks" for all of his good gifts. This fits the familiar paradigm of praising God for who he is ("honor him as God") and for what he has done ("give thanks").

Adam and Eve turned from honoring their Creator as uniquely God, and instead of giving thanks for all the "very good" (Gen 1:31) things that God had made and placed into their care (Gen 1:28), they desired more, even though it meant disobeying him and attempting to usurp his unique position. Thus, in Rom 1 Paul is really describing the situation surrounding the fall, as well as the ensuing consequences in all following generations. At the root of the problem of sin was (and is) an issue of worship, a failure to honor God as God and to give him thanks.

From the perspective of the entire book of Romans, we see that in fact Paul is painting this dark picture of fallen humans' state in Rom 1 so that the light of the gospel will shine all the more brilliantly as he develops it in the chapters to come.[1] And indeed, we see already in Rom 1 a clear indication that that is where Paul is heading: for in the verses immediately preceding those we have looked at, he speaks of the "gospel" being "the power of God for salvation to everyone who believes," and that as a result one can indeed become "righteous" (1:16–17). Paul is promising nothing less than the restoration of worship through Christ and the reversal of our downward spiral of sin (1:18–32) through the power of God's redeeming love displayed in the gospel. By God's gracious saving work (which Paul will expound beginning in Rom 3), it will indeed be possible for men and women to "honor him as God" and to "give thanks." Because of these "mercies of God" (as Paul will summarize the preceding chapters in 12:1), believers will be urged to present their entire selves to God as a fitting and appropriate "spiritual service of worship."

---

1. Or, as Christopher Wright puts it, Paul presents the "bad news" before explicating the "good news" (*Mission of God*, 180).

And so, in one of the darkest chapters in the Scriptures, we find embedded a gleaming jewel, a precious and beautiful description of what worship truly is and should be: attitudes and acts whereby we

*honor him as God*
*and*
*give thanks.*

## Others' Definitions of Worship

Webster's 1913 dictionary defines worship in this way:

> The act of paying divine honors to the Supreme Being; religious reverence and homage; adoration, or acts of reverence, paid to God, or a being viewed as God.

C. E. B. Cranfield rightly reminds us of the different ways we use the English word *worship* (all of which are reflected to different degrees in the definitions below):

> We may distinguish three uses of the word "worship"; (*i*) to denote a particular element of what is generally referred to as worship, namely, <u>adoration;</u> (*ii*) to denote generally the public worship of the religious community gathered together and also the private religious exercises of the family and the individual; and (iii), in a still wider sense, to denote the whole life of the community or of the individual viewed as service of God.[2]

Here is a sampling of how different Christian authors have sought to define worship. These expressions can provide a rich devotional experience in themselves, with their commonality of focus yet diversity of inflection:

> Exactly what is worship? I like King David's definition. "Oh, magnify the LORD with me, and let us exalt his name together!" (Ps. 34:3). Worship is the act of magnifying God. Enlarging our vision of him. . . . Of course, his size doesn't change, but our perception of him does.[3]

---

2. Cranfield, "Divine and Human Action," 387.

3. Lucado, *Just Like Jesus*, 84.

The best biblical definition of worship I know is to "glory in his holy name" (Ps 105:3), that is, to revel in the unique wonder of who he is and has revealed himself to be.[4]

Worship is the activity of the new life of a believer in which, recognizing the fullness of the Godhead as it is revealed in the person of Jesus Christ and His mighty redemptive acts, he seeks by the power of the Holy Spirit to render to the living God the glory, honor, and submission which are His due.[5]

Worship is to feel in the heart and express in some appropriate manner a humbling but delightful sense of admiring awe and astonished wonder and overpowering love in the presence of that most ancient Mystery . . . which we call Our Father Which Art in Heaven.[6]

Worship is both a life lived and an event in which to participate. In and through worship, believers, by grace, center their lives (heart, soul, mind and strength) on the Lord, humbly glorifying God in response to His attributes, His acts, and His Word.[7]

Worship is the gift of participating through the Spirit in the incarnate Son's communion with the Father.[8]

Worship is honor and adoration directed to God.[9]

Worship is the celebrative response to what God has done, is doing, and promises to do.[10]

Our worship is a thankful, joyful appropriation of Christ and of His Worship of the Father, through the Spirit, so that all that is of Christ is ours by Grace through the Spirit.[11]

[Worship is] faith expressing itself in obedience and adoration.[12]

Worship is the echo of the supremacy of God in the heart of the believer.[13]

---

4. Stott, *Christian Basics*, 119.

5. Rayburn, *O Come*, 20–21.

6. Tozer, *Worship*, 4–6.

7. Hall, "What's in the Middle?"

8. J. Torrance, *Worship, Community*, 30.

9. MacArthur, *Worship*, 14.

10. Burkhart, *Worship: A Searching Examination*, 17.

11. D. Torrance, "Word of God," 12.

12. D. Peterson, *Engaging with God*, 283.

13. Piper, "Worship and World Missions."

Worship is the submission of all our nature to God. It is the quickening of conscience by His holiness; the nourishment of mind with His truth; the purifying of imagination by His beauty; the opening of the heart to His love; the surrender of will to His purpose—and all of this gathered up in adoration, the most selfless emotion of which our nature is capable and therefore the chief remedy for that self-centeredness which is our original sin and the source of all actual sin.[14]

Worship is the celebration of being in covenant fellowship with the sovereign and holy triune God, by means of the reverent adoration and spontaneous praise of God's nature and works, the expressed commitment of trust and obedience to the covenantal responsibilities, and the memorial reenactment of entering into covenant through ritual acts, all with the confident anticipation of the fulfillment of the covenant promises in glory.[15]

Worship is an act of the understanding, applying itself to the knowledge of the excellency of God, and actual thoughts of his majesty. . . . It is also an act of the will, whereby the soul adores and reverenceth his majesty, is ravished with his amiableness, embraceth his goodness, enters itself into an intimate communion with this most lovely object, and pitcheth all his affections upon him.[16]

Worship is a lifestyle of humble service that culminates corporately at least once a week, where God's chosen people join with the heavenly chorus to praise Him for His vast attributes, confess our inabilities, affirm His grace, yield to His instruction, celebrate His mercies and respond to His covenantal call.[17]

The essence of worship . . . is the inner act of the heart treasuring God as infinitely valuable.[18]

Worship is a voluntary act of gratitude offered by the saved to the Savior, by the healed to the Healer, and by the delivered to the Deliverer.[19]

Worship in the Bible is the due response of rational creatures to the self-revelation of their Creator. It is an honoring and

14. Temple, *St John's Gospel*, 68.
15. Ross, *Recalling the Hope of Glory*, 67–68.
16. Charnock, *Works*, 1:298.
17. Chapell, "Worship as Gospel Representation."
18. Piper, "Magnifying God with Money."
19. Lucado, *In the Eye of the Storm*, 163.

glorifying of God by gratefully offering back to Him all the good gifts, and all the knowledge of His greatness and graciousness, that he has given. It involves praising Him for what he is, thanking Him for what he has done, desiring Him to get Himself more glory by further acts of mercy, judgment, and power, and trusting Him with our concern for our own and others' well-being. . . . As worship will be central in heaven (Rev 4:8–11; 5:9–14), so it must be central in the life of the church on earth, and it should already be the main activity, both private and corporate, in each believer's life (Col 3:17).[20]

In the Old Testament as well as elsewhere worship is a reciprocal exchange between God and his people (this is also how Luther's famous definition formulates it: "that God may speak to us in his holy word and we to him in prayer and song of praise"). Something happens from God to man and vice versa.[21]

Worship is the expression of relationship in which God the Father reveals himself and his love in Christ, and by his Holy Spirit administers grace, to which we respond in faith, gratitude and obedience.[22]

Worship is a strategy for living whereby we interrupt our preoccupation with ourselves and attend to the presence of God in all of life.[23]

What is worship? We answer: First, it is the action of the new nature seeking, as the sparks fly upward, to return to the Divine and heavenly source from which it came.[24]

The inner essence of worship is experiencing Christ as a more satisfying treasure than anything death can take or life can give (Phil 1:20–23).[25]

[Worship is] the human activity of giving God the glory, of praising the creator for his goodness and power, his judgments and his mercy both past, present and future.[26]

20. Packer, *Concise Theology*, 98–99.

21. Westermann, *Elements*, 187.

22. Schaper, *In His Presence*, 15–16.

23. Attributed to Eugene Peterson.

24. Pink, *Gospel of John*, on John 4:24.

25. Piper, "Devil Can Do Exposition."

26. N. T. Wright, "Worship and the Spirit."

D. A. Carson offers perhaps the most comprehensive, refined, and satisfying definition of Christian worship in the opening chapter of his edited volume *Worship by the Book*—a definition that he then unpacks throughout his opening chapter:

> Worship is the proper response of all moral, sentient beings to God, ascribing all honor and worth to their Creator-God precisely because he is worthy, delightfully so. This side of the Fall, human worship of God, appropriately responds to the redemptive provisions that God has graciously made. While all true worship is God-centered, Christian worship is no less Christ-centered. Empowered by the Spirit and in line with the stipulations of the new covenant, it manifests itself in all our living, finding its impulse in the gospel, which restores our relationship with our Redeemer-God and therefore also with our fellow image-bearers, our co-worshipers. Such worship, therefore, manifests itself both in adoration and in action, both in the individual believer and in corporate worship, which is worship offered up in the context of the body of believers, who strive to align all the forms of their devout ascription of all worth to God with the panoply of new covenant mandates and examples that bring to fulfillment the glories of antecedent revelation and anticipate the consummation.[27]

In ch. 5 we will also work inductively towards a definition of worship.

In worship we *honor* God and *give thanks*. (Rom 1:21)

---

27. "Worship under the Word," in Carson, *Worship by the Book*, 26.

# 3

## STUDYING THE THEOLOGY OF WORSHIP

### What Is a Theology?

F irst of all, what is a theology? The Bible, as you know, is not constructed like a school textbook, theme by theme; rather, it is a collection
of different kinds of literature: history, letters, poetry. The work of the
theologian is to search out all that the Bible teaches on a particular aspect
of God's truth; and then to pull that information together and organize it,
so that the student of theology can gain an understanding of the Bible's
total teaching on that subject. This helps us understand the place of that
subject in *God's* story.

Hence a theology of the Holy Spirit, or *Pneumatology*, is what the
Bible teaches on the Holy Spirit across the panorama of biblical revelation. A theology of Christ, or *Christology*, is the Bible's teaching about
the person and work of Christ throughout its pages. A theology is simply
another way of saying a *biblical understanding* of a topic or theme.

### A Theology of Worship

A theology of *worship* is, then, simply *what the Bible teaches about worship*—pulling together what the Bible has to say about worship in its
various parts (by teaching, by example, and by principle) and bringing
that information together and structuring it to help us get our minds

around God's revelation on the subject of worship—in other words, to arrive at a biblical understanding of worship.

> Worship is the supreme and only indispensable activity of the Christian Church. It alone will endure, like the love for God which it expresses, into heaven, when all other activities of the Church will have passed away. It must therefore, even more strictly than any of the less essential doings of the Church, come under the criticism and control of the revelation on which the Church is founded. An enquiry into the meaning, or essence, of worship will necessarily be a theological one.[1]

## Why Is a Theology of Worship Important?

There are at least six reasons that a *theology* (that is, a *biblical understanding*) of worship is important:

### 1. A theology of worship is important because God's word tells us *who God is*.

God, after all, is the *subject* of our worship; worship is *about him*. We must worship him *as he really is*; and we learn who he really is primarily through the pages of Scripture. God's word tells us who God is, what he is like; so it is there that we need to look in order to understand the God whom we worship. True worship is a fitting *response* to the God who makes himself known through the *revelation* of Scripture. (More about that in ch. 4.)

> Now we must not worship without study, for ignorant worship is of limited value and can be very dangerous. We may develop "a zeal for God, but not according to knowledge" (Rom. 10:2) and do great harm to ourselves and others.[2]

---

1. Nicholls, *Jacob's Ladder*, 9.
2. Willard, *Divine Conspiracy*, 362.

## 2. A theology of worship is important because God's word tells us *what God wants.*

God is not just the *subject* of worship; he is also the *object* of worship: worship is *for him.* It is for his pleasure; and he has every right to tell us how he wants us to worship him. And we learn that from God's word: it is there that God tells us what he wants.

> We must discover from his own self-revelation in Scripture what pleases him. We cannot simply determine for ourselves what is honouring to him. . . . The worship of the living and true God is essentially an engagement with him on the terms that he proposes and in the way that he alone makes possible.[3]

## 3. A theology of worship is important because God's word is *our guide.*

> Your Word is a lamp to my feet
> and a light to my path. (Ps 119:105)

God's word is to be our guide in *every* area of life; and so certainly in this important area of worship, we need biblical guidance.

## 4. A theology of worship is important because God's word tells us that *all of life is to be worship.*

> I appeal to you therefore, brethren, by the mercies of God,
> to present your bodies as a living sacrifice,
> holy and acceptable to God, which is your spiritual worship.
> (Rom 12:1)

This key New Testament verse on worship, which we will come back to again and again, teaches us that worship involves a total commitment of one's life in every area to the worship of God and is an appropriate response to God for all that he's done for us in Jesus Christ. Because God's word tells us that all life is to be worship, a biblical understanding of worship will have implications *for our entire lives.*

---

3. D. Peterson, *Engaging with God,* 19–20.

5. A theology of worship is important because God's word is *our only unchanging standard.*

> Forever, O LORD,
> Your Word is settled in heaven. (Ps 119:89)

People change, cultures change, traditions and preferences change; only God's word does *not* change. We need a standard for our worship that does not shift and change with adjustments in culture or times, but rather remains true and steadfast and unchanging—and we find that in God's word. The Bible leaves room for change and variety, but God's revelation is supreme. It has been said that "tradition is a wonderful servant, but a terrible master": there is much we can learn from the faith and the practices of previous generations, but it dare not be our final authority (as in "the way we've always done it"). We must always hold our worship practices under the scrutiny of God's unchanging standards as found in Scripture.

> The form and expression of the liturgy itself, at any given time, must be subject to the criticism of theology. . . . The rites by which we celebrate the liturgy need constantly to be realigned to their purpose and end by the discipline of a theology-grounded revelation. . . . And since, in the most conservative of liturgical traditions, changes do in any case take place from time to time, it must be the task of theology to scrutinize the changes that are taking place in response to pastoral or evangelistic needs, to ensure that they do not drag away the liturgy from its anchoring in the one revelation.[4]

6. A theology of worship is important because it is only God's word that can give us *a unified understanding of worship.*

Around the world there are multitudes of denominations and a huge variety of practices and styles of worship. That is not necessarily a bad thing: we will consider towards the end of this book what a rich and God-honoring diversity of worship practices there are; the God who created a world of such beautiful diversity delights in manifold creativity.

But underneath it all, it is important that we have a basic, unchanging, unified understanding of the foundations of worship. That will be

4. Nicholls, *Jacob's Ladder*, 10.

the focus of this book: What are the essentials of worship? What does *not* change from place to place (even while there is much that *does* change)?

The conviction underlying this book is that, in the light of the many worship controversies plaguing and dividing the church in our day, Christ's body desperately needs a *unifying*, biblical, theological understanding of worship, a common understanding that allows for great variety yet holds to a shared commitment to the foundational principles and purposes behind all true Christian worship.

> If our worship need not be uniform . . . it must be one in at least those matters which involve the essence of worship.[5]

So for all these reasons, it is important to have a theology or a biblical understanding of worship:

1. God's word tells us *who God is.*

2. God's word tells us *what God wants.*

3. God's word is *our guide* in all areas of life.

4. God's word tells us that *all of life* is to be worship.

5. God's word is our only *unchanging standard.*

6. Only God's word can give us a *unified understanding* of worship.

## The Importance of Worship for Theology: Theology Is a Means to an End

Having considered *the importance of theology for worship*, let us for a moment consider the converse: *the importance of worship for theology.*

Biblical knowledge is *not* an end in itself. As we will see, God reveals himself to us *so that* we might know him and worship him. As J. I. Packer reputedly put it: "The purpose of theology is doxology—we study in order to praise."

> But worship must be added to study to complete the renewal of our mind through a willing absorption in the radiant person who is worthy of all praise. Study without worship is also dangerous, and the people of Jesus constantly suffer from its effects,

5. Nicholls, *Jacob's Ladder*, 67.

especially in academic settings. To handle the things of God without worship is always to falsify them.[6]

There should be no theology without doxology. There is something fundamentally flawed about a purely academic interest in God. God is not an appropriate object for cool, critical, detached, scientific observation and evaluation. No, the true knowledge of God will always lead us to worship, as it did Paul. Our place is on our faces before him in adoration.[7]

This point speaks to an occupational hazard of all formal and informal study of the Scripture—whether in a pastor's sermon preparation, a student's Scripture study in Bible school or seminary, or a layperson's personal devotional Bible reading: the danger of taking in information about God but neglecting to "complete the cycle" by turning back to God in praise for the things he has shown us about himself in his word. Head *plus heart* must enter in; we must have a worship perspective on all our biblical study, or we short-circuit its true goal: the praise of God.

During my first semester in seminary in 1977, I took a required course on Old Testament Introduction. For that course we had to read a very, very thick book; and it was an amazing work of scholarship. Many pages were half-filled with footnotes, with hundreds of sources referenced. What a scholar! But the problem was that the man did not appear to love the things he was talking about; he did not seem to love the God of whom he wrote about with such insight. And I remember thinking: "What a tragedy, what a waste of study, if it doesn't lead us back to the God whom we're studying about."

And so it is vital, in all our biblical study, that we see that study is always a means to an end and not the end in itself. It is always to lead us back to God. We learn about God, so that we can praise him more fully. As Packer put it, the purpose of theology is to lead us to doxology.

Theology, a biblical understanding, is important for our worship, but it is also important in all our study to have a worship perspective and not let the study be an end in itself. This corrective is also needed because historically many Protestant churches since the Reformation have emphasized doctrine and teaching over worship. "The Protestant

6. Willard, *Divine Conspiracy*, 362–63.
7. Stott, *Romans*, 311–12.

practice of doctrine needs to recover a more explicit doxological dimension."[8]

So while we focus in this book on the importance of a biblical understanding of worship, let us remember to always keep before us also the importance of a worshipful perspective in all our study of the Bible (and, as we will see later in ch. 4, let us always be careful to "complete the cycle" of theology and doxology).

## What This Book Is Not

This book does not undertake a detailed history of worship or of liturgical practice. There are many fine volumes on those subjects, many of which will be referenced in the text.

Neither does this book attempt a prescription for detailed forms or styles of worship. It seeks to be decidedly nonsectarian as it mines the text of Scripture for underlying and overarching principles of worship.[9]

## What This Book Is

1. An exploration of the biblical and theological foundations of worship

2. An examination of the centrality of worship to all of life and ministry (not just Sunday morning)

3. An attempt to highlight unifying truths in the midst of the current debate: to be part of the solution, not part of the problem! To dig out from the Scriptures foundational understandings of worship, those things that should remain true in every culture and church setting

4. An affirmation of the considerable freedom that the New Testament seems to give individual churches to apply the foundational truths

---

8. Wainwright, *Doxology*, 219.

9. When I teach on worship overseas, my regular disclaimer is that "I have not come to tell you exactly how to do worship in your culture, for I am not from your culture. What I *can* share with you are biblical principles of worship that, precisely because they are *biblical*, by definition transcend culture." My students' responsibility has been, then, to take those principles and apply them in their own context. Similarly, this book does not deal a lot with specific practices of worship—because of its deliberate nonsectarian and transcultural intent.

to its practice of worship, and a call to give grace to other churches that may *apply* the truths differently

5. An encouragement to the reader to think about and evaluate styles of worship in the light of foundational biblical truths

---

Worship is *about* God and *for* God.

---

# *Part 2*

# Foundations

# 4

# REVELATION AND RESPONSE:
## The Paradigm of True Worship

The most foundational of all principles underlying true worship is the principle of *revelation* and *response*. It is the pattern of all true worship; in fact, as we will see, it is the pattern of all of God's interactions with humankind.

We can worship God because he has *first* revealed himself to us. Worship is always a response, a response to God first showing us himself.[1] We can represent the pattern visually in this way:

Revelation                  Response

Revelation is of course from God to us, followed by our response to him.

---

1. Christopher Wright suggests that behind both the Great Commandment (Matt 22:37) and the Great Commission (Matt 28:18–20) is "the Great *Communication*—the revelation of the identity of God, of God's action in the world and God's saving purpose for all creation" (*Mission of God*, 60 [emphasis original]).

## A Crucial Order

Now the *order* of these arrows is *absolutely* crucial: God always speaks *first*, or we could never know him. Hebrews 1:1–2 says:

> Long ago, at many times and in many ways, God spoke to our fathers by the prophets, but in these last days he has spoken to us by his Son.

We can know God because he has *spoken*. William Nicholls writes:

> Our worship is our answer to God who has first addressed us. . . . Man worships the God who has made Himself known, and that worship is to be governed, both in fact and in form, by this revelation. We "praise His holy Name"—that is, we worship Him in his self-revelation. If God had not revealed Himself, we could not praise Him.[2]

Worship is always a *response*; until God has shown us himself, we have nothing to say to him.

The order of the arrows is absolutely crucial because other religions get it exactly *backwards*:

Other religions/Pelagianism

In the absence of a direct revelation from God, people have always tried to figure out: *What do we need to do? What do I need to offer to God? What do I need to give to him so that he'll be good to me?* This was the problem also with the heresy of Pelagianism in the early church: placing the onus of initiative on the part of humanity to somehow reach God through one's own efforts. Augustine combatted Pelagianism by emphasizing the orthodox Christian view:

Christianity/Augustinianism

2. Nicholls, *Jacob's Ladder*, 37.

True Christianity speaks of *God's initiative*. It is not what we do to reach God. It is not a guess. It is not us trying to figure out something. It is not a leap in the dark. It is not acting out of ignorance. But rather, it is a *response* to God, because he has taken the initiative to *reveal* himself to us. As David Peterson puts it: "Acceptable worship does not start with human intuition or inventiveness, but with the action of God."[3] Similarly, Robbie Castleman writes: "The basic pattern of biblical worship . . . is that it is God who initiates the encounter, not the worshiper."[4]

Or, in the words of the apostle John, "We love because he *first* loved us" (1 John 4:19).

## A Biblical Pattern

We see the pattern of revelation and response throughout Scripture (and hence we will see it throughout this book), for it is in fact basic to all the ways God relates to us as human beings.

Time and time again in the biblical story, we see God taking the initiative to call men and women into relationship with, and service to, himself. In Gen 3, for example, after disobeying God and eating from the tree, Adam and Eve hide themselves from God (vv. 8b, 10); but God *goes looking for them* (v. 9). Abraham is a pagan whom God calls to establish a new people for his name (Gen 12:1–3). In Exod 3, Moses is not in the desert drawing up plans for rescuing his people from Egypt—he is just tending sheep; but God calls Moses and sends him to be the divine instrument in the Lord's hand. Similarly, David has no royal pretensions whatsoever as he tends his father's sheep; but God steps in and makes it clear that he has chosen David to be king over Israel (1 Sam 16:12–13). And the apostle Paul obviously has a complete and unexpected reversal of course (directionally, spiritually, and vocationally) after Jesus appears to him and commissions him on the road to Damascus (Acts 9). How many other examples can you think of from the pages of Scripture where God takes the initiative to break into people's lives? (This is also this author's story, and probably yours as well.)

---

3. D. Peterson, *Engaging with God*, 36.
4. Castleman, *Story-Shaped Worship*, 37.

## The Biblical Pattern of Redemption

The primacy of God's initiative is likewise foundational to his work of redemption in both testaments.

### The Biblical Pattern of Redemption under the Old Covenant

God *reveals* himself to Abraham and makes (and reiterates, throughout Abraham's life) a series of promises (Gen 12:1–3; 15:5, 7, 18–21; 17:1–8; 22:15–18). Abraham *responds*, by first going where God shows him; and then, significantly, we read that Abraham "*believed* the LORD, and he counted it to him as righteousness" (Gen 15:6). Abraham was justified by responding in faith to God's revealed promises (as Rom 4:1–5 makes clear). (See p. 146.)

It is crucial to recognize that the Mosaic law and its sacrificial system were *not* a way of salvation for the people of Israel. The law was to be a way of life for a people whom God had *already* redeemed by his own sovereign and powerful initiative in the exodus. This perspective is clearly seen in Exod 20, where God through Moses gives the nation the Ten Commandments. Crucially, this delivery of the Ten Commandments does *not* start with Commandment One, but rather with God saying:

> "I am the LORD your God, who brought you out of the land of Egypt, out of the house of slavery." (Exod 20:2)

Then, and only then, does he proceed with "You shall have no other gods before me" and the other nine commandments. In other words, God is in essence saying to the people: "I *have* redeemed you; now this is how I want you to live in *response*."

Redemption from Egypt          Law, sacrificial system
(Exod 20:2)                    (Exod 20:3ff.)

Audrey Nash makes the same point: "The commandments were not a ladder to get to God, but showed an already redeemed people how to live as God's people";[5] as does James Torrance:

5. Nash, *Old Testament Story*, 31.

The liturgies of Israel were God-given ordinances of grace, witnesses to grace. The sacrifice of lambs and bulls and goats were not ways of placating an angry God, currying favor with God as in the pagan worship of the Baalim. They were God-given covenantal witnesses to grace.[6]

Torrance makes the broader assertion, citing Dietrich Bonhoeffer, that *"the indicatives of grace always precede the imperatives of law and obligation."*[7] This speaks likewise to the divine initiative in accord with his gracious nature. And we see this in Exod 20 above: "I . . . *have brought* you out of . . . slavery" (indicative); and now "you *shall have* no other gods before me" (imperative). In essence: "I *have done* this . . . so now, in response, *do* this."

### *The Biblical Pattern of Redemption under the New Covenant*

God's initiative in his redeeming work through Christ is clearly articulated by Paul in Eph 2:8–9:

> For by grace you have been saved through faith. And this is not your own doing; it is the gift of God, not a result of works, so that no one may boast.

This is immediately followed in v. 10 by:

> For we are his workmanship, created in Christ Jesus for good works, which God prepared beforehand, that we should walk in them.

Salvation by grace
through faith (Eph 2:8–9)

Response of works
(Eph 2:10; 1 Cor 6:20)

Once again we see what God *has done* (indicative), followed by what God *commands* in response (imperative). Similarly we read in 1 Cor 6:20: "You *have been* bought with a price; therefore *glorify* God in your body." Or, as the old hymn puts it, "Jesus paid it all, all to him I owe."

---

6. J. Torrance, *Worship, Community*, 60.

7. J. Torrance, *Worship, Community*, 70 (emphasis added).

## The Biblical Pattern of Worship

As mentioned above, worship is always a *response* to God's prior activity in revealing himself and showing himself gracious to us. As Christopher Cocksworth writes: "In worship the God who speaks is spoken to in return."[8] We find this pattern of worship through the Scriptures as well, as a few examples will demonstrate.

### The Fall

It has often been observed that Rom 1 is Paul's *theological commentary on Gen 3*; Gen 3 tells us what *happened*, and Rom 1 tells us what it *meant*.[9] In this light, we can see that in the fall Adam and Eve refused to respond faithfully to the revelation they had been given by God:

For his invisible attributes, his eternal power and divine nature, have been *clearly seen*, being *understood* through what has been made. (Rom 1:20)

For even though they knew God, they *did not honor him as God or give thanks*. (Rom 1:21)

They . . . worshiped and served the creature rather than the Creator. (Rom 1:25)

REVELATION   RESPONSE

Adam and Eve's fall into sin was *not* a result of ignorance or insufficient information: "they *knew God*." Rather, it was a refusal to give God the honor, thanks, and worship that he alone was due. (More on this in ch. 7.)

So at the very beginning of the biblical story there is a breakdown of the proper response to God's gracious revelation of himself. This, in

8. Cocksworth, *Holy, Holy, Holy*, 28.

9. This is what Morna Hooker says: "The sequence of events outlined in Rom. 1 reminds us of the story of Adam as it is told in Gen. 1–3. Of Adam it is supremely true that God manifests to him that which can be known of him (v. 19); that from the creation onwards, God's attributes were clearly discernible to him in the things which had been made, and that he was thus without excuse (v. 20). Adam, above and before all men, knew and allowed his heart to be darkened (v. 20). Adam's fall was the result of his desire to be as God, to attain knowledge of good and evil (Gen 3:5), so that, claiming to be wise, he in fact became a fool (v. 21). Thus he not only failed to give glory to God but, according to rabbinic tradition, himself lost the glory of God which was reflected on his face (v. 23). In believing the serpent's lie that his action would not lead to death (Gen. 3:4) he turned his back on the truth of God, and he obeyed, and thus gave his allegiance to a creature, the serpent, rather than to the creator (v. 25)" ("Adam in Romans 1," 77–78).

fact, is the central conflict of the Bible and indeed of all human history; we then see God working through human history to return to himself the proper worship of which he is alone worthy (finally fulfilled, of course, in the book of Revelation.) We will consider this in more depth in part 3.

### Altars in Genesis

One vivid example is observed by Robbie Castleman. She points out that at the time of the Old Testament patriarchs, all the surrounding peoples were also building altars and offering sacrifices on them. What they were hoping to do with these altars and these sacrifices was to invoke their gods, to appease them, to placate them, in hopes that the gods would be merciful to them, would make their crops bountiful, would give them victory in battle, etc. In the absence of direct revelation, they were left to guess at what they should do to gain favor with their gods. This is the pattern of other religions, as we have already seen, getting the order backwards:

CANAANITE ALTARS

Built to: invoke appease placate | In hopes of: mercy blessing

Castleman points out that in the book of Genesis, we find *exactly the opposite* situation: in every case that Noah, Abraham, Isaac, and Jacob built altars, it was only *after* God had appeared and spoken to them, and always in *response* to his self-initiated communication with them.

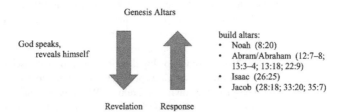

Genesis Altars

God speaks, reveals himself

build altars:
• Noah (8:20)
• Abram/Abraham (12:7–8; 13:3–4; 13:18; 22:9)
• Isaac (26:25)
• Jacob (28:18; 33:20; 35:7)

Revelation    Response

They built altars and sacrificed and worshiped God *in response* to God's *prior* speaking to them. Castleman states:

The importance of this distinction cannot be overstated. These altars were not erected to get a god's attention or to try to gain a god's favor but to mark the site of an encounter with the God who had revealed Himself to humans.[10]

## Abraham's Worship

As we have seen, God took the initiative to reveal himself to Abraham, calling him and making promises to him (Gen 12:1–3). God spoke to Abraham, showing him different aspects of his nature through names such as *El Shaddai* (God Almighty) and *Jehovah Jireh* (the LORD who sees/provides) and revealing himself through theophanies. And in response, we see Abraham's walk of worship, believing God (and that being counted towards him as righteousness [Gen 15:6]), building altars, and calling on the name of the Lord. God reveals his "name" (his nature), and Abraham responds in worship by calling on that name, that nature, those attributes, which God has revealed to him.

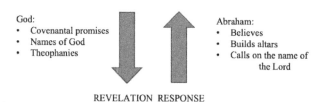

God:
- Covenantal promises
- Names of God
- Theophanies

Abraham:
- Believes
- Builds altars
- Calls on the name of the Lord

REVELATION  RESPONSE

10. Castleman, *Story-Shaped Worship*, 37. Her entire statement is: "Most Old Testament scholars acknowledge that these were altars compiled of rocks upon which an animal would be sacrificed in a way similar to that of neighboring Canaanites. However, what is noteworthy and counter to the surrounding culture is that many patriarchal altars were erected not to evoke a divine encounter but to commemorate such an encounter when God had met someone in a surprising way. The importance of this distinction cannot be overstated. These altars were not erected to get a god's attention or to try to gain a god's favor but to mark the site of an encounter with the God who had revealed himself to humans. To serve or to worship this God who proved himself faithful is a foundational idea for the practices of God's people. Christians do not worship or serve God to either merit or encourage divine faithfulness. Worship, mission, witness and all Christian service is a *response* to the God who has demonstrated his faithfulness already. The basic pattern of biblical worship evident in these texts is that it is God who initiates the encounter, not the worshiper. . . . Worship is a response to the call of God. Worship happens at the initiative of God's grace and is only made possible by his mediating presence on the worshiper's behalf. Throughout Scripture, biblical worship is increasingly marked by the need for God to provide the efficacious grace that makes worship acceptable and pleasing to him" (*Story-Shaped Worship*, 37).

## Psalms

A few examples from Psalms:

48:10 As is your Name, O God,⬇ ⬆ *so* is your praise to the ends of the earth.
(Praise to God is lifted up in response to his self-revelation.)

96:4 Great is the LORD ⬇ ⬆ and [therefore] greatly to be praised.
(Great praise is the commensurate response to God's greatness on display.)

⬆150:2 Praise him . . .
*according to* his excellent greatness. ⬇
(We praise him precisely for all the ways in which
he has shown himself to be excellently great.)

## Romans 12:1

This is one of the most important New Testament worship passages. After eleven chapters of expounding theologically about God's wondrous work in the world through Christ, Paul turns in Rom 12 to *application* after these amazing chapters of theology. So he says:

> I appeal to you therefore, brethren, by the mercies of God [i.e., in response to all that has gone before in the epistle], to present your bodies as a living sacrifice, holy and acceptable to God, which is your spiritual worship.

Paul says that an appropriate *response* to all those mercies that God has revealed, and that Paul himself has just expounded, is to present one's body (i.e., that is one's entire self) to God as a living sacrifice and as an offering of worship. *Worship* is the appropriate *response* to God's gracious initiative in showing his mercy to us in Jesus Christ.

Romans 12:1

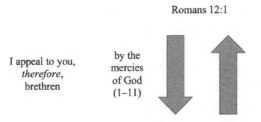

I appeal to you, *therefore,* brethren | by the mercies of God (1–11) | to present your bodies as a living sacrifice, holy and acceptable to God, which is your spiritual *worship.*

Revelation   Response

*Second Corinthians 1:20*

Here's another beautiful passage, where *with two little words* Paul sums up the whole of God's redemptive purposes for us. In Jesus Christ, he writes, all the promises of God are "Yes": God's gracious initiative towards us is, in effect, saying Yes to us in Jesus Christ. And, Paul goes on, because God has said Yes to us in Jesus Christ, all that is left for us to do is to say "Amen" in *response*. And all our worship, all our service, all our walk are simply ways of saying Amen to God, because by his gracious initiative he has said Yes to us in Christ. There is a fuller treatment of this passage on pp. 240–44.

2 Corinthians 1:20

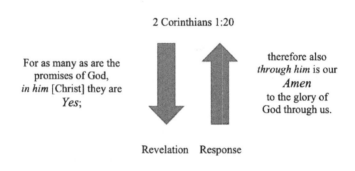

For as many as are the promises of God, *in him* [Christ] they are *Yes*;

therefore also *through him* is our *Amen* to the glory of God through us.

Revelation   Response

*Hebrews 10:19–22*

This is another of the most important New Testament worship passages. The writer has arrived at a summary application, after many chapters of expounding the superiority of Christ and of the new covenant (to Jewish believers who were in danger of returning to Judaism because of persecution). And he says "Therefore": because of what God has done and because what God is doing (as he has expounded in the letter up until this point); because we have confidence to enter the holy place by the blood of Jesus; because we have this great priest still over the house of God (the Lord Jesus interceding for us): because all that is true (*indicative*), we are to "draw near" (*imperative*), we are to respond by taking full advantage of the unique access we have to the Father because Jesus Christ has opened the way for us and is interceding for us in the Father's presence. So our worship is a *response* to what God has accomplished.

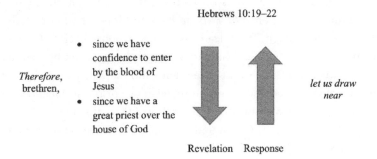

Hebrews 10:19–22

*Therefore, brethren,*

- since we have confidence to enter by the blood of Jesus
- since we have a great priest over the house of God

*let us draw near*

Revelation   Response

*Hebrews 2:12*

We will deal with this amazing little verse in more depth in ch. 26. The writer of Hebrews is quoting from Ps 22, but nevertheless says that these are the words of Jesus himself. Speaking to the Father, Jesus says, "[Father,] I will proclaim your name to my brethren, and in the midst of the congregation, I will sing your praise." Jesus is the agent of God's *revelation* to us (proclaiming to us the Father's *name*, or nature); *and* Jesus is the agent of our *response* back to God. As God, Jesus can mediate God's revelation to us; and as a human, he can mediate our response back to God; we see Jesus in the middle of both of those activities. This suggests the remarkable truth (which we will explore further in ch. 26) that this basic pattern of revelation and response, that we have seen weaving its way through all the Scriptures, finds its ultimate fulfillment in the person and ministry of Jesus Christ. *Jesus himself* is the ultimate fulfillment of the biblical pattern of revelation and response!

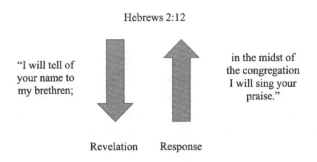

Hebrews 2:12

"I will tell of your name to my brethren;

in the midst of the congregation I will sing your praise."

Revelation     Response

God reveals himself to us through Christ; and it is through Christ that we offer our response of worship back to him—Jesus, our Mediator and our great High Priest, leads us in our response back to God. Jesus Christ, as both God and human, is the bridge between heaven and earth, between God and us, between deity and humanity *in both directions*: showing us God and then leading us in our response back to God. "Christian worship is grounded in the reality of the action of God toward the human soul in Jesus Christ and in man's responsive action through Jesus Christ."[11]

## Summary

So we see through these examples (and many more could be given, and indeed we will see many more as this book goes along in its examination of the Scriptures) that *"revelation and response" is the biblical pattern of worship*. But it always begins with *God's initiative*, showing us himself and showing himself gracious to us. As William Nicholls puts it:

> Our worship is our answer to God who has first addressed us. . . . Man worships the God who has made Himself known. . . . All our worship is but our response to the self-giving of God in revelation and redemption.[12]

Worship is always a *response* to the prior initiative of God towards us. We do not offer up our services, our sets, and our songs in hopes that by saying or singing or doing the right thing, God will be obligated to "show up" and bless us. John Witvliet states it even more starkly:

> Christian worship is not obeisance by which we appease a divine tyrant. We do not sing loud or pray hard in order to generate divine favor—a perfect theology of worship if we wanted to worship Baal.[13]

Rather, we gather under God's grace in grateful recognition of all the blessings he has conferred upon us in Christ. We lift our praises, not out of fear that we're going to miss something or lose out or not gain status with God. Instead we rest, we bask in the status we enjoy with him as his beloved children, because we are in Christ by his mercy.

11. Hoon, *Integrity of Worship*, 77.

12. Nicholls, *Jacob's Ladder*, 37, 53.

13. Witvliet, "What to Do," 242.

## Practical Implications for Our Worship

### The Word in Worship[14]

Because God's revelation is primary, "we must recognize the indispensable place of Scripture in both public and private devotion. It is the Word of God [revelation] which calls forth the worship of God [response]."[15] Edmund Clowney adds:

> In every task of the church, the ministry of the Word of God is central. It is the Word that calls us to worship, addresses us in worship, teaches us how to worship and enables us to praise God and to encourage one another.[16]

### The Problem

But the word of God is not central in many of our services. Douglas Smith writes:

> Why is it that many who would claim to be heirs of the Reformation, or who would at least call themselves "Bible-believers," have so little of the Bible in their public worship services?[17]

We who are Protestants love to proudly claim that we are "people of the book," yet too often (in the author's own experience) the worship service is predominantly sets of songs with little or no Scripture read— at least until the preacher gets up for the sermon.[18] A liturgical service (Catholic, Orthodox, or Anglican) probably includes ten times as much Scripture as the average free-church Protestant service—because in these liturgical traditions the Bible passages are built right into the liturgy. Free churches have to be more intentional to make sure the Scriptures have a prominent place.

14. For more on this subject, see Principle 4 in ch. 39.

15. Stott, *Romans*, 311.

16. Clowney, *Church*, 199.

17. D. Smith, "Sola Scriptura."

18. The author has sat in a number of services where the first word of Scripture heard was thirty to forty minutes in—when the sermon began.

*What's at Stake*

There may be devastating unintended consequences of neglecting the reading of Scripture in our services. We may be unwittingly suggesting that the Bible is not really all that important to living the Christian life—we just need to love Jesus, and praise Jesus, and all will be fine. (We of course don't believe that, but we need to be careful not to imply it.)

> When the role of Scripture in worship is negligible, when Scripture is used only to launch a sermon, what is communicated is that the Bible is marginal in Christian life, too. The use we make or fail to make of Scripture in our worship says far more about Christian discipleship than we may realize.[19]

*The Biblical Mandate*

Paul instructed Timothy (and thereby all pastors) to "devote yourself to the public reading of Scripture" (1 Tim 4:13) and "let the word of Christ dwell richly among you" (Col 3:16).

> Recovering the centrality of scripture in our worship makes it clear that we understand the Bible to be God's Word to God's people here and now. Scripture is read, not just for a sermon text, but to hear what word God addresses to the gathered congregation.[20]

The Bible is the word *of God*, and when it is read it is the God of the universe wanting to speak to his precious people. What a privilege to hear him speak to us![21]

*More of the Word*

So more of the Scripture is called for, in both our private and our public worship. In our services, that may mean:

---

19. White, "Making Our Worship," 38.

20. White, "Making Our Worship," 38.

21. For more reflections on the leader's spoken guidance of the congregation in the worship service, see appendix 1, "Think before You Speak!"

- Printing (if your church uses a bulletin) or projecting a verse or verses (if it is a thematic service, verses relating to the day's theme) for people to see and meditate on as they enter the service

- Evaluating the songs we sing on the basis of Scripture

- Choosing songs to go with Scripture, not Scripture to go with songs!

- Using the Scriptures in different and creative ways: read, sing, recite, pray, memorize, act out

- Reading longer passages of Scripture, not just isolated verses

- Using unison, responsive, antiphonal readings

- Having someone read from the midst of congregation

- Assembling original responsive readings

This last point is exceedingly easy with the resources available to us today: computer Bible concordances make it very simple to search for verses on a particular theme; and then they can be arranged into a responsive reading that powerfully demonstrates what God has to say about that theme in many different places in his word.

In other words, "devote yourself to the public reading of Scripture"—but do not always do it exactly the same way! Bring some creativity to bear on the presenting of the word of God before his people.

Tim Keller notes:

> C. S. Lewis once told a young writer: "Instead of telling us a thing is 'terrible,' describe it so that we'll be terrified. Don't say it was a 'delight,' make us say 'delightful' when we've read the description. You see, all those words ('Horrifying,' 'wonderful,' 'hideous,' 'exquisite') are only saying to your readers, 'Please, will you do my job for me.'"
>
> Lewis complains that authors of gushy and sentimental words are tyrannical because they tell the readers how they must feel rather than letting the subject work on them in the same way it did the author.
>
> Sentimental worship leading works in exactly the same way that Lewis describes. With typical comments "Isn't He just wonderful?" "Isn't it such a blessing?"—the leader tells people how they ought to feel about God instead of telling them about God.[22]

22. Timothy J. Keller, "Reformed Worship in the Global City," in Carson, *Worship by the Book*, 209–10; citing *Letters of C. S. Lewis*, 271.

Let God speak through his word! And may his people take heart from the privilege of hearing from their Creator and Redeemer as they hear.

## *The Call to Worship*[23]

In fact, from our study of revelation and response it should be clear that we need to let God have the first word. We have nothing to say to him until he speaks! As Nicholls puts it, "Our worship is our answer to God who has *first* addressed us. Man worships the God who has made Himself known."[24]

Far from being a remnant of "traditional" or "liturgical" worship (as some contemporary worship advocates claim), a Call to Worship is a powerful statement at the front of the service that it is God who is inviting us into his presence, and not we inviting him (he never left!).[25] Bryan Chapell says:

> The host of the worship service is divine. We do not invite him to be present. He invites us to, "Come before him" (Ps 100:2). God calls us from all other preoccupations to join the people he has redeemed in recognition, praise and service of his omnipresent glory. Because the call to worship is from God, we are reminded that he always initiates; we respond. This is a profound truth not only for our salvation, but also for our worship of the One who saves us. The call to worship is not simply a perfunctory greeting of human cordiality, but is at once a weighty responsibility and a joyful privilege. . . . The traditions of each church and occasion will help determine the appropriateness of gathering people from stray thoughts and conversations with informal words of welcome (e.g., "Good morning. How good to have you here in God's house!"), but the privileges and responsibilities of the call to worship that actually commences our focus on revering God are too good to displace with comments regarding the weather and yesterday's football game. . . . God does not simply invite us to a party of friends, or a lecture on religion, or a concert of sacred music—he invites us into the presence of the King of the Universe before whom all creation will bow and for whom all heaven now sings. With the call to worship God's people are invited to participate in the wondrous praise that already and

23. For more on this subject, see appendix 2, "Whose Gathering Is It, Anyhow?"

24. Nicholls, *Jacob's Ladder*, 37 (emphasis added).

25. "Worship is a dialogue, but the initial call comes from God who begins the conversation" (Paquier, *Dynamics of Worship*, 8).

eternally enraptures the hosts of heaven. This awesome news and great privilege should be reflected with appropriate enthusiasm and joy by the worship leader in the call to worship. Such a call will typically lead directly into a corporate or choral hymn of praise as God's people respond to the blessings of worship into which they are called.[26]

So let us not start our services by saying, "Let's just praise the Lord!" Rather, let us reflect the biblical dynamic by first hearing from God and about God: theology leading to doxology. For many years our church referred to this Call to Worship as the "Scriptural Invitation." The first word the congregation heard from up front was the word of God, inviting us to "draw near" (Heb 10:22).

> By using the words of Scripture as a call to worship, the leader automatically urges God's people to respond to his disclosure of his own nature and purposes. This pattern established by the call to worship shapes the rest of the worship service. We do not approach God on our terms, but his. When he speaks, it is our obligation and privilege to respond appropriately in praise, prayer, repentance, testimony, encouragement of others, and service to what he declares about himself. This corporate dialogue in which we as God's people respond to God's revelation is the sacred rhythm of covenant worship that begins with the call to worship.[27]

So we see that the biblical pattern of revelation and response can and should be reflected from the very start and throughout the service.

## The Dialogue of Worship

And so worship involves a cycle, a "sacred rhythm" (in Chapell's words above) of revelation and response.[28] Worship is in fact a *dialogue* between God and his people. And in any healthy dialogue, one side does not do all the talking. We need to listen to God, and not just talk (and sing) to him. Both parts are important (and as we saw in Heb 2:12, Jesus himself is actively involved in both).

---

26. Chapell, "Call to Worship," 1–2.

27. Chapell, "Call to Worship," 2.

28. "The distinctive genius of corporate worship is the two-beat rhythm of revelation and response. God speaks; we answer. God acts; we accept and give. God gives; we receive" (Martin, *Worship of God*, 6).

There are two aspects to worship, God's address to us and our response to His address. The former consists particularly in the reading and preaching of the Word, and the latter in adoration, reception, thanksgiving, and prayer.[29]

Scripture should constitute the very content for much of what we say, sing, and pray in worship. When this is the case, Scripture permeates the service from beginning to end. Scripture forms the basis for all of worship.[30]

Balance is important. This is true in our private worship, where through Bible reading (↓ revelation) and then adoration and prayer (↑ response) we have the privilege of dialoguing with (hearing from *and* speaking to) God. And it is vital in corporate worship—that we hear God speak through his word and respond back to him. We can represent the dialogue of worship with a series (rather than a single set) of alternating arrows:

Some elements of the service are more *revelation* in nature:

Call to worship
Scripture readings
Preaching
Scripture songs
Songs about God's character and acts

And some are more *response* in nature:

Songs of praise, lament, etc.
Prayer
Confession
Meditation
Lord's Supper
Commitment

Those who plan services need to give careful thought to the need for balance in this dialogue of worship.[31]

29. Murray, "Church," 239.

30. Cherry, *Worship Architect*, 80.

31. "A Christmas Festival of Lessons and Carols," which originated in the Anglican Church but is now celebrated annually in many kinds of churches, of course also displays this balanced rhythm of revelation (the "lessons") and response (the "carols").

## Completing the Cycle

We need to be careful to complete the cycle of revelation and response or, as John Stott calls it, of theology and doxology.[32] Neither should stand on its own. As noted earlier, J. I. Packer reputedly insisted that "the purpose of theology is doxology. We study in order to praise."

### No Theology without Doxology

Similarly, as we have also seen earlier, John Stott writes:

> There should be *no theology without doxology*. There is something fundamentally flawed about a purely academic interest in God. No, the true knowledge of God will always lead us to worship, as it did Paul. Our place is on our faces before Him in adoration.[33]

We see in the book of Romans a beautiful example of how indeed "the true knowledge of God" led Paul to worship. In chs. 1–11, Paul had been laying out some of the most profound theology ever written, through the inspiration of the Holy Spirit. And then suddenly it seems that he could contain himself no longer: at the end of ch. 11, he burst forth in praise. His theology led him to doxology, and he exclaimed:

> Oh, the depth of the riches and wisdom and knowledge of God! How unsearchable are his judgments and how inscrutable his ways!
> "For who has known the mind of the Lord,
> or who has been his counselor?
> Or who has given a gift to him
> that he might be repaid?"
> For from him and through him and to him are all things.
> To him be glory forever! Amen. (11:33–36)

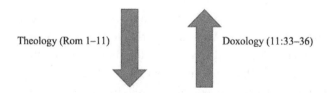

Theology (Rom 1–11)          Doxology (11:33–36)

32. From the Greek, *theology* is literally a "word about God," and *doxology* is "a word of praise."

33. Stott, *Romans*, 311–12 (emphasis added).

Paul was not just a great theologian; he was a great worshiper as well! And what God had revealed to him, which he laid out in these early chapters, made him burst forth in praise for the wonder and wisdom of this God who had dealt so graciously with humankind. This theology inevitably led him to doxology.

In our study of the Bible also, we must be careful always to wed theology with doxology. In ch. 3 we referenced the occupational hazard in all realms of biblical study (Bible college, seminary, personal study, even sermon preparation) that we miss the forest for the trees by concerning ourselves with learning the facts and the doctrines of the text, without then turning it back to God in praise for what we have learned about him.

When I was studying music at the university, I worked in the choral department of a large music store in my town. The manager of that department was a leading authority on sacred choral music. He knew everything on the subject. Somebody would come in and say, I need something of this sort for a particular occasion, and he would go right to the files and pull out multiple suggestions. He knew who wrote what, who set which Scripture texts, who the publisher was, what was really good and what was less so. It was astonishing. However, he was a vulgar and profane man who had no love for God and no love for the church, while at the same time being an authority on *sacred* choral music. That was simply an academic pursuit, an area of specialization, for him. What a tragedy! He missed the forest for the trees; there was no doxology to go with the theology.

No theology without doxology. "The *purpose* of theology is doxology; we study in order to praise." That is true on all levels, not just for adults, but for children, youth, all the way up. We are not just teaching Bible stories or Bible facts or how to find references in the Bible. We teach our young people to know the Bible, *so that* they will learn to love the God of the Bible.

Bible knowledge is meaningless unless we turn what we have learned back to God in praise for the things we have seen of him. We must give our response to revelation. We want to bring forth the responsive doxology from the theology. And so we teach the Bible: to children, to youth, to adults, to draw forth the praise of their hearts. And we read and preach the Scriptures in corporate worship as well, to engender a gathered response of praise among the people of God.

## No Doxology without Theology

John Stott in the same passage quoted above goes on to say:

> There can be *no doxology without theology*. It is not possible to worship an unknown god. All true worship is a response to the self-revelation of God in Christ and Scripture, and arises from our reflection on who he is and what he has done. The worship of God is evoked, informed and inspired by the vision of God. Worship without theology is bound to degenerate into idolatry. Hence the indispensable place of Scripture in both public and private devotion. It is the Word of God which calls forth the worship of God.[34]

Or, as the Scottish preacher Eric Alexander states, "God needs to be known before He can be worshiped."[35]

This goes back to the necessity of significant Scripture use in our services, as well as to the importance of worship leaders and planners receiving Bible training so they can handle the Scripture competently in their ministry. God's people need to "praise him *according to* his excellent greatness" (Ps 150:2). This is the pattern throughout the psalms. The psalms are of course full of praise, but that praise never just comes out of the blue. The psalmists always state a *reason* for praising God: for his work in creation, for his mighty works of rescue and redemption, for his steadfast love. He is then praised for these things.

## The Cycle Completed

Stott goes on to summarize both sides of his argument by stating, "As I believe Bishop Handley Moule said at the end of the last century, we must 'beware equally of an undevotional theology and of an untheological devotion.'"[36]

Bob Kauflin writes:

> In the best worship songs, the two elements are combined: subjective lyrics express the heart's response to lyrics that state objective truth about God with clarity, precision, poeticism, and power.[37]

34. Stott, *Romans*, 311 (emphasis added).
35. Alexander, "Worship: Old Testament Pattern."
36. Stott, *Romans*, 312.
37. Kauflin, "Praise Choruses."

He is calling for wholehearted praise, but which rises out of (and is re-sponding to) a clear biblical vision of the majesty and goodness of God.

A vivid example of this can be found in Stuart K. Hine's familiar hymn "How Great Thou Art." In the first verse of this great hymn, the lyricist reflects on the wonders of God seen in creation:

O Lord, my God, when I in awesome wonder
Consider all the worlds Thy hands have made:
I see the stars, I hear the rolling thunder,
Thy power throughout the universe displayed:

Then the refrain praises God in response:

Then sings my soul, my Savior God, to Thee:
"How great Thou art, how great Thou art!"
Then sings my soul, my Savior God, to Thee:
"How great Thou art, how great Thou art!"

Similarly, verse 3 considers the grace of God demonstrated in the cross of Christ:

And when I think that God, His Son not sparing,
Sent Him to die, I scarce can take it in;
That on the cross, my burden gladly bearing
He bled and died to take away my sin:

And the refrain again responds with praise:

Then sings my soul, my Savior God, to Thee:
"How great Thou art, how great Thou art!"
Then sings my soul, my Savior God, to Thee:
"How great Thou art, how great Thou art!"

We can help to complete the cycle by:

1. Balancing elements of revelation and response
   One seminary professor has his students mark a service bulletin or schedule with up and down arrows according to the nature of each part (and horizontal arrows as well, for body-life/fellowship-type functions in the service).

2. Using Scripture as a lead-in to singing
   A practical example: how much more powerful, if we are going to sing a song about the holiness of God, to first read from Isa 6:3: "Holy, holy, holy is the LORD of hosts; the whole earth is full of his glory!" And then we sing the song in response to what God has said in his word about his holiness: our doxology is based on theology.

3. Allowing for a significant response after preaching
   Rather than a quick closing of the service (because no time remains, or because it is lunchtime), plan a significant time for prayer (silent reflection is especially effective after a challenge from the pulpit), singing, and perhaps a call to commitment.

4. Regarding the entire service as worship
   This means rejecting the duality of worship/sermon, and seeing the entire service as *a ministry of the word and of worship*.

The dynamic of the dialogue of worship, and the need to complete the cycle, was clearly understood by Martin Luther. On the door into the sanctuary of the Castle Church in Wittenberg, Germany (on the opposite side of the church from the famous door where he posted his Ninety-Five Theses in 1517, which touched off the Protestant Reformation), there is inscribed a quotation from Luther.

**Castle Church**

The Restored "Wittenberg Door"

The Luther Quote[38]

Translated from the German, the quote says:

"It should always happen
in this house of God
that *the Lord speaks to us*
through his holy Word,

and that *we then speak to him*
with our prayers
and songs of praise."

## The Foundation of Foundations for Worship

The most basic of all foundations for our worship is, then, *the word of God*. For the word is the record of God's special revelation, and it is that revelation that calls forth the response of worship.

38. Above three photos by author.

John Stott writes:

> To worship God . . . is to "glory in his holy name" (Ps 105:3),
> that is, to revel adoringly in who he is in his revealed character.
> But before we can glory in God's name, we must know it. Hence
> the propriety of the reading and preaching of the Word of God
> in public worship, and of biblical meditation in private devo-
> tion. These things are not an intrusion into worship; they form
> the necessary foundation of it. God must speak to us before we
> have any liberty to speak to him. He must disclose to us who he
> is before we can offer him what we are in acceptable worship.
> The worship of God is always a response to the Word of God.
> Scripture wonderfully directs and enriches our worship.[39]

Similarly, Constance Cherry points out:

> Scripture should constitute the very content for much of what
> we say, sing, and pray in worship. When this is the case, Scrip-
> ture permeates the service from beginning to end. Scripture
> forms the basis for all of worship.[40]

And Ligon Duncan notes:

> Our motto for public worship in our congregations ought to be:
> "Read the Bible, preach the Bible, pray the Bible, sing the Bible."[41]

True worship will always be *biblical* worship.[42]

## Additional Resources (Details in Bibliography)

- Brink and Witvliet, *The Worship Sourcebook*
- Cherry, *The Worship Architect*
- Crider, *Scripture-Guided Worship: A Call to Pastors & Worship Leaders*
- Furr and Price, *The Dialogue of Worship: Creating Space for Revelation and Response*

---

39. Stott, *Contemporary Christian*, 174.

40. Cherry, *Worship Architect*, 80.

41. Duncan, "Foundations," 65.

42. That is why the worship study section of the Evangelical Theological Society took the name *Biblical Worship* (etsworship.wordpress.com).

- Ron Man, "Worship and the Word" (audio and outline)
- Witvliet, "Isaiah in Christian Liturgy"

## Quotes on the Place of Scripture in Worship

Why is it that many who would claim to be heirs of the Reformation, or who would at least call themselves "Bible-believers," have so little of the Bible in their public worship services? . . .

I looked in vain, last Sunday, as I glanced down the bulletin for any mention of biblical lessons. Finally, when I had just about given up hope of any use of scripture in the service, a couple of verses were read as an introduction to the sermon. . . . If we really believe, as we profess, that scripture is central to the Christian life, then it ought also to be central in our worship life. That Sunday bulletin is an important statement of faith. If the bulletin makes it clear that scripture is an important part of Christian worship, then we can be sure people will get the message that the Bible is crucial in shaping their lives as Christians. But, when the role of scripture in worship is negligible, when scripture is used only to launch a sermon, what is communicated is that the Bible is marginal in Christian life, too. The use we make or fail to make of scripture in our worship says far more about Christian discipleship than we may realize.

The first step toward making our worship more biblical is in giving the reading of God's Word a central role in Christian worship on any occasion. . . . Recovering the centrality of scripture in our worship makes it clear that we understand the Bible to be God's Word to God's people here and now. Scripture is read, not just for a sermon text, but to hear what word God addresses to the gathered congregation.[43]

Word and worship belong indissolubly to each other. All worship is an intelligent and loving response to the revelation of God, because it is the adoration of his Name. . . . Preaching is making known the Name of the Lord, and worship is praising the Name of the Lord made known.[44]

Whatever our denomination (or "non-denomination"), if we believe the Bible, we need to intentionally integrate Scripture into the public gathering of God's people. Most Bible-believing churches will have Scripture read in the sermon or just before

43. White, "Making Our Worship," 38.
44. Stott, *Between Two Worlds*, 31.

it, at the least. But many churches will have no more Scripture than that. There are multiple ways to use Scripture in the service, including as transitions to hymns. But one of the best ways of showing the centrality of God's written revelation is by the regular, systematic, public reading of God's Word.[45]

The Bible is not simply read aloud in order to convey information, to teach doctrine or ethics or history, though of course it does that too. It is read aloud as the effective sign that all that we do is done as a response to God's living and active word, the word which, as Isaiah says, accomplishes God's purpose in the world, abiding for ever while all flesh withers like the grass. The place of scripture in Christian worship means that both in structure and content God's initiative remains primary, and all that we do remains a matter of response.[46]

> Revelation and Response is the pattern of all of God's interactions with humankind, and of all true worship

45. D. Smith, "Sola Scriptura."
46. N. T. Wright, "Freedom and Framework."

# 5

# THE GOD WE WORSHIP

B ecause worship is *about* God, and worship is *for* God (see ch. 3 above), when we study worship it makes sense that we should begin by considering the person of God—this God whom we worship. We will do that in this chapter, building on what we have already seen about the biblical pattern of worship: revelation and response/theology and doxology.

Bob Sjogren observes that when high schoolers receive their copy of their school yearbook, the first thing every one of them invariably does is to turn to one's own picture. It is a very natural and normal thing, Sjogren states, for a student to want to see how his or her photo turned out in this very public arena.[1]

---

1. (We would all do the same!) I have adapted this idea for use in classes overseas (where school yearbooks may not be a concept the students understand). At this point in the course, I have the entire class stand and arrange themselves for a group photo. After taking the photo, I go around and show the photo to each student. Then I ask them, "What is the very first thing you looked at when I showed you the photo of the class?" Invariably, of course, each student must acknowledge looking first at his or her own photo. I explain how normal and natural this is, but then pivot towards warning against this approach to the Bible.

**Springbrook High School, Silver Spring, Maryland, Class of 1970**
**(Author appears in center of second to last row.)**

However, Sjogren laments, too many Christians take the same approach to the Bible; he calls this our "yearbook theology." We turn to the
Bible and look first for *ourselves*. But the Bible is not primarily about us;
it is about *God*. It is God's book, God's story. We do not even turn up until
the very end of Gen 1 (vv. 26–28), as the climax of an enormous flurry of
creative activity by God.[2]

The Bible is not about me. It is important to look first for God because
it is his book and his story. In fact, the Bible is *the story of God's glory*.[3]

## The Story of God's Glory

What do we mean when we talk about the glory of God? Some would say
his holiness, some his majesty, some his absolute sovereignty. God's glory
encompasses all of this, and more. It is not a single attribute of God, as
is, for instance, his love or his wisdom or his power. It is not *an* attribute

2. See Sjogren and Robison, *Cat & Dog Theology*. The title plays on the contrasting
traits of cats ("you exist to serve me") and dogs ("I exist to serve you"), and the book
urges a God-centered rather than a me-centered view of life.

3. See the wonderful article by Steve Hawthorne, "Story of His Glory."

of God, but rather, it is the sum of *all* his attributes, all his perfections, all those things that make him God, all his "God-ness." In that sense, it is the greatest subject of all!

God's glory speaks of his complete and utter perfection in every way. John Piper defines and describes the glory of God as "the beauty of the full panorama of His perfections . . . and the perfectly harmonious way they are expressed in creation and history."[4] It is all of the ways in which God is holy and majestic and sovereign; it is, in Piper's words again, "his greatness, his beauty, and his worth on display."[5]

When we come to the Bible, we find that there are *hundreds* of references throughout its pages to the glory of God. The Bible is indeed *the story of his glory.*[6]

## God's Glory in Creation

God created all things for his glory:

> There is one God, the Father, from whom are all things and for whom we exist. (1 Cor 8:6)

> [God,] for whom and by whom all things exist . . . (Heb 2:10)

> For from him and through him and to him are all things. To him be glory forever. Amen. (Rom 11:36)

David exclaims that "the heavens declare the glory of God" (Ps 19:1). That is why the heavens are there; that is why God put them there: to show something of his glory. But not only did God create the heavens for his glory, he created *us* for his glory as well:

> "Bring my sons from afar
> and my daughters from the end of the earth,
> everyone who is called by my name,
> *whom I created for my glory,*
> whom I formed and made." (Isa 43:6–7)

Sometimes untaught Christians can think something like: "Maybe God made us because he was lonely, or he didn't feel complete, or he needed somebody to love." And, of course, all those things are terribly

---

4. Piper, *Providence*, 43–44.

5. Piper, *Providence*, 44.

6. For a more comprehensive survey of "Biblical Texts to Show God's Zeal for His Own Glory," see Piper, *Let the Nations Be Glad*, 41–46.

wrong. God is God. He is complete in and of himself. He does not lack anything. He does not need anything.[7] In fact, the doctrine of the Trinity tells us that before the creation of the universe, God himself existed *in community*, in an eternal community of love and fellowship among Father, Son, and Holy Spirit (see John 17:24).

God did not *need* to create us, but he *did* create us to show forth his glory in us, as those created in his image.[8]

## God's Glory and the Fall

The glory of God was at issue in the fall as well. Here again is that passage in Rom 1 where Paul explains the fall of Adam and Eve into sin:

> For although they knew God, they *did not glorify him as God* or give thanks to him,
> but they became futile in their thinking, and their foolish hearts were darkened.
> Claiming to be wise, they became fools, and exchanged *the glory of the immortal God*
>     for images resembling mortal man and birds and animals and creeping things. . . .
> They exchanged the truth about God for a lie
>     and worshiped and served the creature rather than the Creator, who is blessed forever! Amen. (Rom 1:21–23, 25)

The fall was a terribly wrong decision about the glory of God. Adam and Eve were created for God's glory; but in the fall, they did not give him the glory he deserved. Instead they turned to honor images and creatures (including themselves), and led the entire human race down that path.

Romans 3:23 reflects the same perspective:

> All have sinned and fall short of the glory of God.

Because of sin, we fail to show forth the glory of God as we were created to do.

---

7. Paul said: "The God who made the world and everything in it, being Lord of heaven and earth, does not live in temples made by man, nor is he served by human hands, *as though he needed anything*, since he himself gives to all mankind life and breath and everything" (Acts 17:24–25).

8. And the creation command to Adam and Eve to "be fruitful and multiply and fill the earth" (Gen 1:28) meant they were to fill the earth with image-bearers of God!

John Piper has written, "The essence of sin is the belittling of God's glory."[9] Adam and Eve decided they wanted things their way, not God's; and so do we. Even though they *knew* God, they did not give him the glory or give thanks, but they went their own way and worshiped and served the creature rather than the Creator.

## God's Glory in Israel

As God's special covenant people, the nation of Israel was to reflect God's glory as well:

> "You are my servant, Israel, in whom I will be glorified." (Isa 49:3)

## God's Glory Seen in Jesus Christ

Of course, the ultimate display of God's glory is found in the person of Jesus Christ:

> And the Word became flesh and dwelt among us,
> and we have seen his glory, glory as of the only Son
> from the Father, full of grace and truth. (John 1:14)

> God . . . has spoken to us by his Son. . . .
> He is the radiance of the glory of God
> and the exact imprint of his nature. (Heb 1:1–3)

We see the glory of God in Jesus Christ throughout the life and ministry of Christ:

1. His preincarnate glory

   > "And now, Father, glorify me in your own presence with the glory that I had with you before the world existed." (John 17:5)

2. His incarnate glory foretold

   > Isaiah said these things because he saw his glory and spoke of him. (John 12:41)

3. His incarnation

---

9. Piper, *Pleasures of God*, 158.

And the Word became flesh and dwelt among us, and we have
seen his glory, glory as of the only Son from the Father. (John 1:14)

4. His ministry

This, the first of his signs, Jesus did at Cana in Galilee, and manifested his glory. (John 2:11)

5. His suffering and death

But we see him who for a little while was made lower than the
angels, namely Jesus, crowned with glory and honor because of
the suffering of death, so that by the grace of God he might taste
death for everyone. (Heb 2:9)

6. His resurrection

who through him are believers in God, who raised him from
the dead and gave him glory, so that your faith and hope are in
God. (1 Pet 1:21)

7. His ascension

He was manifested in the flesh,
    vindicated by the Spirit,
    seen by angels,
    proclaimed among the nations,
    believed on in the world,
    taken up in glory. (1 Tim 3:16)

8. His exaltation

"And now, Father, glorify me in your own presence with the
glory that I had with you before the world existed." (John 17:5)

9. His second coming

They will suffer the punishment of eternal destruction, away from
the presence of the Lord and from the glory of his might, when
he comes on that day to be glorified in his saints. (1 Thess 1:9–10)

## God's Glory Seen in Redemption

This great passage about the blessings of our redemption from Eph 1
mentions the glory of God three times:

Blessed be the God and Father of our Lord Jesus Christ,
> who has blessed us in Christ with every spiritual blessing in
> the heavenly places,
> even as he chose us in him before the foundation of the
> world,
> that we should be holy and blameless before him.
In love he predestined us for adoption to himself as sons through
> Jesus Christ,
> according to the purpose of his will
> *to the praise of his glorious grace,*
> with which he has blessed us in the Beloved. . . .
In him we have obtained an inheritance, having been predestined
> according to the purpose of him who works all things ac-
> cording to the counsel of his will,
> so that we who were the first to hope in Christ might be
> *to the praise of his glory.*
In him you also, when you heard the word of truth, the gospel
> of your salvation,
> and believed in him, were sealed with the promised Holy Spirit,
> who is the guarantee of our inheritance until we acquire
> possession of it,
> *to the praise of his glory.* (Eph 1:3–6, 11–14)

*To the praise of his glorious grace, to the praise of his glory, to the praise of his glory.* God not only *created* us for his glory, but he *redeemed* us for his glory as well. John Piper says that this passage shows that "the ultimate goal of God in initiating the entire plan of salvation before creation was that he would be praised for the glory of his grace."[10] He sees Paul as showing us:

- Our *predestination* for the praise of God's glory (1:4–6)

- Our *existence* for the praise of God's glory (1:12)

- Our *inheritance* for the praise of God's glory (1:14)[11]

Paul says this in Rom 15 as well:

> For I tell you that Christ became a servant to the circumcised to
> show God's truthfulness
> in order to confirm the promises given to the patriarchs,
> and in order that the Gentiles *might glorify God for his mercy.*
> (Rom 15:8–9)

10. Piper, *Providence*, 55.
11. Piper, *Providence*, 55.

God redeems that he might receive *glory* for his mercy and his grace; he created us for his *glory*, and redeemed us for his *glory*.[12]

We have already considered Rom 1, and all the implications of the fact that even though Adam and Eve "knew God, they did not *glorify* him as God or give thanks to him." We saw the cascade of negative results that resulted from this wrong decision about God's glory.

But we find that, when Christ comes and redeems us by his grace, he puts all those things right that went so terribly wrong in the fall. In the terminology of Rom 1, Christ redeems us:

- So that we can once again *glorify* God as God and give thanks.

- So that we can exchange images and idols for the *glory* of the incorruptible God.

- So that we can exchange the lie for the truth of God.

- So that we can worship and serve the Creator once again rather than the creature.

## God's Glory and Sanctification

God *created* us for his glory; he *redeemed* us for his glory; and he wants us to *live* for his glory:[13]

> Whether you eat or drink or whatever you do, do all to the *glory* of God. (1 Cor 10:31)

(We will come back to this key verse again and again, as it speaks powerfully to the truth of worship being *all of life*.)

In Jesus's description of himself as the true Vine in John 15, and our need to be connected to him as branches if we are to bear fruit, he further remarks:

> By this my Father is *glorified*, that you bear much fruit and so prove to be my disciples. (John 15:8)

12. John Piper observes the emphasis of the verse: "Paul does not say, 'Christ became a servant in order that the Gentiles might *receive mercy*.' He says, 'Christ became a servant in order that the Gentiles might glorify God for receiving mercy.' The ultimate aim of the gospel is God—God glorified for his mercy" ("Gospel Worship").

13. "This is why you came into the world. This is why God made you, and redeemed you: in order that you might live for his glory alone. That is the key to worship" (Alexander, "Worship: Chief End").

Jesus is saying that when we bear fruit, the Father is *glorified* because we are showing that we are his disciples and bear fruit in our lives by being connected, and *only* by being connected, to the Vine, who is Jesus Christ. So our fruit gives God *glory*, because it shows that fruit as Jesus's disciples comes only through and with the empowerment that he gives through Christ.

Peter makes an analogous point:

> As each has received a gift, use it to serve one another, as good stewards of God's varied grace: whoever speaks, as one who speaks oracles of God; whoever serves, as one who serves by the strength that God supplies—in order that in everything God may be *glorified* through Jesus Christ. To him belong glory and dominion forever and ever. Amen. (1 Pet 4:11)

Our service, our fruit, our ministry: no one can ever say, "I did it myself"; but rather, "I did it by the strength that God supplies." God receives the *glory* for what we accomplish in his name. Or, as John Piper puts it: "*We get the grace; and God gets the glory.*"

## God's Glory in the Church

> To him be glory in the church and in Christ Jesus throughout all generations, forever and ever. Amen. (Eph 3:21)

God *created* us for his glory. He *redeemed* us for his glory. He wants us to *live* for his glory. He wants his glory to be seen in *Israel* (under the old covenant) and in the *church* (under the new covenant). And, ultimately, in *heaven*.

## God's Glory in Heaven

> And the city has no need of sun or moon to shine on it, for the *glory* of God gives it light, and its lamp is the Lamb. (Rev 21:23)

In the new Jerusalem the glory of God illumines and fills all.

> To him who sits on the throne and to the lamb be blessing and honor and *glory* and dominion forever and ever! (Rev 5:13)

Heaven is the place where the *glory* of God is finally acknowledged and celebrated above all.

## The Story of His Glory

We thus get a little glimpse of how the Bible, from the beginning to end, is *the story of God's glory*. Paul summarizes this truth for us magnificently in the grand doxology we have looked at already:

> For *from* him
> and *through* him
> and *to* him are all things.
> To him be *glory* forever. Amen.
> (Rom 11:36)

What a powerful statement! All things have their origin in him. All things remain in existence through him. He is the goal and purpose of all things: everything is created and intended to display and vindicate his infinite *glory*.

The Bible is the story of God creating us for his glory; redeeming us for his glory; wanting us to live for his glory and give him glory through all of our lives; and, finally, filling all of heaven with his glory (Rev 21:23).[14]

And so, as we come to the Bible, it is important to remember that it is not about us. Primarily it is about *God and his glory*:

> Not to us, O LORD, not to us, but to your name give glory. (Ps 115:1a)[15]

## The Glory of God and Worship

### Defining Worship

Since worship is about God and for God, and since we have begun our study by looking at the person of God and considering his all-encompassing glory, it stands to reason that we can now define worship in terms of what we have just been considering:

> *Worship is our response to the glory of God—*
> *all that we are responding to all that God is.*

14. Christopher Wright adds this perspective:
"'Glory be to the Father, and to the Son, and to the Holy Ghost,
    As it was in the beginning, is now, and ever shall be,
    World without end, Amen.'
This is not just a liturgically conventional way to end prayers and canticles. It is a missional perspective on history past, present and future, and one day it will be the song of the whole creation" (*Mission of God*, 64).

15. See also Piper, "Biblical Texts."

The glory of God, as we have seen, speaks of all that God is in his infinite perfections. And worship is all the ways in which we respond to that glory. Or, to unpack it a bit further, worship is:

1. Recognizing the glory of God with our *minds*

2. Cherishing the glory of God with our *hearts*

3. Proclaiming the glory of God with our *mouths*

4. Celebrating the glory of God in *all of life*

It is important to know *about* the glory of God, but that is not enough. James 2:19 says: "You believe that God is one; you do well. Even the demons believe—and shudder!" Even the demons recognize the glory of God, but they don't love it or love him—they don't worship him. We must not only *recognize* God's glory, but *cherish* it. And then we are to *proclaim* it, personally and corporately, and also *celebrate* it, live in its light, in all of life:

> Whether you eat or drink or whatever you do, do all for the glory of God. (1 Cor 10:31)

> You have been bought with a price, therefore glorify God in your body. (1 Cor 6:20)

Glorifying God, giving God glory, is what worship is all about. See the parallel of "worship" and "glorify" in Ps 89:6:

> All the nations you have made shall come
> and *worship* before you, O Lord,
> and shall *glorify* your name.

## Responding to God's Glory

Worship is our appropriate *response* to all the ways in which God has demonstrated his glory throughout the scriptural *revelation*.

REVELATION      RESPONSE
God reveals     We respond
his glory.      in worship.

God reveals his glory, and our response is then to give God glory in worship. Because, as we have seen, worship is about God: it is about his glory. And so Ps 29 says:

> Ascribe to the LORD, O heavenly beings,
>     ascribe to the LORD glory and strength.
> Ascribe to the LORD the glory due his name;
>     worship the LORD in the splendor of holiness. (Ps 29:1–2)

We "ascribe" to the Lord; we do not (and cannot) *add* to his perfect glory. According to the dictionary, to "ascribe" means to "regard a quality as belonging to." And so, we recognize and attribute to God "glory and strength . . . the glory due his name."

## Magnifying and Glorifying God

Similarly, Ps 34:3 tells us to

> magnify the LORD with me,
> and let us exalt his name together!

John Piper explains vividly what it means to magnify the Lord:

> *Magnify* and *glorify* are very similar in their meaning biblically. . . . But, oh, how ambiguous the word magnify is. Does it mean magnify God like a microscope magnifies or like a telescope magnifies? A microscope makes little teeny things look bigger than they are, and a telescope makes gigantic things that to the naked eye look little look more like what they really are.
>
> Now, which way are you called upon to magnify God? The answer is like a telescope, not a microscope. It is blasphemy to magnify God like a microscope: "Oh, poor God. He is so teeny, and so small, I must now make him look bigger than he is." That's blasphemy. But in fact, in this world after the fall, God to most people is either not on their radar screen at all, or a little tiny dot that might show through the smog of sin every two or three weeks with just a little twinkle that you might say exists—but with zero significance.
>
> Your calling is you are on planet Earth to put a telescope to the eye of the world. That's why you exist. By your behavior, your parenting, the way you do your job, the way you worship, and

the way you handle your things in life, everyone should read off of your life, "God is great." That's why you exist.[16]

God is perfect in his glory, and we cannot add to it; but we can declare it, celebrate it, proclaim it, magnify it. We ascribe to the Lord the glory due his name. As we have seen in Ps 150:2, we "praise him according to his excellent greatness." He has revealed all the ways in which he is excellently great; and we praise him accordingly, in response to that. Peter writes:

> You are a chosen race, a royal priesthood, a holy nation,
>     a people for God's own possession,
> that you may proclaim the excellencies of him
>     who has called you out of darkness into his marvelous light.
> (1 Pet 2:9)

Worship is proclaiming the excellencies of the God who has revealed those excellencies to us.

## About and for God

Worship is *about* God—about his glory; and worship is also *for* God—for his glory.

> I will give thanks to you, O Lord my God, with all my heart, and will *glorify* your name forever. (Ps 86:12)

> Now may the God who gives perseverance and encouragement grant you to be of the same mind with one another according to Christ Jesus so that with one accord you may with one voice *glorify* the God and Father of our Lord Jesus Christ. (Rom 15:5–6)

> Fear God, and *give him glory* . . . ;
>     worship him who made the heavens and the earth
>     and sea and springs of waters. (Rev 14:7)

## Joining in with God's Own Purpose

Eric Alexander, a great Scottish preacher, made this statement that well summarizes what we have been talking about in this section:

> There was only one end for which God created and formed the world and made us, and that is for his own exclusive *glory* and

16. Piper, "Why Am I Here?"

honor. [He created us for his glory.] There is only one end for
which our Lord redeemed his people, and that was to bring him
a revenue of *glory*. [He redeemed us for his glory.] And when
you and I find the thirst that God implants within our souls, it
is only going to be satisfied when our souls are set on the same
longing that God himself has for his *glory* and honor. [He wants
us to live for his glory.][17]

In other words, when we seek to glorify God, we are following him in his
*own* purpose of bringing glory to himself.

Christians sometimes struggle with the truth that God seeks his
own glory above all else. After all, they may think, "Aren't we taught that
it is self-centered to seek one's own glory above everything else? How
then can God want that?" How would you answer that question?

God is different from us. He is in a category by himself. And (unlike
us, when we seek to exalt ourselves) there is simply nothing greater than
God for him to seek to glorify! C. S. Lewis explains that, in loving us, God
wants the very best for us and wants us to desire what is the very best for
us. And the very best thing for us is *God and his glory*. Therefore, our own
pleasure and satisfaction in God is central, because what is most fulfilling
to us is what brings him the most glory. As John Piper likes to say, "God
is most glorified in us when we are most satisfied in him." That is why he
created us, that is why he redeemed us—to know and enjoy and reflect
and celebrate his glory.[18]

## Worshiping the God of Glory

So worship is *our response to the glory of God*, because "from him and
through him and to him are all things. To him be glory forever. Amen."

That is the God we worship. We worship the God of glory forever.

> Worship is our response to the glory of God—all that we are
> responding to all that he is.

---

17. Alexander, "Thirsting for God" (emphases added).
18. On this theme of seeking his own glory above all else, see Piper, "Why God."

# Part 3

# The Centrality of Worship
# in God's Program

I have often travelled overseas to teach this material on worship as a one- or two-week course in a Bible school or a seminary. Sometimes I hear that before my arrival a student has wondered out loud how on earth this teacher is going to talk about worship for an entire week, or even two!

But normally by the end of the course that student as well as the entire class has realized what a huge theme in Scripture worship is! In this part we are going to look at that big picture of worship as a central, even unifying, theme of the Bible.

> The theme of worship is far more central and significant in Scripture than many Christians imagine. It is intimately linked with all the major emphases of biblical theology such as creation, sin, covenant, redemption, the people of God and the future hope. Far from being a peripheral subject, it has to do with the fundamental question of how we can be in a right relationship with God and please Him in all we do. One way or another, most of the books from Genesis to Revelation are concerned with this issue.[1]

6. Everyone Worships

7. The Centrality of Worship in Creation and the Fall

8. The Centrality of Worship in Redemption and the Gospel

9. The Centrality of Worship in Missions

---

1. D. Peterson, *Engaging with God*, 17–18.

# 6

## EVERYONE WORSHIPS

I t has often been noted that the problem in our world is not that some people do not worship. *Everybody* worships; all people worship something or someone. The problem in our world is that there are many competing worships; and so many people worship the wrong thing.

### Competing Worships

In the story and film *The Wizard of Oz*, we read of Dorothy, a girl from Kansas who gets swept up by a tornado and finds herself marooned in a far-off country. She wants desperately to get home, and is told about a great wizard living in the Emerald City who is great and powerful and therefore might be able to help her. The story traces Dorothy's adventures along with her friends (a lion, a scarecrow, and a tin woodsman) as they try to get to the Emerald City so that the great wizard can solve all their problems.

But when they finally get to the city and gain entrance to the wizard, they learn that he is a fake, a fraud. He is a normal man hiding behind a curtain and using a microphone, smoke, fire, and levers to make himself seem formidable.

The writer Max Lucado compares this story to humankind's fruitless pursuit of fulfillment and happiness in all the wrong places. He says, "You don't need what Dorothy found. . . . You don't need to carry the burden of a lesser god, a god on a shelf, a god in a box, or a god in a bottle. No, you need a God who can place 100 billion stars in our galaxy, and 100 billion galaxies in the universe."[1]

The James Webb telescope, which went online in 2022, has shown more vividly than ever before the vastness and complexity of the universe. Eric Alexander tellingly writes of "the greatest throwaway line [i.e., understatement] in all of literature: 'He also made the stars (Gen 1:16)'"![2]

## The God We Need

*That* is the God we need: the Creator. That is a God who can meet the deepest longings of our hearts because he made us and put those longings within us. That is a God who deserves our worship and our adoration.

John Piper said: "The great hindrance to worship is not that we are pleasure-seeking people, but that we are willing to settle for such pitiful pleasures."[3] God wants us to seek ultimate pleasure, which can be found in him alone. In Ps 16:11 David declares to God, "In *your* presence there is fullness of joy; at *your* right hand are pleasures forevermore." The essence of sin, Piper maintains, is trying to put anything in the place of God to find meaning in our lives. "The human heart," John Calvin insisted, "is an idol factory."[4]

The world dangles before us competing visions of what the good life means: lots of things to buy, lots of money, lots of pleasure, lots of friends, lots of success, etc. And sometimes even we Christians can be lured into thinking we need some of these things to make us happy. God says through the prophet Jeremiah:

> My people have committed two evils: they have forsaken me, the fountain of living waters and hewed out cisterns, broken cisterns that can hold no water. (Jer 2:11–13)

All the competing worships, all the false claims, all the things we want to put in place of God because we think they can give us satisfaction: these are like broken, leaky cisterns that cannot handle our expectations. Only God can.

---

1. Lucado, *Traveling Light*, 16.

2. Alexander, *Our Great God*, 36.

3. Piper, *Dangerous Duty of Delight*, 49.

4. Calvin, *Institutes*, 1:11.8.

## For Reflection

What false worships do you see people pursuing in the culture around you? What competing worships (broken cisterns) do you struggle with in your own life?

Now let us turn to the Scriptures to see the true way of worship.

> *Everyone* worships something;
> it is crucial that we worship the right thing.

# 7

# THE CENTRALITY OF WORSHIP IN CREATION
# AND THE FALL

## Creation

The most basic truth we can learn about God is that he is the Creator. In fact, it is, of course, the *very first* truth we learn about God in the Bible:

> In the beginning, God created the heavens and the earth. (Gen 1:1)

And everything else in the biblical narrative follows from that.

Because God is the Creator, it means that everything that is not God was made by God. There are only two categories of existence: (1) there is *God*, and (2) there is *everything else*. In the words of A. W. Tozer:

> He is Lord of all being. . . . He is Lord of the concept of being. He is the Lord of all possibility of being. He is that, and that is He. And He is the Lord of all actual existence, and He is the Lord.[1]

As Chris Wright puts it:

> All other reality . . . is created by God and therefore is dependent on God for existence and sustenance. The creation is contingent on God. It cannot and would not exist without God. God did and could exist without it. This essential ontological duality

---

1. Tozer, "Reason We Exist," 53.

between two orders of being (the created order and the uncreated God) is foundational to the biblical worldview.[2]

N. T. Wright adds:

> God creates "that which is not God" out of generous love in order that he may then, in the end, fill it, flood it, drench it, with his love and his glory.[3]

## A Fundamental Distinction

So that means that there is a fundamental distinction between God and everything else. God is utterly unique, and there is no one like him:

> The most fundamental distinction in all reality is presented to us in the opening verses of the Bible. It is the distinction between the Creator God and everything else that exists anywhere. God alone is uncreated, self-existent, noncontingent. God's being depends on nothing else outside God's own self.[4]

The Old Testament writers understood this, and they constantly proclaimed that their God, the Creator, was totally unlike the false gods of the surrounding nations:

> There is no one like the LORD our God. (Exod 8:10)
>
> O God, who is like you? (Ps 71:19)
>
> O LORD, there is none like you, nor is there any God besides you. (1 Chr 17:20)

God himself makes these claims as well:

> I am God, and there is no other; I am God, and there is no one like me. (Isa 46:9)
>
> I am the LORD, that is my name; I will not give my glory to another. (Isa 42:8).

God is saying, "My name is mine alone, my glory is mine alone, my worship is mine alone." This fundamental distinction between God and everything else is why idols are such terrible things: because it is taking

2. C. Wright, *Mission of God*, 163.

3. N. T. Wright, *Case for the Psalms*, 136.

4. C. Wright, *Mission of God*, 163.

something that God has made and giving it the worship that only God deserves. God is in his own category as the Creator.[5]

This fundamental distinction between God and everything else is the foundation of true worship: as Creator, he is the only one deserving of worship, as the twenty-four elders in Rev 4 declare:

> The twenty-four elders fall down before him who is seated on the throne and worship him who lives forever and ever. They cast their crowns before the throne, saying,
> "Worthy are you, our Lord and God,
>    to receive glory and honor and power,
>    *for you created all things,*
>    and by your will they existed and were created."
> (Rev 4:10–11)

And the psalmist similarly extends the invitation:

> O come, let us worship and bow down.
> Let us kneel before the LORD *our Maker.* (Ps 95:6)

So right from the beginning of the scriptural revelation, in Gen 1:1, we are shown that God is the Creator, and therefore alone is worthy of worship.

## Worship God!

Jumping from the very beginning of the biblical account to its very end, we read in Rev 22:

> I, John, am the one who heard and saw these things. And when I heard and saw them, I fell down to worship at the feet of the angel who showed them to me, but he said to me, "You must not do that! I am a fellow servant with you and your brothers the prophets, and with those who keep the words of this book. Worship God." (Rev 22:8–9)

John is so amazed at the magnificent angel who is showing him the visions that he himself wants to worship that angel. But the angel rejects that, and in just two words in the very last chapter of the Bible summarizes what one might say is the call, the invitation of the *entire* Bible. *Worship God.* As we have seen, everybody worships something; what is all important is that we worship the right thing. The angel declares that we must worship *God.*[6]

---

5. "The world with all its sophisticated learning seeks to eliminate the idea of creation and thereby rob the Creator of his honor" (Ross, *Recalling the Hope of Glory,* 78).

6. "At the conclusion of . . . the canon, we hear the purpose and meaning of the

## The Fall

Worship was central in creation. God created us to worship him.[7] Now we want to consider how the issue of worship was at play in the fall of humans into sin as well. The fall was a *challenge* to the fundamental distinction that makes worship what it is: that fundamental distinction between God and everything else; his unique glory that means he is the only one worthy of worship.[8]

## Satan's Prideful Fall

Many commentators hold that in Isa 14 the author is talking about Lucifer, that created angel who fell into sin and became who we know now as Satan. And in Isa 14 we see that at the root of Lucifer's rebellion against God was the attitude displayed in his words:

> How you are fallen from heaven,
>     O Day Star, son of Dawn!
> How you are cut down to the ground,
>     you who laid the nations low!
> You said in your heart,
>     "I will ascend to heaven;
> above the stars of God
>     I will set my throne on high;
> I will sit on the mount of assembly

---

entire Bible summed up in the refrain of the Apocalypse: 'Worship God!' (Rev 14:6–7; 19:20; 22:9)" (Hahn, "Canon," 225).

7. The garden of Eden is described as a sort of temple (where God meets with humans), with Adam as priest: "The LORD God took the man and put him in the garden of Eden to work it and keep it" (Gen 2:15). "The author's intent [is] to depict creation as a fashioning of a cosmic temple, which, like the later tabernacle and Temple, would be a meeting place for God and the human person made in his image and likeness. . . . The biblical authors' intent [is] to describe creation as a royal temple building by a heavenly king. The human person in these pages is intentionally portrayed as a royal firstborn and high-priestly figure, a kind of priest-king set to rule as vice-regent over the temple-kingdom of creation" (Hahn, "Canon," 225–6). See also similar treatments by Gregory Beale, *Temple and the Church's Mission*; Allen Ross, *Recalling the Hope of Glory: Biblical Worship from the Garden to the New Creation*; and Gordon J. Wenham, "Sanctuary Symbolism in the Garden of Eden Story."

8. "The primary and most crucial distinction is that between the Creator and the creation itself. Not surprisingly, therefore, it is that distinction which comes under attack when the mysterious power of evil makes its appearance in that profoundly simple, yet simply profound, narrative of Genesis 3" (C. Wright, *Mission of God*, 164).

in the far reaches of the north;
I will ascend above the heights of the clouds;
*I will make myself like the Most High.*'" (Isa 14:12–14)

Instead of acknowledging God's unique glory, he says that he wants to be like him: "I will make myself *like the Most High.*" That is of course a revolt against the created order. *No one* can be "like the Most High." Lucifer is seeking (futilely, of course) to violate that fundamental distinction between God and everything else. As a created being, his rightful place was to bow before his Creator; and that is what he refused to do.

## Humankind's Prideful Fall

We find something very interesting when we then look at the account of the fall of humankind in Gen 3. When Satan in the form of the serpent tempts Eve, we see that the temptation that Satan dangles before Eve is *the same temptation to which he himself fell*:

For God knows that when you eat of it your eyes will be opened, and *you will be like God*, knowing good and evil. (Gen 3:5)

Satan wanted to make himself "like the Most High," and the same temptation (to "be like God") is what caused Adam and Eve to fall into sin as well. John Gill puts it this way: "'I will be like the Most High'; so Satan affected to be, and this was the bait he laid for our first parents, and with which they were taken."[9] And George MacDonald states that "the one principle of hell is, I am my own."[10]

Satan tells Eve that she and Adam can be "like God" if they eat the fruit. And so in their pride, they take and eat (v. 6) and fall into sin, with the most profound implications for the entire human race. Derek Kidner powerfully adds:

So simple the act, so hard its undoing. God will taste poverty and death before "Take and eat" become verbs of salvation.[11]

9. Gill, *Book of Isaiah*, on Isa 14:14.

10. MacDonald's fuller statement: "[The] Father is good, perfectly good; and . . . the crown and joy of life is to desire and do the will of the eternal source of will, and of all life. . . . The one principle of hell is, 'I am my own, my own king and my own subject. My own glory is my chief care; my ambition, to gather the regards of men to the one center, myself. The more self-sufficing I feel or imagine myself, the greater I am. I will be free with the freedom that consists in doing whatever I am inclined to do, from whatever quarter may come the inclination'" ("Kingship").

11. Kidner, *Genesis*, on Gen 3:6.

Going again to Rom 1 (see ch. 4), we see Paul's commentary on what has transpired:

> For the wrath of God is revealed from heaven against all ungodli-ness and unrighteousness of men, who by their unrighteousness suppress the truth. For what can be known about God is plain to them, because God has shown it to them. For his invisible at-tributes, namely, his eternal power and divine nature, have been clearly perceived, ever since the creation of the world, in the things that have been made. So they are without excuse. (Rom 1:18–20)

The preceding is equally true of humankind in general as well of Adam and Eve in particular. So too the following:

> Although they knew God, *they did not honor him as God* or give thanks to him. (Rom 1:21a)

Adam and Eve did not act out of ignorance. They *knew God*, they walked with him in the garden, they had "clearly perceived" in the things he had created, "his invisible attributes, namely, his eternal power and divine nature." And so they were "without excuse" (v. 20).

They did not honor or glorify him *as God* or give thanks. In other words, they wanted to be like God; and in so doing, they didn't give God the honor and the glory that he and he alone deserves. And so they fell into sin and led the whole human race with them.

The paradigm of revelation and response broke down in the fall. God had revealed himself to Adam and Eve, but they did not respond appropriately.

For his invisible attributes, his eternal power and divine nature, have been *clearly seen*, being *understood* through what has been made. (Rom 1:20)

For even though they knew God, they *did not honor him as God or give thanks*. (Rom 1:21)

They . . . worshiped and served the creature rather than the Creator. (Rom 1:25)

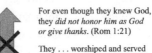

REVELATION   RESPONSE

## Turning to False Worship

Adam and Eve denied the foundation, the presupposition of true wor-ship, which is the uniqueness of God and his glory, that he is the only one we must worship. And the inevitable result of denying the foundation of *true* worship is *false* worship:

> They became futile in their thinking, and their foolish hearts were darkened. Claiming to be wise, they became fools, and *exchanged the glory of the immortal God for images* resembling mortal man and birds and animals and creeping things. Therefore God gave them up in the lusts of their hearts to impurity, to the dishonoring of their bodies among themselves, because they *exchanged the truth about God for a lie* and *worshiped and served the creature rather than the Creator*, who is blessed forever! Amen. (Rom 1:21b–25)

God alone is God; there is no one like him; he is the only one deserving of worship. Adam and Eve exchanged that truth for Satan's lie, that they could be like God. And because they accepted that lie, they worshiped and served the *creature*, including themselves, rather than the *Creator*.[12]

## The Central Issue

The crucial understanding that we need to draw from all this is:

*Worship was the central issue in the fall.*

The issue before Adam and Eve was "*Whom* are you going to worship (and honor, and give thanks to, and obey)? Are you going to worship the God who created you, or are you going to want to be like God and try to retain some of the worship and glory for yourself?"

This is how important, how central, worship is to the biblical story; the central issue in the fall of humankind, the main conflict of the Bible, the main conflict of human history, is over this issue: *Whom are you going to worship?*

And, in fact, that is the most important issue in human existence, the crucial question facing every generation, and every man, woman, and child in the world today: *Whom are you going to worship?* Who is going to be at the center of your life? Who is going to be on the throne of your heart?

---

12. "Humans have indeed breached the Creator-creature distinction. Not that humans have now *become* gods but that they have chosen to *act as though they were*—defining and deciding for themselves what they will regard as good and evil. Therein lies the root of all other forms of idolatry: we deify our own capacities, and thereby make gods of ourselves and our choices and all their implications" (C. Wright, *Mission of God*, 164).

## The Bible's Story: Beginning to End

So we see at the very beginning of the Bible, just three chapters in, the tragedy that falls on the human race. And the entire trajectory of the Bible is God acting in human history to restore to himself the worship and glory that he alone deserves. In the book of Revelation we see that worship and glory fully restored, in great scenes of worship around the throne of God and great views of God's glory filling all in all. And we have seen the angel's climactic declaration, in the very last chapter of the Bible, that John, and we, must "worship God" *only*.

As we have seen, the problem is not that there are many people in the world who do not worship. Everybody worships. What is all important, as the angel in Rev 22:9 reminds us, is *whom* you worship. And God, the Creator, is the *only* one worthy of worship.

That is how important, how central a theme worship is in the Bible. God created us to worship him; in the fall Adam and Eve, and in their steps we, denied him the worship that he alone deserves. The entire biblical story is God acting at infinite cost to himself, the cost of his own beloved Son, to restore people to the place of worship:

> The mission of God is ultimately to restore his whole creation to what it was intended to be—*God's* creation, ruled over by redeemed *humanity*, giving glory and praise to its Creator.[13]

Whom are you going to worship? Worship *God*.

---

The most important question in human existence is:
"Whom are you going to worship?"

---

13. C. Wright, *Mission of God*, 165. Scott W. Hahn, in his article "Canon, Cult and Covenant: The Promise of Liturgical Hermeneutics," gives a fascinating overview of the entire spectrum of biblical revelation as centered in and heading towards worship. He writes: "There is a liturgical reason and purpose for the creation of the world and the human person, and there is a liturgical 'destiny' toward which creation and the human person journey in the pages of the canonical text. At each decisive stage in God's covenant relations with humanity, the divine-human relationship is expressed liturgically and sacrificially. . . . The human person is *homo liturgicus*, created to glorify God through service, expressed as a sacrifice of praise. (Hahn, "Canon," 213).

# 8

## THE CENTRALITY OF WORSHIP IN
## REDEMPTION AND THE GOSPEL

I f worship was the central issue in the fall, then it stands to reason that
it is also at the center of God's solution to the problem of the fall and
sin in his plan of redemption.

### Redemption

#### The Second Adam

Jesus Christ is sometimes called the Second Adam, based on these Pauline texts:

> For if, because of one man's trespass, death reigned through that
> one man, much more will those who receive the abundance of
> grace and the free gift of righteousness reign in life through the
> one man Jesus Christ. (Rom 5:17)

> Thus it is written, "The first man Adam became a living being";
> the last Adam became a life-giving spirit. (1 Cor 15:45)

Through one man, Adam, sin came into the world; so through one man,
Jesus, salvation came to the world.

When we read in Matthew about Satan tempting Christ in the wilderness, the climactic temptation revolves around worship:

> Again, the devil took him to a very high mountain and showed
> him all the kingdoms of the world and their glory. And he said to
> him, "All these I will give you, if you will fall down and *worship*
> me." (Matt 4:8–9)

Imagine the "absurd insolence"[1] of this *created being* saying to the one through whom the worlds were made, "I want you to worship me!"[2]

Jesus is being confronted with what we have seen to be the question of the ages, the question that Adam and Eve tragically answered wrongly: *Whom are you going to worship?*

However, Jesus, the *Second* Adam, answers the question *rightly*:

> Then Jesus said to him, "Be gone, Satan! For it is written,
> 'You shall worship the Lord your God and him only shall
> you serve.'" (Matt 4:10)

---

1. C. Wright, *Mission of God*, 147.

2. Eric Alexander expands on the supreme irony as well as the profound significance of this account: Jesus is "the essential, prototypical man; and he is here in the wilderness, as it were, fighting our battle. It is impossible not to see, when you read this account, the reference back to Genesis 3, where Satan meets the first Adam . . . and this encounter between Satan and the Last Adam—who has come a Second Adam, to the fight and to the rescue. And very significantly Martin Luther says, 'This is Jesus Christ, the proper Man and the Mighty Savior, who is summoning the Prince of hell out into the battlefield and giving him notice of his ultimate downfall.'

"Now the history of salvation therefore views this as one of the most significant moments in the developing revelation of Jesus as our Savior. The climax of it of course comes when Satan assaults our Lord in the whole area of his worship. . . .

"[Satan] was an angel, created by God for a purpose which the writer of the Epistle to the Hebrews clarifies for us in the last verse of chapter 1, when he says: 'Are not all angels ministering spirits sent to serve those who will inherit salvation?' Again, in Hebrews 1:6, 'When God brings his firstborn into the world, he says, "let all God's angels worship him."' . . .

"Here is Satan—a rebellious, fallen angel—coming into the presence of the Lord of glory who has given him being; and he seeks—he who was formed to worship the Lord of Glory—he seeks so to contort and distort [Jesus'] life that he will worship Satan, instead of Satan to ministering to him. Oh, how would we say with the prophet, 'How you are fallen, Lucifer, son of the morning. How you are fallen' [Isa 14:12]. There are few more ugly, grotesque pictures in the Bible, my friends, than the picture of Satan himself seeking to bring Jesus to bow at his feet, and to divert the worship that belonged to God to him. . . .

"It is equally grotesque when you and I as the adopted sons and daughters of the King of glory, redeemed by his precious blood, brought to him by his grace, begin to yield to the temptation to see our lives lived for anything other than to worship God and him exclusively. . . .

"That is one of the remarkable things about this incident. It is really the basic issue of whom we are worshiping—the Creator or the creature. God or self. It is the issue that we need to clarify and by God's grace to settle every day of our lives" ("Worship: Chief End").

And then Jesus, through his redeeming work, enables us to become the kind of faithful followers that God wants us to be, to worship and serve him alone.

## Worshipers out of Rebels

A. W. Tozer makes an amazingly insightful comment along these lines:

> Why did Christ come? Why was he conceived? Why was he born? Why was he crucified? Why did he rise again? Why is he now at the right hand of the Father? The answer to all these questions is in order that he might *make worshipers out of rebels*; in order that he might restore us again to the place of worship we knew when we were first created.[3]

In Tozer's view, the entire thrust of Christ's coming and of his redeeming work was to *enable us to become the worshipers we were created to be* instead of the rebels we had become.

## Undoing the Fall

Going back to the downward cascade of ill effects of the fall in Rom 1:21–25, let us consider how all the things that went so horribly wrong in the fall are made right again through the redeeming work of Jesus Christ:

| Rom 1:21–25 | The Reversal in Christ |
| --- | --- |
| They did not honor God as God or give thanks. | Christ enables us to honor God as God and give thanks. |
| They became futile in their thinking and their foolish hearts were darkened. | Christ enlightens our thoughts and our hearts. |
| Claiming to be wise, they became fools. | Christ gives us his wisdom when we acknowledge our foolishness. |
| [And they] exchanged the glory of the immortal God for images resembling mortal man and birds and animals and creeping things. | Christ enables us to exchange our images and idols for the glory of God. |
| They exchanged the truth about God for a lie. | Christ enables us to exchange Satan's lie for the truth about God. |
| [And they] worshiped and served the creature rather than the Creator. | Christ enables us to worship the Creator rather than the creature. |

3. Tozer, *Worship*, 19 (emphasis added).

## Seeking Worshipers

Jesus says to the Samaritan woman in John 4:23:

> But the hour is coming, and is now here, when the true worship-
> ers will worship the Father in spirit and truth, for *the Father is*
> *seeking such people to worship him.*

The Father is seeking worshipers. Jesus came to make worshipers out of rebels, to make us true worshipers, because that is what the Father is seeking. And Jesus makes that possible through his redeeming work.

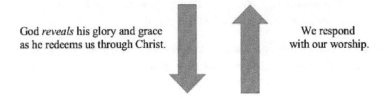

God *reveals* his glory and grace
as he redeems us through Christ.

We respond
with our worship.

## The Gospel

One succinct summary of the gospel is given to us by Paul in 1 Cor 15:

> Now I would remind you, brethren, of the gospel I preached
> to you, which you received, in which you stand, and by which
> you are being saved, if you hold fast to the word I preached to
> you—unless you believed in vain.
>     For I delivered to you as of first importance what I also
> received: that Christ died for our sins in accordance with the
> Scriptures, that he was buried, that he was raised on the third
> day in accordance with the Scriptures. (1 Cor 15:1–4)

However, there is another angle from which we can look at the gospel as it relates to worship. As we have seen, we were created to be worshipers of God; in the fall we refused to give him the worship that he alone deserves; through the work of redemption, Jesus enables us to become the worshipers that God originally intended us to be.

## A Call to Worship

One way of looking at the gospel, then, is as *a call to worship*: a call to turn from the false worships that sin has led us into, to the true worship that Christ makes possible.

There are a few New Testament passages that speak directly to this idea of the gospel as a call to turn from false worship to true worship. In 1 Thess 1, Paul is commending the faithfulness of the Thessalonians and the reputation they have among other believers:

> For they themselves report concerning us the kind of reception we had among you, and how you *turned to God from idols* to serve the living and true God. (1 Thess 1:9)

Coming to Christ through the gospel involved turning to God and away from idols. They turned from the *false worship* of idols to the *true worship* of the living God.

Similarly, in Acts 17:22–31 Paul calls the Athenians to turn from "the objects of your worship" (v. 23) to "the God who made the world and everything in it, being Lord of heaven and earth" (v. 24).

In Acts 14, we see Paul and Barnabas on their missionary journey, and we read of their forced departure from Iconium and arrival in Lystra:

> When an attempt was made by both Gentiles and Jews, with their rulers, to mistreat them and to stone them, they learned of it and fled to Lystra and Derbe, cities of Lycaonia, and to the surrounding country, and there they continued to *preach the gospel.*
>
> Now at Lystra there was a man sitting who could not use his feet. He was crippled from birth and had never walked. He listened to Paul speaking. And Paul, looking intently at him and seeing that he had faith to be made well, said in a loud voice, "Stand upright on your feet." And he sprang up and began walking. And when the crowds saw what Paul had done, they lifted up their voices, saying in Lycaonian, "The gods have come down to us in the likeness of men!" Barnabas they called Zeus, and Paul, Hermes, because he was the chief speaker. And the priest of Zeus, whose temple was at the entrance to the city, brought oxen and garlands to the gates and wanted to offer sacrifice with the crowds. (Acts 14:5–13)

The people are so amazed at the healing of the crippled man that they want to offer up worship to the two missionaries.

> But when the apostles Barnabas and Paul heard of it, they tore
> their garments and rushed out into the crowd, crying out, "Men,
> why are you doing these things? We also are men, of like nature
> with you, and we bring you *good news*, that you should turn
> from these vain things to a living God, who made the heaven
> and the earth and the sea and all that is in them." (Acts 14:14–15)

In similar fashion to the angel's reaction to John's proffered worship in Rev 22:9 ("You must not do that! I am a fellow servant with you
and your brothers the prophets"), Barnabas and Paul cry out, "Men, why
are you doing these things? We also are men, of like nature with you."
Then they proclaim that their role is as God's spokesmen to *preach the
gospel* to them. (The phrase here "bring you good news" is the same word
translated "preach the gospel" in 14:7; the Greek word is *euangelizō*, from
which we get "evangelize.") We preach the gospel to you, they say; and
observe how they describe this gospel they have come to share:

> . . . that you should turn from these vain things to a living God,
> who made the heaven and the earth and the sea and all that is
> in them.

The gospel they preached was a call to turn "from these vain things"
(their *false worship* of Zeus and Hermes, and of Barnabas and Paul) to
*true worship* of a living God. This God deserves their worship because he
is the Creator, the one "who made the heavens and the earth and the sea
and all that is in them."

And in Rev 14, an angel has the same message for all on earth:

> Then I saw another angel flying directly overhead, with an
> eternal *gospel* to proclaim to those who dwell on earth, to every
> nation and tribe and language and people. And he said with a
> loud voice, "Fear God and give him glory, because the hour of
> his judgment has come, and *worship* him who made heaven and
> earth, the sea and the springs of water." (Rev 14:6–7)

On this passage David Peterson writes:

> This "eternal gospel" summons the whole creation to acknowl-
> edge God as creator, lord of history and judge of all. It recalls
> the vision of Revelation 4 and the claim of the heavenly host
> that he alone is worthy to receive "glory and honour and power"
> from everything that he has made. . . . The doctrine of creation is
> given as the primary reason for honouring God as God or wor-
> shipping him. . . . In line with other New Testament passages,

Revelation 14:6–7 suggests that evangelism may be viewed as *a call to worship God appropriately.*[4]

## Saved To, Not Just From

So the gospel is a call to turn away from false worship (of whatever form) to worship of the one true God, the Redeemer. Sometimes we are prone to think of the gospel in primarily negative terms, as simply rescuing us *from* sin, and death, and hell (and thank God it does all those things). But the gospel does not just rescue us *from* something, but also *to* something. The goal of the gospel is to enable us to be able to draw near to God in fellowship and worship:

> Therefore, brethren, since we have confidence to enter the holy places by the blood of Jesus, by the new and living way that he opened for us through the curtain, that is, through his flesh, and since we have a great priest over the house of God, *let us draw near* with a true heart in full assurance of faith, with our hearts sprinkled clean from an evil conscience and our bodies washed with pure water. (Heb 10:19–22)

Hence the title of this book. We have confidence to enter by the blood of Jesus; and so the invitation is to *draw near to God*, to come close, to enjoy that personal fellowship with him that has been made possible through the gospel, through the redeeming work of Christ.

The gospel saves us *from* something, but also *to* something: a personal relationship with God.

> The triune God has eternally desired to bless His people with the greatest possible gift, and the greatest possible gift He can give is nothing other than the enjoyment of His own eternal, fecund [fruitful] fellowship. Communion in the Son's eternal life of love, glory and giving with the Father in the Spirit constitutes the ultimate blessing of the gospel.[5]

Or, as Fanny Crosby's hymn "To God Be the Glory" puts it:

> O come to the Father through Jesus the Son
> and give him the glory, great things he hath done!

---

4. D. Peterson, "Worship and Evangelism."

5. Köstenberger and Swain, *Father, Son and Spirit*, 178.

To allow us to come close and give to God the worship that he and he alone deserves: the gospel enables us to do that. The gospel is *a call to worship*, from false worship to true worship.

## Summary

In summary, we have seen in the last two chapters:

1. God is the Creator, unique in his glory and alone worthy of worship.

2. The fall usurped God's claim to exclusive worship.

3. Christ came to undo the effects of the fall and to enable true worship.

4. The gospel then is a call to all humankind to come to the Father through Christ, a call to worldwide worship, to the glory of God.

> Christ came and died so that we might become the worshipers we were created to be, instead of the rebels we had become.

# 9

## THE CENTRALITY OF WORSHIP IN MISSIONS


From the perspective of the previous chapter, we can regard missions simply as *taking to the whole world the call of the gospel to true worship*, for the glory of God among the nations. As Jesus said to his disciples post-resurrection, "as the Father has sent me, so I am sending you" (John 20:21).


### God, Missions, and Worship

#### Missions Is for God

The Scottish preacher Eric Alexander makes a startling, perhaps even controversial, claim; yet it is one that is consistent with what we have already seen about the glory of God and the centrality of worship:

> The *ultimate missionary compulsion* is not simply that there are people who are dying without knowing Christ, nor is it that God has given us the Great Commission to go out into the world; it is that there are areas of the world . . . where *God is being robbed of His glory.*
>
> That is why when Paul went to Athens, a missionary situation if there ever was one to him, and found people bowing down before idols . . . Paul had what in the Greek of the New Testament seems to mean a *paroxysm*—a cardiac arrest is how

some people think of it. Why was he so upset? It was because God was being robbed of His glory.[1]

Now, Alexander is not downplaying the need of the world's peoples for Christ, nor the seriousness of the Great Commission. But he is looking beyond those things to *a God-centered view of missions*: as a call to worship for the glory of God.

God, who said "my glory I give to no other" (Isa 42:8), sees that glory ignored and denied by multitudes of people the world over. As we saw in the fall, men and women rob God of his glory by refusing to "honor him as God or give thanks to him" (Rom 1:21), and by having "worshiped and served the creature rather than the Creator" (Rom 1:25). So many who owe their very lives and every breath wake up morning after morning and live their lives in a way that in effect says to God, "I don't need you!"

In missions, we aim to go and reach people for Christ, in obedience to the Great Commission (Matt 28:18–20). But ultimately, we want to reach people for the sake of *God*. We want people to become the worshipers God created them to be, instead of the rebels they have become.

## Worship as the Goal of Missions

John Piper, in his book *Let the Nations Be Glad: The Supremacy of God in Missions*, spends the entire first chapter talking about worship as it relates to missions. In fact, his opening sentences make an astounding claim—one that, when I first read it, exploded in my mind and heart and caused me to reevaluate the way I saw missions, and worship, and even God. He writes:

> Missions is not the ultimate goal of the church. Worship is. *Missions exists because worship doesn't.* Worship is ultimate, not missions, because God is ultimate, not man.[2]

Piper is *not* saying missions is unimportant; after all, this is an entire book on missions that he is writing. But what he *is* saying is that missions is a terribly important *means* to an even greater *end*: worship. Piper adds:

1. Alexander, "Worship God" (emphases added). Similarly, John Stott wrote: "The highest of missionary motives is neither obedience to the Great Commission (important as that is), nor love for sinners who are alienated and perishing (strong as that incentive is, especially when we contemplate the wrath of God . . .) but rather zeal—burning and passionate zeal—for the glory of Jesus Christ" (*Romans*, 53).

2. Piper, *Let the Nations Be Glad*, 35 (emphasis added).

When this age is over, and the countless millions of the redeemed fall on their faces before the throne of God, missions will be no more. It is a temporary necessity. But worship abides forever.[3]

As we have seen in our study, God created us to be worshipers; we became rebels; God sent his Son to redeem us and make us worshipers once again. We saw that the gospel is a call to men and women and children to turn from false worship to true worship. And missions is taking that call to all the world and saying to the nations, "Great is the LORD, and greatly to be praised" (Ps 96:4), so that God will receive more glory by more people lifting his name in worship.

Piper expands on this God-centered view of missions:

> Worship . . . is the goal of missions because in missions we simply aim to bring the nations into the white-hot enjoyment of God's glory. The goal of missions is the gladness of the peoples in the greatness of God: "The LORD reigns; let the earth rejoice; let the many coastlands be glad!" (Ps 97:1). "Let the peoples praise Thee, O God; let all the peoples praise Thee! Let the nations be glad[4] and sing for joy!" (Ps 67:3–4).[5]

As can be seen in these verses above, this is a *biblical* emphasis, not one originating with Piper. In the book of Psalms especially, we find repeatedly the call for the nations to give God their worship:

> Let the peoples praise you, O God;
>    let all the peoples praise you!
> Let the nations be glad and sing for joy,
> For you judge the peoples with equity
>    and guide the nations upon earth.
> Let the peoples praise you, O God;
>    let all the peoples praise you! (Ps 67:3–5)

> May all kings fall down before him,
>    all nations serve him! (Ps 72:11)

> Ascribe to the LORD, O families of the peoples,
>    ascribe to the LORD glory and strength! (Ps 96:7)

---

3. Piper, *Let the Nations Be Glad*, 35. Christopher Wright agrees: "Praise will be the dominant reality of the new creation, whereas, since God's mission to redeem his whole creation will be complete, our derivative mission within history will be at an end. . . . So, yes, mission exists because praise does not, for mission means bringing those who do not yet praise the living God to do so" (*Mission of God*, 134).

4. Piper draws the title for his book from this verse.

5. Piper, *Let the Nations Be Glad*, 35.

Kings of the earth and all peoples,
> princes and all rulers of the earth!
Young men and maidens together,
> old men and children!
Let them praise the name of the LORD,
> for his name alone is exalted;
> his majesty is above earth and heaven. (Ps 148:11–13)

Piper comments on how this point of view is also seen in Rom 15:

> For I tell you that Christ became a servant to the circumcised to show God's truthfulness, in order to confirm the promises given to the patriarchs, and in order that the Gentiles might glorify God for his mercy. (Rom 15:8–9)

Piper says:

> The aim was worship. . . . Notice: It's not just that the Gentiles might *receive* God's mercy or simply *experience* God's mercy, but that they *glorify God* for his mercy. The aim of the gospel among the nations is not man-centered. Paul does not say, "Christ became a servant in order that the Gentiles[6] might *receive mercy.*" He says, "Christ became a servant in order that the Gentiles might glorify *God* for receiving mercy." The ultimate aim of the gospel is God—God glorified for his mercy.[7]

And so the goal of missions is for the peoples to give God the glory and the praise and the worship that he deserves.[8] What Piper's book did was to remind the church of this biblical emphasis, and in this way has had a major impact on thinking about missions and its task. Here is an example of how one missions organization shaped its vision statement to reflect this understanding:

> Christar workers participate by planting churches in these least-reached communities, *where he is yet to be worshiped.*[9]

6. The Greek word for Gentiles (*ethnē*), from which we get such English words as "ethnic," is also sometimes translated as "peoples" or "nations."

7. Piper, "Gospel Worship" (emphasis original).

8. Christopher Wright concurs: "Praise is the proper and primary stance or mode of existence of the created order to its Creator. So inasmuch as our mission is a part of our creaturely response to our God, praise must be a primary mode also" (*Mission of God*, 134).

9. See https://www.christar.org/ (emphasis added).

The goal of their organization is to plant churches in difficult areas so that people there might become worshipers of God.

And another missions organization similarly states as its purpose:

> To Every Tribe exists *to extend the worship of Christ* among all peoples by mobilizing the church, training disciple-makers, and sending missionary teams to plant churches among the unreached.[10]

## Worship as the Fuel of Missions

Piper also makes the point that worship is not just the *goal* of missions. It is also the *fuel* of missions. He writes:

> Passion for God in worship precedes the offer of God in preaching. You can't commend what you don't cherish.[11]

In other words, you cannot go and tell others that "great is the LORD, and greatly to be praised" (Ps 96:4) until you have first recognized the Lord's greatness in your own heart and have greatly praised him. Then, and only then, can you be a faithful witness, one who can say, "Taste and see that the LORD is good" (Ps 34:8), because you have tasted of that goodness yourself. You must first of all be a worshiper before you can go and become an advocate for worship among the nations.[12]

Amy Carmichael was a great missionary pioneer to India in the nineteenth century. Once on her mission compound she had a new chapel built, and this chapel had a big steeple at the front and a smaller steeple at the back.

---

10. See https://www.toeverytribe.org/ (emphasis added).

11. Piper, *Let the Nations Be Glad*, 35.

12. "In another equally biblical sense we could say that mission exists because praise does. The praise of the church is what energizes and characterizes it for mission, and also serves as the constant reminder we so much need, that all our mission flows as obedient response to and participation in the prior mission of God" (C. Wright, *Mission of God*, 134).

Someone asked her why there was a larger steeple at the front, and a smaller one in the rear, and she replied, "That's to remind us that worship must always precede service."

We must first be worshipers before we go to serve; truly fruitful service will grow out of a heart of worship, not just a sense of duty or responsibility. Jesus said, "Seek first the kingdom of God and his righteousness, and all these things will be added to you" (Matt 6:33). Tozer concurs: "God meant that a convert should learn to be a worshiper, and after that he can learn to be a worker."[13]

And thus worship fuels missions. Edmund Clowney at the Urbana youth missions conference in 1976 put it this way:

> Praise his name. We are called to doxological evangelism. If we
> do not praise his name, we do not preach the gospel.[14]

The priority of worship must fuel our outreach. Eric Alexander said this at Urbana five years later, in 1981:

> Worship and mission are so bound together in the economy of
> God that you really cannot have one without the other. No one can
> truly worship God and at the same time have an apparently total
> indifference to whether anyone else is worshiping him or not.[15]

So if we are true worshipers, we are going to share God's heart for the worship of the nations. Another mission agency summarized its ministry perspective in a similar way:

- We *worship*.
- We love.
- We go.[16]

## Worship Leads to Missions Leads to Worship!

And so in the purposes of God, worship and missions inevitably intertwine in this way. N. T. Wright observes this about the book of Acts:

---

13. Tozer, *Worship*, 10.
14. Clowney, "Declare His Glory."
15. Alexander, "Mission and Vision."
16. See www.crossworld.org (emphasis added).

It is in this context, that of the church worshipping in the power of the Spirit, that the major new advances in mission take place. Classically, this is expressed at the start of [Acts] 13, where during worship, prayer and fasting the Spirit instructs the church in Antioch to set apart Barnabas and Saul for fresh work. And that work consists, not least, of calling pagans to acknowledge and worship the creator God, the God of Israel.[17]

## All about God

That is a God-centered view of the gospel, a God-centered view of building the church, a God-centered view of the work of missions. It is all ultimately for God, and about God and his glory. As we have seen so far in this book, the God that we worship is the God of glory. It is all about him and his glory: God's glory in creation, God's glory rejected in the fall, God restoring the affirmation of his glory through the work of Christ, God's glory filling the heavens. God earnestly desires his glory to be seen and acknowledged and lifted up among all the nations.

### God and the Nations

### God's Goal for the Nations

The psalmist in Ps 67 is asking God to bless the Jewish nation:

> May God be gracious to us and bless us
> and make his face to shine upon us. (v. 1)

But he does not stop there; God's blessing on them as a nation is not an end in itself:

> *That* your way may be known on earth,
> your saving power among all nations. (v. 2)

As we will see when we look at the call of Abraham on pp. 144–45, it was always in God's mind and heart to bless all the nations through Israel. That is what Israel often neglected. They liked being God's special, chosen people, but they so often forgot that they were to be a light to the nations.

However, the psalmist has not forgotten. He understands the role of Israel to show forth God's "way" and "saving power" to the world, so that:

17. N. T. Wright, "Worship and the Spirit."

Let the peoples praise you, O God;
  let all the peoples praise you!
Let the nations be glad and sing for joy. (vv. 3–4a)

This is God's goal for the nations: that he might receive the praise, the glory of peoples all around the earth.

## God's Sufficiency for the Nations

In Psalms we read:

All the ends of the earth will remember
  and turn to the LORD,
and all the families of the nations
  will worship before you. (Ps 22:27)

Be still, and know that I am God;
  I will be exalted among the nations,
  I will be exalted in the earth. (Ps 46:10)

All nations whom you have made
  shall come and worship before you, O LORD,
And they shall glorify your name. (Ps 86:9)

God *will* accomplish all his purposes for the nations. This is a crucial truth, as A. W. Tozer makes clear:

Probably the hardest thought of all for our natural egotism to entertain is that God does not need our help. We commonly represent Him as a busy, eager, somewhat frustrated Father hurrying about seeking help to carry out His benevolent plan to bring peace and salvation to the world. The God who worketh all things surely needs no help and no helpers.

Too many missionary appeals are based upon this fancied frustration of Almighty God. An effective speaker can easily excite pity in his hearers, not only for the heathen but for the God who has tried so hard and so long to save them and has failed for want of support. I fear that thousands of young persons enter Christian service from no higher motive than to help deliver God from the embarrassing situation His love has gotten Him into and His limited abilities seem unable to get Him out of.[18]

Tozer is of course being satirical: in effect, he is saying, "Poor God: if we don't help, he'll never accomplish his purposes for the world." And

18. Tozer, *Knowledge of the Holy*, 34.

that of course is *not* what our sovereign God is like. He does not *need* to use us to fulfill his will in creation. But he *wants* to use us; he *loves* to use us. Let us serve him with the right perspective—rather than thinking we are somehow getting him out of a jam.

Missions is *God's* work,[19] and he *will* accomplish his work, whether or not we get on board. He *wants* to use us; but he does not *have* to use us. Rather, it is our privilege to join him in his great quest for true worshipers from every tribe, tongue, people and nation, a quest that Rev 7 shows us will be marvelously fulfilled:

> After this I looked, and behold, a great multitude that no one could number, from every nation, from all tribes and peoples and languages, standing before the throne and before the Lamb, clothed in white robes, with palm branches in their hands, and crying out with a loud voice, "Salvation belongs to our God who sits on the throne, and to the Lamb!" And all the angels were standing around the throne and around the elders and the four living creatures, and they fell on their faces before the throne and worshiped God, saying, "Amen! Blessing and glory and wisdom and thanksgiving and honor and power and might be to our God forever and ever! Amen." (Rev 7:9–12)

19. This is the major emphasis of the book *The Mission of God* by Christopher Wright. He states: "In . . . trying to come to a biblical definition of what we mean by mission, we are in effect asking the question, *Whose mission is it anyway?* The answer, it seems to me, could be expressed as a paraphrase of the song of the redeemed in the new creation. 'Salvation belongs to our God, who sits on the throne, and to the Lamb' (Rev 7:10). Since the whole Bible is the story of how this God, 'our God,' has brought about his salvation for the whole cosmos . . . we can affirm with equal validity, 'mission belongs to our God.' *Mission is not ours; mission is God's.* . . . It is not so much the case that God has a mission for his church in the world but that God has a church for his mission in the world. Mission was not made for the church; the church was made for mission—God's mission" (62). And later he writes: "It was not the case that Paul chose to have a mission to the nations on behalf of Israel's God. It is that the God of Israel chose Paul for his mission to the nations" (123, citing Paul's own view of his task and calling in Acts 22:14–15 and 26:17–18). And again: "So all our missional efforts to make God known must be set within the prior framework of God's own will to be known. We are seeking to accomplish what God himself wills to happen. This is both humbling and reassuring. It's humbling inasmuch as it reminds us that all our efforts would be in vain but for God's determination to be known. We are neither the initiators of the mission of making God known to the nations nor does it lie in our power to decide how the task will be fully accomplished or when it may be deemed to be complete. But it is also reassuring. For we know that behind all our fumbling efforts and inadequate communication stands the supreme will of the living God, reaching out in loving self-revelation, incredibly willing to open blind eyes and reveal his glory through the treasures of the gospel delivered in the clay pots of his witnesses (2 Cor 4:1–7)" (129–30).

## God's Call to the Nations

Let the peoples praise you, O God;
    let all the peoples praise you!
Let the nations be glad and sing for joy. (Ps 76:3–4)

Kings of the earth and all peoples,
    princes and all rulers of the earth!
Young men and maidens together,
    old men and children!
Let them praise the name of the LORD,
    for his name alone is exalted
    his majesty is above earth and heaven. (Ps 148:11–13)

God's call to the nations is for them to recognize him as their Creator, to honor and glorify and praise and worship him. That is why he created the peoples of the earth, and why he sent his Son to die, that they might find life in him.

## Our Role

We are to be God's spokespersons, heralds, ambassadors. We are to proclaim:

Praise the LORD, all nations!
Extol him, all peoples! (Ps 117:1)

We are to join in with God in his great purpose for the world:

God is pursuing with omnipotent passion a worldwide purpose of gathering joyful worshipers for himself from every tribe and tongue and people and nation. He has an inexhaustible enthusiasm for the supremacy of His name among the nations. Therefore, let us bring our affections into line with His, and, for the sake of His name, let us renounce the quest for worldly comforts, and join His global purpose.[20]

## For God and His Glory among the Nations

At the 2010 Global Consultation on Music and Missions in Singapore, I delivered a plenary address entitled "Creative Arts, Missions, and

---

20. Piper, *Let the Nations Be Glad*, 62.

Worship" as an attempted synthesis of these great themes.[21] I summarized my conclusions with this illustration—

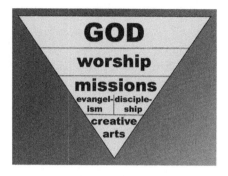

—and with this explanation:

Why should we use the creative arts?
*In order to contextualize and focus the message of missions.*

Why should we do missions (evangelism and discipleship)?
*So that God might receive the worship of all peoples.*

Why should the peoples worship God?
*Because he is supremely worthy of all praise.*

And Ps 96 summarizes well the themes we have been considering as we looked at the relationship between worship and the gospel and missions:

| | |
|---|---|
| O sing to the LORD a new song; sing to the LORD, all the earth! Sing to the LORD, bless his name; | *Worship* |
| tell of his salvation from day to day. Declare his glory among the nations, his marvelous works among all the peoples! | *Missions* |
| For great is the LORD, and greatly to be praised; he is to be feared above all gods. For all the gods of the peoples are worthless idols, but the LORD made the heavens. (Ps 96:1–5) | *Turn from false to true worship* |

21. A video digest of the event can be found at https://www.youtube.com/watch?v=zV48DR4uX7w. See also Ron Man, "Creative Arts."

## Great Commission and Great Commandment

Another way to see the dependent relationship between missions and worship is to compare the Great Commission and Great Commandment.[22]

The *Great Commission* is of course the name we give to the resurrected Christ's final charge to his disciples in Matt 28:

> All authority in heaven and on earth has been given to me. Go therefore and make disciples of all nations, baptizing them in the name of the Father and of the Son and of the Holy Spirit, teaching them to observe all that I have commanded you. (Matt 28:18–20)

The *Great Commandment* was Jesus's response to the question asked him about the greatest commandment in the Old Testament law:

> You shall love the Lord your God with all your heart and with all your soul and with all your mind. This is the great and first commandment. (Matt 22:37)

When we compare these two statements (see the chart below) we see some striking differences.

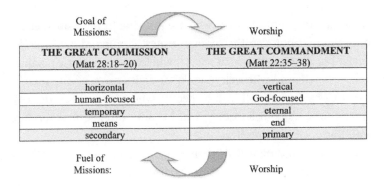

| Goal of Missions: | Worship |
| --- | --- |

| THE GREAT COMMISSION (Matt 28:18–20) | THE GREAT COMMANDMENT (Matt 22:35–38) |
| --- | --- |
| horizontal | vertical |
| human-focused | God-focused |
| temporary | eternal |
| means | end |
| secondary | primary |

| Fuel of Missions: | Worship |
| --- | --- |

1. The Great Commission by definition is *horizontal* and *focused on humans*: we are to go to the nations and make disciples. The Great Commandment, on the other hand, is purely *vertical* in its focus: we are to love God with all our being (which is simply another way to speak of worship).

22. As quoted before, Christopher Wright adds that "behind both [is] the Great *Communication*—the revelation of the identity of God, of God's action in the world and God's saving purpose for all creation" (*Mission of God*, 60 [emphasis original]).

2. The Great Commission, like missions, is *temporary* and limited to this present age; the love for God of which the Great Commandment speaks will continue into eternity.

3. So we see that the Great Commission is a crucially important *means* to an even greater *end*: the fulfilling of the Great Commandment in the lives of people.

There is one more way to demonstrate this relationship. Consider the process of disciple-making as laid out in the Great Commission itself: we are to go and make disciples of all nations by: (1) *baptizing* (probably representative of the whole process of evangelism, whereby we share the gospel and bring converts into the fellowship of the body of Christ through baptism); and (2) *teaching* them to obey *all* that Jesus commanded (which is the process of discipleship). The climax of this teaching process is the disciple's obedience to Christ's commands; and *Jesus himself* said that the *most important* of his commands was "to love the Lord your God with all your heart, soul, mind, and strength." So in fulfilling the Great Commission, disciple-makers are ultimately leading their disciples to live according to the Great Commandment: to be worshipers first and foremost.

Not only that, but disciples who are growing in their obedience to not only the first but also the *second* greatest commandment (to "love your neighbor as yourself" [Matt 22:39]) will learn to see those neighbors as God sees them and will seek to make disciples from among them. So the Great Commission will lead to people who seek to obey the Great Commandment, and in so doing will become disciple-makers, Great Commission agents, themselves.

This understanding will also help us to see in proper context the two aspects of the Great Commission, evangelism and discipleship, in terms of their ultimate purpose: we might say that the end goal of evangelism is to *win more worshipers for God* (from among the nations); and that the final purpose of discipleship is to *build better worshipers of God*—those who love God with ever more of their heart, soul, mind, and strength. Missions, in both its evangelism and discipleship aspects, has as its *ultimate* aim that *more worship* be offered up to God, for his glory.

---

"Missions exists because worship doesn't." (John Piper)

# 10

## THE CENTRALITY OF WORSHIP IN ALL OF LIFE

In this chapter we want to look closely at John 4, one of the most important passages on worship in the New Testament. It is so important because in John 4 *Jesus himself* teaches about worship. (The word for worship is used *nine* times in vv. 20–24.)

### Old-Covenant Barriers between God and the People

In the Old Testament sacrificial system, there were barriers between the individual Israelite and God.

At the tabernacle, the people could enter only the courtyard. The priests alone could offer the sacrifices; and only they could enter the holy place, to burn incense, offer prayers, and attend to the lampstand and the table of shewbread. The high priest alone could go into the holy of holies, once a year on the Day of Atonement. (A veil or curtain separated the holy of holies from the holy place in the tabernacle, and later in the temple.) The holy of holies was where God dwelled in the midst of his people; when the construction of the tabernacle was completed, we read:

> Then the cloud covered the tent of meeting, and the glory of the
> LORD filled the tabernacle. (Exod 40:34)

The glory of God was present among his people; but at the same time the setup demonstrated that God was so holy, and the people were so sinful, that the people could not come close to him.

Tabernacle of Israel, by Philip De Vere[1]

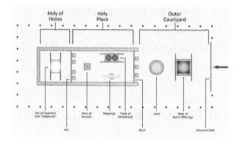

Layout of the Tabernacle, by Adik86[2]

## Jesus, the Great Barrier-Breaker

Jesus came to break down the barriers between God and humans. That is why we read that when Jesus died "the curtain of the temple was torn in two, from top to bottom" (Matt 27:51), signifying that Jesus had removed by his death the barrier of sin between God and the people. A tremendous new-covenant truth that we will examine in more detail later is that we now have *direct access* to God through Jesus Christ (see Heb 10:19–22).

As we turn now to John 4, we see Jesus breaking down other sorts of barriers as well.

1. See https://creativecommons.org/licenses/by-sa/3.0.
2. See https://creativecommons.org/licenses/by-sa/3.0.

## Jesus Breaks Down Geographical Barriers

[Jesus] left Judea and departed again for Galilee. And he had to pass through Samaria. (John 4:3–4)

The Samaritans were despised by the Jews,[3] for several reasons:

1. They were half-breeds, descended from the intermarriage of Jews and Gentiles (which was forbidden by the law).

2. They rejected all of the Old Testament except for the first five books.

3. They had established their own system of worship on Mount Gerizim in their territory.

The land of Samaria was situated between Judea in the south and Galilee in the north. A Jew traveling from Judea to Galilee, or vice versa, would go to great lengths to avoid going through Samaria by crossing over the Jordan River and going up (or down) the other side, before crossing back over.

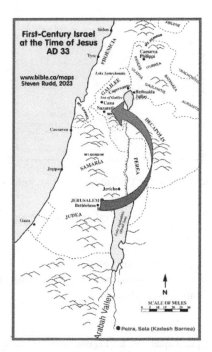

**First-Century Israel at the Time of Jesus, AD 33, by Steven Rudd**

3. That is what makes Jesus's parable of the good Samaritan in Luke 10 so ironically striking.

So it is interesting that John tells us that Jesus "*had to* pass through Samaria" (v. 4). In one sense, of course, he did not *have* to: he could have gone around, like every other Jew would have done. John seems to be implying that Jesus had to pass through Samaria because *the Father had a divine appointment for him to keep there.*[4] And so, to do the Father's will, Jesus breaks down the artificial geographical barrier erected by the Jews and goes right through Samaria.

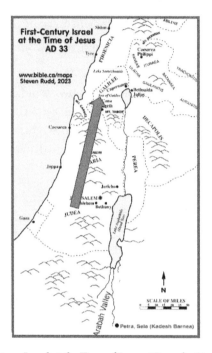

First-Century Israel at the Time of Jesus, AD 33, by Steven Rudd

## Jesus Breaks Down Social and Ethnic Barriers

So he came to a town of Samaria called Sychar, near the field that Jacob had given to his son Joseph. Jacob's well was there; so Jesus, wearied as he was from his journey, was sitting beside the well. It was about the sixth hour.

4. As Jesus later in the chapter will tell his disciples, "My food is to do the will of him who sent me and to accomplish his work" (John 4:34). And that work in this case is accomplished by Jesus through his saving conversation with the woman at the well and through the fact that "many Samaritans from that town believed in him because of the woman's testimony" (v. 39).

> A woman from Samaria came to draw water. Jesus said to her, "Give me a drink." (For his disciples had gone away into the city to buy food.) The Samaritan woman said to him, "How is it that you, a Jew, ask for a drink from me, a woman of Samaria?" (For Jews have no dealings with Samaritans.) (John 4:5–9)

In that culture it was not acceptable for a man to talk to a woman in public, and even less acceptable for a Jew to talk to a Samaritan. But Jesus was not concerned about the contrived social and ethnic prohibitions; he simply saw the woman as a human being, and a needy one at that.

## Jesus Breaks Down Spiritual Barriers

> Jesus answered her, "If you knew the gift of God, and who it is that is saying to you, 'Give me a drink,' you would have asked him, and he would have given you living water." The woman said to him, "Sir, you have nothing to draw water with, and the well is deep. Where do you get that living water? Are you greater than our father Jacob? He gave us the well and drank from it himself, as did his sons and his livestock." Jesus said to her, "Everyone who drinks of this water will be thirsty again, but whoever drinks of the water that I will give him will never be thirsty again. The water that I will give him will become in him a spring of water welling up to eternal life." The woman said to him, "Sir, give me this water, so that I will not be thirsty or have to come here to draw water." (John 4:10–15)

Jesus wants to offer her living water, and she does not quite understand: she seems interested only in getting water to drink. But Jesus is able to look beneath her immediate, surface desire and speak to her real need—her *spiritual* need. He reaches out to offer her the living water of salvation.

## Jesus Breaks Down Religious Barriers

> Jesus said to her, "Go, call your husband, and come here." The woman answered him, "I have no husband." Jesus said to her, "You are right in saying, 'I have no husband'; for you have had five husbands, and the one you now have is not your husband. What you have said is true." The woman said to him, "Sir, I perceive that you are a prophet. Our fathers worshiped on this mountain, but you say that in Jerusalem is the place where people ought to worship." Jesus said to her, "Woman, believe me, the

> hour is coming when neither on this mountain nor in Jerusalem
> will you worship the Father." (John 4:16–21)

Jesus's insight into the woman's marital situation leads her to bring up what is in effect a religious question. She refers to her people's worship on Mount Gerizim and the Jews' worship in Jerusalem; and her implied question is: "Which is correct? Which group is doing worship in the right way and the right place?"

And, as so often happens, Jesus answers this question in an unexpected and surprising way. He says, "The hour is coming" (and, in fact, "is now here" [v. 23]) when *neither* place is the appointed venue for worship of the Father. Jesus says, in effect, "I am changing the rules. With my coming everything is different."

## Worship "in spirit and truth"

> You worship what you do not know; we worship what we know, for salvation is from the Jews. But the hour is coming, and is now here, when the true worshipers will worship the Father in spirit and truth, for the Father is seeking such people to worship him. God is spirit, and those who worship him must worship in spirit and truth. (John 4:22–24)

In v. 23 (and again in v. 24) Jesus says that true worship will be worship "in spirit and truth." And the word *in* here is the same preposition as in v. 21, making the contrast even more clear: neither "*in* this mountain nor *in* Jerusalem will you worship the Father," but rather, "the true worshipers will worship the Father *in* spirit and truth."

Jesus seems to be inaugurating a major lessening of the importance of *where* or *when* one worships, and a wholesale magnifying of the importance of *how* one worships: "in spirit and truth."

## Worship "in spirit"

Many English translations render the word *spirit* in vv. 23–24 with a lowercase *s*, while other versions capitalize the word. And this is representative of the fact that, two thousand years after the fact, there is still a lot of debate and no consensus on whether Jesus is referring here to the "spirit" of humans, that is, to the inner, immaterial part of our being, or whether the Holy Spirit is in view.

While the Holy Spirit certainly plays a key role in worship (as we will examine in ch. 25), the fact that Jesus is referring to the human spirit here seems to be supported by his words in v. 24: "God is *spirit*, and those who worship him must worship in spirit and truth." In other words, God is a spiritual, immaterial being, and therefore people will connect with him primarily on a spiritual, immaterial level.[5]

"Worship in spirit" then refers to the fact that worship must come from the inside out (a prominent theme we will be coming back to again and again in our study). It must be sincere and genuine, from the heart.

And here Jesus may well have in mind an implicit contrast with the Jews. Jewish worship did follow the Old Testament prescriptions for worship; they worshiped according to God's revealed truth. *But* Jesus regularly criticized the Jewish leaders because of the merely *external* nature of their worship (for outward show):

> Beware of practicing your righteousness before other people in order to be seen by them, for then you will have no reward from your Father who is in heaven. Thus, when you give to the needy, sound no trumpet before you, as the hypocrites do in the synagogues and in the streets, that they may be praised by others. . . . And when you pray, you must not be like the hypocrites. For they love to stand and pray in the synagogues and at the street corners, that they may be seen by others. (Matt 6:1–2, 5)

> And in his teaching he said, "Beware of the scribes, who like to walk around in long robes and like greetings in the marketplaces and have the best seats in the synagogues and the places of honor at feasts, who devour widows' houses and for a pretense make long prayers. They will receive the greater condemnation." (Mark 12:38–40)

> Then Jesus said to the crowds and to his disciples, "The scribes and the Pharisees . . . preach, but do not practice. . . . They do all their deeds to be seen by others." (Matt 23:1–3, 5)

> Woe to you, scribes and Pharisees, hypocrites! For you clean the outside of the cup and the plate, but inside they are full of greed and self-indulgence. You blind Pharisee! First clean the inside of the cup and the plate, that the outside also may be clean.

5. Dallas Willard writes: "God is spirit and exists at the level of reality where the human heart, or *spirit*, also exists, serving as the foundation and source of our visible life. It is there that the individual meets with God 'in spirit and in truth'" (*Divine Conspiracy*, 194). A compelling, and perhaps conclusive, defense of this view on a grammatical basis may be found in Tim Ralston's paper "Ambiguity of 'in Spirit.'"

> Woe to you, scribes and Pharisees, hypocrites! For you are like whitewashed tombs, which outwardly appear beautiful, but within are full of dead people's bones and all uncleanness. So you also outwardly appear righteous to others, but within you are full of hypocrisy and lawlessness. (Matt 23:25–28)[6]

> You hypocrites! Well did Isaiah prophesy of you, when he said: "This people honors me with their lips, but their heart is far away from me. But in vain do they worship me, teaching as doctrines the precepts of men." (Matt 15:8–9)

God detests lip service in the absence of heart worship; he hates outward shows of religiosity without genuine and sincere inner devotion, the letter of the law without its spirit.[7] True worship must begin on the inside and be genuine and sincere. That is, worship in *spirit*.

## Worship "in truth"

But, Jesus says, worship must not only be "in spirit," it must also be "in truth." That is, it must be in God's way; as we saw in ch. 4, it must be a response to God's revelation.

Here we have an implicit criticism of Samaritan worship. False worship, we have seen, comes from trying to worship God in the absence of, or ignoring, God's revelation. And, as we saw above, that is what the Samaritans had done. Jesus said to the woman:

> You worship *what you do not know*; we worship what we know, for salvation is from the Jews. (4:22)

The Samaritans may have been very sincere, even enthusiastic, in their worship. But they worshiped what they did not know; their worship was not a response to God's revelation. They had devised their own form and place of worship while rejecting most of the Old Testament and God's revealed will concerning Jerusalem as the place where he was to be worshiped. (At least, Jesus says, the Jews had the advantage of worshiping "what we know," because salvation was "from the Jews," as the recipients and caretakers of God's revelation.)

6. See also the parable of the Pharisee and the tax collector in Luke 18:9–14.

7. We see this also in the Old Testament prophets, where God condemns the rituals and sacrifices of the people (even though externally they were in accordance with the Mosaic law) because of their *externality* in the absence of heartfelt adoration. (See, for instance, Amos 5:21–24.)

True worship must be "in truth," according to God's revelation. And of course, that means above all that true worship will be *through Christ*, God's ultimate revelation, who is himself *the Truth* ("I am the Way, and the *Truth*, and the Life" [John 14:6]). This is hinted at in our passage:

> The woman said to him, "I know that Messiah is coming (he who is called Christ). When he comes, he will tell us all things." Jesus said to her, "I who speak to you am he." (John 4:25–26)

David Peterson writes, "In effect, the exalted Christ is now the 'place' where God is to be acknowledged and honoured . . . rather than a renewed temple in Jerusalem or on some other holy mountain."[8]

## Worship "in spirit *and* truth"

So worship must be sincere and from the heart ("in spirit"), but also according to God's revelation" ("in truth"). Jesus is saying that *both* of those aspects are necessary.[9] That is true in our day as well.

Our worship must be *in spirit*, genuine and sincere, heartfelt, from the inside out. For there are institutions and groups in our world that may have an outward veneer of Christian tradition and practice, may sing the great hymns of the faith, may perhaps even recite the Apostles' Creed weekly—but the people maybe have not accepted Christ as their Savior and do not pursue him within a genuine heart of devotion (though of course only God can judge that).

Our worship must also be *in truth*, according to God's revelation in Christ. For there are many people in our world who are very sincere in their religious beliefs and practices, but do not know or reject God's truth and God's Savior. There is no question that suicide bombers are very devoted and committed to what they consider an act of obedience and worship; but once the deed is done, they of course immediately realize how utterly wrong they have been. Their devotion is, tragically, not according to God's truth.

These are the twin dangers to true worship, as Eric Alexander puts it:

8. D. Peterson, "Worship and Evangelism."

9. Paul may perhaps be alluding to this same idea when he writes: "I will pray with my spirit, but I will pray with my mind also; I will sing praise with my spirit, but I will sing with my mind also" (1 Cor 14:15).

> What are the two great enemies of true worship throughout the whole of history? . . . Are they not the errors of Gerizim on the one hand and Jerusalem on the other? Zeal without knowledge, on the one hand, and knowledge without zeal, on the other; sincerity without truth, or truth without heart, in worship.[10]

So both are necessary. "The true worshipers will worship the Father in spirit *and* truth" (4:23). Jesus says it must be according to God's revealed truth, which ultimately means, of course, that worship must be through Jesus Christ, and it must be genuine and sincere and from the heart. God wants our *hearts.*

## God Wants Our Lives

God also wants our *lives.* In the important worship verse we have already seen, Rom 12:1, we read:

> I appeal to you therefore, brethren, by the mercies of God, to present your bodies as a living sacrifice, holy and acceptable to God, which is your spiritual worship.

Paul seems to be here applying Jesus's teaching from John 4: if it is not so much a matter of *where* or *when* you worship, but *how* you worship; if worship in its deepest nature is in *spirit* and *truth*, and is not limited to a *place* like Mount Gerizim or Jerusalem—then worship must be *all of life.* For you can worship in any place, at any time, as long as it is in spirit and truth.

And so Paul says that, as an appropriate *response* to all "the mercies of God" we have received through Christ (as he has just expounded in Rom 1–11), we are to offer up our "bodies" (that is, our entire lives) as a fitting sacrifice of worship.

This is a crucial New Testament perspective on worship: that it is the response of our entire lives in thankful praise to the one who has redeemed us through Christ:

> You were bought with a price. So glorify God in your body. (1 Cor 6:20)

> So, whether you eat or drink, or whatever you do, do all to the glory of God. (1 Cor 10:31)

---

10. Third sermon ("John 4–3"), in Alexander, "Acceptable Worship."

Note: this does *not* mean that there are no longer any holy times or holy places—but rather that *every* time and *every* place is holy to the Lord![11]

God wants a life and a lifestyle of worship. Christians need to realize that they should not depend on their pastor or worship leader to be solely responsible for providing them their weekly allotment of worship. Rather, every believer is to be walking in a life and a lifestyle of worship all during the week. And when we do that, we come to church with hearts already filled with love for God, and that will make the corporate gathering that much more powerful and special than if they come empty.

Now, sometimes we do all come to church empty, and God in his grace will meet us there. But the *normal* pattern for the *healthy* Christian is a daily walk of worship, which then fills and strengthens and empowers the corporate gathering as well as our individual lives.

## The Father Is Seeking Worshipers

One important final observation may be made from John 4. Jesus said to the woman:

> But the hour is coming, and is now here, when the true worshipers will worship the Father in spirit and truth, for *the Father is seeking such people to worship him.* (John 4:23)

The Father is seeking *worshipers.*[12] That is what he wants first and foremost from every one of us. As we have seen, that is why he created us, and that is why he redeemed us.

Jesus never said, "The Father is seeking *pastors,*" or "The Father is seeking *missionaries,*" or "The Father is seeking *Christian businessmen and -women.*" Jesus said, "The Father is seeking *worshipers.*" That is what he wants in every one of our lives. That is why Jesus said:

> Seek first the kingdom of God and his righteousness, and all these things will be added to you. (Matt 6:33)

Many young Christians are seeking after "God's will for my life." *This is unequivocally God's will for your life*: he wants you to be a *worshiper.*

---

11. Paraphrasing a point made in "Worship under the Word," in Carson, *Worship by the Book,* 40.

12. Eric Alexander notes: "God was seeking that woman, sending the Lord Jesus Christ to the well—and her to the same well to meet him. That is the whole point of the incident. When Jesus saw that woman he was seeking a worshiper" (*Our Great God,* 133).

And, as in Matt 6:33, if we will go hard after that, we can trust God to lead us into the areas of vocation and service he has for us. But first, and above all, we must be worshipers.

Adrian Rogers puts it this way:

> The Father seeks to commune with you in worship. He is not looking for your money, your glory, or your strength. He is looking for your heart. C. S. Lewis said, "It is in the process of being worshiped that God communicates his presence to men." If you are not worshiping God, but you are serving him (or so you think), you are making a big mistake. To pray without worship is mockery. To sing without worship is sounding brass. To work without worship is an insult to God. To teach without worship is ignorance. To serve without worship is hypocrisy. To witness without worship is perjury. God wants your worship.[13]

At the same time, we must remember that becoming a worshiper is not something we can do entirely in our own strength. *Worship is not a work; it is a gift!* Worship is not something we do to gain acceptance from God. We can worship because of God's gracious initiative, because of what God has done for us through the Lord Jesus Christ. And the worship that truly pleases God is something our great High Priest, the Lord Jesus, leads us into and empowers us for. (Much more about this crucial truth in ch. 26.)

The Father is seeking worshipers. But we have a living Lord and the Holy Spirit to help activate that in us.

---

The Father is seeking worshipers. (John 4:23)

---

13. Rogers, "Worship."

# 11

## THE CENTRALITY OF WORSHIP IN HEAVEN

The Letter to the Hebrews and the book of Revelation are the great worship books of the New Testament (as the book of Psalms is to the Old Testament). Gloer says of Revelation:

> There is no book in the New Testament in which worship plays so prominent a role. The reason for this prominence is found in John's conviction that the question of worship is the fundamental and ultimate question of human existence in time and in eternity. "Worship determines the shape of human life and guarantees as well as defines life in the hereafter."[1]

> Then I looked, and I heard around the throne and the living creatures and the elders the voice of many angels, numbering myriads of myriads and thousands of thousands, saying with a loud voice,
> "Worthy is the Lamb who was slain,
>     to receive power and wealth and wisdom and might and honor and glory and blessing!"
> And I heard every creature in heaven and on earth and under the earth and in the sea, and all that is in them, saying,
> "To him who sits on the throne and to the Lamb
>     be blessing and honor and glory and might forever and ever!"
> And the four living creatures said, "Amen!" and the elders fell down and worshiped. (Rev 5:11–14)

1. Gloer, "Worship God!," 47; quoting Thompson, "Worship in Revelation," 47.

In this great worship scene in heaven, we see God the Father on the throne, along with the Lamb of God; then around them the angelic creatures referred to as the "four living creatures" (Rev 4:6–8), the (probably) angelic beings called the "twenty-four elders" (4:4), "myriads of myriads" of angels (5:11), and finally "every creature in heaven and on earth and under the earth and in the sea, and all that is in them" (5:13).[2]

## The Business of Heaven

The point is that these groups are all gathered (concentrically, it seems) around the throne, and all are focused on God and the Lamb and giving them praise. This is the business of heaven: a preoccupation with God, his glory, and his worship.[3] There are no side conversations. Nothing else is going on. All are focused on God and his glory, and that is a model for *our* worship as well: worship (as we have seen) is *about* God and *for* God, and our single-minded focus in worship should also be on the God of glory.

Yes, in corporate worship we also build one another up, as we join our hearts and voices (see Eph 5:19, "addressing *one another* in psalms and hymns and spiritual songs"); but our main purpose, our main focus, our main preoccupation should be God.

So this picture of worship in heaven, with its utter preoccupation with God and his glory, is a model for our earthly worship, as we prepare to one day join that great scene around the throne.

## Heavenly Worship Now

But the New Testament gives us another perspective on heavenly worship: it is not only our future, but also our present privilege.

---

2. More on the great scenes of worship in Revelation in ch. 23.

3. Note too the previous great scene of worship in Rev 4: the "four living creatures" continue the refrain in praise of God's holiness ("Holy, holy, holy is the Lord God Almighty," v. 8) that Isaiah had heard from the seraphim in his heavenly vision more than seven centuries previously (Isa 6:3). And, similarly, we see the worship of "twenty-four elders": "And whenever the living creatures give glory and honor and thanks to him who is seated on the throne, who lives forever and ever, the twenty-four elders fall down before him who is seated on the throne and *worship* him who lives forever and ever" (Rev 4:9–10).

[God] raised us up with [Christ] and seated us with him in the heavenly places in Christ Jesus. (Eph 2:6)

We are not only on earth (as "strangers and exiles" [Heb 11:13]) but are also positionally/spiritually already in heaven, for Paul tells us that "our citizenship is in heaven" (Phil 3:20). And the writer of Hebrews writes of a heavenly position that believers have already obtained:

> You *have come* to Mount Zion and to the city of the living God, the heavenly Jerusalem, and to innumerable angels in festal gathering, and to the assembly of the firstborn who are enrolled in heaven, and to God, the judge of all, and to the spirits of the righteous made perfect, and to Jesus, the mediator of a new covenant, and to the sprinkled blood that speaks a better word than the blood of Abel. (Heb 12:22–24)

My US passport carries these words:

> The Secretary of the United States of America hereby requests all whom it may concern to permit the citizen/national of the United States named herein to pass without delay or hindrance and in case of need to give all lawful aid and protection.

In other words, as a citizen of the United States I am due the rights and privileges that come from being a citizen of my country; and passports of other nations carry such verbiage also.

Now, since we are citizens of *heaven*, we have the rights and privileges that come from *that* status. That means that, in a very real sense, we can take part *now* in the worship of heaven—that land where we truly belong.

Corporate worship, in this understanding, is actually not something that *begins* and *ends* at the appointed times; rather, when we gather we are *joining in* with that worship that is always going on around the throne.

---

A preoccupation with God and his glory
is the business of heaven.

---

# 12

# WORSHIP IS CENTRAL

## A Unifying Theme

A nd so we have seen what a huge, central, pivotal theme worship is in the Scriptures. In fact, worship ties the entire biblical story together:

> The human person [has been shown] from the first pages of Genesis to the last of Revelation to be liturgical by nature, created and destined to live in the spiritual house of creation, as children of a royal and priestly family that offers sacrifices of praise to their Father-Creator with whom they dwell in a covenant of peace and love. . . . The story of the Bible is the story of humankind's journey to true worship in spirit and truth in the presence of God. That is the trajectory, the direction towards which narrative leads.[1]

God created us to worship him and to enjoy his presence. In the fall we refused to give him the worship that only he deserves, and turned to false worship of all kinds. From then on, the biblical narrative relates God's work throughout human history to restore to himself the worship of all creation.

God sent his Son to redeem us and thus enable us to become the worshipers of God that we were created to be, instead of the rebels against God that we had become. The gospel message may then be seen as a call

1. Hahn, "Canon," 225–26.

(a worldwide call, in missions) to all humankind to turn from false worship to true worship of the Creator God.

Once we have turned to true worship through Christ, worship then encapsulates the response of our entire lives to the glory of God displayed in creation and redemption.

And in the great scenes of worship in Revelation, we see the final consummation of God's purposes to receive unto himself the worship of all, and the fulfillment of the angel's charge (and the entire Bible's command) to "worship *God*" (Rev 22:9).

> John's vision of the last things is not meant to be an end in itself. It is a vision in the service of a far more fundamental call, the call to "Fear God and *worship* him who made heaven and earth" (14:7). Indeed, in this the last book in the Bible, we have "the last word on worship."[2]

## Others' Testimony to the Centrality of Worship

- John MacArthur: *Worship: The Ultimate Priority*
- John Piper: "Worshiping God is the number one duty of every human being."[3]
- A. P. Gibbs: *Worship: The Christian's Highest Occupation*
- Bruce Leafblad: "The worship of God is the most blessed of all earthly vocations. There is no higher or nobler task to which we can give our energies and devote our time. God is first. God is worthy. And we are privileged to enjoy personal fellowship with Him. . . . If God is to be first in our life, worship must get top priority."[4]
- G. Campbell Morgan: "The supreme thing is worship."[5]

---

2. Gloer, "Worship God!," 35 (emphasis added); quoting E. Peterson, *Reversed Thunder*, 57. "At the conclusion of our liturgical reading of the canon, we hear the purpose and meaning of the entire Bible summed up in the refrain of the Apocalypse: 'Worship God!' (Rev 14:6–7; 19:10; 22:9)" (Hahn, "Canon," 225).

3. Piper, "You Shall Worship."

4. Bruce Leafblad, foreword, in Allen and Borror, *Worship*, 10.

5. Morgan, "Psalm 96:9."

- Martin Luther: "After having faith, we can do nothing greater than to praise and honor God and to extol, preach, and sing his name, magnifying it in every way we can."[6]

- Eric Alexander: "Why has God designed and purposed that our great destiny is to know Him? What is the knowledge of God for? Why does God mean us to know Him and to grow in the knowledge of God? And there is only one answer that Scripture gives us to that: and that is that we might worship Him. Everything will disappear as we enter His presence and glory, except this. It is the chief business of the church of Jesus Christ in this world, because it is the permanent occupation of the church of Jesus Christ in the world to come, that we should worship God. So says Jesus to the woman of Samaria: The Father is seeking worshipers. When God began to seek you and then find you in Jesus Christ, and drew you to Himself, he was seeking worshipers. The apostle Paul tells us that it is the mark of the people of God, one of the great marks of those who are his true circumcision in Philippians 3:3f.: we are the circumcision, that is the true people of God, who worship God in the Spirit, rejoice in Christ Jesus, and have no confidence in the flesh. . . . What is the ultimate activity of the people of God? It is that we might spend ourselves, heart and soul and mind and strength, in worshiping Him."[7]

- Eric Alexander: "I well remember many years ago, when I was just a theological student, being in a lunch-hour service in the city of Glasgow in the city center, which I had been taken to by a friend because the speaker was the already quite legendary Martyn Lloyd-Jones from London. And Dr. Lloyd-Jones began his sermon that day with a question, as he frequently did. 'If I were to ask you,' he said, 'what was the greatest activity in which the people of God could ever engage; if I were to ask you what was the highest ambition that any man or woman created by God could ever have; if I were to ask you what would remain when every other activity in this world has fallen away—what would you say?'

  "And he proposed a considerable list of answers to his question which were manifestly not the right one, and then came ultimately to the answer.

---

6. Luther, *Treatise on Good Works*, §18.
7. Alexander, "Worship God!"

"'The answer,' he said, 'to my question is to render to God the *worship* that belongs by right to him. There is nothing in the whole universe that is of more significance than that. That is why God created the world: in order that it might be a theater in which he would be worshiped and adored. That is why God called and redeemed a people: in order that they might worship and glorify him. That's why God is perfecting the church of Jesus Christ in this age in order that they might be prepared to be worshipers in heaven with the church glorified. And when you focus it down to your own life, this is why God has made you. This is why God has given you a tongue and lips and a voice; this is why God has created every faculty of your being, that it might be engaged in the proper worship of Almighty God.'"[8]

- Billy Graham: "The purpose of this Christian society called the 'church' is, first: to glorify God by our worship. We do not go to church just to hear a sermon. We go to church to worship God."[9]

- James K. A. Smith: Worship "is the fundamental vocation of being human."[10]

- J. I. Packer (attributed to): "The purpose of theology is doxology; we study in order to praise."

---

| Worship is central because *God* is central. |
| --- |

---

8. Alexander, "Worship: Chief End."

9. Graham, *Peace with God*, 194.

10. J. Smith, *Desiring the Kingdom*, 162.

# Part 4

## Worship in the Old Testament[1]

1. Two fine Old Testament scholars have produced comprehensive studies of biblical worship, and their expertise results in especially detailed treatments of the Old Testament material: Allen P. Ross, *Recalling the Hope of Glory: Biblical Worship from the Garden to the New Creation*; and Daniel I. Block, *For the Glory of God: Recovering a Biblical Theology of Worship*. The reader is referred to these excellent works for further study of worship in the Old Testament.

# 13

## IMPORTANT THEMES AND VOCABULARY IN OLD TESTAMENT WORSHIP

### *Theme*: Worship as Response↑

A s we have already seen in ch. 4, the divine initiative is prominent throughout Scripture: "Acceptable worship does not start with human intuition or inventiveness, but with the action of God."[1] "All our worship is but our response to the self-giving of God in revelation and redemption."[2]

Thus we see this divine initiative operating in the Old Testament. "Again and again, the Old Testament makes the point that the Holy One can be approached only in the way that he himself stipulates and makes possible.[3]

### Worship as ↑ Response to ↓ Revelation

Then Moses said to God, "If I come to the people of Israel and say to them, 'The God of your fathers has sent me to you,' and they ask me, 'What is his name?' what shall I say to them?" God

---

1. D. Peterson, *Engaging with God*, 26.
2. Nicholls, *Jacob's Ladder*, 53.
3. D. Peterson, *Engaging with God*, 35.

said to Moses, "I AM WHO I AM." And he said, "Say this to the
people of Israel: 'I AM has sent me to you.'" (Exod 3:13–14)

God is revealing himself, his nature with this name: "I AM WHO I AM."
That is, "I am the self-existent One. I have no cause, no beginning. I am
God. There is no one like me, the Creator." The people's worship is going
to be in *response* to this *revelation* of himself through Moses.

## Worship as ↑ Response to Redemption

Say therefore to the people of Israel, "I am the LORD, and I will
bring you out from under the burdens of the Egyptians, and I
will deliver you from slavery to them, and I will redeem you
with an outstretched arm and with great acts of judgment."
(Exod 6:6)

[God] said, "But I will be with you, and this shall be the sign for
you, that I have sent you: when you have brought the people out
of Egypt, you shall *serve* God on this mountain." (Exod 3:12)

The word *serve* is also often translated as "worship" in the Old Testament. God is saying, "When I bring you out of Egypt, in response to my
redeeming work in your life as a nation, you shall worship me."

## Worship as ↑ Response to Covenant Relationship

"I will take you to be my people, and I will be your God, and you
shall know that I am the LORD your God, who has brought you
out from under the burdens of the Egyptians." (Exod 6:7)

God is going to form a special covenant relationship with this people. In
fact, the phrase "the LORD our God" occurs 440 times in the Old Testament! Obviously this is a central concept. And in response to that covenant relationship, they will give him their worship.

The entire sacrificial system, as it is presented in the Old Testament, is comprised within the covenant between the Lord and
His people; God has taken the initiative, having both prescribed
and provided the means of access to himself. Worship was thus
Israel's response to the covenant relationship and the means of
ensuring its continuance.[4]

---

4. Davies, "Worship," 851.

As we considered in ch. 4, throughout the Old Testament we see God acting first, and worship as a ↑ *response* to his gracious ↓ initiative.

## *Theme:* God's Grace, Lovingkindness, Mercy

Perhaps you have heard unbelievers (or even untaught believers) say something like: "The God of the Old Testament is a God of hate and violence, and the God of the New Testament is a God of love." But *God does not change*, and the Old Testament is full of demonstrations of God's love, grace, and mercy, represented especially by a special, beautiful, and powerful Hebrew word:

חֶסֶד

*ḥesed*

The word *ḥesed* is used 248 times in the Old Testament; about half of those occurrences are in Psalms, and 26 times in Ps 136 alone (as part of a repeated refrain). Obviously a *very* important word, it is usually rendered (depending on the translation) as "steadfast love" or "lovingkindness" or "mercy." *ḥesed* combines the idea of love and loyalty. It speaks of God's faithfulness to those who are in covenant with him, his *loyal love*. And throughout the Old Testament we see God being faithful to his covenant people Israel, even though they time and time again turn away from him.

## Examples

A few of the many instances of this key Old Testament covenant word:

> You shall not make for yourself a carved image, or any likeness of anything that is in heaven above, or that is in the earth beneath, or that is in the water under the earth. You shall not bow down to them or serve them, for I the LORD your God am a jealous God, visiting the iniquity of the fathers on the children to the third and the fourth generation of those who hate me, but showing *steadfast love* to thousands of those who love me and keep my commandments. (Exod 20:4–6)

> The LORD passed before him and proclaimed, "The LORD, the LORD, a God merciful and gracious, slow to anger, and

abounding in *steadfast love* and faithfulness, keeping *steadfast love* for thousands, forgiving iniquity and transgression and sin. (Exod 34:6–7)

And Solomon said, "You have shown great and *steadfast love* to your servant David my father, because he walked before you in faithfulness, in righteousness, and in uprightness of heart toward you. And you have kept for him this great and *steadfast love* and have given him a son to sit on his throne this day." (1 Kgs 3:6)

Yet our God has not forsaken us in our slavery, but has extended to us his *steadfast love* before the kings of Persia, to grant us some reviving to set up the house of our God, to repair its ruins, and to give us protection in Judea and Jerusalem. (Ezra 9:9)

Surely goodness and *mercy* shall follow me all the days of my life, and I shall dwell in the house of the LORD forever. (Ps 23:6)

Many are the sorrows of the wicked,
    but *steadfast love* surrounds the one who trusts in the LORD.
(Ps 32:10)

He loves righteousness and justice;
    the earth is full of the *steadfast love* of the LORD. (Ps 33:5)

Bless the LORD, O my soul,
    and all that is within me,
    bless his holy name! . . .
Who redeems your life from the pit,
    who crowns you with *steadfast love* and mercy. . . .
The LORD is merciful and gracious,
    slow to anger and abounding in *steadfast love.* . . .
For as high as the heavens are above the earth,
    so great is his *steadfast love* toward those who fear him; . . .
But the *steadfast love* of the LORD is from everlasting to everlasting on those who fear him,
    and his righteousness to children's children.
(Ps 103:1, 4, 8, 11, 17)

The LORD is gracious and merciful, slow to anger and abounding in *steadfast love.* (Ps 145:8)

But let him who boasts boast in this, that he understands and knows me, that I am the Lord who practices *steadfast love*, justice, and righteousness in the earth. For in these things I delight, declares the LORD. (Jer 9:24)

As can be seen in these references, God's *hesed* is *basic to who he is*. He is "abounding in steadfast love" to those in covenant relationship with him—including, of course, us!

## A Repeated Refrain

Psalm 136 was obviously written to be used in the public worship of Israel. A priest would exclaim the first half of every verse, and the people would respond in each instance with the repeated refrain:

> Give thanks to the LORD, for he is good,
>    for his *steadfast love* endures forever.
> Give thanks to the God of gods,
>    for his *steadfast love* endures forever.
> Give thanks to the LORD of lords,
>    for his *steadfast love* endures forever [etc.].

To a people who did not have their own copy of the psalm, this would be a powerful teaching tool, as well as to their children: the clear proclamation and reminder (over and over, for twenty-six verses) of the Lord's everlasting, loyal love to them as his covenant people.

## David's Enduring Confidence

David, when he was running for his life in the wilderness of Judah after his son Absalom had rebelled against him, composed a profound statement of trust in God in Ps 63. (In fact, one writer has pointed out that, in spite of David's desperate situation, there is no request in the entire psalm; there is only *praise*.) And he proclaims:

> Because your *steadfast love* is better than life,
>    my lips will praise you. (Ps 63:3)

David was running for his life, but still he could rejoice in God's *hesed*, because he held it to be *better than life* itself.

And so, we see what a crucial theme in the Old Testament is this concept of God's *hesed*. God ↓ *reveals* his *hesed*, and it is a powerful motivation for the ↑ *response* of praise.

## *Theme:* Worship of the Heart (Spiritual Sacrifices)

When many of us think about worship in the Old Testament, our minds go first to the tabernacle/temple and its sacrifices, rituals, ceremonies, and festivals—the *external* trappings of worship under the Mosaic covenant. However, these externals are actually of *secondary* importance when it comes to the worship that God desires from his people under the old covenant. He is looking for an *inner reality*, without which the external observances are of no value to him.

> The theology of the Old Testament shows that the special place in which God is present is the hearts of the people who invoke him.[5]

## A Surprisingly Common Emphasis

This unexpected truth is nevertheless plainly evident throughout the Old Testament. We can feel the force of God's own priority by examining a wide array of passages:

> The LORD said to Moses, "Speak to the people of Israel, that they take for me a contribution. From every man *whose heart moves him* you shall receive the contribution for me." (Exod 25:1–2)

> Now, Israel, what does the LORD your God require from you, but to *fear* the LORD your God, to *walk* in all his ways and *love* him, and to serve the LORD your God *with all your heart and with all your soul*? . . . Circumcise therefore the foreskin of your *heart.* (Deut 10:12, 16a)

> Samuel said, "Has the LORD as much delight in burnt offerings and sacrifices as in *obeying* the voice of the LORD? Behold *to obey is better than sacrifice,* and to heed than the fat of rams." (1 Sam 15:22)

> For the LORD sees not as man sees: man looks on the outward appearance, but *the LORD looks on the heart.* (1 Sam 16:7)

> O LORD, who shall sojourn in your tent? Who shall dwell on your holy hill? He who walks blamelessly and does what is right and speaks truth *in his heart.* (Ps 15:1–2)

> Sacrifice and meal offering you have *not* desired; my ears you have opened; burnt offering and sin offering you have *not* required. . . . I delight to do your will, O my God; your law is *within my heart.* (Ps 40:6)

5. Allmen, *Worship*, 241.

> Hear, O my people, and I will speak;
> O Israel, I will testify against you.
> > I am God, your God.
> Not for your sacrifices do I rebuke you;
> > your burnt offerings are continually before me.
> I will *not* accept a bull from your house or goats from your folds.
> For every beast of the forest is mine, the cattle on a thousand
> > hills.
> I know all the birds of the hills, and all that moves in the field
> > is mine.
> If I were hungry, I would not tell you,
> > for the world and its fullness are mine.
> Do I eat the flesh of bulls or drink the blood of goats?
> Offer to God *a sacrifice of thanksgiving*
> > and perform your vows to the Most High. . . .
> The one who offers *thanksgiving as his sacrifice* glorifies me.
> (Ps 50:7–14, 23a)

For you do *not* delight in sacrifice, otherwise I would give it; You are *not* pleased with burnt offering. *The sacrifices of God are a broken spirit; a broken and a contrite heart,* O God, you will not despise. (Ps 51:16–17)

I will praise the name of God with song and magnify him with *thanksgiving.* And it will *please the* LORD *better* than an ox or a young bull with horns and hoofs. (Ps 69:30–31)

Bless the LORD, O my *soul,* and all that is *within me,* bless his holy name! (Ps 103:1)

May my *prayer* be *counted as incense* before you; the lifting up of my hands as the evening offering. (Ps 141:2)

Then the LORD said, "Because this people draw near with their words and honor me with their lip service, but they remove their *hearts* far from me, and their reverence for me consists of tradition learned by rote . . ." (Isa 29:13)

For I delight in loyalty *rather than sacrifice,* and in the knowledge of God *rather than burnt offerings.* (Hos 6:6)

Tear your *hearts* and not your garments. (Joel 2:13)

With what shall I come to the LORD and bow myself before the God on high? Shall I come to him with burnt offerings, with yearling calves? Does the LORD take delight in thousands of rams, in ten thousand rivers of oil? Shall I present my firstborn for my rebellious acts, the fruit of my body for the sin of my soul? He has told you, O man, what is good; and what does the LORD require of you but to *do justice*, to *love kindness*, and to *walk humbly* with your God? (Mic 6:6–8)

We have considered so many different passages in order to see what an important priority this is, even in the Old Testament with all its external rites and practices: God places priority on the *internal reality of worship, on sincere devotion* as a necessary prerequisite. As C. S. Lewis puts it, it is not as though God "really needed the blood of bulls and goats."[6]

As H. H. Rowley shows, the *heart* of sacrifice in the Old Testament was its expression of the worshipers' self-surrender to God:

> The efficacy of the ritual act was believed to depend on its being the expression of the spirit of the offerer.... It must be the organ of the approach of men to God in the sincerity of their confession before it could be the organ of God's approach to them in delivering them from their iniquity and in restoring them to righteousness.[7]

## A Powerful Example

One more remarkable passage along these lines is found in 2 Chronicles: King Hezekiah (one of the declining number of kings in Judah who "did what was right in the sight of the LORD" [2 Chr 29:2]) led the people in a revival of devotion to God and reinstituted the Passover after generations of neglect. We read in ch. 30:

> And many people came together in Jerusalem to keep the Feast of Unleavened Bread in the second month, a very great assembly. They set to work and removed the altars that were in Jerusalem, and all the altars for burning incense they took away and threw into the brook Kidron. And they slaughtered the Passover lamb on the fourteenth day of the second month. And the priests and the Levites were ashamed, so that they consecrated themselves and brought burnt offerings into the house of the LORD. They took their accustomed posts according to the Law of Moses the man of God. The priests threw the blood that they received from the hand of the Levites. For there were many in the assembly who

6. C. S. Lewis, "On Church Music," 123.

7. Wainwright, *Doxology*, 400; citing H. H. Rowley, *Worship in Ancient Israel*, 113, 143.

had not consecrated themselves. Therefore the Levites had to slaughter the Passover lamb for everyone who was not clean, to consecrate it to the LORD. For a majority of the people, many of them from Ephraim, Manasseh, Issachar, and Zebulun, *had not cleansed themselves, yet they ate the Passover otherwise than as prescribed.* For Hezekiah had prayed for them, saying, "May the good LORD pardon everyone *who sets his heart to seek God,* the LORD, the God of his fathers, *even though not according to the sanctuary's rules of cleanness." And the LORD heard Hezekiah and healed the people.* And the people of Israel who were present at Jerusalem kept the Feast of Unleavened Bread seven days with great gladness, and the Levites and the priests praised the LORD day by day, singing with all their might to the LORD. (2 Chr 30:13–21)

We see that although a majority of the people had not followed God's explicit instructions for ritual cleansing in preparation for taking the Passover, yet had taken it anyway ("otherwise than as prescribed"; "not according to the sanctuary's rules of cleanness"), Hezekiah boldly asks God to forgive them on the basis of their zeal for worshiping the Lord through the Passover ("everyone who sets his heart to seek God"). And, astonishingly, God overlooks *his own rules* and shows the priority he places on sincere *hearts* of worship.

## The New Testament Witness

We see this priority upheld in the New Testament.

Jesus often criticized the Jewish leaders because of the externality of their religious observances, performing rituals to be seen by others, in the absence of heart-felt devotion to God.

Beware of practicing your righteousness before other people *in order to be seen by them*, for then you will have no reward from your Father who is in heaven.

Thus, when you give to the needy, sound no trumpet before you, as the hypocrites do in the synagogues and in the streets, *that they may be praised by others.* Truly, I say to you, they have received their reward. . . . And when you pray, you must not be like the hypocrites. For they love to stand and pray in the synagogues and at the street corners, *that they may be seen by others.* Truly, I say to you, they have received their reward. (Matt 6:1–2, 5)

And as Jesus reclined at table in the house, behold, many tax collectors and sinners came and were reclining with Jesus and his disciples. And when the Pharisees saw this, they said to his disciples, "Why does your teacher eat with tax collectors and sinners?" But when he heard it, he said, "Those who are well have no need of a physician, but those who are sick. Go and learn what this means: '*I desire mercy, and not sacrifice.*' For I came not to call the righteous, but sinners." (Matt 9:10–13)

And the Pharisees and the scribes asked him, "Why do your disciples not walk according to the tradition of the elders, but eat with defiled hands?" And he said to them, "Well did Isaiah prophesy of you hypocrites, as it is written,
> 'This people honors me with *their lips*,
> but *their heart* is far from me;
> *in vain* do they worship me,
> teaching as doctrines the commandments of men.'"
(Mark 7:5–7; see also Matt 15:7–9)

Jesus condemned this kind of worship as being "in vain," i.e., worthless.[8]

On the other hand, Jesus commended expressions of worship that came *from the inside out:*[9]

And one of the scribes came up and heard them disputing with one another, and seeing that he answered them well, asked him, "Which commandment is the most important of all?" Jesus answered, "The most important is, 'Hear, O Israel: The Lord our God, the Lord is one. And you shall love the Lord your God with all your heart and with all your soul and with all your mind and with all your strength.' The second is this: 'You shall love your neighbor as yourself.' There is no other commandment greater than these." And the scribe said to him, "You are right, Teacher. You have truly said that he is one, and there is no other besides him. And *to love him with all the heart and with all the understanding and with all the strength,* and to love one's neighbor as oneself, is *much more than all whole burnt offerings and sacrifices.*" And when Jesus saw that he answered wisely, he said to him, "You are not far from the kingdom of God." (Mark 12:28–33)

---

8. Jesus's decrying of the Jewish leaders as "hypocrites" (Matt 6:2, 5, 16; 15:7; 22:18; 23:13, 23, 25, 27, 29; 24:51; Mark 7:6; Luke 12:56; 13:15) grew out of his "emphasis upon the moral significance of the inmost heart before God" (Willard, *Divine Conspiracy*, 191).

9. "Our heart is who we really are. Jesus therefore made repeated and unmistakable distinctions between our face to the world and our person before God" (Willard, *Divine Conspiracy*, 191).

Note that Jesus commended the scribe above *because he embraced Jesus's own priority*. (See the fuller treatment of this passage on pp. 220–22.)

> He also told this parable to some who *trusted in themselves* that they were righteous, and treated others with contempt: "Two men went up into the temple to pray, one a Pharisee and the other a tax collector. The Pharisee, standing by himself, prayed thus: 'God, I thank you that I am not like other men, extortioners, unjust, adulterers, or even like this tax collector. I fast twice a week; I give tithes of all that I get.' But the tax collector, standing far off, would not even lift up his eyes to heaven, but beat his breast, saying, 'God, be merciful to me, a sinner!' I tell you, this man went down to his house justified, *rather than the other*. For everyone who exalts himself will be humbled, but the one who humbles himself will be exalted." (Luke 18:9–14)

Jesus said that the tax collector was *justified* because of the attitude of his *heart*; and the Pharisee was *not justified*, because his heart was full of pride as he offered up merely *external* things.

> Jesus looked up and saw the rich putting their gifts into the offering box, and he saw a poor widow put in two small copper coins. And he said, "Truly, I tell you, this poor widow has put in more than all of them. For they all contributed out of their abundance, but she out of her poverty put in all she had to live on." (Luke 21:1–4)

Jesus remarkably stated that the widow "put in *more than all of them*," because her gift of two small coins (all she had) expressed the complete devotion of her heart. Her offering was more: not in *quantity*, but rather in *quality*. God does not *need* our money; he desires that we give as an expression of our heart for him.

Paul, Peter, and the author of Hebrews echo this theme as well:

> For no one is a Jew who is merely one *outwardly*, nor is circumcision outward and physical. But a Jew is one *inwardly*, and circumcision is a matter of the *heart*, by the Spirit, not by the letter. His praise is not from man but from God. (Rom 2:28–29)

> As you come to him, a living stone rejected by men but in the sight of God chosen and precious, you yourselves like living stones are being built up as a spiritual house, to be a holy priesthood, to offer *spiritual sacrifices* acceptable to God through Jesus Christ. (1 Pet 2:4–5)

Through [Christ] then let us continually offer up *a sacrifice of praise* to God, that is, the fruit of lips that acknowledge his name. (Heb 13:15)

External religion and outward expressions without an internal reality are meaningless to God. God is always more concerned about the worship of the heart.

It is, of course, all too possible for us to "go through the motions" in our public and even our private worship, when God is really looking for our heart. It is all too possible to eat the bread and drink the cup in a rote manner while being numb to the spiritual significance of Christ's death for us and the privilege of remembering his sacrifice in this way that he commanded. Baptism also gains true meaning only if it is undergone as a public expression of a spiritual transaction that only God can perform.

And in our worship debates also we must be mindful of this same principle. For most debates, disagreements, and conflicts concerning worship in our churches revolve around external things: practices, tradition, styles, instruments, etc. But God is much, much more concerned that we approach him with genuine hearts of worship. He does not have favorite styles, songs, instruments, or building types! (That should be obvious from the enormous variety of practices in the church worldwide.) He is looking for, and at, our *hearts*. Indeed, "Man looks on the outward appearance, but the LORD looks on the heart" (1 Sam 16:7).

## *Theme:* Calling on the Name of the Lord

It is commonly recognized that a person's name in the Bible is very significant and can often say a lot about a person's nature or character or reputation. So too *God's* name speaks of who he is in his unique holiness.[10] (In fact, as we will see when we talk about Abraham, God reveals himself through a variety of titles and names, which show different aspects of his nature.) That's why the third commandment forbids using his name in vain (that is, in a flippant way): because it is his name that speaks of his nature as the sole One deserving worship.

10. God says: "I am the Lord; that is *my name*; my glory I give *to no other*, nor my praise to carved idols" (Isa 42:8). God calls his people by *his name* (2 Chr 7:14); and he leads (Ps 23:3), forgives (Ps 25:11), delivers (Ps 79:9), and has mercy (Isa 48:9; Ezek 20:9, 22) "for *his/my name's sake.*"

If we remember the biblical pattern of revelation and response, we see that God in Scripture is revealing *his name*; and there are numerous instances in the Old Testament of people "calling on the name of the Lord," which simply means responding to this God who has made his name known. So this response of "calling on the name of the Lord" is another Old Testament way of referring to personal and public acts of worship.

<table>
<tr><td>God reveals his<br>*name* (his nature,<br>character).</td><td></td><td></td><td>People call on<br>the *name* of the<br>Lord.</td></tr>
</table>

So, for example, after God revealed himself to Abraham in Gen 12:1–3 and sent him to the land he would show him, we read that upon arriving in this land: "And there Abraham built an altar to the Lord and *called upon the name of the Lord*" (Gen 12:8). (Note too the stark contrast to the previous chapter, when the inhabitants of Babel conspired to "make a name *for ourselves*" [Gen 11:4].)

Other examples of "calling on the name of the Lord" as *worship*:

> To Seth also a son was born, and he called his name Enosh. At that time people began to *call upon the name of the* LORD. (Gen 4:26)

> And [Abram] journeyed on from the Negeb as far as Bethel to the place where his tent had been at the beginning, between Bethel and Ai, to the place where he had made an altar at the first. And there Abram *called upon the name of the* LORD. (Gen 13:3–4)

> So [Isaac] built an altar there and *called upon the name of the* LORD and pitched his tent there. And there Isaac's servants dug a well. (Gen 26:25)

> Oh give thanks to the LORD; *call upon his name*;
>    make known his deeds among the peoples! (1 Chr 16:8)

> Pour out your anger on the nations
>    that do not know you,
>    and on the kingdoms
>    that do not *call upon your name*! (Ps 79:6)

> Oh give thanks to the LORD; *call upon his name*;
>    make known his deeds among the peoples! (Ps 105:1)

Because he inclined his ear to me,
therefore I will *call on him* as long as I live. (Ps 116:2)

I will offer to you the sacrifice of thanksgiving
and *call on the name of the LORD.* (Ps 116:17)

For at that time I will change the speech of the peoples
to a pure speech,
that all of them may *call upon the name of the LORD*
and serve him with one accord. (Zeph 3:9)[11]

Calling on the name of the Lord, in response to God's revelation of his name, of his nature, is then another way to speak of worship.[12]

## *Theme:* The Presence of God

The fifth and final theme is the theme of *God's presence.* This major theme in the Old Testament centers around God's special presence in the midst of his chosen people Israel in the tabernacle and later in the temple. His people (or at least the priests) are said to come "before the Lord" or "before the face of the Lord" 236 times in the Old Testament (61 times in Leviticus, in the context of ceremonial approach by the priests). (The latter phrase, in Hebrew *lipnē Yahweh*, is a figure of speech called a *synecdoche*, where a part represents the whole—in this case, the Lord's face standing for his whole person.) This promised presence (though mediated through the priests, as we have seen) speaks of God's desire to be in *relationship* with his people.

This is a constant (and even unifying) theme through all of Scripture, as Duvall and Hays observe:

11. Other times the phrase is used of prayer, as someone is entreating the Lord for rescue or salvation (see, for example, 2 Sam 22:4; 1 Kgs 18:24; 2 Kgs 5:11; Ps 18:6; 116:4; Joel 2:32; Acts 2:21; Rom 10:13).

12. This carries into the New Testament as well: "Calling on the name of the Lord is an action and a theme that . . . has deep Old Testament roots. It was the great heritage of Israel's worship. . . . It is significant that Paul's use of the expression here with reference to Jesus [in Rom 10:9, 13: 'If you confess with your mouth, "Jesus is Lord," and believe in your heart that God raised him from the dead, you will be saved . . . for, "Everyone who calls on the name of the Lord will be saved."'] is only one example of a usage that we find in several other places in the New Testament where believers 'call on the name' of Jesus—an action from which Jews would certainly have recoiled in horror as blasphemy, if they had not been convinced that in doing so they were in effect calling on the name of the Lord himself (Acts 9:14, 21; 22:16; 1 Cor 1:2; 2 Tim 2:22)" (C. Wright, *Mission of God*, 121).

The triune God desires a personal relationship with His people and so makes His presence known to establish and cultivate this relationship. . . . This relational presence of God lies at the heart of the Bible's overall message.[13]

The so-called *Aaronic blessing*, which God commands Aaron and his sons to pronounce upon the people, strongly communicates God's heart to be relationally present among his people:

13. Duvall and Hays, *God's Relational Presence*, 325. These authors, as their subtitle *The Cohesive Center of Biblical Theology* implies, see this as the theme of the entire Bible. In their volume they go through the entire Bible, book by book, and show the consistent thread of God's desire to be with us, to have a relationship with us, to make his presence known to us. Some examples:

Gen 2–3: fellowship with God in the garden.
Rom 1:21: They knew God.
And they heard the sound of the LORD God walking in the garden in the cool of the day, and the man and his wife hid themselves from the *presence* of the LORD God among the trees of the garden (Gen 3:8).
Then the LORD said to Jacob, "Return to the land of your fathers and to your kindred, and *I will be with you*" (Gen 31:3).
He said, "*But I will be with you*, and this shall be the sign for you, that I have sent you: when you have brought the people out of Egypt, you shall serve God on this mountain" (Exod 3:12).
I will take you to be My people, and *I will be your God*, and you shall know that I am the LORD your God, who has brought you out from under the burdens of the Egyptians (Exod 6:7).
Then the cloud covered the tent of meeting, and *the glory of the LORD filled the tabernacle* (Exod 40:34).
I will make my dwelling among you, and my soul shall not abhor you. And *I will walk among you and will be your God*, and you shall be my people (Lev 26:11–12).
No man shall be able to stand before you all the days of your life. *Just as I was with Moses, so I will be with you*. I will not leave you or forsake you (Josh 1:5).
As soon as Solomon finished his prayer, fire came down from heaven and consumed the burnt offering and the sacrifices, and *the glory of the LORD filled the temple* (2 Chr 7:1).
[Teach] them to observe all that I have commanded you. And behold, *I am with you always*, to the end of the age (Matt 28:20).
And the Word became flesh and *dwelt among us*, and we have seen his glory, glory as of the only Son from the Father, full of grace and truth (John 1:14).
Even the Spirit of truth, whom the world cannot receive, because it neither sees him nor knows him. You know him, for *he dwells with you and will be in you* (John 14:17).
He has said, "*I will never leave you nor forsake you*" (Heb 13:5).
And I heard a loud voice from the throne saying, "Behold, the dwelling place of God is with man. *He will dwell with them*, and they will be his people, and *God himself will be with them as their God*" (Rev 21:3).

The LORD bless you and keep you; the LORD make His face to shine upon you and be gracious to you; the LORD lift up His face upon you and give you peace. (Num 6:24–26)

## Important Vocabulary in Old Testament Worship

There are many words used for praise and similar expressions in the book of Psalms. For an extensive treatment of these terms, please see Ross, *Recalling the Hope of Glory*, and Block, *For the Glory of God.*

Here we want to only focus on the two main Hebrew words for worship in the Old Testament.

### *ḥistahavah*

The original meaning of this verb carried with it the idea of bowing down in reverence or honor before a mighty person or ultimately, of course, before God. The word came to be used more generally of worship, even when there was not a physical expression involved, but still with the idea of homage, submission, respect, adoration. So in 1 Chr 16:29:

> Ascribe to the LORD the glory due his name;
>   bring an offering and come before him!
> *Worship* the LORD in the splendor of holiness.

*ḥistahavah* is very similar in sense to the primary word for worship in the New Testament, *proskuneō*; and in fact this Greek word is most commonly used to render *ḥistahavah* in the Septuagint (the Greek translation of the Old Testament).

### *ʿabad*

This word is rendered as "worship" or "serve" in various English translations. For instance, God repeatedly says to Pharaoh through Moses: "Let my people go, that they might *worship/serve* me" (Exod 7:16; 8:1, 20; 9:1, 13; 10:3).

The seeming interchangeability of these two translations is clarified by understanding that the *serving* in the biblical writers' minds is not simply *doing activities* for God; rather, it speaks of *an inner attitude of heart allegiance and obedience* (to God, or to a false god). This is clearly seen in statements like Joshua's:

> Choose this day *whom you will serve*, whether the gods your fathers served in the region beyond the River, or the gods of the Amorites in whose land you dwell. But as for me and my house, *we will serve the LORD*. (Josh 24:15)

And similarly:

> You shall not make for yourself a carved image, or any likeness of anything that is in heaven above, or that is in the earth beneath, or that is in the water under the earth. You shall not bow down to them or *serve them*. (Exod 20:4–5)

Once again, there is a close parallel with a New Testament term: in this case, *latreuō*, which is likewise translated "worship" or "serve" in various contexts, and also with the sense of heart allegiance (rather than just religious tasks).

---

God is always more concerned about the worship of the *heart* than about its outward form.

---

# 14

## WORSHIP IN OLD TESTAMENT HISTORY

### *Pentateuch*[1]

> The Bible is the astounding drama of God's love drawing the
> worship of the nations. . . . God ↓ *reveals* his glory *to* all peoples
> so that he may ↑ *receive* glory *from* all creation. This double di-
> mension of glory can help make sense out of an apparent jumble
> of ancient stories.[2]

We now want to survey the Old Testament portion of that drama,
period by period, to see what we can learn about worship.

### The Beginning Period (Gen 1–11)

#### Creation (Gen 1–2)

We have already seen in chs. 5 and 7 how God created humankind to
worship him and reflect his glory.

> In the beginning, there was worship. . . . According to the Bible,
> the ↓ *relationship* between God the sovereign Creator and the
> human beings created in his image is the foundation upon which

---

1. The term is used to refer to the first five books of the Old Testament (Genesis through Deuteronomy) collectively.

2. Hawthorne, "Story of His Glory" (emphasis and arrows added).

all theological concepts rest. As beings created by God, men and women are to ↑ *respond* to him, to pay him due service.[3]

## The Fall (Gen 3)

In ch. 7 we also saw that the central issue in the fall was the issue of worship.

> The sin was between Adam's heart and God. The sin was not first wife abuse. That came soon—as a consequence (Gen 3:12). But it was not first. First was God abuse. And it was not physical. It was spiritual.
>
> Adam hit God. But not with his fist. He hit him with his heart. He said, in effect, "I don't trust you anymore to provide the best life. I think I know better than you what the best life is. I reject your love. I reject your wisdom. I reject you as my all-wise, all-providing Father. I vote for myself as the sovereign in this relationship. I will do it my way." That was man's derision of the greatness and beauty and worth of God. Which was outrageous in proportion to the infinite worthiness of God to be treated otherwise.[4]

Worship, as the English term denotes, is recognizing and celebrating the "worth-ship" of God. That's what Adam and Eve refused to do. "Although they knew God, they did not honor him as God or give thanks to him . . . and [they] worshiped and served the creature rather than the Creator" (Rom 1:21, 25).

## Cain and Abel (Gen 4:1–17)

We see in the very next chapter after the fall that worship, and the family, have already been horribly corrupted by sin. The first murder in the Bible revolves around an act of worship.

When Cain and Abel bring their offerings,[5] God accepts Abel's but not Cain's. And then Cain, in anger at this rejection, slays his brother.

---

3. Hattori, "Theology of Worship," 21 (emphasis and arrows added).

4. Piper, *Providence*, 503.

5. Genesis does not tell us how they knew to bring offerings at all, but we can assume that they received instruction along these lines, either directly from God or through their parents.

Why did God accept Abel's sacrifice and not Cain's? Some interpreters hold that the reason is that Abel brought an animal sacrifice (assuming only a blood sacrifice is acceptable to God), and Cain brought only a grain offering. However, later in the Mosaic law, grain offerings are *commanded*, along with animal sacrifices. In fact, grain offerings are mentioned thirty-four times in Leviticus and sixty times in Numbers! Obviously such offerings are acceptable to God, so this cannot be the reason why Cain's gift was rejected.

Why then was Abel's gift accepted and not Cain's? Hebrews 11 gives us the answer:

> *By faith* Abel offered to God a more acceptable sacrifice than Cain. (Heb 11:4)

It was *the heart of faith* with which Abel made his offering that made it acceptable. (The implication is that Cain did not offer his gift in faith; and we see something of Cain's heart from his response of murderous anger, rather than remorse or shame before God.)

Here we see an illustration of the theme seen in ch. 13 of the priority God places on the *heart attitude of the worshiper*. As Daniel Block puts it: "We tend to think that the gift makes the person acceptable to God; but actually it is the person [specifically, that person's heart attitude] that makes the gift acceptable to God."[6]

## Jubal (Gen 4:21)

> [Jabal's] brother's name was Jubal; he was the father of all those who play the lyre and pipe.

Here we have the first mention of *music* in the Bible.

## The Godly Line: Seth and Enosh (Gen 4:25–26)

> And Adam knew his wife again, and she bore a son and called his name Seth, for she said, "God has appointed for me another offspring instead of Abel, for Cain killed him." To Seth also a son was born, and he called his name Enosh. At that time people began to call upon the name of the LORD.

6. Comment during plenary discussion at the Biblical Theology of Worship Consultation, Calvin Institute of Christian Worship, Grand Rapids, Mar. 20, 2009.

God always had a remnant of faithful worshipers, even while sin and re-bellion also continued.

## Noah and the Flood (Gen 6–8)

The wickedness of humankind in general leads God to destroy the world in a great flood, but he preserves the remnant of Noah and his family.

> So Noah went out, and his sons and his wife and his sons' wives with him. . . . Then Noah built an altar to the LORD and took some of every clean animal and some of every clean bird and offered burnt offerings on the altar. (Gen 8:18, 20)[7]

The first thing Noah did upon disembarking from the ark (in ↑ *response* to God's ↓ *rescue* of him and his family) was to *build an altar* and offer sacrificial *worship*.

## The Tower of Babel (Gen 11)

Men and women in their pride, instead of filling the earth as they were commanded through Adam and Eve (Gen 1:28) and Noah (Gen 9:1), stayed in one place. In direct contradiction to God's instruction, they said, "Come, let us build ourselves a city and a tower with its top in the heavens, and let us make a name for ourselves, *lest we be dispersed over the face of the whole earth*" (Gen 11:4).

We see their sinful pride also in their aim to "make a name for ourselves." Rather than "calling on the name of the Lord" in worship (or depending on God to "make your name great," as God would promise Abraham [Gen 12:2]), they wanted to take matters into their own hands and bolster their own reputation. They did not want to "honor God as God or give thanks to him" (Rom 1:21).[8]

---

7. Unlike most Sunday School pictorial representations of Noah's ark, not all animals came "two by two": Gen 7:2–3 tells us that clean animals and birds came into the ark by *sevens*, so that there would be some for sacrifice.

8. Most commentators agree that the residents of Babel were not so unsophisti-cated to think that their tower could actually reach the heavens; rather, the building would be a monument to their prideful independence of, and rebellion against, God. John Piper writes, "Building a city is the way one avoids being dispersed over the whole earth. And building a tower into the heavens is the way one makes a name for oneself. So the city and tower are the outward expressions of the inward sins. The two sins are the love of praise (so you crave to make a name for yourself) and the love of security

So God responds in judgment: he "confused the language of all the earth. And from there the LORD dispersed them over the face of all the earth" (Gen 11:9).

It is because of this confusion of languages that we have the rise of so many cultures and languages. Missionaries and others have the challenge of spending many years learning another culture and its language; sometimes entire lifetimes are devoted to translating the Scriptures into the hundreds (if not thousands) of different languages in the world.

Yet John Piper brings a fascinating, redemptive perspective to this challenge:

> The praise that Jesus receives from all the languages is more beautiful, because of its diversity, than it would have been if there were only one language and one people to sing.
>
> "And they sang a new song, saying, 'Worthy are you to take the scroll and to open its seals, for you were slain, and by your blood you ransomed people for God *from every tribe and language and people and nation*, and you have made them a kingdom and priests to our God, and they shall reign on the earth'" (Rev 5:9–10).
>
> "After this I looked, and behold, a great multitude that no one could number, from every nation, *from all tribes and peoples and languages*, standing before the throne and before the Lamb, clothed in white robes, with palm branches in their hands, and crying out with a loud voice, 'Salvation belongs to our God who sits on the throne, and to the Lamb!'" (Rev 7:9–10)
>
> It was the spectacular sin on the plains of Shinar that gave rise to the multiplying of languages that ends in the most glorious praise to Christ from every language on earth.[9]

God in his sovereignty can turn even humankind's sin and rebellion, and his judgment against it, to good; he can *multiply his praise* out of the hardest situations. We see that in the life of Joseph:

> His brothers also came and fell down before him and said, "Behold, we are your servants." But Joseph said to them, "Do not fear, for am I in the place of God? As for you, you meant evil against me, *but God meant it for good.*" (Gen 50:18–20)

---

(so you build a city and don't take the risks of filling the earth)" ("Pride of Babel"). Peter Leithart suggests that "God's response to this rebellion is funny. Verse five says, 'Yahweh came down to see the city and the tower.' The 'tower that reaches to the sky' is so far from heaven that the Lord has to 'come down' to see it" (*House for My Name*, 59).

9. Piper, "Pride of Babel."

And above all we see it in the case of the death of Jesus for our salvation:

> This Jesus, delivered up *according to the definite plan and fore-knowledge of God*, you crucified and killed by the hands of lawless men. (Acts 2:23)

> For truly in this city there were gathered together against your holy servant Jesus, whom you anointed, both Herod and Pontius Pilate, along with the Gentiles and the peoples of Israel, to do *whatever your hand and your plan had predestined to take place.* (Acts 4:27–28)

The greatest *sin* of all human history—the slaughter of the innocent Lamb of God—was used by God to effect the greatest *good* in all human history—salvation through that redeeming death.

## The Patriarchal Period (Gen 12–50)

During this period, God begins to work to grow out of one man a special people for himself.

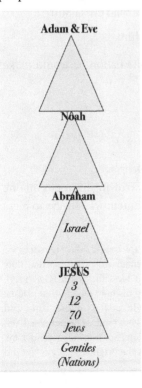

At this point, it is interesting to note a repeating pattern to how God works in human history: through Adam and Eve the human race grows. But then after the flood, God narrows his focus again to one family, that of Noah, and repopulates the earth through them. Then with Abraham, God begins again with one man and one family to develop the nation of Israel. Out of Israel will come the promised one Jesus Christ, who gathers disciples: the inner circle of three (Mark 9:2), the Twelve, the larger group of seventy (Luke 10:1), three thousand Jews on the day of Pentecost (Acts 2:41), and then the following expansion to the Gentiles and the nations (Acts 1:8).

## Abraham

### *The Call of Abram*

As we have seen, God by his own gracious initiative reveals himself to the pagan Abram and completely changes his life trajectory:

> Now the LORD said to Abram, "Go from your country and your kindred and your father's house to the land that I will show you. And I will make of you a great nation, and I will bless you and make your name great, so that you will be a blessing. I will bless those who bless you, and him who dishonors you I will curse, and in you all the families of the earth shall be blessed." (Gen 12:1–3)

If Abram will obey the command to go, God promises to:

1. Make a great nation out of him

2. Bless him

3. Make his name great

4. Make him a blessing

5. Bless those who bless him, and curse those who curse him

6. Bless all the families of the earth through him

We learn in Isa 43 that God's intent for the nation he would make from Abraham was that it be:

> My chosen people,
> the people whom I formed for myself
> *that they might declare my praise.* (Isa 43:20–21)

God was seeking to form *a unique worshiping people.*

We also see that, though God was again narrowing his focus on one man, one family, and one nation, his sovereign intent was always to bless the entire earth through this people.[10]

---

10. "YHWH did not call Israel to himself primarily for Israel's sake. He redeemed the descendants of Abraham and established his covenant with them so that they might bear his name and that through them he might bless the world (Gen 12:3). Deuteronomy 26:19 summarizes their mission as being his holy kingdom of priests: 'He will set you high above all the nations he has made for [his] praise, fame, and honor, and so that you will be a people holy to YHWH your God, as he promised' (cf. Exod. 19:4–6)" (Block, *For the Glory of God*, 39–40). Note: Some scholars render the covenant name of God, Yahweh, as simply YHWH (as the original Hebrew text did not use vowels).

The last phrase of Gen 12:3 ("in you all the families of the earth shall be blessed") is sometimes called the "Great Commission" of the Old Testament. God's heart was always for the nations,[11] and he wanted the nation of Israel to be a pointer to and a testimony of him as the one true Creator God. We saw in ch. 9 the psalmist's godly perspective:

> May God be gracious to us and bless us
> and make his face to shine upon us,
> *that* your way may be known on earth,
> your saving power among all nations. (Ps 67:1–2)[12]

Unfortunately, Israel often forgot this part of its mandate; they were all too ready to enjoy their status as God's chosen people, but in their pride looked down on the benighted nations surrounding them.[13]

---

11. C. Wright, *Mission of God*: "Genesis 12:1–3 . . . is pivotal in the whole Bible because it does exactly what Paul says—it 'announces the gospel in advance' [Gal 3:8]. That is, it declares the good news that, in spite of all that we have read in Genesis 1–11, it is God's ultimate purpose to bless humanity. . . . And the story of how that blessing for all nations has come about occupies the rest of the Bible, with Christ as the central focus. Indeed the closing vision of the canon, with people of every tribe and nation and language worshipping the living God (Rev 7:9–10), clearly echoes the promise of Genesis 12:3 and binds the whole story together" (194–95). "The glorious gospel of the Abrahamic covenant is that God's mission is ultimately to bless all nations" (207). "Matthew begins his gospel affirming Jesus the Messiah as the son of Abraham and ends it with the mission mandate that would encompass all nations" (213).

12. This is one of several texts that Christopher Wright points out as picking up the "all families of the earth will be blessed" promise from Gen 12:3. While most of the Old Testament is of course focused on the growth and history of God's chosen people Israel, Wright highlights a number of texts "that articulate some element of universality, either directly or indirectly echoing the Abraham promise": Gen 18:18; 22:18; 26:4; 28:14; Exod 9:13–16; 19:5–6; Num 23:8–10; Deut 28:9–10; Josh 4:23–24; 1 Sam 17:46; 2 Sam 7:25–26, 29; 1 Kgs 8:41–43; 8:60–61; 2 Kgs 19:19; Ps 22:27–28; 47:9; 67:1–2; 72:17; 86:9; 145:8–12; Is 19:24–25; 25:6–8; 45:22–23; 48:18–19; 60:12; Jer 4:1–2; Zech 8:13 (*Mission of God*, 216, 223–42).

13. "Israel, as God's chosen people, holy nation and royal priesthood [1 Pet 2:9], did not live up to these privileges. God did not give them these blessings in order that they might consume them upon [sic] themselves. He did not create this royal priesthood, this holy nation, for its own sake. But the people became absorbed with their privileges. They heard the 'you are,' but they were deaf to the 'that you may.' They did not listen to God when he told them that he had given them these privileges that they might be a light to the Gentiles and a blessing to the world" (Alexander, *Our Great God*, 136).

## *The Response of Abram*

> So Abram went, as the LORD had told him. . . . Then the LORD appeared to Abram and said, "To your offspring I will give this land." So he built there an altar to the LORD, who had appeared to him. From there he moved to the hill country on the east of Bethel and pitched his tent, with Bethel on the west and Ai on the east. And there he built an altar to the LORD and called upon the name of the LORD. (Gen 12:4, 7–8)

We see Abram's response of obedience to God's call, and then we see that immediately upon arriving in the promised land he builds altars and calls upon the name of the Lord: he responds in *worship*.

## *God's Continuing Revelation to Abraham*[14]

God continued to reveal himself to Abraham through his life, appearing and speaking to him, repeating his promises, and showing various facets of his nature by identifying himself by different names:[15]

- *El Elyon* (God Most High [14:18–19])
- *El Shaddai* (God Almighty [17:1–2])
- *El Olam* (the Everlasting God [21:33])
- *Yahweh Jireh* (the LORD Who Sees/Provides [22:14])

## *Abraham's Life of Faith and Worship*

Abraham was saved, and lived, by faith in the promises of God:

> And [God] brought [Abram] outside and said, "Look toward heaven, and number the stars, if you are able to number them." Then he said to him, "So shall your offspring be." And he believed the LORD, and he counted it to him as righteousness." (Gen 15:5–6)
>
> "Abraham believed God, and it was counted to him as righteousness"—and he was called a friend of God. (Jas 2:23)

14. When God formalizes his covenant with Abram in Gen 17, he changes his name from Abram ("exalted father") to Abraham ("father of a multitude") (17:5).

15. It has been pointed out that all these and other descriptive names given to God in the Old Testament are subsumed and fulfilled by Jesus, "the name that is above every name" (Phil 2:9).

And his life was also characterized by many private and public acts of worship:

1. Sacrifices (Gen 12:7, 8; 13:18; 22:7)

2. Prayer:
   - Praise and thanksgiving (12:8; 13:4)
   - Petition (24:12)
   - Intercession (18:22–23; 20:7)

3. Tithe (14:20)

4. Building of altars (after God appeared to him)
   - Shechem (12:7)
   - Bethel (12:8; 13:3–4)
   - Hebron (13:18)
   - Mt. Moriah (22:9)

### *Abraham's Test of Love*

Genesis 22 relates what is a pivotal event in Abraham's life,[16] and a key moment in Old Testament history.

### THE TEST

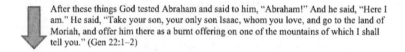

After these things God tested Abraham and said to him, "Abraham!" And he said, "Here I am." He said, "Take your son, your only son Isaac, whom you love, and go to the land of Moriah, and offer him there as a burnt offering on one of the mountains of which I shall tell you." (Gen 22:1–2)

Abraham and Sarah were childless into their old age; this had been a serious trial and test of faith in itself, especially since God had promised to make a great nation out of Abraham. But finally God gave them a son,

16. "Both in structure and concept, this test was strikingly similar to the 'test' in Gen 12:1–7. The latter was the first time God spoke to the patriarch; the former, the last. Both speeches contained the same command, found nowhere else in the Bible ('Go forth/out,' Gen 12:1; 22:2). The first called for a break with Abraham's past; the second, with Abraham's future. Both stressed a journey, an altar, and promised blessings. Thus Genesis 12 and 22 form an appropriate commencement and conclusion, respectively, of the Abrahamic saga" (Kuruvilla, "*Aqedah*," 498).

Isaac, a source of great joy for them in the present as well as their hope for Abraham's future heritage and legacy.[17] Only then God told him to take that son of promise, "your son, your *only* son Isaac, whom you *love*," and to sacrifice him.

What an agonizing test of faith, obedience, allegiance—and love. God is in essence saying to Abraham, "Whom do you love more? Your son, your only son—or *me*?"[18]

It is fascinating to note that here in 22:2 we have the very first use of the word *love* in the Bible; and that this first usage does *not* refer to the love between a man and a woman, but rather to the love of a *father* for a *son*.[19] We are reminded that the first love that ever existed, of which all human loves are simply a reflection, was the eternal love among the members of the Trinity—Father, Son, and Holy Spirit (John 17:24).

### THE RESPONSE OF FAITH AND WORSHIP

 So Abraham rose early in the morning, saddled his donkey, and took two of his young men with him, and his son Isaac. (Gen 22:3)

The Bible, of course, does not give us every detail of everything that happens; at the end of the Gospel of John we read, "Now there are also many other things that Jesus did. Were every one of them to be written, I suppose that the world itself could not contain the books that would be written" (John 21:25). We can only imagine what might have transpired between what we read in v. 2 (the test) and then in v. 3 ("So Abraham rose early").

17. "Indeed, this was a sacrifice not of Isaac, but of Abraham himself—all he hoped for, his future, his life, his seed" (Kuruvilla, "*Aqedah*," 499).

18. Kuruvilla says: "'The father-son relationship is emphasized in the account of Genesis 22: 'father' and/or 'son' is mentioned fifteen times in Gen 22:1–20 (in 22:2 [×2], 3, 6, 7 [×3], 8, 9, 10, 12 [×2], 13, 16 [×2]). The readers are never to forget the relationship. In the only conversation recorded in the Bible between Abraham and Isaac, the latter's words begin with 'my father' and the former's words end with 'my son' (22:7–8)—this is also Abraham's last word before he prepares to slay Isaac ('my son,' is a single word in the Hebrew). The narrator is explicitly creating an emotional tension in the story . . . : a father is called to slay the son he loves" ("*Aqedah*," 501).

19. And again Kuruvilla: "With the entry of this new word into Scripture came an implicit question: Was Abraham's love for Isaac so strong that his allegiance to God had diminished? It appears, then, that this love of Abraham for Isaac was a crucial element in the test—it was this love that was being tested. Would Abraham be loyal to God, or would love for the human overpower love for the divine?" ("*Aqedah*," 501).

The assumption of one commentator about Abraham's "immediate, un-questioning obedience" in v. 3 is too simplistic. It seems unimaginable that Abraham would not have gone through an *immense* spiritual and emotional struggle during the night, before finally stepping out in faith in the morning.[20] Not to mention if he brought Sarah into the picture![21]

> On the third day Abraham lifted up his eyes and saw the place from afar. Then Abraham said to his young men, "Stay here with the donkey; I and the boy will go over there and *worship* and come again to you." (Gen 22:4–5)

It is interesting that in this chapter we also have the first mention of the most common Old Testament word for worship (*ḥistaḥavah*) in the Bible; and it is intriguing that around that theme of worship we have the mingled concepts of obedience, sacrifice (on the mountain where later the Jerusalem temple would be built), fear of the Lord (22:12), total com-mitment, substitution, and love—all of which carry hints of the work of Christ to come.

## The Provision and Promises of God

The angel of the Lord stops Abraham at the last second from carrying out the deed and fulfills the father's words to his son that "God will provide for himself the lamb for a burnt offering" (Gen 22:8) by sending a ram to take the place of Isaac (22:13).

> Abraham called the name of that place, "The LORD will provide [*Yahweh Yireh*]," as it is said to this day, "On the mount of the LORD it shall be provided." (Gen 22:14)

20. As one of my students commented once, "Abraham ended up there [faith and obedience], but likely did not begin there." "By faith Abraham, when he was tested, offered up Isaac, and he who had received the promises was in the act of offering up his only son, of whom it was said, 'Through Isaac shall your offspring be named.' He con-sidered that God was able even to raise him from the dead, from which, figuratively speaking, he did receive him back" (Heb 11:17–19). Apparently the only way Abraham could reconcile the test with the prior promise of God was by concluding that God would resurrect Isaac after he was sacrificed.

21. Kuruvilla similarly highlights what the author (probably Moses) *leaves* out: "'How old was Isaac? Where was Sarah? Where was Moriah? What was Abraham thinking during those three days it took the caravan to approach the mountain? What was going through Isaac's mind?' And so on. The fact is that the author simply does not seem interested in narrating everything that happened" ("*Aqedah*," 492).

God commends Abraham for passing the test:

> Now I know that you fear God, seeing you have not withheld your son, your only son, from me. (Gen 22:12)

And he repeats and even intensifies ("I will *surely* bless you, and I will *surely* multiply your offspring" [Gen 22:15]) his original unconditional promises, on account of Abraham's obedience and demonstration of his love for God:

By myself I have sworn, declares the LORD, because you have done this and have not withheld your son, your only son, I will surely bless you, and I will surely multiply your offspring as the stars of heaven and as the sand that is on the seashore. And your offspring shall possess the gate of his enemies, and in your offspring shall all the nations of the earth be blessed, because you have obeyed my voice. (Gen 22:15–18)

Kuruvilla adds: "One might almost say, 'Abraham so loved God that he gave his only begotten son . . .'"[22] In a certain way, Abraham *does* sacrifice Isaac in terms of holding God in first place in his life and loyalty. We are reminded of Jesus's words:

> Whoever loves father or mother *more* than me is not worthy of me, and whoever loves son or daughter *more* than me is not worthy of me. (Matt 10:37)

## Isaac

We don't have nearly as much material in Genesis about Isaac. But we do see in Gen 26 that God appears to Isaac and repeats to him the promises that he had made to Abraham.

From there [Isaac] went up to Beersheba. And the LORD appeared to him the same night and said, "I am the God of Abraham your father. Fear not, for I am with you and will bless you and multiply your offspring for my servant Abraham's sake." (Gen 26:23–24)

---

22. Kuruvilla, "*Aqedah*," 505. "There is a significant alteration, before and after the test, in how God/angel of Yahweh described Isaac.

Pre-test: 22:2 'your son, your only son, *the one you love*'

Post-test: 22:12 'your son, your only son'; 22:16 'your son, your only son'

The narrative omissions in 22:12 and 16 help clarify the reason for the test. The trifold description of Isaac in Gen 22:2 was to emphasize that this son, this particular one, was the one Abraham *loved*, with a love that potentially stood in the way of his allegiance to, and faith in, God. The subsequent deletion of the phrase, 'the one you love,' was clear indication that Abraham had passed the test" (Kuruvilla, "*Aqedah*," 502).

And Isaac likewise *responds* by building an altar, calling on the name of the Lord and worshiping:

 So he built an altar there and called upon the name of the LORD and pitched his tent there. (Gen 26:25)

## Jacob

Isaac's son Jacob is an interesting figure. In many ways he is a picture of the nation that will be named after him (after his name is changed to Israel [Gen 32:28]): like the later nation, Jacob is called and blessed by God but often chooses to do things his own way. However, God persists in working in Jacob's life, until by the end of his life he becomes a true worshiper of God (see Gen 35 and Heb 11:21).

### Jacob at Bethel (Gen 28:10–22)

A significant event in Jacob's life occurs in Gen 28. Jacob is on the run for his life (Gen 27:41–45) because he has cheated Esau out of his birthright (25:29–34) and out of his father's blessing (27:1–40).

JACOB'S LADDER

*Jacob's Dream,*
by Bartolomé Esteban Murillo (1617–1682)

Along the way he sleeps and dreams:

And he came to a certain place and stayed there that night, because the sun had set. Taking one of the stones of the place, he put it under his head and lay down in that place to sleep. And he dreamed, and behold, there was a ladder [or flight of steps, or ramp] set up on the earth, and the top of it reached to heaven. And behold, the angels of God were ascending and descending on it! (Gen 28:11–12)[23]

Jacob's vision has a fascinating parallel in John 1. Jesus is calling his disciples, and we read:

Jesus saw Nathanael coming toward him and said of him, "Behold, an Israelite indeed, in whom there is no deceit!" Nathanael said to him, "How do you know me?" Jesus answered him, "Before Philip called you, when you were under the fig tree, I saw you." Nathanael answered him, "Rabbi, you are the Son of God! You are the King of Israel!" Jesus answered him, "Because I said to you, 'I saw you under the fig tree,' do you believe? You will see greater things than these." And he said to him, "Truly, truly, I say to you, you will see heaven opened, and the angels of God ascending and descending on the Son of Man." (John 1:47–51)

The wording of Jesus's last phrase in v. 51 is *almost identical* with Gen 28:12, with *one crucial difference*: the angels, instead of "ascending and descending" on a *ladder*, are doing so "*on the Son of Man.*" This is an obvious reference to Gen 28: Jesus seems to be saying, "*I* am the fulfillment of Jacob's vision. In a way that Jacob could not have imagined, *I* am the ladder; *I* am that connection between heaven and earth, between God and humanity." As both divine and human, Jesus is uniquely positioned to be the bridge between God and humans, and humans and God. We will see more of the full significance of that *two-way mediation* for our worship in ch. 26,[24] as William Nicholls suggests in the title of his book, *Jacob's Ladder: The Meaning of Worship.*

Besides the obvious similarity in wording between John 1:51 and Gen 28:12, there are two more hints in the text of John 1 that point towards this interpretation. In v. 48 Jesus tells Nathanael that he saw him when he was "under the fig tree"; we can only speculate, but it is possible

---

23. Peter Leithart notes that, unlike Babel, "Jacob's ladder is the true 'tower' that connects heaven and earth, but it is built by Yahweh, not by Jacob" (*House for my Name*, 63).

24. The angels' two-way movement is also suggestive of our revelation-response arrows, which we will see in ch. 26 are ultimately fulfilled by Christ himself in his two-way mediation.

that Nathanael was *meditating on Gen 28* under the tree, and that it is for that reason Jesus makes the reference to that story in v. 51 (which otherwise seems to come out of the blue). Also, Jesus says of Nathanael in v. 47, "Behold, an Israelite indeed, in whom there is no deceit!" Jacob (later Israel) had a reputation for deceit, so perhaps the Jacob connection is again indicated. (William Temple renders Jesus's words as "Behold an Israelite in whom there is no Jacob"![25])

So, while we cannot say for certain, it certainly seems likely that Jesus has Gen 28 in mind as he talks with Nathanael. And we will see the fuller implications in ch. 26.

## GOD'S COVENANT PROMISES REPEATED

Going back to Jacob's dream in Genesis, we see that in the vision God speaks to Jacob and repeats to him the promises he had previously made to Abraham and Isaac:

> I am the LORD, the God of Abraham your father and the God of Isaac. The land on which you lie I will give to you and to your offspring. Your offspring shall be like the dust of the earth, and you shall spread abroad to the west and to the east and to the north and to the south, and in you and your offspring shall all the families of the earth be blessed. Behold, I am with you and will keep you wherever you go, and will bring you back to this land. For I will not leave you until I have done what I have promised you. (Gen 28:13–15)

## JACOB'S RESPONSE OF WORSHIP

Jacob's heart is stirred by the dream, and we see even at this point in his life the beginnings of a deeper life of worship to come.

### His Heart of Worship

> Then Jacob awoke from his sleep and said, "Surely the LORD is in this place, and I did not know it." And he was afraid and said, "How awesome is this place! This is none other than the house of God, and this is the gate of heaven." (Gen 28:16–17)

### His Act of Worship

So early in the morning Jacob took the stone that he had put under his head and set it up for a pillar and poured oil on the

25. Temple, *St John's Gospel*, 29.

top of it. He called the name of that place Bethel [house of God].
(Gen 28:18–19)

### His Vow of Worship

Then Jacob made a vow, saying, "If God will be with me and
will keep me in this way that I go, and will give me bread to eat
and clothing to wear, so that I come again to my father's house
in peace, then the LORD shall be my God, and this stone, which
I have set up for a pillar, shall be God's house." (Gen 28:20–22)

### *Jacob's Return to Bethel*

In Gen 35, we find a repeat of the now-familiar pattern: God appears to
Jacob and repeats the covenant promises already made to Abraham and
Isaac, and in response Jacob builds an altar and worships:

God appeared to Jacob again, when he came from Paddan-aram, and blessed him. And
God said to him, "Your name is Jacob; no longer shall your name be called Jacob, but
Israel shall be your name." So he called his name Israel. And God said to him, "I am God
Almighty: be fruitful and multiply. A nation and a company of nations shall come from
you, and kings shall come from your own body. The land that I gave to Abraham and
Isaac I will give to you, and I will give the land to your offspring after you." Then God
went up from him in the place where he had spoken with him. (Gen 35:9–13)

And Jacob set up a pillar in the place where he had spoken with him, a pillar of stone. He
poured out a drink offering on it and poured oil on it. So Jacob called the name of the
place where God had spoken with him Bethel. (Gen 35:14–15)

## The Exodus (Exod 1–19)

### God's Initiative in the Exodus

God acts by his own gracious initiative to call and send the sheepherder
Moses (Exod 3) to lead his people out of slavery in Egypt.

And Moses said to the people, "Fear not, stand firm, and see the salvation of the LORD,
which he will work for you today. . . . The LORD will fight for you, and you have only to
be silent." (Exod 14:13–14)

Having heard the cry of His chosen people, weak and suffering in their slavery . . . , He saved them from their bondage in Egypt and bound them to Him in the covenant. Through this experience it became clear that the god of Israel was first of all their Savior-God. He had taken the initiative in their redemption.[26]

## God's Purposes in the Exodus

### Purpose 1: To Show His Power and the Greatness of His Name

#### To Moses and the People of Israel

But on that day I will set apart the land of Goshen, where my people dwell, so that no swarms of flies shall be there, *that you may know that I am the Lord* in the midst of the earth. (Exod 8:22)

Then the LORD said to Moses, "Go in to Pharaoh, for I have hardened his heart and the heart of his servants, that I may show these signs of mine among them, and that you may tell in the hearing of your son and of your grandson how I have dealt harshly with the Egyptians and what signs I have done among them, *that you may know that I am the LORD.*" (Exod 10:1–2)

Israel saw the great power that the Lord used against the Egyptians, *so the people feared the LORD, and they believed in the Lord* and in his servant Moses. (Exod 14:31)

*Who is like you, O LORD,* among the gods?
Who is like you, majestic in holiness,
    awesome in glorious deeds, doing wonders?
You stretched out your right hand;
    the earth swallowed them.
You have led in your steadfast love the people whom you have redeemed; you have guided them by your strength to your holy abode. (Exod 15:11–13)

#### To the Egyptians

The Egyptians *shall know that I am the LORD,* when I stretch out my hand against Egypt and bring out the people of Israel from among them. (Exod 7:5)

---

26. Rayburn, *O Come*, 52.

And I will harden Pharaoh's heart, and he will pursue them, and *I will get glory* over Pharaoh and all his host, and the Egyptians *shall know that I am the* LORD. (Exod 14:4)

And I will harden the hearts of the Egyptians so that they shall go in after them, and *I will get glory* over Pharaoh and all his host, his chariots, and his horsemen. And the Egyptians *shall know that I am the* LORD, when I have gotten glory over Pharaoh, his chariots, and his horsemen. (Exod 14:17–18)

## To Pharaoh

Thus says the LORD, "By this you [Pharaoh] *shall know that I am the Lord*: behold, with the staff that is in my hand I will strike the water that is in the Nile, and it shall turn into blood." (Exod 7:17)

Moses said to Pharaoh, "Be pleased to command me when I am to plead for you and for your servants and for your people, that the frogs be cut off from you and your houses and be left only in the Nile." And he said, "Tomorrow." Moses said, "Be it as you say, so that you may *know that there is no one like the* LORD *our God.*" (Exod 8:9–10)

For this time I will send all my plagues on you [Pharaoh] yourself, and on your servants and your people, so that you may *know that there is none like me in all the earth.* (Exod 9:14)

Moses said to him, "As soon as I have gone out of the city, I will stretch out my hands to the LORD. The thunder will cease, and there will be no more hail, so that you may *know that the earth is the* LORD'*s.*" (Exod 9:29)

But for this purpose I have raised you [Pharaoh] up, *to show you my power.* (Exod 9:16)

## To the Nations

But for this purpose I have raised you [Pharaoh] up, to show you my power, so that *my name may be proclaimed in all the earth.* (Exod 9:16)[27]

27. "When God aims, as he does in Exodus 14:4 and 17, to 'be glorified' for his wondrous triumph over Pharaoh, his aim is that his 'name be proclaimed in all the earth' (Ex. 9:16)—that is, that 'all the nations you have made shall come and *worship* before you, O Lord, and shall *glorify* your name' [Ps 89:6]" (Piper, *Providence*, 95 [emphasis original]). "The one living God wills to be known throughout his whole creation. The world must

You have led in your steadfast love the people whom you have
redeemed;
    You have guided them by your strength to your holy abode.
The peoples have heard; they tremble;
    pangs have seized the inhabitants of Philistia.
Now are the chiefs of Edom dismayed;
    trembling seizes the leaders of Moab;
    all the inhabitants of Canaan have melted away.
Terror and dread fall upon them;
    *because of the greatness of your arm*, they are still as a stone.
(Exod 15:13–16)

For the Lord your God dried up the waters of the Jordan for you
until you passed over, as the Lord your God did to the Red Sea,
which he dried up for us until we passed over, *so that all the peo-*
*ples of the earth may know that the hand of the Lord is mighty,*
that you may fear the Lord your God forever. (Josh 4:23–24)

And, most significant to the unfolding story of redemption, when
the spies go into Jericho before Israel enters the promised land after the
forty years in the wilderness:

Before the men lay down, [Rahab] came up to them on the roof
and said to the men, "I know that the Lord has given you the
land, and that the fear of you has fallen upon us, and that all
the inhabitants of the land melt away before you. For we have
heard how the Lord dried up the water of the Red Sea before
you when you came out of Egypt and what you did to the two
kings of the Amorites who were beyond the Jordan, to Sihon
and Og, whom you devoted to destruction. And as soon as we
heard it, our hearts melted, and there was no spirit left in any
man because of you, *for the Lord your God, he is God in the*
*heavens above and on the earth beneath*." (Josh 2:8–11)

*Forty years* after the exodus, the inhabitants of Jericho were *still* talking
about what God had done in Egypt (as well as his protection of his people
through the years in the wilderness). This report draws out of Rahab's
heart a confession of faith in the true God:

For the Lord your God, *he* is God in the heavens above and on
the earth beneath. (Josh 2:11b)

---

know its Creator. The nations must know their Ruler, Judge and Savior. This is a major
subplot of the exodus narrative in the book of Exodus" (C. Wright, *Mission of God*, 127).

> *By faith* Rahab the prostitute did not perish with those who were disobedient, because she had given a friendly welcome to the spies. (Heb 11:31)

And we read that, after being spared during the destruction of Jericho (Josh 2:12–14; 6:17, 23, 25), Rahab becomes not only part of the nation of Israel, but also the mother of Boaz and the great-great-grand-mother of King David (Matt 1:5–6), thereby making her way into the genealogy of Jesus Christ! What a testimony to the mercy and grace of God, that this Gentile prostitute can find a place in the family tree of the Son of God! Truly, "he is not ashamed to call [us] brethren" (Heb 2:11)!

### Purpose 2: To Judge the False Gods and Worship of Egypt

In the plagues God showed his sovereign might (as the Creator, the one true God) over all the natural forces of Egypt, which the Egyptians believed were controlled by various of their extensive panoply of different gods (there was a god of the Nile, a god of frogs, a god of grasshoppers, etc.).[28] He also confounded Pharaoh's magicians and their dark arts.

> The magicians tried by their secret arts to produce gnats, but they could not. So there were gnats on man and beast. Then the magicians said to Pharaoh, *"This is the finger of God."* (Exod 8:18–19)

> And the magicians *could not stand* before Moses because of the boils, for the boils came upon the magicians and upon all the Egyptians. (Exod 9:11)

> For I will pass through the land of Egypt that night, and I will strike all the firstborn in the land of Egypt, both man and beast; and *on all the gods of Egypt I will execute judgments*: I am the LORD. (Exod 12:12)

> On the day after the Passover, the people of Israel went out triumphantly in the sight of all the Egyptians, while the Egyptians were burying all their firstborn, whom the LORD had struck down among them. *On their gods also the LORD executed judgments.* (Num 33:3b–4)

---

28. "Whoever or whatever the gods of Egypt may be (and the narrator does not even trouble to name them, any more than he names the Pharaoh who claimed to be one of them), the God of Israel is more than a match for all of them" (C. Wright, *Mission of God*, 77).

*Purpose 3: To Form a Unique Worshiping People*

We have seen how this was God's intention even as he called Abraham to make of him a special people:

> My chosen people,
>> the people whom I formed for myself
>> *that they might declare my praise.* (Isa 43:20–21)

We also see God's purpose for this people through Moses's repeated entreaties to Pharaoh:

> Let my people go, *that they might worship me.* (Exod 7:16; 8:1, 20; 9:1, 13; 10:3)

And the psalmist also bears witness to God's intended and completed purpose in the exodus:

> When Israel went out from Egypt,
>> the house of Jacob from a people of strange language,
> *Judah became his sanctuary,*
> Israel his dominion. (Ps 114:1–2)[29]

God brought his people out to establish them as a *unique, worshiping people* out of all the nations of the world.

> [God] had taken the ↓ initiative in their redemption. Their worship was essentially a ↑ response of gratitude to Him.[30]

> The events of the exodus from Egypt bonded Israel together as a worshipping community.[31]

## God's Sovereign Mercy in the Exodus

John Piper offers an important perspective on God's prerogative in rescuing Israel and judging Egypt:

---

29. These verses are paraphrased in the hymn "When Israel Had from Egypt Gone" by J. B. Herbert, in *The Irish Presbyterian Hymnbook*:
> When Israel had from Egypt gone,
> Jacob from men of speech unknown;
> then Judah was his holy place,
> and his dominion Israel's race.

30. Rayburn, *O Come*, 52 (arrows added).

31. Hill, *Enter His Courts*, 35.

At the exodus, God made a name for himself by acting as a God of absolutely free grace. That is, he showed his saving power for people (Israel) who were no more deserving of salvation than the Egyptians. He is who he is, and he saves whom he saves—that is the freedom of grace.[32]

Piper points to the psalmist's recognition of Israel's rebellious nature before and after the exodus:

Both we and our fathers have sinned;
    we have committed iniquity; we have done wickedness.
Our fathers, when they were in Egypt,
    did not consider your wondrous works;
they did not remember the abundance of your steadfast love,
    but rebelled by the sea, at the Red Sea.
*Yet* he saved them *for his name's sake,*
    that he might *make known his mighty power.* (Ps 106:6–8)

And Piper adds:

The situation was not that Egypt deserved to be judged for its arrogance [see Neh 9:10] and Israel deserved to be saved for her righteousness. *Neither* deserved to be saved. But God freely chose to save Israel.[33]

Is there injustice on God's part? By no means! For he says to Moses, "I will have mercy on whom I have mercy, and I will have compassion on whom I have compassion." So then it depends not on human will or exertion, but on God, who has mercy. For the Scripture says to Pharaoh, "For this very purpose I have raised you up, that I might show my power in you, and that my name might be proclaimed in all the earth." So then he has mercy on whomever he wills, and he hardens whomever he wills. (Rom 9:14–18)

## The Mosaic (Sinai) Covenant (Exod 20–Deuteronomy)

God entered into covenant with his people at Mount Sinai, through the mediation of Moses.

---

32. Piper, *Providence*, 105–6.
33. Piper, *Providence*, 104 (emphasis original).

## What God Promised in the Covenant ↓

God promised two main things to his people as his side of the covenant:

1. His special *presence* among his people (see the theme of "The Presence of God" earlier on pp. 134–36)

> Then the cloud covered the tent of meeting, and *the glory of the LORD filled the tabernacle.* (Exod 40:34)

> I will make my dwelling among you, and my soul shall not abhor you. *And I will walk among you* and will be your God, and you shall be my people. (Lev 26:11–12)

And later:

> As soon as Solomon finished his prayer, fire came down from heaven and consumed the burnt offering and the sacrifices, and *the glory of the Lord filled the temple.* (2 Chr 7:1)

2. A special *relationship* with his people

> I am the LORD, and I will bring you out from under the burdens of the Egyptians, and I will deliver you from slavery to them, and I will redeem you with an outstretched arm and with great acts of judgment. *I will take you to be my people, and I will be your God.* (Exod 6:6–7)

> I will also walk among you and *be your God, and you shall be my people.* (Lev 26:12; see also Lev 11:45; 22:33; 25:38; 26:12; Num 15:41; Deut 29:13)

## What God Asked in Return from His Covenant People: Their *Worship* ↑

As we saw above, God redeemed the Israelites from slavery in Egypt in order to form them into a unique *worshiping people.*[34] We can identify at least six aspects of that worship that God asked of them.

---

34. "The exodus was begun with a liturgical act—the celebration of the Passover—and it 'concludes' with the construction of the tabernacle" (Hahn, "Canon," 216).

## 1. Exclusive Worship

As we observed in ch. 4, God did not start the giving of the Ten Commandments with Commandment One, but rather with the statement:

> I am the LORD your God, *who brought you out of the land of Egypt*, out of the house of slavery. (Exod 20:2)

The Ten Commandments and the law, we have already observed, were *not* presented as *a way of salvation*, but rather as a guide to life for a people already redeemed by the gracious initiative of God. As we have seen from James Torrance:

> The liturgies of Israel were God-given ordinances of grace, witnesses to grace. The sacrifice of lambs and bulls and goats were not ways of placating an angry God, currying favor with God as in the pagan worship of the Baalim. They were God-given covenantal witnesses to grace.[35]

The first commandment makes it clear that the people's allegiance and worship was to be directed towards Yahweh alone:

> You shall have no other gods before me. (Exod 20:3)

In fact, the first four of the Ten Commandments directly relate to worship:

---

35. J. Torrance, *Worship, Community*, 60. His brother Thomas expands on this concept: "The whole liturgy was regarded by the OT as an ordinance of grace initiated by God Himself and appointed by Him. It was not an undertaking on the part of man. It was God Himself who provided the sacrifice, and the whole action is described, therefore, in the form of a divinely appointed response to God's Word (Exod. 25:22; Num 7:89). The sacrifices and oblations were not regarded as having any efficacy in themselves, but as having efficacy only in so far as they were liturgical obedience to the divine ordinance. They were designed to point beyond themselves to God's will to be gracious and to pardon. They were essentially witness and were performed within the Tabernacle of Witness or the Dwelling-Place of Testimony. All priestly action within the place of meeting was by way of acknowledgment and witness to God's testimony of Himself in the Covenant. God is not acted upon by means of priestly sacrifice. Priestly action rests upon God's Self-revelation in His Word and answers as cultic sign and action to the thing signified. That is particularly clear in regard to the teaching of the Old Testament about atonement, for the various words used to express expiation or reconciliation are used with God as Subject always, never with God as object (except in describing heathen sacrifice), and are only used with man as subject in the secondary sense of liturgical obedience to God's appointment. It is actually God Himself who performs the act of forgiveness and atonement, but the priestly cultus is designed to answer to His act and bear witness to His cleansing of the sinner" (T. Torrance, *Royal Priesthood*, 3).

1. No other gods (20:3)

2. No physical representations or images (even of the true God) (20:4–6)

3. No using the Lord's name in vain (20:7)

   The Lord's name, as we have seen, speaks of God's character and nature; because his name relates to his perfect holiness, that name should be used only in worshipful ways. Under the Mosaic covenant, certain utensils and other items were designated for use solely in the service of the tabernacle: they were deemed *sacred* objects, set aside for special use; utensils designed for regular use were considered "profane," meaning *common*. Profanity, in our English usage, means to use God's name (which speaks of his holy perfection) in a *common* way—as a flippant exclamation or curse word instead of reserving that name only for expressions of worship. Note too that we as *Christians* carry in that very designation the name of Christ—and we should take care not to take his name in vain by the way we live.

4. Keeping the Sabbath (reserving one day a week for rest and worship) (20:8–11)

The other six of the Ten Commandments deal with how the covenant people are to relate to *one another* (do not lie, steal, commit adultery, etc.). These two parts of the Ten Commandments (1–4: Godward and worship-related; and 5–10: others-related) were in fact reflected by Jesus as he summarized the entire law with what he identified as the Great Commandment (relating to God) and the second Greatest Commandment (relating to others):

> And one of them, a lawyer, asked him a question to test him. "Teacher, which is the great commandment in the Law?" And he said to him, "You shall love the Lord your God with all your heart and with all your soul and with all your mind. This is the great and first commandment. And a second is like it: You shall love your neighbor as yourself. On these two commandments depend all the Law and the Prophets." (Matt 22:35–40)[36]

---

36. The writer of Hebrews also reflects these two Greatest Commandments in the concluding chapter of the epistle: "Through [Christ] then let us continually offer up a sacrifice of praise to God, that is, the fruit of lips that acknowledge his name [Greatest Commandment]. Do not neglect to do good and to share what you have, for such sacrifices are pleasing to God [second Greatest Commandment]" (13:15–16).

## 2. Word-Directed Worship

> Then Moses came and recounted to the people all the words of the
> Lord and all the ordinances; and all the people answered with one
> voice and said, "All the words which the LORD has spoken we will
> do!" Moses wrote down all the words of the LORD. (Exod 24:3–4)

The people's worship was to be guided by the express directions of God.
They did not have to guess who God was or what he wanted. (False religions require a guess like that.) Moses went up on the mountain, came
down with God's instructions, and relayed them to the people; he then
wrote the instructions down as well. The word of God, spoken and written, was to be the standard for their worship.

## 3. Lifestyle Worship

The people were to live as a nation under the direct rule of God: a theocratic nation.[37] Their national lifestyle was to be one of worship and obedience, honoring God in all aspects of society by caring for the poor and
widows, etc.

> You shall be to me a kingdom of priests and a holy nation.
> (Exod 19:6)

David Peterson says of this verse:

> Such terminology suggests that the engagement with God at
> Sinai was to inaugurate a total-life pattern of service or wor-
> ship for the nation. . . . They were chosen to demonstrate what it
> meant to live under the direct rule of God.[38]

## 4. Ritual Worship

Most often people associate Old Testament worship with the array of
complex rituals, sacrifices, ceremonies, and festivals associated with the
tabernacle (and later the Jerusalem temple). And indeed the tabernacle
was the physical and spiritual center of the nation and its worship life.

37. *Theocratic* comes from the Greek words for God (*theos*) and power (*crasis*).
God was to be the ultimate ruler. In a democracy (the Greek *demos* means "people"),
the power is in the hands of the people.

38. D. Peterson, *Engaging with God*, 28.

> The tabernacle was to stand in the centre of the camp and pro-
> vide the means by which all of life was to be related to God. . . .
> In concrete form it expressed the truth that human beings could
> not come into his presence on their own terms.[39]

The sacrificial system of the Mosaic covenant was extremely complex; chapter after chapter in Exodus and Leviticus communicate the
regulations that the people were to follow: how to prepare, what to bring,
what to do, etc. A helpful exercise is to consider the questions: What did
the system and its complexity communicate? Why did God institute such
a complicated system?

Here are some of the likely reasons:

- To show *the holiness and purity of God* (he was set apart in the holy
  of holies)

- To reflect *the beauty and majesty of God* (the grandeur of the tabernacle and its decorations)

- To speak of *the sinfulness of the people* (they could not come close;
  see ch. 10)

- To show *the seriousness of sin* (it was not a simple matter to deal with)

- To demonstrate *the grace of God* (in providing a way to temporarily
  cover sin)

- To provide *a test of the people's obedience* (thus showing a *heart* of
  devotion)

- To produce *a growing frustration in individuals' and the nation's inability to keep the law of God*

This last is a crucial aspect. Over time, a godly Jew would realize
that after offering the *same* sacrifices *year after year* (Heb 9:25; 10:1–3,
11), the people were still not getting any better.[40] In fact, the Old Testament really chronicles the inability of people to live according to God's
standards *in their own strength*—even God's chosen people, who had the
advantage of the presence and revelation of God.

The people of Israel, after Moses had come down from Mount Sinai
and relayed to them God's commands, had rashly promised: "All that
the LORD has spoken we will do!" (Exod 24:3). Yet within a few chapters

---

39. D. Peterson, *Engaging with God*, 32.

40. If a consistent Israelite were to bring an animal for sacrifice every time he or
she sinned, that would surely lead very quickly to running out of animals!

they were worshiping the golden calf (ch. 32)! Israel's history post-Sinai seems to be a wholesale demonstration of the foolhardiness of the people's proclamation at the mountain. The rest of the Old Testament gives testimony to the large-scale devolution of that presumptuous and self-righteous pronouncement—beginning almost immediately with the golden calf incident, continuing with grumblings and worse crimes during the wilderness period and the lawless period of the judges, and later with a host of bad kings and the shocking large-scale neglect (or ignorance) of the law and the Passover for sometimes generations at a time (see 2 Kgs 22:8–13; 2 Chr 30).[41] *Idolatry is never far away from taking center stage in the nation's life.*

The book of Hebrews makes it clear that God intended the Old Testament system to be *temporary*, in preparation for the coming of Christ:

> For since the law has but a shadow of the good things to come instead of the true form of these realities, it can never, by the same sacrifices that are continually offered every year, make perfect those who draw near. (Heb 10:1)

According to Paul, "the law was our guardian [or tutor, schoolmaster] until Christ came" (Gal 3:24). Paul insists that the problem was *not* with the law (it was a perfect representation of the will of God), but rather with the people's *hearts* (Rom 8:2–4). So through the law and the sacrificial system, the devoted Jew would begin to see the inadequacy of the system and to long for a better way.[42] And indeed that better way is foretold in the prophets:

> Behold, the days are coming, declares the LORD, when I will make *a new covenant* with the house of Israel and the house of Judah, not like the covenant that I made with their fathers on the day when I

---

41. In fact, Christopher Wright points out that there is no record in the Old Testament of the Year of Jubilee (commanded by God in Lev 25:8–15) ever being observed (*Mission of God*, 295). He *is* quick to point out that the mere silence of the text does not *prove* that the events did not happen; yet it is still surprising that there is no biblical (or extrabiblical) evidence of such an important event taking place. Wright adds that the Day of Atonement is never mentioned either; and the same could be said of the sabbatical year (Lev 25:3–5): the seventy years of the Babylonian captivity were said to make up for the 490 years of neglecting to let the land rest every seventh year (2 Chr 36:20–21), which apparently also never happened.

42. "They are called to a pure worship of the heart . . . [but] no amount of ethical striving or moral reform can make them holy enough to serve their God. A new covenant is promised as a new exodus and a new creation in which there will be a forgiveness of sins and a divine transformation of the heart (Jer 31:31–34; 32:40; Ezek 36:24–28)" (Hahn, "Canon," 220).

took them by the hand to bring them out of the land of Egypt, my covenant that they broke, though I was their husband, declares the Lord. For this is the covenant that I will make with the house of Israel after those days, declares the Lord: I will put my law *within them*, and I will write it *on their hearts*. (Jer 31:31–33b).

And I will give you *a new heart*, and *a new spirit* I will put within you. And I will remove the heart of stone from your flesh and give you a heart of flesh. And I will *put my Spirit within you*, and cause you to walk in my statutes and be careful to obey my rules. (Ezek 36:26–27)

This new covenant (which would be instituted through Christ's death [Luke 22:20]) would bring with it *divine enablement* to live in obedience to God, in that he would write his law *on their hearts* and put *his Holy Spirit within them*:

For *God* has done what the *law*, weakened by the flesh, could not do. By sending his own Son in the likeness of sinful flesh and for sin, he condemned sin in the flesh, in order that the righteous requirement of the law might be fulfilled in us, who walk not according to the flesh but according to the Spirit. (Rom 8:3–4)

The complex ritual system of the Mosaic covenant would thus help to prepare for the coming of Christ and the new covenant by demonstrating the people's helplessness and dire need for God to intervene in a decisive and redemptive way.

### 5. Testimony Worship

God's plan was simple: God would make His name great and then Israel could make His name known.[43]

Israel's worship was to be a testimony to the nations of how God would bless a people who would worship him as the one true God.

Sing to the Lord, all the earth!
Tell of his salvation from day to day.
Declare his glory among the nations,
    his marvelous works among all the peoples!
For great is the Lord, and greatly to be praised,
    and he is to be feared above all gods.

43. Hawthorne, "Story of His Glory."

> For all the gods of the peoples are worthless idols,
>> but the LORD made the heavens. (1 Chr 16:23–26)

> I will give thanks to you, O LORD, among the peoples;
> I will sing praises to you among the nations. (Ps 57:9)

> May God be gracious to us and bless us
>> and make his face to shine upon us,
> that your way may be known on earth,
>> your saving power among all nations. (Ps 67:1–2)

What is interesting to note, however, is that Israel's worship would be a testimony to the nations *even when they would turn to false worship and idolatry.* Because then God would discipline them, bringing hardship, defeat in battle, etc.

> Israel was told repeatedly that God would destroy them just as swiftly [as the nations they were to displace] if they turned away from His worship to other gods.[44]

And this discipline would be a *testimony* to the nations that *God is so holy that he will judge even his own people when they turn away from him.*

> And many nations will pass by this city [after Jerusalem's destruction by Babylon], and every man will say to his neighbor, "Why has the Lord dealt thus with this great city?" And they will answer, "Because they have forsaken the covenant of the Lord their God and worshiped other gods and served them." (Jer 22:8–9)

Of God sending his people into exile, Isaiah declares:

> But the LORD of hosts is exalted in justice,
> and the Holy God shows himself holy in righteousness. (Isa 5:16)

So Israel's worship *would* be a testimony to the nations, whether their worship was true *or* false. And God would vindicate his name through his future blessing on the people through the new covenant, in spite of their unfaithfulness:

> Therefore say to the house of Israel, "Thus says the LORD God: It is not for your sake, O house of Israel, that I am about to act, but for the sake of my holy name, which you have profaned among the nations to which you came. And I will vindicate the holiness of my great name, which has been profaned among the nations, and which you have profaned among them. And the nations will

---

44. Hawthorne, "Story of His Glory."

know that I am the LORD, declares the LORD God, when through you I vindicate my holiness before their eyes." (Ezek 36:22–23)

## 6. Typological Worship

Finally, the nation's worship would be typological; that is, it would fore-shadow and picture in various ways the coming work of Christ. ("The law has but a shadow of the good things to come instead of the true form of these realities." [Heb 10:1]) This is seen most vividly (at least in retrospect) in the observance of the Day of Atonement. James Torrance summarizes this well:

> In old Israel, as in Israel to this day, the great central act of Jewish worship took place on the Day of Atonement, the *yom kippur*. That was the day in the year which gathered up the worship of every other day. On that day an offering was made which gathered up all the other offerings made daily in the sanctuary, and on that day the worship of all Israel was led by one man, the high priest. Think for a moment of the symbolism of that day. The high priest stands before the people as their divinely appointed representative, bone of their bone, flesh of their flesh, their brother, in solidarity with the people he represents. All that he does, he does in their name; this is symbolized by the fact that he bears their names engraved on his breastplate and shoulders as a memorial before God (Exod 39:7). He consecrates himself for this ministry by certain liturgical acts of washing and sacrifice. Then comes the great moment when he takes an animal, lays his hands on the victim and vicariously confesses the sins of all Israel in an act of vicarious penitence acknowledging the just judgments of God; when the victim is immolated as a symbol of God's judgment, he takes the blood of the vessel, ascends into the Holy of Holies, and there vicariously intercedes for all Israel that God will remember his covenant promises and graciously forgive. He then returns to the waiting people outside with the Aaronic blessing of peace.
>
> The New Testament writers saw this as a foreshadowing of the ministry of Christ, who comes from God to be the true Priest, bone of our bone, flesh of our flesh, in solidarity with all human-ity, all races, all colors, bearing on his divine heart the names, the needs, the sorrows, the injustices of all nations, to offer that worship, that obedience, that life of love to the Father which we cannot offer. In our Lord's high priestly prayer, where he inter-cedes for his people, he says, "For them I sanctify myself, that

they too may be truly sanctified" (John 17:19)—the One for the Many. "Both the One who makes men holy and those are made holy are of the same family. So Jesus is not ashamed to call them brothers" (Heb 2:11). Jesus' whole life of prayer and obedience and love, his whole life in the Spirit, is his self-consecration for us, for he offers, not an animal, but *himself* in death that he might be the Lamb of God to take away the sin of the world, saying Amen in our humanity to the just judgments of God not to appease an angry God to condition him into being gracious, but in perfect acknowledgment of the love of God for a sinful world—to seal God's covenant purposes for humanity by his blood.[45]

Israel's *worship*—exclusive, word-directed, lifestyle, ritual, testimony, typological worship—was to be their ↑ response to the covenant that God ↓ had initiated with them.

> Israel's covenant duty was worship.

---

45. J. Torrance, "Christ in Our Place: The Joy of Worship," in T. Torrance et al., *Passion for Christ*, 44–45. Also: "The earliest Christians were Jews; first-century Jews had Temple-worship in their bloodstream; and the first generation saw, from very early on, that in Jesus and the Spirit they had that towards which the Temple had been an advance" (N. T. Wright, "Worship and the Spirit").

# 15

## WORSHIP IN OLD TESTAMENT HISTORY

### Pre-Exilic Israel

#### (Joshua–2 Chronicles)

W e will now take on a large swath of Israel's history—from the conquest to the Babylonian exile.

### The Conquest (Joshua)

God had two purposes in the conquest of the promised land:

#### 1. The Destruction of False Worship

God's command to go into the promised land and wipe out the Canaanites is troubling to many; but it is important to see it as the judgment of God upon the depraved worship of that land, which often included temple prostitution, child sacrifice, etc.

> God was demolishing systems of false worship in order to preserve the singular devotion of his people and the holiness of His name. Many passages describe the logic of ousting the peoples living in the land because they would swiftly turn the Hebrews "away from following Me to serve other gods" (Deut 4:15–24, 6:13–15, 7:1–8, and many others). . . . Joshua and Moses both voiced the same God-given rationale for the violence of the

conquest: it was, at the core, an annihilation of false worship. God had mandated the destruction so that Israel would never "mention the name of their gods . . . or serve them" (Josh 23:7).[1]

And Moses gave this perspective in anticipation of the conquest:

> Do not say in your heart, after the LORD your God has thrust them out before you, "It is because of my righteousness that the LORD has brought me in to possess this land," whereas it is because of the wickedness of these nations that the LORD is driving them out before you. Not because of your righteousness or the uprightness of your heart are you going in to possess their land, but because of the wickedness of these nations the LORD your God is driving them out from before you, and that he may confirm the word that the LORD swore to your fathers, to Abraham, to Isaac, and to Jacob. Know, therefore, that the LORD your God is not giving you this good land to possess because of your righteousness, for you are a stubborn people. Remember and do not forget how you provoked the LORD your God to wrath in the wilderness. From the day you came out of the land of Egypt until you came to this place, you have been rebellious against the LORD. (Deut 9:4–7)

Before they crossed the Jordan, God had warned the people of Israel that this conquest is not a tribute to their righteousness. They do not deserve a land flowing with milk and honey. They are not destroying the inhabitants because of Israel's superior righteousness, but because of God's justice toward the nations and God's utterly undeserved grace toward Israel.[2]

## 2. The Establishment of True Worship

One thing is clear about the conquest: the point was *pure worship*. God's objective was *not that Israel would be the only people that worshiped him*. His point was *to insure that he was the only God that they worshiped*.[3]

All of Deuteronomy 7 is concerned with the distinctiveness of Israel from the Canaanites, in order to prevent them going down the road of Canaanite idolatry and corrupt religious and social practice. The point of Israel's separation was not ethnic

---

1. Hawthorne, "Story of His Glory."
2. Piper, *Providence*, 119–20.
3. Hawthorne, "Story of His Glory" (emphases added).

exclusiveness (there were all kinds of ways that foreigners could be incorporated into the worship community of Israel) but religious protection.[4]

Be very careful, therefore, to love the LORD your God. For if you turn back and cling to the remnant of these nations remaining among you and make marriages with them, so that you associate with them and they with you, know for certain that the LORD your God will no longer drive out these nations before you, but they shall be a snare and a trap for you, a whip on your sides and thorns in your eyes, until you perish from off this good ground that the LORD your God has given you. (Josh 23:11–13)

In spite of God's repeated warnings, we read that Israel did not follow through on God's command to rid the land of its inhabitants. And, as predicted, the influence of their idolatry would repeatedly drag down the nation throughout the coming centuries, and lead to harsh discipline at the hand of the Lord. (As noted earlier, God would deal justly even with his own people when they turned away from him.)

> They did not destroy the peoples,
>     as the LORD commanded them,
> but they mixed with the nations
>     and learned to do as they did.
> They served their idols,
>     which became a snare to them. (Ps 106:34–36)

## Cycles of True and False Worship (Judges–2 Chronicles)

The rest of the historical books of the Old Testament can be summarized as a series of cycles:

---

4. C. Wright, *Mission of God*, 257.

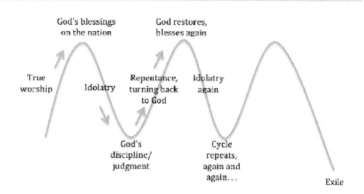

*Israel's fate as a nation always followed its worship.* When the people were worshiping God rightly, God would bless them as a nation. But as happened time and time again, they would eventually turn to idolatry (infected by Canaanite worship because of their failure to totally remove the inhabitants of the land and their religious structures and practices), and God would bring discipline against his people (defeat in battle, failure of crops, etc.)—though always with a view to bringing them to repentance. And repeatedly, when the people of Israel did cry out to the Lord and turn back in repentance, God in his great *ḥesed* (and "for his great name's sake" [1 Sam 12:22]) would forgive them and restore their fortunes. But then the pattern of idolatry, discipline, repentance, and restoration would happen again—and again, and again.

Psalm 105 rehearses the blessings and privileges that God bestowed upon his chosen people. Psalm 106 tells the story of the people's repeated rebelliousness (from when they were in Egypt, on through the exodus and wilderness sojourn, and up until the period we are considering here), and God's repeated mercy:

> Their enemies oppressed them,
>     and they were brought into subjection under their power.
> Many times he delivered them,
>     but they were rebellious in their purposes
>     and were brought low through their iniquity.
> Nevertheless, he looked upon their distress,
>     when he heard their cry.
> For their sake he remembered his covenant,
>     and relented according to the abundance of his steadfast
>     love. (Ps 106:42–45)

Finally the sin of the people became so bad that God took them into exile; but even then it was only a temporary exile (for the Southern Kingdom), and God would allow them to return later.

We see from these cycles that when the people's worship was *right*, then God would *bless* and things would go right for them as a nation; and when the people's worship was *wrong*, then everything went wrong under the *disciplining* hand of God. *Israel's fate as a nation always followed its worship*, since it was the people's *worship* that God desired as their part of the covenant agreement.

## King David

David is a crucial figure in the history of the worship of Israel, and in the history of worship in general, for three reasons:

### 1. David Greatly Developed the Public Worship of the Nation

It is a remarkable fact that, after the establishment by God of the tabernacle and its accompanying worship system through Moses, as recorded in Exodus and Leviticus, there is virtually no mention of music being used in the public worship of Israel for many centuries. The one exception is Num 10:10, where the instruction is given for trumpets to be blown "over" the sacrifices "on the day of your gladness also, and at your appointed feasts and at the beginnings of your months." But as far as songs of praise go, about all we read about are the songs of Moses and Miriam after the crossing of the Red Sea (Exod 15) and the victory song of Deborah and Barak in Judg 5. The worship of the tabernacle itself seems to have been practiced without musical praise.[5]

That situation changes drastically and dramatically with King David. When David establishes Jerusalem as the political and religious capital of Israel, the tabernacle and the ark of the covenant go from being portable, mobile worship sites to being stationary, established worship venues. Interestingly, David leaves the Mosaic tabernacle itself in Gibeon (1 Chr 16:39–43), and puts the ark in a newly constructed tabernacle in Jerusalem (1 Chr 15:1); the sacrifices continue in Gibeon, and there is some musical worship there too (1 Chr 16:40–42), but Jerusalem becomes the

---

5. This is the astute observation of Peter Leithart in *From Silence to Song*, 14, 54.

doxological center of the nation, where daily praises as well as the nation's festivals are celebrated.

And David enriches those celebrations with a huge overhaul of the practice of public worship, most notably by assigning and organizing whole ranks of Levites to be full-time musical ministers, as singers and as instrumentalists, in the service of the people's worship. See especially chs. 15, 16, 23, and 25 of 1 Chronicles for descriptions of these developments. (It has also been pointed out that the stability and peace brought about by David's military victories and settling of Jerusalem allowed for the training of musicians in a way that would have been more difficult before.)

> And they brought in the ark of God and set it inside the tent that David had pitched for it, and they offered burnt offerings and peace offerings before God. . . . Then [David] appointed some of the Levites as ministers before the ark of the LORD, to invoke, to thank, and to praise the LORD, the God of Israel. Asaph was the chief, and second to him were Zechariah, Jeiel, Shemiramoth, Jehiel, Mattithiah, Eliab, Benaiah, Obed-edom, and Jeiel, who were to play harps and lyres; Asaph was to sound the cymbals, and Benaiah and Jahaziel the priests were to blow trumpets regularly before the ark of the covenant of God. Then on that day David first appointed that thanksgiving be sung to the LORD by Asaph and his brothers. (1 Chr 16:1, 4–7)

Peter Leithart has written a fascinating little book entitled *From Silence to Song*, with the appropriate subtitle *The Davidic Liturgical Revolution*. For indeed David, himself a musician, instituted a revolutionary overhaul of the way worship was practiced by the Jewish people. In his book Leithart lays out the grandeur of David's worship reforms, and their huge implications not only for Israel, but also for the church on into our present day. For, as Leithart points out, "when Christians sing hymns and psalms in worship, when we play organs or pianos, guitars or trumpets, we are heirs of David's 'liturgical revolution.'"[6]

What gave David the right to tinker with and expand the Mosaic directives for Israel's worship? Leithart shows from 2 Chr 29:25 (at the later time of Hezekiah) that David had apparently received some sort of revelation from the Lord to that effect, so that his expansive recasting of the Mosaic system was divinely inspired and sanctioned.

---

6. Leithart, *From Silence to Song*, 15.

> And [Hezekiah] stationed the Levites in the house of the Lord
> with cymbals, harps, and lyres, according to the commandment
> of David and of Gad the king's seer and of Nathan the prophet,
> *for the commandment was from the* LORD *through his prophets.*
> (2 Chr 29:25)

Leithart also makes a good linguistic and conceptual case for the Levites' change of role under David's reforms: whereas one of the chief responsibilities assigned by Moses to them was to *lift up* the ark and carry it (Num 4:15; Deut 10:8)—a job no longer necessary because the ark was now a stationary fixture—their role now morphs into one of *lifting up* the Lord in song and praise.[7] The "service" of the tabernacle that they were to carry out (Deut 10:8; there is no mention at all of music in Deuteronomy) now carried a large musical component (1 Chr 16:4–43).

As important as music is now in Christian worship, we can trace that phenomenon back to the influence of David and the reforms he made to heighten the role of music (sung and instrumental) in the public worship of Israel.[8]

## 2. David Was a Tremendous Example of a True Worshiper

David was, of course, far from being a perfect man. He committed some serious sins in his life, with far-reaching consequences.

And yet the overwhelming orientation of his life was: whether he was going through good times (see Ps 23) or hard times (see Ps 63), David knew *the answer was always God.* Perhaps this was one reason the Lord referred to him as "a man after his own heart" (1 Sam 13:14)—because he would turn to God, no matter what the circumstance.

It has been said that a crisis shows what we are really made of. If that is true, David's situation when he wrote Ps 63 certainly qualifies. Our Bibles call this a "psalm of David, when he was in the wilderness of Judah," and most likely this refers to the time later in his life when his son Absalom rebelled against him and David had to flee for his life to the desert. There he sees his bare and parched surroundings as an illustration to him of a life without God; and his heart cries out with longing for God and for the joy of his presence.

---

7. Leithart, *From Silence to Song*, 61.

8. See more development of this theme in Leithart's book, as well as in Man, "King David's Lasting Musical Legacy" and "More on the 'Davidic Liturgical Revolution' in Chronicles."

O God, you are my God; earnestly I seek you;
  my soul thirsts for you;
  my flesh faints for you,
  as in a dry and weary land where there is no water. (Ps 63:1)

That is what David was made of; that is what this crisis brought out in him.[9]

In worldly terms, David has lost it all: his family, his throne, his reputation, his security. He is on the run, far from the tabernacle and the palace, in the dry, barren, dusty desert where he can take no creature comforts for granted. Yet, as Spurgeon puts it, "there was no desert in his heart, though there was a desert around him."[10] Perowne similarly writes:

> It is remarkable that in this Psalm . . . there is no petition. There is gladness, there is praise, there is the most exalted communion with God, there is longing for His presence as the highest of all blessings; but there is not one word of asking for temporal, or even for spiritual good.[11]

David gives us this beautiful expression of a man thoroughly saturated with love and longing for God. He says, in effect: "It's not water I need, not the comfort of my palace, not even the refuge of the tabernacle. I need God!"

It is also striking that, far from Jerusalem and hence removed from any possibility of fulfilling *any* of the Mosaic instructions for worship, David intuitively understood that he still had a personal relationship with God (v. 1, "You are *my* God"; Kidner says that "the simplicity and boldness of 'You are my God' is the secret of all that follows"[12]). David sensed that he could still approach God in worship, even in the wilderness. He doesn't seek to perform a religious or ceremonial duty; rather, he opens his heart to God, thirsts and yearns for him, praises and worships him from his heart.

David looks back on how he has experienced God in the worship of the tabernacle:

9. Note also the tremendous example of Job, who upon losing his children and most of his possessions responded with worship:

> Then Job arose and tore his robe and shaved his head and fell on the ground and *worshiped*. And he said, "Naked I came from my mother's womb, and naked shall I return. The LORD gave, and the LORD has taken away; *blessed be the name of the LORD*." In all this Job did not sin or charge God with wrong. (Job 1:20–22)

10. Spurgeon, *Treasury of David*, on Ps 63:1.

11. Perowne, *Book of Psalms*, 505.

12. Kidner, *Psalms 1–72*, on Ps 63:1.

> So I have looked upon you in the sanctuary,
> beholding your power and glory. (Ps 63:2)

And he turns to this One whom he has come to know in this context. Then, though under threat of death, David joyfully acknowledges that

> your steadfast love [*ḥesed*] is *better than life*. (Ps 63:3)

So we see the flower of David's worship bloom and flourish in the desert. He comes to God, as Eric Alexander puts it, "not to fulfill a duty, but to satisfy an appetite."[13] He exclaims, "My soul thirsts for you, my flesh yearns for you, in a dry and weary land where there is no water" (Ps 63:1). Soul and flesh: the entirety of David's being cries out for God. That's the way David is about God: he wants *God*, and nothing else would do. He longs and thirsts and yearns for God and for the joy of fellowship with him.

David had a tremendous heart for God and is a model for us of a *true worshiper*.

### 3. David Was a Composer of Many Songs for Corporate Worship

David, a musician himself, wrote many songs for use in private and public worship (including at least seventy-three of the psalms). Many of these texts we still set to music and use in worship.

## King Solomon and the Temple

David's son Solomon built the temple in Jerusalem after the basic structure of the tabernacle, only it was much richer in its design and materials. When it was completed and the ark of the covenant was brought into the holy of holies, we read that, similar to what happened at the completion of the tabernacle (Exod 40:34):

> As soon as Solomon finished his prayer, fire came down from heaven and consumed the burnt offering and the sacrifices, *and the glory of the LORD filled the* temple. And the priests could not enter the house of the LORD, because the glory of the LORD filled the LORD's house. When all the people of Israel saw the fire come down and the glory of the LORD on the temple, they bowed down with their faces to the ground on the pavement and worshiped

---

13. Alexander, "Thirsting for God."

and gave thanks to the LORD, saying, "For he is good, for his steadfast love [*ḥesed*] endures forever." (2 Chr 7:1–3)

Again this signifies God's continuing glorious presence among his people.

## The Temple's Purpose

You shall seek the place that the LORD your God will choose out of all your tribes to put his name and make his habitation there. There you shall go, and there you shall bring your burnt offerings and your sacrifices, your tithes and the contribution that you present, your vow offerings, your freewill offerings, and the firstborn of your herd and of your flock. And there you shall eat before the LORD your God, and you shall rejoice, you and your households. (Deut 12:5–7)

The temple was a visible reminder of God's presence among his people and of his saving dominion over all creation. It was where God would ↓ *make himself known* and permit his people to find union with him ↑ *in their worship.*[14]

## The Temple's Magnificence

The temple in Jerusalem was probably the most ornate and beautiful building of its day.

Everything about it ministered to the aesthetic sense of the worship—God is a God of order, beauty, and perfection. Everything about the temple reminded people that the Lord was a holy God and filled them with the hope of glory.[15]

## The Temple's Worship

This magnificent building was dedicated to the worship of the God of glory. Solomon said at the temple's dedication:

But will God indeed dwell on the earth? Behold, heaven and the highest heaven cannot contain you; how much less this house

---

14. Ross, *Recalling the Hope of Glory*, 251 (emphases and arrows added).
15. Ross, *Recalling the Hope of Glory*, 251.

that I have built! Yet have regard to the prayer of your servant and to his plea, O LORD my God, listening to the cry and to the prayer that your servant prays before you this day, that your eyes may be open night and day toward this house, the place of which you have said, "My name shall be there," that you may listen to the prayer that your servant offers toward this place. And listen to the plea of your servant and of your people Israel, when they pray toward this place. And listen in heaven your dwelling place, and when you hear, forgive. (1 Kgs 8:27–30)

The rituals and the ceremonies were even more elaborate than at the tabernacle, building upon David's reforms of Israel's worship and his expansion of the musical component.

It was only in the splendor of the ceremony that the worship of the temple was different from that of the tabernacle. The same sacrifices, offerings, and feasts were observed. The emphasis upon worship through music, both instrumental and vocal, seems to be the only added element. God introduced this emphasis largely through the poetic and musical gifts which He had given to His servant King David.[16]

## The Downward Spiral of Idolatry

Under Solomon's son Rehoboam, the kingdom split into Northern and Southern Kingdoms. Idolatry got worse and worse. Finally, the Northern Kingdom was conquered by the Assyrians and disappeared from history. The Southern Kingdom lasted a little longer, with occasional revivals, notably under Hezekiah (2 Kgs 18–19) and Josiah (2 Kgs 22–23); but it likewise got worse and worse until God sent them into exile too.

## The People

The people of Israel indeed all too often would

draw near with their mouth and honor me with their lips, while their hearts are far from me. (Isa 29:13; Matt 15:7–9)

As we have seen, God despises the kind of worship that is external only, without an internal devotion to him. He rejects even the practices

---

16. Rayburn, *O Come*, 76.

he has himself commanded, when they are not offered up as the expression of the heart:

> What to me is the multitude of your sacrifices?
>     says the LORD;
> I have had enough of burnt offerings of rams
>     and the fat of well-fed beasts;
> I do not delight in the blood of bulls,
>     or of lambs, or of goats.
> When you come to appear before me,
>     who has required of you
>     this trampling of my courts?
> Bring no more vain offerings;
>     incense is an abomination to me.
> New moon and Sabbath and the calling of convocations—
>     I cannot endure iniquity and solemn assembly.
> Your new moons and your appointed feasts
>     my soul hates;
> they have become a burden to me;
>     I am weary of bearing them. (Isa 1:11–14)

> I hate, I despise your feasts,
>     and I take no delight in your solemn assemblies.
> Even though you offer me your burnt offerings and grain offerings,
>     I will not accept them;
> and the peace offerings of your fattened animals,
>     I will not look upon them.
> Take away from me the noise of your songs;
>     to the melody of your harps I will not listen.
> But let justice roll down like waters,
>     and righteousness like an ever-flowing stream.
> (Amos 5:21–24)

## The Rulers

In the books of 1 and 2 Kings, when the writers talk about the different rulers of the Northern and Southern Kingdoms, the reign of each king is always evaluated *according to his worship*. For example:

> In the third year of Hoshea son of Elah, king of Israel, Hezekiah the son of Ahaz, king of Judah, began to reign. He was twenty-five years old when he began to reign, and he reigned twenty-nine years in Jerusalem.... *And he did what was right in the eyes*

*of the* LORD, according to all that David his father had done. He removed the high places and broke the pillars and cut down the Asherah. (2 Kgs 18:1–3)

Manasseh was twelve years old when he began to reign, and he reigned fifty-five years in Jerusalem. And *he did what was evil in the sight of the* LORD, according to the abominations of the nations whom the LORD drove out before the people of Israel. (2 Chr 33:1–2)

Doing "right in the sight of the Lord" means that the king *worshiped God rightly*, and led the people in doing that also. Doing "evil in the sight of the Lord" means that he *fell into idolatry*, and led the people down that path as well.[17]

So every king is evaluated according to his worship: it is his *worship* that makes his reign successful or unsuccessful. When his worship was right, the nation's worship was right. When his worship was wrong, the nation's worship was wrong.

## The Prophets

During this period we have the ministry of many of the prophets, calling the people to repentance and/or warning of impending judgment.

The LORD, the God of their fathers, sent persistently to them by his messengers, because he had compassion on his people and on his dwelling place. But they kept mocking the messengers of God, despising his words and scoffing at his prophets, until the wrath of the LORD rose against his people, until there was no remedy. (2 Chr 36:15–16)

---

*Israel's fate as a nation always followed its worship.*

---

17. Among the kings who were said to have "done right in the sight of the LORD" are David (1 Kgs 15:4; "*except* in the matter of Uriah the Hittite"), Asa (1 Kgs 15:9–11), Jehoash (2 Kgs 12:1–2), Amaziah (2 Kgs 14:1–3), Hezekiah (2 Kgs 18:1–3), Josiah (2 Kgs 22:12), etc. Among the kings who were said to have "done evil in the sight of the LORD" are Nadab (1 Kgs 15:25–26), Baasha (1 Kgs 15:33–34), Omri (2 Kgs 16:24–25), Manasseh (2 Kgs 21:1–2), Zedekiah (2 Kgs 24:18–19), etc.

# 16

## WORSHIP IN OLD TESTAMENT HISTORY
### Exilic and Post-Exilic Israel

### Exilic Worship

#### The Destruction of Jerusalem and the Temple

So God allows the Southern Kingdom to be sent into exile, and Jerusalem is destroyed by the Babylonians in 586 BC.

> Therefore he brought up against them the king of the Chaldeans, who killed their young men with the sword in the house of their sanctuary and had no compassion on young man or virgin, old man or aged. He gave them all into his hand. And all the vessels of the house of God, great and small, and the treasures of the house of the LORD, and the treasures of the king and of his princes, all these he brought to Babylon. And they burned the house of God and broke down the wall of Jerusalem and burned all its palaces with fire and destroyed all its precious vessels. He took into exile in Babylon those who had escaped from the sword, and they became servants to him and to his sons. (2 Chr 36:17–20)

The temple, the most magnificent building in the world, built by Solomon for the worship of God, is destroyed. God allows the building that was built for his praise to be destroyed. And why? Because God does not care about a building if he does not have the *hearts* of the people.

As we have seen, the testimony of this tragic state of affairs would be:

> And many nations will pass by this city, and every man will say to his neighbor, "Why has the LORD dealt thus with this great city?" And they will answer, "Because they have forsaken the covenant of the LORD their God and worshiped other gods and served them." (Jer 22:8–9)

↓ God had made a covenant with his people, and promised his presence among them and a special relationship with them; and ↑ in response he asked for their worship: exclusive, wholehearted, faithful worship. Then when they would turn away to idolatry, God would discipline them in order to bring them to repentance and restoration. After many such cycles (and enduring patience and *ḥesed* on God's part), as we have seen, God finally sends his people into exile.

The glory of God had filled the holy of holies in the tabernacle (Exod 40:34) and later the temple (2 Chr 7:1–3), signifying God's gracious presence among his people. After the exile, Ezekiel sees a tragic vision of God's glory *leaving the temple and then departing from Jerusalem* (Ezek 10:15–19; 11:22–25). Thus far have the people fallen: they have lost God's special presence among them.

## Exilic Worship in the Synagogue

Exiled to Babylon, the people had no temple and thus no way to participate in the sacrificial worship God had established. But they would still gather in smaller groups for worship. Many biblical scholars consider this to be the origin of the Jewish synagogue.

> Before the Babylonian exile, Jewish religious life revolved around the Temple in Jerusalem. When the Babylonians expelled the Jews from Judea, they destroyed the Temple completely. Jewish law stipulated that certain important aspects of Jewish religious life—most notably animal sacrifice—could only be performed at the Temple in Jerusalem. Since the Jews now lacked both a Temple and the ability to go to Jerusalem, changes were needed to retain their cultural and religious identity. The result was the rise of the synagogue among the Jews dispersed throughout the Babylonian Empire. The focus shifted from animal sacrifices, which could only be properly performed at the Temple, to the

study and teaching of the Torah—the Jewish Bible—which became the focal point of worship in the synagogues.[1]

In these meetings, the great *Shema* ("Hear, O Israel: The LORD our God, the LORD is one" [Deut 6:3]) would be recited, and prayers would be lifted up to God. And, significantly, the Law (Torah) would be read aloud, after which *someone would expound on the meaning of the text read.*

This practice of expounding the word of God had enormous implications for the future, becoming *the foundation of Christian preaching* as it extended its influence into the ministry of Jesus Christ, then of Paul, and then into the regular ministry of the church (see Rom 10:14–15; 2 Tim 4:2).

Synagogue gatherings continued even after the people had returned from exile and persisted right into New Testament times. So we see Jesus entering the synagogue in Nazareth and being asked to read, after which he sits to expound the text and shocks the crowd by proclaiming, "Today this Scripture had been fulfilled in your hearing" (Luke 4:21). We see also Paul going first into the local synagogue when he reaches a new city on his missionary journeys, and as a visiting rabbi he would often be asked to give the exposition (which opportunity Paul would take to proclaim Christ from the Old Testament; see Acts 13:15–16; 14:1; 17:1–3, 10–11).

So this aspect of exilic worship had a profound effect on the future of Christian worship.

## Post-Exilic Worship

### The Rebuilding and Restoration

God allowed his exiled people to return after seventy years of captivity (2 Chr 36:20–23). The story of rebuilding the walls and the buildings of Jerusalem and the temple is related in the books of Ezra, Nehemiah, and Haggai.

After the rebuilding of the temple, the priesthood and sacrificial system were reinstituted. However, sadly, we never read about the glory of God filling this new temple (as it had the tabernacle and the first temple). The *next time* we read of the glory of God dwelling in the midst of his people is *in the person of Jesus Christ*:

1. Markey, "What Effects."

> And the Word became flesh and dwelt among us, and we have
> seen his glory, glory as of the only Son from the Father, full of
> grace and truth. (John 1:14)[2]

Importantly, the synagogue system continued even after temple
worship was resumed. Both of these would later influence Christian
worship.

## The Development of Traditions and Legalism

During the rest of the period leading up to the New Testament, the Jewish
leaders developed a complex system of traditions, rules, and regulations
superimposed on the Mosaic law.

Jesus would decry this system of rules because, as he put it, they were

> "teaching as doctrines the commandments of men. You leave
> the commandment of God and hold to the tradition of men."
> And he said to them, "You have a fine way of rejecting the
> commandment of God in order to establish your tradition!"
> (Mark 7:7b–9)[3]

As a result, Jesus said, their worship was "in vain" (Mark 7:7a).

The Sabbath observance, itself commanded in the law, bore much of
the brunt of the Jewish leaders' heavy-handed regulations. They specified

2. Interestingly, the Greek word translated "dwelt" in John 1:14 is closely related
to the Greek word for tabernacle: in essence, "the Word became flesh and *tabernacled*
among us." The tabernacle and temple had been places for God to meet with his people; and that "place" is now the Lord Jesus Christ (John 1:51; 2:11–22) and his church
(2 Cor 6:16; Eph 2:21). N. T. Wright expands on this idea: "What one might say about
the single, holy Temple in Jerusalem, that it was the unique dwelling place of the one
true God, is now to be said of the assemblies of those who meet to worship this God
through Jesus and in the power of the Spirit. The Spirit within the church has, in other
words, taken the place of the Shekinah within the Temple—a replacement all the more
powerful when we consider that nowhere in second-Temple literature do we find the
claim that YHWH has actually returned to take up residence on Mount Zion, and
actually we find strong indications that he has not (e.g. Malachi). Paul's claim fits into
this narrative: YHWH has indeed returned, in the person of Jesus himself [John 1:14]
but also in the person of the Spirit" ("Worship and the Spirit").

3. The law itself was not the problem, but rather all that was presumptuously added
to it by the Jewish leaders. In fact, when asked about the greatest commandment, Jesus
himself responded, "What is *written in the Law*?" (Luke 10:26). And also: "Do not
think that I have come to abolish the Law or the Prophets; I have not come to abolish
them but to fulfill them" (Matt 5:17). But in so doing he had to clear away the tangled
brush that had been allowed to grow around the law and choke out its spiritual intent.

thirty-nine different activities that they claimed amounted to "work" and were therefore forbidden on the Sabbath.[4] For example:

4. The Jewish Mishnah enumerates the thirty-nine categories of activities forbidden on the Sabbath (still observed by many Orthodox Jews): "Here is the list of the 39 *Melachot* (main activities) prohibited on the Shabbat as listed in the *Mishna Shabbat* 73a:

1. *Zoreah*—Sowing (seeding)
2. *Choresh*—Plowing
3. *Kotzair*—Reaping (cutting)
4. *M'amair*—Gathering (bundling sheaves)
5. *Dush*—Threshing
6. *Zoreh*—Winnowing
7. *Borer*—Sorting (selecting, separating)
8. *Tochain*—Grinding
9. *Miraked*—Sifting
10. *Lush*—Kneading
11. *Ofeh/(Bishul)*—Baking/cooking
12. *Gozez*—Shearing
13. *Melabain*—Whitening (bleaching)
14. *Menafetz*—Disentangling, combing
15. *Tzovayah*—Dyeing
16. *Toveh*—Spinning
17. *Maisach*—Mounting the warp (stretching threads onto loom)
18. *Oseh Beit Batai Neirin*—Setting two heddles (preparing to weave)
19. *Oraig*—Weaving
20. *Potzai'ah*—Separating (removing) threads (unweaving)
21. *Koshair*—Tying a knot
22. *Matir*—Untying a knot
23. *Tofair*—Sewing
24. *Ko'reah*—Tearing (unsewing—ripping)
25. *Tzud*—Trapping
26. *Shochet*—Slaughtering (killing)
27. *Mafshit*—Skinning
28. *M'abaid*—Salting/tanning process
29. *Mesharteit*—Tracing (scratching) lines
30. *Memacheik*—Smoothing/scraping
31. *Mechateich*—Cutting (to shape)
32. *Kotaiv*—Writing two or more letters
33. *Mochaik*—Erasing two or more letters
34. *Boneh*—Building
35. *Soiser*—Demolishing
36. *Mechabeh*—Extinguishing (putting out a flame)
37. *Ma'avir*—Kindling (making a fire)
38. *Makeh B'Patish*—Striking the final blow (finishing an object)
39. *Hotza'ah*—Transferring (transporting) from domain to domain (carrying)"
(Torah Tots, "39 Melachot").

> On a Sabbath, while he was going through the grainfields, his disciples plucked and ate some heads of grain, rubbing them in their hands. But some of the Pharisees said, "Why are you doing what is not lawful to do on the Sabbath?" (Luke 6:1–2)

The Pharisees considered this to be an act of "threshing."

Jesus detested this sort of legalistic pickiness, as it missed the whole point of the observance:

> And he said to them, "The Sabbath was made for man, not man for the Sabbath. So the Son of Man is lord even of the Sabbath." (Mark 2:27–28)

The rules for Sabbath-keeping were so minute and burdensome that the conscientious Jew would be so concerned about transgressing one of these small matters that the day could no longer be restful! As a result, its intended purpose would be thwarted, because the day of rest and worship was "made for man."

The entire system piled a heavy burden of legalism upon the people, as Jesus would complain about the scribes and Pharisees:

> They tie up heavy burdens, hard to bear, and lay them on people's shoulders, but they themselves are not willing to move them with their finger. (Matt 23:4)

Jesus came to relieve the people of this kind of unnecessary burden, as he expressed in his beautiful invitation:

> Come to me, all who labor and are heavy laden, and I will give you rest. Take my yoke upon you, and learn from me, for I am gentle and lowly in heart, and you will find rest for your souls. For my yoke is easy, and my burden is light. (Matt 11:28–30)

## Four Hundred Years of Silence

After the close of the book of Malachi, there is no more revelation from God for four hundred years. The *next direct word from God* that Israel receives is when the angel Gabriel appears to Zechariah in the temple in Luke 1 and foretells the birth of John the Baptist. God is moving again among his people, and events quickly escalate from that point on as the coming of Christ approaches.

## Key Worship Take-Aways from Old Testament History

1. Worship was always in ↑ *response* to God's gracious initiative in ↓ *revealing* himself and acting on behalf of his people.

2. God's priority in worship was always the *heart*.

3. God's *ḥesed* (loyal love) was his defining characteristic in all his dealings with his covenant people.

4. The entire Mosaic system was only a preparation for and "a shadow of the good things to come" (Heb 10:1).

5. A big part of this preparation was the indisputable demonstration of the inability (and unwillingness) of the human heart to obey and worship God as he deserved (Exod 24:3).

6. In this way, the need was made clear for a "new covenant," through which God was to provide divine enablement for living by writing his law on the people's hearts and putting his Holy Spirit within them (Jer 31:33; Ezek 36:27).

7. Thus God prepared to bring his Son into the world, to fulfill the law as the great Sacrifice to which it pointed; and to show the way, and be the means, of true worship.

> God does not care about a building if he does not have the hearts of the people.

# 17

# THE PSALMS:
## Israel's Worship Book . . . and Ours

We cannot leave our study of worship in the Old Testament without a closer look at the book of Psalms.[1] It is the great worship book of the Old Testament, and a marvelous gift to the people of God of all ages. Martin Luther reputedly wrote, "No devotional book has ever appeared that is superior to the Psalms."

### The Uniqueness of the Psalms

A very important understanding of Psalms comes from the early church:

> It is reported that Athanasius, an outstanding Christian leader of the fourth century, declared that the Psalms have a unique place in the Bible because most of Scripture speaks *to us*, while the Psalms speak *for us*.[2]

The psalms can help give expression to our feelings, needs, and prayers in a unique way. They address honestly and directly before God all types of life situations, both good and bad. The book is not "a liturgical library,

---

1. An in-depth treatment of the Psalms and their use in Christian worship can be found in Witvliet, *Biblical Psalms*.

2. Bernhard Anderson, *Out of the Depths*, x (emphases added).

storing up standard literature for worship. . . . [It is a] collection of real people's praises and petitions. . . . [The psalms come] straight from life."[3]

Martin Luther wrote:

> Where do you find words more beautifully expressive of joy than in the psalms of praise and thanksgiving? . . . On the other hand, where do you find deeper, more sorrowful, more pitiful words of sadness than in the psalms of lamentation? . . . The Psalter is the book of all saints, and everyone, whatever his situation may be, finds psalms and words in it that fit his situation and apply to his case so exactly that it seems they were put in this way only for his sake.[4]

Plantinga and Rozeboom add: "Psalms are the language we use when we need a voice other than our own."[5] John Goldingay similarly suggests that the assumption of Psalms is that "we do not know instinctively how to talk with God but rather need some help knowing how to do so. . . . The Psalms make it possible to say things that are otherwise unsayable."[6] "The psalms offer [us] a vocabulary for use in honest dialogues with God. . . ."[7] Worship must not be a time of pretend."[8]

## The Structure of the Psalms

Book 1: Pss 1–41 (concluding doxology: 41:13)
Book 2: Pss 42–72 (concluding doxology: 72:18–19)
Book 3: Pss 73–89 (concluding doxology: 89:52)
Book 4: Pss 90–106 (concluding doxology: 106:48)
Book 5: Pss 107–50 (concluding doxology for entire Psalter: Ps 150)[9]

Psalms 146–50 all begin and end the same way: with "Praise the LORD!"— or in Hebrew, Hallelujah! The Hebrew is actually two words, Hallelu-Yah: Hallelu is a plural command, "praise"; and Yah is a shortened form of the name of God, Yahweh. We often use hallelujah as an exclamation of praise, but actually it is a *command* to all of God's people: a command to "praise

---

3. Goldingay, *Psalms*, 1:22.

4. Luther, *What Luther Says*, 1000.

5. Plantinga and Rozeboom, *Discerning the Spirits*, 160.

6. Goldingay, *Psalms*, 1:32, 30.

7. This was true, of course, even of the Lord Jesus, who quoted Ps 22 as he hung on the cross.

8. Kaemingk and Willson, *Work and Worship*, 102, 105.

9. Bernhard Anderson, *Out of the Depths*, 202–3.

the LORD." This Hebrew word for "praise" actually is used thirteen times in Ps 150 (at least twice in every verse); and as such this psalm serves as a sort of exclamation point concluding the entire book of Psalms, and summarizes the call of the entire book to "praise the LORD!"[10]

> Let *everything* that has breath praise the LORD. Praise the LORD!
> (Ps 150:6)[11]

## The Authors of the Psalms

Psalms is a collection of a number of different writers. Seventy-three of the psalms are attributed to David in those psalms' titles. Other authors identified are: Asaph (twelve); Sons of Korah (eleven); Solomon (two); Moses (one: Ps 90); Hernan (one); Ethan (one). The authors of forty-nine of the psalms are not identified.

## The Content of the Psalms

Some psalms were intended for private worship, and some for public worship. The various types of psalms have been classified according to their characteristics and forms:

- Salvation history psalms (trace God's faithfulness in the history of Israel)
- Laments (community and individual)

---

10. The surprising fact has been observed that the psalms have very, very little to say about animal sacrifices. Rather, there is the preponderant emphasis on *heart* worship (which, as we have seen, needed to underlie acceptable sacrifice anyway). "[In the Psalms] worship comes to be seen as a sacrificial offering in thanksgiving for redemption, for deliverance from death. Praise is revealed as the sacrifice by which men and women are to glorify God (Ps. 50:14, 33; 141:2). God is portrayed as desiring that Israel serve him—not with the blood of animals but with their whole hearts, aligning their will with his, making their whole lives a sacrifice of praise and thanksgiving (Ps. 40:6–8; 51:16–17)" (Hahn, "Canon," 219).

11. "The title of the book of psalms in Hebrew is *Tehillim*, 'praises.' This is so even though the largest single category of psalms are the psalms of lament. Praise in the Old Testament was not just about being happy and thankful but about acknowledging the reality of the one living God in the whole of life—including the tough times. So even in those psalms which are mostly in a troubled mode, there is a movement toward praise. Even the whole book of psalms moves from the predominant lament and petitionary psalms in the early sections to the almost complete dominance of praise in the final section" (C. Wright, *Mission of God*, 132).

- Songs of thanksgiving

- Hymns of praise

- Festival songs and liturgies

- Songs of trust and meditation[12]

In addition, we have David's psalm of *confession*, Ps 51 (after his sin with Bathsheba had been exposed):

> Have mercy on me, O God,
>     according to your steadfast love;
> according to your abundant mercy
>     blot out my transgressions.
> Wash me thoroughly from my iniquity,
>     and cleanse me from my sin!
> For I know my transgressions,
>     and my sin is ever before me.
> Against you, you only, have I sinned
>     and done what is evil in your sight,
> so that you may be justified in your words
>     and blameless in your judgment. (Ps 51:1–4)

And then there is David's great psalm of *forgiveness* (after that sin had been confessed and forgiven):

> Blessed is the one whose transgression is forgiven,
>     whose sin is covered. (Ps 32:1)

We can turn to these two psalms to give voice to our own personal prayers of confession and gratitude for forgiveness. And David's intensely personal psalm of trust and rest in the Lord, Ps 23, has of course been appropriated by countless believers over the centuries:

> The Lord is my shepherd; I shall not want. (Ps 23:1)

In addition to these personal and private expressions, many other psalms have found an important place in the corporate praise of the church, for example:

> Make a joyful noise to the Lord, all the earth!
>     Serve the Lord with gladness!
>     Come into his presence with singing!
> Know that the Lord, he is God!

---

12. Bernhard Anderson, *Out of the Depths*, 170–71.

> It is he who made us, and we are his;
> we are his people, and the sheep of his pasture.
> Enter his gates with thanksgiving,
> and his courts with praise!
> Give thanks to him; bless his name!
> For the LORD is good;
> his steadfast love endures forever,
> and his faithfulness to all generations. (Ps 100)

The great variety of moods and emotions expressed in the psalms makes it possible for believers to find a vehicle for their prayers in many, many different circumstances of life.[13]

## The Tone of the Psalms

C. S. Lewis makes a fascinating observation about the psalmists' outlook on life and faith:

> I want to stress what I think that we (or at least I) need more [than instruction about sacrifice]: the joy and delight in God which meet us in the Psalms. . . . These poets knew far less reason than we for loving God. They did not know that he offered them eternal joy; still less that he would die to win it for them. Yet they express a longing for him, for his mere presence, which comes only to the best Christians or to Christians in their best moments. They long to live all their days in the Temple so that they may constantly see "the fair beauty of the Lord" (Ps 27:4). Their longing to go up to Jerusalem and "appear before the presence of God" is like a physical thirst (42). From Jerusalem His presence flashes out "in perfect beauty" (50:2). Lacking that encounter with Him, their souls are parched like a waterless countryside (63:1). They crave to be "satisfied with the pleasures" of His house (65:4). Only there can they be at ease, like a bird in the nest (84:1–3). One day of those "pleasures" is better than a lifetime spent elsewhere (84:11–12).
>
> I have rather—though the expression may seem harsh to some—called this the "appetite for God" than the "love of God."[14]

---

13. Often in teaching this material, I would ask each class member to share what is his or her favorite psalm and why. It was always a rich time of sharing, as students shared about how a particular psalm had lifted them up at an important juncture in their lives; and it was remarkable how practically every student would have a *different* favorite psalm!

14. C. S. Lewis, *Reflections on the Psalms*, 50–51. I have heard a pastor add that

## God in the Psalms

There are three aspects of God primarily portrayed in the psalms:

- His powerful protection[15]
- His gentle care[16]
- His loyal love (*ḥesed*)[17]

## The Poetry of the Psalms

A defining characteristic of Hebrew poetry is its use of a kind of "rhyme" quite unlike what we are used to. Instead of rhyming the sounds at the end of lines, this poetry uses what we might call "concept rhyming": it uses content parallelism to compare and contrast lines of the text. Three main types of parallelism have been classified in the book of Psalms; they are (with examples):

1. *Synonymous parallelism*: The second line restates the content of the first line in a slightly different way.

   > Therefore the wicked will not stand in the judgment,
   > nor sinners in the congregation of the righteous. (Ps 1:5)

2. *Antithetical parallelism*: The second line draws a contrast with the first line.

   > For the LORD knows the way of the righteous,
   > but the way of the wicked will perish. (Ps 1:6)

3. *Synthetic parallelism*: The second line develops further the thought of the first line.

   > As a father shows compassion to his children,
   > so the LORD shows compassion to those who fear him.
   > (Ps 103:13)

---

these amazing expressions of trust and rest in the Lord came long before the invention of anesthetics!

15. K. Bailey, *Good Shepherd*, 35–36.

16. K. Bailey, *Good Shepherd*, 36–37.

17. See the treatment of this theme on pp. 123–25.

A tremendous implication of this sort of poetry is that the parallelisms *can be translated effectively into any language*, in a way that would be impossible with sound rhyming. Thus God in his sovereignty made possible the beauty of this book to be made available to all the nations and cultures of the world!

## The Balanced Perspective of the Psalms

One of the most precious New Testament truths, one that the writer of Hebrews develops at some length, is the fact that in Jesus Christ a holy, transcendent God has come close. Theologians speak of his *immanence*, or nearness, as contrasted with his *transcendence*. (Of course, both are perfectly true of God without contradiction.) There are already hints of this presence and nearness in the Old Testament and, as we have just seen, in Psalms in particular.

When Martin Luther translated the Bible into German for the first time, he made a profound theological point along these lines, simply by his choice of pronouns (including in the book of Psalms). The German language has two different pronouns for the second person singular ("you" in English): an informal/familiar one (*Du*) and a formal/polite one (*Sie*). The polite form was used in addressing everyone but one's own family members and closest friends. Yet Luther used the familiar form in his translation when God was being addressed! There is a world of theology embedded in that single grammatical decision. (Even the "Thees" and "Thous" of the King James Version, while some find them a little stilted and stuffy today, were actually the *familiar* second person pronouns in the English of its day.)

We live in a day when in many churches, not to mention in society as a whole, people have sought to throw off what they consider to be outmoded and stifling formality and have opted for more relaxed, informal forms, practices, dress, etc. The worship and music likewise reflect a more relational age, and the immanence of God is valued and invoked.

In many ways this is a healthy departure from a lifeless traditionalism where God is admired from afar but kept at a distance. Yet a more informal approach to worship should not degrade into a casual one. The psalms give us a balance by showing us the exalted Lord of glory—

O Lord, our Lord,
　　how majestic is your name in all the earth! (Ps 8:1)

The Lord reigns; he is robed in majesty. (Ps 93:1)

—but also giving glimpses of a deeply personal God:

The Lord is *my* shepherd. (Ps 23:1)

O God, you are *my* God. (Ps 63:1)

Let us not forget in our worship that our God who has come close is still the transcendent Lord of glory. He is close, but he is also glorified and holy. He is our friend, but he is also our Lord. We must come with confidence and joy, yet with reverence and awe. Let us boldly "draw near to the throne of grace" (Heb 4:16), but bow our knee to him who sits upon it.

How simply and powerfully the psalmist in 2:11 expresses the delicate balance between God's transcendence and immanence as we come to him in worship:

Rejoice . . . with trembling.[18]

---

Hallelu-jah!

---

18. See Ron Man, "Rejoice with Trembling."

# Part 5

## Worship in the New Testament

# 18

## SIMILARITIES AND DIFFERENCES BETWEEN OLD AND NEW TESTAMENT WORSHIP

T his is an interesting topic to reflect on. There are some profound continuities between the worship of the two Testaments, but some crucial differences.

Please give this some thought. Some possible answers are given in the footnote.[1]

Then, having considered both the many continuities *and* discontinuities between worship in the Old Testament and worship in the New,

*Similarities*
1. Same God (Creator)
2. Centrality of the glory of God
3. Worship as ↑ response to God's ↓ revelation
4. Importance of the Scriptures
5. God's gracious provision of redemption
6. Need for a mediator
7. Sacrifice, priesthood
8. Singing
9. Prayer
10. Giving

*Differences*
1. Many sacrifices/once-for-all sacrifice of Christ
2. Many priests/one High Priest, Mediator; priesthood of all believers
3. Animal sacrifices/spiritual, living sacrifices
4. Worship centrally located (tabernacle/temple)/worship no longer centralized
5. Indwelling Holy Spirit (new covenant)

it might be of interest to listen to a chapel message given by Dr. Mark Bailey, the former president of Dallas Theological Seminary. In "Dispensational Expressions of Worship" he goes even further to detail biblically how the requirements and nature of worship have changed during different periods of biblical history.

Even those who do not hold to the dispensational system of biblical interpretation will find in this message many keen observations about how God's standards and expectations for worship have changed during the various epochs of the history of salvation.[2]

Here is a summary of Dr. Bailey's main points in chart form:

|  | Time | Place | Person | Sacrifice |
|---|---|---|---|---|
| Pre-Law | Anytime | Anywhere | Anyone | Different types |
| Law | Prescribed (daily; feast) | Only at tabernacle or temple | Only the priests | Prescribed |
| Now (John 4) | Anytime | Anywhere; heavenly tabernacle | Through Christ/we are all priests | Spiritual sacrifices, mediated through Christ (selves, praise, works, giving) |
| Millennium | One thousand years | Restored temple | Christ as Priest/King in Jerusalem (Zech 6) | Memorial sacrifices, feasts (Ezek 45) |
| Heaven | Forever | God/Christ *is* the temple | Angels and believers (Rev 4–6) | Praise |

> From more *form* to more *freedom*.

2. M. Bailey, "Dispensational Expressions of Worship." A video of this message can be found on YouTube under the same title.

# 19

## IMPORTANT THEMES IN NEW TESTAMENT WORSHIP

### *Theme*: Inward Worship

J ohn Piper zeroes in on this theme:

> What we find in the New Testament is an utterly stunning degree of indifference to worship as an outward form and an utterly radical intensification of worship as an inward experience of the heart.[1]

When one thinks of worship in the Old Testament, the mind inevitably turns to the Mosaic sacrificial system with its complex of rituals, regulations, and structures. So much of the worship commanded under the old covenant was involved with the careful following of the most detailed instructions and guidelines; chapter after chapter of such prescriptions are found in Exodus and Leviticus.

It is that kind of outward setting of worship that the Samaritan woman at the well in John 4 (as we saw in ch. 10) asks Jesus about: specifically, she asks him to speak to the competing claims of legitimacy of the Jewish system of worship (in Jerusalem) and that of the Samaritans (on Mount Gerizim). Jesus does not avoid the fact that the Jews had been truer to the biblical revelation ("we worship what we know, for salvation

---

1. Piper, "Pursuit of God."

is from the Jews" [v. 22]), but goes on to pronounce that under the new regime he is inaugurating, geographical locale will no longer be the issue at all. It will no longer be a matter of *where* or *when* you worship, but *how* you worship. Worship must originate in the "spirit," in the internal, immaterial part of one's life; and must be in "truth," that is, according to God's revelation.

As we will see here in part 5, the New Testament writers align themselves with Jesus's pronouncement about the priority of worship "in spirit," of worship from the *heart*.

However, we saw in the Old Testament that there too God placed priority on the worship of the heart. If this was the case in the Old Testament, then what indeed is distinctive about the New Testament? Quite simply, that under the old covenant, heart worship was demonstrated by one's obedient adherence to the stipulations of the tabernacle/temple system; and, in the New Testament, that system having been done away with through the work of Christ, the outworking of heart worship is to take place in all of life (see below) rather than through a detailed prescription for public worship.

And so New Testament worship is characterized by "a radical, inward authenticity of worship and an all-encompassing pervasiveness of worship in all of life."[2] True worship, as always, must begin in the heart; but there is an expansion of its outward expression into all of life, so that there is no distinction between the sacred and secular. And that brings us to the next theme.

## *Theme:* Whole-Life Worship

As we saw in ch. 10, the apostle Paul seems to build upon Jesus's declaration in John 4 that worship will be "*neither* in this mountain *nor* in Jerusalem . . . *but* in spirit and truth" (John 4:21, 23). Paul makes a logical application of Jesus's sense when he states in Rom 12:1 (a pivotal passage on worship in the New Testament) that our appropriate response ("therefore") to God for all that he has done for us and given to us in Christ ("by the mercies of God," as detailed in the first eleven chapters of the epistle) is "to present your bodies as a living sacrifice, holy and acceptable to God, which is your spiritual worship." In other words, since worship is not to be limited by time or place (as Jesus declares), it should be all-pervasive.

2. Piper, *Let the Nations Be Glad*, 239–40.

Paul's use of the word *bodies* obviously does not speak merely to external practices of worship (any more than presenting our bodies as a "sacrifice" refers to a blood offering), for he has plenty to say about the inner nature of worship elsewhere in his writings; rather, it speaks of *the whole self.*

This is what is asked of us by God, who has given us everything: *our whole lives,* in grateful response to his magnificent grace. As Paul expressed elsewhere: "You are not your own, for you were bought with a price. So glorify God in your body" (1 Cor 6:19–20). This is of course perfectly consistent with Jesus's call to true discipleship:

> The kingdom of heaven is like treasure hidden in a field, which a man found and covered up. Then in his joy he goes and sells all that he has and buys that field. Again, the kingdom of heaven is like a merchant in search of fine pearls, who, on finding one pearl of great value, went and sold all that he had and bought it. (Matt 13:44–46)
>
> For what does it profit a man if he gains the whole world and loses or forfeits himself? (Luke 9:25)
>
> Jesus said to him, "No one who puts his hand to the plow and looks back is fit for the kingdom of God." (Luke 9:62)

"The command is a radical connection of love and trust and obedience to Jesus Christ in all of life."[3] For the believer, there is no secular place or pursuit, no separation of life into religious and nonreligious areas. D. A. Carson explains in more detail the difference in emphases between the old and new covenants that we just considered above:

> It has always been necessary to love God wholly; it has always been necessary to recognize the sheer holiness and transcendent power and glory and goodness of God and to adore him for what he is. . . .
>
> The way wholly loving God works out under the old covenant is in heartfelt obedience to the terms of that covenant and that includes the primary place given to the cultus [sacrificial system]; and the implications of this outworking include distinctions between the holy and the common, between holy space and common space, between holy time and common time, between holy food and common food.
>
> The way wholly loving God works out under the new covenant is in heartfelt obedience to the terms of that covenant and here the language of the cultus has been transmuted to all of life,

3. Piper, "Our High Priest."

with the implication, not so much of a desacralization of space and time and food, as with a sacralization of all space and all time and all food.[4]

In other words, as we saw in ch. 11, it is not that there are no longer any holy times or places, but rather that *every* time and *every* place is holy to the Lord. ("Whether you eat or drink, or whatever you do, do all to the glory of God" [1 Cor 10:31].)

The implications of this truth are profound for individual believers. It means that each one of us is responsible for a daily walk of worship that allows the presence and influence of God to pervade all our activities and projects and thoughts and dealings with others. We are "to do all to the glory of God" by living for him in all we do, by his power. Worship is not to be confined to a morning quiet time or to a Sunday morning gathering.

The implications are no less profound for pastors and worship leaders. For it means that such leaders are *not* simply purveyors of professional services in the area of worship; suppliers of worship for the people under their charge; sole distributors providing an otherwise unobtainable product. Rather, they are simply to be *facilitators* of a corporate event that *builds upon*, rather than replaces, the individual worship walks of the people. It is simply not fair to place on the shoulders of church leaders the responsibility for "providing worship" for the people of God (still less for "leading them into the presence of God").

This does not at all downplay the importance of corporate worship, but it does put a lot of the onus for its "success" on the shoulders of each individual participant. A more relevant question than "What did I get out of the service today?" might well be "What did I *bring* to the service today?" It is when believers come, not with an empty tank that they hope will be filled, but with hearts brimming with gratitude and devotion from a week of walking with and worshiping God, that our corporate worship can become, by the Spirit's enablement, something truly powerful and more than the sum of its (human and structural) parts.

### *Theme*: Freedom of Form

It is an amazing fact that the New Testament is virtually silent on the matter of form for the church's worship. D. A. Carson writes: "There is no

---

4. "Worship under the Word," in Carson, *Worship by the Book*, 40.

single passage in the New Testament that establishes a paradigm for corporate worship."[5] And Peter Leithart observes: "Though certain isolated 'elements' of worship can be teased out of the New Testament, little is said about the order or significance of these elements. . . . Certainly no book of the New Testament offers anything like a theology of worship, or even much practical guidance."[6]

This is surprising, to say the least. The apostle Paul is writing letters to newly established churches, and we might reasonably expect that as Paul writes he would lay out specific and detailed instructions for these churches' worship (and hence for ours also). Yet that is exactly what he does not do. In fact, Gordon Fee observes that "what comes to us does so for the most part in the form of correction [for instance in 1 Cor 14]. We simply do not know enough to make far-reaching, all-inclusive statements about the nature of worship in the Pauline churches."[7]

Similarly, John Piper makes this astonishing (but true) observation:

> In the New Testament, all the focus is on the reality of the glory of Christ, not the shadow and copy of religious objects and forms. It is stunning how indifferent the New Testament is to such things: there is no authorization in the New Testament for worship buildings, or worship dress, or worship times, or worship music, or worship liturgy or worship size or thirty-five-minute sermons, or Advent poems or choirs or instruments or candles. . . . Almost every worship tradition we have is culturally shaped rather than Biblically commanded.[8]

It must be emphasized, though, that Piper's last statement above does not mean that our worship traditions are wrong; after all, we do need to make many decisions about what worship in our churches is going to look like (in Piper's terms, about our buildings, our worship times, our worship music, the length of the service and the sermon, etc.). But the clear implication is that the New Testament's silence on so many of the details, the absence of specific commands, means that we are allowed *considerable freedom* in the structuring of worship in our churches. Not *total* freedom: there *are* biblical principles (such as we are seeing in this book) to guide us, but also a considerable amount of flexibility. That

5. "Worship under the Word," in Carson, *Worship by the Book*, 55.

6. Leithart, *From Silence to Song*, 106.

7. Fee, *God's Empowering Presence*, 884n13.

8. Piper, "Our High Priest."

explains the huge diversity of different worship forms and practices as you look around the world and down through the centuries.

We will examine this subject in more detail in chs. 36–38, as we consider its implications for the intersection of worship and culture and for the global church.

## *Theme:* Access

As we saw in ch. 10, the old-covenant system of worship, despite its gracious provisions for relating to the covenant-keeping God of Israel (through a temporary covering of sin [Rom 3:24–25] in anticipation of Christ's atoning work), nevertheless was a system that demonstrated strongly the distance that sin had put between God and even his own chosen people. Access to the presence of God (represented in the architecture of the tabernacle/temple) was severely proscribed. The common people were allowed to enter only the courtyard of the tabernacle/temple; one had to be a priest to enter the holy place; while entry into the holy of holies was reserved for the high priest alone, who himself could enter only once a year, on the Day of Atonement (see Lev 16).

The book of Hebrews clearly demonstrates how all the barriers of this old-covenant system were destroyed, and the way into the presence of God made fully available, by the redeeming death of Christ on the cross. That opening of the way into God's presence was powerfully dramatized by the tearing from top to bottom of the temple veil in the Jerusalem temple (the one barring access into the holy of holies, i.e., into the presence of God) at the precise moment of Christ's death (Matt 27:51; Mark 15:38; Luke 23:45). The way into the presence of God was now open by the removal of the barrier of sin by the perfect sacrifice of Christ.

In Heb 10:19 the author climactically turns to make application of the tremendous truths he has been expounding concerning the superiority of Christ, his priesthood, his sacrifice, and the new covenant instituted by his atoning death. He declares:

> *Therefore*, brethren, since we have confidence to enter the holy places by the blood of Jesus, by the new and living way that he opened for us through the curtain, that is, through his flesh, and since we have a great priest over the house of God, *let us draw near* with a true heart in full assurance of faith, with our hearts sprinkled clean from an evil conscience and our bodies washed with pure water. (Heb 10:19–22)

"Christ fulfills and replaces the temple and the whole method of approach to God associated with it."[9] Unlike under the old covenant, that approach is clear and open and direct because of Christ's ministry; and so we are urged to come close "in full assurance of faith" and in the "confidence" we can have because of what Christ has accomplished for us. The writer is saying: You have this wonderful access through Christ (as he has been explaining for ten chapters)—now take full advantage of it! Enjoy to the fullest the advantages that are yours because of the superior benefits of the new covenant.

Christ died, and reigns, to make all this possible:

> For Christ also suffered once for sins, the righteous for the unrighteous, that he might *bring us to God*. (1 Pet 3:18)

> And he came and preached peace to you who were far off and peace to those who were near. For through him we both have *access* in one Spirit to the Father. (Eph 2:17–18)

> Consequently, he is able to save to the uttermost those who *draw near to God* through him, since he always lives to make intercession for them. (Heb 7:25)

> Let us then with confidence *draw near* to the throne of grace, that we may receive mercy and find grace to help in time of need. (Heb 4:16)

Every new-covenant believer has direct access into God's presence through Christ. This is one of the greatest distinctives—and privileges— of New Testament worship! It is the fullest fulfillment of Ps 16:11:

> In your presence there is fullness of joy;
>     at your right hand are pleasures forevermore.

We have access into that very presence through the work of Christ.

> One of the great distinctives and privileges of New Testament worship is the direct *access* every believer has into the presence of God through Christ.

9. D. Peterson, *Engaging with God*, 137.

# 20

## IMPORTANT VOCABULARY IN NEW TESTAMENT WORSHIP

A s we did with the Old Testament, we want to focus on the two most common words for worship in the New Testament.

### *proskuneō*

The Greek word is built out of *pros-* (towards) and *kuneō* (to kiss). The original sense of the word expressed the idea of kissing the ground, in the sense of bowing down to honor, pay homage, or show respect to a person of power or authority.[1] As with the Old Testament term *ḥistahavah* (which is usually translated with *proskuneō* in the Septuagint, the Greek

1. Chris Jack cautions against the error made by some writers and songwriters today of taking this "kiss" part of *proskuneō*'s etymology and therefore emotionalizing it. "The word simply does not signify 'intimacy' or 'mutual affection.' Insofar as these are legitimate facets of our worship, they are not to be derived from this term. . . . *Proskuneō*, important for its frequency of use, emphasizes that worship has to do with honoring God, submitting to him. . . . This, far more than intimacy, is a dominant aspect of biblical worship, yet it is not a major theme, if present at all, in much contemporary talk about worship, or in its expression" (*"Proskuneō* Myth," 95–96). This error is an example of what D. A. Carson calls the "root fallacy": trying to elucidate the meaning of a word by its etymological parts, rather than by its usage (*Exegetical Fallacies*, 28–33). A common example of such a fallacy would be to try to illuminate the meaning of "butterfly" by considering the meanings of "butter" and "fly" (Jack, *"Proskuneō* Myth," 89)! "Pineapple" would be another example.

translation of the Old Testament), *proskuneō* originally carried this sense of a physical act, but then came to mean more generally *worship*, whether or not a physical expression is involved. For instance, *proskuneō* is the word used (nine times!) in John 4 with the general meaning of worship.[2] As the disciples and others come to recognize Jesus as God, they respond in worship:

> And when they got into the boat, the wind ceased. And those in the boat *worshiped* him, saying, "Truly you are the Son of God." (Matt 14:32–33)

> While he blessed them, he parted from them and was carried up into heaven. And they *worshiped* him and returned to Jerusalem with great joy, and were continually in the temple blessing God. (Luke 24:51–53)

And the book of Revelation has great scenes of worship (*proskuneō*) of God and of the Lamb:

> The twenty-four elders fall down before him who is seated on the throne and *worship* him who lives forever and ever. (Rev 4:10)

> And the four living creatures said, "Amen!" and the elders fell down and *worshiped*. (Rev 5:14)

> And all the angels were standing around the throne and around the elders and the four living creatures, and they fell on their faces before the throne and *worshiped* God. (Rev 7:11)

> And the twenty-four elders and the four living creatures fell down and *worshiped* God who was seated on the throne, saying, "Amen. Hallelujah!" (Rev 19:4)

But it is important to recognize an important principle of translation: that is, that there is not necessarily a strict one-to-one correspondence between a word in one language and a single word in another language. That is certainly the case when the Greek Testament is translated into English: scholars talk about a "field of meaning" that a particular Greek word often carries, with different shades of meaning when used in different contexts, hence allowing for (if not necessitating) different translations of that word in different passages.

---

2. It is also used in Revelation, not only of true worship of God and of the Lamb (Rev 4:10; 5:14; 7:11; etc.), but also of *false* worship (of demons, of the dragon, of the beast and his image; see Rev 9:20; 13:4; 14:11; 16:2; etc.).

Along these lines, the word *proskuneō* does not always convey the idea of "worship" when used in the New Testament. It can continue to carry the sense of bowing down in submission, respect, or entreaty. Such seems to be the case in a number of instances in the Gospels, where someone comes to Jesus to make an appeal, but without *yet* recognizing Jesus's deity (and hence that person cannot be said to be "worshiping" him). For instance:

> While he was saying these things to them, behold, a ruler came in and *knelt before* him [*proskuneō*; KJV has "and *worshiped* him"], saying, "My daughter has just died, but come and lay your hand on her, and she will live." (Matt 9:18)

> He answered, "I was sent only to the lost sheep of the house of Israel." But she came and *knelt before* him [*proskuneō*; KJV has "and *worshiped* him"], saying, "Lord, help me." (Matt 15:24–25)[3]

Similarly, there is a common assumption that *proskuneō* should be translated "worship" when the magi visit the baby Jesus in Matt 2:

> Where is he who has been born king of the Jews? For we saw his star when it rose and have come to *worship* him. (Matt 2:2)

> And [Herod] sent them to Bethlehem, saying, "Go and search diligently for the child, and when you have found him, bring me word, that I too may come and *worship* him." (Matt 2:8)

> And going into the house, they saw the child with Mary his mother, and they fell down and *worshiped* him. Then, opening their treasures, they offered him gifts, gold and frankincense and myrrh. (Matt 2:11)

There is no indication that the magi (or Herod) recognized Jesus's deity; rather, it is clearly stated that they were coming *to pay homage to a king.* While Matthew certainly has the perspective of Christ's deity, it seems to be reading back to consider worship being in view in this context. "Pay homage" is in fact the rendering in J. B. Phillips's New Testament in Modern English, the New Revised Standard Version, and the New English Bible.

D. A. Carson concurs:

> "Worship" need not imply that the Magi recognized Jesus' divinity; it may simply mean "do homage." Their own statement

---

3. Even "Lord" in Greek is a form of polite address like "sir," and not necessarily a recognition of deity.

suggests homage paid royalty rather than the worship of Deity. But Matthew, having already told of the virginal conception, doubtless expected his readers to discern something more— viz., that the Magi worshiped better than they knew.[4]

The magi may have consciously only intended "homage"; but Matthew recognizes and perhaps implies that the One who received the homage is indeed deserving of "worship."

David Peterson agrees also:

> Although some English versions view this action as "worship" (*King James Version, Revised Standard Version, New International-al Version*), the statement of the Magi in verse 2 suggests that the meaning is homage paid to royalty rather than the worship of deity (so Phillips, *New English Bible*; cf. 1 Sam 25:23; 2 Kgs 4:36). Of course, Matthew's opening chapter has pointed to Jesus' divine sonship and the evangelist no doubt intended his readers to discern that this homage had a greater significance than the visitors from the East could have imagined. Their attitude to Jesus anticipated the submission of the nations to the risen Lord, which is the essence of discipleship according to Matthew 28:16–20. The immediate context in Matthew 2, however, does not demand that worship of Jesus as Son of God is yet in view.[5]

Another perhaps significant effect of reserving the translation of "worship" for a clearer contextual warrant would be that the *very first* instance of *proskuneō* in the New Testament with the clear meaning of *worship* would be seen to be in Matt 4:9–10—Jesus's monumental commitment to "worship the Lord . . . and serve him *only*" at the outset of his ministry—as the *Second* Adam, in contradistinction to the refusal of the *first* Adam to "glorify God as God" and "serve . . . the Creator" (Rom 1:21, 22–25).[6]

4. Carson, *Commentary on Matthew*, 86; see also 89. R. T. France also is of this opinion: "The nature of the 'homage' of the magi (the verb recurs vv. 8 and 11) is not clearly spelled out, except for the offering of expensive gifts, such as might befit a royal birth. Their 'prostration' (v. 11; literally, 'falling') was a familiar act of homage in Eastern society, a recognition of social superiority. Neither term requires the attribution of divinity to the one so honored, and Matthew's narrative does not indicate that the magi had any such notion (they came looking for a 'king,' not a 'god'), though he might expect his Christian readers with hindsight to read more in the 'worship' of the magi" (*Gospel of Matthew*, 69).

5. D. Peterson, *Engaging with God*, 84–85.

6. John Piper has made an interesting observation about the distribution of *proskuneō* throughout the New Testament: namely, that it occurs twenty-six times in the Gospels, twenty-one times in Revelation, only four times in Acts (none of them referring to *Christian*

## *latreuō*

As we saw in ch. 13, the second most common Old Testament term for worship in the Old Testament, ' *abad*, also has a New Testament counterpart: *latreuō*. Both terms carry the idea of "serve"; but as we saw with ' *abad*, it is the idea of serving God in the sense of the allegiance of one's *heart*: the *inward* aspect that expresses itself in outward service. And so *latreuō* is sometimes translated "worship" and sometimes "serve." Some examples:

> For God is my witness, whom I *serve with my spirit* [inward first!] in the gospel of his Son. (Rom 1:9)

> I appeal to you therefore, brethren, by the mercies of God, to present your bodies as a living sacrifice, holy and acceptable to God, which is your spiritual *worship*. (Rom 12:1)

> For we are the circumcision, who *worship* by the Spirit of God and glory in Christ Jesus and put no confidence in the flesh. (Phil 3:3)

> I thank God whom I *serve*, as did my ancestors, with a clear conscience, as I remember you constantly in my prayers night and day. (2 Tim 1:3)

> How much more will the blood of Christ, who through the eternal Spirit offered himself without blemish to God, purify our conscience from dead works to *serve* the living God. (Heb 9:14)

> Therefore let us be grateful for receiving a kingdom that cannot be shaken, and thus let us offer to God acceptable *worship*, with reverence and awe. (Heb 12:28)

---

worship), twice in Hebrews (in Old Testament quotations), and only once in the writings of Paul (1 Cor 14:25)! Piper's theory about this puzzling phenomenon: "The word did not make clear enough the inward, spiritual nature of true worship. It carried significant connotations of place and form. The word was associated with bodily bowing down and with the actual presence of a visible manifestation to bow down before. So it is prevalent in the Gospels and Revelation where Jesus is physically present to the worshippers, but in the epistles Jesus is not present in visible glory to fall before. Therefore, the whole tendency of the early church was to deal with worship as primarily inward and spiritual rather than outward and bodily; primarily pervasive rather than localized" ("Pursuit of God"). Tom Wells concurs: *Proskuneō* "is uncommon in all of the letters in the New Testament. In part this is due to worship words in Greek often referring to posture, to bowing and kneeling, words that interest narrators such as Matthew and John more than others. (The New Testament is not necessarily indifferent to posture in worship, but its emphasis on inward attitudes naturally suggests different vocabulary)" ("Epistle to the Hebrews," 115–16).

David Peterson summarizes the New Testament's use of *proskuneō* and *latreuō* thus: "The language of worship puts the focus on *submission to God's rule* and *grateful service* in every sphere of life."[7]

## New Testament Use of Old Testament Sacrificial Language

This is an interesting phenomenon: the writer of Hebrews makes it very clear that the old system, the old covenant, has been done away with, being replaced by the much superior new covenant. One might think that, because of that superseding, the writers of the New Testament would shy away from using any language that would be reminiscent of the now defunct system.

And yet that is not the case at all. We see a lot of use of terminology related to the sacrificial system of the Old Testament. However (and this is key), the terms are used now *in a more internalized, spiritualized sense.*[8] This shows that the shadow system of the old covenant has been truly *fulfilled*, not just abrogated.

Some examples of this kind of usage:

I appeal to you therefore, brethren, by the mercies of God, to present your bodies as *a living sacrifice*, holy and acceptable to God, which is your spiritual worship. (Rom 12:1)

Do you not know that you are God's *temple* and that God's Spirit dwells in you? (1 Cor 3:16)

What agreement has the temple of God with idols? For we are the *temple* of the living God. (2 Cor 6:16)

So then you are no longer strangers and aliens, but you are fellow citizens with the saints and members of the household of God, built on the foundation of the apostles and prophets, Christ Jesus himself being the cornerstone, in whom the whole structure, being joined together, grows into a holy *temple* in the Lord. In him you also are being built together into a dwelling place for God by the Spirit. (Eph 2:19–22)

Even if I am to be poured out as *a drink offering* upon *the sacrificial offering* of your faith, I am glad and rejoice with you all. (Phil 2:17)

7. D. Peterson, "Worship and Evangelism." Note that the two terms are used in synonymous parallelism in Matt 4:10.

8. D. Peterson calls this phenomenon "transformed worship terminology" and "sacral terminology used metaphorically" ("Worship and Evangelism").

I have received full payment, and more. I am well supplied, having received from Epaphroditus the gifts you sent, *a fragrant offering, a sacrifice* acceptable and pleasing to God. (Phil 4:18)

For I am already being poured out as *a drink offering*, and the time of my departure has come. (2 Tim 4:6)

You yourselves like living stones are being built up as a spiritual house, to be *a holy priesthood*, to *offer spiritual sacrifices* acceptable to God through Jesus Christ. (1 Pet 2:5)

But you are *a chosen race, a royal priesthood, a holy nation*, a people for his own possession, that you may proclaim the excellencies of him who called you out of darkness into his marvelous light. (1 Pet 2:9)

Through him then let us continually offer up *a sacrifice of praise* to God, that is, the fruit of lips that acknowledge his name. Do not neglect to do good and to share what you have, for such *sacrifices* are pleasing to God. (Heb 13:15)

So we see many examples of the vocabulary connected with the Old Testament sacrificial system being used in the New Testament, but recast and infused with a deeper, more spiritual meaning.[9]

---

"The language of worship [in the New Testament] puts the focus on *submission to God's rule* and *grateful service* in every sphere of life." (David Peterson)

---

9. The concept of *temple* is redefined as denoting, variously, Christ (John 2:19–22), individual believers (1 Cor 6:19), and the body of Christ, the church (Eph 2:19–22). The church as the new temple of God is further described by Peter as "a spiritual house" where believers as "a holy priesthood," "a chosen race," "a royal priesthood," and a "holy nation" are "to offer spiritual sacrifices" (1 Pet 2:5, 9). The tabernacle of the Old Testament is described by the writer of Hebrews as a mere "copy and shadow" of "the greater and more perfect tent (not made with hands, that is, not of this creation)" in heaven (Heb 8:5; 9:11); and John tells us that the glory of God among his people now resides, not in the tabernacle of the temple, but in the person of Jesus Christ, who "became flesh and dwelt [lit., *tabernacled*] among us" (John 1:14).

# 21

## SIGNIFICANT NEW TESTAMENT WORSHIP PASSAGES

### Gospels and Acts

#### Guiding Principles of Worship in the Gospel of Matthew

##### Exclusive Worship

Again, the devil took him to a very high mountain and showed him all the kingdoms of the world and their glory; and he said to him, "All these things I will give you, if you fall down and worship me." Then Jesus said to him, "Go, Satan! For it is written, 'You shall worship the Lord your God, and serve Him only.'" (Matt 4:10)

(Please see also the fuller treatment of this passage on pp. 78–80.)

##### Sincere Worship

"And when you are praying, do not use meaningless repetition as the Gentiles do, for they suppose that they will be heard for their many words." (Matt 6:7)

## Priority Worship

But seek first his kingdom and his righteousness, and all these things will be added to you. (Matt 6:33)

He who loves father or mother more than me is not worthy of me; and he who loves son or daughter more than me is not worthy of me. (Matt 10:37)

## Declaratory Worship

Our Father who is in heaven, hallowed be your name.... Yours is the kingdom and the power and the glory forever. (Matt 6:9, 13)

And those who were in the boat worshiped Him, saying, "You are certainly God's Son!" (Matt 14:33)

Simon Peter answered, "You are the Christ, the Son of the living God." (Matt 16:16)

## Self-Sacrificial Worship

For whoever wishes to save his life will lose it; but whoever loses his life for my sake will find it. (Matt 16:25)

## Humble Worship

Whoever then humbles himself as this child, he is the greatest in the kingdom of heaven. (Matt 18:4)

Whoever exalts himself shall be humbled; and whoever humbles himself shall be exalted. (Matt 23:12)

## Heart Worship

"This people honors me with their lips, but their heart is far away from me. But in vain do they worship me, teaching as doctrines the precepts of men." (Matt 15:8–9)

## Submissive Worship

And he went a little beyond them, and fell on his face and prayed, saying, "My Father, if it is possible, let this cup pass from me; yet not as I will, but as you will." (Matt 26:39)

## Responsive Worship ↓ ↑

But when the crowds saw this, they were awestruck, and glorified God, who had given such authority to men. (Matt 9:8)

And those who were in the boat worshiped him, saying, "You are certainly God's Son!" (Matt 14:33)

## The Rest of Worship (Matt 11:28–30)

As we saw at the end of ch. 16, during the intertestamental period the Jewish leaders added to the Mosaic law a large number of additional rules and regulations—legalistic provisions about Sabbath observances and many other aspects of religious and daily life. Jesus's scathing denunciation of the scribes and Pharisees in Matt 23 included these words:

The scribes and the Pharisees . . . tie up heavy burdens, hard to bear, and lay them on people's shoulders. (Matt 23:2, 4)

And because Christ came and finished the great work, everything necessary for our salvation ("I glorified You on earth, having accomplished the work that you gave me to do" [John 17:4]; "It is finished" [John 19:30]), he is able to extend us grace and give us rest and release from our spiritual burdens and strivings:

Come to me, all who labor and are heavy laden, and I will give you rest. Take my yoke upon you, and learn from me, for I am gentle and lowly in heart, and you will find rest for your souls. For my yoke is easy, and my burden is light. (Matt 11:28–30)

Thus Gregory Nelson's statement about God's resting after creation applies equally well to our present state of rest in the grace of our Lord Jesus Christ: "God does the work; human beings enjoy the results."[1]

The writer of Hebrews likewise speaks of our settled rest in Christ:

So then, there remains a Sabbath *rest* for the people of God, for whoever has entered God's *rest* has also *rested* from his works as God did from his. (Heb 4:9–10)

This is God's grace for our worship. We do not need to worry about whether our worship is "good enough"; when we come in and through and, indeed, with Christ, the Father is always pleased with our worship,

---

1. G. Nelson, *Touch of Heaven*, 30.

because he is always pleased with his Son. (Much more on this later in ch. 26.) Hence *worship is not a work*, not something by which we strive to make ourselves somehow acceptable to the Father.

Worship is always and only a ↑ *response*, a grateful response because of God's merciful ↓ self-*revelation* and gracious initiative in providing for us, and bringing us to, eternal salvation. The great work has been done! We *rest* and bask in the light of God's (unmerited) favor, and offer God our thanksgiving and praise with wonder, joy, freedom, and assurance.

## Seeing Things God's Way (Mark 12:28–34)

The scribes and Pharisees were the object of Jesus's most scathing denunciations (see the whole of Matt 23, and here in Mark 12:38). Jesus condemns them especially for the *externality* of their religion: practicing their rites for public view (Matt 6:1–6; 23:27–28). As we saw in ch. 17, God always detests mere externality of practice without internal reality and is always far more interested in the worship of the heart. (See 1 Sam 15:22; 16:7; Ps 15:1–2; 40:6; 50:13–14; 51:16–17; 69:30–31; 103:1; 141:2; Isa 29:13; Hos 6:6; Joel 2:13a; Mic 6:6–8.)

We saw in ch. 13 how, through the prophets, God criticized the people for the very sacrifices he had himself commanded of them, because they were going through the motions without a true heart devotion to him. As C. S. Lewis pointed out, it is not "that he really needed the blood of bulls and goats";[2] he wanted the sacrifices to be an outward expression of an inward reality.

In this account we see a stark contrast to the usual challenging and critical approach of the scribes to Jesus.

> And one of the scribes came up and heard them disputing with one another, and seeing that he answered them well, asked him, "Which commandment is the most important of all?" (Mark 12:28)

Here we see a rarity in the Gospels: a scribe coming to Jesus with an honest question! Far more often, the scribes and the other Jewish leaders are trying to criticize, entrap, or trick Jesus (see 12:13), and turn the people away from him.

2. C. S. Lewis, "On Church Music," 123.

Jesus answered, "The most important is, 'Hear, O Israel: The Lord our God, the Lord is one. And you shall love the Lord your God with all your heart and with all your soul and with all your mind and with all your strength.' The second is this: 'You shall love your neighbor as yourself.' There is no other commandment greater than these."

And the scribe said to him, "You are right, Teacher." (Mark 12:29–32a)

In some ways, the scribe's reply is quite humorous: *of course* he's right, he's *Jesus!*

The scribe is not taken aback by Jesus's answer (as so often the Jewish leaders were by Jesus's responses), but rather fully endorses Jesus's point of view. And then the scribe goes on to add this profound commentary on the significance of the two Great Commandments that Jesus has just cited:

You have truly said that he is one, and there is no other besides him. And to love him with all the heart and with all the understanding and with all the strength, and to love one's neighbor as oneself, is *much more* than all whole burnt offerings and sacrifices. (Mark 12:32b–33)

Often in the Gospels we find the people "marveling" in wonder at the things Jesus does and the things he says: they are amazed at the power and wisdom of God working through him (see, for example, Matt 8:27; 9:33; Mark 12:17). But on a very few occasions we find Jesus *himself* marveling at the work of God in someone else's heart.[3] Here in Mark 12, Jesus commends the scribe's deep spiritual understanding:

And when Jesus saw that he answered wisely, he said to him, "You are not far from the kingdom of God." (Mark 12:34)

What a commendation indeed! Why is the scribe not far from the kingdom? Because the scribe is *looking at things the way God does;* he has a spiritual perspective in keeping with kingdom values. He sees *the spiritual priority of love for God and for neighbor over all outward expressions of worship.*

---

3. One example is found in Matt 8:8–10: "But the centurion replied, 'Lord, I am not worthy to have you come under my roof, but only say the word, and my servant will be healed.' . . . When Jesus heard this, he *marveled* and said to those who followed him, 'Truly, I tell you, with no one in Israel have I found such faith.'"

One could only wish Mark had told us what happened with the scribe, whether in fact he became a believer in and follower of Jesus. It seems likely, because of the spiritual trajectory he was already on, which Jesus himself identifies. This is surely a sign that the Holy Spirit was already at work in his heart, showing him this most important of spiritual realities.

## Lavish Worship (Mark 14:3–9)

**Clay Jar, by ChildPing[4]**

This beautiful account is framed by signs of the mounting opposition to Jesus during the last week of his earthly life, both from without—

> It was now two days before the Passover and the Feast of Unleavened Bread. And the chief priests and the scribes were seeking how to arrest him by stealth and kill him. (Mark 14:1)

—and even from within the band of disciples:

> Then Judas Iscariot, who was one of the twelve, went to the chief priests in order to betray him to them. And when they heard it, they were glad and promised to give him money. And he sought an opportunity to betray him. (Mark 14:10–11)

Against that backdrop of hostility and treachery, Mark recounts an incident of striking contrast, a beam of light that shines all the brighter for the growing darkness surrounding it. It is the account of a remarkable

---

4. See https://www.shutterstock.com/image-photo/old-big-clay-jar-isolated-on-262172912.

act of love and worship. As G. Campbell Morgan wrote, "There was He, in a dark and desolate land; and lo! out of the heart of a woman, a spring of fresh water sprung for the thirsty Christ! He valued it."[5]

## Action (Mark 14:3)

And while he was at Bethany in the house of Simon the leper, as he was reclining at table, a woman[6] came with an alabaster flask of ointment of pure nard, very costly, and she broke the flask and poured it over his head.

## Reaction (Mark 14:4–9)

### "Some"

Matthew 26:8 identifies these as the disciples, and John 12:4–5 even zeroes in on Judas as the spokesman:

There were some who said to themselves indignantly, "Why was the ointment wasted like that? For this ointment could have been sold for more than three hundred denarii and given to the poor." And they scolded her. (Mark 14:4–5)

Most of those in attendance responded negatively to what they had just observed. The disciples, as usual, totally missed the point. Seeing the event through the world's eyes, they complained of Mary's wasteful extravagance. Why not sell the perfume and spend the money on something *useful*, like helping the poor?

### Jesus

Jesus's response was quite different:

But Jesus said, "Leave her alone. Why do you trouble her? She has done a beautiful thing to me. For you always have the poor with you, and whenever you want, you can do good for them. But you will not always have me. She has done what she could; she has anointed my body beforehand for burial. And truly, I say

5. Morgan, *Gospel According to Mark*, 290.

6. This incident is found in all four Gospels. In Luke 7:37, the woman is termed "a sinner," while John 12:3 identifies her as Mary, the sister of Martha and Lazarus.

to you, wherever the gospel is proclaimed in the whole world, what she has done will be told in memory of her." (Mark 14:6–9)

"Leave her alone!" Far from seeing Mary's act as waste or inappropriate, he commends her and her instinctive act of selfless devotion. ↑ He calls it a "beautiful thing." Mary had a unique opportunity to serve the Lord and express her love for him—and she took full advantage of it. She didn't spend a week praying about it or seeking God's will. She did "what she could"—literally, Jesus is saying, "what she had, she did"—and he rejoiced in her spontaneous display of devotion.

We have ample testimony from the Gospels that Jesus was not one to take the needs of the poor lightly. But on this occasion, he sees a different priority, because "you will always have the poor with you . . . but you will not always have me." In fact, his reaction is a strong testimony to his deity and Messiah-ship; for basically he is saying: "I'm *worth* it; I *deserve* preferential treatment." That would be a remarkably arrogant attitude if Jesus were not in fact who he claimed to be.

Jesus adds that Mary's act has a far deeper significance than even she realized, as she "anointed my body for burial." God rewarded her faithfulness with a very special place in the unfolding story of redemption, and a continuing role as well: "Wherever the gospel is proclaimed in the whole world, what she has done will be told in memory of her." A. T. Robertson writes, "There are many mausoleums that crumble to decay. But this monument to Jesus fills the whole world still with its fragrance."[7] And in the words of an unknown author, "The Lord raises for all time a memorial to her who had done her best to honor him."

And so we fulfill Jesus's words and honor her every time this story is related (including as you read it right now!) about one who gave her best, from the heart, for her Lord. This is one of two gifts that Jesus commends in the Gospel of Mark. The other is the widow's two mites, which Jesus claimed was "more than all those" others gave (Mark 12:43). Obviously, Jesus's approval is not based on the amount given—he doesn't need the money, after all—but on *the heart attitude with which it is given.*

---

7. Robertson, *Word Pictures*, vol. 1, on Mark 14:9.

## A Worthy Example

We need to not only honor Mary, but to follow her example as well. We are called to learn here, not from the scribes or the priests or even the disciples, but from *her* what it means to love and honor the Lord.

It would have fulfilled all the demands of Middle Eastern hospitality for Mary to have anointed the head of Jesus with a few drops of the precious ointment. But her heart was so full of adoration, her focus was so totally on Jesus, that she just gave it all. She broke the bottle, and poured it all out. *What she had, she did.* She held nothing back; she gave it all.

Undoubtedly Mary's act of total commitment and love meant so much to Jesus because it was itself so *Christlike*—it was suggestive of what he was about to do: to give himself *completely* for the sins of the world, to allow himself (as the song puts it below) to be "broken and spilled out" in an act of total selflessness. What *he* had, he did: he had the unique opportunity to give of himself fully for the salvation of humankind, and he did so willingly. "For you know the grace of our Lord Jesus Christ, that though he was rich, yet for your sake he became poor, that you through his poverty might become rich" (2 Cor 8:9). He held nothing back; he gave it all.

The song "Broken and Spilled Out," by Gloria Gaither, draws this same comparison:

> One day a plain village woman, driven by love for her Lord,
> Recklessly poured out a valuable essence, disregarding the scorn.
> And once it was broken and spilled out,
>     a fragrance filled all the room,
> Like a pris'ner released from his shackles,
>     like a spirit set free from the tomb.
>
> (Chorus)
> Broken and spilled out just for love of Thee, Jesus:
> My own precious treasure, lavished on Thee.
> Broken and spilled out and poured at Your feet,
> In sweet abandon, let me be spilled out and used up for Thee.
>
> Lord, You were God's precious treasure,
>     His loved and His own perfect Son,
> Sent here to show me the love of the Father;
>     Yes, just for love it was done!
> And though You were perfect and holy,
>     You gave up Yourself willingly,

And You spared no expense for my pardon,
You were spilled out and wasted for me!

(Chorus)
Broken and spilled out just for love of me, Jesus:
God's most precious treasure, lavished on me.
Broken and spilled out and poured at Your feet,
In sweet abandon, let me be spilled out and used up for Thee.

Mary's act also was a faint reflection of what the Father *himself* was about to do: to give the very best *he* had—his only *Son*—for the salvation of the world (John 3:16). The Father is *the author of lavish giving*: "In him we have redemption through his blood, the forgiveness of our trespasses, according to the riches of his grace, which he *lavished* upon us" (Eph 1:7–8).

## A Lavish Gift of Worship

Mary's act was above all an act of *worship*. The disciples thought it was a wasteful expression; in a certain sense, that's true. Worship doesn't *produce* much that is tangible. But it is worship that puts everything else in its proper perspective and makes sense out of our lives. And so Marva Dawn calls worship a "royal waste of time."[8] It allows us to let God take his proper place as King over our lives.

That means that worship deserves our best, our whole heart, our best energies. Jesus deserves from us a lavish and spontaneous expression of adoration. That will look a little different for each of us, but the point is that we need to get lost in the object of our worship, as Mary did—forgetting ourselves, and turning our focus completely on him.

Most of us carry around an alabaster vial of pure *composure*—and what a valuable commodity it is to us! We cradle that vial, lest we drop it and lose any of that precious self-control. We need to break that vial and let our expressions of love and gratitude and praise come pouring forth. God has lavished his grace upon us and deserves a lavish response of worship in return.

Mary lost her composure, while the disciples kept theirs—and on that occasion Judas was the spokesman for composure! May God save us from that kind of composure. And may he save us from sprinkling just a

8. Dawn, *Royal Waste of Time*.

few drops of worship, thinking we have thereby fulfilled our obligation—and then becoming indignant or condemning, as the disciples did, if the person next to us should give a little more lavish expression of worship to God than we are used to. We dare not despise heartfelt emotion springing out of a genuine response to God and his grace. Leave that to Judas! Our worship should be lavish, poured out without measure from a full heart.

How many of us are fit to stand with Mary, who poured upon her Lord a lavish measure of worship flowing out of a full heart? Are we more like the disciples, with their haughty composure and stale moderation? *What Mary had, she did.* She did what she could—she gave freely of herself to her fullest. Hers was a heart brimming with grateful devotion. She gave her very best.

May we learn to live like her, give like her, *worship* like her!

## The Canticles of Christmas (Luke 1–2)

A canticle is "a scriptural hymn text that is used in various Christian liturgies and is similar to a psalm in form and content but appears apart from the book of Psalms."[9] The four inspired and poetic psalms of praise uttered by different figures in Luke's account of the birth of Christ have been set to music by many different church composers over the centuries (from Monteverdi, to Bach and Mozart, to Dvorak and Bruckner, to William Walton and John Rutter). Often these settings have used the Latin translation (though eventually other languages as well), and so they are often identified by the first word or words of their text in the Latin *Vulgate* translation (see the italicized words below). Together they provide a wonderful look into some key truths that underlie the familiar Christmas story.[10]

Mary's *Magnificat* ("My soul *magnifies* the Lord" [Luke 1:46–55])
   Theme: The Humble Exalted

Zacharias's *Benedictus* ("*Blessed* be the Lord God of Israel" [Luke 1:67–79])
   Theme: A Light in the Darkness

The Angels' *Gloria* ("*Glory* to God in the highest" [Luke 2:14])
   Theme: Glory to God!

9. https://www.britannica.com/topic/canticle.

10. See an exposition of these texts in Ron Man, "Canticles of Christmas."

Simeon's *Nunc Dimittis* (*"Now let* your servant *depart* in peace"
[Luke 2:29–32])
Theme: A Light to the Gentiles

### The Priority of *Heart* Worship (Luke 18:9–14; 21:1–4)

But the tax collector, standing far off, would not even lift up his
eyes to heaven, but beat his breast, saying, "God, be merciful to
me, a sinner!" I tell you, this man went down to his house justified, rather than the other. (Luke 18:13–14a)

Jesus looked up and saw the rich putting their gifts into the offering
box, and he saw a poor widow put in two small copper coins. And
he said, "Truly, I tell you, this poor widow has put in more than all
of them. For they all contributed out of their abundance, but she
out of her poverty put in all she had to live on." (Luke 21:1–4)

(Please see the treatment of these passages on p. 131.)

### Worship in Spirit and Truth (John 4:19–26)

But the hour is coming, and is now here, when the true worshipers will worship the Father in spirit and truth, for the Father is
seeking such people to worship him. God is spirit, and those who
worship him must worship in spirit and truth. (John 4:23–24)

(Please see the treatment of this key passage on pp. 99–110.)

### Ascended on High (Luke 24:50–51; Acts 1:9–11)

And [Jesus] led them out as far as Bethany, and lifting up his
hands he blessed them. While he blessed them, he parted from
them and was carried up into heaven. (Luke 24:50–51)

And when [Jesus] had said these things, as they were looking
on, he was lifted up, and a cloud took him out of their sight. And
while they were gazing into heaven as he went, behold, two men
stood by them in white robes, and said, "Men of Galilee, why do
you stand looking into heaven? This Jesus, who was taken up
from you into heaven, will come in the same way as you saw him
go into heaven." (Acts 1:9–11)

The ascension of Jesus Christ is too quickly skipped over (or ignored) in many churches. Yet it is an event with enormous implications for our lives and for the life of the church. Laura Smit speaks to this:

> Popular conversations about the incarnation tend to focus on the nativity stories and on the earthly life of Jesus. . . . Many think that the ascension really means the shedding of Jesus' human nature, as if Jesus is now simply a spiritual presence who used to be human, someone whom we remember with affection rather than someone we expect to see face to face someday. A full-orbed understanding of the incarnation will also proclaim that the incarnation continues, that it is the incarnate Christ who has ascended. Jesus is our contemporary, not a historical figure from a dead past. He is living now, interacting with us now, and standing now in a human body in the presence of the Father. He is praying for us now, leading our worship now, feeling our pain now, sharing our humanity now.[11]

The implications of Jesus's ascension include:

1. Jesus has been exalted and has taken his place of *rulership* at his Father's right hand (1 Tim 3:16; Col 3:1; Eph 1:20–21).

2. Jesus serves now as our *Advocate and Intercessor* in the Father's presence (1 John 2:1; Heb 7:25).

3. For the first time, *humanity dwells in the Father's presence* in heaven, guaranteeing that we will also follow Jesus there one day (John 14:2–3; 1 Cor 15:23).

4. Jesus went and sent the *Holy Spirit* to dwell in us and with us (John 7:39; 16:7).

5. Christ our Mediator in his continuing humanity and eternal priesthood (1 Tim 2:5; Heb 4:14–15; 5:6; 6:20; 7:17, 21; 8:1; 10:21) serves the heavenly tabernacle (Heb 8:1–2) and actively *leads his people into the Father's presence in worship* (Heb 2:12; 10:19–22).

This last one is, of course, the most important for our purposes here, and will be developed much more fully later in ch. 26.

Michael Farley has summarized the importance of the ascension for our worship thus:

---

11. Smit, "Incarnation Continues."

The ascension is the foundation of the Bible's theology of worship. Jesus' ascension means that he is not only the God and King whom we worship but also the human high priest who leads worship for us and in us through the presence and power of his Spirit. In worship, we experience the union of heaven and earth made tangible and explicit in the concrete actions of worship through which Jesus promises to serve us.

Because the Father receives his death and his life on our behalf, Jesus' ascension signifies that we, too, have access to the Father in heaven (Heb 10:19–25), and from that privileged position, Jesus leads us in every act of worship. He is the ultimate liturgist (Heb 8:2), preacher (Heb 2:12a; Rom 10:14), singer (Heb 2:12b), intercessor (Heb 7:25; Rom 8:34), and table host (Heb 13:9b–10; 1 Cor 10:16).

The God whom we meet in worship and whom we serve in all our lives is the risen, ascended, exalted, and glorified Lord Jesus Christ who reigns over all, and this ought to produce confident peace, joyful hope, and powerful purpose in all that Christians do as we "set our minds on things that are above: where our life is hidden with Christ in God" (Col 3:1). In the specific context of corporate worship, it implies that public liturgy must maintain elements of grandeur and majesty fitting for the King of Kings and Lord of Lords, for the one who calls us and leads us in worship is none other than the resurrected and ascended Lord of glory that John sees in his apocalyptic vision (Rev 1:12–20).[12]

## The Worship of the Earliest Church (Acts 2:42–47)

And they devoted themselves to the apostles' teaching and the fellowship, to the breaking of bread and the prayers. . . . praising God and having favor with all the people. (Acts 2:42, 47)

(Please see the treatment of this passage in chs. 30, 33, and 37.)

> "You shall worship the Lord your God, and serve him only."
> (Matt 4:10)

---

12. Farley, "Jesus' Ascension," 2–3. For more helpful resources on the ascension, see Calvin Institute of Christian Worship, "Ascension Resource Guide"; Milligan, *Ascension and Heavenly Priesthood*; Atkins, *Ascension Now*; and Dawson, *Jesus Ascended*.

# 22

## SIGNIFICANT NEW TESTAMENT WORSHIP PASSAGES

### Epistles

### Worship and the Fall (Rom 1:21–25)

> For although they knew God, they did not honor him as God
> or give thanks to him, but they became futile in their think-
> ing, and their foolish hearts were darkened. . . . They exchanged
> the truth about God for a lie and worshiped and served the
> creature rather than the Creator, who is blessed forever! Amen.
> (Rom 1:21, 25)

(Please see the treatment of this key passage on pp. 73–77; and a fuller
exposition in Ronald Man, "False and True Worship.")

### Paul's Doxology (Rom 11:33–36)

P aul's explanation in Romans of the ramifications of the fall (Rom
1:18–32) and the ensuing blackness of sin that has engulfed the human race (3:9–18, 23) makes the gospel shine all the more brightly as
he expounds on it in the ensuing chapters. He shows how the gospel is

indeed "the power of God for salvation to everyone who believes" (1:16), for through it God has showered upon believers:

- The righteousness of God through faith in Jesus Christ (3:22; 5:19)
- Justification by his grace as a gift (3:24, 26; 4:5; 5:1)
- Redemption (3:24)
- Propitiation (3:25)
- Peace with God (5:1)
- Grace (5:2; 5:15)
- Reconciliation (5:11)
- Salvation as a free gift (5:17; 6:23)
- Life (5:18)
- Eternal life (5:21)
- Newness of life (6:4)
- Resurrection life (6:5)
- Deliverance from condemnation (8:1)
- Life in the Spirit (8:1–11)
- Adoption (8:15)
- Mercy (11:30)

Paul then expounds in chs. 9–11 the mystery of God's purposes for Israel and the Gentiles, and how his grace, mercy, and sovereignty infuse these purposes.

After this profound theological treatise in chs. 1–11 on the gospel and God's work in the world (and before turning to practical applications in chs. 12–16), Paul bursts forth in praise to the wise and utterly sovereign God whose ways he has been privileged to plumb so profoundly:

> Oh, the depth of the riches and wisdom and knowledge of God! How unsearchable are his judgments and how inscrutable his ways!
> "For who has known the mind of the Lord,
>     or who has been his counselor?
> Or who has given a gift to him that he might be repaid?"

For from him and through him and to him are all things.[1] To him be glory forever. Amen. (Rom 11:33–36)

Paul has turned from *theology* to *doxology*, and shown us the intimate and necessary connection between the two. As the late John Stott eloquently put it (partially cited already in ch. 4):

> It is important to note from Romans 1–11 that theology (our belief about God) and doxology (our worship of God) should never be separated. On the one hand, there can be *no doxology without theology*. It is not possible to worship an unknown god. All true worship is a response to the self-revelation of God in Christ and Scripture, and arises from our reflection on who he is and what he has done. It was the tremendous truths of Romans 1–11 which provoked Paul's outburst of praise in verses 33–36 of chapter 11. The worship of God is evoked, informed, and inspired by the vision of God. Worship without theology is bound to degenerate into idolatry. Hence the indispensable place of Scripture in both public and private devotion. It is the Word of God which calls forth the worship of God.
>
> On the other hand, there should be *no theology without doxology*. There is something fundamentally flawed about a purely academic interest in God. God is not an appropriate object for cool, critical, detached, scientific observation and evaluation. No, the true knowledge of God will always lead us to worship, as it did Paul. Our place is on our faces before him in adoration.
>
> As I believe Bishop Handley Moule said at the end of the last century, we must "beware equally of an undevotional theology and of an untheological devotion."[2]

Geoffrey Wainwright agrees:

> The ascription of praise with which a Chrysostom, an Augustine, or a Calvin ended their sermons was no mere formality: It indicated the intention of the sermon itself and its aim of bringing others also to the praise of God on account of what had been proclaimed in Scripture and sermon.[3]

And elsewhere Wainwright points out:

---

1. "God created the world, holds it in existence, and governs all of it for his purposes" (Piper, *Providence*, 698).

2. Stott, *Romans*, 311–12.

3. Wainwright, "Praise of God," 38.

The second-order activity of theology is therefore, at its own level, properly doxological: the theologian is truly theologian when, in his very theologizing, he is listening for the "echo of a voice" and is contributing, even if indirectly, to the human praise of God.[4]

But of course there is nothing indirect about Paul's approach! His full-throated response finds resonance with Isaac Watts's Trinitarian hymn "We Give Immortal Praise," which ends like this:

Almighty God, to Thee
Be endless honours done,
The undivided Three,
And the mysterious One.
Where reason fails, with all her powers,
There faith prevails, and love adores.[5]

After the most profound theological exposition ever written, Paul necessarily comes to the end of himself, and his reason falters before the vastness of God's glory: there he bows the knee in faith and love, and breathlessly exclaims that "from him and through him and to him are all things. To him be glory forever. Amen" (11:36).

## Lifestyle Worship (Rom 12:1)

(Please see the treatment of this key passage in ch. 10.)

## Worship for and from the Nations (Rom 15:8–12)

For I tell you that Christ became a servant to the circumcised to show God's truthfulness, in order to confirm the promises given to the patriarchs, and in order that the Gentiles might glorify God for his mercy. (Rom 15:8–9a)

John Piper offers an important perspective on this passage, and on God's purposes for the nations in general (quoted in part in ch. 9):

The aim was worship. Romans 15:9: "In order that the Gentiles might glorify God for his mercy." Notice: It's not just that the Gentiles might receive God's mercy or simply experience God's

4. Wainwright, *Doxology*, 21.
5. See https://divinehymns.com/lyrics/we-give-immortal-praise-song-lyrics-3/.

mercy, but that they glorify God for his mercy. The aim of the gospel among the nations is not man-centered. Paul does not say, "Christ became a servant in order that the Gentiles might receive mercy." He says, "Christ became a servant in order that the Gentiles might glorify God for receiving mercy."

The ultimate aim of the gospel is God—God glorified for his mercy. Don't fall short of the ultimate aim when you preach the gospel. Don't just offer people mercy. Offer them the greatest gift: a merciful God, and that God glorified for his mercy. Human beings were made finally for God, not mercy. Mercy is a means[,] not an end. Savoring mercy is not the end, savoring God for his mercy is the end.

How does Paul unpack the word "glorify" from verse 9? He does it with four Old Testament quotations in verses 9–12.

As it is written, "Therefore I will praise you among the Gentiles, and sing to your name."

And again it is said, "Rejoice, O Gentiles, with his people."

And again, "Praise the Lord, all you Gentiles, and let all the peoples extol him."

And again Isaiah says, "The root of Jesse will come, even he who arises to rule the Gentiles; in him will the Gentiles hope" (Rom 15:9–12).

Praise, sing, rejoice, praise, extol, hope. Glorifying God for his mercy starts with the emotions of joy (verse 10) and hope (verse 12) in the God of mercy. Joy as you savor the merciful God now, and hope as you happily expect to savor him even more in the future. Then that joy and hope overflow in praise (verse 9, 11) and song (verse 9).

This is the essence of worship: Heartfelt, hope-filled joy in the God of mercy overflowing in fitting outward expressions. The reason I say this is the essence of worship is because I know there are other emotions that are part of worship besides joy. Like the sorrows of confession. But these sorrows are not true worship, unless, at root, they are sorrows for our failures to experience joy in the God of mercy. Therefore, joy in the God of mercy remains the essence of gospel worship. And that is really good news, because in God's design, we get the mercy, God gets the glory. We get the joy, God gets the praise. We revel in hope, God receives the honor. When we call the nations to worship the true God in Christ, that is what we call them to.

And that worship is for all the peoples.[6]

---

6. Piper, "Gospel Worship."

## "From Glory to Glory": God's Glory in Romans

### The Fall

For although they knew God, they did not *glorify* him as God or give thanks to him, but they became futile in their thinking, and their foolish hearts were darkened. Claiming to be wise, they became fools, and exchanged the *glory* of the immortal God for images resembling mortal man and birds and animals and creeping things. (Rom 1:21–23)

### Our Fallen State

For there is no distinction: for all have sinned and fall short of the *glory* of God. (Rom 3:22b–23)

### Our Present Hope
### (from 2 Cor)

But we all, with unveiled face, beholding as in a mirror the *glory* of the Lord, are being transformed into the same image from *glory* to *glory*, just as from the Lord, the Spirit. (2 Cor 3:18)

### Our Future Hope

Through [Christ] we have also obtained access by faith into this grace in which we stand, and we rejoice in hope of the *glory* of God. (Rom 5:2)

The Spirit himself bears witness with our spirit that we are children of God, and if children, then heirs—heirs of God and fellow heirs with Christ, provided we suffer with him in order that we may also be *glorified* with him. For I consider that the sufferings of this present time are not worth comparing with the *glory* that is to be revealed to us. (Rom 8:16–18)

The creation itself will be set free from its bondage to corruption and obtain the freedom of the *glory* of the children of God. (Rom 8:21)

And those whom he predestined he also called, and those whom he called he also justified, and those whom he justified he also *glorified*. (Rom 8:30)

## The Goal of the Church

May the God of endurance and encouragement grant you to live in such harmony with one another, in accord with Christ Jesus, that together you may with one voice *glorify* the God and Father of our Lord Jesus Christ. Therefore welcome one another as Christ has welcomed you, for the *glory* of God. (Rom 15:6–7)

## All Glory to God Forever

For from him and through him and to him are all things. To him be *glory* forever! Amen. (Rom 11:36)

Now to him who is able to strengthen you according to my gospel and the preaching of Jesus Christ . . . to the only wise God be *glory* forevermore through Jesus Christ! Amen. (Rom 16:25, 27)

## "In Remembrance of Me": The Lord's Supper (1 Cor 11:23–26)

(Please see the treatment of the Lord's Supper on pp. 371–75.)

## "Decently and in Order": The Gathering (1 Cor 14)

As pointed out previously, there is precious little in the New Testament by way of specific instructions about how to practice corporate worship in the church. Of the little that one does find, most of it has to do with Paul correcting abuses or imbalances. Such is the case in 1 Cor 14. Here we have Paul emphasizing such priorities as love (v. 1), spirit *and* mind (v. 15), peace (v. 33), decency and order (v. 40), and building up (vv. 4–5, 12, 26); and preferring prophecy over tongues (in the corporate gathering).

### Prophecy over Tongues

For one who speaks in a tongue speaks not to men but to God; for no one understands him, but he utters mysteries in the Spirit. On the other hand, the one who prophesies speaks to people for their upbuilding and encouragement and consolation. The one who speaks in a tongue builds up himself, but the one who prophesies builds up the church. Now I want you all to speak in tongues, but even more to prophesy. The one who prophesies is greater than the one who speaks in tongues, unless someone interprets, so that the church may be built up. (vv. 2–5)

Nevertheless, in church I would rather speak five words with my mind in order to instruct others, than ten thousand words in a tongue. (v. 19)

If, therefore, the whole church comes together and all speak in tongues, and outsiders or unbelievers enter, will they not say that you are out of your minds? But if all prophesy, and an unbeliever or outsider enters, he is convicted by all, he is called to account by all, the secrets of his heart are disclosed, and so, falling on his face, he will *worship*[7] God and declare that God is really among you. (vv. 23–25)

## Church Edification over Self-Edification

The one who speaks in a tongue builds up himself, but the one who prophesies builds up the church. . . . The one who prophesies is greater than the one who speaks in tongues, unless someone interprets, so that the church may be built up. (vv. 4, 5b)

So with yourselves, since you are eager for manifestations of the Spirit, strive to excel in building up the church. (v. 12)

What then, brothers? When you come together, each one has a hymn, a lesson, a revelation, a tongue, or an interpretation. Let all things be done for building up. . . . For you can all prophesy one by one, so that all may learn and all be encouraged. (vv. 26, 31)

## Intelligibility over Unintelligibility

So with yourselves, if with your tongue you utter speech that is not intelligible, how will anyone know what is said? For you will be speaking into the air. There are doubtless many different languages in the world, and none is without meaning, but if I do not know the meaning of the language, I will be a foreigner to the speaker and the speaker a foreigner to me. (vv. 9–11)

If you give thanks with your spirit, how can anyone in the position of an outsider say "Amen" to your thanksgiving when he does not know what you are saying? For you may be giving

---

7. The word here is *proskuneō*—surprisingly, the only time Paul uses the term in his writings.

thanks well enough, but the other person is not being built up. . . . In church I would rather speak five words with my mind in order to instruct others, than ten thousand words in a tongue. (vv. 16–17, 19)

## Order over Confusion

If any speak in a tongue, let there be only two or at most three, and each in turn, and let someone interpret. But if there is no one to interpret, let each of them keep silent in church and speak to himself and to God. Let two or three prophets speak, and let the others weigh what is said. If a revelation is made to another sitting there, let the first be silent. For you can all prophesy one by one, so that all may learn and all be encouraged. (vv. 27–31)
     For God is not a God of confusion but of peace. (v. 33)
     But all things should be done decently and in order. (v. 40)

## The Needed Balance

N. T. Wright speaks helpfully to the balance Paul is calling for:

I am innately suspicious of one standard reading of this passage, that which discovers here a priority of free-form, non-liturgical worship as the genuine Spirit-led phenomenon as opposed to liturgical or set forms, deemed to be less fully spiritual. . . . Of course, the passage does indeed give us a picture of the early worshipping church as enjoying considerable freedom; Paul's arguments against chaotic worship would be irrelevant unless there was an openness to fresh revelations of the Spirit which could in principle lapse into complete disorder. But his argument for unity despite diversity of gifts in chapter 12 . . . , and his argument for order rather than chaos in chapter 14, indicate as well that as far as he is concerned genuine Spirit-led worship will have framework and body to it, not just free-floating and unstructured outbursts of praise and prayer. . . . On the positive side, we must of course say that the order he envisages is an order within which all sorts of new and unexpected things can and should happen. But we should also note the emphasis on mission: one of the key criteria for authentic worship will be that if an outsider enters, he or she will be confronted, not with chaos and apparent gibberish, but with the clear and convicting message of the gospel [vv. 25–26].[8]

## "Yes" and "Amen": God's Program in Two Words (2 Cor 1:20)

### The Gospel in Miniature

Nestled in the opening strains of Paul's Second Epistle to the Corinthians is a statement that plumbs the depths of God's redemptive work through Christ and the relationship with him that we enjoy because of it.

### The Context

The context finds Paul addressing the charge of insincerity to which he found himself vulnerable in Corinth because of changing his plans for revisiting that city. He had redirected his itinerary, and now he wants to make it clear to the Corinthian believers that he is not one to vacillate; he is a man of his word:

> I wanted to visit you on my way to Macedonia, and to come back to you from Macedonia and have you send me on my way to Judea. Was I vacillating when I wanted to do this? Do I make my plans according to the flesh, ready to say "Yes, yes" and "No, no" at the same time? (2 Cor 1:16–17)

The reason Paul finds this so important to emphasize is that he wants them to understand that there is no mixed message and no unclear sound from the trumpet when it comes to the gospel he proclaimed to them. He defends the *messenger* in order to defend the *message*:

> As God is faithful, our word to you is not yes and no. (2 Cor 1:18)

There is unequivocally *one* way of salvation, and this is the message that Paul and his companions, Silvanus and Timothy, preached to the Corinthians—without wavering, without apology, without compromise, without vacillation:

8. N. T. Wright, "Worship and the Spirit."

> For the Son of God, Jesus Christ, whom we proclaimed among you, Silvanus and Timothy and I, was not Yes and No, but in him it is always Yes. (2 Cor 1:19)

They were faithful communicators of God's plan of salvation.

## Yes! ↓

The faithfulness of the messengers is but a dim reflection of the way God himself has dealt with the Corinthians:

> For all the promises of God find their *Yes* in him [Christ]. (2 Cor 1:20a)

God has faithfully fulfilled all his promises in his Son; in Jesus Christ all these promises receive a resounding Yes!

1. All the promises inherent in God's creation of the world for humans to rule over, and in God's creation of humans in his image for fellowship with himself

2. All the promises extended to fallen humans concerning redemption to come, from Gen 3:16 to the sacrificial system of Israel to the Messianic and redemptive prophecies of the Old Testament:

   - The promise to Eve concerning her seed (Gen 3:15)

   - The promise to Abraham concerning his seed and the blessing of the world (Gen 12:1–3; 22:15–18)

   - The promise to Moses concerning the prophet like himself (Deut 18:18)

   - The promise to David concerning his Son who would sit on his throne forever (1 Sam 7:12–13)

   - The promise to Isaiah concerning a virgin-born Child (7:14), eternal King (9:2, 6–7), and suffering Servant whose travails would satisfy God (52:13—53:12)

3. A host of other hints and foreshadowings and types and hopes (cf. Luke 24:25–27; Acts 2:16–36; 3:22–25; 7:2–53; Rom 1:2–3, 16–17; 3:21–26; 1 Cor 5:7–8; 10:1–4; Eph 2:13–14; Heb 1:1–2; 3:5–6; 4:8–9; 7:17–22, 26–28; 8:5; 9:8–15, 24–26; 10:1–18; 11:39–40; 12:18–24; 13:9–10, 11–12, 14; 1 Pet 1:10—12)

All of these promises (and many others) find their *Yes*, their fulfillment, "in him": Jesus himself is the message (see 2 Cor 1:19, "the Son of God, Christ Jesus, who was preached among you by us"): he is the personification of God's stupendous plan for humankind; he is the grand and glorious exclamation point to all that God has revealed about himself; he is the *Yes* to all that God in his grace has intended for us.

## Amen! ↑

God has planned it all and brought it to fruition through the saving work of his Son; it is left for us simply to respond and receive and adore:

> That is why it is through him [Christ] that we utter our Amen to God for his glory. (2 Cor 1:20b)

"That is why" emphasizes that our part is completely and utterly dependent on God's part: he has initiated and consummated his saving purposes on our behalf. Our response is "through him [Christ]," in acknowledgment of God's Yes to us through the redemptive work of Jesus; and that response is summarized by Paul as "our Amen." Paul is using the figure of speech known as *synecdoche*, where a small part is used to represent a much larger whole; by it Paul indicates that *all* of our responses of prayer and praise and worship, which are so often punctuated with a final amen (meaning "it is true" or "so be it"), are expressions of grateful assent and surrender to God's loving purposes for us in Christ.

More than that, our entire lives (which is the true New Testament scope and realm of worship, as we have seen in John 4:23 and Rom 12:1) are to be a confirmation and reflection of the wondrous work God has wrought in us. Our Amen is the full-orbed response of love, with all our heart, soul, mind, and strength (Mark 12:30), to God's Yes to us in Jesus; and this love we express through life- and lifestyle-pervading worship.

## All of Christ

It should be noticed that Jesus Christ is not only the message (2 Cor 1:19); not only is he the fulfillment of the many promises of God (1:20a); not only is he the subject and object of our adoring and grateful response of amen (1:20b): Jesus Christ is also the active *agent* in our response of worship to God for all he has done for us in his Son. Our Amen is not just *to* him, or *for* him—our Amen of response is actually *"through* him" (1:20b). Jesus does not leave us in our (albeit redeemed) frailty and weakness to drum up an appropriate response to God for his magnificent promises and their coming to fruition in his Son; no, Jesus *leads the way* as our Mediator in returning to the Father praise and honor and thanks for his redeeming work, for the "summing up of all things up in Christ" (Eph 1:10 NASB).

And so our own response is but an echo of our High Priest's, and it gives our Maker pleasure—not because we have brought a level or quality or quantity of response appropriate to or worthy of his glory; but because the living Christ himself has made our response for us, and in so doing has made it perfect and worthy and acceptable. That perfect worship that God in his perfection must and does require is effected by our Substitute and is credited to our account; in so doing God is indeed "working in us that which is pleasing in his sight" (Heb 13:21), with the result that "no man may boast" (1 Cor 1:29).

> The perfect human prayer and the perfect human praise are to be found on the lips of Jesus our brother. He is the perfect worshipper in the presence of the perfect God. . . . We are invited to join the prayer and praise of Christ and to allow our voice to be perfected in his.[9]

Our Amen (initiated and carried out through Christ) completes and complements God's Yes to us in Christ; so in Christ the entire duality is carried out and completed: he is the operative force both in the God-to-human movement of Yes ↓ *and* in the human-to-God response of Amen. ↑ Thus in Christ we see the fulfillment of the foundational revelation-response paradigm of Scripture: he is the agent of God's revelation (Yes) and also the agent of our response back to God (Amen). Thus 2 Cor 1:20 brilliantly expresses in microcosm the centrality of Christ and his work. (See also the visual representation on p. 32.)

We will see much more about this dual role of Christ later in ch. 26.

## To the Glory of God

God's plan, its fulfillment in Christ, and the response of worship on our part: all these aspects work together to evoke the "praise of his glory"

9. Cocksworth, *Holy, Holy, Holy,* 158, 161.

(Eph 1:6, 12, 14) through God's sovereign and gracious Yes to us in Jesus Christ and through our humble and never-ending response of Amen.

God has said, "Here is my Son, offered up for your salvation. *Yes!*" We reply, "Thank You, Father. Thank you, Jesus. *Amen!*" And thus God brings great glory to his blessed Name.

## "To the Praise of His Glory": God's Purpose in Redemption (Eph 1:3–14)

After his opening greeting, Paul launches into his epistle by praising God ("Blessed is the God and Father of our Lord Jesus Christ") because he "has blessed us in Christ with every spiritual blessing" (Eph 1:3).

He then enumerates a number of these blessings that make God worthy of praise, namely:

- Election (1:4)
- Love (1:4)
- Adoption (1:5)
- Redemption (1:7)
- Forgiveness (1:7)
- Knowledge of his will (1:9)
- Inheritance (1:11)
- Sealing with the Spirit (1:12)

All these blessings, the "riches of His grace" (1:7), he has "lavished upon us" (1:8).

He has accomplished and bestowed all these things for our good, but ultimately for his honor. As John Piper has often pointed out, our good and his honor are not contradictory, but complementary: "We get the grace, and he gets the glory." Three times Paul reminds us that what God did in Christ, he did "*to the praise of his glorious grace*" (1:6), "*to the praise of his glory*" (1:12, 14). He is deserving of all praise and blessing and worship for what he has so generously and graciously done for us in Christ.

That is why Paul starts by blessing God (1:3), and why he rounds off the first half of his epistle (having delved more deeply into themes he has raised in 1:3–14) with praise as well:

To him be glory in the church and in Christ Jesus throughout all generations, forever and ever. Amen. (Eph 3:21)

God's purpose is to exalt his glory through the exercise of his grace. His aim is the greatness of his name and the gladness of his undeserving people. That is, his aim is the God-exalting, soul-satisfying praise of the glory of his grace. . . . Grace is the consummate expression of God's glory.[10]

## The Ministry of Song (Eph 5:18–20)

There is not nearly as much about musical ministry in corporate worship in the New Testament as there is in the Old. However:

That the singing or chanting of hymns was an integral part of the worship of New Testament churches is clear from Paul's instructions about worship in 1 Cor 14:26. Paul says, "When you come together, each one has a hymn." In Col 3:16 and Eph 5:19 he encourages his readers to sing "psalms, hymns and spiritual songs to God." James also calls on his readers to "sing songs of praise" (5:13).[11]

Ephesians 5:18–20 (along with Col 3:16) does provide a helpful foundation:

And do not get drunk with wine, for that is debauchery, but be filled with the Spirit, addressing one another in psalms and hymns and spiritual songs, singing and making melody to the Lord with all your heart, giving thanks always and for everything to God the Father in the name of our Lord Jesus Christ.

In this passage we see at least eight aspects that should characterize our ministry of song.

### 1. A *Spirit-Filled* Ministry

And do not get drunk with wine, for that is debauchery, but *be filled with the Spirit*. (Eph 5:18)

When someone is drunk, that person is controlled by the influence of alcohol. Paul says that we should be controlled rather by the Spirit of God.

10. Piper, *Providence*, 57, 170.
11. Gloer, "Worship God!," 38.

(A Benedictine hymn goes, "Let us joyfully taste of the sober drunken-ness of the Spirit."[12])

With all the debates about the filling of the Spirit, it's intriguing here that the first result of the filling of the Spirit mentioned by Paul is singing![13]

> For we are the real circumcision, who *worship* by the *Spirit of God* and glory in Christ Jesus and put no confidence in the flesh. (Phil 3:3)

## 2. A *Mutual* Ministry

### Addressing *one another* (Eph 5:19)

There is an important horizontal aspect to our ministry of song in cor-porate worship: it is something we do together. Personal and private worship is an important part of our walk with God, but in the gather-ing of the church we need to be focused on one another as well as on God. This suggests an important corrective to many of our worship con-flicts: congregational worship is to provide a mutual benefit, rather than primarily an individual benefit; hence, the ubiquitous "What's in it for me?" or "What do I get out of it?" attitude with which so many approach corporate worship shows a severe misunderstanding of why we come to-gether. We minister to one another and encourage one another and draw strength from one another as we sing.

## 3. A *Diverse* Ministry

### In psalms *and* hymns *and* spiritual songs (Eph 5:19)

The exact designations of these three categories of song have been widely debated for the past two thousand years, with no indisputable outcome. However, it is quite certain at least that Paul is saying that we should use *different* kinds of songs in our corporate praise. Let us draw from musical riches across stylistic, generational, and national boundaries.

12. Cantalamessa, "Sober Intoxication."

13. N. T. Wright: "Drunkenness is the low-grade and shameful parody of that genuine self-transcendence, enhancement and ennoblement of what it means to be human, which can and should be known when the Spirit fills individuals and whole assemblies and enables them to speak to and sing with one another, making melody with the heart to the Lord, and giving thanks in the name of the Lord to God the Father" ("Worship and the Spirit").

## 4. A *God-Focused* Ministry

Singing and making melody *to the Lord* (Eph 5:19)

Ultimately, of course, our song is directed towards the One who alone is worthy of our praise. We do not sing for our own enjoyment or benefit (though those may well be positive side effects), but at God's bidding and for God's pleasure and glory.

## 5. An *Internal* Ministry

With your *heart* (Eph 5:19)

We are to make melody in our hearts before a song ever reaches our lips. For worship to be God-honoring and God-pleasing, it must be an expression of a devoted heart. Both the Old and the New Testament make it clear that God is far more concerned about the inner attitude of worship than about the external form it takes. Hence, our songs must well up from the inside.

> Man looks on the outward appearance, but the LORD looks on the *heart*. (1 Sam 16:7)

## 6. A *Responsive* Ministry ↑

*Giving thanks* always and for everything to God the Father
(Eph 5:20)

We have a song to sing only because of God's initiative in revealing himself to us and showing himself mighty in saving acts on our behalf. All worship is a grateful ↑ response to God's gracious ↓ self-revelation.

> Praise him for his mighty deeds! (Ps 150:2b)

## 7. A *Christ-empowered* Ministry

*In the name of our Lord Jesus Christ* (Eph 5:20)

Our song pleases God because we come to worship in and through our great High Priest, whose song subsumes and perfects our own. Praying and worshiping in Christ's name is far more than just tacking on Christ's name at the end for maximum effect. Rather, it is acknowledging that it is only in Christ and through Christ, by Christ's priesthood and dressed in Christ's righteousness, that we can draw near to God at all. (Much more on this later in ch. 26.)

> In the midst of the congregation I [Jesus] will sing your [the Father's] praise. (Heb 2:12b)

> Therefore, brethren, since we have confidence to enter the holy places by the blood of Jesus, by the new and living way that he opened for us through the curtain, that is, through his flesh, and since we have a great priest over the house of God, let us draw near with a true heart in full assurance of faith. (Heb 10:19–22)

**Author with unnamed librarian (Ohafia, Nigeria, Mar. 2016)**

She was a small, unassuming woman, librarian of the Presbyterian seminary sponsoring the conference I was speaking at in Nigeria. At the end of one of the sessions, the moderator asked this woman to close the time in prayer. I will never forget how she *started* her prayer: she said, "*In Jesus's name,*" and then went on with her prayer to the Father.

I was struck at what a profound theological insight that simple practice (her regular practice, as I got to hear later) demonstrated. We habitually tack on "in Jesus's name" at the *end* of our prayers, all too often in a rote manner and without reflection on what we are really saying. They are often perfunctory words that punctuate our prayer and (we hope) help it to be effective somehow.

But prayer in Jesus's name (and *worship* in Jesus's name too) is based on the conviction that it is *only in, through, and by Christ* that we enter into the Father's presence with our prayers and our praises. We can come confidently and boldly and with assurance precisely because he has opened and shown us the way to the Father (Heb 10:19–22); and not only that, but in fact Jesus *takes us with him* into the Father's presence! ("Behold, I and the children God has given me" [Heb 2:13].) Jesus represents us before the Father and presents our prayers and our worship to him on the basis of his redeeming work on our behalf. We can be sure that our petitions and praises are *always* accepted because we come *in Christ*.

A. B. Simpson speaks powerfully to this concept:

> "Seeing then that we have a great high Priest, Jesus, the Son of God, let us hold fast our profession. Let us come boldly unto the throne of grace, that we may obtain mercy, and find grace to help in time of need" (Heb. 4:14, 16).
>
> Our great Helper in prayer is the Lord Jesus Christ, our Advocate with the Father, our Great High Priest, whose chief ministry for us these centuries has been intercession and prayer. He it is who takes our imperfect petitions from our hands, cleanses them from their defects, corrects their faults, and then claims their answer from His Father on His own account and through His all-atoning merits and righteousness.
>
> Brother, are you fainting in prayer? Look up. Your blessed Advocate has already claimed your answer, and you would grieve and disappoint Him if you were to give up the conflict in the very moment when victory is on its way to meet you. He has gone in for you into the inner chamber, and already holds up your name upon the palms of His hands; and the messenger, which is to bring you your blessing, is now on his way, and the Spirit is only waiting your trust to whisper in your heart the echo of the answer from the throne, "It is done."[14]

What a bold way to acknowledge these amazing truths, by *beginning* prayer with "in Jesus's name"! It is recognizing that his name—that is, his person and his saving work—is the "key" that opens the door into the Father's presence; his name is the "password" that gives us entrance.

## 8. A *Trinitarian* Ministry

Be filled with the *Spirit* . . . and for everything to God the *Father* in the name of our Lord *Jesus Christ*. (Eph 5:18, 20)

---

14. Cowman, "July 20," quoting A. B. Simpson.

The normal New Testament pattern of worship is seen here as well: we bring our praise *to the Father, through the Son, in the power of the Holy Spirit*.[15]

## "All, and in All": Christ, His Word, and Our Song (Col 3:16)

Colossians 3:16, of course, shows marked similarities to Eph 5:19 (especially the mention of "psalms, hymns, and spiritual songs"), but also provides some unique perspectives on our corporate life and worship.

## The Context: Living in Christ

Paul calls on the Colossian believers (and us) to live with a heavenly perspective, in line with their position in Christ (Col 3:1–3); to reject worldly ways of living (3:5–9); and to reflect the newness of life that is theirs in Christ (3:10). Their new identity in Christ gives them a unity in Christ that supersedes human categories:

> Here there is not Greek and Jew, circumcised and uncircumcised, barbarian, Scythian, slave, free; but Christ is all, and in all. (Col 3:11)

All those distinctions are now meaningless because they are in Christ, and are Christ's: he is their "all," the ground of their being and the fullness of their new existence:

Though being "chosen," "holy," and "beloved" (3:13), living out this reality as a unified church (the "one body" into which they have been called

---

15. N. T. Wright comments: "This, indeed, is one of Paul's more strikingly trinitarian passages, reminiscent of 1 Corinthians 12:4–6, but this time giving not just a parallel between the three members of the Godhead but also a shape and a mutual relation: the Spirit enables worshippers to give thanks to the Father in the name of the Lord Jesus. Here we see, unsurprisingly but still importantly, the roots of developed trinitarian worship, not in a formula to be repeated (though there may be some of those too in Paul) but in the theological interpretation of what happens when Christians gather for worship" ("Worship and the Spirit"). Recent studies have bemoaned the absence of much trinitarian content in most Christian songs of recent decades, that is, the lack of explicit mention of the members of the Trinity and/or a distinguishing of their unique roles (see also ch. 25 for more on the Trinity). Robin Parry did a survey of the songs used most commonly in his denomination (the Vineyard Church) and found that *51.1%* of the songs were what he termed "You Lord" songs—i.e., with just a general reference to "God" or "Lord" without any recognition of the distinct Persons and roles of Father, Son, and/or Holy Spirit! (Parry, *Worshipping Trinity*, 139–46). See also Ruth, "Don't Lose the Trinity!"

in Christ [3:15b]) will call for a number of different qualities (which, if they came naturally, Paul would have no need to command!): compassion, kindliness, humility, meekness, patience, mutual forbearance, forgiveness, love, and gratitude (3:13–15). The peace to be found only in and through Christ must rule in their midst if a motley assortment of redeemed sinners is going to be able to live and function in unity as God intends (3:15a).

## The Challenge: Unity in Christ

This corporate unity will only come about as the "word of Christ" is allowed to "dwell in [them] richly." Paul is not willing to settle for a half-hearted communal gathering: his commands are filled with superlatives, which in turn are grounded in the primary superlative already seen, that of Christ being "all and in all" as the foundation of their unity. These exhortations to excellence include: that the Colossians display love as the *perfect* bond of unity (3:14); the need for Christ's *absolute rule* in their midst (3:15); that the word of Christ dwell *richly* (3:16a) among them; that they bring *all* wisdom to bear on their mutual edification (3:16b); and that indeed *all* that they do, verbally or actively, be done *all* (Paul himself repeats the term) in the name of the Lord Jesus (3:17)—that is, in his way, according to his power, and acknowledging that rule of Christ of which Paul has already spoken.

## The Call: Worshiping through Christ

Let the word of Christ dwell in you richly,
    with all wisdom
        teaching and admonishing one another
            with psalms, hymns and spiritual songs;
    with grace
        singing to God
        in your hearts.[16]
And whatever you do, in word or deed,
    do everything in the name of the Lord Jesus,
    giving thanks to God the Father through him. (Col 3:16–17)

It is surely no accident that in this context, where Paul calls for this kind of unity in the church, he highlights *singing*. For corporate song is

---

16. Layout of v. 16 from grammatical and exegetical study of Detwiler, "Church Music."

ideally suited to illustrating and expressing the *unity in diversity* that is to characterize the body of Christ: many distinct voices (different ranges, tone qualities, etc.), yet joined together in a harmonious chorus of praise to God that is certainly more than the sum of the parts.

Steven Guthrie goes as far as to suggest that our congregational singing not only *illustrates* the unity of the body, but in a real sense *enacts* it. He says of the New Testament churches, such as those in Ephesus and Colossae:

> In its congregational song one would have been able to *hear* the gathered church of Jew and Gentile—with all its various regional accents, all the distinctive pronunciations of aristocrats, slaves, and free people; male and female voices, voices of young and old—all these perceived at once in a single melody. This congregational song is not a *metaphor* of the socially, ethnically diverse church. It is this gathered body; or at least, this body's voice, this body made audible. The church's song is one way the church and the Spirit announce this unity—to one another and to the wider world. It is one way the Spirit reveals this community to its members, and continues to call its members to community. The members of the chorus literally participate in the one Body that is created out of many bodies. As they do, they *instruct* one another, saying: "Listen: this is the body of Christ—a chorus of Jew and Gentile, slave and free. Listen: this is the Image of God—a melody sung by male and female, impoverished and wealthy. Listen: this is the kind of life Christ brings—a harmony resonating through the bodies of these brothers and sisters, so lately aliens and enemies."[17]

It is also deeply significant that Paul identifies this singing as a worthy conduit and reflection of the "word of Christ" dwelling in the congregation's midst. The "word of Christ" should be understood as something far more dynamic than just a word *about* Christ (in Greek grammar, an objective genitive); rather, it suggests that *Christ himself* (a subjective genitive) continues to speak to us through his word and by means of human preachers, teachers, readers—and musicians. (Much more on the "word of Christ" and the role of Christ in our worship later in ch. 26.) It is Christ who should be heard through the readings, through the preaching, and through songs that accurately convey biblical truth. Christ's word is to "dwell" among them, and "richly" at that: it is not just to show up once or twice during the service (during the sermon and perhaps through an "obligatory" Scripture reading); rather, as discussed in ch. 4, the entire

---

17. Guthrie, "Wisdom of Song," 398.

context and content of worship should be word-centered and word-filled. It is this rich word-centeredness that will make even our singing be a rich source of teaching and admonishment and wisdom.

And as diverse as the body of Christ is in its makeup, so the songs sung together should be varied—hence, Paul says, our musical diet in the church should include what he refers to as "psalms, hymns and spiritual songs." As mentioned above under our consideration of Eph 5, much energy and ink have been expended in trying to conclusively delineate these categories of song, with no true consensus having been reached; but one sure conclusion may confidently be drawn, that Paul intends for there to be *different types* of songs. Dare we imagine that in the Colossian church Paul encouraged the inclusion of musical expressions indigenous to the various groups he refers to in v. 11?

Above all, Paul insists, all the actions and words of worship (in the immediate context, though perhaps Paul is looking beyond that to all of life as well) should be done "in the *name* of our Lord Jesus" (17). As noted already in looking at Eph 5, our activities of worship, with all their imperfections and mixed motives, are subsumed and perfected by Christ and offered to the Father, clothed in his righteousness and as part of his perfect offering of worship. And to the extent that we allow our words to be shaped and infused by the "word of Christ," they will be fitting instruments of praise—as the Son speaks in and through us, to the glory of the Father.[18]

## Christ: "All, and in All" (3:11)

Christ our all, Christ our worship, Christ our Mediator and High Priest, Christ our peace, Christ our sure Word spoken into our worship. How reminiscent of the familiar words attributed to Patrick of Ireland:

> Christ be with me, Christ within me,
> Christ behind me, Christ before me,
> Christ on my right, Christ on my left,
> Christ when I lie down,
> Christ when I sit down,

---

18. "Paul's point is that we should sing a variety of songs, all of which summarize and celebrate the 'word of Christ,' that is, the message of the gospel. That means that singing is part of the ministry of God's Word. When a congregation verbalizes truth in song, the Holy Spirit unleashes the double-edged sword of Scripture in our midst" (Merker, *Corporate Worship*, ch. 7 [unpaginated ed.]).

Christ when I arise,
Christ in the heart of every man who thinks of me,
Christ in the mouth of everyone who speaks of me,
Christ in every eye that sees me,
Christ in every ear that hears me.[19]

## A Royal Priesthood Offering Spiritual Sacrifices (1 Pet 2:5, 9)

As noted above in ch. 20, it is interesting to see how the New Testament authors did not shy away from using terms connected to the Old Testament sacrificial system, though investing those terms with more internal, spiritualized meanings. Such is the case here in 1 Pet 2:

> You yourselves like living stones are being built up as a spiritual house, to be a holy priesthood, to offer spiritual sacrifices acceptable to God through Jesus Christ. (1 Pet 2:5)

> But you are a chosen race, a royal priesthood, a holy nation, a people for his own possession, that you may proclaim the excellencies of him who called you out of darkness into his marvelous light. (1 Pet 2:9)

Of course, there are key differences between the national, ethnic Israel and the global, multiethnic church. But in these verses the church is described by Peter with terms and functions highly reminiscent of Israel: a holy priesthood, spiritual sacrifices, a chosen race, a royal priesthood, a holy nation, a people for his own possession. And also similar to Israel, a "people whom I formed for myself that they might declare my praise" (Isa 43:21), the church is to "proclaim the excellencies of him who called you out of darkness into his marvelous light."

This is another example of the ubiquitous *revelation* and *response* pattern in Scripture. God has taken the initiative to ↓ *reveal* his excellencies in his gracious work of calling them out of darkness into light; and their appropriate ↑ *response* is to gratefully proclaim those excellencies he has revealed. God redeems us so that we can reflect back to him (and others) his glory and his grace.

---

"For from him and through him and to him are all things. To him be glory forever. Amen." (Rom 11:36)

---

19. Patrick, "Saint Patrick's Breastplate."

# 23

## ETERNAL PRAISE

### The Great Scenes of Worship in the Book of Revelation

S inclair Ferguson, the great Scottish theologian and preacher, said in a sermon:

> A friend of mine led a tour last year to the seven churches of the book of Revelation. I said, "Did you go to the island of Patmos?" "No," he said, "I asked the people about going to Patmos, and they said, 'It would take you a day to get there, and a day to get back, and when you get to Patmos you don't see anything.'" And I thought to myself, "Tell that one to the Apostle John!"[1]

The aged apostle John, exiled on the island of Patmos, saw and heard a *lot* and tells us about it in the book of Revelation. (Ferguson went on to make application to our worship today: that it is possible to be "in the building" but to "see nothing.")

### Revelation 1

John "was in the Spirit [not just 'in the building'] on the Lord's Day" (1:10), and sees many amazing visions, as we read throughout the book— but none greater than the vision in ch. 1 of the glorified Christ himself.

---

1. Ferguson, "Church's Worship" (Monergism).

Indeed, John starts his account by telling us that what he writes is the "revelation of Jesus Christ" (1:1).

Jean-Jacques von Allmen writes, "The place of worship is essentially the place where Christ is found."[2] Revelation 1 is such a place of worship. John sees a vision of the glorified Christ:

> One like a son of man, clothed with a long robe and with a golden sash around his chest. The hairs of his head were white, like white wool, like snow. His eyes were like a flame of fire, his feet were like burnished bronze, refined in a furnace, and his voice was like the roar of many waters. In his right hand he held seven stars, from his mouth came a sharp two-edged sword, and his face was like the sun shining in full strength. (Rev 1:13–16)

What a picture of glory! And as mentioned earlier in this book, this picture is one we need to be reminded of in an age when much emphasis in corporate worship is on being relaxed and informal, and even casual. If the Lord Jesus were to physically appear in our worship service, he would likely not be dressed in blue jeans, but in shining white robes as we see here. And, rather than chumming it up with him, we would fall at his feet, as did John. We would "rejoice *with trembling!*" (Ps 2:11) ↑.

> ↓ To him who loves us and has freed us from our sins by his blood and made us a kingdom, priests to his God and Father,
> ↑ to him be glory and dominion forever and ever. Amen. (Rev 1:5–6)

## Revelation 4

In this chapter John gets to look into the very throne room of God in heaven:

> After this I looked, and behold, a door standing open in heaven! . . . At once I was in the Spirit, and behold, a throne stood in heaven, with One seated on the throne. And he who sat there had the appearance of jasper and carnelian, and around the throne was a rainbow that had the appearance of an emerald. (Rev 4:1–3)

---

2. Allmen, *Worship*, 241. We already saw in ch. 10, as we looked at John 4, that with the coming of Jesus worship is no longer "in this mountain nor in Jerusalem" (4:21), but "in spirit and truth" (4:23–24); and Jesus of course is "the Truth" (John 14:6). The locus of worship is now Jesus Christ, as Allmen says.

John has reached the very limits of human language in trying to describe the wonder of what he sees: God himself on his throne! He also observes what apparently is a group of angelic creatures whom he calls the "twenty-four elders"—

> Around the throne were twenty-four thrones, and seated on the thrones were twenty-four elders, clothed in white garments, with golden crowns on their heads. (Rev 4:4)

—and another set of angelic creatures, which he calls "four living creatures":

> And around the throne, on each side of the throne, are four living creatures, full of eyes in front and behind: the first living creature like a lion, the second living creature like an ox, the third living creature with the face of a man, and the fourth living creature like an eagle in flight. (Rev 4:6–7)

These remarkable creatures are involved in an equally remarkable activity:

> And the four living creatures, each of them with six wings, are full of eyes all around and within, and day and night they never cease to say,
> "Holy, holy, holy, is the Lord God Almighty,
> who was and is and is to come!" (Rev 4:8)

They praise God, who is holy, who is Lord, who is Almighty, who is the Eternal One.

And, as noted earlier: when Isaiah is granted his vision of the throne room of God, we read in Isa 6 that the seraphim called to one another and said:

> Holy, holy, holy is the LORD of hosts;
> the whole earth is full of his glory! (Isa 6:3)

So in Isa 6 angelic creatures are declaring, "Holy, holy, holy"; and in Rev 4 they are *still* declaring, "Holy, holy, holy"—eight hundred years later! The never-ceasing praise of God—eternal praise.

Then we read:

> The twenty-four elders fall down before him who is seated on the throne and *worship* him who lives forever and ever. They cast their crowns before the throne, saying,
> "Worthy are you, our Lord and God,

> to receive glory and honor and power,
> for you created all things,
> and by your will they existed and were created." (Rev 4:10–11)

The angelic beings, as they bow and worship and cast their crowns, speak of God's supreme worthiness; they consider God worthy of "glory and honor and power" because he is the *Creator*. Eternal praise is to be given to God who is holy, who is eternal, who is worthy, who is the Creator. The eternal praise that continually goes on in heaven is built on this recognition of God's supreme worthiness as our holy, eternal Creator God.

## Revelation 5

In Rev 4, we saw eternal praise offered up to God as *Creator*. In Rev 5, God is given eternal praise because he is also the *Redeemer*.

> Then I saw in the right hand of him who was seated on the throne a scroll written within and on the back, sealed with seven seals. And I saw a mighty angel proclaiming with a loud voice, "Who is worthy to open the scroll and break its seals?" (Rev 5:2)

Then Christ is introduced:

> And one of the elders said to me, "Weep no more; behold, the Lion of the tribe of Judah, the Root of David, has conquered, so that he can open the scroll and its seven seals."
> And between the throne and the four living creatures and among the elders I saw a Lamb standing, as though it had been slain. (Rev 5:5–6)

Here we see something of the wonder and mystery of the incarnation: One who is Lion *and* Lamb, who is God *and* human, who died *yet* who is alive forevermore.

Though Jesus in his *humanity* is actively involved in leading us in our worship of the Father (more on that later in ch. 26), as *God* he is of course also worthy of being worshiped, and that is what we see here in Rev 5. He is worthy of *eternal praise* because:

> You were slain, and by your blood you ransomed people for God
> from every tribe and language and people and nation. (Rev 5:9)[3]

---

3. It is important to remember that, while the unfallen angelic host can acknowledge and praise God for Christ's redeeming work, only redeemed humanity can celebrate it as its *beneficiaries* (and can cry, "Salvation belongs to our God . . . and to the Lamb," Rev

The tremendous scene continues:

> Then I looked, and I heard around the throne and the living creatures and the elders the voice of many angels, numbering myriads of myriads and thousands of thousands, saying with a loud voice,
> "Worthy is the Lamb who was slain,
> to receive power and wealth and wisdom and might
> and honor and glory and blessing!"
> And I heard every creature in heaven and on earth and under the earth and in the sea, and all that is in them, saying,
> "To him who sits on the throne and to the Lamb
> be blessing and honor and glory and might forever and ever!
> And the four living creatures said, "Amen!" and the elders fell down and *worshiped.* (Rev 5:11–14)

The Father and the Lamb are worthy of all praise for the great work of redemption.

## Revelation 7

John sees a "great multitude" with a single, unified message: *eternal praise* to God and to the Lamb.

> After this I looked, and behold, a great multitude that no one could number, *from every nation, from all tribes and peoples and languages,* standing before the throne and before the Lamb, clothed in white robes, with palm branches in their hands, and crying out with a loud voice, "Salvation belongs to our God who sits on the throne, and to the Lamb!" (Rev 7:9–10)

What a sight and sound that will be! We can only imagine: a huge mass of humanity, as far as the eye can see, of incredible diversity, yet all unified in lifting their loud praises to God and to the Lamb! To which the angelic host add their exclamations of eternal praise:

> And all the angels were standing around the throne and around the elders and the four living creatures, and they fell on their faces before the throne and *worshiped* God, saying, "Amen! Blessing and glory and wisdom and thanksgiving and honor and power and might be to our God forever and ever! Amen." (Rev 7:11–12).

---

7:10). Salvation is a wonder "into which angels long to look" (1 Pet 1:12) from the outside.

There is:

- A great *multitude* ("that no one could number")
- A great *diversity* ("every nation, all tribes and peoples and languages")
- A great *sound* ("crying with a loud voice")
- A great *salvation* ("Salvation belongs to our God who sits on the throne, and to the Lamb!")
- A great *praise* ("blessing and glory and wisdom and thanksgiving and honor and power and might")
- A great *God* who is praised ("be to our God forever and ever")

Note that the multitude does *not* cry, "We're saved! We're saved!" But rather, they acknowledge that salvation is all of God, and all of grace: "Salvation *belongs* to our God who sits on the throne, and to the Lamb!" True worship will always be *God-centered*, and focus more on *the Giver* than *the gift*.

## Revelation 14

In this climactic book of the Bible, we see the gospel's call to worship go out one more time to all the earth:

> Then I saw another angel flying directly overhead, with an *eternal gospel* to proclaim to those who dwell on earth, to *every nation and tribe and language and people*. And he said with a loud voice, "Fear God and *give him glory*, because the hour of his judgment has come, and *worship him* who *made heaven and earth, the sea and the springs of water*." (Rev 14:6–7)

The call is for all peoples to worship and give glory to the Creator, the only one worthy of worship.

## Revelation 19

This climactic scene is punctuated repeatedly with cries of "Hallelujah!" As we have seen in ch. 17, this Hebrew term is a plural command to *praise God*, and here it is praise for his great work of final judgment, his final consummation of the "marriage of the Lamb," and the irruption of his eternal rule.

After this I heard what seemed to be the loud voice of a great multitude in heaven, crying out,
"Hallelujah!
Salvation and glory and power belong to our God,
    for his judgments are true and just;
    for he has judged the great prostitute
        who corrupted the earth with her immorality,
    and has avenged on her the blood of his servants."
Once more they cried out,
"Hallelujah!
The smoke from her goes up forever and ever."
And the twenty-four elders and the four living creatures fell down and *worshiped* God who was seated on the throne, saying, "Amen. Hallelujah!" And from the throne came a voice saying,
"Praise our God,
    all you his servants,
        you who fear him,
        small and great."
Then I heard what seemed to be the voice of a great multitude, like the roar of many waters and like the sound of mighty peals of thunder, crying out,
"Hallelujah!
For the Lord our God the Almighty reigns.
Let us rejoice and exult
    and give him the glory,
for the marriage of the Lamb has come,
    and his Bride has made herself ready." (Rev 19:1–7)

## Revelation 21–22

And finally, in the new heavens and new earth, we see that the worship of God will be complete:

The throne of God and of the Lamb will be in it, and his servants will worship him. (Rev 22:3)

And the glory of God will fill all in all:

And the city has no need of sun or moon to shine on it, for the glory of God gives it light, and its lamp is the Lamb. (Rev 21:23)

And night will be no more. They will need no light of lamp or sun, for the Lord God will be their light, and they will reign forever and ever. (Rev 22:5)

And, as we saw in ch. 10 of our study, the angel's stern imperative to John (in the last chapter of the Bible) applies to the *entire* narrative of the Bible, to all of humankind and to all of creation:

Worship *God!* (Rev 22:9)

## Ascriptions of Praise to God in Revelation

Created beings, both human and angelic, give praise to God (or are called to do so) with the following terms:

- Glory (1:6; 4:9, 11; 5:12–13; 7:12; 14:7; 19:1, 7)
- Dominion (1:6)
- Honor (4:9, 11; 5:12–13; 7:12)
- Thanks (4:9; 7:12)
- Power (4:11; 5:12; 7:12; 19:1)
- Wealth (5:12)
- Wisdom (5:12)
- Might (5:12–13; 7:12)
- Blessing (5:12–13; 7:12)
- Salvation (7:10; 19:1)

Often they are heaped one upon another (e.g., "Blessing and glory and wisdom and thanksgiving and honor and power and might be to our God forever and ever!" [Rev 7:12]), as if the ascribers are at a loss to find enough descriptors to give God his due.

Indeed, there can never be enough ways to praise our great God!

---

"Worship God!" (Rev 22:9)

---

# 24

## WORSHIP IN THE BOOK OF HEBREWS

T he Letter to the Hebrews (along with Revelation) is really *the worship book of the New Testament*. Similar to what we see with the Psalms in the Old Testament, Hebrews has more to teach us about worship than any other book of the New Testament, as well as more about the past *and present* priestly ministry of Jesus Christ. In fact, the letter is so richly christological that Noel Due has maintained: "If we take Christ out of Hebrews, we are left with *nothing*.[1]

Hebrews was written to Jewish believers who apparently were in danger of going back to Judaism because of persecution for their faith. So the writer goes to great lengths to demonstrate for his readers the superiority of Christ, and the superiority of the new covenant, over anything found under the old covenant. Basically the message to these wavering believers was: "You have *so much more* in Christ. Why would you *ever* go back?"

As we saw in ch. 10 and again in ch. 14, the old-covenant system was one characterized by barriers between the people and God (because of their sin and because of his utter holiness). And we saw how Christ through his atoning death has removed the barrier of sin and opened the way into the very presence of God for every believer. We have that direct access because of the work of Christ—signified by the veil of the temple being "torn in two, from top to bottom" (Matt 27:51; Mark 15:38;

1. Due, *Created for Worship*, 156.

263

Luke 23:45). This access, as we have seen, is one of the uniquely precious aspects of the new covenant:

> Therefore, brethren, since we have *confidence* to enter the holy places by the blood of Jesus, by the new and living way that he opened for us through the curtain, that is, through his flesh, and since we have a great priest over the house of God, let us draw near with a true heart in full *assurance* of faith, with our hearts sprinkled clean from an evil conscience and our bodies washed with pure water. (Heb 10:19–22)

The writer of Hebrews shows us how in Christ and in the new covenant we have a vastly *better way*, a *better Mediator*, and a *better worship*.

## A Better Way

Here is a list of all the things that the writer of Hebrews says are *better* under the *new* covenant, as contrasted to the old. We have a better:

| | |
|---|---|
| 1:2–14 | spokesman for God (the Son) |
| 2:2–3 | message (salvation) |
| 3:3 | rest |
| 4:15 | High Priest (tempted but sinless) |
| 7:7, 15–17 | priestly order (of Melchizedek) |
| 7:19 | hope |
| 7:21 | priesthood (eternal) |
| 7:22 | covenant (better guarantor) |
| 7:27; 9:26 | sacrifice (priest himself) |
| 7:28 | priest (perfect) |
| 8:2; 9:11 | tabernacle |
| 8:6 | ministry (better covenant) |
| 8:6 | covenant (better promises) |
| 8:6 | promises |
| 8:10; 10:16 | law (written on heart, mind) |
| 8:11 | knowledge of Lord |
| 8:19 | access (to holy place) |
| 9:12; 12:24 | blood |
| 9:12 | redemption (eternal) |
| 9:14; 10:22 | cleansing (of conscience) |
| 9:14–15 | inheritance (eternal) |
| 9:23 | sacrifices |
| 9:24 | holy place (in heaven) |
| 9:26; 10:12, 14 | frequency (once for all) |

| 12:22 | mountain/city (Zion) |
| 12:28 | kingdom (cannot be shaken) |
| 13:9 | food (grace) |
| 13:10 | altar (Christ) |

All of these things are *better* because of Christ and his work. And, again, the implication would be for the original readers: *Why would you ever go back?*

## A Better Mediator

All the "better ways" of the new covenant are built on the foundation of that covenant being founded on and by a *better Mediator*: Jesus Christ.

## The Two Natures and Roles of Christ (Heb 1–2)

First of all, in chs. 1 and 2, the writer speaks of the two natures and roles of Jesus Christ.

### *1. Worship of the Son: His Deity and Authority (Heb 1)*

Chapter 1 of Hebrews focuses on Christ's deity, that he should be worshiped because he is God.

#### HIS DEITY

God . . . has spoken to us by his Son, whom he appointed the heir of all things, through whom also he created the world. He is the radiance of the glory of God and the exact imprint of his nature, and he upholds the universe by the word of his power. . . ."Let all God's angels *worship* him." (Heb 1:1–3, 6)

#### HIS AUTHORITY

Of the Son he says,
"Your throne, O God, is forever and ever,
the scepter of uprightness is the scepter of your
kingdom. . . .
You are the same,
and your years will have no end. . . .

> And to which of the angels has he ever said,
> "Sit at my right hand
> until I make your enemies a footstool for your feet"?
> (Heb 1:8, 12–13)

## 2. Worship by the Son: His Humanity and Priesthood (Heb 2)

Hebrews 2 reminds us of the remarkable fact that while as God Jesus *receives* worship, as a human he also *gives* worship.

### His Humanity

> "You made him for a little while lower than the angels. . . ." For he who sanctifies and those who are sanctified all have one origin. That is why he is not ashamed to call them brethren. (Heb 2:7, 11)

Christ's complete identification with us in his genuine humanity qualifies him to be a priest to offer himself as our substitute and sacrifice, but also to serve as our representative and priest before the Father in worship. (Much more about this later in ch. 26 of this book.)

### His Priesthood

> "In the midst of the congregation I will sing your praise." . . . He had to be made like his brethren in every respect, so that he might become a merciful and faithful high priest in the service of God, to make propitiation for the sins of the people. (Heb 2:12b, 17)

### His Dual Role

These two roles of Christ seen in ch. 1 (as God's spokesman/revealer; cf. "I will tell of your name to my brethren" [Heb 2:12a]) and in ch. 2 (as our priest, making propitiation and leading our worship) are in fact summarized in 3:1:

> Therefore, holy brethren, you who share in a heavenly calling, consider Jesus, the *apostle* and *high priest* of our confession.

As God, Jesus perfectly communicates God's purpose and message (which is what an *apostle* does; he is one who is literally "sent" to do this);

as a human, he is our *High Priest*, offering a propitiating sacrifice on our behalf and leading us to the Father in worship.

> As Apostle, Christ bears witness for God, that he is Holy. As High Priest he acknowledges that witness and says Amen to it. Again as Apostle of God he confesses the mercy and grace of God, his will to pardon and reconcile. As High Priest he intercedes for men, and confesses them before the face of God.[2]

In this way we see our pattern of revelation and response displayed and fulfilled in the person and work of Jesus Christ himself:

**Apostle**  **High Priest**

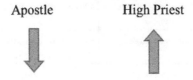

## The Superior Priesthood of Christ (Heb 5–10)

### *Contrasting Two Priesthoods*

The writer of Hebrews contrasts the old-covenant priesthood (the Levitical priesthood or order of Aaron) with the new-covenant priesthood of Christ (in the so-called order of Melchizedek), showing the obvious superiority of the latter in every way:

---

2. T. Torrance, *Royal Priesthood*, 12.

| Levitical Priesthood/Order of Aaron | Priesthood of Christ/Order of Melchizedek |
|---|---|
| Descended from Levi, Aaron (7:5, 11) | Descended from Judah (7:14) |
| Sinful (5:3; 7:27) | "Holy, innocent, unstained, separated from sinners" (7:26) |
| Weak (5:2; 7:28) | Perfect (5:9; 7:28; 10:14) |
| Many, because mortal/temporary (7:2) | One, permanent priesthood (lives forever) (7:24) |
| Could purify only the flesh (9:13) | Can purify the conscience (9:14) |
| Had to offer for own sins (5:3; 7:27; 9:7) | Sinless (7:26) |
| Had to offer same sacrifices repeatedly (5:1; 7:27; 9:25; 10:1, 3, 11) | One sacrifice (7:27; 9:12, 26, 28; 10:10, 12, 14) |
| Offered blood of animals (9:18–22; 10:4) | Offered himself, own blood (7:27; 9:12, 25–26); "better sacrifices" (9:23) |
| Offerings could not make perfect or perfect the conscience (5:9; 7:11, 18; 9:9; 10:1) | Can purify conscience (9:14), perfect those sanctified (10:14) |
| Served shadow tent/tabernacle (8:5; 9:23–24) | Serves true tabernacle (8:2; 9:11, 23–24) |
| Could not take away sins (10:11) | Redeems from sins committed under old covenant (9:15); grants eternal redemption (9:12); saves forever (7:25) |
| Served an imperfect covenant (8:7) | "Guarantor of a better covenant" (7:22; 8:6) |
| Inferior ministry based on inferior promises (8:6) | Better ministry based on better promises (8:6) |

### Christ like Melchizedek

Along with contrasts with the old-covenant priesthood, the writer notes similarities between Christ and the shadowy priest, briefly mentioned in Genesis, named Melchizedek:

> And Melchizedek king of Salem brought out bread and wine. (He was priest of God Most High.) And he blessed him [Abram] and said,
> > "Blessed be Abram by God Most High,
> > Possessor of heaven and earth;
> > and blessed be God Most High,

who has delivered your enemies into your hand!"
And Abram gave him a tenth of everything. (Gen 14:18–20)

It is God who first draws this comparison when he says in Ps 110:4 to the Son:

> The LORD has sworn
>> and will not change his mind,
>>> "You are a priest forever
>>>> after the order of Melchizedek."

This passage is quoted in Heb 5:6; 7:17; and 7:21; and referenced in 5:10; 6:20; and 7:11.

Parallels between Melchizedek and Christ are found in Scripture, including in Hebrews:

- *King of righteousness*: "[Melchizedek] is first, by translation of his name, *king of righteousness*" (Heb 7:2).
  [Jesus]: "By his knowledge shall *the righteous one*, my servant, make many to be accounted righteous, and he shall bear their iniquities" (Isa 53:11).

- *King of peace*: "And then [Melchizedek] is also king of Salem, that is, *king of peace*" (Heb 7:2).
  "[Jesus) himself is our *peace*" (Eph 2:14).

- *Priest forever*: "[Melchizedek] is without father or mother or genealogy, having neither beginning of days nor end of life, but resembling the Son of God he continues a *priest forever*" (Heb 7:3).
  This enigmatic statement has given interpreters fits. The writer is commenting about how little we know about the life of Melchizedek (so little, in fact, that it is all the more remarkable that Hebrews makes so much of him!). But the main emphasis is that Melchizedek's priesthood, like Jesus's, does not come through the Levitical line; undoubtedly he was appointed to his priesthood by God, as was Jesus to his priesthood (5:5). Melchizedek's priesthood *precedes* the Levitical priesthood (7:10), and the writer demonstrates that it is greater (7:4, 6–7, 9–10); so too Jesus's priesthood is greater than the Levitical priesthood (and in fact supersedes it).

- *Descent*: "But this man [Melchizedek] who does not have his *descent* from [Levi]" (Heb 7:6).

"For it is evident that our Lord was descended from Judah, and in connection with that tribe Moses said nothing about priests" (Heb 7:14).

- *King* and *priest*: Both Melchizedek and Jesus are king *and* priest.

There is one more amazing way that Melchizedek is like Jesus, as we can see in the Genesis passage where he appears:

> ↓ Melchizedek *blesses Abraham on behalf of God*: "And he [Melchizedek] blessed him [Abraham] and said, 'Blessed be Abram by God Most High, Possessor of heaven and earth.'" (Gen 14:19)

*and*

> ↑ Melchizedek *blesses God on behalf of Abraham*: "'And blessed be God Most High, who has delivered your enemies into your hand!'" (Gen 14:20)

Melchizedek is the mediator, the agent, of God's blessing on Abraham. *And* he is the mediator, the agent, of Abraham's blessing of God.[3]

This prefigures in a remarkable way *the dual mediating role of Christ*:

> As *God*, he will mediate *between God and humans*; ↓
> and as a *human*, he will mediate *between humans and God*. ↑

And in so doing, Jesus will be fulfilling *at the deepest* level the revelation and response pattern of Scripture! We will look more closely into these incredible truths, and the implications for our worship, in ch. 26.

### Christ Entering the Heavenly Tabernacle as Priest

> Christ . . . entered through the greater and more perfect tabernacle, not made with hands, that is to say, not of this creation; and not through the blood of goats and calves, but through his own blood. (Heb 9:11–12)

---

3. Noted in Willson, "Receiving Jesus as Priest."

### Christ's Ongoing Ministry in the Heavenly Tabernacle as Priest (His Session and Ongoing Ministry)

We have such a high priest, who has taken his seat at the right hand of the throne of the Majesty in the heavens, a minister in the sanctuary and in the true tabernacle. (Heb 8:1–2)

Let us then with confidence draw near to the throne of grace, that we may receive mercy and find grace to help in time of need. (Heb 4:16)

He always lives to make intercession for them. (Heb 7:25)

Who is to condemn? Christ Jesus is the one who died—more than that, who was raised—who is at the right hand of God, who indeed is interceding for us. (Rom 8:34)

### Summary: A Better Priesthood

And every priest stands daily at his service, offering repeatedly the same sacrifices, which can *never* take away sins.

But when Christ had offered for *all* time a *single* sacrifice for sins, he sat down at the right hand of God. . . . For by a *single offering* he has perfected for *all* time those who are being sancti-fied. (Heb 10:11–14)

The former priests were many in number, because they were prevented by death from continuing in office, but he holds his priesthood *permanently*, because he continues forever.

*Consequently*, he is able to save *forever* those who draw near to God through him, since he always lives to make intercession for them. (Heb 7:23–25)

This last statement tells us that Jesus's ongoing intercessory ministry on our behalf guarantees our eternal salvation!

## A Better Worship

Hebrews 10:19–22 begins the final, applicational section of the letter; and this passage itself summarizes important themes as it builds on what has gone before.

*Therefore*, brethren, since we have confidence to enter the holy places by the blood of Jesus, by the new and living way that he opened for us through the curtain, that is, through his flesh, and since we have a great priest over the house of God, let us draw near with a true heart in full assurance of faith, with our hearts sprinkled clean from an evil conscience and our bodies washed with pure water.

## *"Therefore"*

This word shows that the author is turning now to the practical implications of what has gone before concerning the superiority of Christ and his priesthood and of the new covenant as a whole.

## *"Let us draw near* with a true heart in full assurance of faith"

The supreme distinctive and benefit of the new covenant is found in these words: the *access* that every believer has into the very presence of God through the work (past *and* present, as we shall see) of Christ.[4]

This concept of "drawing near" comes from the worship of the Old Testament (and the Greek word used here, *proserchomai*, is the same used in the Greek translation of the Old Testament, the Septuagint), though actually only the priests (and, ultimately, the high priest) could really "draw near" to God. The people could approach only as far as the courtyard outside the curtains enclosing the holy place of the tabernacle (and earlier, only as far as the base of Mount Sinai [Deut 4:11; see Heb 10:1; 12:18]).

Other New Testament uses of this Greek word with the same sense (marked with italics) include:

> Let us then with confidence *draw near* to the throne of grace, that we may receive mercy and find grace to help in time of need. (Heb 4:16)

---

4. Scott Aniol points out: "This idea of drawing near is an important focus of the book of Hebrews, evident by its presence in the three major climaxes of the book. Here in chapter 10:22 we find the second of these climaxes. The first is found in 4:16, which says, 'Let us then with confidence draw near to the throne of grace, that we may receive mercy and find grace to help in time of need.' And the final climax of the book is 12:22, which says, 'but you have come to Mount Zion and to the city of the living God, the heavenly Jerusalem, and to innumerable angels in festal gathering,' and that phrase 'you have come' is a translation of the same Greek term translated 'draw near' in Hebrews 10:22" (*Draw Near*, 2).

But on the other hand, a better hope is introduced, through which we *draw near* to God. (Heb 7:19)

Consequently, he is able to save to the uttermost those who *draw near* to God through him, since he always lives to make intercession for them. (Heb 7:25)

And without faith it is impossible to please him, for whoever would *draw near* to God must believe that he exists and that he rewards those who seek him. (Heb 11:6)

For you have not *come* to what may be touched, a blazing fire and darkness and gloom and a tempest. . . . But you have *come* to Mount Zion and to the city of the living God, the heavenly Jerusalem, and to innumerable angels in festal gathering. (Heb 12:18–22)

*Draw near* to God, and he will draw near to you. Cleanse your hands, you sinners, and purify your hearts, you double-minded. (Jas 4:8)

As you *come* to him, a living stone rejected by men but in the sight of God chosen and precious . . . (1 Pet 2:4)

And the following verses similarly speak of the freedom of access we have into the presence of God:

Through him we have also obtained *access* by faith into this grace in which we stand, and we rejoice in hope of the glory of God. (Rom 5:2)

For through him we both have *access* in one Spirit to the Father. (Eph 2:18)

This was according to the eternal purpose that he has realized in Christ Jesus our Lord, in whom we have boldness and *access* with confidence through our faith in him. (Eph 3:11–12)

Our access, our invitation to draw near, is possible because of *both* the *past* work of Christ ("since we have confidence to enter the holy place by the blood of Jesus" [Heb 10:19]) *and* the *present* work of Christ ("and since we have a great priest over the house of God" [10:21]).

### His Past Work

There are, of course, many references in Hebrews to the past, completed priestly work of redemption accomplished for us by the Lord Jesus through his atoning death on the cross. See Heb 1:3; 2:9–10; 3:1; 5:7–8; 7:26–27; 9:11–14, 23, 26; 10:10, 12–14, 19–20; 12:2, 24; 13:12, 20.

## His Present Work

But, remarkably, the book of Hebrews tells us more about the *present, continuing* priestly ministry of Christ than any other book in the New Testament. As our living high priest:

1. *He leads our worship* (2:12; 3:1; 8:1–2, 6; 10:21; 13:15; more on this later in ch. 26).

2. *He intercedes for us and comes to our aid*:

> For because he himself has suffered when tempted, he is able to *help* those who are being tempted. (Heb 2:18)

> Since then we *have a great high priest* who has passed through the heavens, Jesus, the Son of God, let us hold fast our confession. For *we do not have a high priest who is unable to sympathize with our weaknesses*, but one who in every respect has been tempted as we are, yet without sin. Let us then with confidence draw near to the throne of grace, that we may *receive mercy and find grace* to help in time of need. (Heb 4:14–16)

> Consequently, he is able to save to the uttermost those who draw near to God through him, since he always lives *to make intercession for them*. (Heb 7:25)

> For Christ has entered, not into holy places made with hands, which are copies of the true things, but into heaven itself, now *to appear in the presence of God on our behalf*. (Heb 9:24)

> Who is to condemn? Christ Jesus is the one who died—more than that, who was raised—who is at the right hand of God, who indeed *is interceding for us*. (Rom 8:34)

3. *He guarantees our eternal salvation*:

> Consequently, he is able to save to the uttermost [*or*: forever] those who draw near to God through him, since he always lives to make intercession for them. (Heb 7:25)

"Therefore, *brethren*, since *we* have confidence . . . and since *we* have a great priest . . . let *us* draw near." (Heb 10:19, 21–22)

Together we have been called, and together we are members of one another and of his body:

> For he who sanctifies and those who are sanctified all have one source. That is why *he is not ashamed to call them brethren.* (Heb 2:11)

> "Behold, I and the children God has given me." (Heb 2:13b)

> Therefore *he had to be made like his brethren in every respect,* so that he might become a merciful and faithful high priest. (Heb 2:17)

> Therefore, holy *brethren,* you who *share in a heavenly calling,* consider Jesus, the apostle and high priest of *our confession.* (Heb 3:1)

> Take care, *brethren,* lest there be in any of you an evil, unbelieving heart, leading you to fall away from the living God. (Heb 3:12)

> I appeal to you, *brethren,* bear with my word of exhortation, for I have written to you briefly. (Heb 13:22)

Indeed, the invitation is "let *us* draw near"; while every believer has individual access to God in worship and prayer and fellowship, yet the immediate context of 10:19–25 seems to focus on the corporate gathering:

> And let us consider how to *stir up one another* to love and good works, *not neglecting to meet together,* as is the habit of some, but *encouraging one another,* and all the more as you see the Day drawing near. (Heb 10:24–25)

"Therefore, brethren, since we have *confidence* to enter the holy places . . . let us draw near . . . in full *assurance* of faith." (Heb 10:19–22)

We can draw near freely and without fear because of the gracious saving work of Christ.

> Let us then with *confidence* draw near to the throne of grace. (Heb 4:16)

This was according to the eternal purpose that he has realized in Christ Jesus our Lord, in whom we have *boldness* and access with *confidence* through our faith in him. (Eph 3:11)

In a next-to-last major contrast between the two covenants (the last one comes in 13:9–14), the writer shows the difference between the Israelites' fearful approach to Mount Sinai and our confident and joyful approach to Mount Zion and the presence of God:

For you have *not* come to what may be touched, a blazing fire and darkness and gloom and a tempest and the sound of a trumpet and a voice whose words made the hearers beg that no further messages be spoken to them. (Heb 12:18)

*But* you have come to *Mount Zion* and to the city of the living God, the heavenly Jerusalem, and to innumerable angels in festal gathering, and to the assembly of the firstborn who are enrolled in heaven, and to God, the judge of all, and to the spirits of the righteous made perfect. (Heb 12:22–23)

## Gratitude and Praise

Such confident, abundant access should elicit responses of thankfulness and reverent worship:

Therefore let us be *grateful* for receiving a kingdom that cannot be shaken, and thus let us offer to God *acceptable worship*, with *reverence* and *awe*. (Heb 12:28)

Through him then let us continually offer up *a sacrifice of praise* to God, that is, the fruit of lips that acknowledge his name. (Heb 13:15)

## Conclusion

The writer brings his entire argument into focus in the last chapter of the letter:

Through him [Christ] then let us continually offer up a sacrifice of praise to God, that is, the fruit of lips that acknowledge his name. (Heb 13:15)

The intense *Christ-centeredness* of the book comes to a head here. *In Christ* we have life. *With Christ* we can boldly approach the Father. *Through Christ* we offer our worship.

This truth of our entry through Christ—which is of course central to Christianity—has been highlighted and expounded elsewhere throughout Hebrews, as well in many other parts of the New Testament:

> *Through him* we have also obtained access by faith into this grace in which we stand, and we rejoice in hope of the glory of God. (Rom 5:2)

> No, in all these things we are more than conquerors *through him* who loved us. (Rom 8:37)

> For all the promises of God find their Yes in him. That is why it is *through him* that we utter our Amen to God for his glory. (2 Cor 1:20)

> For *through him* we both have access in one Spirit to the Father. (Eph 2:18)

> I can do all things *through him* who strengthens me. (Phil 4:13)

> And whatever you do, in word or deed, do everything in the name of the Lord Jesus, giving thanks to God the Father *through him*. (Col 3:17)

> You who *through him* are believers in God, who raised him from the dead and gave him glory, so that your faith and hope are in God. (1 Pet 1:20–21)

> In this the love of God was made manifest among us, that God sent his only Son into the world, so that we might live *through him*. (1 John 4:9)

*"Let us draw near": through Christ, in Christ, with Christ.*

---

"Let us draw near in full assurance of faith." (Heb 10:22)

# 25

## THE HOLY SPIRIT AND WORSHIP

### A Beautiful Role

When the Spirit of truth comes, he will guide you into all the truth, for he will not speak on his own authority, but whatever he hears he will speak, and he will declare to you the things that are to come. *He will glorify me*, for he will take what is mine and declare it to you. (John 16:13–14)

The remarkable thing about the ministry of the Holy Spirit is that he is always seeking to point us to Jesus Christ and not to himself. The members of the Trinity—Father, Son, and Holy Spirit—are all equally God and equally glorious. Yet, remarkably, the different members of the Trinity *voluntarily* perform different *roles:*[1] The Father sends the Son (a major theme in the Gospel of John: 4:34; 5:24, 36–38; 6:29; 7:16; etc.); the Son obeys the Father (John 4:34); and the Spirit, as we see here, glorifies Christ (John 16:14).

It is beautiful that the members of the Trinity are so eternally secure in their relationship with one another that there is *never* any sense of competition or of one claiming superiority over the other. They willingly perform their different roles in order to fulfill the purposes of their one, unified divine will. So the Father gives his only begotten Son (John 3:16);

---

1. This truth is reflected to a certain extent in Christian marriage: husband and wife are both *equal* before God spiritually, but perform different *roles.*

Jesus is willing to submit to the Father (Luke 22:42) and to become human and to die (Phil 2:6–8); and the Spirit points always to Christ.

Scripture (which the Spirit himself inspires: Acts 1:16; 28:25; 1 Cor 2:10) does not tell us as much about the Holy Spirit as it does about the Father and the Son; but that is in keeping with the Spirit's own priority to point to Christ and to glorify the person and reputation of Christ, instead of drawing attention to himself. In fact, theologians have sometimes referred to the Spirit as "the shy member of the Trinity," exactly because of this self-effacing aspect of his ministry. His work is usually unseen and therefore somewhat mysterious, and often understood only in retrospect.

J. I. Packer highlights this beautiful aspect of the Spirit's work:

> Think of it this way. It is as if the Spirit stands behind us, throwing light over our shoulder, on Jesus, who stands facing us. The Spirit's message is never, "Look at me; listen to me; come to me; get to know me," but always, "Look at *him*, and see his glory; listen to *him*, and hear his word; go to *him*, and have life; get to know *him*, and taste his gift of joy and peace." The Spirit, we might say, is the matchmaker, the celestial marriage broker, whose role it is to bring us and Christ together and ensure that we stay together.[2]

The question is often asked whether it is appropriate to worship the Holy Spirit. Indeed, the New Testament *never* speaks of the Holy Spirit being *worshiped*, only the Father and the Son, even though the Spirit is equally God and equally glorious. The primary pattern of worship in the New Testament is that of worshiping the Father through the Son in the power of the Holy Spirit.[3] But because the Spirit is also God, it is certainly not wrong to offer him worship and praise; but while there are very few hymns and contemporary songs focusing on the Spirit solely, there are at least more where each member of the Trinity is honored in successive verses. Of course the Holy Spirit generally receives more attention in worship on Pentecost Sunday; and the Sunday after Pentecost is celebrated in liturgical churches as Trinity Sunday. Yet an ongoing focus on worship of the Spirit would seem to be excessive and not in line with the biblical pattern (or with the Spirit's wishes!). In fact, it could be said that

---

2. Packer, *Keep in Step*, 66.

3. Worship of the Son (the Lamb) becomes more prevalent in the book of Revelation, but even there the Holy Spirit is not included: "*To him who sits on the throne and to the Lamb* be blessing and honor and glory and might forever and ever!" (Rev 5:13; see also 7:10).

the clearest sign that the Holy Spirit is vibrantly at work in a church is *not* where the Spirit is the main focus of what is said or sung, but rather where *the person and work of Christ is being exalted* (in line with the Spirit's own priority).[4]

## Glorifying Christ

It has been observed that we never see the Holy Spirit in the New Testament apart from being intimately connected with Christ and his work: "There is no separate activity of the Holy Spirit in revelation or salvation in addition to or independent of the activity of Christ."[5]

How does the Holy Spirit glorify Christ?

## 1. The Holy Spirit glorifies Christ by acting throughout Christ's earthly ministry.

### The Spirit and Christ's Conception

> And the angel answered her, *"The Holy Spirit will come upon you*, and the power of the Most High will overshadow you; therefore the child to be born will be called holy—the Son of God." (Luke 1:35)[6]

### The Spirit and Christ's Baptism

> When Jesus also had been baptized and was praying, the heavens were opened, and *the Holy Spirit descended* on him in bodily form, like a dove. (Luke 3:21–22; see also John 1:32–33)

4. Indeed, I have a friend who used to be the worship pastor at a very charismatic church. But the pastor had written two books, *not* on the Holy Spirit but on *the cross of Christ*!

5. T. Torrance, *Christian Doctrine*, 196.

6. The Holy Spirit shows up throughout the nativity narratives of Luke 1–2, also working in Elizabeth (1:41), Zechariah (1:67), Simeon (2:25–27), and (prophetically) John the Baptist (1:15). Sadly, "The Holy Spirit is the forgotten participant in the Christmas drama. This omission is seen not only in the Christmas card selection at Hallmark, but also in music for the season. There are dozens of shepherd carols, magi carols, angel carols, and Mary and Joseph carols, but precious few that acknowledge the work of the Spirit" (Witvliet, "Singing Our Prayers").

### The Spirit and Christ's Temptations

And Jesus, *full of the Holy Spirit*, returned from the Jordan and was *led by the Spirit* in the wilderness for forty days, being tempted by the devil. (Luke 4:1–2)

### The Spirit and Christ's Ministry

But if it is *by the Spirit of God* that I cast out demons, then the kingdom of God has come upon you. (Matt 12:28)

*The Spirit of the Lord is upon me*, because he has anointed me to proclaim good news to the poor. (Luke 4:18)

In that same hour he *rejoiced in the Holy Spirit* and said, "I thank you, Father, Lord of heaven and earth, that you have hidden these things from the wise and understanding and revealed them to little children." (Luke 10:31)

God anointed Jesus of Nazareth *with the Holy Spirit* and with power. He went about doing good and healing all who were oppressed by the devil, for God was with him. (Acts 10:38)

### The Spirit and Christ's Death

How much more will the blood of Christ, who *through the eternal Spirit* offered himself without blemish to God, purify our conscience from dead works to serve the living God. (Heb 9:14)

### The Spirit and Christ's Resurrection

If *the Spirit of him who raised Jesus from the dead* dwells in you, he who raised Christ Jesus from the dead will also give life to your mortal bodies through his Spirit who dwells in you. (Rom 8:11)

## 2. The Holy Spirit glorifies Christ by continuing Christ's earthly ministry.

Jesus promises to send *another* Helper who in many ways will continue Christ's work, now through his church.

And I will ask the Father, and he will give you *another Helper*, to be with you forever. (John 14:16)

> But *the Helper, the Holy Spirit,* whom the Father will send in my name, he will *teach you* all things and *bring to your remembrance* all that I have said to you. (John 14:26)

> But when *the Helper* comes, whom I will send to you from the Father, *the Spirit of truth,* who proceeds from the Father, he will *bear witness about me.* (John 15:26)

> When the Spirit of truth comes, he will guide you into all the truth, for he will not speak on his own authority, but whatever he hears he will speak, and he will declare to you the things that are to come. He will glorify me, for *he will take what is mine and declare it to you.* (John 16:13–14)

> In the first book, O Theophilus, I have dealt with all that Jesus began to do and teach, until the day when he was taken up, after he had given commands *through the Holy Spirit* to the apostles whom he had chosen. (Acts 1:1)

The clear implication of Acts 1:1 is that Luke intends in his second volume to relate what Jesus will *continue* "to do and teach," only now through the Holy Spirit and his appointed apostles. (More on this in ch. 26). In fact, the giving of the Holy Spirit on the day of Pentecost (Acts 2) is what sets the church in motion, enabling and empowering the "greater works" that Jesus predicted (John 14:12). (Some have suggested therefore that a more appropriate name for the book might be the "Acts of the Holy Spirit.")[7]

### 3. The Holy Spirit glorifies Christ by bringing us to faith in Christ.

It is the Holy Spirit that draws us and brings us into a saving relationship with Christ.

> And when [the Spirit] comes, he will *convict the world* concerning sin and righteousness and judgment. (John 16:8)

> Jesus answered, "Truly, truly, I say to you, unless one is born of water *and the Spirit,* he cannot enter the kingdom of God." (John 3:5)

> But when the goodness and loving kindness of God our Savior appeared, he saved us, not because of works done by us in

---

7. "The fulfillment and realization of the work of the incarnate Son is effected by the coming and indwelling of the Holy Spirit" (T. Torrance, *School of Faith,* civ).

righteousness, but according to his own mercy, *by the washing of regeneration and renewal of the Holy Spirit.* (Titus 3:4–5)

## 4. The Holy Spirit glorifies Christ by giving us assurance of our relationship to God in Christ.

The Spirit works in our hearts to give us confidence in our salvation.

> For you did not receive the spirit of slavery to fall back into fear, but you have received *the Spirit of adoption as sons*, by whom we cry, "Abba! Father!" (Rom 8:15)

> And because you are sons, God has sent the *Spirit* of his Son into our hearts, crying, "Abba! Father!" (Gal 4:6)

## 5. The Holy Spirit glorifies Christ by motivating and empowering our worship of the Father through Christ.

Now we come to the significance of the Holy Spirit for our worship.

> For we are the circumcision, who worship *by the Spirit of God* and glory in Christ Jesus and put no confidence in the flesh. (Phil 3:3)

> And do not get drunk with wine, for that is debauchery, but *be filled with the Spirit*, addressing one another in psalms and hymns and spiritual songs, singing and making melody to the Lord with your heart. (Eph 5:18–19)

One way to understand this is to see the Spirit as the connective tissue between the revelation and response poles of the biblical pattern of worship we have seen throughout this book:

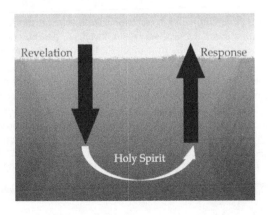

It is the role of the Holy Spirit to take the ↓ revelation of God from our *minds* into *our* hearts and to draw forth our ↑ response.[8]

He does that in bringing us to salvation: we hear the gospel, the truth about the gospel, who God is, who Christ is, what he's done for us. And then the Holy Spirit takes that information (which, after all, people can hear and *not* respond to) into our hearts and makes it real and precious to us and draws us into the response of saving faith.

And in our Christian life, the Spirit takes the truth of God again from our head into our heart. As we learn truths about God, the Holy Spirit brings understanding:

> Now we have received not the spirit of the world, but the Spirit who is from God, that we might *understand* the things freely given us by God. (1 Cor 2:12)

And then he draws forth our response of praise and worship and thanksgiving and honoring of God.

The Spirit takes the *objective* truth about God in Christ and makes it *subjectively* precious to us: objective revelation, subjective response.[9] In this sense, Christ is the *Way* to the Father, but the Holy Spirit is the *Guide*.

Crucially, we can say that we *can* come to the Father because of the ministry of Christ, but we *want* to come to the Father in worship because of the ministry of the Holy Spirit!

The Spirit works to cause us to "be filled with the Spirit, addressing one another in psalms and hymns and spiritual songs" (Eph 5:18–19) so that we can be "teaching and admonishing one another in all wisdom, singing psalms and hymns and spiritual songs" (Col 3:16). The Spirit energizes our corporate praise that we might spur one another on to "grow up in every way into him who is the head, into Christ" (Eph 4:15), as we

---

8. "Worship, as Philip Butin puts it, is a 'trinitarian enactment' in which 'the initiatory 'downward' movement of Christian worship begins in the Father's gracious and free revelation of the divine nature to the church through the Son, by means of the Spirit. . . . The 'upward' movement of human response in worship . . . is also fundamentally motivated by God. Human response—'the sacrifice of praise and thanksgiving'—arises from the faith that has its source in the indwelling Holy Spirit" (Witvliet, *Worship Seeking Understanding*, 146; quoting Butin, *Revelation, Redemption, and Response*, 102). Sinclair Ferguson sees it this way: "The call of God is the proclamation of the gospel of Jesus Christ . . . which is so empowered by the Holy Spirit that it enables or effects the bonding of faith to which the calling of the gospel itself summons us" (*Doctrine of the Holy Spirit*, part 12).

9. "The Holy Spirit subjectively actualizes in us Christ's objective work for us" (Eugenio, *Communion*, 136).

allow "the word of Christ to dwell in [us] richly" (Col 3:16). "When a congregation verbalizes truth in song, the Holy Spirit unleashes the double-edged sword of Scripture in our midst. And the word (sung, prayed, read, and preached) develops the fruit of Christlikeness."[10]

## 6. The Holy Spirit glorifies Christ by producing growth in Christlikeness in us individually and as a church, and giving gifts for the building up of the body.

It is significant to note that the Bible *never* says we're to grow in *Spirit-likeness*. It says we are to grow in *Christlikeness*. And that again is the result of the behind-the-scenes ministry of the Holy Spirit. We often are not consciously aware of the Spirit working in our hearts and lives until we look back and see the fruit that has come because the Holy Spirit has worked quietly within us—showing us Christ and molding us to become more like him.

> If we live by the Spirit, let us also keep in step with [*or*: walk by] the Spirit. (Gal 5:25)

> And we all, with unveiled face, beholding the glory of the Lord, are being transformed into the same image from one degree of glory to another. For this comes from the Lord who is the Spirit. (2 Cor 3:18)

> In him you also are being built together into a dwelling place for God by the Spirit. (Eph 2:22)

> To each is given the manifestation of the Spirit for the common good. (1 Cor 12:7)

Through the Spirit's work, the "have to" of the old covenant becomes the "want to" of the new covenant!

> The law of the Spirit of life has set you free in Christ Jesus from the law of sin and death. For God has done what the law, weakened by the flesh, could not do. By sending his own Son in the likeness of sinful flesh and for sin, he condemned sin in the flesh, in order that the righteous requirement of the law might be fulfilled in us, who walk not according to the flesh but according to the Spirit. (Rom 8:2–4)[11]

---

10. Merker, *Corporate Worship*, ch. 7 (unpaginated ed.).

11. N. T. Wright: In Rom 7, "Paul looks back on his pre-conversion life, and does

## Conclusion

And so we see through all of this *the utter Christ-centeredness of all the Spirit's work*: always pointing us to Christ, wooing us to Christ, rooting us in Christ, growing us in Christ, drawing forth our worship in and through Christ. No wonder Paul and Peter both refer to the third person of the Trinity as "the Spirit *of Christ*" (Rom 8:9; 1 Pet 1:11).

---

The utter Christ-centeredness of all the Spirit's ministry.

---

not suggest that it was misguided, that Torah was not after all worthy of his love and delight. The problem was not with the law, but with the 'self' that was, despite God's call and gift to Israel, nevertheless still in Adam. Unredeemed Torah-worship, Paul is arguing, was proper God-directed worship, but it failed to be lifegiving as it might have been, not because there was anything wrong with Torah but because 'I', the Jew, was still 'in the flesh', part of the solidarity of the old Adam which could not but bring death. The Torah formed, as we have noted, the centre of worship in the synagogue, the direct means of God's living presence with his people. . . . This theme of worship—rightly directed but frustratingly thwarted—then spills over into the dramatic statement of 8:1–11. God has done what the law could not do, acting through the death of his Son to deal with the long and law-enhanced build-up of sin and acting through the Spirit to give the life which the law had longed to give but could not because of the raw material on which it was working. Just as the note of worship in chapter 7 often goes unnoticed, so the note of the Torah's fulfilment often goes unnoticed in 8:5–8: the mind of the flesh is hostile to God's law, cannot submit to it, and cannot please God, but (by clear and strong implication) the mind of the Spirit does submit to God's law, and can and does please him (again, compare 12:1–2). The Spirit thus enables those in Christ to offer God the worship which Torah wanted to evoke, the reality of which synagogue-worship was a frustrated foretaste" ("Worship and the Spirit").

# 26

# JESUS CHRIST AND WORSHIP

With this subject we reach the most profound depths (and heights!) of worship. We will examine some truly transformative truths about the spiritual dynamics of worship.

We begin by considering: What makes worship in the church *good*? Is it the right song or song set? Or the right anointed worship leader? Or the right group of talented musicians? Or the right amount of sincerity?

We are going to see that it is none of those things. In fact, this section should lead us to *repent of the sin of trying to do worship in our own strength*. We simply cannot reach a standard that makes our worship wholly acceptable and pleasing to God—not through our own efforts, however diligent or committed or talented we may be. We need, and have, *Christ's enablement* to make our worship acceptable and pleasing to God.

## How God Works

### Coming Alongside

In Gal 3:3 Paul poses to his readers a *rhetorical question* (one that does not need an answer, because the answer is, or should be, obvious; the person asking such a question is not doing so to get information, but rather to *emphasize a point*). Paul asks:

> Are you so foolish? Having begun by the Spirit, are you now being perfected by the flesh? (Gal 3:3)

The obvious answer is: having begun by the Spirit, *of course* the Galatians are not now being perfected by the flesh! In fact, Paul says it would be "foolish" for them to think that. Later in the same letter he emphasizes:

> If we live by the Spirit, let us also keep in step with [*or*: walk by] the Spirit. (Gal 5:25)

Paul is highlighting an important principle of the Christian faith: God commits himself to complete the good work he has begun in us (Phil 1:6). The Holy Spirit comes alongside to work in us and with us in the process of living the Christian life. This is a crucial distinctive of New Testament Christianity: we are not left alone to progress and grow in the faith in our own strength. This is an emphasis found throughout the Epistles of the New Testament.

Many examples could be given to show what a common (and important) theme this is; here are just a few:

> Likewise the Spirit helps us in our weakness. For we do not know what to pray for as we ought, but the Spirit himself intercedes for us with groanings too deep for words. (Rom 8:26)

We do not even know how to pray sometimes, but at those times the Spirit will come alongside and help us.

> Therefore, my beloved, as you have always obeyed, so now, not only as in my presence but much more in my absence, work out your own salvation with fear and trembling, for it is God who works in you, both to will and to work for his good pleasure. (Phil 2:12–13)

Verse 12 sounds like our growth is up to us ("work out your own salvation"); but then Paul immediately turns and points to God's work within us ("for it is God who works in you").

> But by the grace of God I am what I am, and his grace toward me was not in vain. On the contrary, I worked harder than any of them, though it was not I, but the grace of God that is with me. (1 Cor 15:10)

Paul gives credit to the grace of God for who he is and what he does; even as hard as he worked, he acknowledges the enabling grace of God as propelling his efforts.

> For this I toil, struggling with all his energy that he powerfully works within me. (Col 1:29)

Again, Paul credits the empowering work of God within him.

> But test everything; hold fast what is good. Abstain from every form of evil. Now may the God of peace himself sanctify you completely, and may your whole spirit and soul and body be kept blameless at the coming of our Lord Jesus Christ. He who calls you is faithful; he will surely do it. (1 Thess 5:21–24)

Here Paul is giving instructions as to how we should live ("hold fast what is good. Abstain from every form of evil"). But then he asks and expects *God* to do the faithful work of sanctifying us in holiness.

> For the grace of God has appeared, bringing salvation for all people, training us to renounce ungodliness and worldly passions, and to live self-controlled, upright, and godly lives in the present age. (Titus 2:11–12)

The grace of God trains us for growth.

> Now may the God of peace who brought again from the dead our Lord Jesus, the great shepherd of the sheep, by the blood of the eternal covenant, equip you with everything good that you may do his will, working in us that which is pleasing in his sight, through Jesus Christ, to whom be glory forever and ever. Amen. (Heb 13:20–21)

God wants us to "do his will," yet the writer prays that God himself will *equip* us to do so; we are to live in a manner "pleasing" to the Lord, yet he will work that *in* us.

In all of these verses the common theme is God's promised provision to come alongside us and to help us in living the Christian life. We cannot do it alone, but we do not have to. There are no self-made Christians. No Christian can ever say, "I did it myself." Rather, with Paul we say, "By the grace of God, I am what I am."

## Amazing Grace

*Grace* is the operative principle here. Grace is God doing for us what we could never do for ourselves. In the early church, in his argument against the heretic Pelagius, Augustine expressed it this way: "What God requires, he provides."[1]

This tremendous truth of God's grace is totally unique out of all the religious systems of the world. Every religious system requires something of its followers; but only Christianity claims that *what God requires, he actually provides.*

## Grace for Our Salvation

That is true of our *salvation.* God requires perfect holiness in order to enter heaven. We do not have that in ourselves, but in his grace, Christ has provided that holiness for us: that is *God's grace for our salvation.*

## God's Grace for Our Sanctification

It is also true of our *sanctification* (that is, our growth in our Christian walk). God wants us to live a holy life on earth (1 Pet 1:15–16). We certainly cannot do that ourselves; but, as we have just seen, God has promised to help those who are in Christ in that quest: that is *God's grace for our sanctification.*

## Why God Works That Way

But, we might ask, why would he require something and then provide it for us? Peter gives us the answer:

> As each has received a gift, use it to serve one another, as good stewards of God's varied grace: whoever speaks, as one who speaks oracles of God; whoever serves, as one who serves by the strength that God supplies—in order that in everything *God may be glorified* through Jesus Christ. (1 Pet 4:10–11)

Peter says we are to speak for God and serve him, but we do so by using the gifts and the strength that *he* gives us (1 Cor 12:4–11)—"in order that" *it is God who receives the glory* for what he fulfills in and through us. God provides for us what he requires of us so that he might receive all

---

1. And Augustine's grateful response to this amazing truth was, "And my whole hope is only in Thy exceeding great mercy. Give what Thou commandest, and command what Thou wilt" (*Confessions,* 10.29).

the glory. As John Piper likes to put it, "We get the *grace*; and God gets the *glory*."

What God requires, he provides in Jesus Christ. As Jesus said: "Apart from me you can do *nothing*" (John 15:5). To which Paul adds, "I can do *all things* through him who strengthens me" (Phil 4:13).

### God's Grace for Our Worship

God gives us grace for our *salvation*, and also for our *sanctification*. But also for our *worship*. God deserves, and demands, *perfect worship*. What we will see below is God's wonderful provision for us in that arena as well: what God requires of our worship, he provides *for* us in Jesus Christ. That is *God's grace for our worship*.

## Three Correctives

First, however, we need to clarify and correct three misperceptions about Jesus Christ and his work that sometimes arise. And a right understanding of all these issues is crucial for a New Testament view of worship.

### Misperception #1: Jesus Is Gone!

First is the idea that Jesus is no longer here: that he came to earth, died, rose, and ascended, and now he is back in heaven and far removed from us.

But we have the promise of Jesus:

> And behold, *I am with you always*, to the end of the age. (Matt 28:20b)

Through the Holy Spirit, Jesus is still present and active among us.

### Misperception #2: Jesus Is No Longer a Human

Second is the idea that Jesus came to earth and became a human, but now he has gone back to being God again and is no longer a human being.

However, the biblical doctrine of the incarnation teaches that in Jesus Christ full deity and full humanity were combined in one person *forever.* That means that there is a human being seated at the right hand of the Father in heaven! Paul insists:

> For there is one God, and there is [*not* was, but *is*] one mediator between God and men, the *man* Christ Jesus. (1 Tim 2:5)

One reason this understanding is so important is because of an error that arose during the Middle Ages. In the early church there were heretical teachers who denied the full deity of Christ (especially Arius), making it necessary for the church fathers to make a strong defense that Jesus was in fact God. This crucial defense of Christ's deity eventually led to a downplaying of Christ's full and complete (and continuing) humanity. Hence, in the Middle Ages the church began to develop the idea that access to God was possible only through other human agencies. Thomas and James Torrance put it this way:

> When the Humanity of Christ is depreciated or whenever it is obscured by the sheer majesty of his Deity then the need for some other human mediation creeps in—hence in the Dark and Middle Ages arose the need for a human priesthood to mediate between sinful humanity and the exalted Christ, the majestic Judge and King.[2]

> The medieval Church had tended to substitute the priesthood, the sacrifice, the merits, the intercession of . . . Mary and the saints . . . for the vicarious humanity of the Christ, in a way which obscured the Gospel of grace, the Good News of what God has done for us in Christ.[3]

So the church taught (and the people believed) that one had to go through a priest in order to get to God (much like the old-covenant system), and that in order to have one's prayers heard by God one had to go through the Virgin Mary or one of the saints. One of the major rallying cries of the Reformation then was to restore the biblical concept of the sole priesthood and mediatorship of Christ, without the need

---

2. T. Torrance, *Theology in Reconstruction*, 166. "[Josef] Jungmann . . . showed how anti-Arian motives eventually came to shift the emphasis from the human Christ, or the incarnate Son in His continuing mediatorial function. . . . Jungmann proved conclusively from later liturgies that the liturgical result of the Arian controversy in both East and West was that 'stress was now placed not on what unites us to God (Christ as one of us in His human nature, Christ as our brother), but on what separates us from God (God's infinite majesty)'" (Wainwright, *Doxology*, 63).

3. J. Torrance, "Christ in Our Place," in T. Torrance et al., *Passion for Christ*, 37.

for intermediating agents like priests, saints, or Mary. Again Thomas F. Torrance:

> At the Reformation, this doctrine [justification by Christ] had immediate effect in the overthrow of Roman sacerdotalism—Jesus Christ is our sole Priest. He is the one and only Man who can mediate between us and God, so that we approach God solely through the mediation of the Humanity of Jesus, through his incarnate Priesthood. . . . There was of course no denial of the Deity of Christ by the Reformers—on the contrary they restored the purity of faith in Christ as God through overthrowing the accretions that compromised it; but they also restored the place occupied in the New Testament and the Early Church by the Humanity of Christ, as He who took our human nature in order to be our Priest, as He who takes our side and is our Advocate before the judgment of God, and who once and for all has wrought out atonement for us in His sacrifice on the Cross, and therefore as he who eternally stands in for us as our heavenly Mediator and High-Priest.[4]

The Reformers restored Paul's emphasis that "there is one mediator between God and men, the man Christ Jesus" (1 Tim 2:5), and that therefore we do not have to go through anyone else. Because Jesus is a human, he can represent us before God.

## Misperception #3: Jesus Is No Longer a Priest

Third is the idea that Jesus completed his priestly work when he died on the cross for our sins, and so no longer functions in a priestly role.

However, we saw in our study of Hebrews above that Jesus's high priestly ministry was *not* completed when he offered himself as the once-for-all and once-for-all-time sacrifice for sin. We saw how much the book has to say about the *present*, ongoing priestly ministry of Jesus. The writer makes it clear that "we *have* [not *had*] a great high priest" in Jesus Christ:

> Since then we *have* a great high priest who has passed through the heavens, Jesus, the Son of God, let us hold fast our confession. For we do not *have* a high priest who is unable to sympathize with our weaknesses, but one who in every respect has been tempted as we are, yet without sin. (Heb 4:14–15)

---

4. T. Torrance, *Theology in Reconstruction*, 166.

> Now the point in what we are saying is this: we *have* such a high priest, one who is seated at the right hand of the throne of the majesty in heaven. (Heb 8:1)

> Since we *have* a great priest over the house of God, let us draw near. (Heb 10:21–22)

The writer also makes clear that Jesus (unlike the priests of old) holds his priestly office forever:

> As he says also in another place, "You are a priest forever, after the order of Melchizedek." (Heb 5:6, quoting Ps 110:4; see also Heb 6:20; 7:17, 21)

And the reason this is so important:

> The former priests, on the one hand, existed in greater numbers because they were prevented by death from continuing, but Jesus, on the other hand, because he continues *forever*, holds his priesthood permanently. Therefore he is able also to save *forever* [*or: completely*] those who draw near to God through him, since he always lives to make intercession for them. (Heb 7:23–25 NASB)

As we have seen, our full and eternal salvation is *guaranteed* by the continuing, intercessory priestly ministry of Christ on our behalf.

## Jesus, Our Mediator

### Two-Way Mediation in the Old Testament

In the Old Testament, one finds a double agency of mediation back and forth between God and humanity, which reflects the foundational biblical pattern of *revelation* and *response*.

God spoke to Moses on the mountain, and his responsibility was to go down and faithfully communicate the Lord's *revelation* to the people of Israel; he was God's chosen mediator from himself to the people. Moses's brother Aaron (the first high priest) was to represent, through the sacrificial system, the people in their *response* of worship back to God; he was the appointed mediator from the people to God.

Later in Israel's history one sees a similar pattern: the prophet was to serve as God's mouthpiece,[5] communicating his *revealed message* to the people, as mediator between God and them. The priests continued as mediators between the people and God, representing the people in their worship *response*.

## Two-Way Mediation Fulfilled by Christ

In the New Testament, we learn the wonderful truth that Jesus Christ now fills *both* of those mediatorial roles. As the unique God-man, he mediates both between God and humans (in his deity), and humans and God (in his humanity).

5. We read explicitly that "the word of the LORD came" to the prophets Samuel (1 Sam 15:10), Nathan (2 Sam 7:4; 1 Chr 17:3), Gad (2 Sam 24:11), Jehu (1 Kgs 16:1, 7), Elijah (1 Kgs 17:2, 8; 18:1; 19:9; 21:17, 28), Shemaiah (2 Chr 11:2; 12:7), Isaiah (2 Kgs 20:4; Isa 38:4), Jeremiah (Jer 1:2, 4, 11, 13; 2:1; etc.), Ezekiel (Ezek 1:3; 3:16; etc.), Hosea (Hos 1:1), Joel (Joel 1:1), Jonah (Jonah 1:1; 3:1), Micah (Mic 1:1), Zephaniah (Zeph 1:1), and Zechariah (Zech 1:1, 7).

We saw the suggestion of this in ch. 14, as we considered Jesus's apparent allusion to Jacob's dream in Gen 28:

> Truly, truly, I say to you, you will see heaven opened, and the angels of God ascending and descending on the Son of Man. (John 1:51)

The incarnate Jesus is that unique bridge and connection between God and humanity, between heaven and earth.[6]

## Hebrews 2:12

This two-way mediation as it relates to our worship is beautifully and concisely portrayed in Heb 2:12.[7] Here the writer is quoting from Ps 22:22,[8] though he states that these are *the words of Christ himself*,[9] speaking to his Father:

> *Revelation*: "I will tell of your name to my brethren."
> *Response*: "In the midst of the congregation I will sing your praise."

This remarkable verse takes us to the very heart of worship under the new covenant. As we will see, it shows that Jesus Christ and his present ministry is the ultimate climax and fulfillment of the *revelation* and *response* pattern of Scripture with which we started our study.

---

6. That is why William Nicholls entitled his book *Jacob's Ladder: The Meaning of Worship*.

7. For a fuller treatment of this passage and its implications for our worship, see Ron Man, *Proclamation and Praise*.

8. This familiar psalm foretells the crucifixion of Christ, as he appropriates for himself the opening cry of v. 1 as he hangs on the cross ("My God, My God, why have you forsaken me?" Matt 27:46; Mark 15:34). Verse 22, quoted in Heb 2:12, is the first verse of the second section of the psalm, which looks beyond the suffering of the Messiah to the victory to follow (see Ron Man, *Proclamation and Praise*, 8–12).

9. Besides this, the writer of Hebrews attributes quotations from Isa 8:17 (in Heb 2:13a), Isa 8:18 (in 2:13b), and Ps 40:6–8 (in 10:5–7) as the words of Christ.

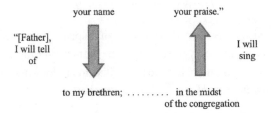

Jesus, as God, is the ultimate *Revealer* of the Father; as a human, he is the ultimate *Responder* to the Father.

## Unpacking Heb 2:12

Let us consider separately the two halves (and directions) of this verse.

↓ "I will tell of your name to my brethren." (Heb 2:12a) ↓

### Jesus's Earthly Mission

The New Testament (especially the Gospel of John) makes it clear that the thrust of Jesus's earthly ministry was to ↓ reveal the Father (his "name," that is, his nature) and to faithfully communicate his message to humankind:

> All things have been handed over to me by my Father, and no one knows the Son except the Father, and no one knows the Father except the Son and anyone to whom the Son chooses to reveal him. (Matt 11:27)

> No one has ever seen God; the only God, who is at the Father's side, he has made him known. (John 1:18)[10]

> I have manifested your name to the people whom you gave me out of the world. Yours they were, and you gave them to me, and they have kept your word. (John 17:6)

> I made known to them your name. (John 17:26a)

> Long ago, at many times and in many ways, God spoke to our fathers by the prophets, but in these last days he has spoken to us by his Son. (Heb 1:1–2a)

10. Here the Greek verb translated "made him known" is related to the English word *exegete*. The Son has "exegeted" the Father for us!

## Jesus's Continuing Ministry

But there are also a number of Scriptures that speak of or imply the *continuation* of Jesus's ministry of revealing the Father *after* his glorification.

Jesus, on the night before his crucifixion, is looking beyond the cross to an *ongoing* role of ↓ revealing the Father:

> I made known to them your name, and *I will continue to make it known,* that the love with which you have loved me may be in them, and I in them. (John 17:26; see also John 16:12–15, 25)

And in Acts 1:1 we read:

> In the first book, O Theophilus, I have dealt with all that Jesus *began* to do and teach.

Luke's clear implication is that in his second volume (the book of Acts— the first volume being, of course, the Gospel of Luke), he will relate what Jesus *continues* "to do and to teach" (only now through the Holy Spirit, through Jesus's chosen apostles, and through his church).

### Christ Working in His Church

John Murray concurs:

> The Gospel [of Luke], in distinction from the Acts, is concerned with what Jesus began to do and teach. So what Luke records in the present treatise [Acts] is what Jesus continued to do and teach. The Gospel of Luke closes with the ascension of Christ into heaven; the book of Acts is therefore concerned with the doing and teaching of Christ from His exalted glory. . . . Prejudice is done to the work of Christ and to our faith in Him when we overlook or even fail to emphasize the continued ministry of Christ in both doing and teaching.
>
> The fact that Jesus continued to teach after His ascension is of paramount importance for the authority of Christ in the teaching of the apostles and in the books of the New Testament. Prior to His ascension Christ's teaching was directly by word of mouth. But afterwards He taught by a different mode. He taught by the ministry of appointed witnesses and inspired writers. The New Testament, all of which was written after Jesus' ascension, is not one whit less the teaching of our Lord than that delivered verbally during the

days of His flesh.[11] How utterly false it is to set up a contrast between the authority of Jesus' spoken words and the authority of
the New Testament as Scripture. The latter is the teaching of Christ
given in His own appointed way after His ascension. . . .

Let us prize with the ardour of our whole soul what Jesus continues to do, and teach. He is the living, acting, and teaching Lord.[12]

William Tait similarly, after reminding us that the risen Lord continued to teach his disciples during the forty days leading up to the ascension (as Acts 1:3 makes clear), adds this insight:

Nor did His ascension put a period to this blessed work: He
has been engaged in it ever since, and is engaged in it still. All
who in any generation, have known the Father's name, and all
who know it now, have learnt it from His teaching. None else
is competent to teach it. For "no man," Jesus Himself declares,
"knoweth the Father save the Son, and he to whomsoever the
Son will reveal Him" (Matt 11:27). This blessed work is Christ's
delight, my brethren. . . . The invisible Father shall never be
known save in and through the Son; and therefore as Jesus shall
delight to teach, His people shall delight to learn of Him.[13]

And Eric Alexander expands on this understanding:

All true ministry in Christ's church *derives* from Christ's ministry. He is the true minister of the tabernacle (Heb 8:2). He is the
shepherd and overseer of our souls (1 Pet 2:25). He's the apostle
and high priest of our profession (Heb 3:1). He is the *diakonos*
[servant] of the circumcision for the truth of God (Rom 15:8).
All the great titles that are used for our ministry are first applied
to Jesus. So it is the ministry of the Lord Jesus Christ which is
continuing in his church. . . . All true ministry derives from him.[14]

## CHRIST SPEAKING TO HIS CHURCH

Here are some testimonies from a variety of sources demonstrating their
understanding of the truth of Christ's continuing proclamation to his
Church in and through his servants:

11. Red-letter editions, beware!

12. Murray, "Living Saviour," 40–41.

13. Tait, *Meditationes Hebraicae*, 160–61.

14. Alexander, *Our Great God*, 141–42.

In Scripture reading and sermon, in sacrament and in liturgical action, Christ proclaims God to man.[15]

The preacher is the servant of the Word. His sermon puts at Christ's disposal the living language of the present day, with its associations with the everyday life of the congregation. It permits Christ to preach His Word through the mouth of the contemporary Church, as He has already through the Apostolic Church.[16]

When the Church is proclaiming the word of God, "Christ is still proclaiming his gospel."[17]

We pray that this would be the preaching moment. For no one can preach unless You first speak; nobody can say anything unless You first give utterance; nobody can do anything unless You first send an anointing. We ask that You would be the preacher this morning, that you would get the glory.[18]

We pray that you won't listen to us, but that you'll listen to Jesus through us.[19]

## THE "WORD OF CHRIST" (ROM 10:14, 17; COL 3:16)

The common rendering of Rom 10:14 is: "How are they to believe in him *of whom* they have never heard?" (e.g., in the KJV, RSV, NIV, ESV, and even the authoritative Bauer-Arndt-Gingrich-Danker *Greek-English Lexicon of the New Testament and Other Early Christian Literature*). However, a more nuanced translation of the grammatical construction is one that is affirmed by exegetical commentators such as C. K. Barrett, C. E. B. Cranfield, Leon Morris, and John Murray, and affords extra support to the view of Christ continuing to speak to his church:

> How then will they call on him in whom they have not believed? And how are they to believe in him *whom* [not: of whom] they have never heard? And how are they to hear without someone preaching? (Rom 10:14)

15. Nicholls, *Jacob's Ladder*, 38.

16. Nicholls, *Jacob's Ladder*, 42.

17. J. D. Crichton, "Theology of Worship," 28, in Jones et al., *Study of Liturgy*, quoting Second Vatican Council, "*Sacrosanctum Concilium*," 7.33.

18. Dr. Frank A. Thomas, prayer before preaching.

19. Highest Call singing group, prayer before presenting program.

Christ is *still* speaking through the agency of servants who faithfully proclaim the message, and through the Holy Spirit, who illumines that message in the hearts of hearers. Morris states, "Christ is present in the preachers; to hear them is to hear Him."[20] And Cranfield agrees: "The thought is of their hearing Christ speaking in the message of the preachers."[21]

We find a continuation of the same idea in Rom 10:17:

> So faith comes from hearing, and hearing through the word of Christ.

Morris concludes:

> It is possible to understand this expression either as referring to the teaching of the historical Jesus passed on in the church or to the teaching of the exalted Lord, the Lord of the church. Probably it is both, for there seems no reason for separating the two.[22]

Indeed, the proximity and connection with v. 14 certainly increases the likelihood that a subjective ("the word that Christ speaks") rather than an objective ("the word about Christ") genitive is at play here.

A similar construction is found in Col 3:16:

> Let the *word of Christ* dwell in you richly, teaching and admonishing one another in all wisdom, singing psalms and hymns and spiritual songs, with thankfulness in your hearts to God.

Commentators are split over whether this is a subjective or an objective genitive, but subjective is certainly a viable possibility (and it is an enriching thought to see a more active role for Christ, "the word of Christ" taken to mean that he is speaking to his people as they gather). Bruce and Ferguson state:

> Christian teaching must be based on the teaching of Jesus Himself; it must be unmistakably "the word of Christ."[23]

> And this is of course the great thing about true preaching among the people of God in the power of the Holy Spirit—that whoever

20. Morris, *Epistle to the Romans*, 390.

21. Cranfield, *Romans*, 2:534.

22. Morris, *Epistle to the Romans*, 392.

23. Bruce, *Ephesians*, 283. The footnote states: "This takes the genitive ["the word of Christ"] to be subjective (the word *proceeding from* Christ); less probably it might be the objective genitive (the word *concerning* Christ)" (emphasis added).

does the preaching is incidental to the One who is truly preaching: our Lord Jesus Christ.[24]

And in the text of the hymn "More about Jesus Would I Know," Eliza Hewitt seems to show an understanding of this same principle:

> More about Jesus; in His Word,
> Holding communion with my Lord;
> *Hearing His voice in every line.*[25]

### Not *Our* Teaching Ministry

This all means that for any of us who are involved with teaching or preaching the word of God, we need to realize that it is in fact *Jesus's* ministry, not ours. We are speaking for and representing him, whose role it is to reveal the Father. *What a high and holy and humbling privilege!*

This dynamic is also suggested by the statue of the nineteenth-century American preacher Phillips Brooks (who also authored the text of the Christmas carol "O Little Town of Bethlehem") outside of Trinity Church in Boston (where he served as rector, 1862–69): there Brooks is seen preaching, with one hand on the Bible and backed up by the figure of Christ:

**Statue of Phillips Brooks, by Augustus Saint-Gaudens**[26]

24. Ferguson, *True Spirituality, True Worship.*

25. See https://www.hymnal.net/en/hymn/h/382.

26. Public domain image from https://commons.wikimedia.org/wiki/Category: Phillips_Brooks_by_Augustus_Saint-Gaudens#/media/File:Phillips_Brooks_by_Augustus_Saint-Gaudens_-_Trinity_Church,_Boston_-_DSC08173.JPG. Thanks to Reggie Kidd for telling me about this statue.

↑ "In the midst of the congregation I will sing your praise."
(Heb 2:12b) ↑

*Jesus, Our Worship Leader*

Even more remarkable, perhaps, are the implications of the second half
of Heb 2:12, where Jesus tells the Father "in the midst of the congregation
I will sing your praise." As our great High Priest, he represents us before
the Father. He not only mediates our response of praise, he participates in
it! This concept plumbs one of the most profound depths of the mystery
of the incarnation: that Jesus Christ, who as God deserves and receives
worship (Heb 1:6), should also as a human be a worshiper himself![27]

> Here lies the mystery, the wonder, the glory of the Gospel, that
> He who is God, the Creator of all things, and worthy of the wor-
> ship and praises of all creation, should become man and as a
> man worship God, and as a man lead us in our worship of God.[28]

When believers gather for worship, Jesus has promised to be in our midst,
lifting up his own praise and leading us in ours.

### HIS PRIESTHOOD OUR ACCESS

As we saw in ch. 24, Christ's continuing priesthood is a major theme in
Hebrews:

> You are *a priest forever* after the order of Melchizedek. (Ps 110:4/
> Heb 5:6; see also Heb 6:20; 7:17)

> Now the point in what we are saying is this: we *have such a high
> priest*, one who is seated at the right hand of the throne of the
> Majesty in heaven, a minister in the holy places, in the true tent
> that the Lord set up, not man. For every high priest is appointed
> to offer gifts and sacrifices; thus it is necessary for this priest also
> to have something to offer. (Heb 8:1–3)

And the writer maintains that we can "draw near" because of the *past*
work of Christ ("*since* we have confidence to enter the holy places by the

---

27. As we saw in ch. 8, Jesus in his earthly ministry countered Satan's temptation
by expressing his own resolve as a worshiper to obey the command of Deut 6:13: "You
shall worship the Lord your God and him only shall you serve" (Matt 4:10).

28. J. Torrance, "Place of Jesus Christ," 351.

blood of Jesus" [Heb 10:19]) *and* because of his *present* work ("*since* we have a great priest over the house of God" [10:21]):

> Therefore, brethren, *since* we have confidence to enter the holy places by the blood of Jesus, by the new and living way that he opened for us through the curtain, that is, through his flesh, and *since* we *have a great priest* over the house of God, let us draw near with a true heart in full assurance of faith, with our hearts sprinkled clean from an evil conscience and our bodies washed with pure water. (Heb 10:19–22)

A crucial function of a priest is *to worship and to lead the people in worship*. "A priest not worshipping, is indeed a contradiction. And God hath sworn and will not repent that Jesus is a Priest forever."[29] A priest who leads worship must himself be a worshiper: true and full mediation (and incarnation) must certainly include this aspect.

Calvin, in his commentary on Hebrews, explains that in 2:12 we see that Christ "is the chief Conductor of our hymns."[30] That he leads the congregation in their praise is not explicitly stated in the verse, but is clearly implied in harmony with the rest of Hebrews and the New Testament. It stands to reason that our Priest is the One who must lead us in offering our sacrifice, which is now identified as a "sacrifice of praise" (Heb 13:15); and this latter verse explicitly states that we make that sacrifice "through him." It is a natural conclusion that our praises would be in conjunction with, motivated by, empowered by, and even led by Christ's praises "in the midst of the congregation" (Heb 2:12b).

### His Worship Our Worship

When Christ our model and brother praises the Father, he leads the way for us. Because we are in union with him, his worship is our worship. Through him we come into the Father's presence in worship; we come clothed in his righteousness, and he bears up our weak offerings of worship and makes them one with his own perfect offering of praise. James Torrance has aptly summarized Jesus's role: "The real agent in all true worship is Jesus Christ."[31]

---

29. Tait, *Meditationes Hebraicae*, 16.

30. Calvin, *Epistle to the Hebrews*, on 2:12. The writer of Hebrews in 8:1 refers to Christ as a "*leitourgos* [liturgist] in the holy places."

31. J. Torrance, *Worship, Community*, 17.

He is not an observer—he is the *Leader* of our worship. As Thomas Torrance explains:

> The Church on earth lives and acts only as it is directed by its heavenly Lord, and only in such a way that His Ministry is reflected in the midst of its ministry and worship. Therefore from first to last the worship and ministry of the Church on earth must be governed by the fact that Christ substitutes himself in our place, and that our humanity with its own acts of worship, is displaced by his, so that we appear before God not in our own name, not in our own significance, not in virtue of our own acts of confession, contrition, worship, and thanksgiving, but solely in the name of Christ and solely in virtue of what He has done in our name and on our behalf, and in our stead. Justification by Christ alone means that from first to last in the worship of God and in the ministry of the Gospel Christ himself is central, and that we draw near in worship and service only through letting Him take our place. He only is Priest. He only represents humanity. He only has an offering with which to appear before God and with which God is well-pleased. He only presents our prayers before God, and He only is our praise and thanksgiving and worship as we appear before the face of the Father. "Nothing in our hands we bring—simply to His Cross we cling."[32]

## Through Christ

New Testament worship is always *through Christ*:

> Behold, I *and* the children God has given me. (Heb 2:13b)

> Consequently, he is able to save to the uttermost those who draw near to God *through him*, since He always lives to make intercession for them. (Heb 7:25)

> *Through him* then let us continually offer up a sacrifice of praise to God, that is, the fruit of lips that acknowledge his name. (Heb 13:15)

> For *through him* we both have access in one Spirit to the Father. (Eph 2:18)

> And whatever you do, in word or deed, do everything in the name of the Lord Jesus, giving thanks to God the Father *through him*. (Col 3:17)

32. T. Torrance, *Theology in Reconstruction*, 167.

Second Corinthians 1:20 (which we considered earlier in ch. 22) is a fascinating conceptual parallel to Heb 2:12:

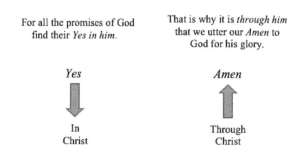

| For all the promises of God find their *Yes in him.* | That is why it is *through him* that we utter our *Amen* to God for his glory. |
| :---: | :---: |
| *Yes* | *Amen* |
| In Christ | Through Christ |

God says Yes to us *in Jesus*; and in response we say Amen to God *through Jesus*. All our Christian life and service and worship can be understood as part of our *Amen* to God because he has said *Yes* to us *in Jesus*; and that Amen is made *through Jesus*. That is the "glory": all of God's work for us in Christ can be summarized as his grand Yes to us, so that all that is left for us to do is to gratefully respond with our Amen of worship and service. Jesus is the Mediator of God's Yes to us, *and also* the Mediator of our Amen in response.

## In Christ

In its essence, New Testament worship centers in Jesus Christ and his two-way mediating ministry. Our worship is in, through, with, and by Jesus Christ. William Nicholls adds:

> Accordingly, the Church's worship will be best conformed to its true nature when its pattern echoes the Christological pattern we have seen in Scripture. In the first place, the Church must be attentive to the proclamation of the Word. . . . The second aspect of Christian worship is our joining in the *latreia* of Christ, offering through Him the sacrifice of praise and thanksgiving to the Father, in the power of the Holy Spirit. . . .
>
> Without the work of Christ, bringing God down to men, and gathering men in Himself before God, there can be no worship at all, and indeed no Church. . . .
>
> Christ [is] the true though invisible Celebrant of all that is done. . . .

Christ is the One in whom Word and response are united.[33]

And as Nicholls well summarizes:

Christ is the essence of worship, and our understanding of the Church's worship must take its starting point from Him. In Him is embodied the downward movement of God's love and grace, as He reveals Himself to man, and reconciles man to Himself; and also the upward movement of man's response, perfectly dependent upon that love, and drawing from it all the resources of strength which are needed to make that response in all circumstances of life, and even in death itself.[34]

## Implications for Our Worship

There are a number of crucial implications and correctives for our understanding and practice of worship from the truths we have been examining in this chapter.

### 1. New-covenant worship is Trinitarian worship.

James Torrance warns against what he terms the quasi-"Unitarian" worship that characterizes much evangelical practice:

Probably the most common and widespread view is that worship is something which we, religious people, do—mainly in church on Sunday. . . . No doubt we need God's grace to help us do it. . . . But worship is what we do before God.

In theological language, this means that the only priesthood is our priesthood, the only offering our offering, the only intercessions our intercessions. Indeed this view of worship is in practice unitarian, has no doctrine of the mediator or sole priesthood of Christ, is human-centered, has no proper doctrine of the Holy Spirit, is too often non-sacramental, and can engender weariness. We sit in the pew watching the minister "doing his thing," exhorting us "to do our thing," until we go home thinking we have done our duty for another week! This kind of do-it-yourself-with-the-help-of-the-minister worship . . . is not trinitarian.[35]

33. Nicholls, *Jacob's Ladder*, 27–28, 36, 39, 40.
34. Nicholls, *Jacob's Ladder*, 26.
35. J. Torrance, *Worship, Community*, 20–21.

Simply put: *we need to repent of trying to do worship in our own strength!* True worship, Torrance insists, is richly Trinitarian:

> The second view of worship is that it is the gift of participating through the Spirit in the incarnate Son's communion with the Father. It means participating in union with Christ, in what He has done for us once and for all, in His self-offering to the Father, in His life and death on the cross. It also means participating in what He is continuing to do for us in the presence of the Father and in His mission from the Father to the world.[36]

"Through the work of the Spirit we are drawn into the life of Christ to participate in his life of love with the Father."[37] Or as John Witvliet puts it:

- The Father *receives* our worship.
- The Son *perfects* our worship.
- The Holy Spirit *prompts* our worship.[38]

## 2. As much as we rightly focus on the past, finished work of Christ, we dare not neglect his *present* ministry.

As we have seen, the book of Hebrews has more to say about his continuing work than any other book in the New Testament:

- He leads our worship (Heb 2:12; 3:1; 8:1–2, 6; 10:21; 13:15).
- He intercedes for us and comes to our aid (Heb 2:18; 4:14–16; 7:25; 9:24; 13:21).

36. J. Torrance, *Worship, Community*, 21. See also Navarro, *Trinitarian Doxology*.

37. Cocksworth, *Holy, Holy, Holy*, 99.

38. "Trinitarian worship offered to the Father, through Christ, in the Spirit conceives of God as the One who acts 'before' us, 'within' us, and 'alongside' of us to receive, prompt, and perfect our worship—divine action in continuity with both past and future divine actions. Trinitarian pastoral concern calls for helping worshipers sense the grace, beauty, and majesty of this vision" (Witvliet, "Prism of Glory," 298). Christopher Cocksworth expands on this idea: "The integrity of the worship which comes from our lips and our hearts is retained—it remains our worship—but it is retuned by the greater integrity of the worship of Christ. The Spirit lifts our prayer and praise into the sphere of Christ's worship to be purified and perfected by His prayer and praise and then presented by Christ to the Father in its new and redeemed form. Our worship is with Christ our brother, in Christ our priest but always through Christ our sacrifice, whose death once for us is the means of our cleansing, renewing and perfecting" (*Holy, Holy, Holy*, 161–62).

- He guarantees our eternal salvation (Heb 7:25).

## 3. The living Christ is present in our midst when we gather for worship.

> We have such a high priest, one who is seated at the right hand
> of the throne of the Majesty in heaven, a minister in the holy
> places, in the true tent that the Lord set up, not man. (Heb 8:1–2)

Nevertheless, through the Holy Spirit he is also present with us "in the
midst of the congregation" (2:12) when the church assembles. Indeed,
he promised, "I am with you always, to the end of the age" (Matt 28:20).

Karen Burton Mains expresses this truth beautifully in her introduction to the hymnal *Sing Joyfully!*:

> We need to remind ourselves, over and over, that the focus
> of Sunday worship must be upon the living Christ among us.
> In truth, if Christ were bodily present and we could see him
> with more than our soul's eyes, all our worship would become
> intentional. If Christ stood on our platforms, we would bend
> our knees without asking. If He stretched out His hands and we
> saw the wounds, our hearts would break; we would confess our
> sins and weep over our shortcomings. If we could hear His voice
> leading the hymns, we too would sing heartily; the words would
> take on meaning. The Bible reading would be lively; meaning
> would pierce to the marrow of our souls. If Christ walked our
> aisles, we would hasten to make amends with that brother or
> sister to whom we have not spoken. We would volunteer for ser-
> vice; the choir loft would be crowded. If we knew Christ would
> attend our church Sunday after Sunday, the front pews would
> fill fastest, believers would arrive early, offering plates would be
> laden with sacrificial but gladsome gifts, prayers would concen-
> trate our attention.
>
> Yet, the startling truth is that Christ is present, through His
> Holy Spirit, in our churches; it is we who must develop eyes to
> see Him.[39]

39. Mains, "Introduction," 5.

## 4. Christ is the essence, enabler, empowerer, channel, guide, activator, offerer,[40] mediator, and perfecter of all true worship.

"The real agent in all true worship is Jesus Christ."[41] Not only is worship *through* Christ; it is also *by* him and even *with* him.

While we sometimes rather glibly speak of worshiping through Christ or praying in the name of Christ, we need to see that it is not worship or prayer simply made *possible* by Christ, but rather, it is worship and prayer *energized, transported, sanctified, and perfected* by Christ as the basis for acceptance by the Father. This is a much more active understanding of the dynamics of worship and prayer than we often acknowledge. Our living and active Savior has not just opened or pointed out the way for us into the Father's presence (Heb 10:19–20); he takes us with him! In the words of Cocksworth: "The invitation of the book of Hebrews is to go where he goes"![42]

Worship is possible only in him and through him, by his grace and in his name. He is the "one mediator between God and men, the man Christ Jesus" (1 Tim 2:5). He is the Ladder between heaven and earth (Gen 28:12; John 1:51), the "bridge across the great divide."

> There is only one true Priest through whom and with whom we draw near to God our Father. There is only one Mediator between God and humanity. There is only one offering which is truly acceptable to God, and it is not ours. It is the offering by which he has sanctified for all time those who come to God by Him (Heb. 2:11; 10:10, 14). There is only one who can lead us into the presence of the Father by his sacrifice on the cross.[43]

---

40. "That is what it means to pray and worship in the name of Jesus Christ 'Mediator, High Priest and Advocate'; He is *the* Offerer of all our worship to God" (T. Torrance, "Mind of Christ," 184).

41. J. Torrance, *Worship, Community*, 17. In the same volume he states, "Whatever else our worship is, it is our liturgical amen to the worship of Christ" (14). And Reggie Kidd insists: "Every group brings its own voice, but no group brings the official voice. One Voice sings above them all, and this Voice sings in all their voices, excluding none. His singular voice is distributed among a plurality of people. Just because there are so many dimensions to His own being, the multiplicity of their voices amplifies His song" ("Bach, Bubba," 9). "He calls us to join his voice and to share in his song" (Cocksworth, *Holy, Holy, Holy*, 159).

42. Cocksworth, *Holy, Holy, Holy*, 157. And Luther, writing on Heb 10:19–22, calls Christ the "ferryman" who takes us to the Father (*Lectures*, 226).

43. J. Torrance, *Worship, Community*, 21.

Jesus is the only Way, but he is an all-sufficient Way. In spite of a huge diversity in worship styles and practices, in music and dress and architecture and forms and customs, from church to church, culture to culture, continent to continent, century to century throughout the history of the church—the fact remains that there is a constant wherever true worship is taking place: it is *the role of the living Christ in the midst of his people, leading their worship.* In light of Jesus's unique role as Worship Leader, perhaps then a new title is needed for those of us who lead the people's praise—"worship facilitator"?? James Torrance stresses that "there is only one way to come to the Father, namely through Christ in the communion of saints, whatever outward form our worship may take."[44]

As Bob Kauflin importantly reminds us:

> No worship leader, pastor, band, or song will ever bring us close to God. . . . Worship itself cannot lead us into God's presence. *Only Jesus himself* can bring us into God's presence.[45]

## 5. Both the proclamation and exposition of God's word *and* the corporate praises of the congregation are done through and by (and are therefore both important aspects of) the effectual mediating ministry of Jesus Christ.[46]

As we have seen, Christ himself is the fulfillment of the biblical pattern of *revelation* and *response* that underlies all true worship (Old and New Testament). We have seen that Christ himself leads both parts in his two-way mediation as the incarnate God-man. That gives both aspects a sublime and holy importance in the corporate gatherings of God's people: not just the *revelation* of God's truth (though that is primary), but also the *response* of the people.

---

44. J. Torrance, "Doctrine of the Trinity," 6.

45. Kauflin, *Worship Matters*, 74.

46. Reggie Kidd has pointed out that, in fact, the ministry of Christ in our worship is to be found in *four* areas: the preaching of the word, singing, prayer, and the Lord's table. He also observes that the early church, through the Middle Ages, came to focus more and more on the table; the Reformation brought its greatest emphasis to the word and preaching; later pietistic movements often centered on prayer (and helped to spawn missionary movements), and in many churches today singing is seen as central—as a "new sacrament," i.e., as a primary vehicle for connecting with God. Kidd sees the need for a balanced view of the "sacramentality" (the presence and activity of Christ) in all four areas (personal conversation).

Some pastors and others consider preaching to be the real focus and goal of the service, and all other parts as only preliminary or preparatory: the Lord Jesus Christ would seem to disagree with that assessment! He thinks the public praises of God's people are so important that he has committed himself to be right in the middle of that practice also, initiating and empowering it and infusing it with the glory of his presence. We do not go to church simply to hear a sermon; rather, we go to dialogue with God, to learn of him and be changed by him, to respond with heart and lips and lives of worship and obedience and service. Ferguson insists that "the dichotomy between worship and preaching is so unbiblical—because the Jesus who leads us in our praises is the same one whose voice is heard by his sheep in the ministry of the Word."[47]

As we saw in ch. 4, the ↓ revelation-response ↑ pattern should be reflected in our services, and the cycle should always be completed. Or, as John Stott incisively puts it, "There can be no doxology without theology. . . . On the other hand, there should be no theology without doxology."[48]

## 6. Our worship is pleasing and acceptable to God not because of its own inherent excellence, but because of (and only because of) the excellence of his Son.

Jungmann identifies the true source of worship's power:

> The Church's prayers of praise to God gain meaning and value only because Christ as high priest stands at her head and joins in them. Through Him, God is constantly paid the highest honor, even without our help, since His divine glorified humanity is the finest flower of creation, the supreme revelation of God.[49]

God accepts and delights in our worship, not because of even our best efforts (we can't impress him with our artistry or even with our spirituality), but because of the Son's continual offering of worship in our place and on our behalf. He gathers up our imperfect expressions of worship into his own perfect one. It is not the excellence of our worship (quality, quantity, or form) that makes it acceptable and pleasing unto

47. Ferguson, "Church's Worship" (Ligonier).

48. Stott, *Romans*, 311–12.

49. Jungmann, *Place of Christ*, 137.

God, but the excellence of his Son, with whom he is eternally well pleased (Matt 3:17; 17:5; 2 Pet 1:17).

We, as worshipers and as worship leaders, do not have to come to public (or private) worship fearing if it will be "good enough," if it will be *acceptable* to God. When we come through and in dependence upon Christ, our worship will *always* be good enough!

And that is indeed *true freedom for those of us involved in worship planning and leading!*[50] What tremendous truth. T. F. Torrance assures us:

> Who does indeed come before God without ulterior motives of some kind corrupting his intention? But to worship and pray through, with, and in Christ is to worship God for God's sake, with the perfection of true worship which Christ is, and not in some secret way for our own sake. Through, with, and in Christ we turn away in penitential self-denial from *our own* acts of worship and prayer in order to rest in the worship and prayer which our Saviour has *already offered* and *continues to offer* to the Father on our behalf.[51]

In other words, as mentioned earlier, we must repent of trying to do worship *in our own strength* and depend on Christ to do *what only he can do*!

Similarly, Robert Webber writes these powerful words:

> Who can love God with his heart, mind, and soul? Who can achieve perfect union with God? Who can worship God with a pure and unstained heart?
>
> Not me! . . . Not you. Not Billy Graham. . . . Not Matt Redman. Not anybody I know or you know.
>
> Only Jesus can. And He does for me and for you what neither of us can do for ourselves.
>
> This is the message that is missing in the literature of contemporary worship.[52] It is too much about what I ought to do and too little about what God has done for me. God has done for me what I cannot do for myself. He did it in Jesus Christ. Therefore my worship is offered in a broken vessel that is in the process of being healed, but is not yet capable of fullness of joy,

---

50. Of course, that does not for a minute mean that we should not carefully plan, prepare, rehearse, and offer to God the best we can offer. But it does mean that such execution is not the grounds for God delighting in our worship.

51. T. Torrance, "Mind of Christ," 211–12 (emphasis added).

52. And, I would maintain, it is also missing in much of the literature of *traditional* worship as well!

endless intense passion, absolute exaltation, and celebration. But Jesus, who shares in my humanity yet without sin, is not only my Savior—he is also my complete and eternal worship, doing for me, in my place, what I cannot do. . . .

He is eternally interceding to the Father on our behalf. And for this reason, our worship is always in and through Christ. . . .

Thanks for Jesus Christ, who is my worship. We are free! And in gratitude, we offer our stumbling worship in the name of Jesus with thanksgiving.[53]

And so, as Heb 10:19–22 encourages us, we can "draw near with a true heart *in full assurance of faith*," having "*confidence* to enter the holy places by the blood of Jesus."

## Conclusion

## "Christ is all, and in all." (Col 3:11)

It has often been said that "Christianity *is* Christ." Likewise it should be clear that "new-covenant *worship* is Christ." Christ is at the core of *biblical worship*. He is the agent of both *theology* and *doxology*. He is the fulfillment of the biblical paradigm of *revelation and response*. He is the Leader of our *proclamation* and of our *praise*.

## God's Grace for Our Worship

Augustine famously confessed: "My whole hope is in Thy exceeding great mercy and that alone. Give what Thou commandest and command what Thou wilt."[54] God expects, deserves, and commands *perfect* worship. None of us is capable of that, but in his grace, God has provided for us in Christ the way to offer up that perfect worship. This is *God's grace for our worship*.

He does not intend for us to operate on a performance basis in our worship any more than in our salvation or sanctification. While we should of course offer our best to God in worship (through studying, practicing, and praying), ultimately that is not the ground of our acceptance before

---

53. Robert E. Webber, "Blended Worship Response," in Engle and Basden, *Six Views*, 130.

54. Augustine, *Confessions*, 10.29.

him. We cannot impress him with our worship! C. S. Lewis warns about our tendency in this regard (as quoted also in ch. 13):

> We must beware of the naïve idea that our music can "please" God as it would please a cultivated human hearer. That is like thinking, under the old Law, that He really needed the blood of bulls and goats. . . . For all our offerings, whether of music or martyrdom, are like the intrinsically worthless present of a child, which a father values indeed, but values only for the intention.[55]

## Worship Is *Not* a Work

> We do not sing loud or pray hard in order to generate divine favor—a perfect theology of worship if we wanted to worship Baal.[56]

We do not offer up our services, our sets, and our songs in hopes that by saying or singing or doing the right thing God will be obligated to "show up" and bless us. We lift our praises, not out of fear that we're going to miss something or lose out or not be accepted by God. Instead we rest, we bask in the status we enjoy with him as his beloved children, because we are in Christ by his mercy.

It is profoundly important to see that *worship is not a work*. It is a grateful and humble gift that we offer to God in response to the grace that he has lavished on us. And even that response is made perfectly acceptable as by grace we offer it to God through Christ our Redeemer and Mediator.

God receives great glory by providing for us what he demands from us. "Worship is a gift we are invited to receive. We are invited to join the prayer and praise of Christ and to allow our voice to be perfected in his."[57]

The all-sufficiency of Christ envelops, enriches, fulfills, and perfects our worship.

> God does not *throw us back upon ourselves* to make our response to His Word. But graciously He helps our infirmities by giving

---

55. C. S. Lewis, "On Church Music," 123.

56. Witvliet, "What to Do," 242.

57. Cocksworth, *Holy, Holy, Holy*, 161.

us Jesus Christ and the Holy Spirit to make the appropriate response *for us* and *in us.*[58]

Adolph Saphir expresses this marvelous truth beautifully in comments on Heb 2:11–12:

> Christians, if Jesus is our brother [11b]; if Jesus and we are both of one [11a]; if Jesus says, "I will sing Thy praise in the midst of the congregation" [12]; if He is the leader of our prayers and praises before the throne of God, then we may approach the Father without fear and without doubt! Christ's peace is our peace, and our worship is the worship of perfect acceptance, of perfect trust and love in union with the Head of the Church. . . . Where is doubt now? For is Jesus in doubt of His acceptance with the Father? . . . Now He presents the Father our sacrifice of thanksgiving, our adoration, our petitions, and the Father hears the voice of Jesus in the voice of the church.[59]

## The Power of True Worship

Whenever true worship happens, it is because Jesus Christ is in the midst of his people, leading them in their praises and presenting them to the Father as part of his own perfect offering of praise. No matter what form or style our worship may take, no matter what language, instruments, architecture, or art forms we may use—*the power of true worship,* in all its wonderfully varied manifestations, is *the living Christ in our midst.*

God accepts and delights in our worship, not because it is so good, so well rehearsed, so sincere (though all these things are important), but because our Lord Jesus presents it to the Father in our place and on our behalf—and the Father is *always* pleased with his Son. It is the Son's excellence that gains the Father's favor.

> We are accepted by God, not because we have offered worthy worship, but in spite of our unworthiness, because He has provided for us a Worship, a Way, a Sacrifice, a Forerunner in Christ our Leader and Representative. This is the heart of all true Christian worship.[60]

---

58. J. Torrance, "Place of Jesus Christ," 359 (emphases added).

59. Saphir, *Great High Priest,* 147.

60. J. Torrance, "Place of Jesus Christ," 352.

## The Joy and Wonder of True Worship

Participation in the relatedness of God is the joy of Christian worship. By giving glory to the Father and the Son and the Holy Spirit we share in the eternal giving and receiving of life and love which constitutes the very being of God.[61]

## Christi!

*Through him* then let us continually offer up a sacrifice of praise to God, that is, the fruit of lips that acknowledge his name. (Heb 13:15)

Johann von Staupitz, Luther's mentor, asked him once, "Luther, what happens if all this works, if you have your Reformation? What happens to the devotions, and to the pilgrimages, and to the relics, and to all the wonderful things of the Church; and to the marvelous, majestic liturgy, with all of its pomp and ceremony; all these things that we've grown up with and that we love so dearly and that are so close to our hearts? What will be left when you're through?"

And Luther said, *"Christ!"*[62]

Christ! He is all we need. He is the Author of life (Acts 3:15); the one Mediator and Bridge between God and humans (1 Tim 2:5; John 1:51); the Founder and Perfecter of our faith (Heb 12:2); our great High Priest (Heb 4:14). And he is *the Leader of our worship* (Heb 2:12). Amen!

Jesus Christ is the Leader of our worship.

---

61. Cocksworth, *Holy, Holy, Holy,* 119.
62. Horton, "Worship."

# Part 6

## Worship in Church History

In this part we will survey developments in worship through the history of the church. This will be a very brief examination of what is, of course, a huge subject, and the reader is directed towards other resources that deal with the subject in far more depth, notably:

- Geoffrey Wainwright and Karen B. Westerfield Tucker, *The Oxford History of Christian Worship*

- James F. White, *A Brief History of Christian Worship*

- James F. White, *Christian Worship in North America: A Retrospective, 1955–1995*

- Lester Ruth and Swee Hong Lim, *Lovin' on Jesus: A Concise History of Contemporary Worship*

- Lester Ruth and Swee Hong Lim, *A History of Contemporary Praise & Worship: Understanding the Ideas That Reshaped the Protestant Church*

We will give special emphasis to the Reformation, because of its importance for evangelical faith and worship.

27. The Pre-Reformation Period and Worship

28. The Protestant Reformation and Worship

29. The Post-Reformation Period and Worship

# 27

# THE PRE-REFORMATION PERIOD AND WORSHIP

## The Apostolic Age (ca. AD 1–100)

**Early Church House Worship (artist unknown)**

## Sparse Information

W e have little detailed information as to exactly what the earliest gatherings of the church might have looked like. We are not told a lot in the Bible, and other historical sources are few as well.

## Relationship to Judaism

We do know that there was considerable *continuity*, at least at first, with Judaism. The first Christians were Jews gathered in Jerusalem from many different nations, as we read in the account of the day of Pentecost in Acts 2. The apostles at first continued to participate in synagogue services and temple ceremonies and feasts (Acts 2:46; 3:1), and we even see them teaching in the temple precinct (Acts 5:20, 42). When the apostle Paul during his missionary journeys would arrive in a new city, he would first go into the Jewish synagogue and begin his teaching ministry there.

But then there was growing *discontinuity* with Judaism in the face of growing rejection by the Jewish leadership and the beginning of the Gentile mission through Paul especially (Acts 13:46–48). The Jerusalem Council (Acts 15) definitively showed that the church was a new work of God and not just an offshoot or a branch of Judaism.

## Influence of Temple *and* Synagogue

We saw in ch. 16 that during the Babylonian captivity the synagogue gatherings were initiated for the exiled Jews to gather and listen to the word of God. And it was pointed out then also that, when the Jews returned from captivity to Jerusalem and rebuilt the temple, reinstituted the sacrifices, and reactivated the priesthood, the synagogue services continued in the communities of Israel.

These two forms of gathered worship (temple and synagogue) continued side by side all the way through the time of Christ and beyond, and both forms would have influence on Christian worship. The influence of the synagogue could be seen in the reading and expounding of Scripture, and the temple's sacrificial aspect would be reflected in the remembrance of Christ's sacrifice in the Lord's Supper. N. T. Wright expresses this phenomenon thus:

> By Paul's day the synagogue theology was well developed: where two or three study Torah, there the Shekinah dwells among them. In other words, for those who cannot easily make the journey to Jerusalem, God has provided another way of meeting him in worship and self-offering. The Torah, read and studied and prayed in the synagogue, is the means of God's presence. Now, for Paul, the Spirit picks up both Temple and Torah and, fulfilling both, transcends both.

The early Christians believed that their Spirit-led worship was the new-covenantal form of that synagogue and temple worship, worshipping the same creator God but filling that worship with new content relating specifically to Jesus crucified and risen.[1]

## House Meetings

Christian gatherings took place mostly in homes (Acts 2:46), especially on the first day of the week, Sunday (in commemoration of the resurrection), and often included common meals culminating in the celebration of the Lord's Supper (1 Cor 11:17–22).

## Included Elements

Elements in these gatherings included "the apostles' teaching [expounding the Old Testament in the light of Christ's coming—see Acts 17:2; 18:28] and the fellowship, the breaking of bread [the Lord's Supper] and the prayers" (Acts 2:42), as well as praise (Acts 2:46) both spoken and sung (Eph 5:18–20; Col 3:16).[2]

## Word/Table Structure

A basic pattern of word and table typified Christian meetings not only during this period, but for many centuries afterwards.[3] (The Lord's Supper was observed in one form or another in virtually every Sunday gathering until the sixteenth century.) This pattern reflects not only the dual influence of synagogue (word) and temple (table), but also of the biblical paradigm of ↓ revelation (word) and ↑ response (table).

---

1. N. T. Wright, "Worship and the Spirit."

2. See a more detailed examination of Acts 2:42, 46 in chs. 30, 33, and 37.

3. See Dix, *Shape of the Liturgy*, 36–37. During the 1980s, this author visited a Brethren church in East Germany during the communist era there. In that church, there were two distinct services on Sunday morning. First was what they called the Service of the Word, and then after a break they reconvened for what they termed the Service of the Table.

## The Patristic Age (ca. AD 100–400)

*The Three Heirarchs*, from Thessaloniki[4]

The patristic age is also known as the age of the *church fathers* (the great early theologians of the church).

## On the Margins

The church was still gathering in small communities. Occasionally there were persecutions, as the new faith collided with Judaism and with Roman emperor worship; in times of persecution, there was often a feeling that the Lord must be going to return very soon.

## Developing Practices

There were evolving traditions. There are a few extant writings from this period that show some patterns emerging in how worship was done.

4. In public domain. See https://www.ebyzantinemuseum.gr/?i=bxm.en.exhibit&id=23.

## Canon, Councils, and Creeds

It was during this period that the canon of Scripture was decided upon by common agreement: that is, which books were considered to be God's inspired word and thus belonged to the New Testament. (There were other writings, often fanciful, that were rejected as uninspired.)

It was also during this time that great church councils were convened that formulated the creeds of the church: the Apostles' Creed, the Nicene Creed, the Chalcedonian Creed. The councils and the creeds that arose from them were in response to various heresies and false teachings that were promoted by some, raising the need for the church to establish once and for all what doctrines undergirded the orthodox Christian faith, especially: the full deity of Christ, the nature of the incarnation and the so-called hypostatic union (the fusion in one person of complete deity and complete humanity in Jesus Christ), and the Trinity.

## Lex Orandi, Lex Credendi

One interesting concept that arose during these debates and councils is represented by the Latin phrase *lex orandi, lex credendi* (literally, "the law of prayer is the law of faith"). As the leaders of the church gathered and formulated the creeds, they would often refer to *already established patterns of worship* as informing what the true doctrine should be.

That is very interesting, because of course now we go to the Bible for the truths upon which to base our worship practices (hence the subtitle of this book is *Biblical Foundations of Worship*). But at that time there was the conviction that, in the absence of a completed canon of Scripture and authoritative creedal statements, the Holy Spirit nevertheless faithfully worked in the church to help it develop appropriate worship practices; and those practices were then themselves appealed to as a reflection of divine truth.

For instance, the *Trinity*, though the word itself does not occur in Scripture itself, was nevertheless implied in Jesus's baptismal command, which certainly was carried over into the early church's practice of the baptismal rite:

> Go therefore and make disciples of all nations, baptizing them in the name of the *Father* and of the *Son* and of the *Holy Spirit*. (Matt 28:19)

And Paul's Trinitarian benediction was probably used in numerous local churches:

> The grace of the Lord *Jesus Christ* and the love of *God* and the fellowship of the *Holy Spirit* be with you all. (2 Cor 13:14)

> The essence of the doctrine of the Trinity was first articulated in worship. Furthermore, during the whole process of the formulation of the doctrine, worship acted as a custodian of the trinitarian revelation of God and as a criterion for judging whether theological statements remained faithful to the way God had shown himself to be.[5]

Another example of early church practice informing doctrinal formulation was how Jesus from early on *was worshiped as God*, though the Christians (as the Jews who seeded the early church) were still firmly monotheistic. Bruce Shelley notes:

> The mystery of the God-man was central to Christian worship long before it became central to Christian thinking. "Deep instinct," J. S. Whale once told the undergraduates at Cambridge University, "has always told the church that the safest eloquence concerning the mystery of Christ is in our praise. The living church is a worshiping, singing church, not a school of people holding all the correct doctrines." Whale meant that the most treasured hymns of the church have always treated Christ as an Object of Worship. You find the beating heart of Christian experience not in the church's creed, but in its music.[6]

Thus the church's worship guided its reflections and conclusions on the unique divine/human nature of Christ.

## Growing Formalism

As the period progresses, we find that worship becomes more formalized, ceremonial, and sacramental. Baptism and the Lord's Supper, and increasingly elaborate rites surrounding them, become more prominent. Infant baptism develops, and in some circles degenerates into the heresy of baptismal regeneration.

This trend towards increased ceremonialism really hearkens back to the rituals of the Old Testament, leaving behind the simpler gatherings and

5. Cocksworth, *Holy, Holy, Holy*, 123.
6. Shelley, *Church History*, 109.

patterns that characterized the very early decades of the church. This trend continued and in fact was magnified into and through the Middle Ages.

## AD 312

In this year a crucial event in the history of the church and of its worship occurred: the conversion of the Roman emperor Constantine. Christianity, which had been a marginalized and sometimes persecuted sect, pitted against the Jewish faith and the pantheon of Roman and Greek gods, suddenly became the official religion of the Roman Empire. Persecutions immediately ceased. Shelley observes: "The [Christian] movement started the fourth century as a persecuted minority; it ended the century as the established religion of the Empire."[7]

It is actually still debated, many centuries later, whether this development was a good thing or not for the church. Christianity had become acceptable: as the state religion, people would naturally identify with it, whether or not it reflected their hearts' reality. The secularizing of the church that has often accompanied this situation prompted Bernard Lewis to exclaim: "Christianity captured the Roman Empire, and was, in a sense, captured by it."[8]

And that state-church pattern continued in most of Europe until recent decades. People in France normally considered that being French meant to be Catholic, and the same was true in Spain and Italy; and to be from one of the Scandinavian countries carried with it the assumption that you were Lutheran. (This identification is less strong in Europe today, but is still a strong influence in other areas, such as in postcolonial Latin America with its enduring Catholic tradition.) This intermingling of the church and state, in terms of a state and official state religion, is something that has often detracted from the witness of the church, because people would just identify with a branch of the church for political or cultural reasons, rather than for any sort of spiritual reason.[9]

---

7. Shelley, *Church History*, 89.

8. B. Lewis, *Middle East*, 33.

9. This prevalent state church pattern in Europe was the reason that the founders of the United States wrote into the Bill of Rights a strong commitment to the division of church and state, insisting that the new nation would have no officially sanctioned religion: "Congress shall make no law respecting an establishment of religion, or prohibiting the free exercise thereof" (Amendment 1).

It is also well documented that the church has often grown more and been more spiritually healthy in contexts of hardship and persecution: witness the explosive growth of Christianity in China under communist rule, and a similar phenomenon in Eastern Europe under the yoke of the Soviet Union.[10] The more difficult living conditions in the Third World and the so-called Global South have undoubtedly contributed greatly to the amazing growth and vigor of the church in those areas recently, as opposed to Christianity's decline in the affluent West.

## The Middle Ages (ca. AD 400–1500)

**Salisbury Cathedral, by Andrew Emptage[11]**

## Rise of Priesthood, Saints, Mariology

As mentioned in ch. 26, the patristic-age debates concerning the true nature of Christ and the need to defend his full deity led to an emphasis on his divine nature at the expense of an appreciation of his full humanity. This neglect led the church to look to other means of mediation than "the one mediator between God and men, the man Christ Jesus" (1 Tim

10. Since the fall of the Soviet Union in 1990, there has been a marked rise of secularism, as well as inroads by various cults, in Eastern Europe.

11. See https://www.dreamstime.com/royalty-free-stock-images-salisbury-cathedral-interior-image11578359.

2:5). And so an understanding arose that one had to go through a priest as a conduit in order to approach God's presence, and that prayer had to be directed to and through one of the saints or to Mary in order for that prayer to reach God.[12]

This is another instance of a return to an Old Testament sort of thinking concerning access to God. As we have seen, the people of Israel could not go directly into God's presence; they had to go through the mediation of the priests, who offered sacrifices to God on their behalf.

Throughout the patristic age and the Middle Ages we see a continuing rise of institutionalism overshadowing the possibility of a personal relationship with God through Christ.

## Ascendance of the Mass, Decline of Preaching

The Mass became increasingly more central in the worship service, and the idea of transubstantiation took hold (though not declared official church dogma until 1551): the teaching that in the Mass the elements are miraculously transformed in their essence (though not in their appearance) into the actual body and blood of Christ.

As the Mass became the central point and focus of the gathering of the church, preaching took on less and less of a role, until by the end of the Middle Ages it had virtually disappeared from services. The Mass became the sole focus.

## Nonparticipation

The services, again hearkening back to an Old Testament model, became more what people *watched*, not what people did or participated in. "Mass was offered *for* the people . . . not celebrated *by* the people."[13]

A large part of this was that the Mass continued to be celebrated in Latin only, which was no longer a language that most people understood (except the priests). Also, the priest would conduct most of the

12. "The medieval Church had tended to substitute the priesthood, the sacrifice, the merits, the intercession of the Church—the vicarious humanity of the *ecclesia* (Mary and the saints)—for the vicarious humanity of the Christ, in a way which obscured the Gospel of grace, the Good the News of what God has done for us in Christ" (J. Torrance, "Christ in Our Place," in T. Torrance et al., *Passion for Christ*, 37).

13. Geoffrey Wainwright, "Periods of Liturgical History," in Jones et al., *Study of Liturgy*, 64.

celebration facing the altar with his back to the people (so that the people could hardly hear him, even if they had understood the Latin).

## No Vernacular Bible

The Bible itself was generally not available to individuals; and was allowed to be only in Latin anyway (which only the priests learned), instead of in the vernacular (the language of the people).

## Church Tradition

The traditions and teaching of the institutional church became increasingly important and eventually came to be held as having equal authority with the Scriptures. That would come to be a central issue in the Reformation, as we will see.

## The Great Schism

In AD 1054 the Western and Eastern Churches split (leading to what are now known as the Roman Catholic Church and the Eastern Orthodox Church). There were some theological issues involved, but the primary cause for the schism was the West's insistence that the bishop of Rome had authority over the entire church, superseding that of the bishop of Constantinople in the East. The bishop of Rome came to be called the pope by the Western Church.

## Corruption in the Church

The supposedly spiritual institution of the church was wracked more and more by controversies and corruption through this period. At times there were two or three rival popes vying for power, each claiming to be the true pope and being favored by one city or another.

Along with the desire for power and influence came the potential for financial gain, and many priests succumbed to the temptation to use their position in this way. A very worldly clergy often were characterized by immorality and commercialism. The sale of "indulgences" (whereby one could supposedly buy a relative's release from purgatory) was one practice decried by Luther and the other Reformers.

## Need for Reformation

Because of all the excesses, corruption, and worldliness surrounding the institutional church, by the end of the Middle Ages there was a widespread feeling that the church was badly in need of reformation.

> Both the tabernacle and the temple influenced early Christian worship.

# 28

# THE PROTESTANT REFORMATION AND WORSHIP

## (ca. AD 1500–1650)

Reformation Wall in Parc des Bastions, Geneva, by InnaFelker[1]

1. See https://www.shutterstock.com/image-photo/reformation-wall-parc-des-bastions
-geneva-225894199.

## The Beginning

T he beginning of the Protestant Reformation is usually traced to
October 31, 1517, the date on which Martin Luther posted his
Ninety-Five Theses to the door of the Castle Church in Wittenberg.[2]

Luther lässt 95 Sätze gegen den Ablass an die Schlosskirche zu Wittenberg
anschlagen den 31 Octbr. 1517, by W. Br. v. Löwenstern[3]

The Ninety-Five Theses were questions, points of disputation, and disagreements that Luther had with the established church of his day.

## The Debt We Owe

The Reformers, at incredible personal cost,[4] championed the truth of
God. They stood against all the political and ecclesiastical authorities of

2. "Reformation Day," October 31, is still a public holiday in Lutheran areas of
Europe, and is also celebrated (or the Sunday before, as Reformation Sunday) by many
different Protestant churches.

3. See https://www.loc.gov/item/2001695713/.

4. Among earlier forerunners of the Reformation, Jan Hus was burned at the stake,
John Wycliffe was declared a heretic, and William Tyndale was strangled. Martin
Luther was eventually excommunicated by the church, Ulrich Zwingli was killed in
battle, and Thomas Cranmer was burned at the stake.

their day, strengthened by faith in God and in his word. In a very real sense, we are involved in the study contained in this book because these Reformers stood for the truth of God's word and helped to return the true faith to the church of Jesus Christ.

Truly they were those "of whom the world was not worthy" (Heb 11:38), whom we rightly honor as true heroes of the faith:

> Remember your leaders, those who spoke to you the word of God. Consider the outcome of their way of life, and imitate their faith. (Heb 13:7)

## A Reformation of Doctrine

It is important to realize that Luther and the other Reformers were not trying to start a new branch of the church, a new religion, or introduce new teachings into the church. They were seeking renewal and restoration, not revolution. They were trying to recover the biblical gospel that had been lost to the church, to restore to the church the New Testament, apostolic teachings about the nature and means of salvation. It was only when the established church rejected them that they had to pull out and start something new.

The apostolic teachings that the Reformers focused on as their rallying cry were concerned with the doctrine of *justification by faith* as summarized and identified by five Latin phrases:

### *Sola scriptura* (The Scriptures Alone)

The Scriptures of the Old and New Testaments are the final and ultimate authority in all matters of faith, doctrine, and life. The traditions and teachings of the church are secondary and must be subjected to the oversight of, and evaluated according to, God's word.

> All Scripture is breathed out by God and profitable for teaching, for reproof, for correction, and for training in righteousness. (2 Tim 3:16)

## *Sola gratia* (By Grace Alone)

Salvation is a free gift of God's grace. One cannot do anything to deserve it or earn it.

> For by grace you have been saved through faith. And this is not your own doing; it is the gift of God, not a result of works, so that no one may boast. (Eph 2:8–9)

## *Sola fide* (By Faith Alone)

This gift of God's grace is received through faith alone, not through works, but merely by acknowledging and accepting the work of Jesus Christ on our behalf.

> A person is not justified by works of the law but through faith in Jesus Christ, so we also have believed in Christ Jesus, in order to be justified by faith in Christ and not by works of the law, because by works of the law no one will be justified. (Gal 2:16)

## *Solus Christus* (In Christ Alone)

It is only through Christ, his righteousness, and his redeeming work on the cross that we receive salvation.

> For there is one God, and there is one mediator between God and men, the man Christ Jesus, who gave himself as a ransom for all, which is the testimony given at the proper time. (1 Tim 2:5–6)

## *Soli Deo gloria* (To God Alone Be the Glory)

God has done all these things in this way that he might receive all the glory.

> ... to the praise of his glorious grace. (Eph 1:6)

> For from him and through him and to him are all things. To him be glory forever. Amen. (Rom 11:36)

God receives all the glory in providing salvation for us by grace, through faith, through the work of Christ, as revealed in the Scriptures to us: these are the great doctrinal emphases of the Protestant Reformation.

## A Reformation of Worship

As crucial as this gospel-restoring reformation of doctrine was, there was also a very important reformation of *worship* as well. As N. T. Wright has summarized it:

> The sixteenth-century Reformers protested against the way in which the Medieval church had turned liturgy and much else besides into a quasi-pagan magic system, which enhanced the power of those who operated it, and did little or nothing to let the true gospel shine out.[5]

## Return to the Word of God

The word of God read and preached was restored to a central role in the worship service. And the Bible was made available to the people translated into their own languages (the invention of the printing press in the fifteenth century made it much more feasible to produce and distribute large numbers of Bibles). Luther himself translated the Bible into German.

> Faith comes from hearing, and hearing through the word of Christ. (Rom 10:17)

## Return to Participatory Worship

As we have seen, the church in the Middle Ages had reverted to an Old Testament model of priestly activity and congregational passivity. The Reformers sought to restore worship to the people.

This was done, first of all, by conducting the service in the language of the people, so that the people could understand and be engaged. The people were encouraged to take an active role in worship as an expression of the "priesthood of all believers" (see 1 Pet 2:9). The development of congregational song was especially important in this.

> Let the word of Christ dwell in you richly . . . singing psalms and hymns and spiritual songs, with thankfulness in your hearts to God. (Col 3:16)

Luther himself wrote numerous hymns for congregational singing, and John Calvin instituted the singing of metrical paraphrases of the psalms.

5. N. T. Wright, *Future of the People*.

## Return to the Sole Priesthood of Christ

As we saw in ch. 26, the efforts in the early centuries of the church to defend the deity of Christ led to a neglect of his full humanity, especially as it related to his mediating role in worship. In the Middle Ages the church assumed the need for a human priesthood to mediate between sinful humanity and the exalted Christ, the majestic Judge and King. Prayer was made to Mary or one of the saints as an intermediary.

The Reformers, on the other hand, insisted with Paul that:

> There is one God, and *one mediator* between man and God, the man Christ Jesus. (1 Tim 2:5)

They stressed the direct access that every believer has into the presence of God, without the need to go through another human mediator (priest, Mary, or saint):

> Therefore, brethren . . . we have confidence to *enter the holy places by the blood of Jesus.* (Heb 10:19)

## Conclusion

And so we see the incredible significance of the Protestant Reformation: how God used the Reformers to restore the apostolic doctrine of justification by grace through faith to the church; and how he used them to bring about a reformation of worship, which encouraged the participation of God's people, the centrality of the word of God, and the importance of our access through Christ and through him alone.

> "There is one Mediator between God and men,
> the man Christ Jesus." (1 Tim 2:5)

# 29

# THE POST-REFORMATION PERIOD AND WORSHIP

## (ca. AD 1650–Present)

**Untitled, by FOTOGRIN**[1]

1. https://www.shutterstock.com/image-illustration/christian-cross-world-map-behind-crucifix-2197722123.

## Broad Movements

T his is a period with a great deal of different developments,[2] and the chart below traces some of the broader historical trends and compares their tendencies:[3]

| Middle Ages | Reformed ($16^{th}$–$17^{th}$ centuries) | Pietism ($17^{th}$–$18^{th}$ centuries) | Revivalism ($19^{th}$ century) | Liberalism ($19^{th}$ century) | Evangelicalism ($20^{th}$ century) | Charismatic Revival ($20^{th}$ century) |
|---|---|---|---|---|---|---|
| Mass | Preaching, doctrine | Devotion, experience | Decision | Social engagement | Teaching | Experience, love |
| Mass-centered | Preaching-centered | Emotion-centered | Music–> Sermon–> Invitation | Formal | Preaching-centered | Emotion-centered |
| –Word | –Worship | –Word | –Edification | –Gospel | –Worship | –Doctrine |
| +Lord's Supper | +Word | +Adoration | +Mission | +Social action | +Doctrine | +Relationships +Worship |

This period is characterized by the multiplication of Protestant confessions and denominations (there are at least nine major branches, and hundreds of distinct groups). The disunity, factionalism, and divisions among Protestants has not always been honoring to Christ (who, after all, prayed "that they may be one" [John 17:11]), but we find different distinguishing characteristics and emphases in different groups. Some are more "left-wing": that is, more radical in their departure from the practices of the church of the Middle Ages; some are more "right-wing" or conservative: hence, closer to the medieval model. In the early centuries of this period, the Anabaptists and the Quakers were the most extreme; Reformed and Methodist groups were more middle-of-the-road; and Lutherans and Anglicans were more conservative, preserving some of the more ceremonial aspects such as found in Roman Catholic worship.

2. Including the modern missionary movement and the enormous expansion of Christianity worldwide. Many of these developments cannot be dealt with in depth here, and the reader is directed to the more extensive historical studies listed at the beginning of ch. 27.

3. Chart adapted in part from Dawn, *How Shall We Worship?*, 108–13.

And in the later centuries, frontier worship and later Pentecostal worship differ greatly from the more formal expressions.

## Broad Trends and Developments

In this section's very quick flyover of a big expanse of history, we want to highlight just a few of the important trends and developments in the area of worship (which will necessarily be broad generalizations with notable exceptions).

### Ascendancy of Preaching, Decline of Worship

The reaction of the Reformers to the Middle Ages' neglect of the word and preaching in worship (and overemphasis on the Mass) led to a healthy reemphasis on the centrality of the Scriptures and their exposition in public worship. The resultant pendulum swing also led to downplaying in many traditions the importance of worship and the frequency of the Lord's Supper (which until the Reformation was practiced in some form in virtually every church gathering).

### Differing Views on "Biblical" Worship

Every Christian group seeks to be *biblical* in its worship practices,[4] but there have been divergent historical streams concerning just what *biblical* worship entails. The view of Calvin, and those who follow him in what has become known as the *regulative principle of worship* (especially Presbyterians and other Reformed groups) was that only what the Bible *specifically mentions in precept or example* should be allowed in public worship. Luther and his heirs (Lutherans, Anglicans, etc.) preferred what is known as the *normative principle of worship*: that anything that is *not specifically forbidden* in Scripture is allowable in worship.

These views have serious implications for what finds its way into corporate worship: such things as drama, videos, dance, etc. Obviously, those

---

4. That is why the study group of the Evangelical Theological Society devoted to the study of worship carries the name of *Biblical* Worship Section (see etsworship.wordpress.com).

who adhere to the normative principle would make allowance for such practices, whereas those who follow the regulative principle would not.[5]

And yet even supporters of the regulative principle are faced with the stark truth (which we touched on in ch. 19, and will examine more closely in chs. 36 and 37) that the New Testament has very, very little to say about the specifics of worship in the church. All kinds of decisions must be made on grounds other than simply what the Bible lays out.[6] There is no one set form in the New Testament that we can just take and apply. So, the regulative principle still leaves a lot of things open to debate and wise judgment (service times, service length, place and form and length of the preaching, music, frequency and mode of communion, etc., etc.).

## The Development of Hymnody

After the Reformers reintroduced congregational singing to the church, succeeding centuries saw rich traditions of songs for worship develop. The priestly chanting of the Middle Ages was replaced by Scripture-based hymns; and, as we have seen, Luther made a notable contribution to this corpus.

Metrical versions of the psalms were encouraged by Calvin and had a far-reaching influence,[7] until Isaac Watts (1674–1748) broke the mold: he rightly observed that if only the psalms were sung, then the person of Christ and his work would never come to expression in the people's song. Watts composed richly lyrical hymn texts that celebrated the work of God and of his Son. Charles Wesley (1707–1788) and others followed in his wake.

The nineteenth century saw the rise of gospel hymnody, focused on an experiential response to the saving work of Christ, which found its way out of evangelistic tent meetings and into the church. And the late twentieth

---

5. Monte Wilson caricatures the extreme regulative principle thus: "Do they use art? It must be a sin. Do they utilize ceremony? Ceremonies are evil. Do they light candles? Candles are of the devil" (Wilson, "Church-o-Rama or Corporate Worship," 74).

6. In fact, on more than one occasion this author has heard or read an impassioned defense of the regulative principle, only for the speaker or writer to then quote *not* from the Bible, but from the Westminster Confession of Faith to illustrate just what those biblically regulated principles are supposed to be! For a balanced treatment of this issue from an insider to the Reformed/regulative perspective, see Gore, *Covenantal Worship.*

7. A few present-day denominations still adhere to this practice of "exclusive psalmody."

saw the development, parallel to the meteoric rise of contemporary praise and worship choruses and songs, of a more traditionally structured sort of modern hymnody from such songwriters as Keith and Kristyn Getty.

## The Enlightenment/Rationalism/Liberalism

The Enlightenment of the seventeenth and eighteenth centuries empha-sized reason over faith, and led to a general skepticism about the supernat-ural aspects of the Christian faith. This led to the German philosophical rationalism of the nineteenth century, which in turn spawned theological liberalism with its denial of miracles, the inspiration of Scripture, and the deity of Christ. This liberalism infected young North American theologians studying in German universities, who then became faculty members at American seminaries and trained future pastors in this way of thinking. Then, as pastors, they brought this teaching to the people in the churches where they ministered.

## Fundamentalism, Evangelicalism, Free Churches

As a reaction to these widespread trends early in the twentieth century, there was the rise of fundamentalism (defending the "fundamentals" of the faith—the virgin birth, inspiration of Scripture, miracles, etc.—from liberal attacks), which in turn became evangelicalism, with its emphasis on the Scriptures and the gospel in contrast to the social issues that pre-dominated in liberal churches.[8] Theologically orthodox faculty left liberal seminaries and founded competing institutions of a more evangelical per-suasion. Many believers left the theologically corrupt "mainline" churches and started new evangelical denominations or independent churches.

## The Neglect of Worship

Evangelicalism's reaction to theological liberalism led to a greater empha-sis on Bible teaching and preaching in the churches. But this necessary reemphasis was another pendulum swing that resulted in again downplay-ing the importance of worship in many churches. That was the situation

8. Of course, the reaction to liberalism (which often tended to focus only on social issues) led evangelicalism to ignore social issues for a long time; thankfully, a more biblical balance seems to be slowly developing.

that A. W. Tozer was addressing in 1961 (as we saw in the preface) when he called worship "the missing jewel" in modern evangelicalism.

## The "Reformation" of Worship

As also noted in the preface, since Tozer wrote in 1961, there has been a tremendous surge in interest in, attention to, and development of worship in the evangelical world. God has moved to restore the proper place of worship in Christ's body.[9]

One major influence was the charismatic movement of the 1960s and beyond. The movement's emphasis on heartfelt and emotional engagement with God in worship helped to reawaken an appreciation for this aspect of worship even in non-charismatic churches (especially in contrast to the pedantic nature of much traditional worship at the time).

The charismatic movement's musical evolution greatly influenced the rise of contemporary worship music, often called "praise and worship music" (this nomenclature itself owing its origins to a characteristic sharp distinction made in charismatic worship between "praise" and "worship").[10]

The so-called worship wars of the 1980s and 1990s were basically fought over issues of musical style and instruments in worship, as the new contemporary worship music movement collided with bastions of traditional church music and worship styles. Often the battle lines were drawn between traditional (usually older) adherents and those (usually the young) who preferred the newer contemporary styles.[11] Sadly, these conflicts led to much division and dissent in churches, even leading to

9. It is interesting to note the developments in worship also during this period in the Catholic Church, which as a result of the Second Vatican Council (1962–65) made allowance for the Mass to be held in the local language (instead of the Latin required since the sixteenth century), placed a greater emphasis on the Bible and preaching, and allowed the use of varied music styles and instrumentation. Mainline Protestant churches also were influenced by the rise of contemporary worship.

10. This distinction is artificial, in this writer's opinion. Biblically, *worship* is a broad, overarching concept (as we have seen in this study), and *praise* is one aspect or subset of worship.

11. Of course, the designation *contemporary* (and even *traditional*, for that matter) is a notoriously fluid category that can refer to a wide range of current expressions. (For that matter, *traditional* can cover quite a spectrum of practices as well.) The "Composers' Datebook" on National Public Radio reminds us that "all music was once new"!

church splits in some instances. More recently, many churches have sought to make peace with the new realities by seeking to blend traditional and contemporary elements, as a way to honor and satisfy all the generations represented in the church and to foster unity by being together in worship, in spite of all the differences in preference. Other churches have chosen to provide separate traditional and contemporary services, largely along generational lines.

The issue of church music continues to be a hot-button issue. In fact, it has been suggested that many evangelicals choose a local church to attend based on its musical offerings, rather than because of the church's preaching or doctrinal stance. All the more reason for churches and their leaders to diligently study what the Bible teaches on worship (and what it leaves open), as a way forward. Hence this book.

## Looking to the Future: A Need for Balance

Too often the increased appreciation for and emphasis on worship in our day has led to a softening commitment to the reading and exposition of the word in corporate worship. We have just observed other pendulum swings, overreactions, and overcorrections of this sort.

As we saw in our study of Heb 2:12 in ch. 26, Jesus himself considers *both* the proclamation of God's word and the praises of the people to be so important that he has committed himself to mediating *both* of those activities in the assembly; so, a balance is called for (though, sadly, too seldom achieved in practice): a balance of revelation and response, theology and doxology, preaching and music; "completing the cycle" in worship, as we considered in ch. 4; seeing the *entire* service as indeed an offering of *worship*: worship through singing, praying, giving, Scripture reading, preaching, partaking at the table.

God has been doing great things in these last decades in restoring the importance of worship to the church of Jesus Christ. This book, and your study of it, are a small part of the grand scope of what God has been doing in and for his church. Let us continue to strive for the kind of balance that will truly give him "glory in the church and in Christ Jesus" (Eph 3:21).

---

There is a continuing need to balance revelation and response, theology and doxology, preaching and corporate praise.

---

# Part 7

## Worship in the Church

H aving considered the broad topic of worship up to this point from
many different angles, and having taken an intentionally nonsectarian approach to the lessons we can learn from the Scriptures, we turn
now finally to focus on the practice of worship on the local church level.

This is, of course, a perilous undertaking, because it is here that we
inevitably run into the issues of taste, preference, and culture that lead
to so much of the debate and (sadly) dissension and even division in
our churches today. There is obviously an incredible diversity of worship
styles, approaches, and practices in our own local context, not to mention
across the world and down through the centuries. In this part we will
seek to carefully distinguish between biblical *nonnegotiables* and allowable *negotiables* as we take a broad view of worship practices across the
church of Jesus Christ. We will definitely need the Scriptures to help us
navigate this minefield!

# 30

# THE NATURE OF WORSHIP IN THE CHURCH

## Jewish Roots

As noted in ch. 27, while we do not have a lot of historical information about worship in the very earliest churches, we can observe that there were influences from Christianity's Jewish roots: both from the synagogue (especially the practice of the reading and expounding of the Scriptures) and from the temple (especially the remembrance of the once-for-all sacrifice of Christ in the celebration of the Lord's Supper).

## The New Testament Witness

There is a little information to be found in the New Testament. In Acts 2, Luke tells us that at the conclusion of Peter's Pentecost sermon "those who received his word were baptized, and there were added that day about three thousand souls" (2:41). And then *in the very next verse* Luke tells us what these new believers regularly did when they got together: "And they devoted themselves to the apostles' teaching and the fellowship, to the breaking of bread and the prayers" (2:42); and a few verses later we read that they were also "praising God" (2:47). They "devoted" themselves to these activities:

- The apostles' teaching
- The fellowship
- The breaking of bread (or the Lord's Supper)

- The prayers

- Praising God

It seems likely that Luke mentions these elements *immediately* after the account of the conversion of the first Christians (and emphasizes that they regularly "devoted" themselves to these) in order to suggest that these were *normative* activities for the church. And in fact, if we consider what elements of worship are found in virtually *every* Christian tradition, across denominations and down through the centuries, we see that these are indeed consistent features (though fleshed out in widely diverse ways):

- The word of God

- Fellowship

- Communion or Lord's Supper

- Prayer

- Praise

These seem to be nonnegotiable *constants* for worship to be truly Christian. (The list is not exhaustive, of course; true worship should also be Christ-centered and gospel-centered, for instance.) As we saw in our look at church history in part 6, around these elements often developed very complex structures; nevertheless, it is important to recognize these consistent elements. (More on this in ch. 37.)

Elsewhere in the New Testament, the element of *singing* is mentioned in Eph 5:18–20; Col 3:16; and 1 Cor 14:26 (though most of 1 Cor 14 revolves around Paul correcting abuses relating to the exercise of prophecy and tongues in the public meetings).

## Church History

The earliest extant account of a Christian worship service dates from about AD 155:

> On the day called Sunday, all who live in cities or in the country gather together to one place, and the memoirs of the apostles or the writings of the prophets are read, as long as time permits; then, when the reader has ceased, the president verbally instructs, and exhorts to the imitation of these good things. Then we all rise together and pray, and, as we before said, when

our prayer is ended, bread and wine and water are brought, and the president in like manner offers prayers and thanksgivings, according to his ability, and the people assent, saying Amen; and there is a distribution to each, and a participation of that over which thanks have been given, and to those who are absent a portion is sent by the deacons. And they who are well to do, and willing, give what each thinks fit; and what is collected is deposited with the president, who succours the orphans and widows, and those who, through sickness or any other cause, are in want, and those who are in bonds, and the strangers sojourning among us, and in a word takes care of all who are in need.[1]

## Later Characterizations

Gordon Lathrop makes these observations about the commonalities of many (if not most) Christian gatherings up to this day:

An assembly of people gathers. The gathering place may be very simple—a hut, a room, a house—or quite elaborate, one of the buildings developed over time from the large public buildings of the late Roman Empire. Singing enables these people to come together, and prayer, often spoken by one who acts as a presider, sums up the sense of the song, interpreting that coming together as being before God. Then, as if this were the principal reason for the gathering, ancient texts are read by one or more readers. Frequently the readings are interspersed with further song. The presider speaks about the meaning of the readings and the meaning of the gathering, and the people respond with yet more song or with an ancient credal text, corporately recited. Another person in the assembly leads prayers for a variety of needs throughout the world. Then gifts of money (and sometimes food) that have been brought by persons in the assembly are collected. Some of the people set a central table—perhaps a simple piece of furniture, perhaps a massive stone—with food, linens, and candles as if for a feast, adding to the growing sense in the meeting that the other principal reason for the gathering is to be this meal. The food set out, however, is simply bread—in one or another form—and a cup of wine. In dialogue with the assembly, the one who presides speaks or sings a formal thanksgiving over the food, and, most commonly aided by others, distributes

1. Justin Martyr, "First Apology of Justin," 185–86. It has been noted that, interestingly, Justin makes no mention of music in this passage; but he does speak of hymns elsewhere in this document.

the food to the assembly for all to eat and drink. Concluding prayers and songs follow, and the assembly is dismissed.

Such a gathering, widely practiced in most of the Christian churches as the principal act of worship, has been especially associated with Sunday, though sometimes it may also occur on other days. It has been practiced, more or less in this form, for a long time, being traceable to the earliest centuries of the Christian movement. In the diverse churches the outline of the assemblies' actions may differ slightly, being intensified with more or less ceremony, led by a single person or by many people, interspersed with more or less communal song, and partly or wholly obscured because of the overlay of rich secondary patterns of action. In all of the churches, other events may be inserted into this outline, especially that washing with water whereby the community adds people to its number. Still, something like this assembly occurs weekly throughout the churches and is treasured as the very heart of Christianity.[2]

James K. A. Smith considers the various components of Christian worship from the perspective of those who have been constituted as "a *royal* priesthood" (1 Pet 2:9) and who "offer to God acceptable worship, with reverence and awe" because we are "grateful for receiving a *kingdom* that cannot be shaken" (Heb 12:28).

| Call to worship[3] | Responding to the invitation of the King |
| --- | --- |
| Greeting | Enjoying the welcome of the King |
| Song | Chanting the language of the kingdom |
| Confession/assurance of pardon | Embracing the hope of the kingdom |
| Creed | Reciting the constitution of the kingdom |
| Prayer | Speaking the language of the kingdom |
| Scripture and sermon | Receiving the instructions of the King |
| Communion | Supping with the King |
| Offering | Embracing the economy of the kingdom |
| Sending | Going as ambassadors of the King[4] |

---

The church: a people "called out."

---

2. Lathrop, *Holy Things*, 1–2.

3. The New Testament word for church is *ekklesia*, literally denoting those who have been "called out."

4. Freely adapted from J. Smith, *Desiring the Kingdom*, 159–207.

# 31

# THE PRIORITY OF WORSHIP IN THE CHURCH

## The Ultimate Goal

A s we saw in ch. 9, John Piper shook up the evangelical world and the missions community with his insistence that:

> Missions is not the ultimate goal of the church. Worship is. Missions exists because worship doesn't. Worship is ultimate, not missions, because God is ultimate, not man. When this age is over, and the countless millions of the redeemed fall on their faces before the throne of God, missions will be no more. It is a temporary necessity. But worship abides forever.[1]

## Piper's Clarification

From the second edition of his book on, Piper has included a new chapter, "Chapter 7—The Inner Simplicity and Outer Freedom of Worldwide Worship," to clarify possible misunderstandings about the above statement. He writes in this chapter:

> I write this final chapter to clarify the first two sentences of chapter 1: "Mission is not the ultimate goal of the church. Worship is." I want to clarify what I mean by "worship," lest any take me to mean merely the gathering of Christians for corporate

---

1. Piper, *Let the Nations Be Glad*, 35.

worship or (still more limiting) that part of the gathering for singing songs and hymns. I love those times and meet God powerfully in them. But to say that missions exists for *that* would be too narrow and far from my meaning. I mean something much more radical and soul-gripping and life-encompassing when I speak of worship as the goal of missions. . . . What makes worship worship is what happens "in spirit and truth"—with or without a place and with or without outward forms. The experience of the heart is the defining, vital, indispensable essence of worship.[2]

## And Yet . . .

Nevertheless, Piper sees corporate worship in the church as a crucial expression of that inner worship of the heart. In fact, as we saw in ch. 9, he goes as far as to state that:

Of all the activities in the church, only one is an end in itself: *worship.*[3]

This is a strong statement, indeed!

You will recall the treatment in ch. 9 comparing the Great Commission and the Great Commandment (in the context of discussing Piper's view that worship is the goal and the fuel of missions). There it was stated that:

2. Piper, *Let the Nations Be Glad*, 239, 243.

3. Piper, "Worship Is an End" (emphasis added).

Robert Wilken concurs: Worship "is not a means which is adapted to attain a certain end—it is an end in itself. . . . When [worship] is rightly regarded, it cannot be said to have a purpose, because it does not exist for the sake of humanity, but for the sake of God. In [worship] man is not so much intended to edify himself as to contemplate God's majesty" ("Angels and Archangels," 13).

So does John Stott:

"It is often said that the church's preeminent responsibility is evangelism. But this is not so, for at least three reasons. First, evangelism comes under the heading of our duty to our neighbor, whereas worship is our duty to God, and our duty to God must take precedence over our duty to our neighbor.

"Second, although all of us are expected to share the gospel with others whenever the opportunity presents itself, evangelism is also a spiritual gift or *charisma* that is given only to some, thus not all Christians are evangelists (see Eph 4:11), but all Christians are worshipers, both in private and in public.

"Third, evangelism is a temporary activity, which will cease when the Lord Jesus comes to consummate his kingdom. But our worship will continue throughout eternity.

"This being so, namely that worship is the church's preeminent duty, we should surely give it our closest attention" (*Living Church*, 34–35).

This understanding will also help us to see in proper context the two aspects of the Great Commission, evangelism and discipleship, in terms of their ultimate purpose: we might say that the end goal of evangelism is to win *more* worshipers for God (from among the nations); and that the final purpose of discipleship is to build *better* worshipers of God—those who love God with ever more of their heart, soul, mind, and strength. Missions, in both its evangelism and discipleship aspects, has as its ultimate aim that more worship be offered up to God, for his glory.

The same conclusion can be brought down to the level of the local church. One could say that the end goal of all the evangelistic/outreach activities of the church (including missions) is to win *more* worshipers for God; and that the end goal of all discipleship activities in the church (everything from children's ministry, to youth groups, to adult small groups and Bible studies, and even preaching itself) is to build *better* worshipers for God: those who love God with ever more of their heart and soul and mind and strength (Matt 22:37). We minister to children, to youth, to adults to help them become worshipers and then to grow in their love for and worship of God. Adapting Piper's phraseology ("Missions exists because worship doesn't"), we could also say that:

- Sunday School exists because worship doesn't.
- Youth groups exist because worship doesn't.
- Evangelism teams exist because worship doesn't.
- Discipleship programs exist because worship doesn't.
- Preaching exists because worship doesn't.

Worship is an end in itself! It is not a means to any other end (except the glory of God).

## The Purpose of the Church

What we see from this is the importance of recognizing *a worship-directed, God-centered purpose for the church*. Through the church's ministries we seek to reach, help, encourage, and disciple people; but ultimately, we do all that *so that* they can reach their created potential as worshipers and lovers of God. As John Stott points out:

The church is essentially a worshipping, praying community. It is often said that the church's priority task is evangelism. But this is really not so. Worship takes precedence over evangelism, partly because love for God is the first commandment and love for neighbor the second, partly because, long after the church's evangelistic task has been completed, God's people will continue to worship.[4]

## Stating the Purpose

This important perspective should make obvious the shortcomings of these examples of actual churches' mission statements:

- Our Mission: To cause God great joy by sharing his love with others as we have seen it in Jesus Christ.

- Our Mission: Developing fully devoted followers of Jesus Christ.

- [First Church] exists in order that we may glorify the Lord God through the means He has established in His Word: Evangelism (introducing people to Jesus Christ) and Edification (building believers to maturity in Jesus Christ).

- For God's glory, [Second Church] is committed to developing disciples in our area and throughout the world so that in all things Christ might have the preeminence.

- To the glory of God: to win, build, and equip disciples of our Lord Jesus through loving, Bible-centered ministry at home and abroad.

These are not bad statements (especially those that focus on God's glory), but worship seems to be neglected in favor of evangelism and discipleship.[5]

Here are some actual examples of more balanced mission statements:

- As a local expression of the universal body of Christ, we desire to corporately love God with all our being by worshipping Him and loving others through relevant ministry both locally and around the world.

---

4. Stott, *Message of 1 Timothy*, 59.

5. It would be an interesting exercise to tweak each of these statements to bring them more into balance.

- [Third Church] exists for the purpose of: magnifying Jesus through worship and the Word; making Jesus known to our neighbors and the nations; and moving believers in Jesus toward maturity and ministry.

- The priorities of ministry of this church flow from the vision of God's glory revealed in Jesus Christ. We exist to savor this vision in *worship* (John 4:23), strengthen the vision in nurture and *education* (1 Cor 14:26, 2 Pet 3:18), and spread the vision in *evangelism, missions*, and *loving deeds* (1 Pet 2:9, 3:15, 5:16; Matt 28:18–20).

- The Mission of [Fourth Church] is to glorify God through joyful worship, to show God's love to all people, to lead them to faith in Jesus Christ, to make them His disciples, and to call them to His service.

## Ministry for God

Every person in ministry (staff or volunteer) should have an ultimate *vertical* purpose to his or her ministry: a purpose of seeking to reflect and demonstrate and display the glory of God in the lives of people; a purpose of building into others (as they seek to also build into their own lives) a preoccupation with God, a loving of him with all the heart, soul, mind, and strength, and a cherishing of him and his glory in lives of worship.

## Others' Testimony to This Perspective

- Eugene Peterson: "The most important thing a pastor does is stand in a pulpit every Sunday and say, 'Let us worship God.'"[6]

- Doug Murren: "I still hold strongly to the biblical conviction that worship is the most important task and purpose for the church."[7]

- A. W. Tozer: "The Christian church exists to worship God first of all. Everything else must come second or third or fourth or fifth."[8]

- William Nicholls: "Worship is the supreme and only indispensable activity of the Christian Church. It alone will endure, like the love

6. E. Peterson, "Business of Making Saints," 22.
7. Murren, "Room for the Sacred," 14.
8. Tozer, *Whatever Happened to Worship?*, 56.

for God which it expresses, into heaven, when all other activities of the Church will have passed away. It must therefore, even more strictly than any of the less essential doings of the Church, come under the criticism and control of the revelation on which the Church is founded."[9]

- John Armstrong: "Any genuine reformation in our time must be one which recovers the highest priority of the church both in heaven and on earth, the worship of God!"[10]

- Billy Graham: "The purpose of this Christian society called the 'Church' is, first: to glorify God by our worship. We do not go to church just to hear a sermon. We go to church to worship God."[11]

- Eric Alexander: "The great motive for ministry is a desire for the glory of God. All ministry comes from him as the head, and all ministry goes back to him as the goal to which we aim."[12]

> "Of all the activities in the church, only one is an end in itself: worship." (John Piper)

9. Nicholls, *Jacob's Ladder*, 9.

10. Armstrong, "How Should We Then," 9.

11. Graham, *Peace with God*, 194.

12. Alexander, *Our Great God*, 149.

# 32

# THE IMPORTANCE OF WORSHIP IN THE CHURCH[1]

Though, as just stated, worship (including worship in the church) is an end in itself, we can identify a number of other values and benefits for the people of God.

## 1. Worship in the Church Honors the Father

This is the end in itself, the ultimate purpose of corporate worship. It serves no higher purpose than this; it is a means to no other end.

God seeks, delights in, and indeed demands our worship. In the corporate gathering we "ascribe to the Lord the glory due his Name" (Ps 96:8), as we acclaim him as Creator and Ruler; we celebrate his supreme worthiness,[2] majesty, and attributes; we proclaim "there is no one like the Lord our God" (Exod 8:10); and we exclaim our wonder at his grace and his great plan for the redemption of humankind (Eph 1:3–14).

---

1. The following points are adapted from Allmen, *Worship*, 111–26; and Dawn, *Reaching Out*, chs. 6 and 7.

2. In fact, our English word *worship* derives from an earlier form denoting "worth-ship."

## 2. Worship in the Church Celebrates Christ

We exalt in the person and work of Christ. We bask in the glory of the gospel, as we tell, again and again, the "old, old story of Jesus and his love."[3] And we commemorate his death on the cross, and remind ourselves of our part in his redemptive work, as we celebrate the Lord's Supper.

## 3. Worship in the Church Draws Us into Fellowship with Christ and with the Father

In corporate worship we draw near to God through, in, and with our Mediator, the Lord Jesus Christ. He grants us access to the Father and takes us with him into the Father's presence (Heb 10:19–22) as he actively leads us in our expressions of praise (Heb 2:12).

## 4. Worship in the Church Foreshadows the Kingdom

Corporate worship reflects the worship of heaven as it looks forward to the time when all creation will continually praise its Maker, when we will "see him as he is" (1 John 3:2), and when we will eat and drink anew with Christ (Luke 22:30). It is a reflection of the worship that even now goes on around the throne of God in heaven (Rev 4–5), and of that ultimate, unending worship of the future.

## 5. Worship in the Church Is Used by the Holy Spirit

In corporate worship the Spirit can act in believers' hearts through the truth proclaimed and sung and prayed, encouraging and engendering a deeper commitment to and growth in the Lord. And unbelievers can also be drawn by the Spirit as they see Christians in worship (1 Cor 14:24–25).

## 6. Worship in the Church Gives Identity to the Church

The church is truly and identifiably *the church* when it is gathered for corporate worship. It is there that we are reminded that though we are

---

3. Hymn quote from William G. Fischer, "I Love to Tell the Story" (https://www.hymnal.net/en/hymn/h/1064).

*in* the world, we are not *of* the world (John 17:14–16)—we are set apart (2 Tim 2:21). And we celebrate our unity in the removal of sociological and ethnic barriers (Gal 3:28).

And yet we are also reminded that we are still *in* the world: we are indeed not gathered all the time, but have a necessary missionary aspect to our lives in the world:

> The life of the Church pulsates like the heart by systole and di-astole. As the heart is for the animal body, so [worship] is for church life a pump which sends into circulation and draws it in again, it claims and it sanctifies. It is from the life of worship . . . that the Church spreads itself abroad into the world to mingle with it like leaven in the dough, to give it savour like salt, to irradiate it like light, and it is toward [worship] that the Church returns from the world, like a fisherman gathering up his nets or a farmer harvesting his grain.[4]

Another similar image would be that of breathing: we breathe in (like the church gathering), and we breathe out (like the church scattering into the world); the process repeats itself over and over and over again. A healthy body must breathe both in *and* out; so too a healthy church body must both gather *and* scatter.

## 7. Worship in the Church Testifies to the World

Corporate worship is a *challenge* to a world system that denies the relevance or even the existence of God. We proclaim in our gatherings what is true reality, the hope of the present and the world's future.

Two examples of this challenge:

1. Once while teaching in Moldova, I attended a Baptist church with an odd feature: the church roof was simply flattened off where a steeple would normally be. I was told that when Moldova was still part of the Soviet Union, the authorities gave permission to the church to build this building, but with the stipulation that it could not have a steeple; this was so that the church would not be too visible to surrounding neighborhoods—because it was recognized to be a challenge to the atheistic Soviet system.

---

4. Allmen, *Worship*, 55.

2. Similarly, the story is told of a man visiting Leningrad (now St. Petersburg) during the Soviet era. The man came upon a beautiful, onion-domed church building; but the church was not on his map. He asked his guide about this and was told that the government did not allow churches to be marked on maps. The man observed that there was indeed one church building noted on his map, but the guide told him that that building was now a museum. The authorities did not allow *live* churches to be on the map, just *dead* ones!

But the testimony of corporate worship is not just a *challenge* to the world, but also an *invitation*: for all are invited to come and "taste and see that the LORD is good" (Ps 34:11), to find redemption and meaning.

## 8. Worship in the Church Nurtures the Character of the Believer

"We become like that which we worship," goes the saying (see Ps 115:4–8). Corporate worship in spirit and truth feeds and nourishes us in the Lord, and motivates our growth in and commitment to him.

## 9. Worship in the Church Builds Christian Community

We do not gather to each have our own little private worship time with the Lord (there are other places and times for that), but together we build ourselves up: as we exercise our gifts for the common good (Eph 4:13–16); as we demonstrate love, kindness, humility, etc. towards one another in the corporate gathering (Col 3:12–15); and as we "let the word of Christ dwell in [us] richly, teaching and admonishing one another in all wisdom, singing psalms and hymns and spiritual songs" (Col 3:16). We are also reminded that we are part of the universal body of Christ, joining with believers from across the world and across the centuries.

## 10. Worship in the Church Reorients Believers to Their True Center

After a week of bombardment by competing worldviews and a panoply of false "worships," corporate worship among God's people reminds us of who, and whose, we are.

We are creatures of short memories. Corporate worship, regularly practiced, calls us back again and again to the divine background and to our life that springs from it.[5]

Worship models and enacts an alternative world of sanity that prevents Israel [and us] from succumbing to the seductive insanities of a world raging against the holiness of Yahweh.[6]

[Sunday worship is] weekly practice at not being God.[7]

## 11. Worship in the Church Prepares Hearts for the Preaching of the Word

Of course preaching is part of worship as well,[8] but of a different kind. As hearts are filled with wonder from the rehearsal of familiar truths through Scripture readings, songs, and prayers, they become more ready to be challenged through the word preached to ascend to new levels of understanding and commitment.

> Corporate worship gives identity to the church.

5. Steere, *Prayer and Worship*, 47.

6. Brueggemann, *Theology of the Old Testament*, 665.

7. Michael Lindvall, cited in Bierma, "Worshipful Service."

8. See Piper, *Expository Exultation*.

# 33

# THE CONTENT OF WORSHIP IN THE CHURCH¹

A bove we saw how Luke seems to outline for us the most basic elements of the corporate gathering in Acts 2:42, 46–47.

## The Word of God ("the apostles' teaching" [Acts 2:42])

In ch. 4 we already considered the importance of the word in worship. The word of God is of supreme importance in the life of the Christian, containing as it does God's revelation of his person, his will, and his ways. The word needs to be pored over, ingested into one's mind and heart, meditated on, and acted upon. It is a unique and precious repository of spiritual truth and guidance and encouragement. There is no aspect of the life of the church or of the individual believer that should not be tied to a scriptural mooring and infused with biblical substance (2 Tim 3:16).

---

1. *Baptism* is an important, but usually not a weekly, feature of corporate worship, and will not be dealt with here. It is, of course, also a subject that has engendered much debate and controversy. The reader is referred to the balanced and fair treatment in Wayne Grudem's *Systematic Theology*, ch. 49; there are also many fine comparative studies. In addition, other elements not handled in this chapter, such as drama, dance, visual arts, etc., may play an impactful role in corporate worship. However, their acceptability and effectiveness will vary according to the cultural context and sensibilities of particular churches. (More on this in chs. 36–38.) So this chapter focuses on more biblically rooted and widely practiced transcultural elements.

The Bible is indeed "a lamp unto my feet, and a light unto my path" (Ps 119:105).

And, as stressed throughout this book, the word is foundational for our worship in all its aspects, including our corporate worship in the church. When Christians gather, it is logical that the word of God should play a central and dominant role. For since worship involves focusing our thoughts and hearts and voices on the praise of God, in ↑ response to his ↓ self-revelation and his gracious saving initiative, we of course need that view of God that the word gives us if our worship is to be "in truth" (John 4:23–24). Our worship can duly honor God only if it accurately reflects what he reveals about himself in his word. Seeing worship as a dialogue of *revelation* and *response* between God and his people[2] means that *both* sides of the equation must be present.[3]

John Stott explains the crucial importance of the word for worship in this way (as quoted earlier):

> To worship God . . . is to "glory in his holy name" (Ps. 105:3), that is, to revel adoringly in who he is in his revealed character. But before we can glory in God's name, we must know it. Hence the propriety of the reading and preaching of the Word of God in public worship, and of biblical meditation in private devotion. . . . The worship of God is always a response to the Word of God. Scripture wonderfully directs and enriches our worship.[4]

Gordon Lathrop agrees:

> The Bible marks and largely determines Christian corporate worship. . . . At the heart of the meeting the Bible is read and then interpreted as having to do with us. Many churches have a large Bible set out on a prominent central reading stand. Some churches give a ceremonial preface to the reading by carrying the book about and honoring it. Furthermore, the text of the Bible provides the source of the imagery and, often, the very form and quality of the language in prayers, chants, hymn texts, and sermons. Psalms are sung as if that ancient collection were intended for our singing. Snatches of old biblical letters are scattered throughout the service, as if we were addressed. Frequently images and texts drawn from the Bible adorn the room

---

2. See Furr and Price, *Dialogue of Worship*.

3. However, it should also be remembered that "the communion between God and human beings is reciprocal, but not symmetrical" (Wainwright, "Praise of God," 39).

4. Stott, *Contemporary Christian*, 174.

where the meeting takes place. To people who know the biblical stories, the very actions of the gathering may seem like the Bible alive: an assembly gathers, as the people gathered at the foot of Mount Sinai, the holy convocation of the Lord; arms are upraised in prayer or blessing, as Moses raised his arms; the holy books are read, as Ezra read to the listening people; the people hold a meal, as the disciples did, gathered after the death of Jesus. To come into the meeting seems like coming into a world determined by the language of the Bible.

In fact, the whole history of worship among Christians might be regarded as a history of the way the book was understood and alive among the churches. Patterns of reading and preaching the parts of the book, of praying in the language of the book, of doing the signs of the book—these are the principal patterns of Christian worship.[5]

So far, so good. However, there are today some imbalances in churches' understanding of the word's proper role in worship.

## The Word "versus" Worship?—The Relationship of Preaching and Corporate Praise

There are a lot of churches where there is a continuing conflict over the proper relationship of preaching and "worship" (an unfortunate and inaccurate dichotomy) in church services.

### "Preliminaries" and Preaching

James F. White and other church historians have pointed out that many American congregations in the Protestant free-church tradition can trace their present worship practices to nineteenth-century revivalism,[6] where music and other activities functioned merely as (and were even called) "preliminaries," designed as a means to "warm up" the audience for the "main event," i.e., the message. As White demonstrates, this pattern, which was widely used for evangelistic meetings, was then carried over into worship services. Sadly, that view of the worship service is alive and well today; even in those churches where Bible teaching has come to take precedence over evangelistic-style preaching, it is now the teaching of

5. Lathrop, *Holy Things*, 15–16.
6. White, *Protestant Worship*, 171–72, 177.

the Bible that is seen as the primary if not sole purpose for gathering.[7] In ch. 26 we saw how this narrow view can rob our corporate services of the richness that Jesus Christ can bring to them in the fullness of his mediatorial role: mediating the truth of God to people, and mediating the worship response of God's people as our High Priest (Heb 2:17; 4:14–15; 5:5; 7:26–28; 8:1–2; 9:11–12; 10:19–22).

There is certainly also a great deal of semantic confusion involved in the controversy. As we have emphasized in this book, *worship* must be understood in its broadest New Testament sense as that which should be a life-pervading, nonlocalized response of the believer to the gracious work of God in his or her life (Rom 12:1; John 4:21–23); all of life, all of our activities are to be done for the glory of God (1 Cor 10:31) and in the name of the Lord Jesus (Col 3:17). As we saw in ch. 32, only worship is an end in itself, an ultimate end.[8] Perhaps "corporate praise" would be a more appropriate term to use in referring to those non-preaching, participatory parts of the service (since "worship" is so global a category, and since *all* of what happens in the service, including preaching, could be termed worship).[9]

Some pastors would hold to what is, in fact, a false dichotomy between the roles served by preaching and corporate praise: that the former handles the word of God while the latter consists simply of singing and such activities. Similarly, in discussions about the revelation/response paradigm that characterizes worship, it is sometimes assumed that only in the sermon does any meaningful communication of *revelation* take place—with the obvious implication that everything else in the service is necessarily *response*.[10] And that response is seen as inherently inferior to revelation[11] (presumably because revelation comes from God, while response is of humanity).

7. Tim Ralston of Dallas Theological Seminary characterizes the view that only a steady and strong diet of Bible teaching is needed for growth in the Christian life as "a dysfunctional view of sanctification" ("Changing Worship").

8. That worship is a bigger and broader category than preaching is clearly demonstrated by the fact that many pastors have *preached about worship*, yet it is nonsensical to think of *worshiping about preaching*; only the lesser can teach about the greater.

9. See Piper, "Preaching as Worship" (*Trinity*).

10. An additional complication is the fact that, by this understanding, basically all of the response in the service would *precede* all the revelation!

11. In all fairness, it should be pointed out that corporate praise has grown in some churches to almost sacramental proportions, to the detriment of the proclaimed word of God; this is likewise an imbalance.

But in fact, the word of God can be and *should* be communicated (explicitly and implicitly) *throughout* the service; a back-and-forth dialogue between the word and the people's response to it should be an ongoing exchange during the entire service. (See ch. 4.) As Bruce Leafblad puts it:

> People don't hear God speak with an audible voice on Sunday morning.... God has appointed spokespersons.... He's been appointing people, not to tell what they think, but to speak what *he* thinks. And that's why we are people of the Book; and that's why the Word must be integrated into the entire service of worship, not just be an act for preaching. The conversation depends on the Word at every point where God speaks in the dialogue.... God isn't limited to one medium of communication.[12]

Response is not an inferior and negligible part of worship. Indeed, God's revelation is prerequisite and foundational to any response; but the fact is that, since Christ mediates *both* the revelation and response parts of worship, they are both of immense value. The high priestly ministry of Jesus in our worship governs and guides both aspects and gives to both an incredible (and complementary) significance.

Despite (or at least in ignorance of) the points mentioned above, many pastors still feel that an elevating of the importance of "worship" (or corporate praise) necessarily means a degrading of the importance of the word of God and of preaching.

### Preaching Serves Worship

Preaching is an integral part of the revelatory side of the dialogue of worship. For the preacher (as others in the service who communicate scriptural truth to the people) *represents God in the dialogue.*[13] He plays a theological role of representing "the God who convenes worship."[14]

John Stott insists on the inseparable connection between preaching and worship:

---

12. Leafblad, "Leading in Worship."

13. In another sense, the preacher represents Jesus Christ in his mediatorial ministry whereby he proclaims the Father's name to his brethren (Heb 2:12). See ch. 26, and also Ron Man, *Proclamation and Praise*, 23, 28, 74–75.

14. Leafblad, "Leading in Worship."

Word and worship belong indissolubly to each other. All worship is an intelligent and loving response to the revelation of God, because it is the adoration of His Name. Therefore, acceptable worship is impossible without preaching. For preaching is making known the Name of the Lord, and worship is praising the Name of the Lord made known. Far from being an alien intrusion into worship, the reading and preaching of the word are actually indispensable to it. The two cannot be divorced. Indeed, it is their unnatural divorce that accounts for the low level of so much contemporary worship. Our worship is poor because our knowledge of God is poor, and our knowledge of God is poor because our preaching is poor. But when the Word of God is expounded in its fullness, and the congregation begin[sic] to glimpse the glory of the living God, they bow down in solemn awe and joyful wonder before His throne.[15]

For worship to be filled with the wonder of God, that wonder must be displayed through the reading and exposition of the mighty acts and ways of God as related to us in Scripture. That's why John Piper refers to preaching as "expository exultation":[16] it should marvel in the greatness of the glory of God, so that our present circumstances and our worries and our worship are all submitted to the mighty hand of God. Worship acknowledges that God is an all-powerful, all-loving, heavenly Father who glorifies himself by satisfying his people.[17]

The ascription of praise with which a Chrysostom, an Augustine, or a Calvin ended their sermons was no mere formality: It indicated the intention of the sermon itself and its aim of bringing others also to the praise of God on account of what had been proclaimed in Scripture and sermon.[18]

Hence, preaching is crucial for God-saturated, God-honoring worship.[19] And worship is the end, the goal, of preaching—as it is of the entire service. Hence Piper's "expository exultation" model—faithful exposition is not the end, but rather a means to achieving the goal of a

15. Stott, *Between Two Worlds*, 82–83.

16. Piper, "Preaching as Worship" (Desiring God, lect. 1).

17. See Piper, *Desiring God*.

18. Wainwright, "Praise of God," 38.

19. But it is a two-way street as well: "Maintaining the centrality of worship in the life of the church is crucial to sustaining integrity in preaching. When worship is central, preaching takes on characteristics that make it an effective means of communicating the gospel" (Gaddy, *Gift of Worship*, 72).

worship response ("exultation") to the God thus seen. The preacher must preach *as* an act of worship (because, after all, "you can't commend what you don't cherish"[20]), and must preach with a view towards engendering worship in others.

Vern Poythress puts it thus:

> We refuse to accept as scriptural a simple dichotomy between praise and preaching. Frankly we do not see how any gospel preacher with a heart in him can *refrain* from praising God as an integral part of his preaching.[21]

And John Piper would agree:

> The overarching, pervasive, relentless subject of preaching is God himself with a view to being worshiped.[22]

> Preaching is meant to be and to kindle God-exalting worship. . . . The mission of all preaching is soul-satisfying, God-exalting worship.[23]

## The Word Neglected in Worship—Benign Neglect in Bible-Believing Churches

The astounding observation has been made as to how little use is made of Scripture in most worship services of most evangelical churches. The irony of course is that those who claim most strongly to stand on the Bible *have so little of it in their worship*. Second Timothy 3:15 ("devote yourself to the public reading of Scripture") should be more than enough warrant!

While the sermon of course takes a prominent role in our services, even preaching consists mostly of talking *about* the Scriptures (often after reading just a very few verses). As noted before, liturgical groups (including Lutherans, Episcopalians, and Roman Catholics) have probably ten times as much actual Scripture in their services (because it is built into their liturgies) as do most Bible-believing, evangelical, free churches!

In too many of these churches the entire first part of the service consists just of music—albeit songs about God and songs reflective of biblical truth (a minimum requirement for songs for worship)—but no Scripture

20. Piper, *Let the Nations Be Glad*, 36.
21. Poythress, "Ezra 3 (Concluded)," 229.
22. Piper, "Preaching as Worship" (Desiring God, lect. 2).
23. Piper, "Preaching as Worship" (Desiring God, lect. 1).

is read at all. This author has experienced this often in both traditional and contemporary services: the problem is pervasive. It would seem crucially important for people in a service, believers and unbelievers, to hear read (and/or printed in a bulletin or flashed on a screen) verses of Scripture chosen to give a clear signal that: "We have come to worship God. The Word is how we know about God, and therefore it is the foundation for all that we do here and for our understanding of why we have come together." Without such a declaration—launching into songs without any context of revelation being set—worshipers make the faulty assumption (consciously or unconsciously) that we invite *ourselves* into God's presence, when in actuality it is only by virtue of his invitation (and his opening the way through the work of Christ) that we may come before him at all.

Once I visited a church where the service consisted of five parts, clearly delineated in the bulletin, and where every part began with a Scripture reading that set the tone for what followed. There was no question that this church saw the central role of Scripture in their worship! As James White puts it, "The first step toward making our worship more biblical is in giving the reading of God's Word a central role in Christian worship on any occasion."[24]

We simply cannot overstate the importance of Scripture for our worship. In Scripture we find the prerequisites for worship, the invitation to worship, the authority for worship, the material for worship, the regulation of our worship, the message of worship, and the end to which worship should lead (see Principle 4 in ch. 39 to see these points unpacked). By all means, let us be as creative as possible to build in Scripture (verses on banners or projected onto a screen as people enter, verses on the bulletin cover, readers' theater, children reciting verses, original Scripture songs, etc.), but let us make sure that the *primacy of the word in worship* is obvious throughout the entire service—not just during the sermon.

> Scripture is read, not just for a sermon text, but to hear what word God addresses to the gathered congregation. Preaching usually builds on that but scripture is read for its own sake as God's Word. . . . It needs to be communicated to all that the centrality of scripture stems from its function as proclamation of God's Word to the gathered people.[25]

24. White, "Making Our Worship," 38.
25. White, "Making Our Worship," 38–39.

Ligon Duncan highlights the centrality of the Scriptures in Christian worship by urging us to "read the Bible, preach the Bible, pray the Bible, sing the Bible and see the Bible."[26]

## The Word Read and Preached in Worship

> And they devoted themselves to the apostles' teaching. (Acts 2:42)

> Until I come, devote yourself to the public reading of Scripture, to exhortation, to teaching. (1 Tim 4:13)

> I charge you in the presence of God and of Christ Jesus, who is to judge the living and the dead, and by his appearing and his kingdom: preach the word; be ready in season and out of season; reprove, rebuke, and exhort, with complete patience and teaching. (2 Tim 4:1–2)

Preaching that is faithfully biblical and expository (laying out the meaning of the scriptural text) is of course a crucial element of the ↓ revelation side of the ↓ ↑ revelation-and-response dialogue of worship. But, as we have seen, we need to let the word of God infuse the entire service.

Scripture readings can be done in a number of different ways (and probably should be, so that the variety helps to hold the people's attention):

1. The pastor, worship leader, or another leader can read.

2. Other readers can be used (for example, a child could be used to read Ps 23).

3. The congregation can read a text aloud together (from a screen or from a printed program): hearing the entire gathering proclaiming God's word together can be very powerful.

4. Responsive readings (put together using an online or published concordance to trace a particular theme through the Scriptures): alternate leader and people, or left and right, or men and women.

5. Dramatic readings/readers' theater: especially with narrative passages.

6. Sung response: for instance, congregation sings the repeated refrain from the second half of every verse of Ps 136.

---

26. To "see the Bible," that is, in the Lord's Supper. Duncan, "Foundations," 65.

More suggestions and guidelines on using the Scripture in worship can be found on pp. 36–37.

For those chosen to do Scripture readings in the service, here are a few recommendations:

1. *Study* and *pray* over the text ahead of time.

2. *Mark* key words and places to pause.

3. When reading:

    - *Don't rush*! (Going too fast is a very common mistake.)

    - Read *expressively*, declaring the text as God's truth: this is the word of God, *God speaking to his people* (encouraging his people, instructing his people, correcting his people).

    - *Emphasize* key words; *pause* between thoughts.

## The Lord's Supper/Communion—"the breaking of bread" (Acts 2:42)

In obedience to Jesus's command (Luke 22:19),[27] his church has always made the ritual remembrance of his substitutionary sacrifice on the cross a central part of gathered worship.[28] In fact, in most traditions the Lord's Supper was celebrated weekly for the first 1500 years of the church. Some groups continue this practice, though many groups now opt for a monthly observance, while others do it quarterly or even less often. (As will be seen later in ch. 37, in the absence of specific biblical instruction as to frequency, there is freedom in this respect.)

> The Lord's Supper is a powerful showing forth of the life and death, the resurrection and ascension of Christ. . . . The Bible calls us to take and eat and drink as well as to hear.[29]

27. Darrell Johnson has observed: "*Eat* and *drink* are the only verbs of worship explicitly commanded by Jesus" (endorsement on back cover of G. Smith, *Holy Meal* [emphasis original]).

28. Most evangelicals recognize this as one of two *ordinances* (along with baptism), as ritual observances ordained by Christ himself as signs and symbols of divine grace effected by God internally in the life of the believer. Other Christian groups add more rituals to these two, and identify them as *sacraments* (i.e., acts that *in themselves* impart divine grace; for instance, the Catholic and Orthodox traditions).

29. White, "Making Our Worship," 40.

We do not come before God in the Eucharist on the ground of what we have done. . . . We come with nothing in our hands but the bread and wine, to feed upon Christ's Body and Blood and find shelter in His sacrifice and oblation on our behalf. . . . We do not have to keep looking over our shoulders to see whether our response is good enough. The very fact that in our response we are called to rely entirely upon the steadfast and incorruptible response of Christ made on our behalf frees us from the anxieties begotten of ulterior motivation and evokes genuine freedom and joy in our responding to God.[30]

## Remembrance

An understanding of the biblical nuance of *remembrance* (Greek *anamnesis*) is key to our understanding of the Lord's Supper. James Torrance explains this concept well:

The word *anamnesis* . . . is of rich liturgical significance in the Bible. It does not mean simply an act of recollection of some remote date of bygone history, as every schoolboy remembers 1066 AD. Rather it means remembering in such a way that we see our participation in the past event and see our destiny and future as bound up with it. So when Jews remember the passover and the exodus from Egypt, they do not think of it simply as an irretrievable date from over 3000 years ago. Rather they remember it in such a way that they confess "*We* are the people whom God brought out of the land of Egypt for *we* were Pharaoh's bondsmen." "*We* are the people with whom God made His covenant, saying 'I will be your God and you shall be my people.'"

In cultic remembrance . . . the past is rendered present; there is a re-*present*-ation of the past so that it lives again in the present time. This, for lack of a better word, we may call a *pre-sentifying* of the past. . . . So at the Last Supper, we do not merely remember the Passion of our Lord as an isolated date from 1900 years ago. Rather we remember it in such a way that we know that *we* are the people for whom our Saviour died and rose again. We are what we are today by the grace of God because of what God did for us then.[31]

---

30. T. Torrance, "Word of God," 158–61.

31. J. Torrance, "Place of Jesus Christ," 355–56.

## Biblical Nuances of the Lord's Supper

Gordon T. Smith, in an insightful little book entitled *A Holy Meal: The Lord's Supper in the Life of the Church*, unpacks seven perspectives gleaned from the major New Testament passages dealing with the Supper—seven angles from which to observe and understand the practice. He summarizes each perspective and passage with a single key word that is the focus of the passage:

- *Remembrance*: The Lord's Supper as a memorial ("do this in *remembrance* of me" [1 Cor 11:24–26]).

- *Communion*: The Lord's Supper as fellowship with Christ and with one another ("a *participation* [*koinonia, fellowship*] in the body of Christ" [1 Cor 10:14–17; 11:27–34])

- *Forgiveness*: The Lord's Supper as a table of mercy ("my blood . . . is poured out for many for the *forgiveness* of sins" [Matt 26:26–28])

- *Covenant*: The Lord's Supper as a renewal of baptismal vows ("this is my blood of the *covenant*" [Mark 14:22–25])

- *Nourishment*: The Lord's Supper as bread from heaven ("my flesh is true food, and my blood is true drink" [John 6:35–58)

- *Anticipation*: The Lord's Supper as a declaration of hope ("I will not eat it/drink it until . . . the kingdom of God" [Luke 22:14–27])

- *Eucharist*: The Lord's Supper as a joyous thanksgiving celebration ("breaking bread in their homes, they received their food with glad and generous hearts" [Acts 2:46–47; see also Matt 26:27; Mark 14:23; Luke 22:17, 19; 1 Cor 11:24])

## The Scope of the Lord's Supper

### Time (Past–Present–Future)

As seen above, at the table we are reminded of the event of Christ's crucifixion, but in its remembrance we draw comfort from the realization that when Jesus died, he died for each of us—thus bringing the significance of the *past* event into our *present* experience.

There is also a crucial *future* aspect as well. Paul writes: "For as often as you eat this bread and drink the cup, you proclaim the Lord's death *until he comes*" (1 Cor 11:26). We look ahead to when we will eat, drink, and enjoy table fellowship with our Savior in the kingdom (Luke 22:16, 18).

> The really distinctive thing about [the Lord's Supper] . . . is its essentially historical and eschatological character. Looking back to an event of the past, it looks forward to the consummation of God's design; and in the present, at each celebration, it finds a creative meeting of the two.[32]

> The [ordinances], as Calvin used to say, bear witness to the fact that Christ is in a manner present and yet in a manner absent. But when Christ is finally present in the *Parousia* we shall no longer need [ordinances]—although we shall still worship.[33]

### Senses

Of all Christian worship practices, the Lord's Supper is the most multisensory: we hear "the old, old story of Jesus and his love"; we see, touch, smell, and taste the elements.

### Emotions

The Lord's Supper is a serious time, but ultimately not a sad one. It is *not* a funeral service for Jesus! Rather, we somberly remember the price paid for our redemption (1 Cor 6:20), yet acknowledge that the work is finished (John 19:30) and that Jesus is our victorious and risen Savior (Rom 1:4), having conquered sin and death (Rom 8:2).

So there is room in the celebration for *serious* reflection, but also for overwhelming *joy* and *gratitude*.

### Personal but Corporate

Participating in the Lord's Supper offers the opportunity for *personal* reflection about one's former state and the glorious reality of all that we are and all that we have because we are in Christ by his redeeming work. And it provides the reminder that in Christ *all* our sins (including our latest ones!) are forgiven thanks to his shed blood.

---

32. Moule, *Worship in the New Testament*, 19.
33. J. Torrance, "Place of Jesus Christ," 364.

Yet at the same time the Lord's Supper is a uniquely *corporate* observance. Many of the activities of worship we can also do when we are alone (Bible study, prayer, even singing); but the Lord's Supper is something we do *together* in the body of Christ.[34]

Much more could be said about the wide range of doctrinal understandings and practices of the Lord's Supper among various Christian groups, and there are many books that address these issues. For a balanced overview, please see ch. 50 in Wayne Grudem's *Systematic Theology*.

## Prayer—"the prayers" (Acts 2:42)

Corporate prayer is an important unifying and focusing activity for the people of God, yet too little time and attention is given to this aspect of worship in many churches.

The pastor or other leader who is going to lead the church in prayer should be diligent to make adequate *preparation* in advance. (Public prayer deserves forethought and planning, as does the sermon or the music.) There is a place for both carefully composed and written-out prayers, as well as unscripted prayers that have been thought out beforehand. There is a place for spontaneous prayers, but using them solely can lead to repetitiousness and triteness.

*Elements* to include in prayer include: praise, thanksgiving, confession, intercession (though not necessarily all in one prayer). *Intercessory prayer* should include known needs within the congregation (as well as its missionaries elsewhere), but should also look outside the walls of the church and bring important global, national, and local issues (and leaders[35]) before God in prayer. The news can inform our congregational prayer; if it is something that is on the minds of the people, bring it before the Lord in prayer! It has often been observed that congregational

---

34. Churches should consider ways to give attention to this corporate aspect during the celebration of the Lord's Supper: perhaps by singing together as the elements are served; perhaps by serving one another the elements; perhaps by looking at our neighbor and reminding him or her as we partake that "this is the body/blood of Christ, given for you."

35. "First of all, then, I urge that supplications, prayers, intercessions, and thanksgivings be made for all people, for kings and all who are in high positions, that we may lead a peaceful and quiet life, godly and dignified in every way" (1 Tim 2:1–2).

prayers (and in fact, services as a whole) were affected dramatically on the Sunday after 9/11.

*Silent prayer* can provide a rich opportunity for the Spirit to work in the lives of the congregation, yet is so often neglected in our churches. There is so little place for silence in our world today! We need to provide time for the people to "be still and know that I am God" (Ps 46:10). It is especially important to give people the opportunity to silently reflect and respond at the conclusion of the sermon; that is the time when the message from the word is freshest in people's minds and hearts, and moving too quickly to a closing song, the announcements, or the benediction can rob people of the most potentially fruitful time for the Lord to work in their hearts before they turn to post-service conversations or lunch.

> Too often, Sunday morning services are run like a television talk show—fast-paced with no "dead air-time." But in doing so, not only do we create an environment conducive to passive entertainment, but also we squeeze out the gaps and spaces that we need and the Holy Spirit uses for reflection, meditation, and conviction. Slow the pace of your service and allow time for reflection, especially after the sermon and at the conclusion of the whole service. Leave little gaps between elements in the service, and leave a long gap after the final word of the benediction and the start of whatever postlude or closing music you use. This will give the congregation time to collect their thoughts, to pray, and to identify what they need to be reassured of or convicted about. If worship is ultimately our service to God with our whole lives, then silence at the end of corporate worship is often where the agenda for our week's worship is set.[36]

*Bidded prayer* (borrowed from the Anglican tradition) is one way to make congregational prayer more participatory than just a chorus of amen at the end. In this form of prayer, the leader will introduce a petition, and then give the congregation time (perhaps thirty seconds) to silently pray for that matter; then the leader introduces another item for silent prayer, etc. These bidded prayers can be for both internal church concerns and external issues.

---

36. Michael Lawrence and Mark Dever, "Blended Worship," in Pinson, *Perspectives on Christian Worship*, 263.

## Music/Singing—"praising God" (Acts 2:47), "psalms, hymns, and spiritual songs" (Eph 5:19; Col 3:16)

(Please see the extended treatment of "The Ministry of Song" on pp. 245–50.)

It must always be remembered that church music is a "functional art."[37] Luther called music "the handmaid of theology"; it must serve the truth that it proclaims. Church music is a means to an end, indeed the most glorious of ends: the worship of Almighty God.

Yet that does not mean that the musical element is negligible, by any means. The Reformers recognized and took advantage of the power of music as a vehicle for communicating truth.

> So effective were Luther's musical reforms . . . that one outraged Jesuit churchman remarked, "The hymns of Luther have killed more souls than his sermons." . . .
>
> Calvin held strong views on the place of music in the spiritual lives of his flock. He was known to quote Plato's maxim that "there is scarcely anything in this world which can more powerfully turn or influence the manners of man than music." He wrote that through song a doctrine might be better known than if it were simply taught, with sound and rhythm aiding the memory.[38]

Stephen Guthrie, in a very illuminating article on this subject, speaks of the unifying and edifying nature of congregational song:

> From the many voices that sing together, a new entity emerges—the voice of the church; a sound which has qualities and properties which the individual voices of which it is composed do not have. And yet, it is also true that the character of the congregational song is constituted and marked by the character of the individual voices singing. The special power of music is not simply that it allows us to hear "one voice." Rather, the special power of music is that here we encounter *"simultaneous voices which are nevertheless also one voice."*[39] One does not hear only "the voice of the Church," but the voice of the Church, *and* the voice of the other individuals singing, *and* one's own voice. . . .

37. Hustad, *Jubilate II*, 22.
38. Fromm, "New Song," 28.
39. Guthrie is here citing Scruton, *Aesthetics of Music*, 339.

There is an analogy of form between the sound of people singing together and the unity to which the church aspires, and for this reason music is a particularly apt vehicle for worship. In Ephesians 5, it is in connection with the command to be filled with the Holy Spirit that Paul urges his readers to sing. Music offers a sounding image of the kind of diversified unity brought about by the Holy Spirit—"*simultaneous voices which are nevertheless also one voice.*" "There are many parts, but one body," is how Paul expresses the same ideal in 1 Corinthians (12:20). It is by the Spirit that Christians are baptized into one Body (1 Cor 12:13); but it is also the Spirit who gives diverse gifts (1 Cor 12:7–11)—who gives to each part of the body its special function, to each voice its distinct part in the great chorus. . . .

This is the point of contact between music and the life of the Church. The unity of the Body of Christ is not a bland, undifferentiated uniformity, but a rich and manifold concord. Music is uniquely equipped to provide an aural image of this kind of community, in which union is not unanimity, nor multiplicity a cacophony.[40]

The power of music to amplify and intensify what is sung means that we have a great responsibility to ensure that what we are singing is infused with biblical truth. That means that song texts (when not directly from Scripture) must be carefully evaluated in terms of theological accuracy.

And the musical vehicle chosen should complement (not overwhelm or contradict) the text that it delivers, and should be presented to the best of our ability, with care and diligent preparation (though musical excellence is not the ultimate goal).[41]

## Readings Other Than Scripture

Church history provides many rich instances of biblically faithful expressions that may be profitably used for solo, unison, or responsive readings in the worship service. Some examples are:

---

40. Guthrie, "Singing, in the Body," 644–45 (emphases original).

41. See appendix 3, "Music for Worship: Excellence as a Means Rather Than an End."

## The Great Creeds of the Church

Powerful expressions of basic orthodox beliefs shared by Christians through the centuries can give a real sense of historical continuity and community (read in unison, of course).

### Nicene Creed (AD 325)[42]

I believe in one God,
    the Father almighty,
    maker of heaven and earth,
    of all things visible and invisible.
I believe in one Lord Jesus Christ,
    the Only Begotten Son of God,
    born of the Father before all ages.
    God from God, Light from Light,
    true God from true God,
    begotten, not made, consubstantial with the Father;
    through him all things were made.
    For us men and for our salvation
    he came down from heaven,
    and by the Holy Spirit was incarnate of the Virgin Mary,
    and became man.
For our sake he was crucified under Pontius Pilate,
    he suffered death and was buried,
    and rose again on the third day
    in accordance with the Scriptures.
    He ascended into heaven
    and is seated at the right hand of the Father.
    He will come again in glory
    to judge the living and the dead
    and his kingdom will have no end.
I believe in the Holy Spirit, the Lord, the giver of life,
    who proceeds from the Father and the Son,
    who with the Father and the Son is adored and glorified,
    who has spoken through the prophets.
I believe in one, holy, catholic and apostolic Church.
    I confess one Baptism for the forgiveness of sins
    and I look forward to the resurrection of the dead
    and the life of the world to come. Amen.

42. See Britannica, "Nicene Creed."

## Apostles' Creed (Fourth Century AD)[43]

I believe in God, the Father almighty,
  creator of heaven and earth.
I believe in Jesus Christ, his only Son, our Lord,
  who was conceived by the Holy Spirit
  and born of the virgin Mary.
He suffered under Pontius Pilate,
  was crucified, died, and was buried;
  he descended to hell.
The third day he rose again from the dead.
He ascended to heaven
  and is seated at the right hand of God the Father almighty.
  From there he will come to judge the living and the dead.
I believe in the Holy Spirit,
  the holy catholic church,
  the communion of saints,
  the forgiveness of sins,
  the resurrection of the body,
  and the life everlasting. Amen.

## Te Deum (ca. AD 387)[44]

This early Latin hymn is a rich expression of praise.

O God, we praise Thee, and acknowledge Thee to be the supreme
Lord.
Everlasting Father, all the earth worships Thee.
All the Angels, the heavens and all angelic powers,
All the Cherubim and Seraphim, continuously cry to Thee:
Holy, Holy, Holy, Lord God of Hosts!
Heaven and earth are full of the Majesty of Thy glory.
The glorious choir of the Apostles,
The wonderful company of Prophets,
The white-robed army of Martyrs, praise Thee.
The Holy Church throughout the world acknowledges Thee:
The Father of infinite Majesty;
Thy adorable, true and only Son;
Also the Holy Spirit, the Comforter.
O Christ, Thou art the King of glory!
Thou art the everlasting Son of the Father.

43. See Britannica, "Apostles' Creed."
44. See Britannica, "Te Deum laudamus."

When Thou tookest it upon Thyself to deliver man,
Thou didst not disdain the Virgin's womb.
Having overcome the sting of death, Thou opened the Kingdom
of Heaven to all believers.
Thou sittest at the right hand of God in the glory of the Father.
We believe that Thou willst come to be our Judge.
We, therefore, beg Thee to help Thy servants whom Thou hast
redeemed with Thy Precious Blood.
Let them be numbered with Thy Saints in everlasting glory.

## Catechisms

These were primers in Christian beliefs, used for instruction of children
and new believers. The question-and-answer format lends itself to use in
responsive readings. One such catechism:

### Heidelberg Catechism (1563)

That this catechism is firmly based on Scripture is shown by the multitude of biblical passages footnoted through the catechism, for example:

> Question 1: What is your only comfort in life and death?
> Answer: That I am not my own,[1] but belong with body and
> soul, both in life and in death,[2] to my faithful Saviour Jesus
> Christ.[3] He has fully paid for all my sins with His precious
> blood,[4] and has set me free from all the power of the devil.[5]
> He also preserves me in such a way[6] that without the will of
> my heavenly Father not a hair can fall from my head;[7] indeed,
> all things must work together for my salvation.[8] Therefore, by
> His Holy Spirit He also assures me of eternal life[9] and makes
> me heartily willing and ready from now on to live for Him.[10]
> *[1] 1 Cor 6:19, 20. [2] Rom 14:7–9. [3] 1 Cor 3:23; Titus 2:14. [4]*
> *1 Pet 1:18, 19; 1 John 1:7; 2:2. [5] John 8:34–36; Heb 2:14, 15; 1*
> *John 3:8. [6] John 6:39, 40; 10:27–30; 2 Thess 3:3; 1 Pet 1:5. [7]*
> *Matt 10:29–31; Luke 21:16–18. [8] Rom 8:28. [9] Rom 8:15, 16; 2*
> *Cor 1:21, 22; 5:5; Eph 1:13, 14. [10] Rom 8:14.*[45]

For focused thematic services, excerpts can be used that focus on
the Trinity, the work of Christ, the ministry of the Holy Spirit, etc.:

> Question 53: What do you believe concerning the Holy Spirit?

45. "Heidelberg Catechism (1563)."

Answer: First, He is, together with the Father and the Son, true
and eternal God.[1] Second, He is also given to me,[2] to make
me by true faith share in Christ and all His benefits,[3] to comfort me,[4] and to remain with me forever.[5]
*[1] Gen 1:1, 2; Matt 28:19; Acts 5:3, 4; 1 Cor 3:16. [2] 1 Cor 6:19;
2 Cor 1:21, 22; Gal 4:6; Eph 1:13. [3] Gal 3:14; 1 Pet 1:2. [4] John
15:26; Acts 9:31. [5] John 14:16, 17; 1 Pet 4:14.*[46]

## Book of Common Prayer (1549, with multiple later revisions)

This is the liturgical guide for the Church of England. Largely written
by Thomas Cranmer, it is richly poetic and prayerful, and packed with
biblical truth:

> Almighty God, unto whom all hearts are open,
>     all desires known, and from whom no secrets are hid:
> Cleanse the thoughts of our hearts by the inspiration of thy Holy
>     Spirit,
> that we may perfectly love thee, and worthily magnify thy
>     holy Name;
> through Christ our Lord. Amen.[47]

Excerpts can be used in different parts of the service, for instance in
introducing communion:

> We do not presume to come to this thy Table, O merciful Lord,
>     trusting in our own righteousness, but in thy manifold and
>     great mercies.
> We are not worthy so much as to gather up the crumbs under
>     thy Table.
> But thou art the same Lord whose property is always to have
>     mercy.
> Grant us therefore, gracious Lord, so to eat the flesh of thy dear
>     Son Jesus Christ,
> and to drink his blood, that we may evermore dwell in him,
>     and he in us. Amen.[48]

---

46. "Heidelberg Catechism (1563)."
47. Church of England, "Order for the Administration."
48. Church of England, "Order for the Administration."

## The Valley of Vision: A Collection of Puritan Prayers and Devotions

This is a recent compilation of deep and rich prayers from the seventeenth, eighteenth, and nineteenth centuries. The first in the collection (giving the whole its name) is:

> Lord, high and holy, meek and lowly,
> Thou has brought me to the valley of vision,
>     where I live in the depths but see thee in the heights;
> Hemmed in by mountains of sin I behold
> Thy glory.

> Let me learn by paradox
>     that the way down is the way up,
>     that to be low is to be high,
>     that the broken heart is the healed heart,
>     that the contrite spirit is the rejoicing spirit,
>     that the repenting soul is the victorious soul,
>     that to have nothing is to possess all,
>     that to bear the cross is to wear the crown,
>     that to give is to receive,
>     that the valley is the place of vision.
> Lord, in the daytime stars can be seen from deepest wells,
> and the deeper the wells the brighter Thy stars shine;

> Let me find Thy light in my darkness,
>     Thy life in my death,
>     Thy joy in my sorrow,
>     Thy grace in my sin,
>     Thy riches in my poverty
>     Thy glory in my valley.[49]

The readings are organized thematically in the collection, which allows them to be excerpted for special service focuses; for instance, this one for New Year's:

> Length of days does not profit me except the days are passed
>     in Thy presence, in Thy service, to Thy glory.
> Give me a grace that precedes, follows, guides, sustains,
>     sanctifies, aids every hour,
> that I may not be one moment apart from Thee,
>     but may rely on Thy Spirit to supply every thought, speak in
>     every word, direct every step, prosper every work, build up

49. "Valley of Vision," in Bennett, *Valley of Vision*, xix.

every mote of faith;
and give me a desire to show forth Thy praise, testify Thy love,
    advance Thy kingdom.
I launch my bark [boat] on the unknown waters of this year,
    with Thee, O Father, as my harbour;
    Thee, O Son, at my helm;
    Thee, O Holy Spirit, filling my sails.

Give me Thy grace to sanctify me,
    Thy comforts to cheer,
    Thy wisdom to teach,
    Thy right hand to guide,
    Thy presence to stabilize.[50]

## New and Old

The above resources are just a few examples of the multitude of different
gems from the centuries of the church. The main point here is to bring
into our worship "what is new and what is old" (Matt 13:52). (This goes
for songs too, of course.) In this way we express continuity with the "faith
of our fathers"; and we can thus honor the devotion of, and declare our
solidarity with, those who came before us. As G. K. Chesterton puts it:

> Tradition is only democracy extended through time. It is trust-
> ing to a consensus of common human voices rather than to
> some isolated or arbitrary record. . . . Tradition means giving
> votes to the most obscure of all classes, our ancestors. It is the
> democracy of the dead. Tradition refuses to submit to the small
> and arrogant oligarchy of those who merely happen to be walk-
> ing about.[51]

---

The word of God must be central in the worship of the church.

---

50. "New Year," in Bennett, *Valley of Vision*, 115.
51. Chesterton, *Orthodoxy*, 38.

# 34

## THE PASTOR AND WORSHIP IN THE CHURCH

### The Pastor's Vital Role in the Worship Life of the Church

Worship is central to the identity and the life of the body of Christ, including, of course, *corporate* worship, as Eduard Schweizer affirms: "Public worship is clearly and openly the place in the congregation's life at which it manifests itself as the Body of Christ."[1] Similarly, William Willimon states: "[Corporate] worship is the center of the Christian community's upbuilding. . . . In worship, all the community's concerns meet and coalesce."[2]

As a result, pastors should see corporate worship life as an important part of their spiritual oversight of their flock. The pastor has the responsibility of publicly cherishing the glory of God and expounding it and inviting others to share in the wonder of wholehearted, and whole-life, worship. Every pastor should have this ultimate *vertical* purpose to ministry: a purpose of seeking to see the glory of God reflected in the lives of the people; a praying and striving towards a preoccupation with God; a loving of God with all the soul, heart, mind, and strength, on the pastor's own part as well as that of the congregation; a private and public cherishing of God in lives of worship. Ultimately ministry is the work of

---

1. Schweizer, "Worship in the New Testament," 205.
2. Willimon, *Worship as Pastoral Care*, 20.

seeking, in the power of the Holy Spirit, to build *more* and *better* worshipers of God (as we have just seen above).

Alas, these goals too often seem elusive in light of what has often been termed the worship wars endemic in so many of our churches. As John Witvliet diagnoses: "The Christian church is deeply divided into communities that rehearse different histories and embody divergent aesthetic preferences."[3] But indeed, "a church at war with itself, or divided into neat cells of parties agreeing to disagree, can't do its work very well."[4] The continuing disunity in many evangelical churches over issues of worship highlights the need for pastors to give strong, informed leadership to their congregations in this area, in order to preserve the unity and witness of the body.

Pastors will need to bring a solid biblical and theological understanding to bear on worship discussions in their churches, if those discussions are not to degrade into mere wranglings over personal opinions, style preferences, and generational proclivities (as, sadly, they so often do). The pastor will also need a firm grasp on historical and contemporary issues in the ongoing worship debates, and a considerable measure of pastoral and practical wisdom in navigating the treacherous waters where so many churches have floundered, to the dishonoring of Christ and his church.[5]

## Points of Worship Engagement for the Pastor[6]

### 1. Be a private worshiper.

This goes without saying. Pastors cannot lead someone where they have not been themselves. Personal spiritual discipline and nurture are foundational to any ministry in the body of Christ, and certainly for the pastor.

3. Witvliet, "Trinitarian DNA."

4. Plantinga and Rozeboom, *Discerning the Spirits*, 118.

5. Because of all these important expectations, theological seminaries and other schools that prepare future pastors need to take seriously their role in educating their students in a deep biblical, theological, cultural, and practical understanding of worship that will help them serve their churches well in ways described below. For more on the school's role, see appendix 4, "Outline for Teaching Worship"; and also Ronald E. Man, "Dallas Seminary Worship Education."

6. And here are some very wise words for those who *listen* to the preacher: "I recently ran across a statement that has stuck with me. It is this: spiritually mature people are easily edified. . . . What does that mean? There are some people who are

"No one should be more passionate for God's glory than the leaders of Christ's church. A church's experience of God will generally not go beyond the worship life of their pastor."[7]

## 2. Sing, pray, and preach out of a walk of worship.

That is, a life of private worship will, and should, show when one is leading the flock in worship. The pastor's personal and private enrichment cannot help but overflow in a deeper, more relevant, and more engaging manner in leading the service.

## 3. Study worship.

The pastor should be a student of worship, so as to give solid biblical guidance to the church in its discussion and practices of worship. The pastor must include this vital area in the ongoing program of biblical, theological and historical inquiry and enrichment. This impetus should begin during seminary training; and it should carry on into ministry as a central spiritual and ministerial focus.

The pastor also needs to be a student not only of worship, but also of the congregation and of the surrounding culture.

---

almost always blessed by sermons. They do not need to be coaxed into a sermon. The introduction, supporting material, and conclusion are not that important to them. The mannerisms, inflections, and voice command of the preacher are not the make it or break it parts of a sermon for them. They listen closely, but to the right stuff, not the side comments or statement a preacher makes that often trip up and cause many listeners to over analyze or get distracted. The irony is these people often have a great deal of Bible knowledge. They should be the pickiest listeners, but they aren't. Why? The easily edified person has a built-in hunger, curiosity, and receptivity to the Word of God. By the time the preacher takes the pulpit, they are ready, Bible open, heart unfurled, happy to take in the Word of God—even when it rebukes.
  1. Don't expect the preacher to be the totality of your spiritual interaction every week.
  2. Pray for God to give you a love for the Bible.
  3. Put to death a critical spirit.
  4. Focus on the content and faithfulness.
  5. Keep short accounts with the preacher if there is a relational issue that is getting in the way" (Thomas, "Easily Edified").
  7. Kauflin, "Worship Matters."

## 4. Preach and teach on worship.

This is a critical lack in most evangelical churches today. There is a crucial need to proclaim a proper biblical perspective on the purpose, principles, and Object of worship. Most worship problems today are issues of discipleship and maturity, not of music styles. This is where the pastor is uniquely postured to challenge the flock to rise above their petty obsessions with personal wants, preferences, and agendas—and to *be the church*, striving for unity (Eph 4:1–3) by considering one another more important than oneself (Phil 1:3), by preferring one another in love (Rom 12:10), and by making concessions to one another for the good of the whole. This will not just happen; pastors need to be actively and continually engaged in calling their people to rise above their inherent selfishness and to see what it means to function practically as the body of Christ—especially in this often heated area of worship.

## 5. Champion worship.

Worship has seen such a huge growth in importance and focus in recent decades that it has been observed that sometimes a pastor may feel intimidated by the worship leader or the leader's ministry. A far better route is for the pastor to nurture a relationship of trust and mutual ministry with the one immediately responsible for leading the corporate praises of the congregation (whether a paid staff member or a volunteer), with a view to presenting a united front to the church. The service should be seen and valued as worship, from beginning to end, and the false dichotomy between preaching and "worship" resisted at every turn.

> The most important thing a pastor does is stand in the pulpit every Sunday and say, "Let us worship God." If that ceases to be the primary thing I do in terms of my energy, my imagination, and the way I structure my life, then I no longer function as a pastor. . . . I cannot fail to call the congregation to worship God, to listen to his Word, to offer themselves to God. Worship becomes a place where we have our lives redefined for us.[8]

> What is needed in congregations today [is] not so much another songbook, a new prayerbook, a fancier sound system, or better worship space, but discerning, nurturing leaders with the instincts to connect specific strategies and practices with a rich

8. E. Peterson, "Business of Making Saints," 22.

spiritual vision of worship and the imagination and persistence
to enable congregations to practice them.[9]

## 6. Help cast a vision for the worship ministry.

The pastor is usually seen as the primary vision-caster for the church,
and pastors should use their platform to promote a unified vision for
worship. They should guide the discussion of the leadership and people
concerning the why, as well as the how and what, of the church's worship.
They should bring their professional expertise in Bible and theology,
church dynamics, and pastoral ministry to bear on the worship issues
with which the church is engaged.

## 7. Help plan worship.

This does not necessarily require musical knowledge. The time of corporate worship (in fact, much more than is usually the case in evangelical
churches today) should revolve around the reading, praying, and singing
of God's word. The pastor can help the congregation immensely to see that
there is a healthy balance of revelation and response in the worship service.

> Far too often, preaching and worship are segregated entities—in
> publications, in seminary curricula, and in the practice of pre-
> paring for worship in local congregations. For centuries, how-
> ever, preaching and worship have been inextricably intertwined.
> Preaching needs worship as its context, and worship needs
> preaching as its anchor. Not infrequently, preachers sense that a
> thoughtful worship service has actually helped "preach" the ser-
> mon, or to make up for a poor one. And musicians, artists, and
> worship leaders regularly observe that unless their contributions
> function as complementary forms of gospel proclamation to the
> sermon, they will end up feeling like second-rate liturgical in-
> terruptions rather than integral elements of Christian worship.
> Whatever liturgical style we adopt, preaching and liturgy need
> to be worked at together.[10]

The pastor explores the meaning of worship and its practice
throughout the Church and guides the parish's musicians and
worship committee theologically and biblically to design the

9. Witvliet, "Beyond Style."
10. Witvliet, "Isaiah in Christian Liturgy," 135–36.

best, most integrated and congruent way to immerse the worshipers in the "glory and strength" of the Lord revealed in the texts for the day.[11]

God has called pastors to feed, lead, care for, and protect the members of the church. . . . Let's not overlook how corporate worship—thoughtfully, passionately, and skillfully led—can be a means of fulfilling those goals. As a pastor, you can feed the church by making sure your worship leader chooses songs for their theologically balanced lyrics, not for their popularity. You can lead the church by directing their attention to what's important and by explaining the role of music in worship. You exercise care when you highlight songs that remind the church of God's promises and faithfulness in the midst of their trials, especially as he has revealed them to us in the gospel. You protect your church from the world by finding songs that remind them of God's holiness and the infinitely superior joy that Christ offers us.[12]

## 8. Model worship publicly.

The most enduring image of this writer's visit to First Evangelical Free Church in Fullerton, California, many years ago, was the level of engagement that then-pastor Chuck Swindoll showed during the time of corporate worship. There was no question as to the value he put on that part of the service (though probably many in the congregation were there primarily to hear him preach). A pastor can set a tremendous example for the congregation of the importance of corporate worship (or, conversely, can set a terrible example through inattention or looking bored or focused only on the preaching spot to come). Congregants will know what pastors value in the service by watching their level of engagement.

A church's response to God's greatness and grace rarely rises above the example of its pastor. Your congregation is watching and listening to you on Sunday, and not just when you preach. What are they learning? What kind of example do you provide for them? If you fiddle with your sermon notes while everyone else is praising God, they may infer that singing is optional. If you look around anxiously to make sure the technical details are being taken care of, they might conclude that the priority of Sunday morning is the performance, not their participation. If

11. Dawn, *How Shall We Worship?*, 148.
12. Kauflin, *Worship Matters*, 251.

you sing halfheartedly, they may assume that passion for God isn't that important. But know this: your church is watching you.[13]

## 9. Help lead worship.

The pastor should not abdicate all worship leadership to the worship pastor or worship leader. The entire service is to be a ministry of the word (Col 3:16), and the pastor can help to shape and guide it by being involved both in its preparation and its implementation. A very strong statement of a high view of corporate worship on the part of a pastor is when that pastor takes an active role in the leading of that part of the service, complementing the worship leader's role (rather than sitting distractedly, waiting for the "main event" of the sermon). This of course does not presume any musical ability; rather, it can take the form of Scripture reading, leading in prayer or responsive readings, and making appropriate pastoral comments along the way.

> Some pastors want to turn the entire area of music and worship over to their worship leader. This is a serious mistake. God has given every pastor the ultimate responsibility of being the worship leader, or lead worshiper, for his church. A pastor may not be a musician, but his love for seeing God's greatness proclaimed and responded to must be something others can learn from and follow.[14]

## 10. Help evaluate worship.

The pastor can play an important pastoral role in the life and ministry of the worship leader by giving careful, constructive feedback (positive as well as negative) on the previous Sunday's service. A ministry of encouragement to the worship leader is crucial.

## 11. Handle the text of Scripture reverently and responsively in sermon preparation.

Sermon preparation is an act of worship! Pastors should ask themselves: "What is God showing me about himself in this text? How should I love

13. Kauflin, *Worship Matters*, 251.
14. Kauflin, "Worship Matters."

and praise him more as a result?" Filtering the text first through one's own life is an important prerequisite to preaching in an open, transparent, and humble manner.

## 12. Preach as an act of worship.

Handling God's word is a serious responsibility, and presenting it to others a holy privilege; when pastors do so they are actively representing Christ, whose ministry it is to proclaim the Father's name to the congregation (Heb 2:12). (See ch. 26.)

> The sermon, if it really is a sermon, is most certainly worship. For the faithful exposition of the Word of God is itself at the same time both Word of God (the divine action of worship) and also hearing of the Word of God (the primary human action of worship), the preacher leading the congregation in its work of hearing.[15]

> Preaching is not just expository, but expository exultation. . . . Christian preaching, as part of the corporate worship of Christ's church, is an expository exultation over the glories of God in his word, designed to lure God's people from the fleeting pleasures of sin into the sacrificial path of obedient satisfaction in him.[16]

> Preaching is not an interruption of worship but an integral part of the liturgy, the work of worship for both preacher and listener.[17]

## 13. Preach as an invitation to worship.

As God's spokesperson on behalf of his inscripturated word, pastors open the text to their people so that they can see God, wonder at his excellencies, and humbly bow before his majesty and grace.

> Preaching is a congregational act of worship, not just a monologue from one individual. . . . Preaching facilitates dialogue between people and God as well as between the preacher and other members of a church. When sermons are delivered by preachers

---

15. Cranfield, "Divine and Human Action," 393.

16. John Piper, in Piper and Edwards, God's Passion, 39.

17. Esbjornson, "Preaching as Worship," 167.

whose purposes are oriented to the glory of God, hearers of the sermons are engaged in a conversation with God.[18]

Preaching is meant by God to catch people up into worship, not to be a practical human application after worship. The aim of preaching is to deal with divorce worshipfully, and to deal with teenagers worshipfully, and to deal with anger worship-fully. Preaching exalts the centrality of God in all of life or it is not Christian preaching. . . . Preaching is meant to be and to kindle God-exalting worship. . . . The overarching, pervasive, relentless subject of preaching is God himself with a view to being worshipped. . . . Preaching is meant to be and to kindle God-exalting worship. . . . The mission of all preaching is soul-satisfying, God-exalting worship.[19]

> The pastor should preach as an invitation to worship.

18. Gaddy, *Gift of Worship*, 72.
19. Piper, "Preaching as Worship" (Desiring God).

# 35

# MANAGING CHANGE IN WORSHIP
# IN THE CHURCH

The "worship reformation" of recent years has led many churches to make changes in their worship styles and practices. That is no small matter, and the way is full of potholes and pitfalls. Therefore, *how* we go about it (if at all) may be more important (and say more about us) than the desired outcome.

Here are some suggested principles to help guide the process:

## The Principle of *Scripture*

The Bible may not give us all the details we need, but it should certainly be our starting point. It gives us the tracks to run on, and we dare not take off "cross-country" into uncharted territory, or we will most certainly end up in a train wreck.

## The Reformation Principle of *Semper Reformanda* (Always Reforming)

We should always be evaluating our worship practices in light of Scripture. That may *or may not* lead us to make changes in our practice of worship, but Scripture should always be the final determinant.

Along those lines, we need also to be reminded that, as R. C. Sproul puts it, the Reformers "were interested, not in innovation, but in renovation. They were reformers, not revolutionaries."[1] What the Reformers had in mind was *not* novelty, not plowing new ground; rather, they stressed the need for continual mid-course corrections to bring our practice back more clearly in line with Scripture.

Let us indeed apply all the creative forces at our disposal to make our worship more interesting, exciting, inspiring—in a way that is profoundly true to Scripture.

## The Principle of *Purposeful Change*

It is so important not to undertake change simply for change's sake. That is not a worthy goal. Any change in our worship must be motivated by a sincere desire to enhance the worship of Almighty God. As Gordon Borror and Ron Allen say in their ahead-of-its-time book *Worship: Rediscovering the Missing Jewel* (1982), we must be a people "more committed to God than to change."[2]

This is where the leadership of the church has a great responsibility to lead in a godly way. "The leaders can reason, 'Our worship is supposed to be a re-presentation of the gospel to those in our spiritual care. So if we are presenting the gospel to them, what are the best ways to communicate the glory and goodness of God with the resources he has given us?'"[3]

## The Principle of *Unity*

In our age of rampant individualism and a pervasive "what's in it for me?" mentality, there must be a deep commitment, on the part of the leadership and the congregation, to avoid pursuing a course of worship change that alienates or disenfranchises one segment of the people in the process. The point is not for one group to "win" and get what it wants; the point is for God to get what *he* wants. And he wants believers to love self-sacrificially and to sublimate one's own desires for the good of the whole. How we need that kind of Christlikeness to pervade our modern-day

---

1. Sproul, *Grace Unknown*, 28.
2. Allen and Borror, *Worship*, 189.
3. Chapell, *Christ-Centered Worship*, 132.

worship debates! It's an issue of maturity, of a godly perspective that chooses "deference over preference."[4]

Worship in a congregation seeping with disunity is hardly pleasing to God—in fact, it is hard to see how it can be worship at all (see Matt 5:23–24).

## The Principle of *Instruction*

Once the leadership has determined a course for the church to take (after much listening to the people), they should deliberately, thoughtfully, and comprehensively explain the *purpose* behind the change(s), being especially careful to show its biblical moorings. The people must be told the *why*, not just the *what* of the anticipated change. (This assumes, of course, the kind of *purposeful* change described above.)

## The Principle of *Incrementalism*

Nothing has been historically messier than an overenthusiastic new pastor deciding to make radical changes in a church's worship overnight; that consistently ends in disaster for the church. A proper concern for the unity of the body will recognize the wisdom of "making haste slowly." Gradual change gives the people time to adjust to new practices; going slowly honors the overriding goals of true worship and unity.[5]

## The Principle of *Prevailing Prayer*

We cannot possibly know all the issues or foresee all the dangers in pursuing worship change. And so we need to beg God for his wisdom and guidance (Rom 8:26–27; Jas 1:5).

The great Reformer John Calvin himself saw the need both for purposeful change in worship and for great care in pursuing it:

> For the upbuilding of the church [worship] ought to be variously accommodated to the customs of each nation and age, [and so] it will be fitting (as the advantage of the church will require) to change and abrogate traditional practices and to

4. A favorite saying of the late Chip Stam.

5. There is a story of a church that was going to introduce the use of the drums in its services. The leadership had the drums sit in the sanctuary for six months before they were ever used, so the people would get used to seeing them there!

establish new ones. Indeed, I admit that we ought not to charge into innovation rashly, suddenly, for insufficient cause. But love will best judge what may hurt or edify; and if we let love be our guide, all will be safe.[6]

Wise advice!

> We must be a people more committed to God than to change.

---

6. Calvin, *Institutes*, 4:10.30.

# 36

## WORSHIP AND CULTURE

*H*ow do we balance the need for biblical fidelity with the need for cultural sensitivity and relevance in our worship?

Churches all over the world face that ongoing and persistent challenge. Matthew Pinson speaks of

> the tension between the need to remain faithful to the gospel and the Christian tradition while at the same time faithfully communicating that Evangel [gospel] in a changing complex cultural milieu that presents mammoth challenges to the continued witness of the Christian church.[1]

But this is not a new issue by any means! The early church faced its own set of cultural and cross-cultural challenges in this regard. Early churches often included Jews, Greeks, Romans, barbarians, masters, slaves, etc., in the same body. Undoubtedly these various groups brought widely different cultural perspectives, preferences, and expectations with them. And yet, unlike today in many parts of the world, there was not the option for a discontented Christian to find another church more to one's liking. There was *the* church at Ephesus, *the* church at Corinth, etc. Believers had to hang in there and work things out![2] And ultimately it was up to the Holy Spirit to forge unity out of the diversity:

1. Pinson, *Perspectives on Christian Worship*, 16.

2. Not that this was easy: the letters of the New Testament make it clear just how many issues and struggles there were in these early churches—even those that had

I therefore, a prisoner for the Lord, urge you to walk in a manner worthy of the calling to which you have been called, with all humility and gentleness, with patience, bearing with one another in love, eager to maintain the unity of the Spirit in the bond of peace. There is one body and one Spirit—just as you were called to the one hope that belongs to your call—one Lord, one faith, one baptism, one God and Father of all, who is over all and through all and in all. But grace was given to each one of us according to the measure of Christ's gift. . . . And he gave the apostles, the prophets, the evangelists, the shepherds and teachers, to equip the saints for the work of ministry, for building up the body of Christ, until we all attain to the unity of the faith and of the knowledge of the Son of God. . . . Speaking the truth in love, we are to grow up in every way into him who is the head, into Christ, from whom the whole body, joined and held together by every joint with which it is equipped, when each part is working properly, makes the body grow so that it builds itself up in love. (Eph 4:1–7, 11–13, 15–16)

## Culture

Churches are not immune from the influences of culture. Every one of us lives in, and is in many respects a product of, the culture in which we live. It is "the air we breathe."

Culture has been defined as "the behaviors and beliefs characteristic of a particular social, ethnic, or age group."[3] Yet a simple way to think of it is simply as *"the way we do things around here."*

This author was once teaching in Vietnam. When the driver picked me up at the hotel in the morning, he had to go left onto the main street. He proceeded to head directly into the oncoming traffic, then slowly worked his way over to the right side of the road! And amazingly, none of the other drivers blew their horns: this was normal, expected behavior. This is the way they turn left around there! This was an aspect of their driving culture that was not out of place in its own context—though it was terrifying to me as an outsider!

---

*Paul* for a teacher! It is not so different today.

3. Adapted from "Culture" at www.dictionary.com.

As Aidan Kavanagh puts it, Christian worship "swims in creation as a fish swims in water."[4] What a person feels to be appropriate or helpful or meaningful is conditioned by his or her own cultural upbringing.

## The Challenges

This brings us back to the question: *How do we balance the need for biblical fidelity with the need for cultural sensitivity and relevance in our worship?* There are two primary challenges that make navigating this issue particularly difficult.

## The Silence of the New Testament

No group consciously seeks to be *unbiblical* in its worship practices. Yet even with a commitment to the Scriptures as our guide for worship, we search the pages of the New Testament in vain for much in the way of specifics of worship (except for some general elements, as seen earlier in ch. 33 and developed later in this chapter), much less structures or liturgies. Even in the Epistles, where we might reasonably expect Paul and the other writers to address these issues as they write to guide and encourage brand new churches, we find frustratingly little. John Piper makes the telling observation, already noted:

> In the New Testament, all the focus is on the reality of the glory of Christ, not the shadow and copy of religious objects and forms. It is stunning how indifferent the New Testament is to such things: there is no authorization in the New Testament for worship buildings, or worship dress, or worship times, or worship music, or worship liturgy or worship size or thirty-five-minute sermons, or Advent poems or choirs or instruments or candles. . . . Almost every worship tradition we have is culturally shaped rather than Biblically commanded.[5]

Piper's startling last statement does not mean that there is something wrong with our worship traditions; rather, it just means that in the absence of clear biblical direction, we must necessarily make choices (about buildings, dress, times, music, etc.), which will inevitably be shaped by our cultural preconditioning.

4. Kavanagh, *On Liturgical Theology*, 4.
5. Piper, "Our High Priest."

We might ask, though: *Why* is the New Testament not more specific about what we are to do in worship? If Jesus or Paul had just laid out the plan, then we could just follow it and avoid so many of our discussions, debates, and dissensions about worship practices.

John Piper suggests this reason: in the Old Testament, there was a "come and see" system.[6]

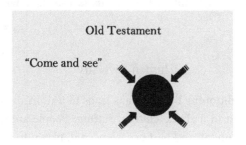

Worship was centralized in a particular time and place. To worship, one had to come to Jerusalem, come to the temple (or before that the tabernacle). And in fact, people from other nations could worship God, but they had to come to Jerusalem, had to become Jews. Worship was centralized in a particular time and place.

And because it was in a particular time and place, the instructions for worship could be *very* detailed. So in Exodus and Leviticus, we find chapter after chapter after chapter of instructions for worship: how to prepare, when to come, what to bring, what to do. It was very specific because it was to be at a specific time and place.

But, as Piper points out, the New Testament is exactly the opposite situation. It is *not* a "come and see" system. It is a "go and tell" system. There is no geographical center to Christianity; but rather the gospel is to go out into every nation, to every people.

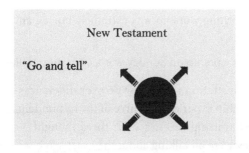

6. Piper, "Our High Priest."

And so perhaps for this reason, Piper suggests, the New Testament leaves things so open regarding worship: so that as the gospel goes out, and the church is planted in different cultures, worship can "breathe the air" of, and find expression in, the various cultures in which the church is planted.

The New Testament leaves room for us to make many choices about our worship practices. But that brings us face-to-face with the second challenge.

## Human Diversity

Cultural preconditioning by no means leads to uniformity of opinion or preferences, even in a single cultural setting. People are different. Personality, temperament, and past experiences all play into a wide range of attitudes, perceptions, and responses.

This writer served with Greater Europe Mission from 2000 to 2008. Every summer, the GEM missionaries from all over the continent would gather for a conference. One year a friend of mine planned and led a Sunday morning worship service during the conference. At the end of the conference, the participants were asked to fill out a survey about different aspects of the conference. There was a question about the Sunday morning worship service. Six people made specific comments about that service, as follows:

1. The Sunday morning service was a real downer.
2. Sunday was powerful for me—a feast of worship. I appreciated the reverence and awe.
3. Sunday morning seemed like a funeral.
4. Sunday was super!!!!!—simple but profound.
5. Sunday morning worship was extremely boring and difficult to sit through.
6. The time of worship on Sunday was a very special blessing.

This is a vivid illustration about how people's differences can affect their response to worship experiences. Three of the respondents thought it was one of the best worship services ever; three thought it was one of the worst. And they were all talking about the exact same service!

## Freedom within Bounds

It is a reasonable assumption that the virtual silence of the New Testament writers on the matters of form and style for worship means that the Lord intends for us to have considerable latitude and flexibility in these areas. But of course this leads to the worship debates that are so common in our day. If the New Testament laid out as detailed a prescription for worship as we find in the Old Testament, there would be hardly any room for debate for churches that desired to be biblically faithful; but it is the latitude allowed that leaves room for differing opinions and (often) conflict.

At the root of most of the current worship debates is the nature of the interface of worship and the culture in which a local church finds itself. The church dares not sell out to the surrounding culture, but cannot ignore it either. It is important in this light to stress that this latitude does not mean *total* freedom—it is certainly not a matter of pulling everything in from the culture, of "anything goes."

So just what is it in the Bible that is supposed to govern and determine our worship? How do we discern the balance? How do we bridge the historical and practical gap between the scriptural mandates and our cultural context? How can our worship be "in" the world but not "of" the world? How do worship and culture intersect? How shall we then worship?

There is *freedom*, but *within bounds*.

The bridge model described in the next chapter has proven helpful in giving biblical guidance, yet at the same time allowing for true biblical freedom.

---

How to be biblically faithful *and* culturally relevant in our worship?

---

# 37

## THE BRIDGE[1]

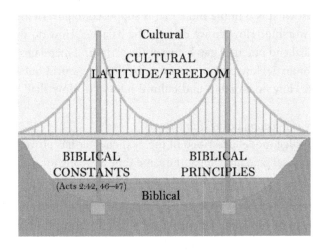

B y way of illustration, this model is based on certain characteristics of a *suspension bridge* (familiar examples of suspension bridges are the Brooklyn Bridge in New York City and the Golden Gate Bridge in San Francisco).

---

1. See also Ron Man, "'The Bridge': Worship between Bible and Culture," ch. 4 in Krabill et al., *Worship and Mission*, 17–25.

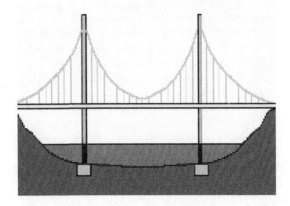

In a suspension bridge, the weight is supported by both the towers and the suspension cable. The towers are sunk deep in the earth and are meant to be as stable and immovable as possible. The suspension cable or span, on the other hand, while sharing a significant portion of the load bearing, nevertheless has by design a great deal of flexibility to expand and contract, thus allowing the bridge to withstand variances in temperature, wind, weight load, etc. It should also be pointed out that, while the stationary columns and the flexible span are both important parts of the bridge's construction, yet ultimately the cable transfers much of the weight of the roadbed and its traffic to the towers, so that the towers are crucial to the bridge's integrity and durability.

What can we then learn about our worship from this illustration? Our worship needs to be supported by firmly rooted biblical foundations, which are illustrated by the two towers. The flexible cable span suggests the liberty that the New Testament seems to allow for individual congregations to constitute their corporate worship. Like any art form, Christian worship allows for much creative expression, but within defined parameters.[2] The Bible gives those parameters as well as that freedom.

2. For example, a painter has unlimited freedom to paint what he or she desires, but *within the constraints* of the frame and the palette of colors.

## The First Tower: *Biblical Constants*

BIBLICAL
CONSTANTS
(Acts 2:42, 46–47)

The first tower suggests an immovable aspect of Christian worship that we could term *biblical constants*. These are nonnegotiables, elements that simply *must* be present for our worship to be considered Christian.

What are these elements? In chs. 30 and 33 we saw that Acts 2 gives us a good starting point:

> So those who received his word were *baptized,* and there were added that day about three thousand souls. And they devoted themselves to the *apostles' teaching* and *fellowship,* to *the break-ing of bread* and the *prayers . . . praising God* and having favor with all the people. (Acts 2:41–42, 47)

We saw that Luke seems to be suggesting a list of normal activities for the people of God when they congregate together:

1. The word of God

2. Fellowship

3. The Lord's Supper

4. Prayer

5. Praise

As noted in ch. 30, a number of commentators have assessed these verses as indeed something more than simply a *description* of what the earliest church did, but perhaps rather a *prescription* of normative practice for the church of all ages. In fact, this writer has often given an overnight assignment to students to list what activities are consistently found in *every* Christian worship service, in every denomination, around the world and down through history—and the results they come up with invariably correspond almost exactly with the list found in Acts 2:42, 47! These indeed seem to be nonnegotiable elements that define and characterize truly Christian worship, and that *must* therefore be represented in some form in every church's corporate gatherings.[3] These *biblical constants* serve as one foundational pillar for our worship.[4]

## The Span: *Flexibility and Freedom*

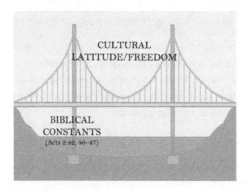

The span of the bridge, with its built-in elasticity and flexibility, represents the *freedom* that the New Testament seems to allow by its virtual silence regarding the specifics of worship: freedom for wise and prudent application of culturally meaningful expressions.

> [We are] free to find place and time and dress and size and music and elements and objects that help us orient radically toward the supremacy of God in Christ.[5]

We have a *biblical* framework (represented by the two towers): we cannot go outside it and still be truly honoring to God; but within that

3. Allowing, of course, for periodic rather than weekly celebrations of the Lord's Supper—though the practice of the early church was certainly weekly if not more often.

4. It should be noted, however, that there are differences of opinion about what belongs in this realm of nonnegotiables. Some see more biblical guidance from the Old Testament for our New Testament worship forms, for instance. For much more on this, see Farley, "What Is 'Biblical' Worship?" See also Meyers, *Lord's Service*; and Chapell, *Christ-Centered Worship*.

5. Piper, "Our High Priest."

framework there is a lot of *freedom* and *latitude* in how we can honor God in our worship.[6]

## Freedom of Form Applied Globally

We certainly can see the application of this principle (consciously or not) in the vast array of worship expressions seen down through the history of the Christian church and in churches around the world today. There has been, and is, an enormous variety in terms of architecture, atmosphere, form, structure, style, dress, music, liturgy, etc. And God, who has created the world and humanity with such incredible diversity, must certainly rejoice in such variety from his people.[7] Piper insists that

> the New Testament is not a manual for worship services. Rather, it is a vision for missions in thousands of diverse people groups around the world. In such groups, outward forms of worship will vary drastically, but the inner reality of treasuring Christ in spirit and truth is common ground.[8]

Tim Keller makes a fascinating point along these lines:

> Why has Christianity, more than any other major religion of the world, been able to infiltrate so many radically different cultures? There is of course a core of teachings . . . to which all forms of Christianity are committed [the biblical framework]. Nevertheless, there is a great deal of freedom in how these absolutes are expressed and take form within a particular culture. Contrary to popular opinion, then, Christianity is not a Western religion that destroys local cultures. Rather Christianity has taken more culturally diverse forms than other faiths.[9]

Similarly, John Piper claims that

---

6. "If we start with the Bible for our principles, then we can allow our cultural practices to be informed by God's truth as we step into the world and subvert the stories that people are daily believing about God, themselves, and the world around them. Cultural *accommodation* is very different from cultural *connection*" (Dan Wilt, "Response to Ligon Duncan," in Pinson, *Perspectives on Christian Worship*, 133).

7. Reggie Kidd in his book *With One Voice* explores the various legitimate expressions of worship found today in the West using categories he calls art music, folk music, and popular music.

8. Piper, *Let the Nations Be Glad*, 247.

9. Keller, *Reason for God*, 45.

Christianity is almost infinitely culturally adaptable . . . because of how little we are told.[10]

## Freedom of Form Applied Historically

Below are some fascinating testimonies from church history, which acknowledge the silence of the New Testament and hence the admissibility of cultural adaptation and change in worship:

### Early Catholicism, AD 596

Pope Gregory I sent Augustine of Canterbury to England as a missionary about AD 596 with this advice: "It seems to me that you should carefully *select* for the English Church, which is still new to the faith and developing as a distinct community, whatever can best please Almighty God, whether you discover it in the Roman Church, or among the Gauls, or anywhere else. . . . From each individual church, therefore, *choose* whatever is holy, whatever is awe-inspiring, whatever is right; then arrange what you have collected as if in a little bouquet according to the English disposition and thus establish them as custom."[11]

### Martin Luther, 1523

This is enough for now about the mass and communion. What is left can be decided by actual practice, as long as the Word of God is diligently and faithfully preached in the church. And if any should ask that all these [forms] be proved from Scriptures and the example of the fathers, they do not disturb us; for as we have said above, *liberty* must prevail in these matters and Christian consciences must not be bound by laws and ordinances. That is why *the Scriptures prescribe nothing in these matters*, but *allow freedom* for the Spirit to act according to his own understanding as the respective place, time, and persons may require it.[12]

---

10. Piper, "Pursuit of God."

11. White, *Brief History*, 44 (emphases added).

12. "Order of Mass and Communion for the Church at Wittenberg," in Luther, *Liturgy and Hymns*, 38 (emphases added).

## Augsburg Confession (Lutheran, 1530)

And to the true unity of the church it is enough to agree concerning the doctrine of the Gospel and the administration of the sacraments. *Nor is it necessary that human traditions, that is, rites or ceremonies, instituted by men, should be everywhere alike.*[13]

## John Calvin, 1536 (already cited in part)

The Master . . . did *not* will in outward discipline and ceremonies to *prescribe in detail* what we ought to do (because he foresaw that this depended on the state of the times, and he did not deem one form suitable for all ages). . . . Because *he has taught nothing specifically*, and because these things are not necessary to salvation, and for the upbuilding of the church ought to be *variously accommodated to the customs of each nation and age*, it will be fitting (as the advantage of the church will require) to *change* and abrogate traditional practices and to establish *new* ones. Indeed, I admit that we ought not to charge into innovation rashly, suddenly, for insufficient cause. But love will best judge what may hurt or edify; and if we let love be our guide, all will be safe.[14]

## Thirty-Nine Articles of Religion (Church of England, 1563)

*It is not necessary that Traditions and Ceremonies be in all places one, or utterly like;* for at all times they have been divers and may be *changed* according to the *diversities* of countries, times, and men's manners, so that nothing be ordained against God's Word. . . . Every particular or national Church hath authority to *ordain, change, and abolish*, ceremonies or rites of the Church, ordained only by man's authority, so that all things be done to edifying.[15]

## Challenge and Conflict Resulting from Freedom of Form

As already noted, the New Testament's virtual silence on the details of worship and the resultant cultural freedom has led to all kinds of

13. Melanchthon, *Augsburg Confession*, art. 7 (emphases added).

14. Calvin, *Institutes*, 4:10.30 (emphases added). Note the care with which Calvin thinks change should be undertaken. (See ch. 35 of this book, "Managing Change.")

15. "Article 34—Of the Traditions of the Church," in "Thirty Nine Articles" (emphases added).

discussions, debates, and disagreements about what is acceptable and what is unacceptable.

## Worship Wars

One familiar example will be the so-called worship wars in North American churches during the late twentieth century. Most of the controversy revolved around worship atmosphere (formal vs. casual) and music (traditional vs. contemporary, organ vs. band).

The late music missionary and ethnomusicologist Tom Avery (1950–2008) once gave a seminar where he drew on his training and field experience to helpfully analyze the issues in these worship wars. Some of his insights were:

1. It is common for people to feel very strongly about the music with which they identify, and to find the music with which they don't identify to be extremely distasteful.

2. We live in a society where different generations may and often do have different musical cultures. (This is caused by the rapid rate of culture change experienced by society, probably unprecedented in the history of the world.)

3. We have people in the same churches who partake of radically different musical cultures.

4. Music is *not* a universal language. It can speak very differently to different groups of people, even within the same church.[16]

To illustrate this last point, Avery humorously but incisively reflected on the polar-opposite reactions of an elderly "Joe Traditional" and a young "Johnny NewSong" as they both experienced a contemporary and then a traditional worship service:

---

16. Avery, "Worship Wars and Ethnomusicology" (emphasis original).

**by Tom Avery, "Worship Wars and Ethnomusicology"**

Disputes about instrumentation, music styles, and texts in worship are nothing new. In the thirteenth century, a controversy supposedly raged whether it was appropriate to bring an organ into the church; some considered it "the devil's instrument"!

"Mindless words, bad theology, emotional tunes." This was a reputed assessment, not about a recent contemporary worship song, but about Isaac Watts's hymn "O God, Our Help in Ages Past" in the eighteenth century!

Vernon Whaley relates this sad account:

> I read about a group of clergy who met at a Christian college in the northern part of Michigan to discuss the appropriate use of instruments in worship. Many felt the instruments were loud, distracting, and in general, a hindrance to the work of the Kingdom. One brother voiced concern and lack of biblical support for the use of any instrument, other than the organ, in the worship of a majestic and holy God. Another pastor stood and gave an extended dissertation of the evils in using instruments associated with the barroom. "How could God be pleased with such a carnal instrument in worship as a piano?" he asked. And one rather divisive and intense moment erupted. In response, a brother called the group to order and asked for a show of hands of those willing to go back to their churches and discipline any member actively engaged in playing church music with saxophones and trumpets. Another brother, the pastor of a large and well-established congregation, stood and lamented the passing of old hymns and spiritual songs. He expressed concern over the perceived lack of respect by a younger, less spiritual group of pastors. He reminded the group of God's gift of heritage.
>
> Others made persuasive arguments for Christian liberty and tolerance. Some told of how God was working in their midst

and reminded everyone to be engaged in a spiritual ministry. A compelling speech by an older pastor dealt with changes taking place in America and how the assembly should meet people at their point of greatest need. He concluded his speech by making a plea for unity and oneness in ministry. The group spent considerable time talking about worship and how the body of Christ across the country struggles with the idea of change.

During the course of their meetings to discuss music practices appropriate for worship, people argued. Some stormed out of the meeting with fury, showing obvious hostility and resentment towards those in authority. Harsh, angry words were spoken by many. The meeting on music and worship was characterized by hurt feelings, harsh and angry words, divisive attitudes, and spiritual casualties.

This historic meeting convened in the fall of 1870. For three days at a small Christian college, sincere pastors and influential men argued about worship. Not once in the recorded minutes is there any indication that these men ever engaged in any form of worship.[17]

Contemporary worship music has of course been a flash point in recent decades. One cartoon has an elderly grandfather showing his grandson his upper arm and explaining: "And I got that scar from the chairman of the board during the second battle of 'Guitars in the Sanctuary' back in '71." Of course, the controversy did not really devolve into violence, but many ministries were hurt by the divisiveness of the debates, and some churches even split over the issue.[18]

## Rays of Hope

John Frame provides a valuable service with his sound, balanced treatment in *Contemporary Worship Music: A Biblical Defense*. His main point is that each song deserves to be judged on its own merits, rather than automatically making assumptions about the entire genre (like all contemporary worship songs are "shallow," "me-centered," etc.).

In fact, there has been a real maturing in the contemporary worship movement over the years. This writer was shocked when in the 1980s he went through the first edition of the *Maranatha! Music Praise Chorus Book* searching for songs for a communion service, and found exactly *one*

17. Whaley, *Dynamics of Corporate Worship*, 95–96.
18. See Hamilton, "Triumph of the Praise Songs."

reference to the death of Christ in the entire collection![19] At that point the emphasis was on Scripture songs (especially setting psalm texts) and songs focusing on the attributes of God; the imbalance may have been an overreaction to so much of nineteenth-century gospel hymnody, which focused almost entirely on the death of Christ to the exclusion of other themes. At any rate, recent years have seen a wider and deeper repertoire of songs being written, with works from (for example) Matt Redman, Chris Tomlin, and Sovereign Grace Music (among many others) dealing with profound biblical truths, including the redeeming work of Christ.

A beautiful story from the "trenches" of the worship wars: this writer once heard Joe Stowell, who was at the time president of Moody Bible Institute, tell about the time the Moody radio network decided to change its standard programming from old-style gospel music to a more contemporary music format. The station received a letter from an older woman who had long been a financial supporter of Moody Radio. Her letter went something like this: "For many years I have supported your programming, and I so enjoyed the music that was broadcast. But now I learn you have decided to change the format to one with more modern music. *However*, I want you to know that if that is what you think is necessary to reach the younger generation, I am behind you one hundred percent. Enclosed is my donation." What a mature response from a believer who understood that it was not all about her!

## Implications of Freedom of Form

### *1. There is no one "right" way to do worship.*

This is an absolutely crucial point, for such an assumption is at the core of many, if not most, conflicts about worship. The fact of the matter is that, in the absence of New Testament specificity about forms, *no* church or denomination can claim to have discovered the one proper way in which to do worship (with the implication that other groups that do things differently are wrong). *It is arrogant to assume to have an inside track to the mind of God in areas where he has chosen to remain silent!*[20]

---

19. A Maranatha! Music board member balances this point with the observation that the services where these songs were used commonly included preaching that was very cross-centered.

20. "To think there is a singularly 'acceptable' way of self-offering, in living sacrifice and utter surrender, that is instituted by God in the Scriptures and is disconnected

In fact, severe disagreements about songs and instruments usually reveal a deeper problem than simply a musical one: they speak more often to *maturity* issues, to people wanting to have things their own way and to sing only the songs *they* like. They are forgetting what it means to be part of the *body of Christ*.

The story is told about two people sitting in church. At the end of some new song being introduced, one turned to the other and said, "I didn't like that song very much." To which the other replied, "So what? It wasn't *for* you!" While a little sarcastic, yet the point is clear: we need to look beyond ourselves and our preferences as the ultimate arbiters of what is acceptable in worship.

*2. God's taste is broader than any of ours!*

We all have preferences when it comes to music, style, etc. But again, we tend to conclude that what *I* think is most honoring to God just happens to coincide with what he himself thinks! When we look worldwide, it seems obvious that God is pleased to accept a huge breadth of different worship expressions.

---

from our 'now' human contribution, imagination, and even innovation, is untenable— at least to me. We all do things in our daily lives that are not 'revealed in Scripture.' . . . I believe in a God who . . . doesn't mind the content of biblical worship being engaged through a wide variety of human expressions of creativity. . . .

"I am not contending that all worship expressions are equal in biblical quality or even devotional efficacy for the community or the disciple. I am contending that the continually stated preference for a style . . . and an ongoing elevation of that style in contradistinction to others begins to *make a preference a prejudice*. It also runs the danger of affirming a narrowing of God's opinion on worship matters that He Himself would not endorse [emphases added]. . . .

"The world is wide in the heart of God when it comes to our ways of connecting with God and others in this dynamic exchange that is living worship. . . . If understanding what is 'biblical' in worship were as straightforward as we evangelicals often make it seem, then why would the church from its earliest years have moved into so many different cultural expressions of worship, all the while reading from the same pages of the Old and New Testament Scriptures?

"I . . . have a problem . . . with a Western cultural overlay being emphatically described as 'biblical,' over and against the diversity in the church today that I personally believe reflects the nature of God and gives Him great and lasting joy" (Dan Wilt, "Response to Ligon Duncan," in Pinson, *Perspectives on Christian Worship*, 133, 131–32, 130–31, 132–33).

### 3. God's priority is the heart of the worshiper.

God does *not* have favorite styles, or favorite instruments, or favorite songs! He is looking for hearts that are devoted to him, regardless of the outward form or expression that may take.

### 4. The promised presence of Christ is key.

As we saw in ch. 26, what makes our worship acceptable and pleasing to God is (along with our hearts) the promised presence of Christ leading us perfectly into the Father's presence.

## Key Factors to Take into Account

### 1. A Church's or Denomination's History and Traditions

While these should not be the final determinants, yet neither should they be ignored. As mentioned above when looking at principles of worship change, it is always a disastrous move to make radical changes in a church's worship practices overnight.

Protestants depart from Catholics by denying that church traditions have equal authority with Scripture. But tradition is *not* the enemy or without value; much can be learned from the way that past generations came to God in worship. The proper perspective is reflected in the statement (author unknown) "Tradition is a wonderful servant, but a terrible master." We can learn much from tradition, but it should never have the final say—only Scripture does.

Or, in the words of Jaroslav Pelikan:

> Tradition is the living faith of the dead, traditionalism is the dead faith of the living. And, I suppose I should add, it is traditionalism that gives tradition such a bad name.[21]

### 2. The Local Cultural Context

We will consider much more on this below, but it is important to realize that the people in our churches are to a large extent a product of their

---

21. Pelikan, *Vindication of Tradition*, 65.

culture in terms of how they look at things, how they respond to different artistic expressions and forms, and what tastes and preferences they come laden with. They "breathe the air" of the culture in which they have grown up, which then shapes what they consider as "normal" or "beautiful" or "moving." Everyone has what is called a "heart language." And that heart language is to be considered when making decisions about forms, styles, music, and other artistic expressions of faith—though not as the final determining factor. Culture is not the enemy either—at least, once it is filtered through the lens of Scripture.

## Biblical? Or Cultural?

### The Critical Need

Recognizing that the New Testament has left so much (though not everything) open, and recalling Piper's observation that "almost every worship tradition we have is culturally shaped rather than Biblically commanded,"[22] it is *absolutely critical* that we learn to carefully examine our worship practices and distinguish what is *biblical* from what is a *cultural* application or decision.

This is vital because most worship conflicts arise from people confusing these two categories: they take an accustomed practice and regard it as normative, the "right way," or even "biblical"—even when it is an aspect that is not directly addressed in the Bible itself! "The way we've always done it" is seen to carry an authority on that basis alone (and hence becomes traditionalism).[23]

### A Case in Point

A good example is the frequency of *communion* in different churches and denominations. Some celebrate the supper weekly, some monthly, others quarterly or less often. Which is correct? Which groups have it wrong?

22. Piper, "Our High Priest."

23. D. Peterson incisively stated: "We all know that music is a great encouragement to snobbery.... We become so familiar with and comfortable with our particular styles of music that we end up saying, maybe overtly sometimes, 'I am not willing to listen to your kind of music. I am not willing to sing one of your silly songs.' We get even more intense than that. We say, 'Your music is not true worship. Your music is not honoring to God'" ("Psalms, Hymns").

The point is that the New Testament *does not specify* how often we are to observe the Lord's Supper. It is not a right or wrong issue. There is freedom for a church and its leadership to decide what is best for that church.

*On the other hand*, what the Bible (in fact Jesus himself) commands is that we practice communion "in remembrance of me." For a church to decide to no longer practice the Lord's Supper at all (as something outmoded, or for whatever reason) would be *wrong*, would be *sin*, because of refusing to obey the explicit command of Scripture.

The Bible is clear as to the necessity of the practice (it is *biblical*) but does not specify the frequency (a *cultural* decision). Similarly, some churches have the people come forward to receive the elements, while some pass them out while the people remain seated. Again, there is *no one right way*, in the absence of explicit biblical teaching on the issue.

### A Helpful Exercise in Discernment

Consider the following list of worship practices to determine whether each is either *biblical* or *cultural*. (In a few cases it may be possible to argue either way, but for the most part the distinction should be clear.)

| Praise | Come up to take communion/giving | Sixty-minute sermon |
|---|---|---|
| Singing | Pass offering plates/bags | Fifteen-minute sermon |
| Choruses | Use offering chests at exits | Prayer |
| Guitars | Dark room | Prayer seated |
| Organ | Sunny room | Prayer standing |
| Loud music | Scripture reading | Prayer with eyes closed |
| Soft music | Responsive readings | Sit on floor |
| Hymns | Candles | Sit on chair |
| Communion | Sermon | When to stand |
| Pass communion trays | Thirty-minute sermon | |

*The Bottom Line*

To reemphasize, many of our worship conflicts would go away if we could learn to differentiate what is explicitly *biblical* in our practices (and therefore *nonnegotiable*) and what is a *cultural* decision (and hence *negotiable*). And we would look at the differing practices of other churches in a different, more accepting light (when negotiable areas are concerned).[24]

## Navigating the Treacherous Waters

The virtual silence of the New Testament as to the specifics of congregation worship practice seems to allow for local churches, as the fundamental unit of the body of Christ on earth, to have considerable autonomy and freedom as individual congregations in working out the issues involving the balance of biblical constants and biblical flexibility in the worship of that church. That does not mean that it is an easy task, however—as recent history has amply demonstrated. The so-called worship wars are symptomatic of the kind of danger into which freedom of this sort can cast us; and we might indeed be left wishing that Paul had just prescribed a set liturgy for all time and left it at that! God obviously wants his people to apply biblical wisdom and discernment in this, as well as in many other areas where he has chosen not to spell everything out for us. As John Piper has put it:

> There is very little in the New Testament about the forms and style and content of corporate worship. . . . God must mean to leave the matter of form and style and content to the judgment of our spiritual wisdom—not to our whim or our tradition, but to prayerful, thoughtful, culturally alert, self-critical, Bible-saturated, God-centered, Christ-exalting reflection driven by a

---

24. Another area of considerable difference of opinion (especially between generations) is about the appropriate *dress* for corporate worship. Once again, this is an area of debate because of the silence of the New Testament on the issue. But actually, in a way Paul *does* speak to what we should wear when we come to worship: "*Put on* then, as God's chosen ones, holy and beloved, *compassionate hearts, kindness, humility, meekness, and patience*, bearing with one another and, if one has a complaint against another, forgiving each other; as the Lord has forgiven you, so you also must forgive. And above all these *put on love*, which binds everything together in perfect harmony" (Col 3:12–14).

passion to be filled with all the fullness of God. I assume this will be an ongoing process, not a one-time effort.[25]

It will take several things for a local church to successfully navigate these treacherous worship waters, among them:[26]

## Leadership

It is this writer's conviction that it is incumbent upon the leadership of individual congregations to study the Scriptures, but also their culture and their congregation, and to prayerfully make decisions about the form that worship will take in their particular church context. "'All things are lawful,' but not all things are helpful. 'All things are lawful,' but not all things build up" (1 Cor 10:23).

## Communication

The careful solicitation of points of view from members of the congregation, while not the last word on worship decisions that must be made by the leadership, is an important step in leading the people as shepherds.

## Teaching

The pastor and other leaders must promote a biblical understanding of worship in the public teaching ministry of the church. And if any kind of change in worship is to be undertaken in the church, it is absolutely essential that the people are told the *why*, not just the *what*, of any change.

## Principle-Based Decisions

This relates to the second tower of the bridge illustration, and also the principles to be outlined in ch. 39: just because the Bible does not give a lot of specifics about worship services does not mean that we have no biblical guidance at all. Clear biblical principles can be discerned, and this gives hope for agreement on a foundational biblical level within, and even among, churches. But principles by definition must be applied, and

25. Piper, "Thoughts on Worship and Culture."
26. See also ch. 35, "Managing Change."

that is where the leaders must devote prayer for wisdom and balance in making application of the principles to their particular local church situation. Also, by definition, principles may be applied *differently* by different people and in different situations; so we must learn to give grace to others in the church who would prefer a different application, and to other churches that apply principles differently to their situation. *Preferences* need to be guided by *principles*.

## Semper Reformanda

As seen in ch. 35, this Latin phrase means "always reforming" and comes to us out of the Reformation; it expresses the importance of regularly and repeatedly subjecting our worship and other practices to the scrutiny of the Scriptures. Culture and traditions change; the Scriptures do not.[27] As we have seen above, a church's traditions should not be ignored when considering worship issues in that church; but neither should they be allowed to assume the level of authority that is appropriate only to the Scriptures. As we have seen, "Tradition is a wonderful servant, but a terrible master."

## Humility and Concern for One Another and for the Unity of the Body

We are called to give up our own prerogatives for Christ ("And he was saying to them all, 'If anyone wishes to come after me, he must deny himself, and take up his cross daily and follow me'" [Luke 9:23]). And we are to sublimate our own desires for the common good ("Do nothing from selfishness or empty conceit, but with humility of mind regard one another as more important than yourselves" [Phil 2:3]; "Let no one seek his own good, but the good of his neighbor" [1 Cor 10:24]). Concessions should be made on all sides ("Be devoted to one another in brotherly love; give preference to one another in honor" [Rom 12:10]).

Relevant here is the perspective Paul gives in 1 Cor 8 to the then-divisive issue of whether to eat meat that had been offered to idols. Basically Paul is saying, "I have no problem eating such meat, because idols are not real (vv. 4–6). *But*, if it will cause my brother to stumble, I will never eat

---

27. "Worship traditions change, and as long as we understand the theology behind our worship, there's nothing wrong with admitting that" (Dan Kimball, "Response to Ligon Duncan," in Pinson, *Perspectives on Christian Worship*, 140).

that meat (vv. 7, 9–13)." Paul saw that in Christ he had the freedom to eat, but also the freedom *not* to eat (v. 8): he saw protecting his brother's walk as a greater priority than taking advantage of his freedom.

So too in our worship: it is not just about giving free rein to our own expression, but of considering others and the good of the body.

*Prayer*

Humility and concern for others do not come naturally! We must ask God for his help. Hence much prayer is needed.

## The Second Tower: *Biblical Principles*

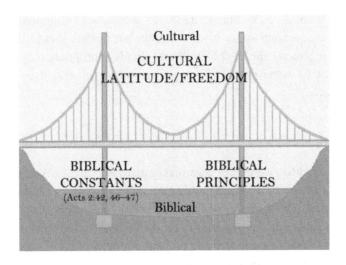

These principles will be enumerated and unpacked in ch. 39.

> There is a *biblical framework* for our worship,
> but also much *cultural flexibility.*

# 38

## WORSHIP AND CULTURE IN THE WORK OF WORLD MISSIONS

### The Wrong Way

I t is recommended that you go to YouTube and observe carefully the opening scene of the 1951 Humphrey Bogart/Katharine Hepburn movie *The African Queen*.

What we see in the opening moments is a brother-and-sister team, who have gone to Africa in the cause of Christ in the early twentieth century, leading worship in a church they have apparently planted. There is no questioning the sincere motivation of these two, who have given their lives to reach these people. However, they are making some real cultural mistakes. They are *dressed like Westerners*; they are leading singing, in *English*, accompanied by a *pump organ* that they have brought with them; and they are using a *musical system* (their own) that is obviously completely foreign to the people—obvious because of the utter cacophony coming out of their mouths. (The church *building* is even built in a much different style than the surrounding huts.) These well-meaning missionaries have brought the gospel *dressed in their own cultural clothing*. They have a very narrow view of what Christianity is and should look like.

The movie then cuts away to show the approach of the Humphrey Bogart figure in his boat, the *African Queen*. This man, we will soon learn, is a scoundrel, and has come to Africa just to make money. Yet in the brief seconds we see him here, he is conversing *in the local language* with the young man with him on the boat and is listening to the fellow play a *local instrument.* The irony here is that the scoundrel is much more culturally attuned to the people than the missionaries!

Sadly, this is how many missionaries used to carry out their ministry in far-off lands (with some notable exceptions). D. T. Niles of Sri Lanka made this plea for relating the gospel to local culture:

> The gospel is like a seed and you have to sow it. When you sow the seed of the gospel in Palestine, a plant that can be called Palestinian Christianity grows. When you sow it in Rome, a plant of Roman Christianity grows. You sow the gospel in Great Britain and you get British Christianity. The seed of the gospel is later brought to America and a plant grows of American Christianity. Now when missionaries came to our lands they brought not only the seed of the gospel, but their own plant of Christianity, flower pot included! So, what we have to do is to break the flower pot, take out the seed of the gospel, sow it in our own cultural soil, and let our own version of Christianity grow.[1]

Similarly, William Wadé Harris, Liberian missionary to the Ivory Coast, said in 1914:

> I have never been to heaven, so I cannot tell you what kind of music is sung in God's royal village. But know this, God has no personal favorite songs. He hears all that we sing in whatever language. It is sufficient for us to compose hymns of praise to Him with our own music and in our own language for Him to understand.[2]

The guidelines of ch. 37 involved with the bridge illustration have direct relevance here—especially the critical need of discerning which elements of our practices are *biblical* (and therefore nonnegotiable) and which are *cultural* (and therefore flexible). Thankfully, recent years have seen amazing progress in the missions community in terms of a more culturally sensitive approach.

---

1. D. T. Niles, quoted in Hawn, *Gather into One*, 32.
2. William Wadé Harris, quoted in Krabill et al., *Worship and Mission*, 146.

## A Better Way

Instead of missionaries bringing the gospel dressed in their own cultural clothing, there is now much more recognition of the need for missionaries to go into a culture and to be *learners and listeners first*; to learn the language and to help translate the Bible into that language; to learn the culture and traditions of the people and become conversant with the artistic expressions built into that culture; and then *and only then* work with converts to carefully develop worship practices that make sense in that culture.

## Contextualization

This is all part of a foundational missions strategy known as *contextualization*. One definition:

> Contextualization, within evangelical Christianity, is communicating the gospel using methods and terms appropriate to a given audience. It represents the understanding that although the gospel message is *abiding and universal*, the cultural contexts in which God revealed it and in which it is delivered are *distinct and different.*[3]

Quite simply, contextualization means *taking the local context into account*. Contextualization is applied to:

## Language

Some missionaries undertake the difficult task of learning the language of the host people, and then working with the people to translate the Bible into that language (sometimes also having to design for the first time a written form of the language; then there needs to be literacy education also).

There are moving videos on YouTube and elsewhere that show different groups receiving their own copies of God's word in their own language for the very first time; people are overcome with emotion when they realize that "God speaks *our* language!"[4]

3. See www.theopedia.com/contextualization (emphases added).

4. "The role of translation is a distinct characteristic in Christian faith . . . unlike other world religions which maintain a sacred tongue of transmission" (Pubols, "Translating God"). "History reveals that Bible translation and the cultural appropriation of the Christian faith it triggers are foundational to deepening understanding and ownership of the gospel. Bible translation creates the appropriate conditions for people to enter an effective dialogue with God within their specific cultural identity"

## Modes of Communication and Preaching

People listen and learn differently in various cultures, and that must be accommodated. For example, a purely oral culture will necessitate its own kind of approach.

## Music and the Other Arts

The missionary who lives among the people and becomes familiar with that culture's various types of artistic expression will thereby communicate a *valuing* and *validating* of those arts. These modes of self-expression have been built into people's souls and experiences from childhood on, and are sometimes referred to as a people's "heart language."

Sometimes we may think of the arts as mere entertainment or a decorative add-on to the weightier matters of life. But in fact, the arts of a culture give powerful expression to the values and the deepest longings of peoples' hearts.[5]

It is also critical to recognize that while music is a universal *phenomenon*, it is decidedly not a universal *language*. There are many different musical systems (the *African Queen* missionaries run into one instance of this); and music communicates very differently to different peoples (and even to different generations, as observed by Tom Avery in the last chapter). One vivid example of this is a song from the Canela people of Brazil. Converted to Christ, this tribe created a song[6] that is polytonal and sounds very harsh and dissonant to Western ears. Outsiders might guess that it is a song of mourning or lament; yet the text of the song is actually "God's word makes me happy"! To the Canela, this is happy music. Many of us would not hear it that way, because *music is not a universal language.*[7]

---

(Kenmogne, "Bible Translation Is Key," 10).

5. An unknown author once described the arts as "a delivery system of philosophy into the culture."

6. You can hear a recording of the song at www.tinyurl.com/canela2.

7. "What are the logical outcomes of thinking of music as a 'universal language'? 1. What it means to me, it probably means to you. 2. There is only 'good/bad' or 'high/low' in this language of music, not different music languages. 3. Since I speak this universal language, I should know what qualifies as a 'high' or 'low' expression. . . .

"Music may be a universal phenomenon, found in virtually every culture around the world. But . . . music, like other art forms, is not a universal language—our responses to music are learned, not intrinsic. . . . Just as in spoken language, music and other arts must be understood in their historical and cultural contexts to be interpreted

One would not introduce Bach organ music in worship in an African tribal village: the form and style would have no meaning for this people. And conversely, some of the most natural cultural expressions of various African villages would be incomprehensible to most northern Europeans. (In many contexts in Africa, drums are the *primary* instrument for worship—not a debated add-on!)

More and more missions agencies are recruiting, training, and sending "arts specialists" to lead the way in evaluating, validating, and embracing local art forms.[8]

## Worship

After a long time in the culture, gaining acceptance and a hearing, missionaries can then help converts evaluate their own music, other arts, and traditions to see what can profitably be brought into an indigenous form of Christian worship for their people. And that has to be a process of discernment, because not everything should be brought into Christian worship. There might be an instrument or a style of music that was formerly used in the context of ancestor or demon worship, for example. Things like that should not be incorporated into their worship, because of the distracting and distasteful associations that practice would have in their minds and hearts.[9]

Positively, many things (musical forms, instruments, other artistic expressions, traditions) *can* be brought into worship in a way that will resonate deeply with the people, exactly because their "heart language" is released to express their newfound faith in Christ. Again, rather than worship being seen as something that is foreign and imported, this strategy communicates to the people: "God likes *our* music!" "God likes *our* arts!"

The story of the Maasai people of Kenya and Tanzania is one of many examples of the power of a contextualized, indigenized, and culturally inflected approach. This people group is known for their distinctive

---

correctly" (Harris, "Great Misconception").

8. See Hall, "Every Team Needs One." An example of the sophisticated training and work of such missionaries can be found in an instructive YouTube video from SIL International that can be accessed at http://tinyurl.com/artscons.

9. The same process should be used in our own local churches when considering different styles of music and other elements drawn from the culture. Strong associations with immoral or degrading practices and lifestyles will certainly distract from worship.

customs, dress, music, and dance. The gospel was not making headway among these people until thoughtful missionaries were able to help them understand that they did not have to give up being Maasai if they became Christians. Many conversions resulted, and the rich cultural heritage of the Maasai now finds expression in their Christian faith.

In the mid-1980s, John Bendor-Samuel, then president of Wycliffe Bible Translators/SIL International, made this remarkable statement in a personal conversation with Frank Fortunato, international music director of Operation Mobilisation:

> Where the missionaries got the new believers to sing the newly translated Scriptures in their own indigenous cultural styles, churches grew *rapidly*. Where that was not happening, churches grew *slowly*.

It should be added that, whether it is considered as a positive or negative thing, the present reality is that Western contemporary music styles are now, because of modern communications, part of the "heart language" of young people all over the world. So in seeking to help people groups fashion their own worship style, it is not reasonable or wise to try to do away with all these Western influences; but neither is it a good idea to lose the traditional elements either. The "psalms, hymns, and spiritual songs" principle of Eph 5:19–20 (see ch. 22) certainly allows for a "both-and" rather than an "either-or" approach when it comes to the question of whether to use indigenous music and instruments or adapted Western songs and instrumentation. Indeed, the generational issues of traditional vs. contemporary music are found in cultures all over the world! So care must be taken to be inclusive rather than exclusive.

## The Ethnodoxology Movement: A New Way of Doing Missions[10]

### A New Professional Field

An outgrowth of the contextualization emphasis in modern missions has been the rise of a new field called *ethnodoxology*.[11] The term was coined in the late 1990s by music missionary Dave Hall, and a recent definition is:

---

10. For an analysis of the movement from the outside, and the ensuing robust debate, see Aniol et al., "Worship from the Nations"; Stallsmith, "Worship from the Nations: Response"; Ron Man, "Culture and Worship."

11. *Ethnomusicology* is a much older term, and refers to the study of the musics of

*Ethnodoxology* is the interdisciplinary study of how Christians in every culture engage with God and the world through their own artistic expressions.[12]

The term is built from two Greek words: *ethnē* (peoples) and *doxologia* (praise). As such, ethnodoxology has to do with how different peoples worship God around the world, using their own local artistic expressions.

## A New Breed of Missionary

Many missionaries who specialize in this sort of arts consultant work now refer to themselves as *ethnodoxologists*.

## A New Fellowship

In 2003, an umbrella group called the International Council of Ethnodoxologists (ICE) was birthed; recently the name was changed to the Global Ethnodoxology Network (GEN). It is not itself a missions agency; rather it is an international network of missionaries and Christian workers, with many different agencies, who are involved in arts-related ministries all over the world. They have banded together for mutual encouragement, resourcing, and cooperation.

GEN's stated vision is:

> The Global Ethnodoxology Network envisions a future in which communities of Jesus followers in every culture engage with God and the world through their own artistic expressions.
>
> We offer networking, training, and resources for the flourishing of biblical and culturally appropriate arts.[13]

---

the world's peoples. It has been employed in Christian missions, as well as being a field of secular study taught in universities.

12. Official definition of the Global Ethnodoxology Network (www.worldofworship.org/about/).

13. The statement continues: "This article, published January 2020 in *Evangelical Missions Quarterly* (Vol. 56, no. 1), explains who we are: https://tinyurl.com/GEN-4EMQ." See www.worldofworship.org/core-values/.

## New Courses

GEN sponsors two traveling courses that are taught in various schools in the US and internationally: (1) Introduction to Ethnodoxology, a one-week survey (offered for undergraduate and graduate credit) that combines biblical foundations, procedures and skills, field studies and experience in crafting multicultural worship;[14] (2) Arts for a Better Future, a one-week intensive practicum in applying principles and techniques to help communities draw on their artistic resources to enrich lives and meet social and spiritual needs.[15]

## New Resources

A growing number of print resources have emerged from the ethnodoxology movement.

The cornerstone volume is *Worship and Mission for the Global Church: An Ethnodoxology Handbook.* More than one hundred practitioners offer "theological reflection, case studies, and practical tools to help the global church appreciate and generate culturally appropriate arts in worship and witness." Its companion volume, *Creating Local Arts Together: A Manual to Help Communities Reach Their Kingdom Goals,* gives a practical seven-step method "to guide an individual or group into a local community's efforts at integrating its arts with the values and purposes of God's kingdom."

Other related resources (more are being added all the time) include:

- C. Michael Hawn, *Gather into One: Praying and Singing Globally*
- C. Michael Hawn, *One Bread, One Body: Exploring Cultural Diversity in Worship*

14. See www.worldofworship.org/introduction-to-ethnodoxology.
15. See www.worldofworship.org/artsforabetterfuture/.

- Brian Schrag and Kathleen J. Van Buren, *Make Arts for a Better Life: A Guide for Working with Communities*

- Brian Schrag and Julisa Rowe, *Community Arts for God's Purposes: How to Create Local Artistry Together*

- Roberta R. King, *Global Arts and Christian Witness: Exegeting Culture, Translating the Message, and Communicating Christ*

## New Global Events

In 2003, an event called the Global Consultation on Music in Missions (GCOMM) was held in Fort Worth, Texas. Three hundred participants from over twenty countries celebrated the use of culturally appropriate arts in the ministry of the church worldwide. (It was actually at this event that ICE was birthed.)

The tremendous response to this event led to a cycle of GCOMM events:

| | |
|---|---|
| 2006 | St. Paul, Minnesota |
| 2010 | Singapore |
| 2013 | Chiang Mai, Thailand |
| 2016 | Nairobi, Kenya |
| 2021 | online |
| 2023 | Fort Worth, Texas |

Before the 2021 event, the name was changed to Global Consultation on Arts and Music in Missions (GCAMM) to better reflect the focus on a wider range of creative arts than just music.[16]

## The Nairobi Statement on Worship and Culture

In 1996 the Lutheran World Federation released a statement that is so rich in its insights and implications that it has been used widely to inform the discussion of the relationship between worship and culture.[17] The statement in summary states that:

16. See gcamm.org/past/ to read more about and view highlights from these events. The website for GCAMM is www.gcamm.org.

17. Lutheran World Federation's Study Team on Worship and Culture, "Nairobi Statement."

Christian worship relates dynamically to culture in at least four ways.

First, it is *transcultural*, the same substance for everyone everywhere, beyond culture.

Second, it is *contextual*, varying according to the local situation (both nature and culture).

Third, it is *countercultural*, challenging what is contrary to the gospel in a given culture.

Fourth, it is *cross-cultural*, making possible sharing between different local cultures.

One way of looking at the interrelation of these four dynamics is:

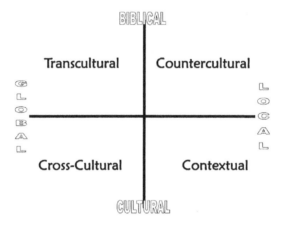

## Transcultural

The main emphasis of this book has been in this area: the foundational unifying truths and principles of worship that, precisely because they are *biblical*, by definition *transcend culture*.

> Churches in every generation and in every context must ask in what ways their worship practice can/should transcend their particular culture, placing them within the universal Christian tradition.[18]

---

18. Lutheran World Federation, "Cartigny Statement on Worship and Culture," in Wilkey, *Worship and Culture*, 33.

## Contextual

Much of this chapter has been devoted to the importance of locally inflected worship forms, so that worship speaks both *from* and *to* people's hearts in ways that reflect and honor their own cultural identity.

> The contextual aspect of worship involves recognizing the cultural particularity of Christian worship—the use of local cultural patterns, images, materials, and terms to make worship meaningful and relevant in specific contexts.[19]

> The apostolic decree of Acts 15 builds cultural diversity into the Christian church forever.[20]

## Countercultural

As already discussed, the freedom of form allowed by the New Testament does *not* mean that "anything goes," that anything can be pulled in from the culture. The associations in people's minds and hearts with particular practices or aspects must always be borne in mind, and decisions made to include or exclude them accordingly.

> There must always be some tension between gospel and culture. . . . The gospel doesn't carry with it a culture of its own. It must always find its place in the culture of the time and place. Nevertheless, it always questions the local culture and holds it accountable before the cross.[21]

## Cross-Cultural

Modern technology and communications has made it possible, much more than ever before, for people to be aware of the rich diversity of Christian worship expressions worldwide. Reflecting some of that diversity locally is a powerful reminder to people that they are part of something much bigger than just one local assembly.

19. Charles E. Farhadian, "Beyond Lambs and Logos," in Farhadian, *Christian Worship Worldwide*, 22.

20. Andrew Walls, "Ephesians Moment," in Farhadian, *Christian Worship Worldwide*, 30.

21. Byars, *Christian Worship*, 110.

While it is clear that each church, within its cultural context, will need to ask these questions for itself and find answers appropriate to its own situation, it also clear that this inquiry will require each church to attend to the experiences of the other churches and to the treasures of other cultures.[22]

## Interplay

The trick is that all four of these aspects are operating *at the same time*! That of course adds a lot of complexity and challenge to the whole endeavor. And, needless to say, different churches will be stronger in certain of these areas than others. Overemphasis of one will lead to imbalance: for instance, being so culturally *contextual* that harmful elements are not sifted out (i.e., not being appropriately *countercultural*); or being so rigidly *transcultural* that there is not enough sensitivity to the local *context* and the heart language of the people; or being contextually so monocultural that due is not given to the rich possibilities of drawing on *cross-cultural* influences.

## The Bottom Line in Worship, Culture, and Missions

To reiterate, the bottom line in applying the freedom, flexibility, and latitude (represented by the span in our bridge illustration) in the work of worship in missions is to insist on *an unchanging message* (biblical), while acknowledging the huge *variety of possible expressions of this message* (cultural). As in all worship, the key in missions applications is to rigorously distinguish between what is *biblical* and what is *cultural*.

> There is an *unchanging message*,
> but *many ways* to communicate and celebrate it.

---

22. Lutheran World Federation, "Cartigny Statement on Worship and Culture," in Wilkey, *Worship and Culture*, 33.

# Part 8

# Conclusion

# 39

## BIBLICAL PRINCIPLES OF WORSHIP

### The Second Tower: Biblical *Principles*

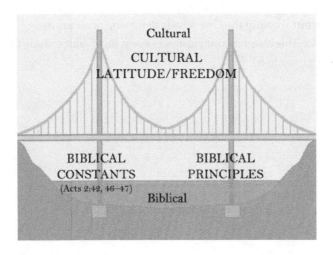

J ust because the New Testament does not give us a lot of specifics about
how to do worship in the local congregation, this most certainly does
not mean that we have no biblical guidance concerning worship. As we
have already stressed, it is *not* "anything goes"! As with so many areas in
our lives not specifically addressed by the Scriptures (be it movies, drugs,

etc.), there most certainly are biblical truths that are applicable and which we must with wisdom and honesty apply to our situation.

The same is true with worship. There are a host of principles that can be drawn from the pages of Scripture to guide us, and to guide the leadership of local churches, in fashioning biblically appropriate yet culturally meaningful expressions of worship. Biblical principles are represented by the second tower in the bridge illustration unpacked in ch. 37. As the second tower does in a physical suspension bridge, these principles give further stability and strength to the (worship) structure as a whole. The first tower (biblical constants) deals with more specific practices; biblical *principles* are, by definition, more general and must be *applied* (and may legitimately be *variously* applied) in different church contexts and cultures.

This chapter develops and unpacks twelve biblical principles—general, *transcultural*, unifying principles—that grow out of our study of the biblical texts throughout this book. We want to stand firmly on biblical ground in the ordering of our worship life as local congregations, while allowing for the variety and freedom that the New Testament allows and avoiding "teaching as doctrine the precepts of men." Above all we want to glorify in our worship the One who is deserving of all praise.

(Note: This chapter could also serve as a stand-alone study for individual or group use.)

Principle 1: God's glory, and our joyful
celebration of it in worship, should be the focus
and goal of all life and ministry.

## Doxological Worship

Whether, then, you eat or drink or whatever you do,
do all to the glory of God. (1 Cor 10:31)

## To the Glory of God

As children of God and citizens of heaven (Phil 3:20), our primary focus in all of life is to be on him who created us and redeemed us and is
committed to conforming us to his image. God has a unique claim on
our allegiance and attention; his lordship is to permeate, more and more,
every corner of our lives. He is the center of our existence, the purpose of
our existence, and the goal of our existence (Rom 11:36). He is both the
subject and the object of our worship.

When we speak of his "glory" we are speaking of the sum total of
all his perfections, the uniqueness of his being, the totality of what dis-
tinguishes him as Creator from his creation and his creatures. (Thus the
concept is very close to that of God's holiness, his complete "otherness.")
His glory is what in its ultimate sense he "will not give to another" (Isa
42:8; 48:11), though he causes faint glimmers of reflected glory to show
forth in his creation and especially in humanity, which bears his image
(Gen 1:26; 1 Cor 11:7). God's glory is also described in Scripture in terms
of light (Isa 60:1, 19; 2 Cor 4:4, 6; 1 Tim 6:16; Rev 21:23).

We cannot add to the glory of God, which is perfect; yet the Scriptures maintain that in some mysterious way the created order (Ps 19:1;
72:19), the course of history (Isa 66:18), and above all the church of Jesus
Christ (Eph 3:21) are all intended to reflect and manifest and display his
glory. As John Piper puts it: "The manifestation of the glory of God is the
meaning of the universe."[1] God's glory is the ultimate goal of every breath
we take, everything we are allowed to do—and should, for us as believers,
be our ultimate motivation in all our endeavors ("Whatever you do, do
all to the glory of God" [1 Cor 10:31]). We must consciously keep this

1. Piper, "Christ and the Meaning."

goal before us and seek to submit all our activities (personal, relational, vocational, spiritual) to that overarching design, in order to bring to our lives value, meaning, and a divine orientation and significance, even in our most mundane involvements.

If this is true through all of life, it is, if anything, even more important to have this perspective as we undertake the work of the church. Human theories, techniques, ideas, systems, tastes, and structures must all be submitted to a compelling and overriding passion for the glory of God.

How quickly we forget whose work, whose church, whose worship service we are involved in! How quickly we seek to supplement the revelation of Scripture with human ingenuity, demographic studies, and how-to seminars. How anxious we are to find gimmicks that will attract people and keep them coming back. Our single-minded focus, in worship and in all our activities, must be on recognizing, reflecting, declaring, and celebrating the glory of God.

He who authoritatively proclaimed "I will build my church" (Matt 16:18) has no need of church growth principles to constrain him in the task to which he has committed himself. And he who proclaimed to the crowds that "no one can come to me, unless it has been granted him from the Father" (as the result of which many in his day withdrew [John 6:65–66]) would hardly see as a priority the comfort of the unchurched visitor—or of the churched attender, for that matter!

Systems of theology, even profoundly biblical ones that were formulated to bring to finite minds some grasp of the infinite scope of God and his ways, sometimes become entrenched to the point where the system may be revered almost as much as the One whom it seeks to honor. At the very least, we are tempted to find our rest in a system: because we desperately (though perhaps not consciously) hope that it might bring a certain predictability and manageability to God; or because our system (invariably the "true" one) helps us feel a little more "in control"—what folly! Having corralled mystery (so we think), we leave little room for God to act and move outside our carefully crafted paradigms.

God in his glory and majesty and holiness and mystery and providential inscrutability supersedes to an infinite degree all attempts to contain or define him. We could more easily catalog snowflakes or classify grains of sand! God has revealed to us many deep and wonderful truths about himself in his word, and in redemption has allowed us to see deep into his heart. But let us never presume to have fathomed the wonder of his person! Let us accept with humility that we are concerning ourselves with holy things that are far beyond us; and let us bow before him who with incomprehensible condescension has called us to be his own. And let us live life, and do church, and approach worship, with a profound sense of awe and gratitude; may we in our earthbound scurrying never lose sight of the One who looks from the heavens in love—that One whose glory is over all (Isa 6:3).

> Let them praise the name of the LORD,
> for his name alone is exalted;
> His glory is above earth and heaven. (Ps 148:13)

May his glory be all our hope and all our aim and all our comfort.

> To him be glory in the church and in Christ Jesus throughout all generations, forever and ever. Amen! (Eph 3:21)

## Others' Observations

In the creature's knowing, esteeming, loving, rejoicing in and praising God, the glory of God is both exhibited and acknowledged; his fullness is received and returned.[2]

The uniqueness at the heart of Christianity is the glory of God manifest in the freedom of grace. God is glorious because he does not need the nations to work for him. He is free to work for them. "The Son of Man came not to be served but to serve and to give his life a ransom for many" (Mark 10:45).[3]

There is only one end for which God created and formed the world and made us, and that is for His own exclusive glory and honor. There is only one end for which our Lord redeemed His people, and that was to bring Him a revenue of glory. And when you and I find this thirst that God implants within our souls, it is only going to be satisfied when our souls are set on the same longing that God Himself has: for His glory and honor.[4]

Our response in leaving a worship service should never be: "What great *worship* we had today!" but rather: "What a great God *we* worshiped today!"[5]

---

2. Jonathan Edwards, "End for Which God Created the World," quoted in Hannah, *To God Be Glory*, 25.

3. Piper, *Let the Nations Be Glad*, 55.

4. Alexander, "Thirsting for God."

5. Author unknown.

## Principle 2: Worship is first and foremost for God.

### GOD-CENTERED WORSHIP

"Worship God." (Rev 19:10; 22:9)

### A Tapescrew Letter

C. S. Lewis's *Screwtape Letters* consist of an imagined correspondence between the senior demon Screwtape and his young nephew Wormwood. Screwtape gives advice on tempting and leading humans astray. Lewis uses this correspondence to make some insightful and often biting observations about the human condition, and how easily we are deceived by the forces of evil.

I am happy to report that a new letter has just been discovered, this time from Screwtape's relative Tapescrew, writing to *his* nephew Woodworm. This letter may shed some light on the state of worship in our churches today.

My dear Woodworm,

In today's world there are some delicious tendencies that make it particularly easy to confuse, distract and divert the Enemy's people from the things on which they should be focused. Some of our unwitting agents among the philosophers and academics have paved the way for the current wonderful situation, whereby the pathetic creatures seem to each go around in their own little bubble, unaware of forces and values that extend beyond the boundaries of their own consciousness and concern.

While there are some isolated voices crying out things like "It's all about him!" these cries are, as it were, cries in the wilderness, and largely fall on deaf ears, thank Badness. There are blissfully few who can crack the barrier of their own self-absorption and truly focus even on other humans, much less on divine priorities and demands. That makes our work so much easier! The worms bounce around inside the shell of self-centeredness that is about all they know; and then they wonder why they feel that they are without a meaning or a purpose that extends beyond themselves! They do the work for us, in many respects, as they so successfully fill their lives with a multitude of sweetly irrelevant pursuits, leaving little time or energy for the Enemy's worrisome projects and plans.

In their churches, this kind of rampant individualism gets carried to hilarious extremes. In a delightfully blind way, these beings can recite creeds and sing songs and pray prayers that speak of the Enemy's sovereign (and, we would say, dictatorial) rule over all things, and then they turn around and act as though they themselves are the center of the universe! It is in their churches, those annoying places intended by the Enemy for corporate brainwashing and mutual encouragement in the perverse ways of holiness and godliness, that we find the most exciting displays of selfishness and narrowmindedness. The smaller the issue, it seems, the more overwrought their emotions become in their stubborn campaign to get their own way! I tell you, we hardly need to whisper a corrupting suggestion into their ears before they are off fighting over the color of the carpet, the brand of coffee served, or even—most thrilling of all—over their worship! And each one with a self-righteous conviction that his or her own convictions or preferences on the matter just happen to exactly coincide with the Enemy's point of view!

I tell you, it warms our devilish hearts when we are able to use worship, of all things, as a way to divide the Enemy's people! The one activity that should unite them the most has become a wonderful seedbed for strife and disagreement. And it's all made possible when they begin to look out for themselves and their interests rather than the Enemy's. And that perspective, I'm happy to report, is everywhere. It's embarrassingly easy to promote among those creatures, and truly is one of our greatest successes!

Affectionately yours,
your uncle Tapescrew

(with apologies to C. S. Lewis)[6]

## Others' Observations

Acceptable worship is by definition theocentric worship. Only the Creator is worthy to be revered and praised by his creatures. It is corporate worship which calls men and women to throw

---

6. Ron Man, "Letter from Tapescrew."

off the engulfing self-absorption that is not only the father of sin, but also the fleshly tendency even of the redeemed; and it is corporate worship which calls believers to refocus on him who is the Giver and Sustainer of life and of life eternal. Our worship must be relentlessly theocentric. God deserves and demands our reverent attention; and our often-frantic existence needs to be regularly and formally drawn back to its reason for being: to honor and bring glory to God. Hymns and choruses which emphasize our human pilgrimage and reactions can be perfectly appropriate responses, but only after God has been lifted up and magnified in our midst.[7]

The primary purpose of worship is the glory of God, not the edification of man; "God must come first, or man's edification will not follow."[8]

[Worship is] man's own act of self-dethronement in God's presence in order that God, not man, may reign.[9]

Worship is the occupation of the heart, not with its needs, or even with its blessings, but with God Himself.[10]

The chief aim of worship is to please God—whether by adoration and praise, prayer and proclamation, confession and offerings, thanksgivings and commitment, or by all of these actions combined. The point of worship is to recognize that "God alone matters." Many battles over worship styles would be eliminated if this answer were kept in mind as the foundational criterion for planning what we do, no matter what forms we use.[11]

Certainly true worship invigorates, but to plan invigoration is not necessarily to order worship. As all that glitters is not gold, so all that makes us feel happy and strong is not worship. The question is not whether a particular liturgical form is used, but whether a God-centered as distinct from man-centered perspective is maintained—whether, in other words, the sense that man exists for God rather than God for man is cherished or lost.[12]

[Worship is] weekly practice at not being God.[13]

7. Ron Man, "Worship for All," 2.

8. Abba, *Principles of Christian Worship*, 13.

9. Bary, *Gospel of Worship*, 37.

10. Gibbs, *Worship*, 14.

11. Dawn, *Reaching Out*, 80.

12. "What about Jacuzzi Worship?," in Packer, *Celebrating the Saving Work*, 207.

13. Michael Lindvall, cited in Bierma, "Worshipful Service."

I don't have any problem with consumer-oriented worship as long as we remember Who the Consumer is.[14]

What is the test of true worship? Peter speaks of "offering spiritual sacrifices *acceptable to God*" (1 Pet 2:5). How do you assess whether worship is real worship or not? Well, says Peter, the test is this: "Is it acceptable to him?" The problem, you see, is that so often in our thinking worship is tested by whether it is "acceptable to *me*." People say, "I didn't get much out of that." But it is not *what I get out of worship* that is the vital thing; it is *what God gets out of it*, because the thing that worship ought to focus on is what is pleasing to him. That is the real issue in biblical, spiritual, God-centred worship.[15]

14. Attributed to Eric Alexander.

15. Alexander, *Our Great God*, 33.

## Principle 3: Worship is a dialogue between God and his people, a rhythm of revelation and response.

### DIALOGICAL WORSHIP

↓ Great is the LORD,
↑ and greatly to be praised. (Ps 96:4)

The rhythm of *revelation* and *response* is characteristic of all God's dealings with humans. And this ordering of these two elements is tremendously significant, for it speaks of the *initiative* that God takes, and the lengths to which he goes, to ensure a relationship with those whom he chooses. Throughout Scripture we see God's revelatory initiative with his people, with the result that all worship, obedience, and service should be seen as a *response* to God's prior activity in revelation and redemption. This is true because, as Eric Alexander states, "God needs to be known before He can be worshiped."[16] Nicholls expands on this idea: "Our worship is our answer to God who has first addressed us. Man worships the God who has made Himself known. We 'praise His holy Name'—that is, we worship Him in His self-revelation."[17]

Calvin speaks also to this natural progression: "The proclamation of God's praises is always promoted by the teaching of the gospel; for as soon as God becomes known to us, His infinite praises resound in our hearts and ears." To which Butin adds (quoted before):

> The initiatory "downward" movement of Christian worship begins in the Father's gracious and free revelation of the divine nature to the church through the Son, by means of the Spirit. In more concrete terms, this takes place in the proclamation of the

16. Alexander, "Worship: Old Testament Pattern."
17. Nicholls, *Jacob's Ladder*, 37.

Word according to Scripture, by the empowerment and illumination of the Spirit. . . . The "upward" movement of human response in worship—focused around prayer and the celebration of the sacraments—is also fundamentally motivated by God.[18]

Worship is a *dialogue* between God and his people: that means that our services should alternate and balance elements of revelation and response: *hearing from God* (through his word, read and sung and prayed and preached) and *replying to him* (with our songs and prayers and confession and the Lord's Supper). Historically, this pattern underlies both Old Testament worship (in covenant establishment and renewal) and Christian worship (in the word-table structure found in most historical liturgies).

But revelation should precede response: we should let God have the first word, and be careful to listen before we speak. Too many services launch right into singing; but that means we are responding before we have heard anything to respond to! This does violence to the biblical pattern, and to God's preeminence. Until we have heard from God, we have nothing to say to him—we must worship him as he really is, not as we (or the songwriters) imagine or hope him to be. In this light, a "Call to Worship" is anything but outdated. Indeed, it is (whether read, or sung, or prayed, or whatever) an acknowledgment that we have come to worship God at his invitation and by and through his word.[19]

## Others' Observations

Biblical faith is uncompromisingly and unembarrassedly dialogical.[20]

Worship is a dialogue, but the initial call comes from God who begins the conversation.[21]

All our worship is but our response to the self-giving of God in revelation and redemption.[22]

---

18. Witvliet, *Worship Seeking Understanding*, 146; quoting Butin, *Revelation, Redemption, and Response*, 102.

19. Ron Man, "Dialogue of Worship."

20. Brueggemann, *Psalms*, 68.

21. Paquier, *Dynamics of Worship*, 8.

22. Nicholls, *Jacob's Ladder*, 53.

The distinctive genius of corporate worship is the two-beat rhythm of revelation and response. God speaks; we answer. God acts; we accept and give. God gives; we receive.[23]

Christian worship is grounded in the reality of the action of God toward the human soul in Jesus Christ and in man's responsive action through Jesus Christ.[24]

Worship depends upon revelation, and Christian worship depends upon the revelation of God in Jesus Christ. Worship, that is to say, begins not from our end but from God's; it springs from the divine initiative in redemption. We come to God because God, in Jesus Christ, has come to us: we love Him because he first loved us: we ascribe to Him supreme worth because he has showed Himself to be worthy of our complete homage, gratitude and trust. Worship is essentially a response, man's response to God's Word of grace, to what he has done for us men and for our salvation.[25]

Since worship is the Church's obedient response to the saving acts of God, these saving acts must be set forth before the response can be evoked. . . . It follows that the Bible, in which God's redemptive action is declared, must be read early in the service if the praise, prayer and offering of the congregation are to be a true response to the divine Word. Failure to grasp this simple principle results in liturgical chaos. . . . When Thanksgiving, Intercession and Offering precede the reading and hearing of the Word of God to which they are essentially the response, the theological basis of worship is destroyed. Worship ceases to be dependent upon revelation.[26]

23. Martin, *Worship of God*, 6.
24. Hoon, *Integrity of Worship*, 77.
25. Abba, *Principles of Christian Worship*, 5.
26. Abba, *Principles of Christian Worship*, 48.

## Principle 4: The word of God must be central in our worship.

### WORD-SATURATED WORSHIP

Praise him according to his excellent greatness. (Ps 150:2)

This principle grows directly out of the previous one, because of the primacy of God's revelation.

The word of God is of supreme importance in the life of the Christian, containing as it does God's revelation of his person, his will, and his ways. The Word needs to be pored over, ingested into one's mind and heart, meditated on, and acted upon. It is a unique and precious repository of spiritual truth and guidance and encouragement. There is no aspect of the life of the church or of the individual believer that should not be tied to a scriptural mooring and infused with biblical substance (2 Tim 3:16–17). The Bible is indeed "a lamp unto my feet, and a light unto my path" (Ps 119:105).

When Christians gather for corporate worship, it is logical that the word of God should play a central and dominant role. For since worship involves focusing our thoughts and hearts and voices on the praise of God, in response to his self-revelation and his gracious saving initiative, we of course need that view of God that the word gives us if our worship is to be "in truth" (John 4:23–24). Our worship can duly honor God only if it accurately reflects what he reveals about himself in his word.

### The Word Neglected

That said, the astounding observation has been made as to how little use is made of Scripture in the worship services of most evangelical churches. The irony, of course, is that those who claim most strongly to stand on the Bible *have so little of it in their worship.* While the sermon takes a prominent role in our services, even preaching consists mostly of talking *about* the Scriptures (often after reading just a very few verses). It must be said that liturgical groups (whether on the more liberal or the more conservative end of the spectrum theologically) have probably *ten times* as much actual Scripture in their services (because it is built into their liturgies) as most evangelical, free churches!

In too many of our churches the entire first part of the service consists just of music, and no Scripture is read at all. This author has experienced this often in both traditional and contemporary services: the problem is pervasive. It would seem crucially important for people in a service, believers and unbelievers alike, to hear (and/or see printed in a bulletin or flashed on a screen) verses of Scripture chosen to give a clear signal that: "We have come to worship God. The word is how we know about God, and therefore it is the foundation for all that we do here and for our understanding of why we have come together." Without hearing such a declaration, worshipers make the faulty assumption (consciously or unconsciously) that we invite *ourselves* into God's presence, when in actuality it is only by virtue of his invitation (and his opening the way through the work of Christ) that we may come before him at all.

As we have already learned from James White, "The first step toward making our worship more biblical is in giving the reading of God's Word a central role in Christian worship on any occasion."[27] We simply cannot overstate the importance of Scripture for our worship. By all means, let us be as creative as possible in building in Scripture (verses on banners or projected onto a screen as people enter, verses on the bulletin cover, readers' theater, children reciting verses, original Scripture songs, etc.), but let us make sure that the *primacy of the word in worship* is obvious throughout the entire service—not just during the sermon. As White adds:

> Scripture is read, not just for a sermon text, but to hear what word God addresses to the gathered congregation. Preaching usually builds on that but Scripture is read for its own sake as God's Word. . . . It needs to be communicated to all that the centrality of Scripture stems from its functions as proclamation of God's Word to the gathered people.[28]

In Scripture we find the prerequisites for worship, the invitation to worship, the authority for worship, the material for worship, the regulation of our worship, the message of worship, and the end to which worship should lead.

27. White, "Making Our Worship," 38.
28. White, "Making Our Worship," 38.

## The Word and the Prerequisites for Worship

The word of God helps to bring us to the point where our approach to God in worship is possible: it teaches us that we are dead in our trespasses and sins (Eph 2:1); it reveals that God has provided for redemption, forgiveness, and eternal life through the work of Jesus Christ; and it presents the opportunity to come by faith into a right relationship with the Father. "The washing of water with the word" (Eph 5:26) provides the spiritual cleanliness that God requires for us to be able to enter confidently into his presence (Ps 15:1–2; Heb 10:19–22; 12:18–24).

## The Word as the Inviter to Worship

God has done everything to make our approach in worship possible; and in his word he extends the invitation (yea, command) to draw near. The Old Testament book of worship, the Psalter, is replete with calls to "praise the LORD!" (Hebrew, *hallelujah*). As the Danish hymn puts it:

> I come, invited by your Word,
> To kneel before your altar, Lord.[29]

## The Word as the Authority for Worship

The fact of the matter is that every aspect of the service should serve to reflect and honor the word of God. The sermon (and the preacher) must be subservient to the word: the word must guide and control the preacher's thoughts and words if the sermon is to communicate God's message and not just the ideas of humans. But also the music must be subservient to the word: the texts must reflect and express biblical truth, and the music itself must be a suitable medium to carry the text; the musician(s) must also be subservient to the word in terms of motivation and execution of the music. In addition, prayers and readings must be consistent with biblical teaching, if not actually taken from Scripture. As John MacArthur puts it, "If we are to worship in truth and the Word of God is truth, we must worship out of our understanding of the Word of God."[30]

29. Kingo, "I Come."
30. MacArthur, *Worship*, 122–23.

## The Word as the Material for Worship

Gary Furr and Milburn Price suggest a number of ways in which the revelation of the Word can be communicated in the service, besides the sermon: Scripture readings of all sorts, music (setting Scripture texts, and also faithfully presenting scriptural truth in paraphrased or freely composed form), symbols (fish, cross, stained glass, etc.), carefully used drama.[31] When Scripture and scriptural truth are pervasive in the service, then the acts of response will properly be understood as response to God's self-revelation through his word.

## The Word as the Regulator of Worship

Worship must be guided and channeled by truth, i.e., be in accordance with what God has revealed about himself and his ways (and, as John 4:25–26 shows, must be through the Son, the Messiah, who *is* the truth [John 15:6]). As Furr and Price state: "This is the perfect blend: emotion regulated by understanding, enthusiasm directed by the Word of God."[32]

## The Word and the Message of Worship

Preaching is part of worship and leads to worship. Indeed, John Piper calls preaching "expository exultation" and explains:

> The all-pervasive, all-important, all-surpassing reality in every text is God. Whether he is commanding or warning or promising or teaching, he is there. And where he is, he is always supreme. And where he is supreme, he will be worshiped.[33]

## The Word and the End of Worship

The word should rightly be exalted in our worship (because it is the word *of God*), but not as an end in itself. For the ultimate goal of worship (as of the church and of our lives as believers) is to display and proclaim and magnify *the glory of God*. The glory of God will be well served in our worship as the word speaks to us of the wonders of his person and

31. Furr and Price, *Dialogue of Worship*, 8–15.
32. Furr and Price, *Dialogue of Worship*, 125.
33. Piper, "Preaching as Worship" (*Trinity Journal*), 36.

his ways—through reading, preaching, praying, singing, meditating, and practicing ordinances that are infused with and reflective of scriptural truth. The word will enable us to obey its own command to "praise him according to his excellent greatness" (Ps 150:2).

## Others' Observations

You cannot read too much Scripture; and what you read you cannot read too carefully, and what you read carefully you cannot understand too well, and what you understand well you cannot teach too well, and what you teach well you cannot live too well.[34]

Since the Bible is the church's source book of knowledge about its salvation, its guidebook for living, and the promise of its destiny, it must be kept central in the church's worship.[35]

The Bible is not simply read aloud in order to convey information, to teach doctrine or ethics or whatever, though of course it does that too. It is read aloud as the effective sign that all that we do is done as a response to God's living and active word, the word that, as Isaiah says, accomplishes God's purpose in the world, abiding forever while all flesh withers like the grass. The place of Scripture in Christian worship means that both in structure and content God's initiative remains primary and all that we do remains a matter of response.[36]

God's Word is the King speaking to his covenant people. When it is read, sung, prayed, and preached, I must quiet my heart, focus my thoughts, and attune my ears. It is the Lord of Glory who speaks.[37]

Our imaginations, our emotions, our clever minds, are "idol factories," as Calvin said, and they will always lead us away from God unless we are constantly judging our worship by the Word.[38]

If the bulletin makes it clear that Scripture is an important part of Christian worship, then we can be sure people will get the message that the Bible is crucial in shaping their lives as Christians. But, when the role of Scripture in worship is negligible,

34. Luther, *What Luther Says*, 1110.
35. Segler, *Christian Worship*, 66.
36. N. T. Wright, "Freedom and Framework."
37. Cabaniss, "Worship and the Word."
38. Horton, *In the Face of God*, 209.

when Scripture is used only to launch a sermon, what is communicated is that the Bible is marginal in Christian life, too. The use we make or fail to make of Scripture in our worship says far more about Christian discipleship than we may realize.[39]

39. White, "Making Our Worship," 38.

## Principle 5: Worship is the responsibility of all God's people.

### PARTICIPATORY WORSHIP

So we Your people and the sheep of Your pasture will give
thanks to You forever. (Ps 79:13)

In a now-famous quote, Kierkegaard stresses that the members of the congregation are the "performers," with God as the "audience" (rather than seeing the congregation as the audience who watch performers on the platform).[40] In other words, worship is something done *by* God's people, not *for* God's people. It is not a spectator sport; hence the title of Robert Webber's book *Worship Is a Verb.* As Don Hustad aptly puts it, "The relevant question is not 'Do you have a *voice?*' but 'Do you have a *song?*'"[41] And *all* believers in Christ have a song to sing in gratitude to their Redeemer.

Congregational participation in corporate worship is in fact a direct application of the biblical doctrine of (and the Reformation reemphasis on) the priesthood of all believers, and thus is in itself a powerful testimony to the nature of the new covenant and the free access of every believer into the presence of God through Jesus our great High Priest.

### The Singing Congregation

Music is a gift of God ideally suited for the praise of the Creator—in heaven and in the church on earth. And *the congregation is the most important singing group in the church* (the wonderful ministry of the gifted musical

---

40. "In the theater, the play is staged before an audience who are called theatergoers; but at the devotional address, God himself is present. In the most earnest sense God is the critical theatergoer, who looks on to see how the lines are spoken and how they are listened to: hence here the customary audience is wanting. The speaker then is the prompter, and the listener stands openly before God. The listener, if I may say so, is the actor, who in all truth acts before God" (Kierkegaard, *Purity of Heart*, 181). There has been some appropriate pushback to this concept, insisting that God is so much more than just a passive recipient in the dialogue of worship (see Principle 3 above). Yet Kierkegaard is certainly right to point the congregation itself away from passive spectating itself, and the leaders up front away from nursing a performance mindset.

41. Hustad, *Jubilate II*, 120.

leaders notwithstanding). Following are some ways the congregation can be brought into a greater participatory role in worship through song:

## 1. Give them credit.

Announcing every hymn number found in the bulletin, or every song title projected on the wall, is almost an insult to the intelligence of the worshiper, and certainly can detract from a worshipful atmosphere. That is not to say that thoughtful words of introduction cannot sometimes set the tone in an effective way; but a rote lead-in that is always the same would be better left out, not to mention a mini-sermon. The bulletin or projection tells the people what to sing; the instrumental introduction tells them in what key and tempo to sing; and the worship leader shows them when to sing—so why not just let them start singing?

## 2. Coach the congregation.

Use the choir or worship team to sing through a song that is unfamiliar, then let the congregation join in the second time. If the tune is not too difficult, it is surprising how quickly the average group can pick it up.

## 3. Model for the congregation.

Expressions of joy or wonder, enthusiasm in singing, and an obvious heart for worship go a long way towards motivating the congregation. In this way the musicians up front truly serve as worship facilitators (and fulfill Kierkegaard's view of them as "prompters" for the audience's "performers").

## 4. Use hymns and songs creatively.

It is remarkable how taking well-known texts and singing them in unfamiliar ways can make those texts come alive to our people. If the text is worth singing, then it is worth being savored and reflected on, not just sung in a lifeless, rote manner. Try changing the tempo and/or dynamic range of hymns or songs (either slower or faster, or louder or softer). Doing a normally lively or majestic setting in a more contemplative way can bring new attention to, and appreciation for, the words being sung.

And there's no law that says all verses of a hymn must be used every time; in fact, if a theme is being developed, very often only one or two verses will pertain to that theme. There are many contemporary harmonizations of classic hymns now available; and there is as well a strong movement towards setting rich old texts to new contemporary tunes.[42]

## 5. Avoid straining their voices.

It has often been pointed out that many contemporary songs, as well as quite a few settings in hymnbooks, are pitched too high for comfortable singing by untrained voices.

Ed Willmington puts it this way:

> It seems that the world is full of tenor worship leaders these days! Think about it! Name a few and see if I'm not right. Great voices, great hearts . . . but tenors! I can't believe how high Chris Tomlin sings *Indescribable!* Great song, but not me in that key! I don't know what your vocal range is, but the average Joe and Jane Pewsitter have about a one octave range: from C to C. Though not all songs have a one octave range, many are very close or smaller. So, if the goal is to encourage congregational participation, then considerable thought should be given to that average C to C range. If you get beyond that range, be ready for people to shut down, stop trying to sing. . . . Adjust *your* comfort and playing ability to what is more important: congregational accessibility and involvement.[43]

People will simply stop singing if the range of the songs makes it uncomfortable to sing for any length of time. It is worth the trouble to transpose music into lower keys (either by hand or by using a music notation software; there are even websites that will automatically transpose chord charts). We want to remove any impediments we can to full participation by God's people in musical praise. Also, just because a song is effective on some solo artist's album does not mean that it is necessarily suited to congregational singing. Rhythms and melodic lines must not be too complex.

42. Some excellent examples may be found in the online RUF Hymnbook, https://www.igracemusic.com/hymnbook/home.html.

43. Willmington, "Worship Leader."

## 6. Do not blow them away.

When sound systems are in use, it is important to use them judiciously so that the congregation is not overwhelmed by the flood of sound from the speakers. It is simply not a fair fight when electronic amplification is in play. When the music from the front is too loud, people will just stop singing, and then what results is a concert rather than a worship service. If the congregation is the most important musical group, then the primary function of those up front is to support and facilitate the singing of the whole body: to help them sing better, not to drown them out.

## 7. Consider a thematic approach.

Long strings of contextually unrelated songs or choruses are not conducive to reflective worship, for there is no time to linger on a single aspect of God's nature or work. There is a power to focusing on and developing a single thematic focus throughout the time of corporate praise (perhaps, though not necessarily, related to the topic of the sermon), for it gives the people time to meditate on and respond to truth.[44]

## 8. Make creative use of the instruments and voices.

Don't have all the instruments play full out all the time; vary the textures by leaving out one instrument or the other on occasion. And a cappella singing can be used in both traditional and contemporary contexts: there is no instrument like the human voice, and no better way to foster a sense of community in our singing.

### The Speaking Congregation

Remember that worship is more than music. As already emphasized repeatedly in this book, the word of God needs to have a prominent (and therefore, in most churches, a much greater) role in our worship.

Churches with pew Bibles or with a single-translation tradition can read Scripture passages aloud together, as can churches with projection capabilities. Responsive readings should not be confined to those found in the back of most hymnals; it is well worth the effort to put together

---

44. See Ron Man, "Power of Thematic Worship."

original responsive readings that incorporate a variety of Scripture texts (and then print or project them for the congregation). This is a wonderful way to help develop a theme in worship by pulling together many related texts to instruct and encourage God's people. Such readings are not too difficult to develop with the use of a Bible concordance (especially a computer concordance that allows for searches of pairings of specific words).

Fearing rote expressions, many nonliturgical churches have eschewed the practice of reciting the historic creeds of the church, the Te Deum, the Lord's Prayer, etc. But precisely because they are therefore less familiar in such churches, they may be used on occasion as effective doctrinal confessions and expressions of worship. (See ch. 33 for more on different kinds of readings that can be used.)

## The Praying Congregation

All the praying in church should not be left to the pastor. Some churches have small-group prayer during a worship service, or use a greeting time for sharing prayer needs. In smaller churches it is possible to have seasons of corporate prayer where different individuals may pray aloud. In larger churches where this is not feasible, the practice of "bidded prayer" can allow for greater participation in prayer. In this practice, borrowed from the Anglican church, the pastor or other leader will successively mention specific areas for prayer, then leave about thirty seconds after each for the people to pray silently about that area; in this way the members of the congregation are truly praying, rather than just listening to one person pray.

## Conclusion

It is imperative that the members of our congregations leave, not just having attended a worship service, but *having worshiped*. It is worth all the creativity and effort we can muster to lovingly draw the people of God into meaningful participation in expressing praise to the God of their salvation.

## Others' Observations

One of Luther's stated goals was the restoration of true worship. He understood the tremendous benefit resulting from hearing the word of God and then uniting as a congregation to offer thanksgiving in song. This stress on congregational participation in worship became a lynchpin of the Reformation.[45]

Oftentimes Free Church Protestants, who speak the most about the priesthood of all believers, are the most guilty of promoting clergy-dominated worship in which the minister does all the preaching, praying, speaking, acting, and leading, and the people do all the passive sitting and listening.[46]

I challenge our worship leaders to consider themselves worship facilitators, not worship performers. The very measure of an effective worship time is not whether we performed well. It is whether or not people engaged well. . . . Contemporary worship without participation is nothing more than a concert with spiritual words.[47]

On most Sundays, the congregation watches, listens, and the only active participation is singing a few hymns. Apart from singing, the only voice that is heard is the minister's. . . . The typical evangelical service is not Reformation worship; it is in important respects closer to the medieval abuses that the Reformers spent themselves to change. Reforming worship demands an end to the clericalisation of evangelical worship and a new emphasis on congregational participation.[48]

If we remember that public worship presents the opportunity to unite with others in gratitude to the King of the cosmos, we will each want to do our best and offer our most excellent singing—our finest performance—and join with all the other saints in thorough participation in the act of worship.[49]

---

45. Fromm, "New Song," 28.

46. Willimon, *Word, Water, Wine*, 123–24.

47. Joe Horness, "Contemporary Worship Response," in Zahl and Basden, *Six Views*, 202.

48. Leithart, "Transforming Worship," 31.

49. Dawn, *How Shall We Worship?*, 78.

## Principle 6: Our worship is acceptable in and through Christ our High Priest.

### CHRIST-LED WORSHIP

In the midst of the congregation I will sing your praise.
(Heb 2:12b)

(See also the extensive treatment of this theme in ch. 26.)

## Towards a Christology of Worship

1. The living Christ is present in our midst when we gather for worship.

   In the midst of the congregation I will sing your praise. (Heb 2:12b)

2. Only in and through Christ can we enter God's presence in worship.

   There is one mediator between God and men, the man Christ Jesus. (1 Tim 2:5)

3. Our worship is pleasing and acceptable to God not because of its own excellence, but because of (and only because of) the excellence of his Son.

   God accepts and delights in our worship, not because of our efforts or our artistry or even our spirituality, but because of the Son's continual offering of worship in our place and on our behalf.

4. The word of God, by which Christ proclaims his Father's name to his brethren, deserves priority and centrality in our worship.

   I will tell of your name to my brethren. (Heb 2:12a)

   How are they to believe in him whom they have never heard? . . . Faith comes from hearing, and hearing through the word of Christ. (Rom 10:14, 17)

5. The corporate praise of God's people, led by Christ himself, is an integral and crucial part of the gathering of the church.

> Let the word of Christ dwell in you richly, with all wisdom teaching and admonishing one another with psalms, hymns and spiritual songs; with grace singing to God in your heart. (Col 3:16)

6. Jesus Christ is himself the ultimate fulfillment of the biblical pattern of *revelation* and *response*.

> ↓ I will tell of your name to my brethren;
> ↑ in the midst of the congregation I will sing your praise. (Heb 2:12)

7. No matter how they may differ in the externals, all true expressions of worship have in common that they are led and mediated by Christ in the power of the Holy Spirit.

> Through him [Christ] we both have our access in one Spirit to the Father. (Eph 2:18)

> For we are the true circumcision, who worship in the Spirit of God and glory in Christ Jesus and put no confidence in the flesh. (Phil 3:3)

8. When we preach or lead worship, we do so representing Christ *whose ministry it is.* He's the preacher; he's the worship leader.

> I will tell of your name to my brethren; in the midst of the congregation I will sing your praise. (Heb 2:12)

9. Because Christ leads us in our worship, we can enter boldly and confidently into God's presence.

> Therefore . . . since we have a great priest over the house of God, let us draw near to God. (Heb 10:19, 22)

10. By his grace God has provided in Christ the worship he requires of us.

> Grant me what You command, and command what You will.[50]

11. Our singing Savior shows us the appropriateness and necessity of our own songs of praise.

> In the midst of the congregation I will sing your praise. (Heb 2:12b)

> I will praise you among the Gentiles, and sing to your name. (Rom 15:9)

---

50. Augustine, *Confessions*, 10.31.

If Christ our Mediator deems it fitting to sing the Father's praises in the midst of the congregation (Heb 2:12) and among the nations (Rom 15:9), how can we do less?

12. We need to repent of doing worship in our own strength.

> Through, with, and in Christ we turn away in penitential self-denial from our own acts of worship and prayer in order to rest in the worship and prayer which our Saviour has already offered and continues to offer to the Father on our behalf.[51]

## Conclusion

All true worship is in and through and by Jesus Christ. This is a supremely unifying understanding of Christian worship in all times and places and styles and forms.[52]

---

51. T. Torrance, "Mind of Christ," 211–12.
52. This section adapted from Ron Man, *Proclamation and Praise*, ch. 5.

## Principle 7: Our response of worship is enabled, motivated, and empowered by the Holy Spirit.

### SPIRIT-ENABLED WORSHIP

We are the true circumcision, who worship in the Spirit of God and glory in Christ Jesus and put no confidence in the flesh. (Phil 3:3)

(See also the extensive treatment of this theme also in ch. 25.)

The Holy Spirit is committed to actualizing our worship in and through Jesus Christ in the body of Christ and in our personal lives.

### Enabled by the Spirit

As we saw in ch. 25, the Holy Spirit's ministry may be seen as an extension of what Christ has done and is doing. The same holds true for worship. "Worship, through the presence and action of the Holy Spirit, is a meeting . . . between Jesus Christ and his people."[53]

In his humanity Jesus Christ is the one Mediator between us and God in our response of worship; he is "in the midst of the congregation," leading us in singing the Father's praise (Heb 2:12). Yet in his humanity he is physically present at the Father's right hand, interceding for us (Heb 7:24) and serving as the Minister in the true sanctuary in heaven (8:1–2). So how can he be present among us as well? (He is omnipresent in his deity, of course, but not in his humanity.) Reggie Kidd suggests that "the union between the Son and the Holy Spirit within the Trinity and the functional . . . representation of the Son by the Holy Spirit mean that when the Holy Spirit ministers among us, Christ Himself is present. . . . Christ sings in the church by means of the Holy Spirit . . . and that's why Christ [in his humanity] can 'be in two places at once.'"[54]

Gerrit Dawson explains this mystery thus:

> The glorified, ascended, still incarnate Jesus is in the Holy Place, within the true tabernacle (Heb 8:2) of which every earthly house of worship is at best a shadow. Yet in the Holy Spirit he is not removed from us. The Spirit is the Spirit of Jesus, and brings

53. Allmen, "Worship and the Holy Spirit," 130.
54. Reggie Kidd, email to author, Aug. 30, 2009.

his presence to us in worship. . . . And the Spirit lifts us up, spiritually, in our worship to the throne of God where Jesus serves as our advocate, priest, intercessor and worship leader. Through the Spirit, then, the ascended Jesus comes to be in our midst and through the same Spirit we are brought in Christ our High Priest into the Father's welcoming presence.[55]

So, as we saw in ch. 25, we might say that Christ is the *Way* and the Holy Spirit is the *Guide*.

## Motivated by the Spirit

As Christopher Cocksworth puts it, "The new humanity of Christ, in which we share by the Spirit, is doxological by nature. He gives glory to the Father in the Spirit. To enter the realm of Christ's humanity is to step into a life of worship."[56] Allmen adds, "Worship is the automatic outcome of the outpouring of the Holy Spirit upon the Church."[57] To be in Christ (2 Cor 5:17; 1 Pet 5:14), and to be indwelt by him (John 14:20; 17:22–23), thus means to be a worshiper; and it is the Holy Spirit who baptizes us into Christ and energizes the process of sanctification by which we grow progressively in Christlikeness—becoming as part of that process more willing and wholehearted worshipers.

The role of the Spirit in worship is to open our hearts to Christ—to take what we know in our heads and drive it into our hearts; to engender thankfulness and praise for his grace, his love, and his presence; and then through and in Christ to lift our praises to the Father. "The Son eternally gives glory to the Father in the Spirit. . . . Christian worship is participation in this . . . life of God through the presence and activity of the Holy Spirit in the life of the believer and in the midst of the fellowship of the Church."[58]

As William Nicholls explains it:

> If the objective basis of our worship is the work of Christ, its subjective basis is the work of the Spirit in the individual members of the Church, enabling them to hear Christ's Word as God's Word, and to participate personally in His response to the Father.[59]

55. Dawson, *Jesus Ascended*, 136.

56. Cocksworth, *Holy, Holy, Holy*, 185.

57. Allmen, "Worship and the Holy Spirit," 130.

58. Cocksworth, *Holy, Holy, Holy*, 189–90.

59. Nicholls, *Jacob's Ladder*, 58.

In other words, we *can* come into God's presence in worship because of the (objective) work of Christ (Heb 10:19–22); but we *want to* come into God's presence because of the (subjective) work of the Holy Spirit in our hearts. The Spirit completes in us the biblical cycle of *revelation* and *response*, taking the ↓ *revelation* of God and driving it home to our hearts, thus drawing forth our ↑ *response* of worship.

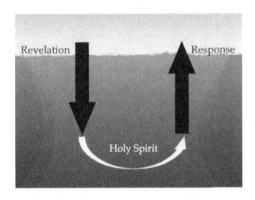

## Empowered by the Spirit

The true power of new-covenant worship rests not in our own efforts to lift to God an appropriate and worthy response of praise; but rather in the continuing mediating ministry of Christ, who offers to the Father, as our Representative and High Priest, a perfect response of praise. And the Holy Spirit empowers our worship thus as he connects us to that perfect offering: by identifying us with Christ (Rom 8:9–11); by assuring us that we are children of God (Rom 8:14–17) and brethren in Christ (Rom 8:17; Heb 2:11); by encouraging us to therefore come boldly into the Father's presence (Heb 10:19–22); and by filling us that we might sing to, praise, and thank the Father through Christ from our hearts (Eph 5:18–20).

The Spirit also empowers our worship by giving gifts to promote the growth, unity, and love of the body (Eph 4:1–16). Sinclair Ferguson states:

> The correlation between the ascension of Christ and the descent of the Spirit signals that the gift and gifts of the Spirit serve as the external manifestation of the triumph and enthronement of Christ [cf. Eph 4:7–8]. . . . Gifts of the Spirit are given to equip the people of God and to enable them to set on display the glory of God, the fullness of Christ, in the temple of God (Eph 4:12, 16).[60]

60. Ferguson, *Holy Spirit*, 207–8.

Here again we see the *Christ-centeredness* of all the Spirit's doings, even in his most distinctive (and debated) contributions. As controversial as the work of the Spirit is in the church today, let us remember two defining and limiting qualifications that Ferguson points out:[61] (1) the primacy of *God's revealed Word* in the ordering and exercise of spiritual gifts (revelation always logically and theologically precedes response); and (2) the goal of *love* (the "more excellent way" of 1 Cor 12:31 and ch. 13). The Spirit's gifts, as all his work, will always seek to glorify Christ and bring honor to the Father.

## Others' Observations

Neither you nor I could ever know anything of Christ or believe in him, or have him as our Lord, except as this is offered to us by the Holy Spirit through the preaching of the Gospel.[62]

Martin Luther . . . told of a time when he was focused intently on the person and work of Christ. The Holy Spirit was there as if in the form of a dove, gently alight on his shoulder, and when Luther turned his attention to the Spirit and away from Christ, the dove flew away.[63]

Almighty God, unto whom all hearts be open, all desires known, and from whom no secrets are hid; Cleanse the thoughts of our hearts by the inspiration of thy Holy Spirit, that we may perfectly love thee, and worthily magnify thy holy Name; through Christ our Lord. Amen.[64]

*O Holy Spirit,*
As the sun is full of light, the ocean full of water,
    Heaven full of glory, so may my heart be full of thee.
Vain are all divine purposes of love
    and the redemption wrought by Jesus
    except thou work within,
        regenerating by thy power,
        giving me eyes to see Jesus,
        showing me the realities of the unseen world. . . .
I bewail my coldness, poverty, emptiness,

---

61. Ferguson, *Holy Spirit*, 208–9.

62. Luther, *Luther's Large Catechism*, art. 3.

63. Harold Best, "Charismatic Worship: A Traditional Worship Response," in Zahl and Basden, *Six Views*, 158.

64. Church of England, "Order for the Administration."

imperfect vision, languid service,
    prayerless prayers, praiseless praises.
Suffer me not to grieve or resist thee.
Come as power,
    to expel every rebel lust, to reign supreme and keep me thine;
Come as teacher,
    leading me into all truth, filling me with all understanding;
Come as love,
    that I may adore the Father, and love him as my all;
Come as joy,
    to dwell in me, move in me, animate me;
Come as light,
    illuminating the Scripture, moulding me in its laws;
Come as sanctifier,
    body, soul and spirit wholly thine;
Come as helper,
    with strength to bless and keep, directing my every step;
Come as beautifier,
    bringing order out of confusion, loveliness out of chaos.[65]


Spirit of Truth, come down,
    Reveal the things of God,
Make Thou to us Christ's Godhead known,
    Apply His precious blood.
His merits glorify,
    That each may clearly see
Jesus, Who did for sinners die,
    Hath surely died for me.
No man can truly say
    That Jesus is the Lord,
Unless Thou take the veil away
    And breathe the living word.
Then, only then, we feel
    Our interest in His blood
And cry with joy unspeakable,
    "Thou art my Lord, my God."
O that the world might know
    The all-atoning Lamb;
Spirit of faith, descend and show
    The virtue of His Name.[66]


65. "Spiritus Sanctus," in Bennett, *Valley of Vision*, 28.
66. Wesley, "Spirit of Truth."

The role of the Holy Spirit in worship is . . . the glorification of Christ and the leading of men to share in His human worship of the Father.[67]

Without the operation of the Spirit Christian Worship would be a merely human act, like heathen . . . worship—human effort and self-exertion before God. Through the Spirit Christian Worship is the act of God in the community.[68]

Genuine worship must be prompted, energized, and brought to fulfillment by the presence and sanctifying power of the Holy Spirit. Without the Holy Spirit worship by human beings remains merely a human activity which has no guarantee of reaching the Father.[69]

Apart from the action of the Holy Spirit, God's self-disclosure in Christ, crucified and risen, is simply religious information that we may take or leave. God moves toward us in Christ, and by the Spirit connects with us, lifting us into God's own life, which is, at its very heart and center, relational Holy Trinity. Worship that is profoundly Christian will be shaped in form and content by a Trinitarian faith.[70]

The Spirit makes known the personal presence in and with the Christian and the church of the risen, reigning Saviour. . . . He empowers, enables, purges, and leads generation after generation of sinners to face the reality of God. And he does it in order that Christ may be known, loved, trusted, honored and praised. . . . The distinctive, constant, basic ministry of the Holy Spirit under the new covenant is . . . to mediate Christ's presence to believers.[71]

Bread and wine are nothing, apart from the Holy Spirit; baptism is nothing, apart from the Holy Spirit; our worship and our liturgies are nothing, apart from the Holy Spirit. But they're everything in the power of the Spirit, because in the power of the Spirit Christ is there to baptize and Christ is there to make the bread and wine a communion in the body and blood of Christ. We're utterly dependent on the Spirit.[72]

---

67. Nicholls, *Jacob's Ladder*, 65.
68. Delling, *Worship in the New Testament*, 23–24.
69. Toon, *Our Triune God*, 32–33.
70. Byars, *Future of Protestant Worship*, 63.
71. Packer, *Keep in Step*, 47, 49.
72. J. Torrance, "Priesthood of Christ."

## Principle 8: Worship is the response of our entire lives to God.

### WHOLE-LIFE WORSHIP

Therefore I urge you, brethren, by the mercies of God,
to present your bodies a living and holy sacrifice,
acceptable to God, which is your spiritual service of worship.
(Rom 12:1)

### Jesus on Lifestyle Worship

As we saw in ch. 10, in John 4 Jesus makes a significant statement about the nature of worship under his lordship. Jesus tells the Samaritan woman that "an hour is coming when neither *in* this mountain nor *in* Jerusalem will you worship the Father" (v. 21), but rather, "an hour is coming, and now is, when the true worshipers will worship the Father *in* spirit and truth" (v. 23). Jesus's redirection of the preposition *in* from speaking of external location to internal focus is a shift of enormous spiritual significance. He is saying that he is changing the rules: no longer is it a matter of *where* or *when* you worship, but *how* you worship. No longer is there a geographical center for the people of God. Worship is now to be everywhere and at every time. As has been said, this is not a devaluing of times and places for corporate worship, but rather a hallowing of *every* time and *every* place as suitable for worshiping God.

### Paul on Lifestyle Worship

Paul develops this thought further in Rom 12:1. As an appropriate response ("Therefore") to all the wonderful "mercies of God" he has been explicating in chs. 1–11 of his epistle, he enjoins believers to present their "bodies," that is their entire lives, to God as living sacrificial gifts of thanksgiving. There is to be no sacred/secular compartmentalization in the lives of Christians. Paul reminds us elsewhere that we have been "bought with a price," and again the fitting response is to "glorify God in your bodies" (1 Cor 6:20). As "temples of the Holy Spirit," both individually (1 Cor 6:19) and corporately as the church (1 Cor 3:16), the place of worship is *always present* with us, and the time for worship is *always now*: "Whether you eat or drink, or whatever you do, do all to the glory of God" (1 Cor 10:31).

## Implications for Us

Since God's "divine power has granted to us all things that pertain to life and godliness" (2 Pet 1:3), that means that we are in possession of all that is necessary for a life and lifestyle of worship. Through the mediating ministry of the living Christ and the enabling, empowering ministry of the Holy Spirit within us, we can enter into the presence of the Father—anywhere, any time. Each believer has a responsibility to cultivate his or her own life of worship (cf. Gal 5:25; Heb 12:14).

This crucial perspective has huge implications for what we do when we gather for corporate worship. It is *not* the responsibility of the pastor or the worship leader to supply or actuate worship for the people of God (only Christ in the power of the Spirit can do that anyway, as we have seen), but merely to facilitate its corporate expression. We should not be in the habit of coming to the service with an empty spiritual "tank," hoping to get it filled in order to be able to face the week *ahead*; the ideal for Christian living is to come to church *out of a week* of daily worship throughout all of life, and then to join hearts and voices together in a corporate expression borne out of the fullness of our spirits. Sunday should be a preparation for our week; but our week should also be a preparation for Sunday! It is true that sometimes we may indeed come spiritually empty and dry; and God in his grace will meet us in our need, and refresh and restore our spirits, and send us into our week with a renewed passion for God. We often need to be reminded, by gathering with like-minded believers, of what is the true center of our lives (since that is constantly being challenged out in the workaday world). But our goal should be to come to church with a heart full of love and devotion to God from walking with him throughout the week.

As quoted before, Jay Thomas wisely counsels:

> Don't expect the preacher to be the totality of your spiritual interaction every week. Sunday services are important, but they should be the high points of an already spiritually alive week for you. That does not mean your week was awesome in every way. It just means you were fighting for faith and seeking God all week. Then, Sundays bolster, affirm, solidify, and remind you that this gospel stuff is all true.[73]

73. Thomas, "Easily Edified."

## A Parable

In the children's story *Stone Soup*, three soldiers are returning home from the war. They approach a village, but the villagers, seeing them coming, scurry to hide all their food, because there is a shortage and they do not want to have to share with outsiders. They tell the soldiers that they have no food to give them.

The soldiers, being rather shrewd fellows, tell the villagers that they will make some "stone soup" and ask simply for a large kettle filled with water. They choose several large, round stones and add them to the kettle, with the curious villagers looking on. Then the soldiers remark, "This soup should be excellent; but if we only had a couple of potatoes, it would be even better." One of the villagers says, "I think I might have a few to spare," and goes off to retrieve some potatoes from her stash. The soldiers add these to the pot, taste the soup, and say: "Wonderful! Now if we just had a few carrots . . ." and someone runs off and gets some. The same happens with onions, and cabbage, and so forth, until a hearty soup has been prepared. The soldiers invite the villagers to join with them in their feast, and the villagers are amazed that such a marvelous soup could be made with just *stones*![74]

In our corporate worship, our rituals, hymns, anthems, even our sermons are like those stones—they are building blocks, a framework, a skeleton. What makes it special and makes it *worship* is when our people come and add to the pot from what has been stored up in their hearts during a week of worshiping and walking with God, a week of loving God and cherishing and savoring his glory—*then* we are ready to worship God *together*. When our corporate adoration is the overflow of *many* hearts rejoicing in the goodness and greatness of God, the Spirit can energize and transform the gathering into something far more than the sum of the parts. And then our congregational worship will truly be a nourishing and invigorating feast for the people of God, and—more importantly—a fragrant aroma to the God of glory, who delights in the worship of his people.

## Others' Observations

> So here's what I want you to do, God helping you: Take your
> everyday, ordinary life—your sleeping, eating, going-to-work,

74. See Brown, *Stone Soup*.

and walking-around life—and place it before God as an offering. (Rom 12:1 MSG)

Have your heart right with Christ, and he will visit you often, and so turn weekdays into Sundays, meals into sacraments, homes into temples and earth into heaven.[75]

How do we become intentional in worship? How do we become participants rather than spectators? [A] friend's mother taught her to go to church with "a full basket, not an empty one."[76]

I believe that we have enough how-to-do-it books and not enough reflection on worship as a total biblical idea. Worship is a subject that should dominate our lives seven days a week. Vitality and meaning will not be restored to Christian gatherings until those who lead and those who participate can recover a biblical perspective on their meetings, seeing them in relation to God's total plan and purpose for his people.[77]

Worship is not just a matter of regularly paying our dues by attending weekly rituals; it is "a soundtrack for the rest of life, the words and music and actions of worship inside the sanctuary playing the background as we live our lives outside, in the world," as Thomas Long writes in *Testimony*. Long says, "The words of worship are like stones thrown into the pond; they ripple outward in countless concentric circles, finding ever fresh expression in new places in our lives."[78]

True worship which God desires embraces the whole of the Christian's life from day to day. . . . Any cultic worship which is not accompanied by obedience in the ordinary affairs of life must be regarded as false worship, unacceptable to God.[79]

"Whether you eat or drink or whatever you do, do all to the glory of God' (1 Cor 10:31). And "whatever you do in word or deed, do all in the name of the Lord Jesus, giving thanks through him to God the Father" (Col 3:17). This is the form of worship commanded in the New Testament. . . . But the New Testament uses those greatest of all worship sentences without any reference to worship services. They describe life.[80]

---

75. C. H. Spurgeon, cited in Patterson, *Serving God*, 147.

76. Mains, "Introduction," 5.

77. D. Peterson, *Engaging with God*, 21.

78. Michael Lindvall, cited in Bierma, "Worshipful Service."

79. Cranfield, *Romans*, 2:601.

80. Piper, "Worship God."

## Principle 9: God is much more concerned with our *heart* than with our *form* of worship.

### HEART WORSHIP

Man looks on the outward appearance,
but God looks on the heart. (1 Sam 16:7)

### A Surprising Truth

In ch. 13, we noted that when it comes to Old Testament worship, our thoughts naturally turn to the minutely detailed instructions (chapter after chapter after chapter) given for the rituals of the Mosaic tabernacle/ temple system. There is such a focus on the externals that one might conclude that outward conformity to his instructions was of paramount importance to God—precisely because he went to such lengths to spell them all out.

However, nothing could be further from the truth! We looked at many Old Testament texts and saw resounding testimony to the priority God placed, even in the old-covenant economy with its complex system of ritual and ceremony, on the worship of the *heart*.

This does not mean that obedience to the prescriptions of the Mosaic law was unimportant. To the contrary: the way for a pious Jew to express a heart of love for God was by obedience to his instructions for ceremonial worship. But the Old Testament writers, and especially the prophets, made it abundantly clear that merely outward conformity to the requirements without an engaged heart meant nothing to God; in fact such offerings and rituals were detestable to him. C. S. Lewis warns us that it would be wrong to think that God "really needed the blood of bulls and goats." What he values rather is "the intention."[81]

### Worship "in spirit"

Jesus continues the prophets' criticism of the Jewish leaders for their external conformity to the law without an inward heart motivation. He

81. C. S. Lewis, "On Church Music," 123.

calls the scribes and Pharisees "whitewashed tombs" (Matt 23:27), "blind guides" (23:16), and "hypocrites" (23:13, 23), who "tithe mint and rue and every herb, and neglect justice and the love of God" (Luke 11:42), who "clean the outside of the cup and the plate, but inside they are full of greed and self-indulgence" (Matt 23:25).

Jesus tells the Samaritan woman at the well in John 4 that true worship must be "in spirit" (4:23, 24). Because "God is spirit" (4:24)—that is, not a physical being but a spiritual one—then our worship must likewise begin in the inner, immaterial part of our being: it must be genuine, from the heart. (First Peter 3:4 shows the close relationship between the human spirit and the heart.) Probably Jesus had the Jewish leaders in mind when he insisted on "worship in spirit" (even as he likely had the theologically wayward Samaritans in view as he advocated "worship in truth").

Jesus, like his Father, has no tolerance for worship that is external only, no matter how carefully and painstakingly performed. Let us take heed!

## A Lifestyle of Heart Worship

In the New Testament the heart, "the inner life, the centre of the personality,"[82] is portrayed as the seat of sin (Rom 1:21; 2:5), saving faith (Rom 10:9–10), assurance (2 Cor 1:22; Heb 10:22), sanctification (2 Cor 4:6; Gal 4:6; Eph 3:17), commitment (1 Thess 2:4), peace (Phil 4:7; Col 3:15), love (1 Tim 1:5; 1 Pet 1:22), obedience (Eph 6:6), and encouragement (Col 2:2; 4:8). As we saw in ch. 19, the New Testament emphasis is on worship as a *lifestyle*; this worship in every time and place is in fact possible because it consists fundamentally of the *heart's* response to God, rather than a set of prescribed rituals, practices, or forms.

The heart is also the wellspring of our corporate worship; Paul exhorts us: "Be filled with the Spirit, addressing one another in psalms and hymns and spiritual songs, singing and making melody to the Lord *with your heart*" (Eph 5:19; see also Col 3:16).

## The Bottom Line

"Man looks on the outward appearance, but God looks on the heart" (1 Sam 16:7). This familiar passage is not often applied to the area of

82. T. Sorg, "Heart," in *NIDNTT* 2:182.

worship, yet it is resoundingly applicable. Most of what we think and talk about when it comes to worship are outward forms and styles, and usually with a very narrow perception of what might be "appropriate" or "acceptable" to God. Yet when we look at the scope of various worship expressions down through the centuries, and across the world (or even across the street!) today, it is quite evident that God has a much, much broader spectrum of taste than any of us can claim to have! And it is the height of arrogance for us to presume (as most of us have, at one time or another) that our own particular set of preferences just happens to coincide with what the Almighty himself favors!

Lewis reminds us that "all our offerings, whether of music or martyrdom, are like the intrinsically worthless present of a child, which a father values indeed, but values only for the intention."[83] God does not have a set of favorite songs or a preferred style. He is looking for *hearts* of worship.

## Others' Observations

> Hence it is perfectly clear that neither words nor singing (if used in prayer) are of the least consequence, or avail one iota with God, unless they proceed from deep feeling in the heart. Nay, rather they provoke his anger against us, if they come from the lips and throat only, since this is to abuse his sacred name, and hold his majesty in derision. . . . Still we do not condemn words or singing, but rather greatly commend them, provided the feeling of the mind goes along with them. For in this way the thought of God is kept alive on our minds.[84]

> Almighty God, unto whom all hearts be open, all desires known, and from whom no secrets are hid: Cleanse the thoughts of our hearts by the inspiration of thy Holy Spirit, that we may perfectly love thee, and worthily magnify thy holy Name; through Christ our Lord.[85]

> True and genuine worship is not to come to a certain place; it is not to go through a certain ritual or liturgy; it is not even to bring certain gifts. True worship is when the spirit, the immortal

---

83. C. S. Lewis, "On Church Music," 123.

84. Calvin, "Of Prayer," §31.

85. Church of England, "Order for the Administration."

and invisible part of man, speaks to and meets with God, who is immortal and invisible.[86]

The lack of worship is a symptom; the lack of true worshipers is the root of the problem. . . . Making changes in the structure of the service itself is just another attempt at dealing with art alone and not with heart. It is we who need the changes.[87]

Music and liturgy can assist or express a worshiping heart, but they cannot make a non-worshiping heart into a worshiping one. The danger is that they can give a non-worshiping heart the sense of having worshiped. So the crucial factor in worship in the church is not the form of worship, but the state of the hearts of the saints. If our corporate worship isn't the expression of our individual worshiping lives, it is unacceptable.[88]

Spiritual worship involves an awareness and perception of God through faith that arises from the heart, from the innermost being of the worshiper.[89]

Music has many benefits. It moves us emotionally. It helps us to reflect on, remember, and be affected by the truth. However, apart from faith resonating in our hearts, we are no closer to God when we sing than when we wash dishes or do homework.[90]

86. Barclay, *Gospel of John*, 1:154.

87. Allen and Borror, *Worship*, 37.

88. MacArthur, *Worship*, 104.

89. Nation, "Essentials of Worship," 6.

90. Kauflin, "Worship Matters."

## Principle 10: Worship should promote the unity and edification of the body.

### Edifying Worship

Do nothing from selfish ambition or conceit, but in humility count others more significant than yourselves. (Phil 2:3)

So then let us pursue what makes for peace and for mutual upbuilding. (Rom 14:19)

### Another Tapescrew Letter

My dear Woodworm,

It's truly delightful to see what havoc we have caused around the world by perverting, of all things, the worship of the Enemy. In insisting that all honor and praise be directed to himself he is certainly setting the creatures up for failure—just because so much of their existence is wrapped up in themselves and their individual wants and desires.

So stay the course! We are seeing marvelous results. Above all, promote the idea that the purpose of worship is each individual's enjoyment, satisfaction, and sense of well-being. This will result in a delightful clash of personalities and temperaments, since of course no two people will agree on what will bring the desired results. The more you can get people to focus on their own needs and preferences (which, after all, should not be too difficult, people being the selfish beings that they are!), the further they will stray from their apostle's admonition to "consider one another more important than yourselves" and to "prefer one another in love." Delightfully, it never even occurs to them that the Enemy might want them to apply these principles to their practice of worship! How successful we have been to keep such dangerous ideas out of their minds! Most of them haven't any clue that worship is for anything other than their personal fulfillment. This is wonderful, because with such a self-focused attitude (which has been easy to exploit, from the Garden until now) they will never realize that worship was intended by the Enemy to focus on himself and to bring him glory (horrors!) and satisfaction. As long as we can keep the Christians looking to themselves and their own personal agendas, rather than to him and his priorities, they will continue to be pathetic, narcissistic beings with little impact in the world.

Needless to say, our efforts to put a wedge between their generations (which has always been relatively easy) has succeeded more wildly than ever in the arena of worship. Each side is utterly convinced that their way is right, that they presume to know exactly what is and what is not acceptable to the Enemy, and that there is nothing at all to learn from the other side. And all the while they hide behind a smokescreen of supposed "biblical warrant" or "cultural necessity," when in reality all their studies of the subject inevitably end up where they started, with their foregone conclusions firmly and immovably in place. What they *like* always turns out to be identical with what they think is appropriate and correct! This is now so widespread that it is seldom questioned, and our work is that much easier for it.

And how delicious it is that, like so many of the Enemy's supposedly "good" gifts, we have been able to twist music to our purposes. Music now separates rather than unites the Enemy's people. They can indeed be a powerful and unified force when they sing together, but we have managed to shift their focus so that even if corporate singing does happen, half of the people are stewing over the song selection, the absence of their favorites, the volume, the types of instruments used, etc. etc. And the other half seem to just be reveling in the fact that their preferences are being at least temporarily satisfied. Hardly anyone focuses on the Enemy as the subject and object of the songs! We owe all of this to our incredibly fruitful efforts to promote radical individualism as the prevailing philosophy of the day. Such chilling concepts as "the good of the whole" and the "health of the body" fortunately never occur to them as they go about their selfish ways.

Our "divide and conquer" strategy seems to be progressing on schedule!

Affectionately yours,
your uncle Tapescrew[91]

## Others' Observations

We've made worship self-centred instead of God-centred. We lobby for what we want: "I don't like the songs," "I don't like the volume." It's as if we're worshipping worship instead of worshipping God. If worship is a decision, then the greatest worship happens when someone who doesn't like a church's music or

---

91. Ron Man, "Tapescrew Letter 4." For more Tapescrew, see Ron Man, "More from Tapescrew" and "Tapescrew Letter 3."

liturgical style prays, "Not my will but yours be done, God—I'll worship you in spite of it."[92]

I fear that attempting to satisfy personal preferences may honor selfishness while further destroying the unity of the church.[93]

Worship that does not contribute to unity is not the worship embraced by Christianity.[94]

If our churches are really going to reflect the diversity that makes up the body of Christ, then everybody is going to have to sing songs they don't like.[95]

The New Testament churches were made up of people of different ages, genders, races and socio-economic levels, who came together because of their common belief in Jesus. Christ gave them their identity and, consequently, their unity. In an era of marketing niches—of builders, boomers, and busters—we have grown accustomed to having things our way. But do we really need single-taste congregations? What would happen if people with different musical tastes got along because of their common commitment to Christ? What a testimony to the outside world![96]

A wise friend had told me that when his heart is unable to worship in a given moment or situation, for whatever reason, he looks around the congregation to find a person most engaged in worship and begins to pray, "Lord, let that person's worship be mine." At times when the worship seems to my musical sensibilities as a diet of cotton candy, I remind myself first, that the worship isn't there for me (so I can "be fed") and second, that there are many in the congregation for whom that musical expression is authentic, even empowering. In turn, this reminds me that I am a small part of a congregation that is so much bigger than me. It has enabled me to transcend the limitations of the styles that I prefer and even to worship, dare I say, "vicariously" through others. It's a great fix for the "me generation."[97]

Maintaining unity among the diversity of the church's membership requires that we defer to one another in love, being willing

---

92. Bullock, "Beyond Self-Centred Worship," 16.

93. Pyne, "Worship in the Bible."

94. Gaddy, *Gift of Worship*, 220.

95. Attributed to Marva Dawn.

96. Bierly, "Sparring over Worship."

97. Attributed to Greg Roig.

to sing one another's music rather than insisting on the music we most enjoy.[98]

We should conclude that in music as in every other area we must seek to love one another, honoring the diversity of the body to protect its unity. As we have seen, diversity presents problems of musical communication. But we can now see that problem is at least in part a problem of love. When sophisticated members of the church insist that worship employ only the most sophisticated music of their own culture, what has happened to their love for those who are poorly educated or of a different cultural stream? Or, from the opposite side of our musical wars: when advocates of contemporaneity want to set the traditions of the church completely aside and replace them with something largely meaningless to the older generation, are they acting in love? Are they honoring their spiritual fathers and mothers?[99]

When I first became a Christian . . . I thought that I could do it on my own, by retiring to my rooms and reading theology, and wouldn't go to the churches and Gospel Halls; . . . I disliked very much their hymns which I considered to be fifth-rate poems set to sixth-rate music. But as I went on, I saw the merit of it. I came up against different people of quite different outlooks and different education, and then gradually my conceit just began peeling off. I realized that the hymns (which were just sixth-rate music) were, nevertheless, being sung with devotion and benefit by an old saint in elastic-side boots in the opposite pew, and then you realize that you aren't fit to clean those boots. It gets you out of your solitary conceit.[100]

The British journalist and author G. K. Chesterton was once asked by the *London Times* to answer the question, "What is wrong with the state of the world?" Submitted amongst the voluminous responses by scholars, statesmen and other famous people who went into great depth about economic inequalities, ineffective political leadership and so on, Chesterton offered a two-word answer that rang loud and clear: "I am." Chesterton was what was wrong with the world.

What's wrong with . . . worship? That's simple. Me. I am what's wrong with . . . worship.

For every service that I take for granted that wherever two or more are gathered I miss an opportunity to meet with God.

98. Frame, *Contemporary Worship Music*, 28.

99. Frame, *Contemporary Worship Music*, 25–26.

100. "Answers to Questions on Christianity," in C. S. Lewis, *God in the Dock*, 52.

For every time I let my personal likes and dislikes rule my being and cloud my judgment. For every time I forget I am a small part in a large Body. For every time I forget worship is more about my personal motivation than it is about what everybody else is doing. For every time I forget worship is more about giving to God than what I personally receive. . . .

Worship is . . . chock full of things that you don't really care for and probably wouldn't do the same way if you were the one making the decisions. But tolerating a bit of what you might not like seems worthwhile in the hope of those moments when the Spirit comes and massages your heart unexpectedly. And those times can be powerful. They can be meaningful. And if taken in proper measure, they have a funny way of drowning out the noise of your own personal worship likes and dislikes.[101]

Sacrifice always goes with spiritual maturity.

A great opportunity to teach this shared sacrifice presented itself at a retreat. I preached on the topic several times that weekend, and between my sermons, our song leader led the congregation in an informal time of singing. He would ask participants to suggest their favorite hymns, and then the group would sing the selections.

At one point, when the song leader asked for a new round of suggestions, I popped up and said, "Why don't we apply this principle of shared sacrifice? From this point on, you can only suggest singing a hymn that is *not* one of your favorites but one that you know is valued by others here."

People looked at me as if I had just shown up, uninvited, to their party.

"Then, let's pass the acid test," I continued, "by singing those songs as passionately as we would our favorites."

Silence, and a profound pause. Then a few, softly-spoken, uneasy suggestions were offered. Before the weekend was out, however, the suggestions came easier and faster. Some huddled to ask others about their preferences. The singing was never better.

Several weeks later, long after the points of my sermon were but faint memories (if that), people were still talking about the great worship times during that weekend. I heard comments: "I didn't realize how satisfying worship could be just by demonstrating love for God and others by intentionally refusing to please ourselves."[102]

101. Di Sabatino, "What's Wrong."

102. M. Lewis, "Can You Teach."

## Principle 11: Young and old need each other in the body of Christ.

### TRANS-GENERATIONAL WORSHIP

Young men and maidens, old men and children:
Let them praise the name of the LORD,
for his name alone is exalted. (Ps 148:12–13; cf. Titus 2:2–8)

## The Discman Syndrome[103]

A few years ago I drove five Christian teenagers to a ski camp. For the first hour or so, they visited and talked excitedly among themselves, and genuinely seemed to enjoy one another's fellowship. Then suddenly all the headphones went on, the Discmans started up, and five teenagers each retired to his or her world and music of preference. You see, one liked country, one liked rock, and I have no idea what the others were into. I must admit I was thankful to be spared having to listen to some of their preferred styles on the car stereo! But I couldn't help but notice how abruptly the fellowship stopped as each young person pursued his or her own musical taste.

It also occurred to me that this is what happens in many churches today. God has called us in Christ into one body (Eph 4:4), and the Spirit is the one who must make us one in all our diversity. The fellowship of the church is intended to be a laboratory where, guided by divine love, we learn to break down barriers (Eph 2:14) and recognize and enjoy the fact that in Christ what bonds us is far deeper and more significant than the trappings of generation, background, culture, and personal preference.

Yet in many churches, when it comes to corporate worship, we find a similar phenomenon to what I experienced in the car that day. Different segments of the body gather at different times, and perhaps even in different places, to pursue musical worship according to their own preferred style. The congregation is divided into musical affinity groups with the admitted purpose of giving people what they want, what they are comfortable

---

103. Obviously the "discman" is seriously outdated technology! But the application endures, regardless of the current form for accessing one's music.

with, and what is most meaningful to them. The melting-pot nature of the church gives way to homogeneous groupings that value choice over unity.

## Unity in Diversity

Can you imagine the early church structuring itself in that way? Surely there wouldn't have been separate services for Jews and for Greeks, for slaves and for free, though their backgrounds and hence their tastes would have undoubtedly shown much variety! What if Acts 2:41–47 had been written in this way?

> So then, those who had received his word were baptized; and there were added that day about three thousand souls.
>
> And they were continually devoting themselves to one of the four electives offered: the apostles' teaching, fellowship, the breaking of bread, or prayer.
>
> And half of those who believed were together, gathering in the temple court at the hour of prayer for traditional worship; and the believers rejoiced in the way things had always been done and in the general sobriety of the proceedings.
>
> And the other half of those who believed were breaking bread from house to house, engaging in new, exciting, and culturally relevant forms of worship with an upbeat heart.
>
> And they all praised God in the form most comfortable to them, and they had favor with some of the people. But others wondered what they truly had in common, since they were divided in what should have been their central unifying activity.

In Corinth Paul taught against the institutional recognition of factions within the church; far from advocating separate services for those of Paul, of Apollos, of Cephas, of Christ (1 Cor 1:12–13), he decried gathering under any banner but that of Christ alone.

It should also be pointed out that in areas of the world today where the church is persecuted, there are rarely any debates about worship styles; rather, God's people are deeply grateful simply for the opportunity to worship with other believers. May we learn from them! Our worship wars grow out of a complacency and arrogance to which we are susceptible because of our spiritual affluence.

Surely the unity of the body should be demonstrated and lived out in a congregation's corporate worship life. Surely the people of God should be challenged to join together as one body and to work towards a unified, corporate expression of praise to the Lord who wants them to be one (John 17:23). Surely the leadership of the church should wrestle with ways to bring the people together, not send them into separate enclaves with "separate but equal" worship forms and styles.

We should be under no illusion that such a pursuit will be easy. It will take much work and prayer on the part of the church leaders and those responsible for worship; most importantly, it will demand a mature response on the part of the people. Rather than vying for what they like or want, their goal must be the good of the whole body. But is that not what being the body of Christ is all about? Is that not how all people will recognize that we are Christ's disciples, from the love and deference we show for one another (John 13:35)? If the body is to "build itself up in love" (Eph 4:12), the area of worship will definitely test the progress of the church towards that goal!

And don't leaders have the right and indeed the responsibility to exhort the congregation to respond in a Christlike, body-edifying way? Sometimes pastors and other church leaders are afraid that if they ask too much of their people—even Christian maturity!—some will become disillusioned and offended and leave for another, less demanding church home. Perhaps we should welcome such departures!

## Blended Worship for a Blended Body?

The fact that the body of Christ is by definition *blended*, not homogeneous (Gal 3:28), might perhaps suggest a direction for our worship. A blended style of worship, which pulls songs and other materials from a wide variety of styles and sources (and historical periods), and which artfully synthesizes them into a tasteful whole, would seem to be one way forward. That will look different from congregation to congregation, and will require a lot of work by gifted and biblically informed musicians, guided by an understanding leader who is firmly committed to the spiritual goal of unified congregational worship. The result will probably need to be a good deal more integrated and complex than simply having different styles of worship represented at different parts of the service; that simply invites people to "check out" during the portion of the service that is not to their liking.

The diversity ideally should extend beyond merely generational preferences (Western traditional and contemporary idioms), and also include expressions of the faith from other lands and cultures, even languages (the "cross-cultural" aspect of worship, as we saw in the "Nairobi Statement" in ch. 38). The availability of these materials in our day is one effect of globalization for which we can truly be thankful.

It cannot be overemphasized that the ultimate goal is not to keep everyone happy. Of course, the goal is not to make them unhappy either! One key is that the people must *continually* be taught about the gravity and importance of what they're doing when they gather for worship, and the significance of moving forward in unity of heart and expression. The importance of this teaching is enormous. For we are redeemed, but not yet glorified, and we will always tend to seek out spiritual shortcuts that demand less effort and self-sacrifice on our part.

## Scaling the Discman Barrier: Corporate Worship in a Compartmentalized World

An encouraging development during our trip to ski camp came when one of the girls in the car plugged some portable speakers into her Discman in order to expose her friends to some of her favorite songs; others then took the opportunity to share some songs they particularly liked too. All of them seemed to be willing to extend themselves just a little over their accustomed boundaries of personal preference, in order to meet one another on some common ground. Shouldn't church be like this?

Of course, at this point I became an involuntary participant also, for up until this point I had retreated as well into my own world (in my case, a world of silence); so it was good for me to enter into this stretching experience too. But the main thing is that *fellowship was restored*, we came back together out of our separate worlds, and we were challenged to meet each other halfway as we learned from one another. *Isn't this what the Lord desires from his church?*

It has been maintained that diverse worship services are needed in a single church in order to serve as entry points into the church for different types of unbelievers. Certainly God can, and apparently has, blessed churches that have moved in that direction, and we should not presume to know what God may or may not choose to use or bless. But have we considered the impact on outsiders of a church that is striving, out of love for the Lord and for one another, to sacrificially grow together in unified worship for the good of the whole?[104]

One of my all-time favorite worship cartoons appeared in 1995 in the pages of *Leadership Journal*.[105] It showed an older woman complaining on the phone to a friend: "They're putting choruses in hymnbooks and projecting hymns onto the screen. It's getting so I can't remember what I'm not supposed to like!"

May God help us to *forget* what we're not *supposed to like!*

## A Parable

And he also told this parable to certain ones who trusted in themselves that their worship style was the only acceptable form:

"Four men went up into the temple to pray, two traditional music directors and two contemporary worship leaders. One of the music directors stood and was praying thus to himself, 'God, I thank thee that I am not like many other church musicians: untrained, unrefined, undignified, or even like these contemporary worship leaders. I program only the finest art music; I present only those works truly worthy of thee.'

"One of the contemporary worship leaders was standing off to the other side, praying like this: 'O Lord, I thank you that I am not like many other church musicians: stuffy, inhibited, stuck in a rut of boring and irrelevant music of the past. I present only the very latest songs and reach people where they're at.'

"In another corner the other music director and the other contemporary worship leader were kneeling and praying together. The music director prayed: 'Lord God, you know how easily the striving for artistic excellence can become idolatrous. When I use my gifts, may I always remember that they come from your hand, and that you delight in all the genuine gifts of worship that your children bring, in all their variety.' The worship leader prayed: 'God, I only know four chords on the guitar, and I am not a polished performer; but I thank you for your grace in allowing me to come near in worship, and for the privilege in leading others to your throne. Thank you for all the different ways that your people can praise you.'

---

104. See also Ron Man, "Biblical Case."

105. By illustrator Tim Liston, the cartoon can be accessed by subscribers at https://www.christianitytoday.com/pastors/2004/may-online-only/mixing-up-church-music-warriors.html. (I was not able to locate the cartoonist to get permission to reprint the cartoon here.)

"I tell you, these last two went away with their offerings of worship received by the Lord, rather than the others; for God is not so much concerned with the style of the musical gifts you bring, as he is with the humility of heart and genuineness of love with which you bring them."

*The one who eats is not to regard with contempt the one who does not eat, and the one who does not eat is not to judge the one who eats, for God has accepted him* (Rom 14:3).[106]

## Others' Observations

Tradition means giving votes to the most obscure of all classes, our ancestors. It is the democracy of the dead. Tradition refuses to submit to the small and arrogant oligarchy of those who merely happen to be walking about. All democrats object to men being disqualified by the accident of birth; tradition objects to their being disqualified by the accident of death. Democracy tells us not to neglect a good man's opinion, even if he is our groom; tradition asks us not to neglect a good man's opinion, even if he is our father.[107]

Some growth experts . . . have said those who pursue blended styles merely take turns "insulting different segments of the congregation." But we believe otherwise: blended styles are the result of shared sacrifice and spiritual maturity. Traditional congregations committed to outreach also must passionately communicate the concept that sacrifice always goes with spiritual maturity.[108]

There are two ways in which a tradition can be abused—either by neglect or by a slavish subservience. The Church which worships a God who was incarnate in human history cannot afford to neglect the heritage of that event; and a Church which worships the God who is a living Spirit cannot allow that heritage to become a dead letter of bondage.[109]

It is natural for us, as for past generations, to feel that "we are the people and wisdom will die with us," but nowhere is the operation of this prejudice so disastrous as in the public worship of God. An illustration of the function of tradition as an enlarger and liberator of our worship lies to hand in our hymnbooks. A

---

106. Ron Man, "Parable."
107. Chesterton, *Orthodoxy*, 64–65.
108. M. Lewis, "Can You Teach."
109. Read, "Reformation of Worship," 79.

hymnbook is a heritage, and within its pages we join an astonishing variety of Christian ancestry at worship.[110]

In our worship it isn't simply a matter of working out how to bring together the traditional with the contemporary. That is important, but it is equally important to ensure that the tradition is celebrated through the lens of the gospel, not uncritically, and that the contemporary is adopted by the same standards. What T. S. Eliot called the "easy commerce of the old and the new" is, as the poem in question ["Little Gidding"] makes clear, not achieved easily or without struggle; but it is there if we will work and pray at it. It isn't a matter of slavishly adopting a particular culture, whether that of Europe in the sixteenth or seventeenth century or of America in the twenty-first; nor is it a matter of slavishly renouncing the one or the other. It is not a matter of saying "this is what this congregation will be comfortable with"; who says you ought always simply to be comfortable in the presence of Almighty God? But nor is it a matter of "this is what this congregation needs to wake them up"; who says it is your place to shock and startle the people of God? There will be shocks, yes, and there will be the deep comfort of the familiar, and good liturgy, planned carefully week by week and year by year, will bring the two together so that they complement and reinforce each other and, most importantly, build up the worshippers in the knowledge and love of God and send them out refreshed for their kingdom-tasks in the world.[111]

Walt Gerber, pastor of the 5000-member Menlo Park Presbyterian Church in Menlo Park, California, calls the blended concept "negotiated sacrifice." Everybody gives a little and everybody gets a lot to keep the body of Christ together.[112]

The Church is the place where generational differences are to be transcended, not reinforced. Where ephemeral fashions and cultural distinctions are subsumed into an eternal perspective, into a kingdom which "endures from generation to generation" (Dan 4:34). Only a church which resists being merely of one generation can be relevant to them all.[113]

Dramatic statements can be made by worship leadership in churches and beyond. First of all, worship leaders of differing approaches could, because of convergent philosophy, talk to each

110. Read, "Reformation of Worship," 70.
111. N. T. Wright, "Freedom and Framework."
112. Attributed to Ken Carter.
113. Veith, "Through All Generations," 9.

other and even lead worship together, making a positive statement to congregations about focusing on God rather than style. A
second unifying gesture would be for younger worship leaders to
seek older, experienced leaders for mentorship. What a great in-
vestment it would be for experienced worship leaders to seek out
and offer to mentor younger leaders. Third, creative worship leaders of all generations could work together to develop convergent
worship elements. Great relationships, enhanced resources, and
inspiring worship elements would emerge from such efforts.[114]

Maintaining unity among the diversity of the church's membership requires that we defer to one another in love, being willing
to sing one another's music rather than insisting on the music
we most enjoy.[115]

The youth of the church will probably prefer a more contemporary style of worship than the older ones. The common solution to this cultural problem is to segregate the youth church
from the adult church. The psalms-hymns-and-spiritual-songs
paradigm begs for a different solution: unity within diversity.
This new paradigm allows the contemporary and the historic to
stand side by side and challenges our hearts to greater love. We
don't have to choose between being reverent or celebrative. Be
reverent and celebrative! Be objective and subjective! Structured
and spontaneous! Testimonial and theological![116]

When the people of God are seen worshipping in both the Old
and New Testaments, it is not by age grouping, marital status, spiritual maturity, or any other division—it is all of God's
people, regardless of differences, coming together to worship
the Lord. When you read of the worship that will happen at the
throne when Christ comes again, it is quite apparent there will
be unified worship focused on who God is.[117]

The church is most able to represent God's intention for the
world when the grand diversity of the human race is at least
partly exhibited in the community assembled at worship. The
purest worship is that which brings together old and young,
adults and children, boomers and gen-Xers and the generations
that bracket them at either end.[118]

---

114. Willmington, "Convergence."

115. Frame, *Contemporary Worship Music*, 28.

116. Gustafson, "Psalms, Hymns, Spiritual Songs," 36, 46.

117. J. Nelson, "Unity in Diversity."

118. Byars, *Christian Worship*, 109–10.

## Principle 12: These truths must be taught and retaught.

### TAUGHT WORSHIP

Finally then, brethren,
we request and exhort you in the Lord Jesus,
that as you received from us instruction as to how you ought
to walk and please God (just as you actually do walk), that you
excel still more.
(1 Thess 4:1)

The above principles need to be repeatedly taught, as we all have the tendency to return to our "default mode" of *what we want and what we like* when it comes to worship. We need to be constantly reminded of what worship is, how it happens, and Whom it is for!

There is a critical need for preaching and teaching on worship in the church.

### The Biblical Need

As we considered in ch. 7, the central question of human history is: *Whom are you going to worship?* Adam and Eve in their rebellion answered the question wrongly, turning instead to self-worship and the worship of created things (Gen 3:1–6; Rom 1:21–25); that is our legacy through Adam (Rom 5:12). Jesus Christ, on the other hand, answered the question rightly when he, himself tempted by Satan, said: "It is written, 'You shall worship the Lord your God and him only shall you serve'" (Matt 4:10). And through his redeeming work he has in turn made possible what A. W. Tozer termed the making of "worshipers out of rebels."[119]

Pastors must take the lead here.[120] And if they are to faithfully communicate the big picture and scope and trajectory of God's written revelation to their congregations, they must tackle the fundamental challenge and call of human history: the appropriate worship of our worthy God.

---

119. Tozer, *Worship*, 23.

120. And pastors' training must prepare them to meet the challenge outlined here: see appendix 4, "Outline for Teaching Worship."

That is pastors' highest calling: to call people to be what God is seeking: worshipers (John 4:23).

## The Theological Need

As we have seen in this book, the biblical paradigm for all of God's dealings with humankind takes on the form of *revelation* and *response*. God always takes the initiative to make himself known and to draw people into relationship with himself (*revelation*); but the cycle is not complete unless there is a complementary *response* on the part of the creature. Worship is in essence the totality of our grateful, obedient response to God's initiative in revelation and redemption.

The goal of preaching and teaching the Scriptures is not knowledge *about* God. Rather, it is to *know God* and to respond to him appropriately with a heart of love and worship. As John Stott puts it: "There should be no theology without doxology. . . . The true knowledge of God will always lead us to worship, as it did Paul. Our place is on our faces before him in adoration."[121]

## The Christological Need

Chapter 26 showed us that our worship is acceptable and pleasing to the Father not because of its quality or excellence or "up-to-dateness," but rather because of the excellence of the Son, in whose perfect offering of praise the Father takes great delight, and therefore in ours as well as it is subsumed and gathered up into Christ's own offering.

This grace-oriented, Christ-exalting, and unifying understanding of the power behind all true worship must be proclaimed loudly over the reigning cacophony behind so much practice of worship in our churches today—where marketing techniques, growth orientation, seeker-driven methods, and a worship-equals-singing posture have been winning the day.

---

121. Stott, *Romans*, 312.

## The Historical Need

Three historical factors have figured strongly into the neglect of worship in many Western churches in the twentieth century and into the twenty-first.

1. The neglect of preaching and doctrine in the church of the late Middle Ages, which gave rise to the Reformation. As so often is the case, the pendulum has swung to the other extreme, with an overbearing emphasis on teaching and preaching as the only important part of the service (which denies the fullness of the revelation-response paradigm of Scripture).

2. The reinforcement of this tendency through the American revivalism of the nineteenth century. In public evangelism meetings, music and singing were seen merely as preliminaries and preparation of the people for the "main event": the message. As James White has pointed out, this orientation was then imported into church services in the American free church as the normal pattern for worship.[122]

3. The evangelical movement of the twentieth century, where we see again the needed defense of the Scriptures, of doctrine, and hence of teaching and preaching in the church. The corporate praises of the people were again subjected to an inferior if not inconsequential position—as merely a warm-up for the evangelistic or expository message. Church and worship leaders need to espouse and model a proper balance of revelation and response in their approach to corporate worship.

## The Contemporary Need

The last several decades have seen an explosion of interest in, and focus on, worship in churches. But at the same time, worship has erupted out of its former benign neglect to become the leading hot button and center of controversy in the church today. What is desperately needed today is the teaching of a unified, trans-denominational, transcultural, biblical understanding of worship, coupled with a call to extend grace to others who may differ in their application of that understanding.

122. White, *Brief History*, 159–61.

## The Cultural Need

At issue in the current worship debates is the interface of worship and culture in the context in which a local church finds itself. The church dare not sell out to the surrounding culture, but cannot ignore it either. Like any art form, Christian worship allows for much creative expression but within defined parameters. The Bible gives those parameters as well as that freedom. This reflects the reality that "worship is the most universal [following unchanging biblical guidelines] and at the same time the most particular [embodying distinct cultural expressions] of the activities in which Christian communities engage."[123]

The New Testament does not give us a lot of specifics about how to do worship in the local congregation, but there are biblical principles (such as those outlined in this chapter) that can be drawn from the pages of Scripture to guide the leadership of local churches in fashioning biblically appropriate yet culturally meaningful expressions of worship. Pastors need to be "read up" and "prayed up" so that they will be able to lead the discussions about worship that will inevitably arise in their churches and guide the leadership in developing what form that church's expression will take within those biblical parameters.

## The Pastoral Need

There is a critical need for pastors to help their congregations to biblically navigate the treacherous worship waters of our day. There is a tremendous (and seemingly irreconcilable) diversity when it comes to people's tastes and preferences in worship. It is "every man for himself," as God's children ignore the biblical injunctions to "not insist on [one's] own way" (1 Cor 13:5); to "consider one another more important than yourself" (Phil 2:3); to "love one another with brotherly affection" (Rom 12:10a); and to "outdo one another in showing honor" (Rom 12:10b). In Byron Anderson's words, we have been "catechized by consumerism."[124]

As we considered in ch. 34, pastors must be "part of the solution, and not part of the problem" by:

1. Being worshipers themselves.

---

123. Erickson and Lindner, "Worship and Prayer," 23.
124. E. Byron Anderson, "Worship and Theological Education," 120.

2. Not abdicating their part in worship planning, leading, and evaluating to the musicians solely.

3. Guiding the church leadership through a careful study of both the biblical guidelines for worship and the corporate culture of their congregation; and then leading the way, in dialogue with the people, in helping the leadership to chart a course for that church's worship life.

4. Being diligent to preach and teach on worship: reminding the people that worship is for God, not for their own entertainment or fulfillment; and calling them to apply biblical principles of church unity, mutual caring, and self-sacrificing love to the church's worship life—in defiance of the rampant individualism of our age that so infuses most of our debates about worship styles and forms.

## The Homiletical Need

According to John Piper:

> Preaching is not conversation. Preaching is not discussion. Preaching is not casual talk about religious things. Preaching is not simply teaching. Preaching is the heralding of a message permeated by the sense of God's greatness and majesty and holiness. . . . The Word of God is to come teaching the mind and reaching the heart; showing the truth of Christ and savoring the glory of Christ; expositing the Word of God and exulting in the God of the Word.[125]

That's why Piper defines preaching as "expository exultation." Preaching is in itself an act of worship and a modeling of worship.

## The Missiological Need

As seen before, John Piper has famously stated: "Missions is not the ultimate goal of the church. Worship is. Missions exists because worship doesn't."[126]

An important corollary understanding of this concept is to see the Great Commandment (Matt 22:35–40) as primary, and the Great Commission (Matt 28:18–20) as a hugely important means to that even greater end. (This idea was expanded on in ch. 9.) The love for God enjoined in

125. Piper, "Why Expositional Preaching."
126. Piper, *Let the Nations Be Glad*, 35.

the Great Commandment is vertical in its focus, purely God-centered and -directed, and is eternal in its scope (hence is, in fact, *worship*); the Great Commission, on the other hand, is by definition human-centered and -directed and (as Piper says about missions) "a temporary necessity."

In addition, we considered that the culmination of the discipleship process involves "teaching them to obey all that [Jesus] commanded [them]" (28:20), and that, according to Jesus himself, the *most important* of those commanded things is in fact the *Great Commandment*!

Hence the ultimate consummation of the Great Commission is teaching disciples to be wholehearted worshipers.

## The Personal Need

Pastors of course want to turn their people's hearts towards God. That means they must turn them towards *worship*. John Stott writes:

> If worship is right because God is worthy of it, it is also the best of all antidotes to our own self-centredness, the most effective way to "disinfect us of egotism," as one writer put it long ago. In true worship we turn the searchlight of our mind and heart upon God and temporarily forget about our troublesome and usually intrusive selves.[127]

As the Westminster Shorter Catechism puts it, "Man's chief end is to glorify God, and to enjoy him forever." God is seeking *worshipers* (John 4:23). That is what he wants first and foremost from every member of the congregation, and that must therefore be the pastor's highest goal.[128]

---

127. Stott, *Christian Basics*, 119.

128. Two other versions of this chapter's treatment of biblical principles of worship are in Ron Man, "Biblical Principles of Worship" and "Biblical Principles of Worship and Their Application." The latter version shows how each principle could be fleshed out in a church's worship (and, in fact, was written in the context of a particular church as an attempt to make specific applications of those principles to that congregation).

# 40

## SUMMARY AND BENEDICTION

### Our Gift to God

R ecommended is an insightful little children's book by Cathy Trzeciak called *Worship: Our Gift to God* (out of print, but used copies are available). The author reflects and summarizes simply and effectively many of the perspectives on worship that we have considered in this book (and summarized in ch. 39).[1]

The title of Trzeciak's book itself is instructive, and reflective of Principle 2 in ch. 39: "Worship is first and foremost for God." It cannot be repeated too often that most of our worship debates and arguments would fade away if we could truly take this principle to heart: worship is primarily *for God*, not for me!

Worship is always a ↑ *response* to God's ↓ *revelation*, a grateful reply to his gracious initiative in our lives. We praise and thank him for who he is, and for all that he has done for us and given to us in the Lord Jesus. It is *our gift to him* for all his good gifts to us!

---

1. The book emphasizes the centrality of worship as "one of the most important things mothers, fathers, boys, and girls can do" (ch. 12), and that "worship can happen anywhere [Principle 8] . . . because worship happens in your heart [Principle 9]" (Trzeciak, *Worship*, 21, 2).

## Benediction

Paul's words in Rom 15:5–6 express beautifully this author's prayer for all of you who have made it through this study, as you go forth as students and teachers and leaders of worship, and as worshipers:

> May the God of endurance and encouragement
>> grant you to live in such harmony with one another,
>> in accord with Christ Jesus,
> that *together* you may *with one voice*
> *glorify the God and Father of our Lord Jesus Christ.*

---

Worship is our gift to God.

---

# Appendix 1

## THINK BEFORE YOU SPEAK!

W orship is a time to address God, to respond to his gracious initiative in our lives with appropriate expressions of praise, adoration, thanksgiving, confession, and joy. The responsibility of the worship leader (and the worship team, or the choir) is to facilitate the process of inviting people into God's presence with their sacrifices of praise; to ease the process by which people connect with the living Christ in the midst of our worship, and then to *get out of the way*!

Our leadership role is fairly obvious in the realm of our musical offerings of praise. I would like to address the issue of what we should and should not *say* when leading worship.

We need to be very careful that the words we speak really enhance and further the purpose for which we have gathered: that is, *worship*. Too much patter and "filler" can get in the way of the people's single-minded focus on God, and can lead to a more human-centered time that leaves the worship leader at the center of attention (which should be the *last* thing we want!). Enthusiasm is one thing; but we don't need to be cute, we don't need to compliment them when they sing well nor harangue them when they don't, we don't need to be an entertainer or a cheerleader or an instructor: we need to be one who *models* an attitude of worship before the people, and who lovingly and gently points them towards God.

A few things to keep in mind when it comes to what we say when leading worship:

1. *We may speak to the people on behalf of God.* Indeed, that is the sobering role in which we as worship leaders find ourselves. What then would God have us say?

God would have us communicate his *word* to his people. Many churches use shockingly little Scripture in their services, including those churches that profess to hold the highest view of the word of God. And yet the truth is that we gather for worship at the invitation and command of the word; the word provides the authority and the substance and the framework for our worship; and if we are going to worship him in truth at all, we must find that truth in Jesus Christ (who *is* the Truth), as he is revealed and presented to us in the pages of the Bible.

In this light, a Call to Worship is anything but outdated. Indeed, it is (whether read, or sung, or prayed) an acknowledgment that we have come to worship God by and through and with his word, for any other source would simply be a pooling of our fallen ignorance.

What do we possibly have to say that can come anywhere near the significance of "This is the word of the Lord"? Ligon Duncan is known for insisting that we should "read the Bible, preach the Bible, pray the Bible, sing the Bible and see the Bible [in the Lord's Supper]."[1]

We need to bring all of our creativity to bear on ways to incorporate more and more of Scripture into our services. And we need to choose our words well, taking advantage of the opportunity to communicate God's revelation—which can only enrich our worship.

2. *We may also speak to God on behalf of the people.* We can lead in prayers of praise and contrition and trust and petition, though much of people's response to God in the service will come in the form of corporate expressions, both sung and spoken.

3. *Avoid stating the obvious!* Too much verbal instruction as to the logistics of the service can distract the worshiper's attention away from God.

In fact, most verbal instructions given in worship are superfluous and unnecessary. For instance, when a song text is flashed up on the screen, will not people assume that they are about to sing that song without being told, "And now we'll sing . . ."? Let's give our people a little

---

1. Duncan, "Foundations," 65.

credit! Let the instrumental introduction begin without a verbal cue, and the flow of worship will be enhanced considerably.

If your congregation uses a bulletin, first see that the ushers ensure that everyone gets one, and then go through the service as it is laid out in the bulletin with a minimum of extraneous verbal guidance. As long as the hymn numbers are there in print, let the instruments set the stage without the leader's litany of "Now let's turn to page number . . ." They really can figure that one out, if they are following along!

Often I have directed the congregation even in a round (such as "You Are My All in All") without a set of verbal instructions (about who sings what when), merely by using large gestures that clearly communicated to the congregation which half of them was to come in at which point.

It is amazing how much the flow[2] and focus of worship can be improved by just letting one thing happen after another—not without preparation or guidance, but with carefully planned alternatives to verbal cues that disturb the continuity.

The greatest compliment I have ever gotten as a worship leader (alas, only twice, I believe) was that *I seemed to disappear*, and *the people saw only Jesus*. That's what we want to happen! And the above hints are just some practical ways to get out of the way and let the Spirit carry our worship.

*Note*: A dear friend, who is blind, reacted to this article by pointing out that for visually impaired people, verbal cues may be the *only* way they have to know what is going on. So I would adjust my comments and recommend that the leader be extremely sensitive to the presence, or possible presence, of such people. Still, the principle would hold of making even verbal instructions brief, to the point, and well thought through.

---

2. See Man, "Flow, Service, Flow."

# Appendix 2

## WHOSE GATHERING IS IT, ANYHOW?
### *Why God Should Have the First Word*

Robert Nordling tells a story about taking his five-year-old son, Jackson, to a young friend's birthday party: All dressed up, brimming with enthusiasm, Jackson rushes into his friend's house to join the festivities. But when his father arrives to pick him up after the party, Jackson looks dejected. "What's the matter, Jackson?" asks his father. "Didn't you enjoy the party?" The answer is a terse no. "But you were looking forward to this party so much! Why didn't you have fun?" Jackson answers, "I didn't get any presents!" To which Dad can only reply, "But Jackson, it wasn't *your* party!"

The lesson Nordling draws from that exchange is this: worship is, so to speak, *God's* party, not ours. And we come primarily not to *receive* (though we certainly do that also), but to *give* to God the presents of our faith, our gratitude, our praise, our confession, and the commitment of our hearts.

God is simultaneously the inviter, the host, and the guest of honor at our worship services. Worship, after all, is God's idea, not ours.

How should that affect how we approach worship, and how we begin worship? We need to recognize that *all* of our movement toward God occurs because God acts first. After all, it is God:

- Who created us

- Who made us able to respond to him as creatures to their Creator

- Who has revealed himself to us through the pages of Scripture, through creation, and through his Son, Jesus Christ

- Who has given us salvation through Christ and drawn us into relationship with himself

## God Initiates

God always initiates; we can only respond. And our primary response is worship. In worship we respond in praise to the glory and greatness God has revealed to us; we respond with thanksgiving for the saving grace God has lavished upon us; we respond in wonder and delight to the relationship God has initiated with us.

Even our response to God depends not on our own strength but on the Holy Spirit working in us. "Are you so foolish?" Paul asks the Galatian believers. "Having begun by the Spirit, are you now being perfected by the flesh?" (Gal 3:3). The obvious answer to Paul's rhetorical question is, of course not! We are saved through the sanctifying work of the Spirit, and we can't be perfected through our own effort! (Paul indicates that it would be foolish for the Galatians even to entertain that thought.) As believers we are in continual need of the Spirit to grow in righteousness and, indeed, to do anything that is truly pleasing to God—including worshiping him.

## God Invites

Our worship is an obedient response to God's invitation. We may invoke God to bless our worship and to make his presence known. But in a greater sense we cannot invite God to be present in our worship. He is always present; we're the ones who stray! Rather, it is God who invites *us* to worship. It is his word that tells us, "Come, let us worship and bow down" (Ps 95:6).

God has revealed himself to us and has established a relationship with us by his power and grace. God delights in that relationship and desires (and deserves) our worship as a means of affirming and strengthening our relationship with him. "Worship the LORD with gladness," says the psalmist, "come before him with joyful songs" (Ps 100:2). Coming to

God is not an option for Christians but rather our obedient response to God's gracious invitation.

The work of Christ has opened the way for us to come into God's presence, as the book of Hebrews makes clear (4:16; 7:19, 25). The writer exhorts us to take full advantage of the free access to the Father that Christ has made available: "Let us draw near to God" with confidence, assurance, and faith (10:22). Our living High Priest has not only made the way clear through his blood (vv. 19–20), but actively leads us (v. 21) into fellowship with God.

## Implications

Those truths have profound implications for how we "come to God in worship." So how should we respond to God's invitation?

Many worship services either begin with some innocuous words of greeting by the worship leader—focused on the weather or on the size of the crowd or on the pleasure the leader has in seeing the people gathered—or else the service launches right into songs written about or to God.

But the question is, *who deserves the first word in worship?* Who deserves to be heard first? That question takes us back to the question of whose gathering it is. The fact is, we have been invited and ushered by God himself into his holy presence. God has taken the initiative and paid the cost. God is the Host of this gathering, the Subject and the Object of our worship. God is the main event, our purpose for gathering.

God doesn't "show up" at worship, as the popular catchphrase goes. Although it's obviously intended to communicate a vivid sense of fellowship with God, let's be careful about suggesting both that God was somewhere else and that we did something to bring him close! As Steve Fry puts it:

> I'm concerned that some of us have perceived worship as a spiritual talisman we employ to get God to show up, rather than seeing worship as a simple response to His grace. . . . If we perceive worship as a mechanism that triggers His presence, we'll inadvertently focus on the act of worship itself instead of the One we are worshiping—worshiping worship if you will.[1]

---

1. Fry, "Unity, Worship, and Presence."

Since God is the Inviter, the Host, and the Honoree, shouldn't we hear first from him? Isn't it infinitely appropriate to hear a word of invitation and welcome and testimony from God himself as the One who has made our gathering both possible and meaningful? Let us hear first from God through his word, and *then* respond to him with our songs, prayers, and words of praise.

## A Biblical Pattern

If we give God the first word, then our worship will reflect the biblical pattern of all God's dealings with humanity. This pattern, evident throughout Scripture, can be represented thus:

### Revelation    Response

God always takes the first step to reveal himself and to initiate a relationship with his creatures; our part is always to respond to God's first move. In our worship, it is ultimately true that until God first speaks to us we have nothing to say to him. We cannot respond appropriately until we have heard something to respond *to*!

This pattern should be incorporated not only at the beginning of the service but throughout as an alternating rhythm of revelation and response, so that our worship becomes a true *dialogue* between God and his people. (An interesting exercise is to take an outline of your worship service and put a down or up arrow beside each element to indicate whether in that part of the service God is speaking to us or we are responding to him; horizontal arrows can also indicate those times when we are speaking to each other for our mutual edification.)

The word can provide a God-centered, divinely focused transition between songs or parts of the service. Consider the difference between these two transitions:

And now we're going to sing "Holy, Holy, Holy." Let's all sing out!

*or*
In the words of Isaiah 6:3, "Holy, holy, holy is the LORD of hosts;
the whole earth is full of his glory!" (followed by singing)

Which is a more powerful lead-in? Which is more likely to enhance the flow of worship and the worshipers' concentration?

We need to hear from God more than God needs to hear from us. And while God deserves and desires and relishes the praises of his people, how much more fervent and heartfelt those praises will be when they are fueled by God's own self-revelation!

Let's honor God and his gracious invitation by always letting him have the first word.

# APPENDIX 3

## MUSIC FOR WORSHIP
### Excellence as a Means Rather Than an End

E xcellence is called for in all of our human endeavors: "Whatever you do in word or deed, do all to the glory of God" (Col 3:17). God is glorified in our creative endeavors when we give of our very best, for our best reflects most closely (though, of course, in a very faint shadow) the image of the One who in his creative acts bestowed on us that image, including the ability to create (undoubtedly the most "Godlike" attribute that a creature can possess).

Actually, all creative activity glorifies God, even that which is poorly or sloppily done, for even our most slovenly effort is infinitely above any random or accidental juxtaposition of raw materials by irrational forces: intention, even of the most misguided sort, bespeaks intelligence and personality. Even the decision to give less than one's best is a divinely enabled response of inestimable wonder, a moral choice of which only God's choicest creations are capable.

But obviously the relatively closer we attain to his standards of beauty and quality and efficiency and exactitude (however many light-years from perfection we inevitably remain), the truer we are to the divine spark within us. Excellence becomes him who is of infinite excellencies!

How much more should these things be true when the creative activities in question are those directly related to the corporate worship of God by his people, when the endeavors speak explicitly and obviously of

God himself, and seek to communicate directly his special revelation and to proclaim overtly his very nature? Then, of all times, we should marshal our greatest concentration, talent, effort and consistency. Certainly a meeting with the Sovereign of the universe deserves as much considered preparation, dignity, and attention as that important job interview, that dinner party, that joyful wedding!

Music is a gift of God specially designed and ideally suited as a vehicle for the praise and adoration of God, and God deserves the very best musical expressions to be lifted up in his honor on the lips of his dear children. The creative act in the making of music for worship in fact parallels very closely the never-ending business of heaven, which is likewise musical worship (Rev 5:9–10). "Music *for* worship" says it all: the end is worship, and the means is music.

But the closer a creation is to God, the greater its potential for evil and idolatry if diverted short of its divine focus (witness Lucifer). And music can all too easily become an idol if the desire for excellence in its performance becomes an end in itself. Even the word *performance* is dangerous, as it implies something presented for an audience that is less proficient in that particular field. In worship, music is *offered* (by the congregation, or on behalf of the congregation) rather than *performed*; it is offered to the One who thought it all up in the first place, to the One who gave it to his creatures that they might with gratitude return it to him. We should offer the best we can (none less than the best of the flock was demanded for sacrifice in the Old Testament); yet, as also in the Old Testament, the heart attitude of the one offering the sacrifice of praise is of far more significance and value to God than the quality of the sacrifice itself. The true end of worship music is the satisfaction and pleasure of One who graciously and gladly receives such gifts, as does the parent who cherishes the intrinsically worthless present from a child because of the expression of relationship and love inherent in that act of giving (to use C. S. Lewis's analogy).

So by all means, let us be careful never to enter into the presence of our transcendent and holy God with musical offerings that are hastily prepared or lazily executed. But let us likewise be careful to realize that all of our best preparation and execution are but widows' mites dropped into the Master's treasury, which he nonetheless welcomes and cherishes.

May we strive to offer to God our musical sacrifices of praise with excellence, and may we be transported by such means to the heavenly end of worship!

# APPENDIX 4

## AN OUTLINE FOR TEACHING WORSHIP IN EVANGELICAL SEMINARIES[1]

T he following is an attempt at a wholistic consideration of the place of worship in the seminary program. While real progress has been made in some areas since the detailed studies of James F. White cited below (now quite dated), yet the need remains in many institutions for a more foundational and thorough commitment to *doxology* as the indispensable partner to *theology*.[2] For, as White puts it, "It is absurd to certify graduates as equipped for pastoral ministry who have not been forced to think through rigorously the Church's most important activity."[3]

This suggested plan develops three basic areas:

1. Overall *emphasis* given to worship in the school

2. *Instruction* in worship provided to the students

3. *Experience* in worship made available to the students

1. Adapted from Ronald E. Man, "Dallas Seminary Worship Education," where a fuller treatment can be found.

2. "No theology without doxology" (Stott, *Romans*, 311). Consider also the perspective of Geoffrey Wainwright (from his full title onward) in his study *Doxology: The Praise of God in Worship, Doctrine and Life; a Systematic Theology*.

3. White, "Teaching of Worship," 317.

## Overall Emphasis

## A Doxological Purpose

L. Gregory Jones has placed theological education within a broader framework:

> Although the formation of Christian leaders is the special focus of theological education, its ability to achieve even this special purpose can only be strengthened when theological education is itself understood as one movement within the faithful formation and education of the entire church for the doxological praise of God.[4]

It is important that the seminary recognize *and articulate* its overriding doxological purpose. That means that the school's purpose, vision, or mission statement should be clearly God-centered, and focus on the glory of God as the ultimate aim of the institution. Many schools opt instead for a statement that is more goal-oriented or pragmatic in nature; or sometimes even in schools that have a more God-directed focus statement, it is downplayed or "assumed" in favor of proclaiming more immediate goals.[5] In either case, Piper cautions us against assuming a doxological purpose silently and articulating instead more immediate or pragmatic purposes and goals; and he sees this on the level of the school's program as well:

> God doesn't like being taken for granted in any course, in any syllabus, in any seminar, in any workshop. . . . God means to be public: "Whether you eat or drink or whatever you do"—whatever course, whatever workshop, whatever seminar, whatever book, whatever article—"do all to the glory of God." Do not neglect the explicit honoring of God in everything you do.[6]

It is appropriate to desire to minister to people, and to train students to go out and minister to others. But that is a means to an end: ultimately it is all for God and his glory. Every seminary (and every church) must articulate a God-centered goal for its existence. It is God's glory that is of

---

4 L. Gregory Jones, "Beliefs, Desires, and the Ends of Theological Education," in Volf and Bass, *Practicing Theology*, 205.

5. Of course, many churches do this with their mission statements as well: articulating a vital yet *secondary* goal, such as "to fulfill the Great Commission," rather than focusing on the ultimate importance of bringing glory to God thereby.

6. Piper, "Training the Next Generation."

paramount importance over anything else—and that perspective must be expressly stated over and over. It is *God* and his purposes we serve in the seminary.

Quite simply, worship must be a central focus in the *seminary* because it is a central focus of the *church*, as Frank Senn expounds:

> But we would also like to assert, both theologically and practically, that everything the Church is and does comes to focus in the liturgy. It is the place where the Church is realized and is visibly seen doing its thing. It is the place where the reality of the Kingdom of God and the eschatological presence of Christ is known, thereby altering our perception of the rest of life and the world around us since we have seen it redeemed in the sacramental celebrations. It is the one place where the fruits of evangelism, education, social ministry and stewardship are collected, offered, transformed, and activated—simultaneously.[7]

Seminaries will faithfully serve the church only if they focus on issues that are relevant and indeed vital to the latter's life and faith:

> The ultimate context of theological education is worship: we reach toward maturity "by meditating on the fact that God is the only one; that the fear of God is the only fear worth having. . . . The central question, in the classroom as well as everywhere else, and even in thinking about the curriculum, is that we come back to the fact that we are expected to know, understand, and love that which has to do with God."[8]

## Worship and Prayer in Every Class

These activities should not be limited to the Practical or Pastoral Theology department, but rather be the atmosphere in every class and every course. The clear message from every professor should be: "We're here to honor the God who is the subject matter of this course." God is to be glorified not just later, when the graduate takes the material out and applies it in ministry—but right here, right now. God means to be honored in the present, "whether we eat or drink or whatever we do." No seminary class should appeal to the head only without taking the heart

7. Senn, "Teaching Worship in Seminaries," 332.

8. Krister Stendahl, "Formation in Theological Education," 32, cited in TeSelle, "Between Athens and Jerusalem," 92.

into account—that would result in an unbiblical dichotomy: "What God has joined let no one put asunder."

## A Worship Response to Truth

Out of the immediately preceding flows the insistence that seminary professors train themselves, and train their students, to always complete the revelation-response (theology-doxology) cycle, making a worship response to truth. Truth unresponded to is not worth much: James says even the demons have the facts straight, that God is one (Jas 2:19); but of course there is no heart response, and that makes all the difference for time and eternity. Revelation always demands a response; theology requires doxology. John Stott quotes Handley Moule: "We must beware equally of an undevotional theology and an untheological devotion."[9]

Kevin Vanhoozer points out:

> Our worship should sharpen our theology, just as our theology should sharpen our worship. Of all the ugly ditches to which we are exposed in seminary education—the ditch between the biblical and theological studies, between theory and practice, between the seminary and the church—none is uglier than the ditch between theology and worship.[10]

Similarly, John Witvliet sees the need in theological education "to overcome the idea that devotional vitality and rigorous learning live in opposition—an opposition unwittingly promoted not only by devotional literature that lacks theological precision, but also by theological teaching and writing that avoids devotional engagement."[11]

Wayne Grudem's *Systematic Theology* exemplifies the wedding of doxology to theology by ending each chapter with a hymn or song of response to the subject of that chapter. If seminary professors can be striving towards balancing theology and devotion in their own lives as well as in their teaching, and be teaching their students to do so, how much healthier will our congregations be!

9. Stott, *Romans*, 312.
10. Vanhoozer, "Worship at the Well," 14.
11. Witvliet, "Teaching Worship."

## Dialogue and Debate

The academy is the place for fresh yet historically rooted discussions concerning vital elements of our faith and practice. This is especially needed in our day in the area of worship; far too often discussions about worship occur merely on the level of styles, tastes, and preferences. Seminaries need to encourage and support healthy academic discussions of various views of and approaches to worship; churches will be all the stronger if the academy provides them with pastors whose understanding of worship has been forged through rigorous engagement with a variety of viewpoints, and who have learned to wield all the exegetical and hermeneutical tools at their disposal to the issues of worship.[12] Frank Senn speaks to this need for interdepartmental engagement with questions of worship.

> We need to take seriously how interdisciplinary our discipline [liturgics] is. We need to know what kind of research is being done in biblical studies, in church history, in constructive theology, and in pastoral theology. We also have contributions to make to our colleagues, reminding them that the sources of cultic data run deep, beyond reason and through the senses, to lay hold on a person totally. Here too are needs which the Church's ministry must meet in ways which may not have been considered before. Perhaps the most urgent professional need, apart from getting liturgiologists appointed to seminary and divinity school faculties, is to open up dialogue between the professor of worship and other members of the faculty. Seminaries do a disservice to ministry students by compartmentalizing each theological discipline. After all, the pastor is expected to draw upon his or her whole theological reservoir in the exercise of ministry. Some aspect of exegetical theology may be needed in a counseling situation. An approach to systematic theology may be needed in an educational forum. Competence in pastoral care may be needed in preparing a sermon. Knowledge of church history may be needed at a church board or committee meeting. Preparing for and presiding in liturgy may require all of the above. There are ways in which the worship professor may

12. This purpose is behind the stated mission of the Biblical Worship section of the Evangelical Theological Society: "The Biblical Worship Section is a forum for evangelical scholarship that analyzes the practice of Christian worship from historical, biblical-theological, and pastoral/practical perspectives. . . . The section aims primarily to encourage and model academic study that supports renewal and reform in the worship of evangelical churches and promotes education about worship in evangelical institutions" (https://etsworship.wordpress.com/about/).

need to demonstrate this in the classroom. Hopefully those in
other disciplines will take liturgical data with equal seriousness
in their own classroom.[13]

## A Balanced, Integrated Curriculum

The ideal is not simply a course or courses inserted into the offerings of
the Practical or Pastoral Theology department; such relegation belies the
foundational importance of worship to the entire course of study in the
seminary. Rather, a more organic effort "to integrate the teaching of worship into the total curriculum"[14] should be aspired to, as a natural outgrowth of and corollary to the institution's overall doxological purpose:

> The foremost element of seminary education today is the dis-
> covery of the full dimensions of Christian worship. . . . Both
> Word and Sacrament, both liturgy and life, both confession of
> sin and confession of faith, both doxology and self-sacrifice,
> both the heart and the head.[15]

This aim of integration also fits well with the seminary's goal of
developing balanced pastoral leaders: "An interdisciplinary approach to
worship is necessary since [they are] forming presiders of worship and
not detached 'experts' in the field of liturgics."[16]

This integration is, sadly, rarely attempted, much less achieved. In
this area Catholics have cast the vision better:

13. Senn, "Teaching Worship in Seminaries," 331–32.

14. White, "Teaching of Worship," 308.

15. R. Nelson, "Seminary—Academy and Chapel," 59.

16. Krosnicki and Gurrieri, "Seminary Liturgy Revisited," 167. To Robert Webber, besides integration is also needed what is, in essence, a little more respect: "The
recognition of worship as a legitimate discipline among the other disciplines . . . it is a
field in its own right" ("Evangelical and Catholic Methodology," in Johnston, *Use of the
Bible*, 140). And indeed, the field of worship itself is by its very nature uniquely interdisciplinary and integrative. Webber remarks: "Indeed it is an interdisciplinary study
demanding expertise in biblical, historical, and systematic theology as well as the arts,
practical expertise, and personal formation" ("Evangelical and Catholic Methodology,"
in Johnston, *Use of the Bible*, 140); White agrees: "The most fascinating thing for me
about the teaching of worship in a seminary is the integrating quality of the subject in
combining theory and practice including several types of theory: theological, historical, scriptural, and sociological. I know of no other seminary discipline that functions
in such a fully integrative fashion" (White, "Teaching of Worship," 309).

53. To achieve greater progress in liturgical study more than a little help will come from its coordination with other disciplines, as the Second Vatican Council recommends. Thus for example, in treating especially the doctrine and practice of the sacraments, there ought to be close cooperation between the liturgy professor and the professors of dogma, moral, and canon law. There should be frequent conversations to foster a fruitful common spirit with everyone working together for the same end in order to avoid frequent repetition of the same things, and, indeed, to avoid contradicting each other.

54. In arranging the class schedule for the theological courses, it would be desirable, if possible, to treat liturgical questions at the same time that theological questions on similar issues are being taught. For instance, at the time that ecclesiology is taught, the liturgy classes would explain the theological nature of the praying Church, and so forth.[17]

Seminaries should give careful thought and study into ways to bring a more holistic approach and more worship emphasis to the educational process:

A further hope is the clarification of the liturgical aspects of other disciplines, especially in biblical, historical, and theological fields. This will come in time as other faculty members explore these dimensions of their work. Books such as Geoffrey Wainwright's *Doxology: The Praise of God in Worship, Doctrine and Life* aid considerably. But it also necessitates that liturgical scholars become more knowledgeable about other fields, too. Bridges are usually built from both banks. Surprisingly, some of the most difficult bridges to build are to the practical fields. It is often harder to convince the people teaching pastoral care, Christian education, evangelism, and even preaching that worship is the heartbeat of what they espouse than it is to relate to the theologians. Aspects of ministry are usually taught in watertight compartments and then students are expected to combine them all in ministry. Yet, faculty cannot even talk to each other intelligently about each other's disciplines. But those bridges must be built so students can see worship as an integral part of all their entire work of ministry.[18]

---

17. Congregation for Catholic Education, "Instruction on Liturgical Formation," pt. 2b, §§53–54.

18. White, "Teaching of Worship," 318.

## Instruction in Worship

## Courses

Along with the integration of worship into the overall curriculum in an organic way, there is still a place for specialized courses in worship. Thus White asserts:

> Courses in worship need to be taught and made available to all ministerial students. That may seem obvious to liturgical scholars but not necessarily to other faculty members, as my survey shows. Furthermore, even in many institutions where worship is taught, a majority of students do not take such courses. . . .
>
> It is absurd to certify graduates as equipped for pastoral ministry who have not been forced to think through rigorously the Church's most important activity. The minimum necessity is that the study of worship be presented as far more than just an option for students who fancy such a thing, as is currently the case at some distinguished ecumenical, Methodist, Presbyterian, and Free Church seminaries.[19]

In other words, it is not enough to make electives in worship studies available in the curriculum. Required courses must be built into the program. White's survey in 1981 (covering the full range of ATS schools in the US and Canada) found the following situation:

> Most seminaries (113 schools or 73%) reach a large majority of students with one or more courses while another 13 (8%) reach a small majority with one or more such courses. Yet there still remain 29 (19%) seminaries, or almost one-fifth, where from about half to no students receive courses in worship. In these cases, including some very distinguished schools, knowledge and skill in worship leadership evidently are not seen as essential to ministry.[20]

It is doubtful that the statistics would be that favorable, even today, in evangelical seminaries, though positive strides have been made in some schools. The higher regard for expository preaching in most of those institutions may still work against the proper value being placed on worship in the minds and in the preparation of those preparing for pastoral ministry. Because of the priority of worship in all life and ministry,

19. White, "Teaching of Worship," 317.
20. White, "Teaching of Worship," 307.

seminarians need to have a thorough grounding in and understanding of worship if they are to serve effectively in the future—especially in the pastorate. There should be therefore, at the very least, one worship course required of all seminarians.

## Course Content

This course (or, preferably, these courses) should include instruction on the biblical teachings on worship (precepts and principles); an overview of the history of Christian worship and liturgy; contemporary case studies for discussion and exercises in enculturating worship practices; and the construction of a personal pastoral philosophy of worship. White suggests the following approach:

> What I consider to be essential information for seminarians in the theological and historical aspects of worship is in print elsewhere so I shall be brief here. It is amazing the amount of convergence we now recognize on what all ministerial students need to know. It seems to me that this includes the history and theology of five items: initiation rites, the liturgical year, the Eucharist, the divine office, and rites of passage. . . . To this I would add instruction in a general theology of worship, sacramental theology in general, and a broad knowledge of the cultic arts, architecture, and pastoral music. I believe some familiarity with these areas is essential equipment for everyone preparing for pastoral ministry. Needless to say, such is often far from present reality.[21]

Along with biblical and historical foundations, there are practical issues that must be dealt with as well. Because of the rapid growth of worship focus, resources, and importance in the church in the last decades, there are some very real opportunities and very real challenges, and students need to be prepared for what some of these are likely to be out in the pastoral ministry. It is an oft-quoted truism that more people select a new church today because of the music than because of the preaching. Pastors-in-training need to be prepared to navigate the potentially treacherous waters of relating to worship staff and the needs and wants of different generations and constituencies.

---

21. White, "Teaching of Worship," 317.

A very helpful resource for elucidating the challenges and the dynamics of interfacing a church's worship with its cultural context is the "Nairobi Statement on Worship and Culture," which was produced by the World Lutheran Federation in 1996. The essence of the statement is as follows:

> Christian worship relates dynamically to culture in at least four ways:
> First, it is *transcultural*, the same substance for everyone everywhere, beyond culture.
> Second, it is *contextual*, varying according to the local situation (both nature and culture).
> Third, it is *counter-cultural*, challenging what is contrary to the Gospel in a given culture.
> Fourth, it is *cross-cultural*, making possible sharing between different local cultures.[22]

Much helpful discussion, debate, and creative thinking could go into a classroom consideration of the implications of applying these four aspects of worship in an integrated way in the local church.

John Witvliet advocates a spiritually holistic approach to worship courses:

> In the past, many worship courses functioned as a kind of introduction to liturgical studies. Yet while introducing students to the vocabulary, methods, and key concepts in liturgical studies is a worthy goal, it is both possible and beneficial to aspire to more. . . . A worship professor is not primarily interested in producing worship professors or liturgical critics but rather worshipers (and, in seminary teaching, pastors and worship leaders) who participate in worship more fully, actively, and consciously as part of a vital, faithful Christian life.[23]

### Course Instructors

James White, writing in the 1980s, gave this assessment of the staffing of worship courses in seminaries:

22. Lutheran World Federation's Study Team on Worship and Culture, "Nairobi Statement."

23. Witvliet, "Teaching Worship."

> For the majority of those teaching worship, it is a secondary discipline. . . . This probably means, in all too many instances, that worship is still a stepchild taught in someone's spare time.[24]

> Beyond the development of scholarship about worship is the need to make the study of worship a vital part of the seminary preparation of future ministers. The great evangelical seminaries have developed impressive faculties in recent years, yet not a single one has on its faculty a person who has completed Ph.D. studies in Christian worship. Until such scholars are trained, worship will either not be taught at all or will be taught by people who have not done advanced study of their subject. Seminaries would hardly tolerate such a situation in ethics, New Testament, or pastoral counseling. A genuine commitment of people and resources is necessary.[25]

This situation has definitely changed for the better, but there is still much room for improvement—especially in the area of full-time, fully credentialed teachers of worship in a course of study required of all (or at least most) of the student body. Once again, Catholics seem to be further ahead in their thinking:

> 51. So that all this will be correctly taught, there ought to be in each seminary a special professor suitably prepared to teach liturgy. As far as possible he should have had his preparation in an institute which has this special purpose. He should have studied theology and history and ought to understand pastoral reality as well as being endowed with a sense of the public prayer of the Church. He should well understand that his work is not simply scientific and technical, but rather "mystagogical," so that he may introduce the students into the liturgical life and into its spiritual character.[26]

Seminaries must look at their staffing plans and build in the acquisition of full-time specialists in worship whenever possible. More and more opportunities are developing for advanced worship studies, so that worship specialists may be available for hire—though careful consideration must be given to finding a person with an open mind and irenic spirit, as well as the requisite academic qualifications.

24. White, "Teaching of Worship," 315.

25. White, "Missing Jewel," 112–13.

26. Congregation for Catholic Education, "Instruction on Liturgical Formation," §51.

Where this is not possible, the development of faculty with a sub-specialty in worship (from the Bible or Theology department, perhaps) is also a feasible approach. In small schools and missions situations, it may be possible to bring in adjunct lecturers to give worship instruction; if no one is available locally, someone could come and teach in a modular format.

In all size schools, it would be valuable to bring in occasional guest lecturers to address the practical issues involving worship in today's churches. Ideal would be to have an effective pastor/worship pastor team come in and address the dynamics of working together.

*Preparation for Worship Teaching*

### Training

For those planning to teach in the area of worship, as well as for faculty members seeking to develop this as a subspecialty, there are an ever-increasing number of opportunities for training in worship. In the past, many evangelical worship scholars got their training in the PhD studies program in worship and liturgics at Notre Dame University.[27] The school has been very open and friendly towards evangelicals (the provost there at one point was himself a Protestant evangelical).

Real progress has been made in recent decades, and today there are many more options. Now there are numerous doctoral programs in worship studies (both PhD and DMin) at evangelical seminaries (not to mention at the bachelor's and master's levels). Both the Robert E. Webber Institute for Worship Studies and Liberty University provide a Doctor of Worship Studies (DWS) program (now accredited) aimed especially at those with MA or MM degrees in music.[28]

There are many online opportunities for further training in worship as well. In addition, there are some substantial conferences, notably the Calvin Institute of Christian Worship's annual Symposium on Worship.[29]

---

27. See www.nd.edu.
28. See www.iws.edu; www.liberty.edu.
29. See https://worship.calvin.edu.

## RESOURCES

Any Internet search will turn up an enormous scope and variety of resources on worship. This author's ministry website, www.worship-resources.org, contains a page of links to a large number of them, as well as an array of articles on worship and access to a free monthly online worship newsletter, *Worship Notes*.

The Calvin Institute of Christian Worship also has a rich trove of worship materials and information available at its website, as does the website of the Robert E. Webber Institute for Worship Studies.

## Experiences in Worship

There is an incredible potential for enhancing the spiritual life, worship understanding, and future ministry of students by exposing them to a wide spectrum of different worship styles, practices, and approaches.

## In the Classroom

As already mentioned, the seminary classroom should be a place where truth is not only learned, but also responded to. The professor, regardless of the course, should bring a worshipful attitude towards the course material, and communicate its content with an air of devotion and consecration. As Bishop Stephen Neill articulates it: "If [seminary professors] really took this as their first vocation—to be men and women of prayer, persons who really have access to the holy place—the students would catch it from them."[30] Time should be given in class for worship and prayer—not only at the beginning, but perhaps on occasion as an interruption to the lecture, when the subject matter may warrant it (as Paul bursts into doxology in Rom 11:33–36 after his profound exposition in the preceding eleven chapters).

The professor could extend this attitude to the coursework outside of class as well: for instance, by assigning journaling (allowing students to respond to the course matter being studied) or group devotional projects as part of the requirements for the course.

---

30. Groh, "Ecumenism's Past and Future," 572.

## In Chapel

It would be hard to overestimate "the chapel's significance for all those who are educating and being educated in theology."[31] Far from being an optional extra, or a distraction from or interruption in the seminary program, it should be seen as an integral part of the life of the institution, as Robert Duke maintains:

> The worship life of a seminary is a corporate activity involving the whole community: faculty and students together. In this sense, it is integral to the curriculum and ought not to be considered as an extracurricular function of some separate, pious group within the seminary.[32]

Similarly, Robert Nelson holds that "the chapel should surely inform the academy with the viewpoint, attitude, and appreciation of what is valid and valuable in the curriculum."[33]

For the seminary as a worshiping community (though not a church, we should hasten to add), the chapel performs a special function of providing a corporate venue for celebrating the God whose worth and glory are the subject and object and raison d'être of the institution. Vanhoozer states:

> Our corporate worship is a means for articulating, transmitting, and receiving the vision that we believe in and reflect on in the classroom. Chapel may be our last best hope for integrating what otherwise risks staying departmentalized. . . . Corporate worship . . . is . . . precisely what we need to sustain us during our sojourn in the groves of Academe.[34]

And chapel is also a vital link in the total formation of students in preparation for ministry, as Gregory Jones expresses:

> Seminaries need to attend to the process of forming students as much as, if not more than, the process of transmitting information to students. . . . One result of such an understanding might lead seminaries to become more attentive to the character and

---

31. R. Nelson, "Seminary—Academy and Chapel," 55.
32. Duke, "Seminary Worship," 42.
33. R. Nelson, "Seminary—Academy and Chapel," 59.
34. Vanhoozer, "Worship at the Well," 16.

quality of seminary-sponsored worship while also encouraging classroom study of Christian worship and prayer.[35]

The potential here is that of making "the experience of worship, so universal yet so particular, an essential element in a comprehensive program of formation intended to continue theological education outside the classroom."[36]

## The Chaplain

There must be "a person or persons responsible for the worship leadership of the seminary community."[37] A staff or faculty member should be put in charge of the chapel program's development and implementation—and that not simply as one more added responsibility to an already too-full schedule. Rather the school should demonstrate its valuing of the chapel program by building into that person's job description sufficient time and resources to allow for careful (and prayerful) planning and quality execution. In assessing the results of his survey into seminary worship, James White saw the need similarly (though his data is of course outdated):

> I also asked whether schools designated a faculty or staff person with responsibility for directing the worship life of the community. The affirmatives were surprisingly high here: 126 (of 176 or 72%) persons said "yes" as contrasted to 50 (28%) "no." That means that in the majority of seminaries this work is regarded as a specific function. As to names and titles, a wide variety appeared: worship chairman, spiritual director, chaplain, dean of the chapel, spiritual life coordinator, coordinator of liturgical activities, director of liturgy were representative. The bottom line was how much this work was regarded as part of a teaching load. It split almost evenly: it was for 59 (of 129 replies or 46%) and not for 70 (54%). . . . But the fact that almost half the individuals responding indicated worship leadership was considered part of the teaching load is significant and other schools may want to reflect on this.[38]

35. L. Gregory Jones, "Beliefs, Desires, and the Ends of Theological Education," in Volf and Bass, *Practicing Theology*, 203.

36. Erickson and Lindner, "Worship and Prayer," 24.

37. E. Byron Anderson, "Worship and Theological Education," 118.

38. White, "Teaching of Worship," 314.

## *The Chapel Services*

Here is a unique opportunity to provide enriching and varied experiences of worship as a seminary community,[39] which can also serve a didactic purpose of exemplifying some of the possibilities inherent for creative use of different traditions. "With a little greater intentionality, seminaries and divinity schools might find it possible to use the worship service as occasion for exposure to widely diverse forms of piety and liturgical life."[40] The chapel services themselves should be carefully designed to give a full and varied diet of worship elements and structures—not simply consist of a song or two followed by the speaker. Lesher writes of the potential:

> That is what I hope for seminary worship: a solid commitment to and a grounding in the western worship tradition, the catholic shape of worship as it has been recovered in the *Lutheran Book of Worship*—and then—a faithful, reverent, ambitious, creative, collaborative, community-wide attempt to experience in the seminary worshipping community, a variety of ways of making the essence of Christian worship cross the boundaries of cultures and speak its essential message and meaning with authenticity and power. Is that not the way, in a multicultural, multipreferential church, to equip worship leaders to be both grounded in the essentials and open in style, so that ministry and worship can be truly contextual and effective?[41]

This potential was in the past not realized often enough: "While many institutions, even small denominational seminaries, have an increasingly ecumenical and global student body, drawn from diverse denominations and cultures, this diversity is seldom reflected in a fully intentional way in worship practices."[42] There should be a healthy representation of the full spectrum of backgrounds found in the seminary community itself; but

---

39. With an appropriate emphasis on worship as a seminary *community*, it might be helpful as an expression of equality before the Lord for the faculty and staff to sit intermingled with the students in the chapel, rather than having reserved places of privilege up front—the latter arrangement communicates a hierarchicalism that runs contrary to the intended spirit of the event.

40. Erickson and Lindner, "Worship and Prayer," 28.

41. Lesher, "On Worship," 401–2.

42. Erickson and Lindner, "Worship and Prayer," 24.

then extend far beyond that as well into other traditions.[43] Real progress has been made in this area too in recent years.

Other faculty should be involved in the designing and leading of chapel worship programs—and not just members of the Pastoral or Practical Theology department. Exegetes, theologians, church historians, etc., all have vital and necessary contributions to make in enriching the worship program of the seminary. E. Byron Anderson makes this point well:

> If seminary sponsored worship is to be part of the formational theological curriculum, as I have argued it must be, the shape and practice of such worship must be part of any discussions of the theological curriculum. That is, the shape and practice of worship must be part of and managed by the theological faculty in honest conversation with the norms and theological traditions of the seminary, its sponsoring institutions, and the ecumenical Church as these norms and traditions are brought to bear in the mission and purpose of the school.[44]

Away with the divide between the Bible/Theology and the Practical/Pastoral Theology departments!

Students also should be involved. While of course the goal is genuine worship, the program can also serve as a laboratory for students to try their hand and gain experience at planning and leading worship. (Musical aptitude is not necessary.) Why not require all students to have at least one such experience during their seminary career? White sees the advantages of such student involvement, while cautioning as well:

> In many cases, syllabi indicate that course requirements include planning, preparing, and conducting actual chapel services. In some instances, such leadership is critiqued after the service or discussed in class. There is always danger in making seminary worship too clinical, too self-conscious in looking over one's shoulder to see what one is doing. On the other hand, many possibilities will never be encountered unless students experience them first in seminary worship. Much can be shown in actual worship services that can only vaguely be glimpsed in class.[45]

---

43. As should be the case in churches as well, care should be taken to explain the meaning of unfamiliar forms, actions, and words, so that understanding prevails and not just novelty.

44. E. Byron Anderson, "Worship and Theological Education," 127.

45. White, "Teaching of Worship," 309–10.

"Nothing else can so transform the church, nurture its ministries, and revitalize its fellowship as the encounter God makes available to us through worship."[46] The same could certainly be said for the life of the seminary! A vital worship life on campus can serve only to build students and faculty spiritually, and give added weight and conviction to the subject matter of study.[47] As White rightly asserts, "The classroom has to be balanced by the chapel. A strong worship life in the seminary is as basic as a good library in equipping men and women for ministry."[48]

## In Churches

Another invaluable experience that seminary could provide would be a concerted (and required) program of visiting the worship services of many different types of churches. This would instill in the students a greater appreciation for the wide variety of legitimate worship expressions, and help develop greater discernment about worship practices which may be biblically questionable.

These church visits would preferably be preceded by a historical and theological study of the particular tradition to be observed; and in addition the visits should be followed by an evaluation, either in written form or by way of group discussion.

## In Personal Life

White reminds us that "worship is a basic part of the whole personal being of all in Christian ministry, both ordained and lay."[49] And so if seminaries are to be instruments of the Lord used by him in the formation and preparation of their students in a holistic way, the individual as well as the corporate worship needs of each student must not be overlooked. As Stephen Neill expresses it:

46. Loscalzo and Mims, "Worship Leadership," 198.

47. It must be pointed out that the seminary as (hopefully) a worshiping community should never, however, be allowed to substitute for the student's (or faculty member's) active involvement in a local congregation. As Gordon Smith points out, the comparatively homogeneous grouping that makes up a seminary community does not accurately reflect the generational and occupational diversity that characterizes, enriches, and stretches the body of Christ (G. Smith, "Managing the Tension").

48. White, "Teaching of Worship," 318.

49. White, "Teaching of Worship," 318.

> You can't force spiritual development; any attempt to do so by regimentation is counterproductive. Yet the atmosphere at the seminary must be an atmosphere of prayer and worship if it's to be effective. My definition of a seminary is a fellowship of adoration, study and witness. Adoration comes first.[50]

Seminary study too easily and too often becomes a spiritually deadening time in the life of the student; and the seminary should do everything in its power to counteract this tendency. Spiritual formation programs and groups of course have been designed with this in mind. But again care must be taken to not just add one more program to the student's already busy schedule; rather time must be built into the program for the student to be able to breathe spiritually and to respond in devotion to the spiritual truths being learned (as discussed already). Instruction and encouragement in spiritual disciplines *along with* time allowed for their application can produce rich dividends; without the time to practice these things, the result may just be frustration and feelings of guilt.

A dedicated day of prayer once a year or once a semester could also help, as could the encouragement (or even scheduling of) times for personal spiritual retreats.

## Conclusion

As has been seen, *the need is great and the time is now for including worship in the seminary curriculum.* This matter needs to be taken seriously by the administrations and faculties of all theological institutions preparing students for Christian ministry—especially pastoral ministry in the church. Appropriate emphasis must be given to worship in the ethos and atmosphere of the institution as a whole; focused instruction in the theology, history, and practice of worship must be provided; and a rich palette of worship experiences must be offered, both on and off campus.

Seminaries can and should play a major role in addressing and alleviating the worship challenges facing the church today. Such institutions exist to serve the church, God's primary human instrument for his work in the world today; and the church will not be well served unless seminaries attack head-on the problems in worship being faced in many (if not most) local congregations; and their graduates will not be well

50. Groh, "Ecumenism's Past and Future," 572.

served unless they are given some fundamental understanding in this area so that they can truly lead their flocks through the fog that so often surrounds the worship debates.

The call to the seminary is, in a nutshell: "*No theology without doxology.*"[51] For "great is the LORD, and [therefore] greatly to be praised" (Ps 96:3).

51. Stott, *Romans*, 311.

# BIBLIOGRAPHY

Abba, Raymond. *Principles of Christian Worship*. New York: Oxford University Press, 1966.

Alexander, Eric. "Acceptable Worship: Sermons on Worship from John Chapter 4." Eric Alexander, n.d. https://www.ericalexander.co.uk/sermons/acceptableworship.php.

———. "Do Not Do It/Worship God." Presentation at Philadelphia Conference on Reformed Theology, Philadelphia, Apr. 24, 1998.

———. "Mission and Vision." Presentation at Urbana 81 conference, Urbana, IL, 1981. https://tinyurl.com/EAUrbana.

———. *Our Great God and Saviour*. Carlisle, PA: Banner of Truth Trust, 2010.

———. "Thirsting for God." iHeart, Nov. 14, 2016. https://www.iheart.com/podcast/256-more-of-god-please-31024294/episode/eric-alexander-thirsting-for-god-38066971/.

———. "Worship God!" Sermon at First Evangelical Church, Memphis, n.d. https://worship-resources.org/2023/07/31/worship-god-revelation-1910-sermon-eric-alexander/.

———. "Worship: The Chief End of Man." Presentation at Philadelphia Conference on Reformed Theology, Philadelphia, Apr. 26, 1998.

———. "Worship: The Old Testament Pattern." Presentation at Philadelphia Conference on Reformed Theology, Philadelphia, Apr. 25, 1998.

Allen, Ronald Barclay, and Gordon Borror. *Worship: Rediscovering the Missing Jewel*. Eugene, OR: Wipf & Stock, 2000.

Allmen, Jean-Jacques von. "Worship and the Holy Spirit." *Studia Liturgica* 2 (1963) 124–35.

———. *Worship: Its Theology and Practice*. London: Lutterworth, 1968.

Anderson, Bernhard W. *Out of the Depths: The Psalms Speak for Us Today*. Philadelphia: Westminster, 1974.

Anderson, E. Byron. "Worship and Theological Education." *Theological Education* 39 (2003) 117–30.

Aniol, Scott. *Draw Near: The Heart of Communion with God*. Eugene, OR: Wipf & Stock, 2020.

Aniol, Scott, et al. "'Worship from the Nations': A Survey and Preliminary Analysis of the Ethnodoxology Movement." *Artistic Theologian* 3 (2015) 2–21.

Armstrong, John. "How Should We Then Worship?" *Reformation & Revival* 2 (Winter 1993) 9–22.

Atkins, Peter. *Ascension Now: Implications of Christ's Ascension for Today's Church.* Collegeville, MN: Liturgical, 2001.

Augustine. *Confessions.* Translated by J. G. Pilkington. Logos Library, n.d. http://www. logoslibrary.org/augustine/confessions/1029.html.

Avery, Tom. "Worship Wars and Ethnomusicology." Presentation at Global Consultation on Music in Missions, St. Paul, MN, July 11–15, 2006.

Bailey, Kenneth E. *The Good Shepherd: A Thousand-Year Journey from Psalm 23 to the New Testament.* Downers Grove, IL: IVP Academic, 2014.

Bailey, Mark. "Dispensational Expressions of Worship." Chapel message at Dallas Theological Seminary, Dallas, Jan. 12, 2010. https://tinyurl.com/BaileyDisp. https:// voice.dts.edu/chapel/dispensational-expressions-of-worship-mark-l-bailey/.

Barclay, William. *The Gospel of John.* The New Daily Study Bible. Louisville, KY: Westminster John Knox, 2017.

Bary, Richard de. *The Gospel of Worship.* London: Ivor Nicholson & Watson, 1934.

Beale, Gregory K. *The Temple and the Church's Mission: A Biblical Theology of the Dwelling Place of God.* New Studies in Biblical Theology. Downers Grove, IL: IVP Academic, 2004.

Bennett, Arthur, ed. *The Valley of Vision: A Collection of Puritan Prayers and Devotions.* Edinburgh: Banner of Truth Trust, 1975.

Bierly, Steve. "Sparring over Worship." *Leadership* (Winter 1997) 2–8.

Bierma, Nathan. "Worshipful Service." *Reformed Journal,* Jun. 1, 2006. https:// reformedjournal.com/worshipful-service/.

Block, Daniel Isaac. *For the Glory of God: Recovering a Biblical Theology of Worship.* Grand Rapids: Baker Academic, 2016.

Brink, Emily, and John D. Witvliet. *The Worship Sourcebook.* 2nd ed. Grand Rapids: Faith Alive Christian Resources, 2013.

Britannica, The Editors of Encyclopedia. "Apostles' Creed." *Encyclopedia Britannica,* July 20, 1998; last updated May 19, 2023. https://www.britannica.com/topic/ Apostles-Creed.

———. "Nicene Creed." *Encyclopedia Britannica,* July 20, 1998; last updated May 19, 2023. https://www.britannica.com/topic/Nicene-Creed.

———. "Te Deum laudamus." *Encyclopedia Britannica,* July 20, 1998; last updated Feb. 19, 2022. https://www.britannica.com/topic/Te-Deum-laudamus.

Brown, Marcia. *Stone Soup: An Old Tale.* New York: Aladdin, 1986.

Bruce, F. F. *The Epistles to the Colossians, to Philemon, and to the Ephesians.* NICNT. Grand Rapids: Eerdmans, 2008.

Brueggemann, Walter. *The Psalms and the Life of Faith.* Minneapolis: Fortress, 1995.

———. *Theology of the Old Testament: Testimony, Dispute, Advocacy.* Minneapolis: Fortress, 2012.

Bullock, Geoff. "Beyond Self-Centred Worship." *Renewal Journal* 6 (1995) 15–20.

Burkhart, John E. *Worship: A Searching Examination of the Liturgical Experience.* Philadelphia: Westminster, 1982.

Butin, Philip Walker. *Revelation, Redemption, and Response: Calvin's Trinitarian Understanding of the Divine-Human Relationship.* New York: Oxford University Press, 1995.

Byars, Ronald P. *Christian Worship: Glorifying and Enjoying God.* Foundations of Christian Faith. Louisville, KY: Geneva, 2000.

———. *The Future of Protestant Worship: Beyond the Worship Wars.* Louisville, KY: Westminster John Knox, 2002.

Cabaniss, Craig. "Worship and the Word Go Hand in Hand." Crosswalk, Apr. 15, 2003. https://www.crosswalk.com/faith/spiritual-life/worship-matters-worship-and-the-word-go-hand-in-hand-1195514.html.

Calvin Institute of Christian Worship. "Ascension Resource Guide." Calvin, 2011. https://worship.calvin.edu/resources/resource-library/Ascension-Resource-Guide.

Calvin, John. *Calvin: Institutes of the Christian Religion.* Edited by John T. McNeill. Louisville, KY: Presbyterian, 1960.

———. *Commentaries on the Epistle to the Hebrews.* Translated by John Owen. Grand Rapids: Eerdmans, 1949.

———. "Of Prayer: A Perpetual Exercise of Faith: The Daily Benefits Derived from It." CCEL, n.d. https://www.ccel.org/ccel/calvin/prayer.html.

Cantalamessa, Raniero. "The Sober Intoxication of the Word and Spirit." Adoremus, Jan. 12, 2017. https://adoremus.org/2017/01/sober-intoxication-word-spirit/.

Carson, D. A. *Commentary on Matthew.* The Expositor's Bible Commentary 8. Grand Rapids: Zondervan, 1984.

———. *Exegetical Fallacies.* 2nd ed. Grand Rapids: Baker, 1996.

———, ed. *Worship by the Book.* Grand Rapids: Zondervan, 2002.

Castleman, Robbie F. *Story-Shaped Worship: Following Patterns from the Bible and History.* Downers Grove, IL: IVP Academic, 2013.

Chapell, Bryan. "The Call to Worship." Box, n.d. https://tinyurl.com/bchapell.

———. *Christ-Centered Worship: Letting the Gospel Shape Our Practice.* Grand Rapids: Baker Academic, 2009.

———. "Worship as Gospel Representation." Unpublished manuscript, n.d.

Charnock, Stephen. *The Works of Stephen Charnock.* 5 vols. Edinburgh: Banner of Truth Trust, 2010.

Cherry, Constance M. *The Worship Architect: A Blueprint for Designing Culturally Relevant and Biblically Faithful Services.* 2nd ed. Grand Rapids: Baker Academic, 2021.

Chesterton, G. K. *Orthodoxy.* Scotts Valley, CA: CreateSpace, 2015.

The Church of England. "The Order for the Administration of the Lord's Supper or Holy Communion." In *The Book of Common Prayer.* Cambridge: Baskerville, 1762. www.churchofengland.org/prayer-and-worship/worship-texts-and-resources/book-common-prayer/lords-supper-or-holy-communion.

———. "Thirty Nine Articles of Religion." Anglican Communion, n.d. https://www.anglicancommunion.org/media/109014/Thirty-Nine-Articles-of-Religion.pdf.

Clowney, Edmund P. *The Church.* Contours of Christian Theology. Downers Grove, IL: IVP Academic, 1995.

———. "Declare His Glory among the Nations." Presentation at Urbana 76 conference, Urbana, IL, 1976. https://tinyurl.com/EClowney.

Cocksworth, Christopher. *Holy, Holy, Holy: Worshipping the Trinitarian God.* London: Darton, Longman and Todd, 2004.

Cohen, David. J., and Michael Parsons, eds. *In Praise of Worship.* Eugene, OR: Wipf & Stock, 2010.

Congregation for Catholic Education. "Instruction on Liturgical Formation in Seminaries." EWTN, 2003. https://www.ewtn.com/catholicism/library/instruction-on-liturgical-formation-in-seminaries-2003.

Cowman, Charles E. "July 20: Our Helper in Prayer." In *Streams in the Desert: 366 Daily Devotional Readings*, edited by James Reimann, 219. Grand Rapids: Zondervan, 2016.

Cranfield, C. E. B. *A Critical and Exegetical Commentary on the Epistle to the Romans*. 2 vols. ICC. New York: T. & T. Clark International, 2004.

————. "Divine and Human Action: The Biblical Concept of Worship." *Interpretation* 12 (Oct. 1958) 387–98.

Crider, Joseph R. *Scripture-Guided Worship: A Call to Pastors & Worship Leaders*. Fort Worth, TX: Seminary Hill, 2021.

Crosby, Fanny. "To God Be the Glory," 1875. https://hymnary.org/text/to_god_be_the_glory_great_things_he_hath.

Cummings, Brian, ed. *The Book of Common Prayer: The Texts of 1549, 1559, and 1662*. New York: Oxford University Press, 2011.

Davies, J. G. "Worship." In *A Dictionary of Biblical Tradition in English Literature*, edited by David Lyle Jeffrey, 851–53. Grand Rapids: Eerdmans, 1952.

Dawn, Marva J. *How Shall We Worship? Biblical Guidelines for the Worship Wars*. The Vital Questions Series. Wheaton, IL: Tyndale, 2003.

————. *Reaching Out without Dumbing Down: A Theology of Worship for the Turn-of-the-Century Culture*. Grand Rapids: Eerdmans, 1995.

————. *A Royal Waste of Time: The Splendor of Worshiping God and Being Church for the World*. Grand Rapids: Eerdmans, 1999.

Dawson, Gerrit Scott. *Jesus Ascended: The Meaning of Christ's Continuing Incarnation*. Phillipsburg, NJ: P&R, 2004.

Delling, Gerhard. *Worship in the New Testament*. Philadelphia: Westminster, 1962.

Detwiler, David F. "Church Music and Colossians 3:16." *BSac* 158 (Sep. 2001) 347–69.

Di Sabatino, David. "What's Wrong with Contemporary Worship?" *Worship Leader* (May–Jun. 2002) 62.

Dix, Dom Gregory. *The Shape of the Liturgy*. 2nd ed. London: Dacre, 1949.

Due, Noel. *Created for Worship: From Genesis to Revelation to You*. Fearn, Scot.: Mentor, 2005.

Duke, Robert W. "Seminary Worship." *Theological Education* 2 (Autumn 1965) 42–46.

Duncan, J. Ligon. "Foundations for Biblically Directed Worship." In *Give Praise to God: A Vision for Reforming Worship: Celebrating the Legacy of James Montgomery Boice*, edited by Philip Graham Ryken et al., 51–73. Phillipsburg, NJ: P&R, 2003.

Duvall, J. Scott, and J. Daniel Hays. *God's Relational Presence: The Cohesive Center of Biblical Theology*. Grand Rapids: Baker, 2019.

Engle, Paul E., and Paul B. Basden, eds. *Six Views on Exploring the Worship Spectrum*. Counterpoints. Grand Rapids: Zondervan, 2004.

Erickson, John H., and Eileen W. Lindner. "Worship and Prayer in Ecumenical Formation." *Theological Education* 34, Supplement (1997) 23–29.

Esbjornson, Robert. "Preaching as Worship." *Worship* 48 (1974) 164–70.

Eugenio, Dick. *Communion with the Triune God*. Princeton Theological Monograph Series Book 204. Eugene, OR: Pickwick, 2014.

Farhadian, Charles E., ed. *Christian Worship Worldwide: Expanding Horizons, Deepening Practices*. Calvin Institute of Christian Worship Liturgical Studies Series. Grand Rapids: Eerdmans, 2007.

Farley, Michael A. "Jesus' Ascension and Christian Worship." Central Pres Worship, May 15, 2012. https://centralpresworship.files.wordpress.com/2020/05/ascension-jesus-ascension-and-christian-worship-farley.pdf.

———. "What Is 'Biblical' Worship? Biblical Hermeneutics and Evangelical Theologies of Worship." *JETS* 51 (Sep. 2008) 591–613.

Fee, Gordon D. *God's Empowering Presence: The Holy Spirit in the Letters of Paul*. Grand Rapids: Baker Academic, 2011.

Ferguson, Sinclair B. "The Church's Worship." Ligonier, Jan. 19, 2006. https://www.ligonier.org/learn/conferences/orlando-2006-national-conference/the-churchs-worship.

———. "The Church's Worship." Monergism, Jan. 26, 2006. https://tinyurl.com/SinclairF.

———. *The Doctrine of the Holy Spirit*. MP3 series. https://www.monergism.com/doctrine-holy-spirit-mp3-series.

———. *The Holy Spirit*. Contours of Christian Theology. Downers Grove, IL: IVP Academic, 1996.

———. *True Spirituality, True Worship*. Audio CD. Lookout Mountain, GA: Covenant College Press, 2004.

Flemming, Dean E. *Contextualization in the New Testament: Patterns for Theology and Mission*. Downers Grove, IL: IVP Academic, 2005.

Forrest, Benjamin K., et al., eds. *Biblical Worship: Theology for God's Glory*. Grand Rapids: Kregel, 2021.

Frame, John M. *Contemporary Worship Music: A Biblical Defense*. Phillipsburg, NJ: P&R, 1997.

France, R. T. *The Gospel of Matthew*. NICNT. Grand Rapids: Eerdmans, 2007.

Fromm, Chuck. "New Song: The Sound of Spiritual Awakening (A Study of Music in Revival)." Paper presented to Oxford Reading & Research Conference, Jul. 1983. https://buddysheets.tripod.com/newsongthesoundofspiritualawakening.htm.

Fry, Steve. "Unity, Worship, and the Presence of God." *Discipleship Journal* (Nov.–Dec. 2002) 56.

Furr, Gary, and Milburn Price. *The Dialogue of Worship: Creating Space for Revelation and Response*. Faithgrowth. Macon, GA: Smyth & Helwys, 1998.

Gaddy, C. Welton. *The Gift of Worship*. Nashville: Broadman, 1992.

Gibbs, Alfred P. *Worship: The Christian's Highest Occupation*. Dubuque, IA: ECS Ministries, 2013.

Gill, John. *Book of Isaiah*. Exposition on the Entire Bible. Sioux Falls, SD: Graceworks Multimedia, 2011.

Gloer, W. Hulitt. "Worship God! Liturgical Elements in the Apocalypse." *Review and Expositor* 98 (Winter 2001) 35–57.

Goldingay, John. *Psalms*. 3 vols. BCOTWP. Grand Rapids: Baker Academic, 2006.

Gore, R. J., Jr. *Covenantal Worship: Reconsidering the Puritan Regulative Principle*. Phillipsburg, NJ: P&R, 2002.

Graham, Billy. *Peace with God: The Secret of Happiness*. Reprint, Nashville: Thomas Nelson, 2017.

Groh, John E. "Ecumenism's Past and Future: Shifting Perspectives (An Interview with Bishop Stephen C. Neill)." *Christian Century* (Jun. 4, 1975) 568–72.

✗ Grudem, Wayne A. *Systematic Theology: An Introduction to Biblical Doctrine*. 2nd ed. Grand Rapids: Zondervan Academic, 2020.

Gustafson, Gerrit. "Psalms, Hymns, and Spiritual Songs: A Paradigm for the Church of the Future." *Worship Leader* (May–Jun. 1996) 34–36, 46.

Guthrie, Steven R. "Singing, in the Body and in the Spirit." *JETS* 46 (Dec. 2003) 633–46.

———. "The Wisdom of Song." In *Resonant Witness: Conversations between Music and Theology*, edited by Jeremy Begbie, 382–407. The Calvin Institute of Christian Worship Liturgical Studies. Grand Rapids: Eerdmans, 2011.

Hahn, Scott W. "Canon, Cult and Covenant: The Promise of Liturgical Hermeneutics." In *Canon and Biblical Interpretation*, edited by Craig G. Bartholomew, 7:207–35. Scripture and Hermeneutics Series. Grand Rapids: Zondervan, 2006.

Hall, Dave. "Every Team Needs One: The Essential Role of the Worship-Arts Leader in Church-Planting." *Mission Frontiers* 23 (Jun. 2001) 23–25. www.missionfrontiers. org/pdfs/23-2.pdf.

———. "What's in the Middle?" Unpublished manuscript.

Hamilton, Michael S. "The Triumph of the Praise Songs: How Guitars Beat Out the Organ in the Worship Wars." *Christianity Today*, Jul. 12, 1999. https://www. christianitytoday.com/ct/1999/july12/9t8028.html.

∨ Hannah, John D. *To God Be the Glory*. Today's Issues. Wheaton, IL: Crossway, 2000.

Harris, Robin. "The Great Misconception: The 'Universal Language' of Worship." *Worship Leader*, Oct. 7, 2015. https://worshipleader.com/leadership/worship-theology/the-great-misconception.

∠ Hattori, Yoshiaki. "Theology of Worship in the Old Testament." In *Worship: Adoration and Action*, edited by D. A Carson, 21–50. World Evangelical Fellowship Faith and Church Study Unit. Eugene, OR: Wipf & Stock, 2002.

∨ Hawn, C. Michael. *Gather into One: Praying and Singing Globally*. Calvin Institute of Christian Worship Liturgical Studies Series. Grand Rapids: Eerdmans, 2003.

———. *One Bread, One Body: Exploring Cultural Diversity in Worship*. Bethesda, MD: Alban Institute, 2003.

Hawthorne, Steve. "The Story of His Glory." *Mission Frontiers*, May 1, 1993. https:// www.missionfrontiers.org/issue/article/the-story-of-his-glory.

"The Heidelberg Catechism (1563)." Westminster Seminary California, n.d. https:// www.wscal.edu/about-wsc/doctrinal-standards/heidelberg-catechism.

Herbert, J. B. "When Israel Had from Egypt Gone (Psalm 114)." In *The Irish Presbyterian Hymnbook*, edited by Public Worship Committee, no. 26. Norwich, UK: Canterbury, 2004.

∠ Hill, Andrew E. *Enter His Courts with Praise! Old Testament Worship for the New Testament Church*. 2nd ed. Grand Rapids: Baker, 2012.

Hooker, Morna Dorothy. "Adam in Romans 1." In *From Adam to Christ: Essays on Paul*, 73–84. Eugene, OR: Wipf & Stock, 2008.

Hoon, Paul Waitman. *The Integrity of Worship: Ecumenical and Pastoral Studies in Liturgical Theology*. Nashville: Abingdon, 1971.

∨ Horton, Michael Scott. *In the Face of God*. Dallas: Word, 1996.

———. "Worship: The New Testament Pattern." Presentation at Philadelphia Conference on Reformed Theology, Philadelphia, Apr. 25, 1998.

Hustad, Donald P. *Jubilate! Church Music in the Evangelical Tradition*. Carol Stream, IL: Hope, 1981.

———. *Jubilate II: Church Music in Worship and Renewal*. Carol Stream, IL: Hope, 1993.

Jack, Chris. "The *Proskuneō* Myth: When a Kiss Is Not a Kiss." In *In Praise of Worship*, edited by David J. Cohen and Michael Parsons, 84–97. Eugene, OR: Wipf & Stock, 2010.

Johnston, Robert K., ed. *The Use of the Bible in Theology: Evangelical Options*. Louisville, KY: John Knox, 1985.

Jones, Cheslyn, et al., eds. *The Study of Liturgy*. Revised ed. New York: Oxford University Press, 1992.

Jungmann, Josef Andreas. *The Place of Christ in Liturgical Prayer*. Translated by Geoffrey Chapman. Classics of Liturgy. Collegeville, MN: Liturgical, 1965.

Justin Martyr. "The First Apology of Justin." In *The Apostolic Fathers with Justin Martyr and Irenaeus*, edited by Alexander Roberts et al., 159–87. Vol. 1 of *ANF*. New York: Scribner's Sons, 1903.

Kaemingk, Matthew, and Cory B. Willson. *Work and Worship: Reconnecting Our Labor and Liturgy*. Grand Rapids: Baker Academic, 2020.

Kauflin, Bob. "Praise Choruses: Mainly Man-centered?" *Worship Matters* (blog), Dec. 30, 2003. https://www.scribd.com/document/262238024/Hymns-vs-Praise-Choruses.

———. *Worship Matters: Leading Others to Encounter the Greatness of God*. Wheaton, IL: Crossway, 2008.

———. "Worship Matters: Pastors and Worship Leaders, Part 4." Crosswalk, Feb. 26, 2003. https://www.crosswalk.com/faith/spiritual-life/worship-matters-pastors-and-worship-leaders-part-4-1187423.html.

Kavanagh, Aidan. *On Liturgical Theology*. Reprint of The Hale Memorial Lectures of Seabury-Western Theological Seminary 1981. New York: Pueblo, 1992.

Keller, Timothy J. *The Reason for God: Belief in an Age of Skepticism*. New York: Riverhead, 2009.

Kenmogne, Michel. "Bible Translation Is the Key to a Christian Faith 'at Home' in Any Culture." *Evangelical Missions Quarterly* 58 (Sep. 2022) 10–14.

Kidd, Reggie. "Bach, Bubba, and the Blues Brothers." *Reformed Journal* 18 (1998) 8–9, 17.

———. *With One Voice: Discovering Christ's Song in Our Worship*. Grand Rapids: Baker, 2005.

Kidner, Derek. *Genesis*. Kidner Classic Commentaries. Downers Grove, IL: IVP Academic, 2019.

———. *Psalms 1–72: An Introduction and Commentary on Books I and II of the Psalms*. TOTC. London: IVP Academic, 1973.

Kierkegaard, Søren. *Purity of Heart Is to Will One Thing*. Translated by Douglas Steere. New York: Harper and Brothers, 1948.

King, Roberta R. *Global Arts and Christian Witness: Exegeting Culture, Translating the Message, and Communicating Christ*. Mission in Global Community. Grand Rapids: Baker Academic, 2019.

Kingo, Thomas. "I Come, Invited by Thy Word." Translated by J. C. Aaberg. https://hymnary.org/text/i_come_invited_by_thy_word.

Knox, Ronald. *Enthusiasm: A Chapter in the History of Religion with Special Reference to the Seventeenth and Eighteenth Centuries.* New York: Oxford University Press, 1961.

Köstenberger, Andreas J., and Scott R. Swain. *Father, Son and Spirit: The Trinity and John's Gospel.* New Studies in Biblical Theology 24. Downers Grove, IL: IVP Academic, 2008.

Krabill, James R., et al., eds. *Worship and Mission for the Global Church: An Ethnodoxology Handbook.* Pasadena, CA: William Carey, 2013.

Krosnicki, Thomas A., and John A. Gurrieri. "Seminary Liturgy Revisited." *Worship* 54 (1980) 158–69.

Kuruvilla, Abraham. "The *Aqedah* (Genesis 22): What Is the Author *Doing* with What He Is *Saying?*" *JETS* 55 (2021) 489–508.

Lathrop, Gordon. *Holy Things: A Liturgical Theology.* Minneapolis: Fortress, 1999.

Leafblad, Bruce. "Leading in Worship." Presentation at worship conference, Southwestern Baptist Theological Seminary, Fort Worth, TX, 1995.

Leithart, Peter J. *From Silence to Song: The Davidic Liturgical Revolution.* Moscow, ID: Canon, 2003.

————. *A House for My Name: A Survey of the Old Testament.* Moscow, ID: Canon, 2000.

————. "Transforming Worship." *Foundations* 38 (Spring 1997) 27–34.

Lenski, R. C. H. *The Interpretation of the Acts of the Apostles.* Minneapolis: Fortress, 2008.

Lesher, William E. "On Worship." *CurTM* 22 (Oct. 1995) 401–2.

Lewis, Bernard. *The Middle East: A Brief History of the Last 2,000 Years.* New York: Scribner, 1995.

Lewis, C. S. *God in the Dock: Essays on Theology and Ethics.* Edited by Walter Hooper. Reprint, Grand Rapids: Eerdmans, 2002.

————. "On Church Music." In *Christian Reflections*, 117–23. Grand Rapids: Eerdmans, 2014.

————. *Reflections on the Psalms.* San Francisco: HarperCollins, 2017.

Lewis, Michael. "Can You Teach an Old Church New Tricks?" *Leadership* (Summer 1993). https://www.christianitytoday.com/pastors/1993/winter/93l3023.html.

Lim, Swee Hong, and Lester Ruth. *Lovin' on Jesus: A Concise History of Contemporary Worship.* Nashville: Abingdon, 2017.

Loscalzo, Craig A., and Lloyd L. Mims III. "Worship Leadership." In *Preparing for Christian Ministry: An Evangelical Approach*, edited by David P. Gushee and Walter C. Jackson, 191–204. Grand Rapids: Baker, 1996.

Lucado, Max. *In the Eye of the Storm* and *The Applause of Heaven.* Nashville: Thomas Nelson, 2011.

————. *Just Like Jesus.* Nashville: Word, 1998.

————. *Traveling Light: Releasing the Burdens You Were Never Intended to Bear.* Nashville: Thomas Nelson, 2013.

Luther, Martin. *Lectures on Titus, Philemon, and Hebrews.* Edited by Jaroslav Pelikan. Luther's Works 29. Saint Louis, MO: Concordia, 1968.

————. *Liturgy and Hymns.* Edited by Jaroslav Pelikan and Helmut T. Lehmann. Luther's Works 53. Saint Louis, MO: Concordia, 1965.

————. *Luther's Large Catechism: With Study Questions.* Edited by Paul Timothy McCain and Rodney L. Rathmann. St. Louis, MO: Concordia, 2010.

———. *Treatise on Good Works*. Edited by Scott H. Hendrix. Luther Study ed. Minneapolis: Fortress, 2012.

———. *What Luther Says: A Practical In-Home Anthology for the Active Christian*. Edited by Ewald M. Plass. Saint Louis, MO: Concordia, 2006.

Lutheran World Federation's Study Team on Worship and Culture. "Nairobi Statement on Worship and Culture Full Text." Calvin, Jan. 1996. https://worship.calvin.edu/ resources/resource-library/nairobi-statement-on-worship-and-culture-full-text/.

✓MacArthur, John. *Worship: The Ultimate Priority*. Chicago: Moody, 2012.

MacDonald, George. "Kingship." In *The Unspoken Sermons: Series I, II, III*, 242–45. Scotts Valley, CA: CreateSpace, 2016.

Mains, Karen Burton. "Introduction." In *Sing Joyfully!*, edited by Jack Schrader, 3–6. Carol Stream, IL: Tabernacle, 1969.

✓Man, Ron. "The Biblical Case for Blended Worship." https://worship-resources.org /2023/02/18/the-biblical-case-for-blended-worship/.

———. "Biblical Principles of Worship and Their Application to Local Church Ministry." Worship Resources, n.d. https://worship-resources.org/2023/02/18/biblical-principles-of-worship-and-their-application-to-local-church-ministry/.

———. "Biblical Principles of Worship (One-Page Summary)." Worship Resources, n.d. https://worship-resources.org/2023/02/21/biblical-principles-of-worship/.

———. "The Canticles of Christmas (Luke 1–2)." *Worship Notes* 2 (Dec. 2007). https:// worship-resources.org/2007/12/30/2-12-december-2007-the-canticles-of-christmas/.

———. "Creative Arts, Missions, and Worship." Plenary address at Global Consultation on Music and Missions, Singapore, 2010. https://worship-resources. org/2023/06/25/creative-arts-missions-and-worship/.

———. "Culture and Worship: A Response to Scott Aniol and a Contribution to the Ongoing Debate." Box, Apr. 2020. https://worship-resources.org/2023/06/25/ culture-and-worship-a-response-to-scott-aniol-and-a-contribution-to-the-ongoing-debate/.

———. "The Dialogue of Worship." *Worship Notes* 1 (May 2006). https://worship-resources.org/2006/05/25/1-5-may-2006-the-dialogue-of-worship/.

———. "Flow, Service, Flow." https://worship-resources.org/2023/06/08/flow-service-flow/.

———. "King David's Lasting Musical Legacy." *Worship Notes* 4 (Oct. 2009). https:// worship-resources.org/2009/10/01/4-10-october-2009-song-in-scripture-i/.

———. "A Letter from Tapescrew (with apologies to C. S. Lewis)." *Reformed Worship*, Sep. 2009. https://www.reformedworship.org/article/september-2009/letter-tapescrew. (Also at https://worship-resources.org/2023/06/09/a-letter-from-tapescrew-with-apologies-to-c-s-lewis/.)

———. "More from Tapescrew." *Reformed Worship*, Sep. 2010. https://www. reformedworship.org/article/september-2010/more-tapescrew.

———. "More on the 'Davidic Liturgical Revolution' in Chronicles." *Worship Notes* 5 (Sep. 2010). https://worship-resources.org/2010/08/01/5-7-july-2010-song-in-scripture-viii-more-on-the-davidic-liturgical-revolution-in-chronicles/.

———. "Music for Worship: Excellence as a Means Rather Than an End." *Church Musician Today*, Mar. 1999. https://worship-resources.org/2023/06/09/music-for-worship-excellence-as-a-means-rather-than-an-end/. See also appendix 3.

———. "A Parable." *Church Musician Today*, May 1999. https://worship-resources. org/2023/06/09/a-parable/.

———. "The Power of Thematic Worship." https://worship-resources.org/2023/06/09/the-power-of-thematic-worship/.

———. *Proclamation and Praise: Hebrews 2:12 and the Christology of Worship*. Eugene, OR: Wipf & Stock, 2007.

———. "Rejoice with Trembling." *Church Musician Today*, Sept. 1998. https://worship-resources.org/2023/05/16/rejoice-with-trembling-psalm-211/.

———. "Revelation and Response: The Paradigm of True Worship." Presentation at Evangelical Theological Society conference, Atlanta, Nov. 2015. https://tinyurl.com/RevandResp.

———. "Tapescrew Letter 3." Worship Resources International, n.d. https://worship-resources.org/2023/06/09/tapescrew-letter-3/.

———. "Tapescrew Letter 4." Worship Resources International, n.d. https://worship-resources.org/2023/06/09/tapescrew-letter-4/.

———. "To God Alone Be the Glory." *Worship Notes* 1 (Mar. 2006). https://worship-resources.org/2006/03/25/1-3-march-2006-to-god-alone-be-the-glory/.

———. "Whose Gathering Is It, Anyhow? Why God Should Have the First Word." *Reformed Worship*, Mar. 2008. https://www.reformedworship.org/article/march-2008/whose-gathering-it-anyhow. (Also at https://worship-resources.org/2023/06/09/whose-gathering-is-it-anyhow/.) See also appendix 2.

———. "Worship and the Word." Presentation at Calvin Symposium on Worship, Grand Rapids, 2009. https://worship.calvin.edu/resources/resource-library/symposium-2009-worship-and-the-word/.

———. "Worship for All of God's People: Bridging the Generation Gap." https://worship-resources.org/2023/06/09/worship-for-all-of-gods-people-bridging-the-generation-gap.

———. "Worship in Eden: What We Had, What We Lost, What Was Restored." *Worship Notes* 14 (Oct. 2019). https://wornotes.wordpress.com/2019/10/31/worship-in-eden-what-we-had-what-we-lost-what-was-restored/.

———. "Worship in Old Testament History (Part 7)." *Worship Notes* 7 (Jul. 2012). https://wornotes.wordpress.com/2012/07/31/worship-in-old-testament-history-part-7/.

Man, Ronald E. "Dallas Seminary Worship Education for Future Pastors." DMin diss., Dallas Theological Seminary, 2009. https://worship-resources.org/2023/07/16/dallas-seminary-worship-preparation-for-future-pastors-d-min-dissertation/.

———. "False and True Worship in Romans 1." *BSac* 157 (Mar. 2000) 26–34. (Also at https://worship-resources.org/2023/06/08/false-and-true-worship-in-romans-118-25/.)

*Maranatha! Music Praise Chorus Book*. Costa Mesa, CA: Maranatha! Music, 1983.

Markey, Dell. "What Effects Did the Babylonian Exile Have on the Jewish Religion?" Classroom, Jun. 25, 2018. https://classroom.synonym.com/effects-did-babylonian-exile-jewish-religion-7222.html.

Martin, Ralph P. *The Worship of God: Some Theological, Pastoral, and Practical Reflections*. Grand Rapids: Eerdmans, 1982.

Melanchthon, Philip. *Augsburg Confession* (1530). Translated by Gerhard Friedrich Bente. https://en.wikisource.org/wiki/Augsburg_Confession#Article_VII:_Of_the_Church.

Merker, Matt. *Corporate Worship: How the Church Gathers as God's People*. Edited by J. Ligon Duncan. Building Healthy Churches. Wheaton, IL: Crossway, 2021. Kindle.

Meyers, Jeffrey J. *The Lord's Service: The Grace of Covenant Renewal Worship*. Moscow, ID: Canon, 2003.

Milligan, William. *The Ascension and Heavenly Priesthood of Our Lord*. Reprint, Eugene, OR: Wipf & Stock, 2006.

Morgan, G. Campbell. *The Gospel According to Mark*. New York: Revell, 1927.

―――. "Psalm 96:9: Worship, Beauty, Holiness." Precept Austin, n.d. https://www.preceptaustin.org/westminster-pulpit-g-campbell-morgan-2.

Morris, Leon. *The Epistle to the Romans*. Grand Rapids: Eerdmans, 1988.

Moule, C. F. D. *Worship in the New Testament*. Bramcote, UK: Grove, 1989.

Murray, John. "The Church—Its Identity, Functions and Resources." In *The Claims of Truth*, vol. 1 of *Collected Writings of John Murray*, 237–44. Edinburgh: Banner of Truth Trust, 1982.

―――. "The Living Saviour." In *The Claims of Truth*, vol. 1 of *Collected Writings of John Murray*, 40–43. Edinburgh: Banner of Truth Trust, 1976.

Murren, Doug. "Room for the Sacred." *Worship Leader* (Mar.–Apr. 1996) 14, 40.

Nash, Audrey. *Old Testament Story: Seeing the Old Testament as a Whole*. Milton Keynes, UK: AuthorHouse, 2008.

Nation, Garry D. "The Essentials of Worship: Toward a Biblical Theology of Worship." *Journal of the American Academy of Ministry* 5 (Winter–Spring 1997) 5–20.

Navarro, Kevin J. *Trinitarian Doxology: T. F. and J. B. Torrance's Theology of Worship as Participation by the Spirit in the Son's Communion with the Father*. Eugene, OR: Pickwick, 2020.

Nelson, Gregory P. *A Touch of Heaven: Finding New Meaning in Sabbath Rest*. Nampa, ID: Pacific, 1999.

Nelson, Jerry. "Unity in Diversity—Many Members Yet One Body." Unpublished manuscript, n.d.

Nelson, Robert J. "The Seminary—Academy and Chapel." *Theological Education* (1964) 53–62.

Nicholls, William. *Jacob's Ladder: The Meaning of Worship*. Louisville, KY: John Knox, 1955.

Packer, J. I. *Celebrating the Saving Work of God*. Vol. 1 of *The Collected Shorter Writings of J. I. Packer*. Carlisle, PA: Paternoster, 1998.

―――. *Concise Theology: A Guide to Historic Christian Beliefs*. Carol Stream, IL: Tyndale, 2001.

―――. *Keep in Step with the Spirit: Finding Fullness in Our Walk with God*. Revised and enlarged ed. Grand Rapids: Baker, 2005.

Parry, Robin. *Worshipping Trinity: Coming Back to the Heart of Worship*. Carlisle, UK: Paternoster, 2005.

Paquier, David. *Dynamics of Worship: Foundations and Uses of Liturgy*. Philadelphia: Fortress, 1967.

Patrick. "Saint Patrick's Breastplate (Abbreviated Extracts)." Daily Prayers, n.d. https://www.daily-prayers.org/angels-and-saints/prayers-of-saint-patrick-of-ireland/.

Patterson, Ben. *Serving God: The Grand Essentials of Work & Worship*. Revised ed. Downers Grove, IL: InterVarsity, 1994.

Pelikan, Jaroslav. *The Vindication of Tradition: 1983 Jefferson Lecture in the Humanities*. New Haven, CT: Yale University Press, 1992.

Perowne, J. J. S. *The Book of Psalms: A New Translation with Introductions and Notes Explanatory and Critical*. Vol. 1. London: Bell and Sons, 1885.

Peterson, David. *Engaging with God: A Biblical Theology of Worship.* Downers Grove, IL: IVP Academic, 2002.

———. "Psalms, Hymns, and Spiritual Songs: Does the Bible Direct Us in the Choice of Musical Styles?" Presentation at the Institute for Christian Worship, Southern Baptist Theological Seminary, Louisville, KY, Apr. 14, 2005.

———. "Worship and Evangelism." David G. Peterson, 2009. https://davidgpeterson. wordpress.com/worship/worship-and-evangelism/.

Peterson, Eugene. "The Business of Making Saints." *Leadership* (Spring 1997) 21–28.

———. *The Message: The Bible in Contemporary Language.* Colorado Springs: NavPress, 2005.

———. *Reversed Thunder: The Revelation of John and the Praying Imagination.* Reprint, San Francisco: HarperSanFrancisco, 1991.

Pink, Arthur Walkington. *Exposition of the Gospel of John.* Grand Rapids: Ministry Resources Library, 1975. https://www.gracegems.org/Pink/exposition_of_the_ gospel_of_john.htm.

Pinson, J. Matthew, ed. *Perspectives on Christian Worship: 5 Views.* Perspectives. Nashville: B&H Academic, 2009.

Piper, John. "Biblical Texts to Show God's Zeal for His Own Glory." Desiring God, Nov. 24, 2007. https://www.desiringgod.org/articles/biblical-texts-to-show-gods-zeal-for-his-own-glory.

———. "Christ and the Meaning of the Universe." Desiring God, Mar. 21, 2008. https:// www.desiringgod.org/articles/christ-and-the-meaning-of-the-universe.

———. *The Dangerous Duty of Delight: Daring to Make God Your Greatest Desire.* Colorado Springs: Multnomah, 2011.

———. *Desiring God: Meditations of a Christian Hedonist.* Colorado Springs: Multnomah, 2011.

———. "The Devil Can Do Exposition, but He Can't Preach." Desiring God, Sep. 13, 2018. https://www.desiringgod.org/messages/the-devil-can-do-exposition-but-he-cant-preach.

———. *Expository Exultation: Christian Preaching as Worship.* Wheaton, IL: Crossway, 2018.

———. "Gospel Worship: Holy Ambition for All the Peoples to Praise Christ." Desiring God, Jan. 31, 2017. https://www.desiringgod.org/messages/gospel-worship.

———. *Let the Nations Be Glad! The Supremacy of God in Missions.* 3rd ed. Grand Rapids: Baker Academic, 1993.

———. "Magnifying God with Money." Desiring God, Dec. 14, 1997. https://www. desiringgod.org/messages/magnifying-god-with-money.

———. "Our High Priest Is the Son of God Perfect Forever." Desiring God, Dec. 8, 1996. https://www.desiringgod.org/messages/our-high-priest-is-the-son-of-god-perfect-forever.

———. *The Pleasures of God: Meditations on God's Delight in Being God.* Revised and expanded ed. Sisters, OR: Multnomah, 2000.

———. "Preaching as Worship: Meditations on Expository Exultation." Desiring God, Nov. 2–3, 1994. https://www.desiringgod.org/series/preaching-as-worship-meditations-on-expository-exultation.

———. "Preaching as Worship: Meditations on Expository Exultation." *Trinity Journal* 16 (Spring 1995) 29–45.

———. "The Pride of Babel and the Praise of Christ." Desiring God, Sep. 2, 2007. https://www.desiringgod.org/messages/the-pride-of-babel-and-the-praise-of-christ.

———. *Providence*. Wheaton, IL: Crossway, 2020.

———. "The Pursuit of God in Corporate Worship." Desiring God, Nov. 11, 2011. Session 1 of Gravity and Gladness Seminar. https://www.desiringgod.org/messages/gravity-and-gladness-session-1.

———. "Thoughts on Worship and Culture." 1990. https://www.desiringgod.org/articles/thoughts-on-worship-and-culture.

———. "Training the Next Generation of Evangelical Pastors and Missionaries." Address given at the Evangelical Theological Society Annual Meeting, Orlando, 1998. https://www.desiringgod.org/messages/training-the-next-generation-of-evangelical-pastors-and-missionaries.

———. "Why Am I Here?" Desiring God, Nov. 6, 2017. https://www.desiringgod.org/messages/when-i-dont-desire-god-part-1/excerpts/why-am-i-here.

———. "Why Expositional Preaching Is Particularly Glorifying to God." Desiring God, Apr. 27, 2006. https://www.desiringgod.org/messages/why-expositional-preaching-is-particularly-glorifying-to-god.

———. "Why God Is Not a Megalomaniac in Demanding to Be Worshiped." Evangelical Theological Society Annual Meeting, Providence, RI, Nov. 20, 2008. https://tinyurl.com/piperets.

———. "Worship and World Missions: A Pastoral Strategy." Desiring God, Feb. 9, 1988. https://www.desiringgod.org/messages/worship-and-world-missions-a-pastoral-strategy.

———. "Worship God." Desiring God, Nov. 9, 1997. https://www.desiringgod.org/messages/worship-god--2.

———. "Worship Is an End in Itself." Desiring God, Sep. 13, 1981. https://www.desiringgod.org/messages/worship-is-an-end-in-itself.

———. "Worship: The Feast of Christian Hedonism." Desiring God, Sep. 25, 1983. https://www.desiringgod.org/messages/worship-the-feast-of-christian-hedonism.

———. "You Shall Worship the Lord Your God." Desiring God, Sep. 8, 1985. https://www.desiringgod.org/messages/you-shall-worship-the-lord-your-god.

Piper, John, and Jonathan Edwards. *God's Passion for His Glory: Living the Vision of Jonathan Edwards, with the Complete Text of* The End for Which God Created the World. Wheaton, IL: Crossway, 1998.

Plantinga, Cornelius, and Sue A. Rozeboom, eds. *Discerning the Spirits: A Guide to Thinking about Christian Worship Today*. Calvin Institute of Christian Worship Liturgical Studies Series. Grand Rapids: Eerdmans, 2003.

Poythress, Vern S. "Ezra 3, Union with Christ, and Exclusive Psalmody." *WTJ* 37 (1975) 74–94.

———. "Ezra 3, Union with Christ, and Exclusive Psalmody (Concluded)." *WTJ* 37 (1975) 219–35.

Public Worship Committee. *The Irish Presbyterian Hymnbook*. Norwich, UK: Canterbury, 2004.

Pubols, Heather. "The Translating God." *Evangelical Missions Quarterly* 58 (Sep. 2022) 7.

Pyne, Robert A. "Worship in the Bible and in Church History: Some Observations." Unpublished manuscript, Northwest Bible Church, Dallas, n.d.

Ralston, Tim. "The Ambiguity of 'in Spirit': Addressing Disparate Approaches." Evangelical Theological Society Annual Meeting, Colorado, Nov. 2011. https:// etsworship.files.wordpress.com/2011/10/in-spirit-article.pdf.

———. "Changing Worship—Calming the Conflict." Chapel message, Dallas Theological Seminary, Dallas, 1994.

Rayburn, Robert G. *O Come, Let Us Worship: Corporate Worship in the Evangelical Church*. Reprint, Eugene, OR: Wipf & Stock, 2010.

Read, D. H. C. "The Reformation of Worship." *SJT* 8 (Mar. 1955) 64–79.

Robertson, Archibald Robertson. *Word Pictures in the New Testament*. 6 vols. Grand Rapids: Baker, 1933.

Rogers, Adrian. "Worship." Love Worth Finding Daily Devotional, Mar. 27, 2004. https://www.lwf.org. Post removed.

Ross, Allen P. *Recalling the Hope of Glory: Biblical Worship from the Garden to the New Creation*. Grand Rapids: Kregel, 2006.

Ross, Melanie C., and Mark A. Lamport, eds., *Historical Foundations of Worship: Catholic, Orthodox, and Protestant Perspectives*. Worship Foundations. Grand Rapids: Baker, 2022.

Rowley, Harold Henry. *Worship in Ancient Israel: Its Forms and Meaning*. London: SPCK, 1981.

Ruth, Lester. "Don't Lose the Trinity! A Plea to Songwriters." Robert E. Webber Institute for Worship Studies, Feb. 1, 2006. https://iws.edu/2006/02/lester-ruth-dont-lose-the-trinity/.

Ruth, Lester, and Swee Hong Lim. *A History of Contemporary Praise & Worship: Understanding the Ideas That Reshaped the Protestant Church*. Grand Rapids: Baker Academic, 2021.

Saphir, Adolph. *The Great High Priest: An Exposition of the Epistle to the Hebrews*. Reprint, Charleston, SC: BiblioLife, 2009.

Schaper, Robert N. *In His Presence: Appreciating Your Worship Tradition*. Nashville: Thomas Nelson, 1984.

Schrag, Brian. *Creating Local Arts Together: A Manual to Help Communities Reach Their Kingdom Goals*. Pasadena, CA: William Carey, 2012.

Schrag, Brian, and Julisa Rowe. *Community Arts for God's Purposes: How to Create Local Artistry Together*. Littleton, CO: William Carey, 2020.

Schrag, Brian, and Kathleen J. Van Buren. *Make Arts for a Better Life: A Guide for Working with Communities*. New York: Oxford University Press, 2018.

Schweizer, Eduard. "Worship in the New Testament." *Reformed and Presbyterian World* 24 (Mar. 1957) 197–205.

Scruton, Roger. *The Aesthetics of Music*. Oxford: Oxford University Press, 2009.

Second Vatican Council. "*Sacrosanctum Concilium*: Constitution on the Sacred Liturgy." Adoremus, Dec. 4, 1963. https://adoremus.org/1963/12/sacrosanctum-concilium/.

Segler, Franklin M. *Christian Worship: Its Theology and Practice*. Nashville: Broadman, 1967.

Senn, Frank. "Teaching Worship in Seminaries: A Response." *Worship* 55 (1981) 325–32.

Shelley, Bruce L. *Church History in Plain Language*. Updated 4th ed. Nashville: Thomas Nelson, 2013.

Sjogren, Bob, and Gerald Robison. *Cat & Dog Theology: Rethinking Our Relationship with Our Master*. Revised ed. Downers Grove, IL: InterVarsity, 2003.

Smit, Laura A. "The Incarnation Continues: Recovering the Importance of the Ascension." *Reformed Worship*, Mar. 2006. https://www.reformedworship.org/article/march-2006/incarnation-continues-recovering-importance-ascension.

Smith, Douglas. "Sola Scriptura and Service Planning." Gazing at Glory, Oct. 31, 2008. http://glorygazer.blogspot.com/2008/10/sola-scriptura-and-service-planning.html.

Smith, Gordon T. *A Holy Meal: The Lord's Supper in the Life of the Church*. Grand Rapids: Baker Academic, 2005.

———. "Managing the Tension between Church and Academy." Lecture given at the Institute for Excellence in Christian Leadership Development, Osijek, Croatia, Apr. 5, 2006.

Smith, James K. A. *Desiring the Kingdom: Worship, Worldview, and Cultural Formation*. Vol. 1 of *Cultural Liturgies*. Grand Rapids: Baker Academic, 2009.

Sproul, R. C. *Grace Unknown: The Heart of Reformed Theology*. Grand Rapids: Baker, 1997.

Spurgeon, C. H. *The Treasury of David: Containing an Original Exposition of the Book of Psalms; A Collection of Illustrative Extracts from the Whole Range of Literature; A Series of Homiletical Hints upon Almost Every Verse; and Lists of Writers upon Each Psalm*. Peabody, MA: Hendrickson, 2011.

Stallsmith, Glenn. "Worship from the Nations: A Response to Scott Aniol." *Ethnodoxology: A Global Forum on Arts and Christian Faith* 3 (2015). https://artsandchristianfaith.org/index.php/journal/article/view/25.

Steere, Douglas V. *Prayer and Worship*. Richmond, IN: Friends United, 1978.

Stott, John R. W. *Between Two Worlds: The Challenge of Preaching Today*. Reprint, Grand Rapids: Eerdmans, 2017.

———. *Christian Basics: A Handbook of Beginnings, Beliefs and Behaviour*. Grand Rapids: Baker, 1991.

———. *The Contemporary Christian: An Urgent Plea for Double Listening*. Leicester, UK: InterVarsity, 1993.

———. *The Living Church: Convictions of a Lifelong Pastor*. Nottingham, UK: IVP, 2007.

———. *The Message of 1 Timothy and Titus: The Life of the Local Church*. Bible Speaks Today. Leicester, UK: InterVarsity, 1996.

———. *Romans: God's Good News for the World*. Bible Speaks Today. Downers Grove, IL: InterVarsity, 1994.

Tait, William. *Meditationes Hebraicae, or, a Doctrinal and Practical Exposition of the Epistle of St. Paul to the Hebrews*. London: Seeley, Burnside and Seeley, 1845.

Temple, William. *Readings in St John's Gospel: First and Second Series*. Christian Classics. London: Pendlebury, 2018.

TeSelle, Sallie. "Between Athens and Jerusalem: The Seminary in Tension." *Christian Century* 93 (Feb. 4, 1976) 89–93.

Thomas, Jay. "Easily Edified." Gospel Obsessed, Feb. 17, 2012. https://gospelobsessed.com/2012/02/17/easily-edified/.

Thompson, Marianne Meye. "Worship in the Book of Revelation." *Ex Auditu* 8 (1992) 45–54.

Toon, Peter. *Our Triune God: A Biblical Portrayal of the Trinity*. Vancouver, BC: Regent College Press, 2002.

Torah Tots. "The 39 Melachot." Torah Tots, n.d. https://www.torahtots.com/torah/39melachot.htm.

Torrance, David W. "The Word of God in Worship." *Scottish Bulletin of Evangelical Theology* 1 (1983) 11–16.

Torrance, James B. "The Doctrine of the Trinity in Our Contemporary Situation." In *The Forgotten Trinity*, edited by Alisdair I. C. Heron, 3:3–17. London: Inter-Church, 1991.

———. "The Place of Jesus Christ in Worship." In *Theological Foundations for Ministry: Selected Readings for a Theology of the Church in Ministry*, edited by Ray S. Anderson, 348–69. Grand Rapids: Eerdmans, 1979.

———. "The Priesthood of Christ." Presentation at Perichoresis conference, n.p., n.d. Audiotape.

———. *Worship, Community and the Triune God of Grace*. Downers Grove, IL: IVP Academic, 1997.

Torrance, Thomas F. *The Christian Doctrine of God, One Being Three Persons*. 2nd ed. T&T Clark Cornerstones. London: T. & T. Clark, 2016.

———. "The Mind of Christ in Worship: The Problem of Apollinarianism in the Liturgy." In *Theology in Reconciliation: Essays towards Evangelical and Catholic Unity in East and West*, 139–214. Grand Rapids: Eerdmans, 1975.

———. *Royal Priesthood*. 2nd ed. Edinburgh: T. & T. Clark, 1993.

———. *The School of Faith: Catechisms of the Reformed Church*. Eugene, OR: Wipf & Stock, 1996.

———. *Theology in Reconstruction*. Reprint, Grand Rapids: Eerdmans, 1975.

———. "The Word of God and the Response of Man." In *God and Rationality*, 137–64. New York: Oxford University Press, 1971.

Torrance, Thomas F., et al. *A Passion for Christ: The Vision That Ignites Ministry*. Eugene, OR: Wipf & Stock, 2010.

Tozer, A. W. *The Knowledge of the Holy: The Attributes of God, Their Meaning in the Christian Life*. San Francisco: Harper & Row, 1978.

———. "The Reason We Exist." In *Worship: The Reason We Were Created: Collected Insights from A. W. Tozer*. Chicago: Moody, 2017.

———. *Whatever Happened to Worship?* Camp Hill, PA: Christian, 1985.

———. *Worship: The Missing Jewel*. Camp Hill, PA: Christian, 1992.

Trzeciak, Cathy. *Worship: Our Gift to God*. St. Louis, MO: Concordia, 1986.

Vanhoozer, Kevin. "Worship at the Well: From Dogmatics to Doxology (and Back Again)." *Trinity Journal* 23NS (2002) 3–16.

Veith, Gene Edward. "Through All Generations." *For the Life of the World* 2 (Mar. 1998) 7–9.

Volf, Miroslav, and Dorothy C. Bass, eds. *Practicing Theology: Beliefs and Practices in Christian Life*. Grand Rapids: Eerdmans, 2002.

Wainwright, Geoffrey. *Doxology: The Praise of God in Worship, Doctrine and Life; a Systematic Theology*. New York: Oxford University Press, 1984.

———. "The Praise of God in the Theological Reflection of the Church." *Interpretation* 39 (1985) 34–45.

Wainwright, Geoffrey, and Karen B. Westerfield Tucker, eds. *The Oxford History of Christian Worship*. New York: Oxford University Press, 2006.

Webber, Robert E. *Worship Is a Verb: Eight Principles Transforming Worship*. 2nd ed. Peabody, MA: Hendrickson, 1996.

Wells, Tom. "The Epistle to the Hebrews and Worship." *Reformation and Revival* 9 (Spring 2000) 115–29.

Wenham, Gordon J. "Sanctuary Symbolism in the Garden of Eden Story." *Proceedings of the World Congress of Jewish Studies* 9 (1986) 19–25.

Wesley, Charles. "Spirit of Truth, Come Down." Hymnary, 1746. https://hymnary.org/hymn/HLMC1969/228.

Westermann, Claus. *Elements of Old Testament Theology*. Atlanta: John Knox, 1982.

Whaley, Vernon M. *The Dynamics of Corporate Worship*. Ministry Dynamics for a New Century Series. Grand Rapids: Baker, 2001.

White, James F. *A Brief History of Christian Worship*. Nashville: Abingdon, 1993.

———. *Christian Worship in North America: A Retrospective, 1955–1995*. Reprint, Eugene, OR: Wipf & Stock, 2007.

———. "Making Our Worship More Biblical." *Perkins Journal* (Fall 1980) 38–40.

———. "The Missing Jewel of the Evangelical Church." In *Christian Worship in North America: A Retrospective: 1955–95*, 103–14. Collegeville, MN: Liturgical, 1997.

———. *Protestant Worship: Traditions in Transition*. Louisville, KY: Westminster/John Knox, 1989.

———. "The Teaching of Worship in Seminaries in Canada and the United States." *Worship* 55 (1981) 304–32.

Wilken, Robert Louis. "Angels and Archangels: The Worship of Heaven and Earth." *Antiphon* 6 (2001) 10–18.

Wilkey, Gláucia Vasconcelos, ed. *Worship and Culture: Foreign Country or Homeland?* Grand Rapids: Eerdmans, 2014.

Willard, Dallas. *The Divine Conspiracy: Rediscovering Our Hidden Life in God*. San Francisco: HarperSanFrancisco, 1998.

Willimon, William H. *Word, Water, Wine, and Bread: How Worship Has Changed over the Years*. Valley Forge, PA: Judson, 1980.

———. *Worship as Pastoral Care*. Nashville: Abingdon, 1990.

Willmington, Edwin M. "Convergence: Coming to a Worship Service Near You." *Theology, News, & Notes* [Fuller Seminary] (Spring 2006) 11.

———. "The Worship Leader and the Vocal Range of Congregational Songs." Worship Resources International, n.d. https://worship-resources.org/2023/07/13/the-worship-leader-and-the-vocal-range-of-congregational-songs-ed-willmington/.

Willson, Sanders L. "Receiving Jesus as Priest." Sermon preached at Second Presbyterian Church, Memphis, TN, n.d.

Wilson, Monte E. "Church-o-Rama or Corporate Worship." Highway, 1998. From *The Compromised Church: The Present Evangelical Crisis*, edited by John Armstrong (Wheaton, IL: Crossway, 1998). https://www.the-highway.com/church_Wilson.html.

Witvliet, John D. "Beyond Style: Asking Deeper Questions about Worship." Alban Institute, Jan. 24, 2007. https://alban.org/archive/beyond-style-asking-deeper-questions-about-worship/.

———. *The Biblical Psalms in Christian Worship: A Brief Introduction and Guide to Resources*. The Calvin Institute of Christian Worship Liturgical Studies Series. Grand Rapids: Eerdmans, 2007.

———. "Isaiah in Christian Liturgy: Recovering Textual Contrasts and Correcting Theological Astigmatism." *Calvin Theological Journal* 39 (2004) 135–56.

———. "Prism of Glory: Trinitarian Worship and Liturgical Piety in the Reformed Tradition." In *The Place of Christ in Liturgical Prayer: Trinity, Christology, and*

*Liturgical Theology*, edited by Bryan D. Spinks, 268–99. Collegeville, MN: Liturgical, 2008.

———. "Singing Our Prayers, Praying Our Songs: Historical and Cross-Cultural Music in the Context of Worship." Unpublished manuscript, n.d.

———. "Teaching Worship as a Christian Practice: Musing on Practical Theology and Pedagogy in Seminaries and Church-Related Colleges." *Reformed Journal* (blog), Jun. 1, 2006. https://reformedjournal.com/teaching-worship-as-a-christian-practice-musing-on-practical-theology-and-pedagogy-in-seminaries-and-church-related-colleges/.

———. "The Trinitarian DNA of Christian Worship: Perennial Themes in Recent Theological Literature." *Colloquium Journal* [Institute of Sacred Music, Yale University] (Autumn 2005). https://ism.yale.edu/sites/default/files/files/The%20Trinitarian%20DNA%20of%20Christian%20Worship.pdf.

———. "What to Do with Our Renewed Trinitarian Enthusiasm: Forming Trinitarian Piety and Imagination through Worship and Catechesis." In *Trinitarian Theology for the Church: Scripture, Community, Worship*, edited by Daniel J. Treier and David Lauber, 237–53. Wheaton Theology Conference Series. Downers Grove, IL: IVP Academic, 2009.

———. *Worship Seeking Understanding: Windows into Christian Practice*. Grand Rapids: Baker Academic, 2003.

Wright, Christopher J. H. *The Mission of God: Unlocking the Bible's Grand Narrative*. Downers Grove, IL: IVP Academic, 2006.

Wright, N. T. *The Case for the Psalms: Why They Are Essential*. New York: HarperOne, 2013.

———. "Freedom and Framework, Spirit and Truth: Recovering Biblical Worship." NT Wright, 2002. https://ntwrightpage.com/2016/04/05/freedom-and-framework-spirit-and-truth-recovering-biblical-worship-2/.

———. *The Future of the People of God*. Christian Audio, 2006. https://christianaudio.com/the-future-of-the-people-of-god-nt-wright-audiobook-download.

———. "Worship and the Spirit in the New Testament." NT Wright, Feb. 21–23, 2008. https://ntwrightpage.com/2016/04/25/worship-and-the-spirit-in-the-new-testament/.

Zahl, Paul F. M., and Paul Basden, eds. *Six Views on Exploring the Worship Spectrum*. Counterpoints. Grand Rapids: Zondervan, 2004.

# SUBJECT INDEX

Aaron, mediator between the people
 and God, 294–95
' abad, 136–37, 214
Abram/Abraham, 26–27, 144–50
 call of, 144–45
acceptable worship, 276, 287, 310, 313,
 314, 316, 350, 366–67, 411, 415,
 443, 470, 476
 in Christ, 316, 461
access. See drawing near to God.
Alexander, Eric, 43, 57n, 62–63, 68,
 79n, 86–87, 91, 108, 109n,
 116–17, 145n, 179, 179, 299,
 356, 441, 445, 446,
all of life worship. See whole-life
 worship.
Allmen, Jean-Jacques von, 256, 357–61,
 464, 465
altar/altars, 29–30, 141, 146, 147, 149
Anglicanism. See Church of England.
Apostles' Creed, 107, 325, 380
Apostolic Age, 321–23
arts in missions, 96, 426–27, 429
ascension, See: Jesus Christ, ascension of.
assurance, 263–64, 275–76, 283, 314,
 504
 from Holy Spirit, 283, 466
Augustine, 24, 233, 290, 290n, 314,
 367, 462
Augustinianism, 24

Babel, Tower of, 24, 133, 141–42, 152n
balance, need to, biblical fidelity and
 cultural relevance, 398–99

baptism, 326n
believers as temple, 215–16, 216n
Bible
 the foundation of foundations for
 worship, 46–47
 in vernacular, 336
 not in vernacular, 330
 the story of God's glory, 51–63
 worship according to, 164
 worship as unifying theme of, 77,
 114–17, 262
 biblical constants of worship, 347–48,
 406–7
 biblical or cultural, 418–9
blended worship, 485–86
Book of Common Prayer, 382, 467, 476
Bridge, the, 404–22, 422, 437

Cain and Abel, 139–40
Call to Worship (element of worship
 service), 37–39, 350, 447, 500
call to worship, the gospel as, 82–85,
 86, 260
Calvin, John, 68, 304, 337, 341, 367,
 377, 396–97, 410, 476
Calvin Institute of Christian Worship,
 520
Carson, D. A., 11, 109, 210, 205–6,
 206–7, 212–13
Castleman, Robbie, 25, 28–29
catechisms in corporate worship,
 381–82
centrality of worship, 65–117
ceremonialism, 326–27

# SCRIPTURE INDEX

## Mark

Made in the USA
Las Vegas, NV
23 December 2024

15308554R00350